The Two Horizons New Testament Commentary

Joel B. Green and Max Turner, *General Editors*

Two features distinguish THE TWO HORIZONS NEW TESTAMENT COMMENTARY series: theological exegesis and theological reflection.

Exegesis since the Reformation era and especially in the past two hundred years emphasized careful attention to philology, grammar, syntax, and concerns of a historical nature. More recently, commentary has expanded to include social-scientific, political, or canonical questions and more.

Without slighting the significance of those sorts of questions, scholars in THE TWO HORIZONS NEW TESTAMENT COMMENTARY locate their primary interests on theological readings of texts, past and present. The result is a paragraph-by-paragraph engagement with the text that is deliberately theological in focus.

Theological reflection in THE TWO HORIZONS NEW TESTAMENT COMMENTARY takes many forms, including locating each New Testament book in relation to the whole of Scripture — asking what the biblical book contributes to biblical theology — and in conversation with constructive theology of today. How commentators engage in the work of theological reflection will differ from book to book, depending on their particular theological tradition and how they perceive the work of biblical theology and theological hermeneutics. This heterogeneity derives as well from the relative infancy of the project of theological interpretation of Scripture in modern times and from the challenge of grappling with a book's message in Greco-Roman antiquity, in the canon of Scripture and history of interpretation, and for life in the admittedly diverse Western world at the beginning of the twenty-first century.

THE TWO HORIZONS NEW TESTAMENT COMMENTARY is written primarily for students, pastors, and other Christian leaders seeking to engage in theological interpretation of Scripture.

Revelation

John Christopher Thomas and Frank D. Macchia

WILLIAM B. EERDMANS PUBLISHING COMPANY
GRAND RAPIDS, MICHIGAN

© 2016 John Christopher Thomas and Frank D. Macchia
All rights reserved

Published 2016 by
Wm. B. Eerdmans Publishing Co.
2140 Oak Industrial Drive N.E., Grand Rapids, Michigan
49505

Library of Congress Cataloging-in-Publication Data

Names: Thomas, John Christopher, author. | Macchia, Frank D., 1952-
Title: Revelation / John Christopher Thomas, and Frank D. Macchia.
Description: Grand Rapids, Michigan: William B. Eerdmans Publishing Company, 2016. |
    Series: The two horizons New Testament commentary
    Includes bibliographical references and index.
Identifiers: LCCN 2015034476 | ISBN 9780802825544 (paperback)
Subjects: LCSH: Bible. Revelation — Commentaries. |
    BISAC: RELIGION / Biblical Commentary / New Testament.
Classification: LCC BS2825.53 .T46 2016 |
    DDC 228/.07 — dc23 LC record available at http://lccn.loc.gov/2015034476

www.eerdmans.com

This commentary is dedicated to our daughters —
Paige Diane Thomas Scaperoth
Lori Danielle Thomas Brown
Desiree Verena Macchia
Jasmine Xian Macchia

Contents

Preface	xv
Abbreviations	xxi

INTRODUCTION — 1

Structure and Nature of the Book — 1
- Literary Markers Recognized by a First-Time Hearer of Revelation — 2
- Revelation as Visionary Drama — 7
- Revelation as Christian Prophecy — 10
- Revelation and the Apocalyptic Tradition — 11
- Revelation as Intertext — 14
- The Canonical Location and Function of Revelation — 15

Audience — 17
- Geographic Location — Asia Minor — 17
- The Johannine Community — 19
- OT Literature (Intertextuality) — 20
- People of the Spirit — 20
- Women — 21
- Witness and Persecution — 22
- Opponents and Opposition — 23
  - Cosmic Opposition — 23
  - Concrete Expressions of Opposition — 24

Contents

Date	26
Internal Indicators	26
External Evidence	32
A Modest Proposal with regard to Date	34
Authorship	35
John the Prophet	36
Writing in the Spirit	38
John the Prophet and the Other Johannine Literature	39
John in Early Christian Tradition	41
Revelation and Its Streams of Influence: The History of Effects	44
Disastrous Interpretations of Revelation	44
Other Johannine Apocalyptic Documents	47
Art	50
Music	53
Poetry	58
Film	62
Commentaries	64
COMMENTARY	73
Prologue (1:1-8)	73
"In the Spirit on the Lord's Day" (1:9–3:22)	79
The Inaugural Vision of Jesus (1:9-20)	79
The Seven Prophetic Messages to the Seven Churches of Asia (2:1–3:22)	85
To the Angel of the Church in Ephesus (2:1-7)	85
To the Angel of the Church in Smyrna (2:8-11)	94
To the Angel of the Church in Pergamum (2:12-17)	98
To the Angel of the Church in Thyatira (2:18-29)	103
To the Angel of the Church in Sardis (3:1-6)	112
To the Angel of the Church in Philadelphia (3:7-13)	118
To the Angel of the Church in Laodicea (3:14-22)	126

Contents

"In the Spirit in Heaven" (4:1–16:21)	135
The Inaugural Vision of Heaven, the One Who Sits on the Throne, the Lamb, and the Scroll Sealed with Seven Seals (4:1–5:14)	135
The Opening of the Scroll Sealed with Seven Seals (6:1–8:5)	154
The Opening of the First Six Seals (6:1-17)	155
The Interlude of the 144,000 and the Great Multitude (7:1-17)	164
The Opening of the Seventh Seal and the Golden Altar (8:1-5)	175
Seven Angels with Seven Trumpets (8:6–11:19)	179
The Sounding of the First Six Trumpets (8:6–9:21)	179
The Interlude of the Little Scroll and the Two Witnesses (10:1–11:14)	191
The Sounding of the Seventh Trumpet (11:15-19)	210
The Struggle of God's People in Cosmic Perspective (12:1–14:20)	214
Signs in Heaven: The Woman Clothed with the Sun, and the Red Dragon (12:1–13:1a)	214
The Two Beasts (13:1b-18)	229
The Lamb and the 144,000, the Harvest and the Winepress (14:1-20)	250
Seven Angels with Seven Bowls of Plagues (15:1–16:21)	266
Another Great Sign in Heaven: The Seven Angels (15:1-8)	266
The Pouring Out of the Seven Bowls (16:1-21)	277
"In the Spirit" — Carried to a Wilderness (17:1–21:8)	291
The Woman on the Beast: Babylon the Whore (17:1-18)	291
The Destruction of Babylon (18:1-24)	306
From Babylon the Great to the New Jerusalem — from the Last Judgment to the New Creation (19:1–21:8)	325
Rejoicing in Heaven and on Earth and the Marriage Supper of the Lamb (19:1-10)	325
The King of Kings and Lord of Lords (19:11-16)	337
Victory over the King's Enemies (19:17-21)	343
The Thousand-Year Reign (20:1-6)	348
Satan's Final Rebellion and Defeat (20:7-10)	357
The Final Judgment (20:11-15)	360
The Descent of the New Jerusalem (21:1-8)	363

Contents

"In the Spirit" — Carried to a Great High Mountain:
    The Description of the New Jerusalem (21:9–22:5)   373

Epilogue (22:6-21)   391

THEOLOGICAL HORIZONS OF REVELATION   405

God   405
  Revelation and Biblical Theology   405
    Revelation   406
    Gospel of John and 1–3 John   412
    Matthew and Mark   413
    Luke and Acts   414
    Paul   415
    Other New Testament Voices   417
    Conclusion   417
  Revelation and Systematic Theology   418
    The Sovereign God of Classical Theism   419
    Doxology: The Point of Departure   423
    The Sovereign God of Resurrection   425
    The Sovereign God of Love and Grace   427
    The Sovereign God in Holiness   431
    The Sovereign God at War   433
    Conclusion   436

Christ   437
  Revelation and Biblical Theology   437
    Revelation   437
    Gospel of John and 1–3 John   445
    Matthew and Mark   447
    Luke and Acts   451
    Paul   452
    Other New Testament Voices   454
    Conclusion   456
  Revelation and Systematic Theology   457

Christological Method	457
Worship and the Mediation of the Lamb	460
Christ and the Challenge of Pluralism	466
Toward a Nonviolent Christology	470
Word of the Father and Man of the Spirit	472
Conclusion	474
Holy Spirit	**475**
Revelation and Biblical Theology	475
Revelation	475
Gospel of John and 1–3 John	479
Matthew and Mark	480
Luke and Acts	481
Paul	482
Other New Testament Voices	483
Conclusion	484
Revelation and Systematic Theology	485
The Need for Discernment	485
The Deity and Person of the Spirit	490
The Witness to the Nations	494
The Spirit of Life	496
Conclusion	499
Church	**500**
Revelation and Biblical Theology	500
Revelation	501
Gospel of John and 1–3 John	509
Matthew and Mark	511
Luke and Acts	513
Paul	515
Other New Testament Voices	518
Conclusion	519
Revelation and Systematic Theology	520
The Trinitarian Founding of the Church	520
The Worship of the Saints	525
Missionary Ecclesiology	526

Contents

The Witness of the Martyrs	529
Israel and the Nations	532
Conclusion	536

Salvation — 537
- Revelation and Biblical Theology — 537
  - Revelation — 537
  - Gospel of John and 1–3 John — 543
  - Matthew and Mark — 547
  - Luke and Acts — 550
  - Paul — 552
  - Other New Testament Voices — 559
  - Conclusion — 563
- Revelation and Systematic Theology — 564
  - Salvation, Trinity, and Divine Pathos — 564
  - Atonement: Exclusion and Embrace — 569
  - An Ecumenical Geometry of Salvation — 578
  - Conclusion — 583

Eschatology — 584
- Revelation and Biblical Theology — 584
  - Revelation — 585
  - John — 594
  - Matthew and Mark — 597
  - Luke and Acts — 600
  - Paul — 603
  - Other New Testament Voices — 607
  - Conclusion — 609
- Revelation and Systematic Theology — 609
  - The Necessity of Eschatology — 610
  - The Question of Apocalyptic — 613
  - The Delay of Christ's Coming — 618
  - The Ultimate Embrace — 620
  - Uttering the Unutterable — 621
  - Conclusion — 623

Bibliography	625
Index of Names	637
Index of Subjects	642
Index of Biblical and Other Ancient References	647

Preface

Every book has a story, and this book has a particularly long and winding one. We should perhaps confess from the outset that we never intended to write a commentary such as this on the book of Revelation. Having grown up in the apocalyptic tradition of Pentecostal spirituality, where the return of Jesus occupied a not insignificant place in the theological heart of the movement as part of the fivefold gospel that proclaims Jesus as Savior, Sanctifier, Holy Spirit Baptizer, Healer, and Soon Coming King, we were keenly attuned to the importance of eschatology and the unrivaled role played in it by the book of Revelation. This doctrine was the subject of countless sermons, lessons, lectures, and prophecy talks that we encountered, not to mention films, books, tracts, and larger-than-life charts! All of these combined to create within us a robust respect for those who could divine their way through current events by means of biblical prophecy. Rumors about government checks mistakenly sent to unsuspecting citizens that bore the number 666 circulated with a surprising degree of regularity, likewise the naming of world leaders who seemed to fit characteristics of the "antichrist," speculations about the relationship between the ten kings of Rev 17 and the European Common Market (as it was known in those days), as well as fears with regard to bar codes and more — all combined to create a heightened sense of interest in signs of the coming end of the world.

But despite our early interest and sympathy with such attempts to understand end-time prophecy, problems with "the script" began to emerge. Too many prophetic predictions and pronouncements by those "in the know" proved to be off the mark, with little acknowledgment of mistaken notions and little to no reflection about the significance of such missteps. As we began our interpretive and spiritual journey further into biblical studies, we discovered that a straightforward reading of Scripture often proved not to fit the interpretations we were hearing; rather, it became apparent that interpreters were forcing Scripture into a preexisting template. Eventually we learned that some specific words essential to this narrative, like "antichrist," did not appear in Revelation at all nor elsewhere in Scripture with their popular meaning. At the same time, we found certain academic approaches to Revelation were often beholden to their own "scripts," discounting portions or emphases of the text that did not fit with their own more nuanced interpretations. Not surprisingly, the Apocalypse remained for us a closed book, about which we thought it best simply to steer clear.

It was Rick Moore who first mentioned that I (John Christopher Thomas) should one day turn my attention to the Apocalypse, a suggestion I laughingly dismissed. But as I look back, Rick's words proved to be a catalyst in helping me to discern that God was calling me to this fascinating part of Scripture. Other encouragements would follow. One day in chapel at the seminary where I teach, Vladimir Mourashkine, a student from the former Soviet Union, gave a testimony about his life and ministry. Vladimir, who had experienced imprisonment and other forms of persecution at the hands of the Communist government for being a Pentecostal Christian, began to rehearse the history of Russia by means of the story line found in Revelation. Although there were aspects of the story that did not seem to fit for me as well as they did for him, I was enraptured by his words and began to think more deeply about how the book sounds and what it means in parts of the world where people do not have the luxury of speculating leisurely about end-time events. The other event that had a significant impact on me was reading Richard Bauckham's *The Theology of the Book of Revelation*. This was far and away the best work I had ever read on Revelation, and it gave me reason to ponder the book more intently from a literary and theological vantage point. The cumulative effect of these events caused me to be open to the possibility of working on this distinctive book of the NT.

The very first person to whom I verbalized the conviction that the Lord was preparing me to do something on Revelation was my friend Max Turner, who (along with Joel Green) promptly offered me the opportunity to contribute a volume to Eerdmans' Two Horizons New Testament Commentary (THNTC) series. But the offer was not to write on Revelation — it had already been assigned to someone else! Not long after agreeing to work with the THNTC project on the other volume, however, I was asked to consider writing the volume on Revelation instead, as plans with a different author had fallen through. As I began work on the commentary, I soon enlisted my good friend Pentecostal theologian Frank Macchia to join me in the endeavor — a partnership that has been enjoyable and enriching from the beginning.

Preface

I (Frank D. Macchia) first entered the project while giving lectures at the Pentecostal Theological Seminary, Cleveland, Tennessee, where my friend Chris Thomas (as his friends call him) taught New Testament studies. He asked me to sit in on his seminar, which happened to be on the theology of the Apocalypse. The lively discussion of which I was privileged to be a part and the sermon I preached from Revelation that night at his church were the sparks that inspired him to ask me if I would be willing to join him in writing this commentary. I was initially hesitant to do so. After all, systematic theologians rarely consider participating in a biblical commentary. More typically, they write monographs on issues of Scripture and theology relating to the history of doctrine or some contemporary intellectual challenge. Three factors, however, made the project appealing to me. In the first place, I knew that systematic theology has at times been renewed by discoveries in the field of biblical studies, including recent studies on Revelation. Second, so much of the book of Revelation theologically seems to move against the stream of where Christian theology has gone over the past several decades. Themes of divine sovereignty or wrath are hardly topics of constructive theological work today, except perhaps as ideas to be critically assessed or avoided. Engaging in theological reflection on major topics of theology in the light of the message of Revelation was a challenge that was hard for me to resist. I assumed from the beginning that Revelation had a liberating message from the first chapter to the last, and my detailed study in this book has only confirmed that assumption. Third, the prospect of working with Chris was equally hard to forgo. I knew of his gifts as a New Testament scholar and was excited to join my reflective work in biblical and systematic theology to a stellar commentary on the text of Revelation. I have not been in any way disappointed. Moreover, his stimulation and encouragement with every chapter submission were invaluable. Please note that, in citing Scripture in the "Theological Horizons" section, I follow the NIV translation, with occasional minor modifications.

I am especially grateful to my wife, Verena, for her loving support as I worked hard over the last several years thinking theologically about Revelation. Without her constant encouragement, my scholarship would not at all be possible. My daughters, Desiree and Jasmine, had to endure patiently not having me as attentive to their needs as I normally would be because of the long hours I spent on this manuscript. I am grateful to them. My good friends Amos Yong and Dale Irvin, as well as students and colleagues at Vanguard University, Costa Mesa, California, were gracious conversation partners throughout the project (especially participants in my Theology of the Apocalypse seminar during the spring term of 2013), and I'm sure that my department chair, Rich Israel, looked the other way more than once as he found my office door locked and/or unoccupied while I hunkered down to bring my thoughts to print. I was also pleased to present some of my work at the 2011 Abbott Lectures (Pentecostal Theological Seminary) and in a paper given in San Francisco at the 2012 annual meeting of the Society of Biblical Literature (Hermeneutics of Christian Scripture section).

WHEN IT BECAME CLEAR that the draft of the commentary we produced was over the word limits to be included in the THNTC series, Eerdmans graciously consented to allow me (JCT) to publish the longer version through the Centre for Pentecostal Theology Press, without Frank's theological essays, to be followed by this THNTC version, which, including Frank's fine theological contributions, fit better within the size envisioned for the THNTC volumes. We are grateful to series editors Joel Green and Max Turner, as well as Eerdmans Publishing itself, for their longsuffering, consent, and support.

The completion of this commentary, written over the course of about a decade, would not have been possible without the generous provision of periodic study leaves offered by the Pentecostal Theological Seminary as part of the research provisions attached to the Clarence J. Abbott Chair of Biblical Studies, which has been my privilege to hold since its inception. I would especially like to thank for their support Steven Jack Land, who has been the seminary president during this period, as well as James P. Bowers, followed by Sang-Ehil Han, who each served as vice-president for academics during a good portion of this period.

For the most part the commentary portion was written at Tyndale House in Cambridge and at the Centre for Pentecostal Theology on the grounds of the Pentecostal Theological Seminary. Both of these research facilities are ideal places for such work. The writing process itself has been the most exhilarating and exhausting experience of my life! At so many points I have simply been overwhelmed by the literary artistry and theological depth found in Revelation. I found it to be an overpowering vision that subverts any temptation to make it manageable or to tame its contents. My own attempt has been to offer a literary and theological reading of the text that seeks to discern the effect of the text on its hearers, both implied and actual. The reader should note that, unless otherwise indicated, all citations of Scripture in the commentary section are my own translation.

This work has taken place within the local communities of which I am part. At my local church, the Woodward Church of God in Athens, TN, I have experienced extended and numerous times of prayer for this and the various research projects with which I am involved, dialogue with those in the community about the process and the results, and times of interaction where insights from a variety of sources have been processed. Here, I have had the opportunity to teach and preach through Revelation on several occasions. Just as it is difficult to put into words the effects one's family has upon one's scholarship, so it is difficult for me to describe the community's role. For I have learned that the Spirit can and does speak in and through a variety of unexpected contexts and individuals. It has amazed me over the years that in my local church, a congregation where there is a place for many of those on society's margins (the poor, the severely mentally challenged, ex-convicts, ex-addicts, those who have suffered racial discrimination, etc.), the Spirit speaks about certain issues that, while not always directly related to my scholarly work, often have a profound impact upon it. At the seminary the project has been helped along by careful readings of the developing drafts by my students over the years, as well as the resulting intensive conversations about the meaning of Revelation and the hearing here proposed. Such dialogue has taken place in the Apocalypse seminar that has been offered on a yearly basis, as well as the Abbott lectures and various Ministers Week seminar presentations.

It has also been my happy privilege to have been invited to share portions of this work at a variety of venues both academic and popular, including the Society for Pentecostal Studies, the Society of Biblical Literature, Bangor University (Bangor, Wales), Institutul Teologic Penticostal (Bucharest, Romania), Regent University (Virginia Beach, VA), Southeastern University (Lakeland, FL), and Renovatus (Charlotte, NC). These opportunities have also led to improvements in the text.

Finally, I should like to thank a variety of people for their assistance along the way. My colleagues at the Pentecostal Theological Seminary, where I have served full-time since 1982, have contributed to the creation of a wonderful environment in which to pursue constructive Pentecostal theology. Students of my Apocalypse seminar have been energetic dialogue partners, spotting all manner of errors in the drafts, questioning points of interpretation, offering helpful suggestions, as well as prodding me to rethink certain conclusions. Their contributions are hard to overestimate, and I thank them here for their dialogue. Special mention should be made of Steven Spears and Trina Sills, who meticulously read the manuscript, calling my attention to the many aspects in need of revision, as well as Steffen Schumacher, for his careful reading of parts of the manuscript. Thanks are also due to graduate assistants Larry Fleckner, Christopher Brewer, Andy Dimbi, and Sarah Cassell, also doctoral student David Johnson, for work on the indexes for this project. Special thanks are also due Craig Noll of Eerdmans for his detailed and meticulous editing of the manuscript.

My partner on the THNTC volume, Frank Macchia, has contributed very much indeed to this commentary. He has read the whole manuscript carefully more than once, has engaged me in constructive dialogue all along the way, and graciously encouraged me at every phase of the journey. Frank is my dear friend, brother in the Lord, and model constructive Pentecostal theologian.

My friend and colleague Lee Roy Martin is also worthy of special mention. He has been my dialogue partner on this and many other projects — always cheerful, always constructive, always dependable, and always ready with a helpful comment. In fact, he created an exquisite stained glass of the Apocalypse for me, the image of which appears on the back cover of the CPT Press commentary. He has also contributed to the project in many ways less visible, and I am indebted to him very much indeed. I have often thought that everyone needs a friend like Lee Roy. I have been blessed by our partnership in this endeavor, for which I here offer my heartfelt, public thanks.

The greatest debt of thanks is due my family. My parents, Wayne and Betty Fritts, have been a constant source of encouragement to me and my family, offering spiritual, emotional, and financial support, without which my academic study of Scripture would not have been possible. Their lives have been models of the best of Pentecostal spirituality, and they will never know how deeply their living testimonies have impacted me, my brother Mark, and our extended family, who rise up and call them blessed. The role of my wife, Barbara, in this project has been enormous. She is strong, industrious, hardworking, athletic, independent, beautiful, and deeply spiritual. Barb has sacrificed a great deal for this and many other projects without complaint, creating a home environment that has freed me to pursue the research and writing to which I have felt called. I thank her for all she has done and for what she means to me in our thirty-fifth year of married life together. I should also like to thank our children, Paige, Lori, David (Paige's husband), and Chad (Lori's husband), for bringing great joy to our lives, taking interest in my Revelation work, living with our frequent separations, and celebrating the completion of the work with me. Barb and I love them more than life itself and thank God for them daily as they continue their journey through life. We could not be prouder of their professional accomplishments and their spiritual development.

OUR PRAYER IS THAT this reading of Revelation and the resulting theological reflection will assist the church to rediscover and reappropriate this extremely important book in the canon of Scripture. May the Lord use it as he sees fit.

Abbreviations

ACCS   Ancient Commentary of Christian Scripture
ATR   *Anglican Theological Review*
BAGD   Walter Bauer, William F. Arndt, F. William Gingrich, and Frederick W. Danker, *A Greek-English Lexicon of the New Testament and Other Early Christian Literature* (Chicago: University of Chicago Press, 2nd edition, 1958)
BCOT   Baker Commentary on the Old Testament
BZNW   Beihefte zur Zeitschrift für die neutestamentliche Wissenschaft
CBQ   *Catholic Biblical Quarterly*
CNT   Commentaire du Nouveau Testament
CTJ   *Calvin Theological Journal*
CTM   Calwer theologische Monographien
ECNT   Exegetical Commentary of the New Testament
EDNT   Horst Balz and Gerhard Schneider, eds., *Exegetical Dictionary of the New Testament* (3 vols. Grand Rapids: Eerdmans, 1990-1993).
EQ   *Evangelical Quarterly*
EUSST   European University Studies
HTR   *Harvard Theological Review*
ICC   International Critical Commentary
Int   *Interpretation*
JBL   *Journal of Biblical Literature*
JETS   *Journal of the Evangelical Theological Society*
JPTS   Journal of Pentecostal Theology Supplement
JSNT   *Journal for the Study of the New Testament*
JSNTS   Journal for the Study of the New Testament Supplement
JTS   *Joournal of Theological Studies*
MBPS   Mellen Biblical Press Series

NCCS	New Covenant Commentary Series
NDT	Das Neue Testament deutsch
NIBC	New International Bible Commentary
NICNT	New International Commentary on the New Testament
NIDNTT	Colin Brown, ed., *New International Dictionary of New Testament Theology* (3 vols. Grand Rapids: Zondervan, 1975-78)
NIGNT	New International Greek New Testament
NovT	*Novum Testamentum*
NRT	*La nouvelle revue théologique*
NTM	New Testament Message
NTS	*New Testament Studies*
PTMS	Pittsburgh Theological Monograph Series
PTR	*Princeton Theological Review*
SBL	Society of Biblical Literature
SNTSMS	Society for New Testament Studies Monograph Series
TDNT	Gerhard Kittel and Gerhard Friedrich, eds., *Theological Dictionary of the New Testament* (trans. Geoffrey W. Bromiley; 10 vols; Grand Rapids: Eerdmans, 1964-)
TynB	*Tyndale Bulletin*
WBC	Word Biblical Commentary
WUNT	Wissenschaftliche Untersuchungen zum Neuen Testament
ZNW	*Zeitschrift für die neutestamentliche Wissenschaft*

Introduction

The book of Revelation is the most sensual document in the NT, filled with references to things seen, heard, smelled, touched, and even tasted! Its holistic sensory invitation has proven to be an embrace hard to resist for many, whether they be artists, musicians, preachers, filmmakers, visionaries, revolutionaries, ascetics, or religious enthusiasts. Yet its wide appeal, particularly on a popular level, is met with a skeptical response on the part of many with academic training in theology, who often write the book off as the domain of the lunatic fringe. For it is at the same time a book that purports to reveal things that shall soon take place, but its message is conveyed in such symbolic and cosmic language that there are nearly as many interpretations of the book as there are interpreters!

The purpose of this introduction is to aid readers in their reading of the text of Revelation and the commentary that follows. Here we give primacy of place to the text of the book and the introductory issues that arise from the text. The introduction begins with a section devoted to the structure and nature of Revelation, which gives way to an examination of what can be known about the audience of this book, and then on to issues of date and authorship. Owing to the effect of this text upon a wide variety of individuals, the introduction concludes with a section identifying some of the major streams of influence that can be traced back to Revelation.

Structure and Nature of the Book

Revelation is perhaps the most literarily complex and sophisticated document in the NT. A close reading reveals a vast array of extraordinarily impressive literary devices, which testify to the intricate design and brilliance of the

Introduction

work.¹ When discussing the literary character and structure of Revelation, it is important to remember that the document was apparently written to be heard while it was being read aloud (1:3). Part of the genius of the work is that the clues as to its structure seem to communicate at a couple of different levels. On the one hand, some of the literary devices are apparent on one's first exposure to the document; on the other hand, many of these dimensions emerge slowly as the book is repeatedly read and heard over a prolonged period of time. Like so many other aspects of the text of Revelation, the blessing promised to those who hear the words of this prophecy promises more than meets the eye (or ear, in this case). It is not an overstatement to say that each hearing or reading of Revelation brings discoveries of connections and nuances previously unnoticed. Given the breadth and depth of its imagery, little wonder that it has fueled the imagination of so many interpreters.

Literary Markers Recognized by a First-Time Hearer of Revelation

Several aspects of the structure emerge after an initial encounter with the text of Revelation. It is clear from an initial hearing of the book that Revelation begins with a prologue. From this prologue the hearer learns that this Apocalypse of Jesus Christ, given by God to John, is a prophecy that results in a blessing for those who read, hear, and keep the things written in it (1:3). After these initial words, the prologue proceeds with a formula normally found at the beginning of an epistle. Here the standard A (author) to B (recipient) greeting occurs, with John being identified as the author, and the seven churches in Asia as the recipients. The greeting continues in expanded Christian fashion with the bestowal of grace and peace upon the readers. The prologue moves to a doxology and concludes with two prophetic words.

Another feature of the book's structure, apparent from an initial encounter with the text, is the role and prominence of the Spirit. Soon after mention of the seven spirits before the throne (1:4), a pattern begins to emerge in which the Spirit plays a significant role. At four strategic locations (1:10; 4:2; 17:3; 21:10) the phrase ἐν πνεύματι (*en pneumati*, "in the Spirit") occurs. Each occurrence

---

1. The most extensive study of the structure of Revelation is that of R. Bauckham, *The Climax of Prophecy: Studies on the Book of Revelation* (Edinburgh: T&T Clark, 1993), 1-37. As will be apparent, much of what follows in this section is informed by this excellent essay. For a critique of Bauckham's work, cf. P. Prigent, *L'Apocalypse de Saint Jean* (CNT 14; Geneva: Labor & Fides, 2000), 71-74. For additional discussions on the structure of Revelation, cf. F. D. Mazzaferri, *The Genre of the Book of Revelation from a Source-Critical Perspective* (Berlin: Walter de Gruyter, 1989), 330-65, and D. E. Aune, *Revelation 1-5* (WBC 52A; Dallas: Word, 1997), xc-cv.

stands at the beginning of a new section of the book, and together they serve as the major structural markers in Revelation. Significantly, this phrase appears for the first time immediately after the close of the prologue.

Other major structural components one encounters in an initial hearing of Revelation are several series of sevens. There are seven prophetic messages to the seven churches of Asia (2:1–3:22), seven seals (6:1–8:5), seven trumpets (8:6–11:19), and seven plagues (15:1–16:21).[2] Obviously, these series are an important dimension of the text and contribute something to the overall structure of the book. In this regard, the first series of seven (messages) are unnumbered in their delineation and are not formally connected to the other series of sevens. It is also significant that this first series of sevens is followed immediately by the second occurrence of the phrase *en pneumati* ("in the Spirit"), indicating the beginning of a new section of Revelation. The other three series of sevens are each individually enumerated in their description (first, second, third, etc.), and each of these series is formally connected to the others. To illustrate by means of computer software language, when one clicks on the icon of the seventh seal, the seven trumpets appear (8:1-2). Likewise, though not quite as explicit, when one clicks on the icon of the seventh trumpet (11:15-19), following the interlude of chapters 12–14, the seven bowls emerge (15:1). Thus, it would appear that these three series of sevens stand together structurally in the book. Confirming this idea is, immediately after the seventh bowl of plagues is poured out, the phrase *en pneumati* occurring for a third time, indicating the onset of the next major section in Revelation.

Additional structural markers that first-time hearers of Revelation will notice come in the form of the interludes that appear between the sixth and seventh seals (7:1-17) and between the sixth and seventh trumpets (10:1–11:14). In each case, these interludes seem to interrupt the flow of the document, at the least delaying the action being described. At the same time, such interludes draw attention to significant theological aspects of the text.[3] Similarly, chapters 12–14 appear to interrupt the flow of the document, dividing the description of the seven trumpets (8:6–11:19) from that of the seven bowls (15:1–16:21). While chapters 12–14 do interrupt the flow of the document, they do have a structural significance, for they are connected thematically to the first two interludes, and the story line of 12–14 converges in 15:1 with the story line left off at 11:19. Suffice it to say at this point that these interludes would also make a structural impression upon first-time hearers of Revelation.

---

2. Reference is also made to seven thunders (10:3-4), but unlike the others mentioned, they are sealed up and not written down.

3. J. L. Resseguie, *The Revelation of John: A Narrative Commentary* (Grand Rapids: Baker, 2009), 53.

Introduction

Near the end of the book the hearer encounters a contrast between two cities: Babylon, the great whore (17:1–21:8), and New Jerusalem, the bride of Christ (21:9–22:5). These sections are each marked by one of the seven angels with bowls of plagues speaking to John (17:1; 21:9), the phrase *en pneumati* ("in the Spirit," 17:3; 21:10), and near-identical introductory statements (17:1-3; 21:9-10). Thus, the climax of the book is reached with a description of the destruction of Babylon and the descent from heaven and description of the New Jerusalem.

A final structural dimension of Revelation readily distinguishable to the first-time hearer is the book's concluding epilogue (22:6-21). Not only does the epilogue serve as a balance to the opening prologue, but numerous terms and themes found in the prologue also reappear in the epilogue, offering an inclusio effect for the hearer.

The following structure emerges from the above clues available to first-time hearers:

1:1-8	Prologue	
1:9–3:22	"In the Spirit on the Lord's Day"	
	1:9-20	The Inaugural Vision of Jesus
	2:1–3:22	The Seven Prophetic Messages to the Seven Churches of Asia
		2:1-7 To the Angel of the Church in Ephesus
		2:8-11 To the Angel of the Church in Smyrna
		2:12-17 To the Angel of the Church in Pergamum
		2:18-29 To the Angel of the Church in Thyatira
		3:1-6 To the Angel of the Church in Sardis
		3:7-13 To the Angel of the Church in Philadelphia
		3:14-22 To the Angel of the Church in Laodicea
4:1–16:21	"In the Spirit in Heaven"	
	4:1–5:14	The Inaugural Vision of Heaven, the One Who Sits on the Throne, the Lamb, and the Scroll Sealed with Seven Seals
	6:1–8:5	The Opening of the Scroll Sealed with Seven Seals
		6:1-17 The Opening of the First Six Seals
		7:1-17 The Interlude of the 144,000 and the Great Multitude
		8:1-5 The Opening of the Seventh Seal and the Golden Altar
	8:6–11:19	Seven Angels with Seven Trumpets
		8:6–9:21 The Sounding of the First Six Trumpets
		10:1–11:14 The Interlude of the Little Scroll and the Two Witnesses
		11:15-19 The Sounding of the Seventh Trumpet
	12:1–14:20	The Struggle of God's People in Cosmic Perspective

12:1–13:1a Signs in Heaven: The Woman Clothed with the Sun, and the Red Dragon
13:1b-18 The Two Beasts
14:1-20 The Lamb and the 144,000, the Harvest and the Winepress
15:1–16:21 Seven Angels with Seven Bowls of Plagues
15:1-8 Another Great Sign in Heaven: The Seven Angels
16:1-21 The Pouring Out of the Seven Bowls
17:1–21:8 "In the Spirit" — Carried to a Wilderness
17:1-18 The Woman on the Beast: Babylon the Whore
18:1-24 The Destruction of Babylon
19:1–21:8 From Babylon the Great to the New Jerusalem — from the Last Judgment to the New Creation
19:1-10 Rejoicing in Heaven and on Earth and the Marriage Supper of the Lamb
19:11-16 The King of Kings and Lord of Lords
19:17-21 Victory over the King's Enemies
20:1-6 The Thousand-Year Reign
20:7-10 Satan's Final Rebellion and Defeat
20:11-15 The Final Judgment
21:1-8 The Descent of the New Jerusalem
21:9–22:5 "In the Spirit" — Carried to a Great High Mountain: The Description of the New Jerusalem
22:6-21 Epilogue

Given this basic structure, which emerges from an initial exposure to Revelation, what other significant elements may be discerned from a more intensive engagement with the text? In addition to this broad structure, there are a number of places where the whole document, large sections, or smaller sections are connected to one another by means of similar or, in some cases, identical vocabulary or themes. For example, a comparison of the language of 1:1-3 with that of 22:6-7 reveals that these verses constitute an inclusio that bounds the entire book.

> The revelation of Jesus Christ, which God gave him to show his servants what must soon take place. He made it known by sending his angel to his servant John, who testifies to everything he saw — that is, the word of God and the testimony of Jesus. Blessed is the one who reads the words of this prophecy, and blessed are those who hear it and take to heart what is written in it, because the time is near. (1:1-3)

The angel said to me, "These words are trustworthy and true. The Lord, the God of the spirits of the prophets, sent his angel to show his servants the things that must soon take place." "Behold, I am coming soon! Blessed is he who keeps the words of the prophecy in this book." (22:6-7)

A variety of terms used to describe Christ near the beginning of the book — "his eyes were like flames of fire" (1:14; 2:18), "from his mouth came a sharp two-edged sword" (1:16; 2:12, 16), he will rule "with an iron scepter" (2:26-27), he is the "faithful and true witness" (3:14) — converge in one passage near its end in describing the King of Kings and Lord of Lords (19:11-16). A final example of a literary device that serves to hold the entire book together is the occurrence of seven beatitudes, found at various places throughout the book (1:3; 14:13; 16:15; 19:9; 20:6; 22:7, 14).

Not only does one find techniques that help knit the entire book together, one also sees a similar phenomenon within a major section of the book. An example occurs in 4:1–16:21. This section, which is devoted primarily to the three series of sevens, is held together in part by a recurring phrase that expands in intensity as the section unfolds. Specifically, the "flashes, sounds, and thunder" that come from the throne in 4:5 become the "thunder, sounds, flashes, and earthquake" that come to earth from heaven when the angel casts down fire from the altar in 8:5. And then when God's temple in heaven opens in 11:19, there come "flashes, sounds, thunder, earthquake, and great hail." This recurring theme culminates in 16:18-21 when, after a voice from the throne says "It is done," there come "flashes, sounds, thunder," an earthquake greater than any experienced on earth before, and hailstones weighing 100 pounds (ταλαντιαία, *talantiaia*) each. Significantly, these phenomena do not occur together elsewhere in the book. Similarly, the interlude of chapters 12–14 is bounded on either side by great signs in the heavens. The interlude begins with "a great sign was seen in heaven" (12:1), and its conclusion gives way to "and I saw another great and marvelous sign in heaven" (15:1). In like fashion the ending of one section and beginning of another section can be conveyed by the occurrence of the same phrase on two separate occasions. The close of the central major section (4:1–16:21) and beginning of the next section (17:1–21:8) are signaled by the appearance of "It is done" in 16:17, while the close of the latter and beginning of the final major section in the book (21:9–22:5) are likewise signaled by "It is done," in 21:6. Additionally, the same term can occur in a given section to convey a sense of movement from one ultimate domain to another. On seven occasions beginning with 13:1 through 15:2, the term εἶδον (*eidon* "I saw") occurs and is used to convey a sense of movement from the sea, beside which the dragon stood, to the sea of glass, beside which stood those who had been victorious over the beast. The text says:

> And I saw a beast coming *out of the sea.* (13:1)
> And I saw another beast coming *out of the earth.* (13:11)
> And I saw . . . the Lamb standing *upon Mount Zion.* (14:1)
> And I saw another angel flying *in mid-air.* (14:6)
> And I saw . . . one like the Son of Man sitting *upon a cloud.* (14:14)
> And I saw another great and marvelous sign *in heaven.* (15:1)
> And I saw what looked like *a sea of glass, beside which* were standing those who had been victorious over the beast. (15:2)

Another characteristic of the literary structure of Revelation is, on at least three occasions, two sections that come together at a transition point in the book overlapping with one another. This is the case where the seven seals give way to the seven trumpets (8:1-5), where the story line of the cosmic interlude converges with the story line of the seven bowls of plagues (15:1-4), and where the description of the New Jerusalem gives way to the epilogue (22:6-11). Such phenomena remind the hearer that, while major movements within the book may be discerned, the document stands together as a single visionary drama.

Revelation as Visionary Drama

Insofar as, through repeated hearings and readings of the book, the structure of Revelation emerges as a visionary drama, what would be conveyed to its hearers with regard to the kind of literature that is being heard and read? While differing aspects of this question receive more extensive treatment below, it is important initially to gain a sense of the way in which a hearer may have understood the document as a whole.

One of the first things evident to the hearer about the literary nature of Revelation is that it is designed for "oral enactment."[4] While it is legitimate to note that the document had to be read publicly owing to John's absence on Patmos, such an explanation of the act of reading does not take into sufficient account the dramatic characteristics of Revelation. At every turn, there are indications that the book is designed for oral enactment.[5] Evidence for this observation includes many of the literary features noted in the discussion with regard to the book's structure, but it is not confined to them. In addition

---

4. For this designation, cf. D. L. Barr, "The Apocalypse of John as Oral Enactment," *Int* 40 (1986): 243-56.

5. The following observations are based in large part on the work of Barr, "The Apocalypse of John as Oral Enactment," and S. S. Smalley, *Thunder and Love: John's Revelation and John's Community* (Milton Keynes, UK: Word, 1994), cf. esp. 103-10.

Introduction

to the utilization of various numbered series (sevens, threes, and twos), the multiple use of the *en pneumati* ("in the Spirit") phrase, and the employment of periodic interludes, there are numerous other indicators. For example, the images and places used to convey the message of the book are both intriguing and memorable. To this feature we might add the first person address of both John and Jesus, the generous use of hymns, and, at each stage of the book, a fuller revelation about Jesus. The liberal use of colors in Revelation tends to confirm that the work is designed for oral enactment. By way of illustration, the relatively colorless Fourth Gospel, which mentions only white and purple, pales in comparison with the colors of Revelation, which include gold/yellow, white, scarlet, red, purple, silver, green, and black. Given the dramatic characteristics of Revelation, some interpreters have gone so far as to argue that it was constructed to be staged in ways not unlike the Greek tragedies.[6]

The point of these observations is to underscore the fact that, first and foremost, the hearers and readers of Revelation would have experienced this document as the oral enactment of a visionary drama. It is important to take up the issue at this point, for discussions that attempt to ascertain the literary genre of Revelation sometimes lose sight of this rather basic understanding of the document.

Part of the power of this visionary drama is that it creates for its hearers and readers a symbolic world offering an alternate version of reality to that experienced by the Asian churches in the Roman world.[7] This alternate reality offers heaven as the vantage point from which to assess the reality of this world and its powers. The significance of such an alternate reality is difficult to overestimate, for it empowers its hearers and readers to confront their present reality as faithful witnesses who have an active role to play in the conversion of the nations, which lies before them. But there is more. The hearers and readers are not only invited to hear or view this symbolic world, but also to experience it by means of participation. For throughout this oral enactment, the hearers and readers find themselves responding vicariously along with John as he turns, sees, hears, and looks. As the visions of the one who sits on the throne and of the Lamb unfold, the hearers and readers find themselves in the spontaneous acts of worship that erupt on numerous occasions.

The logical place for such oral enactment is the context of worship within the

---

6. In addition to the work of Smalley, cf. E. Dansk, *The Drama of the Apocalypse* (London: T. Fisher Unwin, 1894); E. W. Benson, *The Apocalypse: An Introductory Study of the Revelation of St John the Divine* (New York: Macmillan, 1900), 4-41; R. R. Brewer, "The Influence of Greek Drama on the Apocalypse of John," *ATR* 18 (1935-36): 74-92; and J. W. Bowman, "The Revelation to John: Its Dramatic Structure and Message," *Int* 9 (1955): 436-53.

7. On this proposal, cf. R. Bauckham, *The Theology of the Book of Revelation* (Cambridge: Cambridge University Press, 1993), 10.

community. Not only would this be consistent with the common practice found across early Christianity of reading significant communiqués before the entire community (1 Thess 5:27; Eph 6:21; Col 4:16; Phlm 2), but it would also be the most appropriate context for hearing, testing, and discerning prophetic utterances. This would be true both of prophetic utterances of a spontaneous nature and of prophetic messages (including visions) that, while experienced outside the context of the community's worship, would be brought to it for the appropriate response.[8]

This phenomenological understanding of Revelation, as orally enacted visionary drama, goes a long way toward defining for the hearers and readers the kind of literature Revelation is. Within this understanding of how the hearers and readers would experience Revelation as visionary drama, other questions with regard to the issue of the literary genre of the book may be pursued.

Technically, this visionary drama takes the form of a circular letter to the seven churches of Asia (1:4, 11; 22:16). The book bears the marks of the standard A (author) to B (recipient) greeting near the beginning of the book (1:4) and concludes with the epistolary formula "May the grace of the Lord Jesus be with you all" (22:21). Although the content of Rev 2–3 is sometimes described as the seven letters to the seven churches, in point of fact Revelation is a single circular letter that includes seven prophetic messages to the seven churches of Asia. This literary device means that, while each church is informed by the specific message addressed to it, at the same time they are all informed by *all* the prophetic messages, which are to be read by all the churches. The theological reason that such a visionary drama takes the form of an epistle is owing to the command received by John in his inaugural vision.

> That which you see, write in a book and send it to the seven churches, to Ephesus and to Smyrna and to Pergamum and to Thyatira and to Sardis and to Philadelphia and to Laodicea. (1:11)

Among other things, the epistolary form, as does the command to write in a book everything seen, serves to reinforce the idea that this visionary drama stands together and is to be heard and read as a whole. John is told at the beginning to write down in a book all the things he sees, which conveys to the hearers and readers that John is to embark on a journey. For those who care to join him in this journey, perhaps his book will give the impression of being a travelogue.[9]

---

8. On the liturgical context of Revelation, cf. J.-P. Ruiz, *Ezekiel in the Apocalypse: The Transformation of Prophetic Language in Revelation 16,17–19,10* (EUSST 23; Frankfurt: Lang, 1989), 184-89.

9. For this idea, cf. R. W. Wall, *Revelation* (NIBC, NTS 18; Peabody, MA: Hendrickson, 1991), 13.

Introduction

Revelation as Christian Prophecy

A number of indicators in the text reveal that this visionary drama, which takes the form of a circular letter, is a piece of early Christian prophecy. Such an identification comes very early in the book, where John describes the volume as "the words of this prophecy" (1:3). This description is repeated near the close of the book as well, where again Revelation is referred to as "the words of this prophecy" (22:7). These phrases form an inclusio that bounds the book on either side, indicating how the entire epistle is to be heard and read. This identification of Revelation as a prophecy is also confirmed by the words of the angel who instructs John, "Do not seal up the words of this prophecy" (22:10). Finally, the book closes with a set of warnings that further underscore the book's description of itself as a prophetic book.

> I witness (to) all who hear the words of the prophecy of this book: if anyone adds unto them, God will add upon them the plagues written (described) in this book. And if anyone takes away from the words of the book of this prophecy, God will take away his part of the tree of life and the city of the saints (holy ones), which are written (described) in this book. (22:18-19)

Not only does the book describe itself as prophecy, but also a number of passages in the book look very much to be individual prophetic utterances. These include the following:

- the words of God in 1:8 — "I am the Alpha and Omega . . . who is, and who was, and who is to come";
- the prophetic messages of Jesus to the seven churches in 2:1–3:22;
- the words of the Spirit in 14:13 — "Yes," says the Spirit, "in order that they might rest from their labor; for their works follow after them";
- the words of Jesus in 16:15 — "Behold, I come as a thief! Blessed is the one who stays awake and keeps one's garments (pure), in order that he might not walk naked and they see his private parts"; and
- the numerous words of Jesus in 22:7-20.[10]

In addition to the overt descriptions of the book as prophecy and examples of prophetic utterances in the book, several textual indicators suggest that the context from which the book originates is itself a prophetic one. Mention is

---

10. Another possible prophetic utterance from the risen Jesus is found in 13:9-10, while 2:21 is sometimes taken as reference to an earlier (unrecorded) prophetic word given by John.

made in the book of at least one rival prophet(ess) (2:20). Other statements make it clear that John does not function alone in his prophetic activity, for he and others are addressed near the end of Revelation by an angel who says, "I am a fellow servant with you and your brothers the prophets" (22:9). This same group (possibly including the OT prophets) may well be in view a few verses earlier when the angel makes reference to "the Lord, the God of the spirits of the prophets" (22:6). Other references to these prophets in Revelation include 11:18; 16:6; 18:20, 24 (cf. also references to prophets in 10:7 and 11:10). Taken together, this textual evidence makes one thing very clear: the prophecy that is Revelation comes from a prophetic community. This fact, in and of itself, would add some understanding to the public reading of "the words of this prophecy" to the community.

Finally, it should also be noted that this prophecy has a number of affinities with OT prophecy. Not only does Revelation resemble a number of OT prophetic books in formal ways (i.e., by inclusion of call narratives and the emphasis upon the Word of God and the visions),[11] but it also exhibits a similar prophetic consciousness on the part of the author.[12] In fact, it appears that John so sees himself as heir to the OT prophetic tradition that he, as the OT prophets before him, inherits earlier prophecies, the reinterpretation of which figures prominently in his own prophecy. This may be illustrated by the way in which the prophecy concerning Babylon in Rev 18:1–19:8 echoes every message against Babylon found in the OT, as well as two messages against Tyre.[13] Owing to the many similarities between Revelation and the OT prophetic tradition, John's own sense of prophetic consciousness, and the scope and magnitude of Revelation, one writer has described the book as "the climax of prophecy."[14]

Revelation and the Apocalyptic Tradition

It is also clear from several aspects of the text of Revelation that there is some kind of relationship between Revelation and the apocalyptic tradition. In fact, for some interpreters the evidence for this is so strong that it is not uncommon to find commentaries that address the issue of apocalyptic as its first order of

---

11. On this issue, cf. esp. Mazzaferri, *The Genre of the Book of Revelation from a Source-Critical Perspective*, 259-378.

12. On the issue of prophetic consciousness, cf. the very helpful works by A. J. Heschel, *The Prophets* (2 vols.; Peabody, MA: Hendrickson, 2003), and R. D. Moore, "The Prophetic Calling: An Old Testament Profile and Its Relevance for Today," *JEPTA* 24 (2004): 16-29.

13. Bauckham, *The Theology of the Book of Revelation*, 5.

14. Cf. Bauckham, *The Climax of Prophecy*.

business.[15] What evidence is there for seeing a relationship between the two, and what is the nature of the relationship?

Perhaps one of the most significant clues that Revelation has strong connections to the apocalyptic tradition is its being the first document we know of to use the word ἀποκάλυψις (*apokalypsis*, "revelation") as part of its title. Whatever the relationship between this book of prophecy and the apocalyptic tradition may be, many later documents follow Revelation in using the word *apokalypsis* as part of its title. While there is some debate as to the precise meaning of the phrase "an apocalypse of Jesus Christ" (an issue that will be addressed later), it should be noted that there is some degree of circularity in assuming that this document, from which an entire genre of literature takes its name, is an apocalyptic document, merely because the word "apocalypse" is part of its title.[16]

Assessing the nature of the relationship between Revelation and the apocalyptic tradition is complicated because the broad boundaries and specific characteristics of the apocalyptic genre are anything but fixed; they are still greatly debated within the scholarly community.[17] Despite the inherent obstacles involved in ascertaining the relationship between Revelation and the apocalyptic tradition, perhaps the following observations will be of some assistance in sorting out this difficult issue.

First, it should be noted that Revelation is similar to the apocalyptic tradition in several respects. The fantastic imagery employed in Revelation, among other things, reminds one of the imagery of a number of other apocalyptic documents. This similarity suggests, at the least, that Revelation and a variety of apocalyptic documents draw from the same conceptual well.[18] Like the broader apocalyptic tradition, Revelation conveys a transcendent perspective about this world and its history, allowing hearers and readers the opportunity to view this world and its history from the perspective of heaven. Revelation also shares with other apocalyptic documents an interest in the question, Who is Lord over the world?[19] In addition, Revelation is decidedly eschatological in orientation.[20]

---

15. Cf., for example, J. Sweet, *Revelation* (London: SCM Press, 1990), 1-5.

16. For a similar point, cf. G. Linton, "Reading the Apocalypse as an Apocalypse," in *SBL Seminar Papers* (Atlanta: Scholars Press, 1991), 174-82.

17. Perhaps the most widely used set of criteria for defining the genre are those proposed by J. J. Collins, "Toward the Morphology of a Genre," *Semeia* 14 (1979): 1-20. Cf. also the perceptive comments of Linton, "Reading the Apocalypse as an Apocalypse," 178-85.

18. E. Schüssler Fiorenza, *Revelation: Vision of a Just World* (Minneapolis: Fortress Press, 1991), 23, notes, "Revelation employs stock images, conventional *topoi* or places, scriptural figures, and proofs, as well as literary techniques developed in apocalyptic literature."

19. Bauckham, *The Theology of the Book of Revelation*, 7-9.

20. Schüssler Fiorenza, *Revelation: Vision of a Just World*, 24-25.

At the same time, there are decided differences between Revelation and what has come to be known as the apocalyptic tradition. One of the best-known differences is that the author of Revelation writes in his own name, unlike the documents normally considered as part of the apocalyptic tradition, which are pseudonymous with regard to authorship. If Revelation is to be considered as part of the apocalyptic tradition, it stands virtually alone in this regard.[21] Perhaps this anomaly is to be explained by John's considering his work to be a book of prophecy, or perhaps it has something to do with his closer temporal proximity to the time of Jesus' earthly ministry.

Another difference between Revelation and the apocalyptic tradition is evident in the use of visual symbolism. Generally speaking, there is more visual symbolism in Revelation than (other) apocalyptic texts. At the same time, there is a virtual absence of angelic interpretation present in Revelation, as opposed to other apocalypses. Additionally, the generally short and self-contained vision normally found in only one part of an apocalyptic document virtually encompasses the whole of this one. A final difference is that, unlike the book of Daniel, for example — where Daniel is instructed by the angel to "close up and seal up the words of the scroll until the time of the end. . . . Go your way, Daniel, because the words are closed up and sealed until the end of time" (Dan 12:4, 9) — John is instructed, "Do not seal up the words of the prophecy of this book, because the time is near" (Rev 22:10).[22] Revelation is an open book rather than a closed one.

Given the differences and similarities of Revelation to the apocalyptic tradition, what might be concluded about the nature of their relationship? It is important to remember that the hearers and readers of this book would not make the kind of hard and fast distinctions between the prophetic and apocalyptic genres that contemporary students of Scripture sometimes do.[23] It is clear that John and his hearers would be familiar with a number of the symbols, imagery, and language found in apocalyptic documents of the time. However, the use of similar imagery does not necessarily imply a literary dependence but suggests that these ideas were in the air breathed by John and his audience. They often draw from the same conceptual well but utilize the concepts to suit their own purposes. In other words, regardless of the ambiguity surrounding the relationship of Revelation to the apocalyptic tradition, it appears that the hearers of Revelation would move easily in this apocalyptic conceptual world.[24]

21. The other possible exception to this practice also comes from a Christian writer, the Shepherd of Hermas.
22. Bauckham, *The Theology of the Book of Revelation*, 9-12.
23. G. K. Beale, *The Book of Revelation: A Commentary on the Greek Text* (NIGNT; Grand Rapids: Eerdmans, 1999), 37.
24. Bauckham, *The Climax of Prophecy*, 38-91. On the relationship between prophecy and

Introduction

Revelation as Intertext

If there are questions about the extent of the relationship of Revelation to the apocalyptic tradition, there are no such questions with regard to its relationship to the OT. Revelation is overflowing with OT imagery, ideas, and vocabulary. Yet, unlike in many NT documents, by most reckonings there is not a single direct quotation of the OT in this book. A reading of Revelation reveals that its utilization of the OT is not primarily concerned with respecting the OT context of a given idea, thought, or term.[25] At the same time, the hearer of Revelation soon discovers that the OT is more than a language arsenal from which the writer constructs his own theological statement or prophetic vision.[26]

Rather, the relationship between Revelation and the OT is a much more dynamic phenomenon. Revelation is better seen as an intertext where a variety of texts (including those of the writer, John!) converge and/or intersect. The intersection of OT texts, ideas, imagery, and vocabulary with John's visionary experience results in an intertext where echoes and allusions to the OT (among other things) provide shape and definition of meaning to the vision that is Revelation. Sometimes these allusions are like loud voices calling out to the hearers, while at other times they are no more than mere whispers to which the hearers' ears must be attuned or they will be missed altogether. Such a dynamic understanding of the relationship between Revelation and the OT means that no mere listing of allusions or echoes to the OT does justice to this dimension of Revelation. For everything found in Revelation is influenced, in one way or another, by the OT.[27] Specifically, one must ask how the OT context interacts with the NT context.[28] Discernment of these echoes and allusions is called for here, perhaps in ways not unlike the discernment called for in the receiving and recording of this prophecy by John and the task of the circle of prophets mentioned earlier. However, it is safe to say that any hearers or readers of Revelation who neglect the voice of the OT do so at their own peril.

---

apocalyptic, cf. the helpful comments by R. D. Moore, "Joel" (manuscript), 8-10, to appear in *The Book of the Twelve* (ed. J. C. Thomas; Blandford Forum, UK: Deo Publishing).

25. Contra Beale, *The Book of Revelation*, 76-99.

26. Contra E. Schüssler Fiorenza, *Revelation: Justice and Judgment* (Philadelphia: Fortress Press, 1985), 135.

27. Cf. the helpful comments by F. J. Murphy, *Fallen Is Babylon: The Revelation to John* (Harrisburg, PA: Trinity Press International, 1998), 28.

28. S. Moyise, *The Old Testament in the Book of Revelation* (JSNTS 115; Sheffield: Sheffield Academic Press, 1995), 19.

The Canonical Location and Function of Revelation

Whatever the historical events that resulted in the current New Testament canon, it is clear that the interpretive role and influence of a given book have significance within the structure of the overall canon. In this section we consider certain observations about the role and function of Revelation in the New Testament canon.

First, though, we should note that not all groups of Christians include Revelation as part of their canon.[29] It should also be observed that, while Revelation stands last in the vast preponderance of canonical lists, the book follows the Gospels in a few listings.[30] Two reasons may account for such a location. First, since Revelation contains so many words of the resurrected Jesus, we can understand how it made some sense to locate the book after the documents that give careful attention to his "pre-ascension" words.[31] At the same time, the close affinity that exists between the Fourth Gospel and Revelation may also account for the latter being drawn to a position in closer canonical proximity to the former.[32]

Owing to its unique standing as the last book in the biblical canon, Revelation functions on several canonical levels. The best way to approach this topic is perhaps to structure these canonical reflections in a way that moves from Revelation's function in connection with the books in closest canonical proximity to its broader function in the metanarrative of the whole Bible.

Revelation is quite obviously connected canonically to the Epistles, the documents that precede it in the NT; as noted earlier, it too takes the form of an epistle. In this regard, Revelation furthers a number of concerns and themes found among both the letters of Paul and those that come from other voices. Of the specific concerns addressed, Revelation continues the theme of false teaching that is more than of passing interest in a large number of the epistles. Among other things, Revelation makes clear both that false teaching is dangerous to the Christian community and that anyone who identifies with it will share in the destruction that awaits the evil triumvirate of Satan, the beast,

---

29. R. W. Wall and E. E. Lemcio, *The New Testament as Canon: A Reader in Canonical Criticism* (JSNTS 76; Sheffield: JSOT Press, 1992), 276, observe, "Today, there are still some non-Chalcedon (i.e., Nestorian) Christian communions who reject the canonicity of Revelation and follow the Peshitta, an ancient Syriac version of the Bible that excludes Revelation along with 2 Peter, 2-3 John, and Jude."

30. B. M. Metzger, *The Canon of the New Testament: Its Origin, Development, and Significance* (Oxford: Clarendon Press, 1987), 295.

31. Metzger, *The Canon of the New Testament*, 295.

32. A suggestion made by J. Painter in private conversation.

and the false prophet. Revelation also continues the emphasis of several of the epistles on the return of Jesus.

The canonical function of Revelation may also be seen in its connections to the Johannine literature that precedes in the NT. First, one of the great points of both continuity and development is the presentation of Jesus. On the one hand, the image of Jesus as the (paschal) Lamb of God found in the Fourth Gospel (1:29) also appears in Revelation (5:6). On the other hand, the revelation of Jesus in Revelation includes a development of this image to such an extent that it is not uncommon for students of Scripture to speak of the Wrath of the Lamb as a way of describing the Lamb's identity in this book.[33] Second, the pneumatology of the Fourth Gospel, which places a great deal of emphasis upon the role of the coming Paraclete,[34] and that of 1 John, where the Spirit's role in prophetic activity comes into focus,[35] gives way to a more full-blown prophetic pneumatology in Revelation.[36]

The canonical function of Revelation also extends to its relationship with the Gospels, located at the other end of the NT. The major sections devoted to the return of Jesus in Matthew (24–25), Mark (13), and Luke (21) in some ways serve to anticipate the more extended discussion of this topic in Revelation. Here too, the full implications of the Messiah's coming for both the Jewish people and the nations, announced in Matt 1, are made explicit in the imagery of Revelation (cf. especially the relationship between the 144,000 and the innumerable multitude in ch. 7).

In addition, the canonical function of Revelation can also be seen at the metanarrative level of the Bible. First, the book serves as a fitting conclusion to the story of humanity's rebellion against God. This story, which began so long ago in Genesis, is completed by a vision of God's reign and rule established completely. Second, in Revelation a number of God's purposes for his creation are redeemed, especially through the thousand-year reign. Third, in many ways Revelation functions as the fulfillment and completion of all biblical prophecy that came before it. Finally, through this book it becomes apparent that many of the judgments of God, which were longed for so long by his people, will not ultimately take place until the end of time.[37]

---

33. Sweet, *Revelation*, 50-52.

34. Cf. J. C. Thomas, *The Spirit of the New Testament* (Leiderdorp, Neth.: Deo Publishing, 2004), 157-74.

35. Cf. J. C. Thomas, *1 John, 2 John, 3 John* (London: T&T Clark, 2004), 13-14, 123-41, 197-214, 249-64.

36. Cf. R. C. Waddell, *The Spirit of the Book of Revelation* (JPTS 30; Blandford Forum, UK: Deo Publishing, 2006).

37. For some of these ideas about Revelation's canonical function on the level of metanarrative, cf. R. Wall, *The New Testament as Canon*, 280-82.

Audience

What might be known of the audience to whom these words of prophecy were written? Unlike a number of other NT letters (both circular and specific), the text of Revelation gives some specific information as to the identity of its intended audience. This information includes the names of the cities in Asia Minor where the churches are located to whom the seven prophetic messages are addressed in chapters 2–3.

Geographic Location — Asia Minor

The interpreter of Revelation has good reason to believe that the prophecy's intended audience includes churches in the cities of Ephesus, Smyrna, Pergamum, Thyatira, Sardis, Philadelphia, and Laodicea. This geographic location is confirmed by John's writing from the island of Patmos, which is just off the coast of Asia Minor in the Aegean Sea.

This listing of these specific cities informs the interpreter of Revelation in several ways. When these seven cities are located on a map of Asia Minor, one discovers that, in their textual order, they are not haphazardly arranged but take on a certain shape. One who follows the textual order of these cities on a map of Asia Minor would begin with Ephesus in the south, go due north to Smyrna, and then on due north to Pergamum. From Pergamum, the northernmost city in the list, one would go southeast to Thyatira, due south to Sardis, southeast to Philadelphia, and then southeast again to Laodicea. While there may be literary and theological reasons for this particular order, an issue to be taken up later, it is often noted that the textual order of these cities is owing to their location on an ancient trade and postal route.[38] (See map on page 18.)

This list of churches found in Revelation is informative in other ways as well. On the one hand, an examination of this list reveals that several of these cities are also known from other early Christian writings. Paul writes a (circular) letter to the church at Ephesus and indicates that he has written the church at Laodicea, instructing the church at Colossae to exchange letters with this congregation (Col 4:16). Ignatius is known to have written letters to the churches at Ephesus, Smyrna, and Philadelphia. Polycarp served as the bishop of Smyrna, while Melito functioned in that capacity at Sardis. On the other

---

38. Cf. the work of W. Ramsay (*The Seven Letters to the Seven Churches of Asia and Their Place in the Plan of the Apocalypse* [London: Hodder & Stoughton, 1904], 183-96), which has influenced a number of scholars on this topic.

Introduction

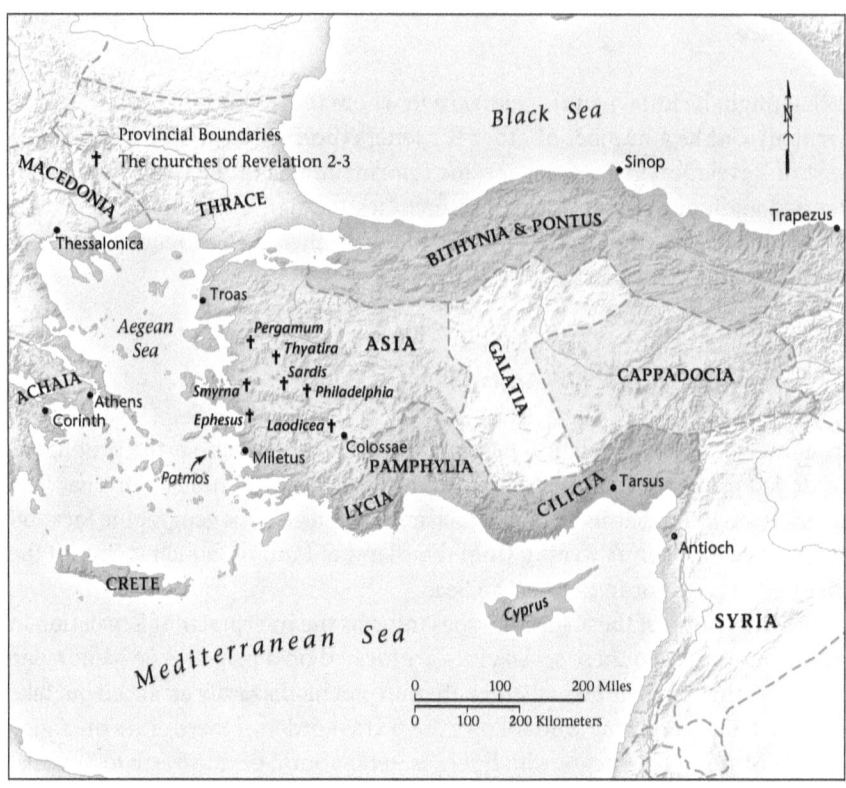

hand, other churches in Asia Minor were located in cities not mentioned in Revelation. Paul refers to the church in Hierapolis (Col. 4:13), where Papias later served as bishop, and Ignatius wrote letters to the churches in Tralles and Magnesia.[39]

John makes no mention of certain prominent churches and cities (Colossae, Hierapolis), while including others that seem to be less prominent within early Christian circles (Thyatira), which suggests that the seven churches listed in Revelation should not be taken to imply that he knows of these seven and no more. Rather, such selectivity suggests that these seven churches serve as representatives of other (unnamed) churches. Since seven is a sign of completion in Revelation, it appears that these seven churches represent all (Johannine) churches. Consequently, the mention of these seven churches suggests that Revelation is intended to be heard by all the churches of Asia Minor.

39. J. R. Michaels, *Interpreting the Book of Revelation* (Grand Rapids: Baker, 1992), 35-36.

The Johannine Community

Not only do the seven cities listed in Revelation reveal something about the book's intended audience, but the identity of the audience is also brought into sharper focus by inquiring as to the relationship of Revelation to other Johannine documents found in the NT. Specifically, the question may be asked, How is Revelation connected to what most scholars describe as the Johannine community?

Few NT works are more similar in expression than 1 John and the Fourth Gospel.[40] It thus appears likely from the close literary and theological affinities between the Fourth Gospel and the Johannine Epistles that these documents come from the same community or circle, if not the same hand. In the case of the Fourth Gospel, the Beloved Disciple is identified as the one who wrote these things, though it is clear from the third person language used that other hands were involved. In the case of 2 and 3 John, the author explicitly identifies himself as "the Elder," clearly an (if not *the*) authoritative leader in the community. It is likely that 1 John is also the result of the Elder's literary activity.[41] To speak of the Johannine community, then, is to speak of the individuals and congregations over which the Beloved Disciple and/or the Elder offered spiritual oversight.[42]

Three pieces of evidence suggest that Revelation and its audience(es) are part of this Johannine community. First, a careful comparison of the language of Revelation with that of the Fourth Gospel reveals that, although a number of linguistic differences exist between the two documents, they exhibit so many kinds of similarities that it is more than safe to assume these documents come from the same family or community.[43] Second, there are a number of points at which one can detect certain theological affinities between Revelation and the Johannine literature.[44] As noted earlier, both the Fourth Gospel

---

40. According to R. E. Brown, *The Epistles of John* (Garden City, NY: Doubleday, 1982), 21, not even Luke and Acts are as similar to one another as are 1 John and the Fourth Gospel!

41. For my thoughts on this issue, cf. Thomas, *1 John, 2 John, 3 John*, 4-10.

42. The most helpful work on this topic is M. Hengel's *The Johannine Question* (London: SCM Press; Philadelphia: Trinity Press International, 1989). Cf. also his more extensive treatment *Die johanneische Frage: Ein Lösungversuch* (Tübingen: J. C. B. Mohr [Paul Siebeck], 1993).

43. Cf. esp. the carefully detailed analysis by J. Frey, "Erwägungen zum Verhältnis der Johannesapokalypse zu den übringen Schriften des Corpus Johanneum," in *Die johanneische Frage*, by Hengel, with J. Frey, 326-429. Prigent (*L'Apocalypse de Saint Jean*, 26) describes Frey's work as follows: "L'étude, remarquablement documentée, bénéficie d'instruments de travail, notamment d'ordre statistique, qui manquaient à ses grands devanciers. Ses résultats sont donc plus précis, plus objectifs et donc plus fiables."

44. Y. Simoens, *Apocalypse de Jean: Apocalypse de Jésus Christ* (Paris: Éditions Facultés Jésuites de Paris, 2008), xii, and S. S. Smalley, *The Revelation to John* (Downers Grove, IL: InterVarsity Press, 2005), 4.

Introduction

and Revelation regard Jesus as the (paschal) Lamb of God. Though differently nuanced, the issue of witness or testimony is another point of theological affinity, as it is prominent in the Fourth Gospel, as well as Revelation.[45] There are also certain similarities of thought in these major Johannine documents reflected in the understanding of the unity and diversity of God. Third, an obvious indicator that Revelation is part of the Johannine community is the fact that all of these documents are either directly or indirectly tied to the name John, though Revelation is the only document in which the name appears in the text itself.[46]

OT Literature (Intertextuality)

The intertextual nature of the document also reveals something about the audience implied by Revelation. The frequency with which OT imagery and allusions appear within the book suggests that the hearers and readers are not only well versed in the OT (being expected at times to pick up on some very faint allusions) but that the Jewish Scriptures were revered as authoritative within the community. Such familiarity and respect suggest that the heritage of Israel is regarded in some sense as the heritage of the community as well.

People of the Spirit

In addition to being people of the OT, the text suggests that the readers are people of the Spirit as well. This aspect of the hearers' identity is supported by two pieces of textual evidence. It is clear that the hearers implied by the text have some understanding of the Spirit's activity. Such an understanding includes both the affinity the hearers appear to have with John's experiences of being "in the Spirit" at various points and the ability to discern pneumatic speech (2:7, 11, 17, 29; 3:6, 13, 22)[47] and to enter into "pneumatic [πνευματικῶς, *pneumatikōs*] interpretation" (11:8). Not unrelated to this awareness of the Spirit's activity is the prophetic activity that permeates the document. Not only is the audience aware of prophetic figures in its midst, but there are also indications

---

45. This important Johannine theme is also found in 1 John 1:2, 5:6-12, and 3 John 3, 6, 12.

46. On the significance of titles in NT documents, cf. M. Hengel, *Studies in the Gospel of Mark* (trans. J. Bowden; Philadelphia: Fortress Press, 1985), 64-84.

47. Cf. Ruiz (*Ezekiel in the Apocalypse*, 195-99), who goes on to suggest that several other verses (13:9-10, 18; 17:9, as well as 1:20; 10:7; 17:5, 7) are also evidence for this phenomenon (pp. 200-214).

that the hearers themselves are viewed as participants in such prophetic activity. Whether or not the text implies a belief in the "prophethood of all believers," it does suggest a deep level of participation within the community of a variety of (if not all) individuals.[48]

Women

Another dimension of the audience's identity appears to be revealed by the significant role that women play in Revelation. The first of four references to women in this book occurs early on, in 2:20, where reference is made to a woman named Jezebel, who speaks of herself as a prophetess but who actually teaches and deceives "my servants" to commit sexual immorality and eat food sacrificed to idols. That she represents a real person within the community is suggested by her being given an opportunity to repent, though she refuses to do so. This interpretation is confirmed by the judgment that awaits her and her children. Despite the symbolic nature of her name (what the resurrected Jesus calls her, "Jezebel," as opposed to what she calls herself, "prophetess"), her existence reveals that the prophetic figures in this prophetic community include women. For she is condemned, owing not to her gender, but to her deception. The next reference to a female occurs in Rev 12, where we find reference to a woman clothed with the sun. While her identity is debated, her strategic location in salvation history is clear. Somewhat like psychedelic imagery, this woman changes forms as she conveys characteristics of a variety of female figures to include Eve, Israel, Mary, and the church. The third female image to appear in Revelation is found in Rev 17–18, Babylon the great whore. This image gives way in Rev 19 and following to the bride of Christ, New Jerusalem.

Such depictions indicate that women are included within the audience implied by this text, confirming the picture of the role of women within the Johannine community that emerges from an examination of the Fourth Gospel, where every female character serves as an exemplary model of belief. Though Revelation includes negative images of women, they are never denigrated because of their gender but are assessed on the basis of their behavior and relationship to God.[49]

---

48. Cf. esp. the helpful discussion by D. Hill, *New Testament Prophecy* (Atlanta: John Knox Press, 1979), 87-93, and P. Poucouta, "La mission prophétique de l'Église dans l'Apocalypse johannique," *NRT* 110 (1988): 38-57.

49. The reference to those "not defiled by women" in 14:4 is taken up in detail in the commentary below.

Introduction

Witness and Persecution

The prominence of the theme of witness or testimony against the backdrop of a hostile environment implies that at least certain parts of the intended audience of Revelation are familiar with the necessity of bearing witness in the face of opposition and the distinct possibility that such activity could lead to various forms of persecution, including death. While it might be going too far to say that the entire community experienced persecution, and while the external evidence for the extent of such persecution is very much debated, the text makes clear that the audience is familiar with persecution owing to their witness. One of the primary pieces of evidence for this conclusion is the way in which the prominent witnesses within Revelation all experience death. This theme begins in 1:5 with the description of Jesus Christ, who is called ὁ μάρτυς ὁ πιστός (*ho martys ho pistos*, "the faithful witness"). The fact that being a "faithful witness" involves death is made clear in the next phrase, which describes him as "the firstborn of the dead." That such "faithful witness" is not confined to the work of Jesus but extends to his followers as well is confirmed in 2:13 by mention of Antipas, ὁ μάρτυς μου ὁ πιστός μου (*ho martys mou ho pistos mou*, "my faithful witness"). In order that the point not be missed, the relationship between "faithful witness" and death is again underscored in the text, where the reference to Antipas is followed by the words "who was put to death among you." Lest it be thought that Antipas's "faithful witness" was a one-off event, Rev 11:1-13 speaks of two witnesses who are protected by God until their witness is completed, at which point the beast overcomes and kills them (v. 7). They, like their Lord, are vindicated by being raised from the dead and taken up to heaven while their enemies look on (vv. 11-13). This theme of the cost of faithful witness may also be found in the poetic words about believers found in 14:4, where it is said, "These follow the Lamb wherever he leads."

In addition to the connection between faithful witness and death is John's own appearance on Patmos, which was because of "the word of God and the testimony of Jesus." Several times in the seven prophetic messages of chapters 2–3, there are indications that the hearers have experienced or will experience opposition owing to their belief. This includes hardships (2:3), afflictions, slander, imprisonment (2:8-10), death (2:13), and little strength (3:8). To this evidence might be joined the admonitions to "overcome" found at the end of each prophetic message (2:7, 11, 17, 26-28; 3:5, 12, 21), the words of encouragement to the hearers found at various points throughout the book (13:9; 14:13; 16:15), and the frequent reference to those who have given their lives, shed their blood, or were "warred against" for the sake of the Lamb (6:9-11; 7:14-17; 12:17; 14:12; 16:6; 17:6; 18:24; 19:2; 20:4-6). While questions remain about the extent of the community's acquaintance with persecution, the audience envisioned by the text appears to understand that their identification with the testimony of Jesus could and perhaps would lead to persecution.

Opponents and Opposition

If the text of Revelation suggests that persecution and suffering are part of the audience's horizon, what does it reveal about the source of this opposition? This question must be answered in two parts, for the text envisions the antagonists in cosmic terms that take concrete expression in the world of the audience.

Cosmic Opposition

On the cosmic level, the opposition faced by the community is primarily the evil triumvirate of Satan, the beast, and the false prophet (the other beast). At many points this evil trinity parodies what is said of the one who sits on the throne, the Lamb, and the seven Spirits of God. The ultimate figure standing behind the opposition to the believers is Satan. In two texts (12:9; 20:2) he is identified more fully as the great dragon, the ancient serpent, the devil. He orchestrates religious opposition by means of "the synagogue of Satan" in Smyrna (2:9) and Philadelphia (3:9). Not only is he able to cause the church to suffer by having some of them imprisoned (2:10), but also, in a parody of God, he has a throne, and where he lives is where "my faithful witness" Antipas died (2:13). Apparently, his "deep secrets" are the source of false teaching (2:24). Satan is the one who opposes and seeks to destroy the woman clothed with the sun, her male child, and the rest of her seed (12:1-13). However, he loses his place in heaven at the hands of Michael (12:7-12), an event that fills him with fury to oppose more completely the church (12:12). As a result, the dragon gives his power and throne and great authority to the beast (13:2), which results in worship of the dragon and the beast (13:4). The relationship between the dragon and the other beast is indicated by the latter's speaking like a dragon (13:11). The unity of the dragon, the beast, and the false prophet is underscored by demon spirits coming from each of their mouths performing miraculous signs (16:13). Satan's work is that of deceiving the nations (20:3, 7-8). However, he is thrown into the Abyss for a thousand years (20:2) and ultimately into the lake of fire (20:7-10).

Satan is joined in opposing God and his people by the beast, whose very first mention is in connection with killing the two witnesses who prophesy in 11:7. There the beast comes up from the Abyss, but in 13:1 he comes up out of the

Introduction

sea. Receiving his power from the dragon, he parodies the Lamb by having a fatal head wound that is healed (13:3) and, like the dragon, is worshipped (13:4), a practice facilitated by the other beast (13:11-17). The number of the beast is 666 (13:18), but those who receive his mark will be punished by God (14:9-11; 16:2), as will the beast himself (16:10). By way of contrast, the beast, his image, and his number are overcome by those standing beside the sea of glass (15:2). The relationship of the beast to Babylon the Great, the mother of whores, is made clear in chapter 17, where the woman is found riding the back of the beast (vv. 3, 7). The astonishment he causes is because, in a parody of God, he is described with the words "he was, he is, and he comes" (vv. 8, 11). His close relationship with the ten kings who have not yet received a kingdom is also underscored (vv. 11-14, 16-17). However, the beast's opposition to the Lamb is futile, as he is thrown into the lake of fire (19:20), sharing Satan's fate (20:10), while those put to death by him "live and reign" (20:4).

The third member of the evil triumvirate, the "other beast," comes up out of the earth. Looking like a lamb and sounding like a dragon, his authority comes from the first beast, which he uses to cause all the earth's inhabitants to worship the first beast, going so far as to set up an image of the beast, which he causes to speak (13:11-15). He performs great signs, causing fire to fall from heaven, deceiving the inhabitants of the earth (v. 14). His efforts result in a complete control of economic activity, so that anyone wishing to buy or sell must have the mark of the beast in one's hand or on one's forehead (vv. 16-17). Along with the dragon and the beast, demon spirits come from the mouth of "the false prophet" (16:13), and he shares their fate in the lake of fire (19:20; 20:10).

Joining the evil triumvirate as the other major cosmic opponent in Revelation is Babylon the Great, who is identified as ἡ μήτηρ τῶν πορνῶν (*hē mētēr tōn pornōn*, "the mother of sexual immorality"). She sits upon many waters (peoples, multitudes, nations, and languages). Elaborately dressed (17:4), she is drunk on the blood of the saints (v. 6), committing sexual immorality with the nations and kings of the earth (18:3), though she is eventually betrayed by her "partners" (17:16-17). She is the great city that rules over the kings of the earth. Her destruction and the mourning it causes are described in some detail in chapter 18.

Concrete Expressions of Opposition

The opposition faced by the audience also takes concrete expression in the text of Revelation. While all opposition is understood to have a cosmic explanation, at numerous points it is possible to discern certain concrete expressions of the opposition faced by the church. These primarily take three forms. First, at any number of places it appears that the image of Rome is discernible. Perhaps the most likely example of such a reference comes in chapter 17, where the seven heads of the beast upon which the woman, Babylon the Great, sits are seven hills. The reference to the seven hills of Rome may well be present. The mention that these seven hills are seven kings may also be a possible allusion to Roman rulers, especially with the mysterious words that "five have fallen, one is, and the other is yet to come" (17:10). The relationship between the beast and Nero, who both suffer fatal head wounds, may also direct the readers' attention to Rome and its opposition to the church.[50] Finally, there also appears to be a rather direct, scathing economic critique of Rome and its power in chapter 18.[51]

There are also hints that the audience of Revelation faced concrete opposition in the form of its relationship with the Jewish community. As already noted, the audience of Revelation appears to have a clear appreciation for its Jewish heritage. Not only does its presumed familiarity with the OT point in this direction, but also the way in which certain "Christian" details are grounded in Jewish roots. At the same time, there is clear tension reflected in the book with the broader Jewish community. The pejorative description "the synagogue of Satan," found twice (2:9; 3:9), carries with it the accusation that there were those who claimed to be Jews but were not. The church at Smyrna is slandered by this "Jewish" community (2:9). This group may even have been regarded as having the power to cause the imprisonment of members of the church (v. 10). The opposition offered the church at Philadelphia by this "Jewish" community is such that the risen Christ speaks words of vindication (3:9). While it might be going too far to argue that the audience of Revelation as a whole is in a struggle with the Jewish community, it seems reasonable to suggest that it is in some conflict with the broader Jewish community, revolving around the issue of identity.

A final concrete expression of opposition to the audience is perhaps the clearest of the three, namely, the threat of false teaching, false prophets/prophetesses, false apostles, and immoral behavior. In point of fact, it appears from the seven prophetic messages in Rev 2–3 that the churches are beset by these problems more than by any other opposition. The church at Ephesus is praised for not tolerating evil individuals, testing those who claimed to be apostles but were not (2:2), and hating the works of the Nicolaitans (2:6). Conversely, the church at Pergamum is rebuked for having some in its midst who keep the teaching of Balak (idolatry and sexual immorality) and the teaching of the Nicolaitans (2:14-15). The church at Thyatira struggles with the woman who

---

50. Cf. Bauckham, *The Climax of Prophecy*, 384-452.
51. Cf. Bauckham, *The Climax of Prophecy*, 338-83.

Introduction

calls herself a prophetess but whom the risen Jesus calls Jezebel (2:20-25). Her works include sexual immorality and eating food sacrificed to idols. Those who commit sexual immorality with her will be punished with her. The theme of false teaching and false prophecy continues as Revelation describes the activities of the dragon, the beast, the false prophet, and the great whore. The temptation of the church to capitulate to these activities is conveyed in part by John's astonishment at the appearance of Babylon the Great (17:6). When the inhabitants of the world saw the healing of the beast's wounded head, they were astonished and in turn worshipped the beast (13:3-4). When John saw the great whore, he was astonished and was immediately rebuked by the angel, who asked, "Why are you astonished at her?" and then explained the mystery of the woman (17:6-7). Clearly, such opponents were an ongoing part of the reality faced by the audience of Revelation.

Date

The date of Revelation is a notoriously difficult issue to sort out, for the evidence may be read in at least three different ways. The dominant view for the better part of eighteen centuries was that the document was written sometime during the reign of Domitian (81-96 CE). In the last century a fair number of scholars held that the book emerged earlier, at the time of the emperor Nero (sometime between 64 and 70 CE). A still more recent proposal has sought to combine the evidence for both of these views, arguing that the vision was experienced sometime during the time of Nero but was written down much later, during the time of Domitian. What accounts for such wide divergence of dates among interpreters? Part of the answer to this question is the uncertainty that accompanies almost every piece of relevant evidence. One soon discovers that the interpretive challenges one faces, as with so many other aspects of Revelation, are no less great here.

Internal Indicators

Given its similarities at a number of points to the OT prophetic literature, it is somewhat surprising to find that in Revelation there is an absence of any internal dates, unlike some of the prophetic literature. This is all the more surprising in the light of John's naming himself as the author rather than using a pseudonym, an unusual if not unique phenomenon among apocalyptic documents. Yet despite this lack of internal references to date, several texts within

Revelation could provide textual clues that may reveal something about the date of the document. While more extensive exploration of the verses in question must await discussion in the commentary proper, we briefly survey each clue here. Some of the more prominent include:

- the mention of seven kings in Rev 17:9-11,
- the present tense reference to the temple in Jerusalem in 11:1,
- the use of the term Babylon to refer to Rome,
- the relationship between the beast with the wounded head and the legend that Nero would return,
- the use of the language "the twelve apostles" in 21:14,
- the identity of the persecutor of the church,
- the relationship of the worship of the beast and emperor worship in chapter 13, and
- the Sitz im Leben of the seven churches in chapters 2–3.

On the face of it, one of the clearest internal indicators with regard to date is the mention of seven kings in Rev 17:9-11. Of the seven kings, who are the seven hills upon which the great whore sits, "five have fallen, one now is, the other is not yet," and when this one comes, it is necessary for him to remain a little while. The beast who was and is not, is an eighth king, being one of the seven. Since this list may be thought to refer to Roman leaders (i.e., the seven hills), it might seem a simple matter to count down the list of Roman emperors until one arrives at the sixth one — and now we have discovered the date of composition. A number of complications, however, face the interpreter, as the chart[52] on page 28 reveals:

The chart lists all the Roman emperors from Julius Caesar to Trajan, while the letters across the top of the chart represent different ways in which the emperors may be numbered. Does one begin with Julius Caesar (as in A, B, and H) or Augustus (as in C and D) or Gaius (as in E) or Nero (as in F) or Galba (as in G)? Are the three so-called minor emperors included (as in A, C, E, F, and G) or excluded (as in B, D, and H)? Does one count only those emperors deified by the Roman Senate or who claimed divinity for himself (as in H)? From an examination of the list, it is apparent that a variety of attempts can be made to determine which figure is to be identified as the sixth king, with little scholarly consensus. Suffice it to say that the reference to the seven kings in Rev 17 is not

---

52. This chart is a slight modification of one by D. E. Aune, "Notes to 'Revelation to John (Apocalypse),'" in *Harper Collins Study Bible* (New York: HarperCollins, 1993), 2330, also cited by Murphy, *Fallen Is Babylon*, 44.

Introduction

Roman Emperor	A	B	C	D	E	F	G	H
Julius Caesar (101-44 BCE)	1	1						1
Augustus (27 BCE–14 CE)	2	2	1	1				2
Tiberius (14-37 CE)	3	3	2	2				
Gaius (37-41 CE)	4	4	3	3	1			
Claudius (41-54 CE)	5	5	4	4	2			3
Nero (54-68 CE)	6	6	5	5	3	1		
Galba (June 68-Jan 69 CE)	7		6		4	2	1	
Otho (Jan-Apr 69 CE)	8		7		5	3	2	
Vitellius (Apr-Dec 69 CE)			8		6	4	3	
Vespasian (Dec 69-June 79 CE)	7		6	7	5	4	4	
Titus (79-81 CE)		8		7	8	6	5	5
Domitian (81-96 CE)				8		7(8)	6	6
[Neronic antichrist]							7(8)	
Nerva (96-98 CE)								7(8)
Trajan (98-117 CE)								

sufficient by itself to determine the date of the book's composition. Rather, one might observe that, if one can determine the date of the book on other terms, the list of kings can be manipulated to fit it.

Mention of the temple in Rev 11 might also be thought to help establish the date of Revelation. The present tense reference to the temple could suggest that it was still standing in Jerusalem at the time of the book's composition, thus, arguing for a date of composition before 70 CE. This literal reading of the text, however, does not square with the details, for the dimensions of the temple described in chapter 11 reveal that this temple is not the Herodian structure but appears to resemble the one described in Ezek 40–48.[53] Neither is it altogether clear that the temple described in Rev 11 is actually located in Jerusalem.

The use of the term Babylon to refer to Rome might also have some bearing on the topic of date, since it appears that such references to Rome do not appear in apocalyptic documents until after 70 CE. Part of this suggestion seems to be based upon the parallel of Babylon destroying Jerusalem in 586 BCE and now, a second time, Babylon (Rome) destroying Jerusalem.[54] While such evidence would seem to indicate that the book was written after 70, a reference to "Babylon," apparently with reference to Rome, is found in 1 Pet 5:13, a book widely thought to have been written in the 60s.

---

53. Beale, *The Book of Revelation*, 21.
54. Beale, *The Book of Revelation*, 18-19.

Another tantalizing reference in the text with regard to establishing the date of the book is the reference to the beast with the wounded head that has been healed (13:3, 12). On one level, the reference is a clear parody of the Lamb who looked as if he had been slain in chapter 5, but on another level numerous interpreters have seen a not-so-subtle reference to a legend that emerged sometime after Nero's death that he would come back to life. Obviously, this myth could not have occurred before Nero's death in 68 CE. It appears, however, that this rumor did not circulate widely until near the end of the first century, when various impostors turned up claiming to be Nero![55]

It is also possible that the phrase "the twelve apostles" occurring in the description of New Jerusalem in 21:14 reveals something about the date of Revelation. Here several points should be made. While reference to "the Twelve" does appear on occasion in the Fourth Gospel (6:67, 70-71; 20:24), in the Johannine literature there are no occurrences of the term ἀπόστολος (*apostolos*, "apostle"), except for its proverbial use in John 13:16, outside of Revelation, where it occurs three times: in Rev 2:2, referring to those who claimed to be apostles but were not, and in 18:20 and 21:14. At the same time, while the term "apostle" occurs frequently in other strands of NT thought, the term "the twelve apostles" is relatively rare, occurring only in Matt 10:2 and the textually uncertain Luke 9:1 and 22:14. The term is also found in the title of the *Didache*.[56] Taken together, this evidence appears to indicate that the designation appears for the first time in the last quarter of the first century CE, perhaps implying a later date for Revelation.

As noted earlier, the audience envisioned by the text of Revelation is one familiar with persecution. If the specific persecution that lies behind the text were identifiable, it would be possible to be more certain about the date of the document. Before looking at specific examples of persecution, it should be remembered that the extent of the persecution envisioned by the text is not altogether clear. While in the seven prophetic messages some persecution has been experienced and more is anticipated, for the most part, the suffering of the Christians comes from the hands of the "Jewish community" rather than the Romans.[57] However, if Roman persecution is part of the landscape, as the book may suggest, then two primary options present themselves.

It is well known that Nero initiated a severe persecution of Christians. According to Tacitus (*Annals* 15.44), in order to divert the blame from himself for the fire that devastated Rome, Nero blamed and persecuted the Christians:

---

55. On this whole question, cf. Bauckham, *The Climax of Prophecy*, 407-41.
56. Aune, *Revelation 1-5*, lxiv.
57. Aune, *Revelation 1-5*, lxvi.

Introduction

Therefore, to scotch the rumour, Nero substituted as culprits, and punished with the utmost refinements of cruelty, a class of men, loathed for their vices, whom the crowd styled Christians. Christus, the founder of the name, had undergone the death penalty in the reign of Tiberius, by sentence of the procurator Pontius Pilatus, and the pernicious superstition was checked for a moment, only to break out once more, not merely in Judea, the home of the disease, but in the capital itself, where all things horrible or shameful in the world collect and find a vogue. First, then, the confessed members of the sect were arrested; next, on their disclosures, vast numbers were convicted, not so much on account of arson as for hatred of the human race. And derision accompanied their end: they were covered with wild beasts' skins and torn to death by dogs; or they were fastened on crosses, and when daylight failed were burned to serve as lamps by night. Nero had offered his Gardens for the spectacle, and gave an exhibition in his Circus, mixing with the crowd in the habit of a charioteer, or mounted on his car. Hence, in spite of a guilt which had earned the most exemplary punishment, there arose a sentiment of pity, due to the impression that they were being sacrificed not for the welfare of the state but to the ferocity of a single man.[58]

Suetonius (*Nero* 16.2) simply observes, "Punishment was inflicted on the Christians, a class of men given to a new and mischievous superstition."[59]

Clearly these texts indicate that a persecution of Christians did take place under Nero, a figure who could be called or likened to a beast in non-Christian documents[60] and about whom a legend arose of his return after his death. This sort of evidence makes an early date appealing. However, evidence for a persecution that extends to Asia (Minor), leading to exile, is still not forthcoming for this period. Consequently, while appealing, such evidence does not prove conclusive with regard to the date of Revelation.

There is also some evidence of a persecution of Christians under Domitian. In addition to the uncomplimentary picture of Domitian that emerges from the Roman historians Tacitus and Suetonius, there are a few other pieces of relevant information. Melito of Sardis (quoted in Eusebius, *Ecclesiastical History* 4.26.9-10) reminds his reader, Marcus Aurelius, that Christians got on quite well with Rome for the most part, with two ominous exceptions: "The only emperors who were ever persuaded by malicious men to slander our teaching

---

58. Cited according to the translation of J. Jackson, *Tacitus*, vol. 4 (London: Heinemann, 1962), 283-85.

59. Cited according to the translation of J. C. Rolfe, *Suetonius*, vol. 2 (London: Heinemann, 1965), 111.

60. Cf. Philostratus, *Life of Apollonius* 4.38, and perhaps the *Sibylline Oracles* 5.343.

were Nero and Domitian, and from them arose the lie, and the unreasonable custom of falsely accusing Christians. But their ignorance was corrected by your pious fathers, who wrote many rebukes to many, whenever they dared take new measures against Christians."[61]

Tertullian (*Apology* 5.4) specifically states that Domitian was involved in the persecution of Christians but that he eventually relented: "Domitian, too, a man of Nero's type in cruelty, tried his hand at persecution; but as he had something of the human in him, he soon put an end to what he had begun, even restoring again those whom he had banished."[62]

The closest one comes geographically to evidence of a persecution of Christians in Asia (Minor) is found in the written correspondence between Pliny, Trajan's legate in Bithynia, and the emperor (Pliny's *Letters*, 10.46-47). These letters reveal several things about the nature of the persecution. It is clear from the correspondence that Pliny is not at all certain about how to proceed with his interrogations and decisions, indicating that there was no formal policy on the matter, a fact that Trajan confirms in response. It is also obvious that a number of Christians had been put to death as a result of the investigations. Not only were suspects interrogated, but some were also tortured in order for Pliny to get to the truth of the matter. Pliny indicates that formal worship of Trajan's statue and the images of the gods, along with cursing Christ, was treated as sufficient evidence that such ones were no longer considered Christian, a strategy with which Trajan agrees. This evidence, which may be dated somewhere around 111 CE, is almost fifteen years removed from the reign of Domitian. Unlike the evidence regarding Nero and Domitian, however, this evidence of persecution is not far removed geographically from the churches mentioned in Revelation.

It may be tentatively concluded that, while the evidence for persecution at various periods might be of some assistance in constructing general attitudes with regard to the persecution of Christians in this general time frame, it does not in and of itself settle the issue of the date of Revelation.

The emphasis upon worship of the dragon and beast, combined with the implicit identification of the beast with Rome, might be taken as evidence that, at the time of the book's composition, the community was faced with enforced emperor worship. Part of the problem in using this topic to gain leverage on the issue of date is that solid evidence for such a practice is very late. In point

---

61. Cited according to the translation of K. Lake, *Eusebius*, vol. 1 (London: Heinemann, 1926), 391. Cf. also Melito Fragment 1 in *Melito of Sardis: On Pascha and Fragments* (ed. and trans. S. G. Hall; Oxford: Clarendon Press, 1979), 65.

62. Cited according to the translation in *The Writings of Tertullian*, vol. 1 (ed. A. Roberts and J. Donaldson; Edinburgh: T&T Clark, 1869), 64. This passage from Tertullian is also cited by Eusebius (*Ecclesiastical History* 3.19-20).

of fact, Pliny offers the earliest unequivocal testimony of such a practice, and even it does not seem yet to be a formal practice. This is not to suggest that such temptation was not part of the audience's horizon, but again to note that such a possibility does not settle the issue of date.

Finally, it is possible that the condition of the seven churches described in chapters 2-3 could provide clues as to the date of the document's composition.[63] Such an investigation is notoriously dangerous and fraught with the challenges of getting the interpretive "cart before the horse," creating a life setting to read the text over against. While it is possible that these descriptions can bring clarity to a variety of issues once a date has been established, such an approach cannot speak definitively to the issue.

The ambiguity of much of the internal evidence thus makes a decision with regard to date difficult if not impossible. There are so many uncertainties and the attempt to reconstruct the original life setting so hypothetical that certainty on the matter is perhaps beyond the reach of the interpreter. On balance, however, the internal evidence tends to favor a later date of composition, if only slightly.

External Evidence

The external evidence is hardly more helpful than the ambiguity of the internal textual indicators with regard to date. What may be said with certainty is that Revelation was known to exist by 135 CE, based on the words of Justin Martyr in *Dialogue with Trypho* (81.4):

> And further, there was a certain man with us, whose name was John, one of the apostles of Christ, who prophesied, by a revelation that was made to him, that those who believed in our Christ would dwell one thousand years in Jerusalem; and that thereafter the general, and, in short, the eternal resurrection and judgment of all men would likewise take place.[64]

It is also possible that Revelation was known by Papias, who is cited as bearing witness to its genuineness by Andreas of Caesarea in his *Preface to Revelation*, written sometime in the sixth or seventh century.

---

63. Cf. C. J. Hemer, *The Letters to the Seven Churches of Asia in Their Local Settings* (JSNTS 11; Sheffield: JSOT Press, 1986), 2-5.

64. Cited according to the translation found in *The Ante-Nicene Fathers*, vol. 1 (ed. A. Roberts and J. Donaldson; Grand Rapids: Eerdmans, 1989), 240.

Regarding, however, the divine inspiration of the book [i.e., the Revelation of John], we think it superfluous to speak at length, since the blessed Gregory (I mean the Theologian) and Cyril, and men of an older generation as well, namely Papias, Irenaeus, Methodius, and Hippolytus, bear witness to its genuineness.[65]

If this testimony does indeed go back to Papias, it would indicate that Revelation was known to exist perhaps as early as 115 CE. While Irenaeus (*Against Heresies* 2.22.5; 3.3.4) states that John lived into the time of Trajan, Clement of Alexandria (quoted in Eusebius's *Ecclesiastical History* 3.23.5-6; cf. also Clement's *Who Is the Rich Man That Is Saved?* 42) gives some evidence as to the timing of John's days on Patmos when he notes:

> For after the death of the tyrant he passed from the island of Patmos to Ephesus, and used also to go when he was asked, to the neighbouring districts of the heathen [ἐθνῶν], in some places to appoint bishops, in others to reconcile with whole churches, and in others to ordain some one of those pointed out by the Spirit.[66]

From the context, it appears that the tyrant in question is Domitian. Such a statement would suggest that Revelation was written (or experienced) sometime during the reign of Domitian (81-96 CE). This testimony would appear to be in agreement with Irenaeus's statement (*Against Heresies* 5.30.3), which seems to place the appearance of Revelation in the reign of Domitian:

> If it were necessary that his [the antichrist's] name should be distinctly revealed in this present time, it would have been announced by him who beheld the apocalyptic vision. For that was seen no very long time since, but almost in our day, toward the end of Domitian's reign.[67]

All in all, the external evidence is quite meager but would appear to confirm, if ever so slightly, suspicions that Revelation was written down near the end of the first century CE.[68]

---

65. Cited according to the translation of M. W. Holmes, *The Apostolic Fathers: Greek Texts and English Translations* (Grand Rapids: Baker, 1992), 577.
66. Cited according to the translation of Lake, *Eusebius: The Ecclesiastical History*, 1:243 (3.23.5-6).
67. Cited according to the translation found in *The Ante-Nicene Fathers*, 1:559-60. For the critical questions surrounding the meaning of this quote, cf. Aune, *Revelation 1-5*, lviii-lix.
68. Beale, *The Book of Revelation*, 4.

Introduction

A Modest Proposal with regard to Date

Although the evidence, both internal and external, slightly favors a late date, it appears from the text that, with perhaps one exception, John has been intentional (and successful) in disguising the date of composition from the hearers and readers. In other words, it appears that the text may intend to conceal rather than reveal the date of its composition. If so, it would seem to be more in keeping with the S/spirit of the text to respect its intentional ambiguity and look one more time for any internal indicators that might shed light on the intentions of the text.

The closest Revelation comes to offering a date for its composition may be a phrase found in 1:10, where John says, "I was in the Spirit on the Lord's Day." It is commonly thought that this phrase, τῇ κυριακῇ ἡμέρᾳ (*tē kyriakē hēmera*, "on the Lord's Day"), is simply an early equivalent for "Sunday." Evidence offered in support of this interpretation is the meaning this phrase seems to have in documents in some close temporal proximity to Revelation (i.e., *Did.* 14.1; Ign., *Magn.* 9.1; and *Gos. Pet.* 35, 50). On this view, Rev 1:10 is the earliest example of the evolution of this term. The accuracy of this explanation would be hard to disprove or deny, though the traditional Johannine designation for Sunday is τῇ ... μιᾷ τῶν σαββάτων (*tē mia tōn sabbatōn*, "on the first day of the week"). But at the same time, in a book known for its pregnant imagery, it is possible that the hearers and readers are being given more than a detail about the day of the week on which John experiences the revelation. This statement may also convey something else about the date of the document (or of the experience). By means of the phrase "on the Lord's Day," John may be giving his writing an eschatological date.

On this reading, the phrase *tē kyriakē hēmera* might very well cause the hearer to think of the OT idea of יום יהוה (*yom Yahweh*, "the Day of the Lord/Yahweh"). But the hearer is not likely to see here simply a reference to the OT "Day of the Lord," but to that day as the Lord's Day, when Jesus himself will appear to resurrect the righteous dead. As ever, the intertext that is Revelation is the point of convergence of various "texts" (people, ideas, experiences, written texts). Here the convergence includes the OT idea of the "Day of the Lord," John's experience "in the Spirit," the person of the resurrected Jesus, and the anticipation of his return and the resurrection of the dead. This intertextual understanding of the phrase goes some way toward explaining why John does not simply utilize the OT language *yom Yahweh*, for it is that day and more! Origen comes close to this understanding when he uses ἐν τῇ μεγάλῃ κυριακῇ (*en tē megalē kyriakē*, "on the great Day of the Lord") to describe the resurrection of all, which follows Jesus' resurrection "on the third day."[69] Not only would this reading of "the Lord's Day" be consistent with the rich symbolism of the document, but it would also dovetail nicely with the eschatological context in which Rev 1:10 is located, between vv. 7-8 and vv. 12-20.[70]

What would be the significance of this date for the book? Simply that the Lord's Day relativizes all other days, indicating that the only day that matters is the Lord's Day, the end of all days.[71] The convergence of this dimension of the phrase, with the emerging understanding of this term as a designation for Sunday, would also not be without significance for the writer and his community.

Authorship

In contrast to the issue of date, determining the authorship of Revelation is a bit more straightforward, for unlike the four gospels, Acts, Hebrews, and 1–3 John, all anonymous documents, Revelation actually names its author. In

---

69. Origen, *Commentary on John* 10.35.

70. On the significance of the place of 1:10 in the narrative of Revelation for this understanding of "the Day of the Lord" and other aspects of the question, cf. A. Bacchiocchi, *From Sabbath to Sunday: An Historical Investigation into the Rise of Sunday Observance in Early Christianity* (Rome: Pontifical Gregorian University Press, 1977), 123-30.

71. At this point it might prove beneficial to consider this very phenomenon within the prophetic literature of the OT, for such a practice is not wholly without precedent. The typical way by which the date of an OT prophetic book is revealed is by means of the phrase "the word of the Lord came to [a certain prophet] in the days of [a certain] king[s]" (cf. Jer 1:2-3; Ezek 2:3; Hos 1:1; Amos 1:1; Mic 1:1; Zeph 1:1; Hag 1:1; Zech 1:1). However, on occasion, a book does not contain this phrase and, consequently, does not make reference to the reign of a certain king. With the book of Joel it appears that this lack of an internal indicator of the book's date is an intentional device to draw attention to "the day of the Lord." Cf. the perceptive comments of R. D. Moore ("Joel" [manuscript], 6, to appear in *The Book of the Twelve*), who notes:

> My alternative suggestion is that Joel intentionally refrains from assigning a date, not because he wants to establish a "dehistoricized" liturgy relevant for all time, but rather because he sees the Day of the Lord eclipsing all of time and all of our days to the point of rendering them irrelevant — irrelevant enough to be left unspecified. Refusing to tell us in the first verse, as we would expect, that the word of the LORD came to Joel *"in the days of (a certain) king,"* Joel seems deliberately to accentuate this omission in the second verse by prefacing the prophetic word with the question, "Has anything like this happened *in your days or the days of your father?*" . . . This day is so much bigger than the big days (viz., royal coronations) by which time has previously been calculated, that it blows away the entire dating system to become for Joel the new referent point for all future generations (cf. 1:3).

Given Revelation's self-conscious identification with the prophetic literature, perhaps a similar phenomenon may be at work here.

Introduction

point of fact, four times does this author identify himself as John, twice in the prologue (1:1, 4), once at the beginning of the inaugural vision (1:9), and once in the epilogue (22:8). However, no other appellations are given to describe this individual. No titles or additional names are used, nor does the author claim to be a physical relative of Jesus or some other authoritative figure within early Christianity. Yet, despite the scarcity of descriptive titles, much may be learned about the author from the text.

John the Prophet

Primarily, the text reveals that John is regarded as, and regards himself to be, a prophetic figure. Though he never technically calls himself a prophet in the text, there are numerous indicators that he does indeed fulfill this function. The book begins with a description of the revelation of Jesus Christ given by God to "his servant John," who testifies of the things he saw and heard (1:2). The next verse (v. 3) identifies the content of what John wrote as "the words of this prophecy." One of the primary hints as to John's prophetic identity is the description, on at least two occasions, of John's prophetic commissioning. The first of these commissionings is in 1:9-20, where John, "in the Spirit on the Lord's Day," hears a loud voice that twice instructs him to write what he sees and hears (vv. 11, 19). The second commissioning occurs in chapter 10, where John is instructed to take the open scroll from the hand of the angel and to eat it (vv. 8-9). After ingesting the scroll, he is instructed, "You must prophesy again" (v. 11). This call narrative mirrors OT call narratives, especially that of Ezekiel, virtually establishing that John is indeed a prophet.[72] John's prophetic activity is communicated to the hearer by means of his book being closely identified with "the word of God," "the testimony of Jesus," and he is repeatedly being said to be "in the Spirit" during the experience of the revelation.[73] Rev 19:10 plays a significant role in this understanding, where it is stated, "The testimony of Jesus is the Spirit of prophecy." John's prophetic identity is also made known by his instructions to engage in the prophetic activity of measuring the temple (ch. 11) and by the utilization of prophetic formulas that are also found among the classic prophets.[74]

---

72. On this whole matter, cf. Mazzaferri, *The Genre of the Book of Revelation from a Source-Critical Perspective*, 264-96.

73. Cf. Mazzaferri, *The Genre of the Book of Revelation from a Source-Critical Perspective*, 296-317.

74. Cf. Mazzaferri, *The Genre of the Book of Revelation from a Source-Critical Perspective*, 317-30.

Not only is there evidence of John's own identity as prophet, but as noted earlier, there are also signs of prophetic activity within the community from which Revelation comes. The presence of a rival prophetess on the concrete level (2:20), along with the appearance of the false prophet on the cosmic level (16:13; 19:20; 20:10), are negative testimony that the community was indeed accustomed to prophetic activity. But such negative evidence does not stand alone, for the community represented by Revelation knows of other prophetic figures functioning within the community, such as John's brother prophets (22:6, 9). Prophetic activity seems to have been so widespread that it is possible for Revelation to use "prophets" to describe the activity of faithful members of the community: "the prophets and the saints" (11:18), "saints and prophets" (16:6), and "the saints and the prophets" (18:24).[75] The prophetic nature of the community would say much, not only about John's identity, but also about the way he would function as part of it. Hints in the text suggest that the brother prophets (if they need be distinguished from others in the community) might have a role in the reading (hearing and keeping) of the text at different meetings in various locations across the community. Perhaps prophetic instruction accompanied the successive multiple readings of Revelation, but well within the boundaries set by the warning with which the book concludes (22:18-19). No doubt such activity would involve the kind of "pneumatic" interpretation called for in Revelation itself. The role of the other prophetic figures within the community in the composition of the book is difficult to determine. Part of the difficulty here is owing to questions about the way in which the book was composed. Was it experienced in a short period of time, and then written up shortly thereafter, as the text suggests? Or is it the product of an extended time of reflection, as the complex literary structure would suggest? On the former view, the involvement of other members of the prophetic community would perhaps be limited to discerning responses when the prophecy is read and heard by the community in times of worship. On the latter view, it might not be hard to imagine that John's own prophetic activity is joined by others, as together the implications of the vision(s) and their intertextual significance are creatively constructed.[76]

The text may also reveal two other aspects of the author's identity. First, it appears that John was from a Jewish home, as his knowledge of the OT and

---

75. Bauckham, *The Climax of Prophecy*, 84.

76. On the extent of the activity of the prophetic community, cf. Bauckham, *The Climax of Prophecy*, 83-91. The idea that Revelation was written down some time after it was experienced is found as early as Victorinus, *Commentary on the Apocalypse of the Blessed John*, in his comments on 10:11.

his appreciation for the Jewish heritage would seem to make clear.[77] Second, if Rev 1:9 speaks of banishment, then something else about John's social location is revealed. Since banishment under the Romans was reserved for royalty and members of the priesthood, the implication is that John may have come from a priestly family, as Polycrates testifies (Eusebius, *Ecclesiastical History* 5.24.3).[78]

Writing in the Spirit

The text of Revelation indicates that John experiences this revelation while "in the Spirit" and that, while "in the Spirit," he is commanded to write what he sees and hears. It is clear from this and other dimensions of the text that John regards the document as carrying a spiritual authority; one might even say that he seems to regard the words of this prophecy as an "inspired" document. To speak of writing "in the Spirit" in a discussion of authorship would therefore appear to be most appropriate. But what does it mean to write "in the Spirit"?

Obviously, given that John is "in the Spirit" when he is given the command to write and that "in the Spirit" he experiences the revelation, there is a very tight interplay between the experiences of seeing and hearing and the experience of writing. But can anything else be said of this phenomenon? While it is possible to treat John primarily as an exegete of OT Scripture[79] or to view him as a passive instrument who simply records what is seen or heard in an automatic fashion, neither of these conceptions appears to fit the situation envisioned by the text.

The text says that John saw a vision. But what did he see, and how much of what he saw made sense to him because of who he was? The concrete dimensions of his visionary experience notwithstanding, does John see the vision he does because of who he is and how he is formed? If some other early Christian experienced the revelation, would it look the same, or would it take a different form? Or does the Spirit use *John's* knowledge of the OT for the vision to take

---

77. Contra R. K. MacKenzie, *The Author of the Apocalypse: A Review of the Prevailing Hypothesis of Jewish-Christian Authorship*, (MBPS 51; Lewiston, NY: Edwin Mellen Press, 1997).

78. On this aspect of John's identity, cf. M. Hengel, *The Johannine Question*, 125-26.

79. Note Waddell's perceptive criticism of one such approach in *The Spirit of the Book of Revelation*, 85. "In conclusion, I have a few concerns with Beale's hermeneutics. Although I highly value Beale's detailed analysis of John's use of the Old Testament in the Apocalypse, at the end of the day, as a Pentecostal, I find it inadequate. He leaves insufficient room for John to be recording an actual vision as opposed to solely exegeting Scripture. When I read the text, I assume John is interpreting and relaying an experience in the Spirit, albeit not void of Old Testament allusions. The Apocalypse ought not be reduced solely to a contextually sensitive exegesis."

the form it does? If so, then the intertext that is John's life, his acquaintance with the OT, apocalyptic traditions, the Jesus tradition, his worshipping community, and the experience of the revelation itself is used "in the Spirit" to produce the text of Revelation. On this understanding, we can view Revelation as the point of dynamic convergence and intersection of all that John is, including the revelation he experiences. Consequently, it is precisely because of John's knowledge of the OT, the apocalyptic tradition, the Johannine Jesus tradition, and the worshipping community of which he is a part that enables him to write "in the Spirit." One might go so far as to say that John's life is such that he is especially prepared for this prophetic activity, which the Spirit integrates into a profound "inspired" text. On this view, the tension between (1) the text's claim that this is a visionary experience and (2) the document's intricate design and literary complexity, which suggest that it is the product of a long period of time, gives way to the Spirit's encountering John in such a way that the convergences take place before his very eyes (and ears). Perhaps the phenomenon of glossolalia and its interpretation in contemporary Pentecostalism might function as an analogy, where the Spirit speaks through an individual believer in ways that draw upon all that he or she is, while not obliterating his or her heritage or personality.[80]

John the Prophet and the Other Johannine Literature

Understanding the relationship between Revelation and the Fourth Gospel and 1–3 John has presented a perennial challenge to NT interpreters. Though commonly identified as part of the Johannine community, there is some question whether Revelation was an integral part. A brief comparison indicates some of the reasons for these attitudes.

On the one hand, there are numerous points of continuity among the documents. In both the Fourth Gospel and Revelation a great deal of emphasis is placed upon the issue of witness or testimony. The anticipation of persecution owing to one's witness found in the Fourth Gospel (16:1-4) gives way in Revelation to the reality of such persecution (2:3, 9-10, 13). "Word of God" is a theme common to the three major community documents (Fourth Gospel, 1 John, and Revelation). It has already been noted how the pneumatology shows signs of development from the Fourth Gospel to 1 John to the full-blown prophetic pneumatology of Revelation. A final example is the way in which the "revelation of Jesus Christ," to which Revelation is devoted, accomplishes this task by following the revelation of his identity by means of the imagery of the

---

80. On this analogy, cf. also S. Moyise, *The Old Testament in the Book of Revelation*, 40.

Introduction

Lamb. The paschal overtones of the lamb imagery in the Fourth Gospel (1:29; 19:33-34), while present in Revelation (5:6), are supplemented by a vision of the wrath of the Lamb (6:16-17), who is powerful in battle.

On the other hand, there are several differences between these documents. Perhaps the most notable differences to readers of the Greek NT are those of vocabulary, phraseology, style, and syntax.[81] Some of these differences in vocabulary and style were noted as early as the third century. Such differences may be taken to imply that the hands of different writers are to be detected in these documents. At the same time, the grammatical style of Revelation is very curious, and there may be more than one way to interpret the evidence. Quite clearly there are significant differences between these texts. One of the results emerging from additional analyses of the grammar of the book, however, is the belief by some that the style of Revelation reflects the author's intention to confront the hearers and readers with a style that replicates that of the OT prophets. Such a device would not only have implications with regard to the prophetic genre of the book[82] but also have affective and dispositional implications for its hearers as well.[83] In keeping with what has earlier been observed about John "writing in the Spirit," it might not be going too far to ask whether it is not rather the prophetic experience itself that explains the employment of the prophetic language and style found in Revelation.[84] Such an interpretation would fit nicely both with John's immersion in the OT prophetic literature and the phenomenology of his prophetic experience, while leaving open issues related to authorial intent.[85]

The differences between the documents are indeed enough to suggest that different writers produced the Fourth Gospel and 1–3 John, on the one side, and Revelation, on the other. Yet, if the style of Revelation is an intentional strategy or the result of John's prophetic experience, and there are substantial similarities between the documents, then one should not assume that the author is incapa-

---

81. The most comprehensive study on this topic to date is Frey, "Erwägungen zum Verhältnis der Johannesapokalypse zu den übrigen Schriften des Corpus Johanneum," 326-429. Cf. also the still influential work of R. H. Charles, *The Revelation of St. John*, vol. 1 (ICC; Edinburgh: T&T Clark, 1920), xxix-xxxi.

82. F. J. A. Hort, *The Apocalypse of St. John*, vol. 1 (London: Macmillan, 1908), xxxviii; C. G. Ozanne, "The Language of the Apocalypse," *TynB* 16 (1965): 3-9; Ruiz, *Ezekiel in the Apocalypse*, 224, 518, 529.

83. A. D. Callahan, "The Language of the Apocalypse," *HTR* 88 (1995): 453-70.

84. I am indebted to my colleague R. D. Moore for this observation. Cf. also G. R. Osborne, *Revelation* (ECNT; Grand Rapids: Baker, 2002), 4.

85. In any case, Revelation's grammatical style is not without theological significance. Cf. Resseguie, *The Revelation of John*, 49-53.

ble of writing in different styles.[86] Such differences in writing style do seem to occur in Luke, where the first two chapters appear more Semitic in nature than do the chapters that follow.[87] In addition, there is always the possibility that other hands were involved in assisting the writer in the process of composition.

John in Early Christian Tradition

How does this emerging picture of the author of Apocalypse fit with the testimony about authorship found in the early church? The earliest extant witness is that of Justin Martyr (*Dialogue with Trypho* 81.4), cited in the discussion on date above. There it was seen that Justin identifies the author as "John, one of the apostles of Christ." It would appear safe to assume that Justin believes that John the son of Zebedee wrote Revelation. Part of the strength of Justin's testimony is that he actually lived in Ephesus for a while in the first half of the second century. Similar testimony continues to be found among various early Christian writers. Tertullian identifies the author as "the apostle John" (*Against Marcion* 3.14.3; 3.24.4), as do Clement of Alexandria (*Who Is the Rich Man That Is Saved?* 42) and Hippolytus (*De Antichristo* 18, 36-42).

The evidence from Irenaeus is in some ways the most extensive and, at the same time, perhaps the most frustrating. For while Irenaeus may believe that the son of Zebedee wrote Revelation, he never actually calls him an apostle, preferring simply to use the name John without other attribution (*Against Heresies* 1.26.3; 4.14.2; 5.26.1), or the Fourth Gospel designation "the Lord's disciple" (*Against Heresies* 4.20.11).

Not everyone in the early church agreed with such an assessment. Perhaps the best known of the dissenting voices is that of Dionysius. whom Eusebius quotes extensively on this subject (*Ecclesiastical History* 7.25.1-27). In this testimony Dionysius notes that some not only reject John as the author but even go so far as to attribute it to Cerinthus, his archenemy (7.25.2-3). Dionysius says:

> That, then, he was certainly named John and that this book is by one John, I will not gainsay; for I fully allow that this book is by some holy and inspired person. But I should not readily agree that he was the apostle, the son of Zebedee, the brother of James, whose are the Gospel entitled according to

86. Beale, *The Book of Revelation*, 35.
87. As G. B. Caird (*The Revelation of Saint John* [London: A&C Black, 1966], 5) observes, "Because a man writes in Hebraic Greek, it does not inevitably follow that this is the only Greek he is capable of writing. He may have adopted this style for quite deliberate reasons of his own, as Luke appears to have."

Introduction

John and the Catholic epistle. For I form my judgement from the character of each and from the nature of the language and from what is known as the general construction of the book, that [the John therein mentioned] is not the same. (7.25.7-8a)[88]

Dionysius goes on to point out the following differences: Revelation names its writer, the gospel and epistles do not (7.25.8b-11); the gospel and epistles share numerous ideas and vocabulary, while Revelation is utterly different (7.25.17-24); and the style and grammar of the gospel and epistles are in faultless Greek, while that of Revelation "is not accurate" and employs "barbarous idioms" that are too many to number (7.25.25-26). Lest he be misunderstood, Dionysius adds, "For I have not said these things in mockery (let no one think it), but merely to establish the dissimilarity of these writings" (7.25.27).[89]

Given the testimony cited above, the question must be raised whether John the son of Zebedee can be identified with the John of Revelation. While it is theoretically possible to make this identification, there are at least three complications that should be noted.[90] First, there is no evidence until the latter half of the second century that the son of Zebedee was ever in or near Ephesus. Ignatius, writing to the church at Ephesus ca. 110-15, makes no mention of John but goes to great lengths to demonstrate his own close relationship to Paul. Although others claim (Irenaeus, in particular) that both Polycarp and Papias had a personal relationship with the son of Zebedee, neither Polycarp nor Papias makes such a claim. Second, some evidence exists suggesting that John the son of Zebedee was martyred early in the church's history. In Mark 10:39 Jesus appears to prophesy the martyrdom of both James and John, while Papias, as quoted by Philip of Side (ca. 430), states that both James and John were killed by the Jews.[91] Third, if the son of Zebedee were the author, it would indeed be odd that he never identifies himself as an apostle and is so reticent to use apostolic language. Only three times does the term *apostolos* appear in Revelation. Once the term is used to describe "those who claim to be apostles but are not" (2:2), once it appears in a voice (from heaven?) celebrating the downfall of Babylon (18:20), and once it appears in the description of New Jerusalem, where the names of the twelve apostles of the Lamb are said to appear

---

88. Cited according to the translation of K. Lake, *Eusebius: The Ecclesiastical History*, vol. 2 (London: Heinemann, 1932), 199.

89. Cited according to the translation of K. Lake, *Eusebius: The Ecclesiastical History*, 2:209.

90. Cf. the relevant discussion in Thomas, *1 John, 2 John, 3 John*, 7-8, from which this section draws.

91. The statement of Papias is also recorded by Georgius Monachus (in the ninth century) and is supported by Syriac and African martyrologies.

on the twelve foundations of the wall of the city (21:14). In this last text it appears that the author of Revelation sees himself as distinct from this "foundational" group (from another generation?). In the end, there seems to be little reason to identify the author of Revelation as the son of Zebedee.

Is it possible to identify the author of Revelation with John the Elder, who is sometimes identified as the Beloved Disciple, the author of the other Johannine documents?[92] Such an identification would explain the relationship between the name John, which appears in the text of Revelation and the titles of the gospel and epistles. It would further explain the virtual absence of apostolic language in the Johannine literature and the treatment of the apostles as a foundational group at some distance from the author. It would perhaps also explain why the son of Zebedee, an apostle, is not mentioned by Ignatius in his letter to the Ephesians. On this view the Elder, not being one of the Twelve, would perhaps not be on the Ignatian radar screen. This identification would also have in its favor the fact that both John the Prophet and John the Elder could independently be placed in, or around, Asia. The former is of course placed off the coast of Asia near the book's beginning and clearly knows a number of the churches in Asia, as the seven prophetic messages imply. The latter appears to be one of the Asiatic sources from which Papias of Hierapolis (*Ecclesiastical History* 3.34.2) draws. Papias appears to have actually interviewed the Elder, perhaps in Asia, where he is said to have interviewed Philip (3.39.8-17). Such an explanation is possible, but is it plausible? The answer to this question will depend in large part on how one accounts for the differences in vocabulary, phraseology, style, and syntax that exist between the Johannine documents. If John the Prophet is thought to be John the Elder, such an identification would require that either John purposely adopted a style different from his normal one or that such a style was generated from his prophetic experience. Or it would require that he composed Revelation himself, while relying on the assistance of others in the composition of the Fourth Gospel and 1–3 John, which the texts themselves may imply.[93] But in the end, it is impossible to be certain about this identification. Consequently, perhaps the best course of action is simply to hear the voice of John the Prophet alongside the other Johannine voices, content with the knowledge that they come from the same community if not the same hand.[94]

---

92. On the relationship between the Beloved Disciple, the Elder, and the authorship of the Fourth Gospel and 1–3 John, cf. the discussion in Thomas, *1 John, 2 John, 3 John*, 8-10, and in Hengel's *The Johannine Question*.

93. G. D. Fee (*Revelation* [NCCS; Eugene, OR: Cascade Books, 2011]) makes a similar argument in defense of authorship by the son of Zebedee.

94. As for the likelihood of various leaders in the community bearing the same name, note

Introduction

Revelation and Its Streams of Influence: The History of Effects

Revelation has had an extraordinary influence upon a variety of hearers and readers throughout the centuries. Not only do the varied responses generated by Revelation reveal something of the document's power, but they also suggest that attention paid to specific responses will enrich one's own grappling with this remarkable text. In this section, the book's effective history is selectively reviewed by surveying a few examples from the following categories: disastrous interpretations of Revelation, other apocalyptic "Johannine" documents, art, music, poetry, film, and commentaries.

Disastrous Interpretations of Revelation

When pondering the effective history of Revelation, perhaps one of the first things to cross the interpreters' minds is what we could call the disastrous interpretations of the book that have occurred over the centuries. Of the many such interpretations, I choose three as representative and describe their results, all of which involve the loss of life owing to the interpretations espoused.

During the sixteenth century a convergence of influences produced one of the most bizarre and tragic events in the effective history of Revelation. Within a decade of the infamous Peasant Revolt of 1524-25, with which the influential Reformation figure Thomas Müntzer became involved, and the devastating defeat in the battle of Frankenhausen, where Müntzer was captured and eventually put to death, another social uprising occurred, fueled in part by the fire of Revelation, namely, the acquisition and transformation of the city of Münster. The seeds for the establishment of the Anabaptist kingdom of Münster may be found in the thought and writings of the prophetic figure Melchior Hoffmann, whose commentary on Revelation identified the emperor as the dragon, the pope as the beast, and the monks as the false prophets. Owing to various prophetic encounters and experiences, Hoffmann became convinced later in his life that (1) he was the Elijah that was to come and that the corresponding Enoch was either Cornelius Poldermann of Middleburg or Caspar Schwenckfield; (2) the spiritual Jerusalem was the present Christian community, which he identified with Strassburg; (3) the downfall of Babylon (i.e., all priests) must take place before the coming of the Lord; (4) an earthly theocracy must be established in the intervening period; and (5) violence could be used in

---

that in the Fourth Gospel there were three women at the foot of the cross who shared the name Mary (19:25) and two disciples named Judas.

the annihilation of the godless.⁹⁵ Though Hoffmann's views proved too much for the authorities in Strassburg, leading to his arrest there, his teaching won many adherents from the populace in the city of Münster in Westphalia. Upon Hoffmann's arrest, a Dutch baker from Haarlem named Jan Matthys became the inspirational leader of the movement, identifying himself as Enoch who is to come and sending word that it was time to raise the 144,000 warriors of which Rev 7 and 14 speak.⁹⁶ Seizing control of the city council, he and his followers sought to establish the New Jerusalem by, among other things, driving from the town all Catholics and Protestants who refused rebaptism. As a result of the various proceedings, an army from the bishop of Münster surrounded the city. Though being victorious in previous encounters, this time Matthys and several followers were killed in a skirmish just outside the city walls. It appears that at this point one of his "apostles," Jan Bockelson, became the unchallenged ruler of the kingdom, pronouncing himself king of the city, eventually instituting the practice of polygamy,⁹⁷ and seeking to export this eschatological movement to other cities throughout Europe.⁹⁸ The kingdom died a somewhat rapid death, however, falling in 1536, along with the capture, torture, and execution of its king. Thousands lost their lives as a result of these disastrous interpretations of Revelation.

During the summer of 1969, Los Angeles, California, was shocked by the ruthless ritualistic murders that occurred on Saturday, 9 August, of Steven Earl Parent, Voytek Frykowski, Abigail Folger, Sharon Tate Polanski, and Jay Seabring, and on the following night, the murders of Leno and Rosemary La-Bianca. Though baffling to police investigators for some time, the bizarre clues of the murder scene would serve to reveal the motives for these horrendous acts. As Deputy District Attorney Vincent Bugliosi would discover, these terrible acts were in part the result of the disastrous interpretation of the book of Revelation by Charles Manson.⁹⁹ The illegitimate son of a teenage mother who repeatedly abandoned him, Charles Manson would spend most of his life in a variety of institutional settings, owing both to his frequent abandonment and to the local, state, and federal crimes that he committed. Upon his release after

---

95. K. Deppermann, *Melchior Hoffman: Social Unrest and Apocalyptic Visions in the Age of Reformation* (ed. B. Drewery; trans. M. Wren; Edinburgh: T&T Clark, 1987), 254-62.

96. Deppermann, *Melchior Hoffman*, 336.

97. G. H. Williams, *The Radical Reformation* (Philadelphia: Westminster, 1962), 511, notes that the practice of polygamy might not be unrelated to the desire to fill out the number of 144,000 as quickly as possible.

98. A. W. Wainwright, *Mysterious Apocalypse* (Nashville: Abingdon, 1993), 90-92.

99. Much of what follows draws upon Vincent Bugliosi (with Curt Gentry), *Helter Skelter: The True Story of the Manson Murders* (New York: Norton, 1974 [1994]), 320-28.

the completion of a ten-year prison sentence, Manson gathered a number of followers, who became known as the Manson Family, over whom he exerted near total and absolute control. As the deputy district attorney who prosecuted the case discovered, the motivation for these savage murders was grounded in Manson's interpretation of the book of Revelation. For Manson, Rev 9 held the key. He identified the four angels of this chapter, who would kill a third of humankind, as referring to the four-member rock band the Beatles. The following details confirmed this interpretation for Manson: (1) the four angels would, like the locusts who arise from the Abyss, have the faces of men; (2) hair as that of a woman, an obvious reference to the long-haired look of the Beatles; (3) fire coming from their mouths, taken as a reference to the influence of their words; and (4) breastplates of fire, seen as a reference to their electric guitars. Manson thought of himself as the angel who held the key to the bottomless pit, from which all manner of evil would arise and which would be a place of refuge for him and his followers. This hermeneutical key enabled Manson to interpret a number of songs from the Beatles' so-called White Album (officially entitled simply "The Beatles") as prophesying an imminent racial war in which blacks would rise in revolt against white oppression. Manson hoped to initiate this cataclysmic bloodbath, which he called Helter Skelter, a phrase he took from the Beatles' song by that title, by directing murderous activities that would gain national, if not global, attention. In the end, his apostles of murder savagely butchered seven people in Los Angeles. When questioned by the deputy district attorney about his role in the murders, Manson responded, "It's the Beatles, the music they are putting out. They're talking about war."[100]

Finally, one of the better-known disastrous interpretations of Revelation resulted in the horrendous events that took place on 19 April 1993 in Waco, Texas. Here, eighty members of a religious group known as the Branch Davidians met their death in a fiery confrontation with the Federal Bureau of Investigation following an extended siege of the community.[101] With roots deep in Seventh-day Adventist thought, and more specifically the "Shepherd's Rod" movement, the leader of this group had come to have specific ideas about his own prophetic role, as well as the identity of the second beast of Rev 13 and 17. The son of an unwed teenage mother, Vernon Wayne Howell struggled in, and eventually dropped out of, high school, owing in part to dyslexia. After claiming

---

100. Barry Miles, *Paul McCartney: Many Years from Now* (New York: Henry Holt, 1997), 488-90.

101. Much of what follows draws heavily from K. G. C. Newport, *Apocalypse and Millennium: Studies in Biblical Eisegesis* (Cambridge: Cambridge University Press, 2000), 197-236, who offers an excellent theological analysis of Koresh and the events that led to the horrible events of 19 April 1993.

a born-again experience in a Baptist church, he made his way to the church of his mother, the Seventh-day Adventist Church. He followed this trajectory to the Shepherd's Rod movement, and then to Davidian Seventh-day Adventism, a group from which the Branch Davidians came, and located on property they called Mount Carmel. Eventually assuming leadership of the group, Howell later changed his name to David Koresh, drawing upon the biblical name David, as well as the name Cyrus (from Heb. כורש), who he said came to destroy Babylon, a task in which he would share. While his interpretations drew heavily from the traditions to which he was heir, Koresh seemed to sharpen the somewhat standard identification of the lamb-like beast of Rev 13 as the United States of America. Consequently, his extended confrontation with governmental representatives such as the Bureau of Alcohol, Tobacco, Firearms, and Explosives, and later the FBI, reinforced this identification for Koresh, especially when his compound was surrounded by the lamb-like beast, who, he was convinced, sought to persecute and kill him. At the end of an extended siege, the FBI moved on the compound, and when the smoke cleared from the resulting fires, eighty members of the community, including women and children, were dead, including Koresh, who died from a gunshot to the head.

But the effective history of Revelation is far richer than a chronicling of its disastrous interpretations, as is seen in the following sections.

Other Johannine Apocalyptic Documents

One of the places where the influence of Revelation may be seen is its role in generating other Johannine apocalyptic literature. Although this aspect of the book's effective history is not always fully appreciated, it is not surprising that Revelation has acted as a catalyst in the production of other Johannine apocalyptic documents.[102]

The first document that may safely be identified as being located in the Johannine apocalyptic trajectory is a work known as the *Second Apocalypse of John (2AJ)*.[103] Structurally, this book (which may be dated as early as ca. 400 or as late as the ninth century)[104] takes the form of a series of questions raised by "righteous John" and answered by "our Lord Jesus Christ." The temporal

---

102. On this topic, cf. esp. J. Court, *The Book of Revelation and the Johannine Apocalyptic Tradition* (JSNTS 190; Sheffield: Sheffield Academic Press, 2000).

103. Court (*The Book of Revelation and the Johannine Apocalyptic Tradition*, 32-65) provides the Greek text of the *2AJ*, an English translation, as well as a useful commentary.

104. For the evidence in favor of this later date, cf. A. Whealey, "The Apocryphal Apocalypse of John. A Byzantine Apocalypse from the Early Islamic Period," *JTS* 53 (2002): 533-40.

Introduction

location of this apocalypse is "after the ascension" on Mount Tabor, the traditional site of Jesus' ascension (*2AJ* 1). The influence of the Revelation of John is evident at many places throughout the document. After praying for seven days, the heavens are opened, and John sees a book sealed with seven seals (2-3). Later, this book is opened by the Lamb (18-19). The imagery of Revelation (esp. ch. 21) is also quite apparent at the close of the *2AJ* (27), where the nature of existence in heaven is described in some detail. Many of the issues addressed in the *2AJ* are very much what one might expect to be of interest to those who know Revelation and other early Christian documents dealing with various eschatological topics. For example, one of the first topics discussed in the *2AJ* concerns ὁ ἀρνητῆς (*ho arnētēs*, "the denier"), also known as ὁ ἀντίχριστος (*ho antichristos*, "the antichrist"). Specifically, there is a description of his physical appearance (7) and the length of his reign (8). Other topics addressed include the nature of the resurrection body (10-11), the descent of the heavenly things to earth (17), the order of divine judgment upon the Greeks, the Heretics, the Hebrews, and the baptized (20), the depth of the Underworld, where the unclean spirits and the Adversary are located (20), and the proportionality of punishment, based upon one's social location (24).

Another apocalyptic text that stands within Revelation's stream of influence is the *Apocalypse of St. John Chrysostom (AStJC)*.[105] This document, whose date appears to be somewhere between the sixth and eighth centuries, resembles the *2AJ* in that it too takes the form of a dialogue between Jesus and John the Theologian, again known as "righteous John." Unlike *2AJ*, the fifty-one verses that compose the *AStJC* are not as concerned with eschatological details as they are with contemporary issues of relevance. The first issue raised by John and addressed by Jesus deals with the number of different kinds of sins and the identification of those sins deemed to be unforgivable (1-4). This initial discussion is followed by one devoted to how one's actions honor or dishonor Sunday (5-10), which evolves into a discourse on the nature and purpose of fasting (8-19). Of particular interest is the use of the word for Sunday in the *AStJC*, being the same word as found in Rev 1:10, when John says, "I was in the Spirit on the Lord's Day [κυριακῇ, *kyriakē*]." The final thirty-two verses of this document are devoted to explanations about a variety of liturgical practices (20-51). These issues range from an explanation of the symbols of the church, the individuals involved in worship, words and phrases used in worship, and even the length of hair for men and women involved in baptism and communion.

---

105. Court (*The Book of Revelation and the Johannine Apocalyptic Tradition*, 74-103) provides the Greek text of the *AStJC*, an English translation, as well as a useful commentary.

The *Third Apocalypse of John (3AJ)* continues to give evidence of Revelation's influence upon other Johannine apocalyptic documents. Like the first two documents described in this section, this book also incorporates the dialogue format, only in this case the dialogue takes place between St. John the Theologian and James the Lord's brother. The primary focus of *3AJ* is the fate of sinners and the righteous.[106] After an introductory question as to when the soul leaves the body (1), there is an extended description of the fate of unrepentant sinners (2-10). Angelic guides lead sinners to torment that lasts forever, including the river of fire and the worm that never dies. The next major section of *3AJ* (11-35) focuses upon the fate of the righteous, who, full of light, pass over the torments of the unrepentant. Worthy of mention from this section is the catalog of sinners who are offered as examples of recipients of God's grace as a result of their repentance (23-27). Included in this list are Peter, who denied the Lord three times (23); Mary the prostitute, who had sinned indiscriminately with 1,703 men; Manasseh, who killed his own son; 40 elders, as well as Isaiah; the thief on the cross, who had committed 99 murders (24); David, who sinned with Bathsheba, one of 100 women he kept (25); Andrew of Crete, who committed incest with his own mother but later became a bishop (26); and Cyprian, who was born of a race of demons and destroyed 1,300 children before his conversion and call as a bishop (27). The document concludes with a warning that there is no opportunity for repentance or forgiveness after one's death (35). Clearly, the document's major emphasis is upon the importance of repentance and God's free forgiveness.

A final document to be mentioned in this section devoted to Revelation's influence upon later Johannine apocalyptic texts is the *Coptic Apocalypse of John (CAJ)*.[107] This work, which appears to date from the eleventh century, continues the now-familiar dialogue format found in the previous three books described. On the Mount of Olives, just before the ascension of Jesus, John the apostle and the Holy Virgin request that he be taken to heaven by Jesus in order to see all the mysteries contained therein. Granting his request, Jesus entrusts John to "a great cherubim" [*sic*] covered with eyes who could answer all John's questions, for the words of the Father are hidden within the cherubim (2). John's journey includes a visit to the seven heavens. Here he discovers that water, which existed before the creation of heaven and earth (3), is scarce at times owing to the sin of humanity. He finds that Michael is an unrivaled angelic being whose name

---

106. Court (*The Book of Revelation and the Johannine Apocalyptic Tradition*, 108-31) provides the Greek text of the *3AJ*, an English translation, as well as a useful commentary.

107. Court (*The Book of Revelation and the Johannine Apocalyptic Tradition*, 137-63) provides E. W. Budge's English translation of the *CAJ*, as well as Court's own useful commentary.

Introduction

is found upon the garments of all angels who come to earth because his name keeps such ones from being led astray by the devil (7). John discovers that Eve was hidden in Adam's rib from his creation and separated from him later (13). He finds that after Solomon had the demons reveal the origins of illness and their remedies, he inscribed them on a wall of the temple. Hezekiah plastered over this information, and when he was found in need of healing, Hezekiah prayed and was sent the prophet Isaiah with the remedy (14). Finally, John is told that God determines a soul's destiny and that animals also have souls, though they always remain on earth (18).

Art

The influence of Revelation upon countless artists is hard to overestimate. In fact, it is not going too far to say that artists have been among the most attentive interpreters of Revelation. The reason for this is not difficult to ascertain, for the book's aesthetic beauty speaks very powerfully to those with artistic sensibilities and connects with them at very deep levels. Thus, while the sometimes bizarre imagery of Revelation can serve to frighten off certain textually inclined individuals, this same imagery often proves to be an irresistible invitation to the imaginations of various artists who devote their energies to artistic conceptualizations of Revelation. The influence of Revelation in the realm of art is so vast, the challenges involved in attempting to describe artistic depictions without benefit of the visual images themselves so great, that one could almost despair of attempting to include a section in this part of the introduction devoted to history of effect. The significance of this voluminous evidence, however, necessitates the inclusion of a survey of the art inspired by Revelation, despite the limitations of the presentation.

The effective history of Revelation in art can be detected as early as the depictions of scenes from Revelation found within the catacombs in Rome. Here, among the numerous representations drawn from both the OT and the NT, appear to be drawings inspired by Revelation. One example is a picture of Christ the Judge, surrounded by stacks of books, the basis of the judgment of the dead (cf. Rev 20:12), and sheep, which represent the elect.[108] Other depictions informed by Revelation include the conquering Christ entering the holy city in triumph and Christ teaching the multitude in the heavenly Jerusalem.[109]

---

108. J. Stevenson, *The Catacombs: Life and Death in Early Christianity* (Nashville: Thomas Nelson, 1985), 107-8.
109. Stevenson, *The Catacombs*, 114-16.

One of the ways to gain entry into the art of Revelation in general is to become aware of the variety of media used in creating these artistic depictions. These media include the following (with an example of the medium provided within parentheses):

- illuminated manuscripts (*The Trinity Apocalypse*, Trinity College Library, Cambridge),
- oil paintings (Raphael's *The Vision of Ezekiel*),
- stained glass (the Great East Window of York Minster),
- frescoes (Correggio's Painted Cupola, Giovanni Evangelista at Parma),
- mosaics (the Triumphal Arch of S. Maria Maggiore in Rome),
- relief sculptures (*Majestas Domini*, Chartres [Eure-et-Loir], Notre Dame, Portail Royal), and
- tapestries (The Brussels Tapestries).[110]

Another avenue by which to gain some understanding of the effective history of Revelation in the realm of art is to give some attention to the scenes from Revelation that are most often depicted. One of the more popular scenes among artists is the attempt to depict John near the beginning of his visionary experience. Sometimes the focus is upon John taking the book from the angel or writing in it, though often these scenes include some aspect of the vision that awaits John. One of the best examples is the well-known fifteenth-century altarpiece by Hans Memling *(St. John the Evangelist on Patmos).* In this oil on wood painting, John sits writing in the foreground, while in the background many of the prominent aspects of the vision are depicted.

Another very popular theme among artists of Revelation is the vision of heaven in chapters 4–5. Also prominent are depictions of angelic beings. Not surprisingly, special attention is given to the seven angels with the seven trumpets (8:2), the sounding of which accompanies significant events on the earth, the seven angels with the seven bowls of judgment (ch. 15), as well as the angels who accompany and/or speak with John during the course of the visionary drama. Equally influential are the images of the opening of the seven seals and the Four Horsemen, who accompany the opening of the first four of these seals. Other prominent images of Revelation to be found in art include the four living beasts, the woman clothed with the sun, the beast and the dragon, and Babylon

---

110. All these examples may be found in N. Grubb's *Revelations: Art of the Apocalypse* (New York: Abbeville Press, 1997), a small but helpful introduction to the art of Revelation, and in a more exhaustive treatment by F. van der Meer, *Apocalypse: Visions from the Book of Revelation in Western Art* (New York: Alpine Fine Arts, 1978).

Introduction

the harlot. As could be expected, much attention is devoted to depictions of the new heaven and new earth.

Yet another way to gain some appreciation for the art inspired by Revelation is to give attention to a few individual contributions of special significance. Some of the most exquisite and moving artistic depictions of scenes from Revelation are to be found in a group of illuminated manuscripts that contain a commentary on the book of Revelation written sometime during the eighth century by Beatus, a resident of the Benedictine abbey of Santo Turibio at Liébana, Spain. The commentary Beatus produced could more properly be considered a catena, a collection of comments from a variety of earlier writers.[111] Several illuminated manuscripts appeared over the next few hundred years that illustrate a number of scenes from Revelation. It appears that the original cycle of illustrations consisted of 108 somewhat disparate images. Of these, one illustration accompanies each chapter of text as well as an introductory image. These illustrations are among the most beautiful and emotive devoted to Revelation.[112]

In 1498 Albrecht Dürer produced a series of fifteen woodcuts based on Revelation, which brought him immediate fame. These black-and-white depictions are staggering in terms of their vision, intricacy, and detail. Introduced by a depiction from *The Life of John*, where John is in a cauldron of oil, they include many of the major scenes from Revelation. His work, considered by many to have superseded everything that preceded it, inspired other scenes by later artists in order to complement those offered by Dürer.

Perhaps the single, best-known artistic depiction generated by Revelation is *The Adoration of the Lamb*, by Jan van Eyck, which is part of the Ghent Altarpiece. While any artistic depiction of a scene from Revelation involves interpretation on the part of the artist(s), the integrative vision that produces *The Adoration of the Lamb* may be without rival. The focal point of the scene, as the name indicates, is the Lamb standing upon an altar with his blood from an open wound flowing directly into a chalice. He is surrounded by angels, two of whom continually minister incense around him, while twelve others are given to other forms of adoration. For example, two of the twelve stand on either side of a large wooden cross that they gently embrace, a crown of thorns in the hand of one and a spear in the hand of the other. In the background is a sunlike sphere, the rays of which disperse in all directions, from which the Spirit as a dove descends. All around the Lamb are groups of saints who worship

---

111. According to Beatus's preface, these included the writings of "Jerome, Augustine, Ambrose, Fulgentius, Gregory, Tyconius, Irenaeus, Apringius and Isidore."

112. On the Beatus cycle, cf. van der Meer, *Apocalypse*, 108-27. Cf. also J. Williams, *The Illustrated Beatus: A Corpus of the Illustrations of the Commentary on the Apocalypse* (5 vols.; London: Harvey Miller Publishers, 1994-2003).

him. These include the martyrs, confessors, virgins, apostles, prophets, pilgrims, and soldiers of the cross. In the foreground is the fountain of the water of life, which the death of the Lamb makes available to all who believe (Rev 22:1-2). The indescribable beauty of *The Adoration of the Lamb* makes it one of the most magnificent pieces of the artistic effective history of Revelation.[113]

Music

When reflecting upon Revelation's effective history in the realm of music, one of the first compositions to come to mind is the "Hallelujah Chorus" in G. F. Handel's *Messiah*. Written over a twenty-four-day period in 1741 (21 August through 14 September 1741),[114] this ambitious oratorio in three parts covers the life of Christ beginning with the nativity and concluding with the apocalyptic vision of the Lamb of God glorified in heaven. *The Messiah,* along with *Israel in Egypt,* consists entirely of texts taken from Scripture.[115] It reaches its climax at the end of part 2, in the crescendo entitled "Hallelujah." Relying heavily upon Rev 19:6, from which the title "Hallelujah" comes, the chorus incorporates the well-known phrase "for the Lord God Omnipotent reigneth" as a repeated refrain. This refrain then gives way to additional words that come from Rev 11:15, "The kingdom of this world is become the kingdom of our Lord and of His Christ, and He shall reign forever and ever." As the chorus draws to its climatic conclusion, the words "King of Kings and Lord of Lords," also from Rev 19:16, are incorporated into the vigorous, almost overpowering integration of words from these texts, words that are brought together in an extraordinary marriage of lyrics, voices, notes, and instruments. The influence of Revelation upon *The Messiah* is not limited to its effect upon the "Hallelujah Chorus" but continues to be seen in the oratorio's very last chorus, entitled "Worthy Is the Lamb That Was Slain," with which the whole composition concludes. On this occasion it is Rev 5:12-13 that provides the lyrics:

> Worthy is the Lamb that was slain, and hath redeemed us to God by his blood, to receive power, and riches, and wisdom, and strength, and honour, and glory, and blessing.

---

113. For an extensive discussion of van Eyck's *Adoration*, cf. van der Meer, *Apocalypse,* 236-57.

114. The autograph score of *The Messiah* bears these dates, written in German in Handel's own hand, at the beginning and the end of the manuscript, respectively. J. Tobin, *Handel at Work* (New York: St. Martin's Press, 1964), 2.

115. E. Smith, "Handel's English Librettists," in *The Cambridge Companion to Handel* (ed. D. Borrows; Cambridge: Cambridge University Press, 1997), 103.

Introduction

Followed by:

> Blessing and honour, glory and pow'r, be unto Him, be unto Him that sitteth upon the throne, and unto the Lamb.

It is even possible that the "Amen" of Rev 5:14 inspires its repeated use as *The Messiah* concludes. When one hears *The Messiah*, first performed in Dublin and regularly at the Foundling Hospital in London for charitable purposes,[116] the effect of the text of Revelation is unmistakable. However, it is possible not only to detect Revelation's effect upon *The Messiah* but also to know something of this text's effect upon the composer himself. For it is said that, upon the completion of the "Hallelujah Chorus," Handel commented to his servant, "I think I did see all Heaven before me and the Great God Himself."[117]

The effective history of Revelation upon music may also be observed in the hymns of Charles Wesley (1707-88).[118] The son of an Anglican cleric (Samuel) and a mother (Susanna) fiercely devoted to religious training, Charles worked closely with his better-known brother John. On 21 May 1738, three days before John's experience of the assurance of his salvation (when his heart was "strangely warmed"), Charles had his own religious awakening. Often referred to as the poet of the Methodist movement, Charles eventually penned more than 6,000 hymns. Rich in biblical content and theological reflection, a significant number of these hymns clearly show the impact of Revelation. For example, in the 1904 edition of *The Methodist Hymn-Book*, more than 110 of Charles's hymns make explicit reference to the words and/or imagery of the book of Revelation. Some of the hymns reflect a single idea such as the "cleansing blood of Jesus," found in Rev 1:5 (cf. Hymn 525.1 [verse 1]; 708.5; 709.4); "following the Lamb wherever he leads," in Rev 14:4 (541.1; 787.1; 788.1; 857.2); or "come quickly, Lord Jesus," from Rev 22:20 (66.6; 291.4; 529.5; 546.4; 554.2; 829.6). The ideas and wording of Revelation are so embedded in the hymns of Wesley that such examples could be offered almost ad infinitum. In addition to traces of Revelation's effective influence across a wide range of compositions, a number of Wesley's hymns are devoted wholly to a specific text or an amalgam of texts from Revelation. The three examples selected for inclusion here each

---

116. A. Hicks, "Handel and the Idea of an Oratorio," in *The Cambridge Companion to Handel*, 157, and D. Burrows, "Handel's Oratorio Performances," in *The Cambridge Companion to Handel*, 265.

117. Tobin, *Handel at Work*, 2.

118. On the eschatological views of Charles Wesley, cf. esp. Newport, *Apocalypse and Millennium: Studies in Biblical Eisegesis*, 119-49. Newport confines his fine study to the prose of Charles Wesley.

reveal something of the extent to which Revelation penetrated Charles Wesley's very soul.

The first example (Hymn 200) offers Wesley's meditation upon the prophetic word contained in Rev 1:7:

> 1 Lo! He comes with clouds descending,
>   Once for favored sinners slain;
>   Thousand thousand saints attending,
>   Swell the triumph of his train:
>   Hallelujah!
>   God appears on earth to reign.
> 2 Ev'ry eye shall now behold Him
>   Robed in dreadful majesty;
>   Those who set at nought and sold Him,
>   Pierced and nailed him to the tree,
>   Deeply wailing, deeply wailing,
>   Shall the true Messiah see.
> 3 The tokens of His passion
>   Still his dazzling body bears;
>   Cause of endless exultation
>   To His ransomed worshippers:
>   With what rapture
>   Gaze we on those glorious scars!
> 4 Yea, Amen! let all adore thee,
>   High on Thy eternal throne;
>   Saviour, take the power and glory,
>   Claim the kingdom for Thine own;
>   Jah, Jehovah,
>   Everlasting God, come down![119]

Another example (Hymn 802) is a moving reflection upon the description of those who passed through the great tribulation described in Rev 7:13-17:

> 1 What are these arrayed in white,
>   Brighter than the noonday sun?
>   Foremost of the sons of light,
>   Nearest the eternal throne?
>   These are they that bore the cross,

---

119. *The Methodist Hymn-Book* (London: Wesleyan Conference Office, 1904), 78.

Introduction

> Nobly for their Master stood;
> Sufferers for His righteous cause,
> Followers of the dying God.
>
> 2 Out of great distress they came,
> Washed their robes by faith below
> In the blood of yonder Lamb,
> Blood that washes white as snow:
> Therefore are they next the throne,
> Serve their Maker day and night;
> God resides among His own,
> God doth in His saints delight.
>
> 3 More than conquerors at last,
> Here they find their trials o'er;
> They have all their sufferings passed,
> Hunger now and thirst no more;
> No excessive heat they feel
> From the sun's directer ray,
> In a milder clime they dwell,
> Region of eternal day.
>
> 4 He that on the throne doth reign,
> Them the Lamb shall always feed,
> With the tree of life sustain,
> To the living fountains lead;
> He shall all their sorrows chase,
> All their wants at once remove,
> Wipe the tears from every face,
> Fill up every soul with love.[120]

A final example (Hymn 848) draws upon the concluding chapters of Revelation, focusing upon the future reward and place of abode awaiting the saints:

> 1 Away with our sorrow and fear!
> We soon shall recover our home,
> The city of the saints shall appear,
> The day of eternity come:

---

120. *The Methodist Hymn-Book*, 303.

From earth we shall quickly remove,
    And mount to our native abode,
The house of our Father above,
    The palace of angels and God.

2 Our mourning is all at an end,
    When, raised by the life-giving word,
We see the new city descend,
    Adorned as a bride for her Lord:
The city so holy and clean,
    No sorrow can breathe in the air;
No gloom or affliction of sin,
    No shadow of evil is there.

3 By faith we already behold
    That lovely Jerusalem here;
Her walls are of jasper and gold,
    As crystal her buildings are clear;
Immovably founded in grace,
    She stands as she ever hath stood,
And brightly her Builder displays,
    And flames with the glory of God.

4 No need of the sun in that day,
    Which never is followed by night,
Where Jesus's beauties display
    A pure and a permanent light:
The Lamb is their light and their sun,
    And lo! By reflection they shine,
With Jesus ineffably one,
    And bright in effulgence divine.[121]

Other Wesley compositions heavily influenced by Revelation include Hymns 227 and 848.

Though many other examples could here be offered,[122] the work of Han-

---

121. *The Methodist Hymn-Book*, 321-22.

122. Though the effective history of Revelation in the so-called mainline churches is often hard to discern, it has recently been demonstrated that the music known in this tradition reveals that, even here, Revelation is not without influence. Cf. the very helpful work of C. R. Koester, *Revelation and the End of All Things* (Grand Rapids: Eerdmans, 2001), esp. 33-38.

del and Charles Wesley illustrates the powerful influence of Revelation in the realm of music.

Poetry

The first example here offered of the effective power of Revelation in the world of English poetry comes from the so-called *Gawain*-Poet. Writing near the close of the fourteenth century in the Northwest Midlands of England, the *Gawain*-Poet produced four works contained in a single medieval manuscript. The name *Gawain* comes from the first poem in the manuscript, "Sir Gawain and the Green Knight." The similarity of dialect and vocabulary, among other things, leads most scholars to conclude that these four works come from the same author.[123] The effect of Revelation is quite pronounced in the most ambitious of the *Gawain* pieces,[124] a poem entitled "The Pearl." This influence is seen in the occasional direct references to "the Apostle John" or to "the Apocalypse," the numerous direct quotations of the book, and a variety of other more subtle appearances of the language and imagery of Revelation. One extended passage illustrates something of the extent of the theological integration of Revelation into the poetry of the *Gawain*-Poet. The passage is devoted to reflection upon the relationship between Christ and his bride, the church.

> 64
> O spotless Lamb who doth defeat
> All ills, my dearest Destiny
> Chose me His mate, although unmeet
> At first had seemed that unity
> From the world of woe I did retreat.
> He called me to His company:
> "Come hither to me, my belovéd sweet;
> There is no mote nor spot in thee."
> Might and beauty He gave to me.
> In His blood He rinsed my robes before
> He crowned me clean in virginity,
> Adorning me in pearls so pure.

---

123. On this and other introductory questions, cf. esp. A. Putter, *An Introduction to the* Gawain-*Poet* (London: Longman, 1996), 1-37.
124. Putter, *An Introduction to the* Gawain-*Poet*, 147.

65
Why, spotless bride who flames so bright,
Possessed of royalty rich and rife,
What kind of Lamb is He who might
Wed thee and take thee to his wife?
Above all others thou climbedst the height
To lead with Him so noble a life!
So many, comely combed, did fight
For Christ and live in constant strife,
And all those dear ones thou didst drive
Out from that marriage and so assure
Thy place alone, so bold and blithe,
A peerless maid, matchless and pure.

66
"Spotless," quoth that merry queen,
Unblemished I am, without a blot,
And that I might bear with stately mien,
But "unmatched queen," that said I not.
All wives of the Lamb in bliss we have been,
A hundred and forty thousand lot,
As in the Apocalypse it is seen.
St. John saw them gathered all in a knot,
On the hill of Sion, that seemly spot.
The Apostle saw them, in his vision's dream,
Arrayed for the wedding on that hill top,
The fair new city, Jerusalem.[125]

Another witness to the effective history of Revelation comes from the work of William Blake (1757-1827). Perhaps "the best poetry in English since Milton," Blake's work is widely known for its beauty, masterful design, and minute articulations.[126] Traces of Revelation's influence can be detected throughout much of the Blake corpus. For example, in "The Marriage of Heaven and Hell" (plate 19), one encounters the phrase "seven houses of brick," which refers to the seven churches of Rev 2–3. It is sometimes argued that, if Oothoon's search

---

125. *The Pearl* (trans. and ed. S. Deford et al.; New York: Appleton-Century-Croft, 1967), 65-67.

126. H. Bloom, *Blake's Apocalypse: A Study in Poetic Argument* (Garden City, NY: Doubleday, 1963), 9.

for Theotormon were successful in "Vision of the Daughters of Albion," there would be no more sea (Rev 21:1). Clear reference to Rev 11 is made in a passage from "Milton: The First Book" (plate 24, lines 59-62):

> The witnesses lie dead in the Street of the Great City;
> No Faith is in all the Earth: the Book of God is trodden under Foot:
> He sent his two Servants Whitefield & Westley: were they Prophets
> Or were they Idiots or Madmen? shew us Miracles.[127]

Also informed by Revelation (21–22) are the descriptions and measurements of Jerusalem in "Jerusalem: Chapter 1" (plates 12-13). By far the composition with the greatest concentration of Apocalypse imagery, however, is Blake's epic "The Four Zoas." Not only is the title taken from the four living beasts of Rev 4:6 (τέσσαρα ζῷα, *tessara zoa*), but there are also references to a number of terms and topics also found in Revelation. For example, the numerology of Revelation is reflected in "The Four Zoas: Night the First":

> Then they Elected Seven, called the Seven
> Eyes of God & the Seven lamps of the Almighty;
> The Seven are one within the other, the Seventh is named Jesus
> The Lamb of God blessed forever. . . .[128]

In addition to the numerology, descriptive terms like "the Synagogue of Satan" and "the Harlot of the Kings of Earth," also known as "Mystery the Harlot," frequently appear. Throughout the piece special standing is given to "the Lamb of God," who, among other things, creates for himself a bride and wife. While numerous other observations could be made about the effect of Revelation upon the poetry of Blake, perhaps something of the creative integration of these powerful images in his vision might best be captured in a passage from "The Four Zoas: Night the Eighth":

> We now behold the Ends of Beulah & we now behold
> Where Death Eternal is put off Eternally
> Assume the dark Satanic body in the Virgin's womb
> O Lamb divin[e] it cannot thee annoy O pitying one
> Thy pity is from the foundation of the World & thy Redemption

---

127. From *The Complete Poetry and Prose of William Blake* (ed. D. V. Erdman; New York: Doubleday, 1988), 118.

128. From *The Complete Poetry and Prose of William Blake*, 312-13.

Begun Already in Eternity
Come then O Lamb of God
Come Lord Jesus come quickly.[129]

Revelation's effective history in the realm of poetry is also evidenced within the Pentecostal tradition in a composition that appeared in 1907, written by an individual identified simply as Bro. A. Beck. The poem, entitled "The First Resurrection," was inspired by the words of Rev 20:6, "Blessed and holy is he that hath part in the first resurrection; On him the second death has no power."

"The First Resurrection"

Behold the sight most wonderful;
From every grave beneath the skies,
From ocean depth and mountain peak,
   The righteous dead arise.

With bodies glorified they come,
With faces radiant and sublime;
With shouts of victory ascend,
   All in a moment's time.

Changed in the twinkling of an eye,
Immortal bodies they put on;
Swifter than any lightning's ray
   And brighter than the sun.

Oh, what vast and joyous host,
When dead and living are called out,
From silent grave, and worldly crowd,
   At the archangel's shout.

No wicked one amongst that host,
Shall rise to life on that great day;
The flowers above their graves still bloom,
   Over their lifeless clay.

---

129. From *The Complete Poetry and Prose of William Blake*, 377.

Introduction

> In that great resurrection morn,
> Oh, grant us all a standing place;
> That we with all the Bloodwashed saints
> May see Thy blessed face.¹³⁰

Film

While the effective history of Revelation in the medium of film is vast, this brief section focuses upon two distinct celluloid interpretations that find their raison d'être in the book of Revelation. Distinct in their emphases and target audiences, each film exhibits clear signs of Revelation.

One motion picture that draws heavily upon Revelation is *End of Days*, a dark Arnold Schwarzenegger film. Timed for release to coincide with the turn of the millennium, the imprint of Revelation is obvious throughout. The premise of the film is that a female baby, born twenty years before the turn of the millennium, is dedicated and prepared to bear a child fathered by Satan upon his release from the Abyss. This tale of struggle at the cosmic level draws upon Revelation at a number of points as the story unfolds. Perhaps the clearest sign of Revelation's effect upon the film is the way in which Rev 20:7 serves as a refrain throughout the piece. The words of this verse ("And when the thousand years have ended, Satan will be loosed from his prison") appear as early as the opening credits and are read by the viewer or heard from the lips of various characters in the film on several occasions. In fact, the viewer is not permitted to allow the importance of Revelation to go unnoticed as part of the mystery of these words is revealed when Jericho (Schwarzenegger's character) actually reads them from the Bible. The release of Satan, accompanied by explosions and earthquake-like phenomena, is depicted as a phantom-like presence who searches New York City until the right man is found, of whom Satan takes possession. The plot develops as the powers of Satan are manifested and the diverse strategies of the church are unveiled. Satan's identity is developed in ways clearly indebted to Revelation, as both serpent and hideous beast are associated with either his activity or an image he takes on at some point. While the adulterous activities of the great πόρνη (*pornē*, "whore") of Rev 17–18 find no place in the film, the sexual immorality of this female figure appears to be lived out in the figure of Satan, who is sexually immoral from his first appearance to his last one. The purpose of his release, "to deceive the nations," is represented by the numerous individuals he co-opts

---

130. *Apostolic Faith* (ed. William J. Seymour; Los Angeles, CA), 1.8 (May 1907): 2.

or attempts to seduce in order to accomplish his goal. The witnesses of the church, who seek to oppose Satan at every point, meet fates similar to that of the witnesses found in Revelation. The gematria of the beast's number (666) is inverted (999) in this movie in order to produce the meaning that Satan's release coincides with the year 1999. The woman clothed with the sun, whose child the beast opposes in Rev 12, is transformed in this story into Christine York (Christ in New York!), who must be protected from the dragon by God and his agents, so that she *not* become impregnated. Her principal defender, Jericho, though a person on the verge of suicide as the movie opens — who has had a disagreement with God when his wife and daughter are ruthlessly murdered — mirrors Christ in several ways. At one point Satan, seeking the whereabouts of Christine, tempts Jericho with the promise of the return of his dead wife and daughter in exchange for the information. Perhaps the most explicit example of the similarities between Christ and Jericho is the moment in the movie when Jericho, while seeking to protect Christine, is betrayed by his best friend, attacked and beaten by a mob, finally being crucified in a dirty alleyway. Furthermore, near the conclusion of the film, Jericho renounces violence, asks God for strength, and seeks to face Satan through his faith in God/Christ. Despite Satan's attack, which includes Satan's entering him in order to accomplish his purpose for Christine, Jericho successfully fights off these internal struggles and, like Christ, goes to his death in order to save others. Jericho's death not only protects Christine but also culminates in Satan's return to the Abyss.[131] The effect of Revelation upon this film, intended for a mainstream audience, is obvious.[132]

A second film that shows the clear effects of the text of Revelation is *The Omega Code*, a TBN Ministries production. In keeping with a popular line of eschatological thought, this movie traces the rise of a world leader to a position of religious, political, and economic control. In addition to a plot readily recognizable to many (dispensational) students of "Bible prophecy," *The Omega Code* utilizes in its story line the Bible Code, a recent theory that, deep within Scripture, a secret code exists that yields to painstaking numerical and linguistic analysis. The world leader of *The Omega Code*, Stone Alexander (played by Michael York), makes use of the Bible Code to gain dominance of the world. From the beginning of the film, where explicit reference is made

---

131. It is perhaps significant to note that, in contrast to numerous other films in which the effect of Revelation can be detected, the term "antichrist" appears nowhere in *End of Days*.

132. For a somewhat different analysis of this film, cf. R. Walsh, "On Finding a Non-American Revelation: *End of Days* and the Book of Revelation," in *Screening Scripture: Intertextual Connections between Scripture and Film* (ed. G. Aichele and R. Walsh; Harrisburg, PA: Trinity Press International, 2002), 1-23.

Introduction

to the books of Daniel and Revelation, the significance of Revelation is clear. Throughout *The Omega Code* characters and events found in Revelation are highlighted. For example, the two witnesses described in Rev 11 figure prominently at numerous points throughout the film. Not only do they function as prophetic figures, appearing before the world on cable TV, but they are also martyred and humiliated but then raised from the dead. As the story unfolds, messages from the biblical text, discovered by means of the Bible Code, appear on a computer screen. Among the messages having clear reference to Revelation are the following:

- TEN HORNS UNITE UNDER WORLD LEADER
- AROMA OF END ENCHANTS ALL FOR 3½ YEARS
- BLOOD POURS FROM STONE — WORLD WONDERS
- SEVEN HORNS BOW TO WOUNDED HEAD, and
- DAWN OF A NEW MILLENNIUM.

In addition to these messages, which act as a refrain throughout the film, there are the rebuilding of Solomon's temple (based upon an interpretation of Rev 11), the worship of the beast and reference to his (false) prophet, a wound to the head of Alexander and his subsequent recovery, the reading of the text of Rev 13 by the two witnesses, and the appearance in a vision of the Four Horsemen, described in Rev 6. It is difficult to overestimate the significance of this and other films like it,[133] for they represent the thinking and expectations about the end time of a significant number of Christians worldwide.

Commentaries

This subsection concludes the part devoted to Revelation's streams of influence, as well as the introduction proper. The four commentaries surveyed at this point each represent a significant contribution and movement in the study of Revelation over the centuries.

The first extant commentary on Revelation is that by Victorinus, bishop of Pettau (d. ca. 304), written sometime around 260 and preserved by Jerome. This work offers comment on a number of verses in almost every chapter, except 16 and 18. Victorinus's interpretative approach is symbolic in nature, if not allegorical, as the following examples illustrate. Commenting on the open door John saw in Rev 4:1, Victorinus notes, "The New Testament is announced as an

---

133. Cf. also movies based upon the *Left Behind* series of books by Tim LaHaye.

open door in heaven."[134] His comments on the open book in the hand of God continue this thought, "This book signifies the Old Testament, which has been given into the hands of our Lord Jesus Christ, who received from the Father judgment."[135] But perhaps the nature of Victorinus's approach is captured best by his comments on Rev 6:12-14:

> 12"And I saw, when he had opened the sixth seal, there was a great earthquake." In the sixth seal, then, was a great earthquake: this is that very last persecution.
>
> "And the sun became black as sackcloth of hair." The sun becomes as sackcloth; that is, the brightness of doctrine will be obscured by unbelievers.
>
> "And the entire moon became as blood." By the moon of blood is set forth the Church of the saints as pouring out her blood for Christ.
>
> 13"And the stars fell to the earth." The falling of the stars are the faithful who are troubled for Christ's sake.
>
> "Even as a fig-tree casteth her untimely figs." The fig-tree, when shaken, loses its untimely figs when men are separated from the Church by persecution.
>
> 14"And the heaven withdrew as a scroll that is rolled up." For the heaven to be rolled away, that is, that the Church shall be taken away.
>
> "And every mountain and the islands were moved from their places." Mountains and islands removed from their places intimate that in the last persecution all men departed from their places; that is, that the good will be removed, seeking to avoid the persecution.[136]

Victorinus offers an extensive explanation of how the numerical calculation of the number of the beast, found in Rev 13:18, works in Greek, Latin, and even Gothic. For him, there is no doubt as to the identity of the seven hills upon which the woman sits in Rev 17:9. It is "the city of Rome." On the identity of the kings in 17:10-11, he writes:

> 10"And there are seven kings: five have fallen, and one is, and the other is not yet come; and when he is come, he will be for a short time." The time must be understood in which the written Apocalypse was published, since then reigned Caesar Domitian; but before him had been Titus his brother, and

---

134. Cited according to the translation of R. E. Wallis in *The Ante-Nicene Fathers*, vol. 7 (Edinburgh: T&T Clark, 1989), 347.
135. Cited according to the translation of R. E. Wallis in *The Ante-Nicene Fathers*, 7:349.
136. Cited according to the translation of R. E. Wallis in *The Ante-Nicene Fathers*, 7:351.

Introduction

Vespasian, Otho, Vitellius, and Galba. These are the five who have fallen. One remains, under whom the Apocalypse was written, Domitian, to wit. "The other has not yet come," speaks of Nerva; "and when he is come, he will be for a short time," for he did not complete the period of two years.

11"And the beast which thou sawest is of the seven." Since before those kings Nero reigned.[137]

In his more extensive comments on Rev 20:1-6 Victorinus appears to argue for an earthly millennial reign of Christ, at the end of which Satan will be released for a period of three and one-half years. He goes on to say:

> I do not think the reign of a thousand years is eternal; or if it is thus to be thought of, they cease to reign when the thousand years are finished. But I will put forward what my capacity enables me to judge. The tenfold number signifies the decalogue, and the hundredfold sets forth the crown of virginity: for he who shall have kept the undertaking of virginity completely, and shall have faithfully fulfilled the precepts of the decalogue, and shall have destroyed the untrained nature or impure thoughts within the retirement of the heart, that they may not rule over him, this is the true priest of Christ, and accomplishing the millenary number thoroughly, is thought to reign with Christ; and truly in his case the devil is bound. But he who is entangled in the vices and the dogmas of heretics, in his case the devil is loosed. But that it says that when the thousand years are finished he is loosed, so the number of the perfect saints being completed, in whom there is the glory of virginity in body and mind, by the approaching advent of the kingdom of the hateful one, many, seduced by that love of earthly things, shall be overthrown, and together with him shall enter the lake of fire.[138]

The second commentary to be considered comes from (the Venerable) Bede (ca. 672-735).[139] Bede's work, which is a running commentary on every verse in Revelation, is over 40,000 words long. Several aspects of this volume merit comment.

As far as can be determined, Bede is the first interpreter to offer a seven-part structure for Revelation. His view of the structure is roughly as follows:

---

137. Cited according to the translation of R. E. Wallis in *The Ante-Nicene Fathers*, 7:358.
138. Cited according to the translation of R. E. Wallis in *The Ante-Nicene Fathers*, 7:359.
139. The Venerable Bede (Venerable Beda), *The Explanation of the Apocalypse* (trans. E. Marshall; Oxford: James Parker, 1878).

Preface 1:1-8
1. 1:9–3:22
2. 4:1–7:17
3. 8:1–11:18
4. 11:19–15:8
5. 16:1-21
6. 17:1–18:24
7. 19:1–22:21

In the commentary itself, however, Bede's work takes the form of three books (Book 1: 1-8; Book 2: 9-14; Book 3: 15-22). In a letter he explains this move by saying that three short books relieve the mind of the readers better than seven. Bede is clearly indebted to interpreters before him. There are places where his interpretative decisions mirror those of Victorinus. He not only cites the interpretive rules of Tyconius in his letter to Eusebius, but he also quotes Tyconius some ten times in the body of the commentary. Generally, Bede sees recapitulation at work in Revelation, specifically mentioning that the story is recapitulated at several points (4:1; 8:1; 9:20; 11:18; 20:1). Like Victorinus before him, much of the interpretive approach could be described as spiritual or even allegorical in nature. He offers some "philological" evidence in his exposition, as for example when he gives a definition of the meaning of the names of six of the seven churches in Rev 2–3. The four living creatures are the Evangelists, and when they preach, everyone falls down. The book in the hand of the one who sits on the throne, described in chapter 5, is the Bible; the writing on the outside is the OT, while the writing on the inside is the NT. At a number of points Bede sees the symbols of Revelation as pointing to the heretics with which the church is confronted. They are identified as the pale horse in Rev 6 and one of the trumpets in Rev 8. There are extensive explanations offered for the order and significance of the twelve tribes of chapter 7 and the jewels found in the description of the New Jerusalem in chapter 21. The theophanic element of lightning is identified on several occasions as referring to the working of miracles. Those playing harps are those who have been crucified. Mention of the sea of glass refers to baptism, as does mention of the first resurrection in 20:5. Apparently influenced by Tyconius and Augustine, Bede interprets the thousand-year reign as the present time, that is, what remains of the sixth day, at the end of which Satan is loosed for 3½ years. The liars mentioned in 21:8 are those who claim to be Jews but are not.[140]

---

140. On Bede and others, cf. the discussion by G. Kretschmar, *Die Offenbarung des Johannes: Die Geschichte ihrer Auslegung im 1. Jahrtausend* (CTM 9; Stuttgart: Calwer, 1985), 116-22.

Introduction

The third commentary to be discussed is the *Expositio in Apocalypsim*,[141] by the medieval abbot Joachim of Fiore (ca. 1135-1202). This commentary, which is considered the abbot's greatest work, incorporates earlier writing on Revelation entitled the *Enchiridion super Apocalypsim*. Following an introduction, the commentary is divided into eight books, each devoted to a section of Revelation.

Book 1   1:1–3:22 — Letters to the Seven Churches
Book 2   4:1–8:1 — The Opening of the Seven Seals
Book 3   8:2–11:18 — The Seven Trumpet Blasts
Book 4   11:19–14:20 — The Two Beasts
Book 5   15:1–16:17 — The Seven Bowls
Book 6   16:18–19:21 — The Destruction of Babylon
Book 7   20:1-10 — The Millennium
Book 8   20:11–22:21 — The Heavenly Jerusalem.

These eight parts of Revelation correspond to the seven special times (eras) of the church, followed by the eighth, which corresponds to the glorification of the heavenly Jerusalem.[142] Crucial to Joachim's interpretation is his understanding of redemptive history as being divided into three eras or statuses, namely, the era of the Father, the era of the Son, and the era of the Holy Spirit. While these eras have distinct points at which they begin and end, they also overlap with one another. Joachim, who produced a number of works entitled *Liber Figurarum* ("Book of Figures"), by which he taught theological truths, conveyed this reality as three successive circles that overlap with one another. They are arranged in such a way, however, that all three converge at the centermost part, signifying the unity of the Father, Son, and Holy Spirit. The age of the Father can be traced from Adam until Christ's first advent, the age of the Son begins there, and the age of the Spirit is still to come. Within these three eras the seven ages of redemptive history may be fitted. The first five (Adam, Noah, Abraham, David, and Babylonian Exile) occurred in the age of the Father, the sixth (John the Baptist) in the age of the Son, with the seventh awaiting the beginning of the era of the Spirit.

Part of Joachim's contribution is the employment of historical referents in the interpretation of Revelation. For example, in his discussion of the beast with seven heads found in Rev 12 and following, Joachim offers these identifications set out in the chart that follows:

---

141. For the text, cf. Joachim of Fiore, *Expositio in Apocalypsim* (Frankfurt: Minerva, 1964).
142. Cf. the website of the International Center for Joachimist Studies, in San Giovanni in Fiore, www.centrostudigioachimiti.it/Benvenuti/benvenutieng.asp.

Head	Person	Persecution by	Time period reflected
1.	Herod	Jews	Apostles
2.	Nero	Pagans	Martyrs
3.	Constantius	Heretics	Doctors
4.	Muhammad	Saracens	Virgins
5.	Mesomoth	Son of Babylon	Conventuals
6.	Saladin	Spiritual men	In Joachim's time
7.	Gog	Second antichrist	End of time

As the chart indicates, these historical identifications enable the reader to make their way through redemptive history. The mention of Joachim's contemporary Saladin (1138-93) as the sixth head of the beast reveals something of the eschatological expectancy of Joachim's thinking, for Saladin was the Muslim leader who recaptured Jerusalem from the Crusaders. From Joachim's perspective, the seventh head could appear at any time, signaling the end of time and the beginning of the age of the Spirit in earnest. Challenging the amillennial views of interpreters like Tyconius and Augustine, Joachim's work fueled the fire for millennial expectation in numerous later interpreters.[143]

A final commentary to be mentioned in this survey is by Allan A. Boesak.[144] Writing during the time of apartheid in South Africa, Boesak combines an analysis of the text that focuses on the message of the book for John, as well as its contemporary significance. Following an extensive introductory chapter, the rest of the book is divided into seven chapters, entitled:

The Blessing
The Scroll
The Seven Seals Opened
The Woman and the Dragon
The Beast from the Sea and the Beast from the Earth
The Fall of Babylon
The End and the Beginning.

---

143. In addition to the website mentioned above, cf. also the helpful discussions of Joachim by Wainwright, *Mysterious Apocalypse*, 49-53, and J. Kovacs and C. Rowland, *Revelation* (Oxford: Blackwell, 2003), 17-19. For excerpts of Joachim's work in English, cf. *Apocalyptic Spirituality: Treatises and Letters of Lactantius, Adso of Montier-en-Der, Joachim of Fiore, The Franciscan Spirituals, Savonarola* (New York: Paulist Press, 1979), 97-148.

144. A. A. Boesak, *Comfort and Protest: Reflections on the Apocalypse of John on Patmos* (Edinburgh: St. Andrew Press, 1987).

Introduction

Boesak sees Revelation as underground protest literature written within the context of a persecuted church. Bringing considerable attention to historical issues of introduction, Boesak argues that ultimately such issues are of secondary importance for readers of the book. For example, though he will argue vigorously for a date of composition sometime during the reign of Domitian, in comparison to the context of the "oppressed" reader, this point is relatively inconsequential. He comments:

> The arguments around the different hypotheses seem to lead always to an effort to establish the truth about judging the *degree* of oppression that was meted out by one or another emperor. Whether it was Nero or Domitian or even Galba (as John A. T. Robinson suggests) is ultimately of secondary importance. To the suffering people of God it did not really matter who they suffered under. What mattered is that they suffered. . . . It is the fact that the weak and the destitute remained oppressed which provides the framework for understanding and interpreting history.[145]

Describing his work as "biblical exegesis from the underside," Boesak writes specifically with the black South African church in mind. He notes:

> For people who face situations like these, the Apocalypse is an exciting, inspiring, and marvellous book. It is a book which, in our sociopolitical situation, is a constant call to conversion and change. It is prophetic, historical, contemporary. But we shall have to learn to read it differently. We shall have to do away with those sterile escape mechanisms and dead-end arguments about numbers and symbols and signs by which the real message is so often paralyzed.[146]

Boesak's reading is one in which the text of Revelation, its first-century context, and the context of the black South African church interact on an almost constant basis. Examples of the power of this interaction abound, as the following citations reveal. Note his comments on the meaning of the song in Rev 5:12:

> On a Sunday afternoon young black Christians pick up this ancient song and make of it a new song as they dance around a police vehicle just after a student has been arrested at our church service. . . . In translation it goes something like this:

---

145. Boesak, *Comfort and Protest*, 25.
146. Boesak, *Comfort and Protest*, 38-39.

> "It is broken, the power of Satan is broken!
> We have disappointed Satan, his power is broken.
> Alleluia."

As we sing, the song is picked up by others. The police somewhat confused, somewhat bewildered, somewhat scared, release our friend. Others join us as we march, singing and dancing, back into the church. This is a new song, a freedom song, and the power of it, the sheer joy of it, the amazing truth in it captivate and inspire thousands upon thousands throughout South Africa. For although the seals of the scroll must still be opened, the scroll is not in the hands of Caesar but in the hands of the Lamb. And we will sing this new song until "every creature in heaven and on earth and under the earth and in the sea, and all therein," will say (5:13):

> "To him who sits on the throne and to the Lamb be blessing and honour and glory and might for ever and ever!"[147]

Boesak's interpretation of the "souls under the altar" in 6:9-10 is no less insightful.

> The martyrs are dead, but their witness is still alive. Their voices can still be heard; they still inspire the church. They remind the church of what it means to be faithful to Jesus the Messiah, of the price one must pay for testimony to the one true God. They remind the church also of the true character of the powers of this world. The church must not forget who and what it is facing.[148]

To interpreters who are repelled by the vengeful nature of the martyrs' prayer, Boesak responds:

> People who do not know what oppression and suffering is react strangely to the language of the Bible. The truth is that God *is* the God of the poor and the oppressed. . . . The oppressed do not see any dichotomy between God's love and God's justice. Why is there this division between the God of the Old Testament and the God of Jesus? Why, on this point, does white Western Christianity go back to the heresy of Marcion?[149]

On the identity of the number of the beast, Boesak says:

---

147. Boesak, *Comfort and Protest*, 61-62.
148. Boesak, *Comfort and Protest*, 68.
149. Boesak, *Comfort and Protest*, 72.

> For the key here is not who the beast is; the church knows that. Neither is the key whether we begin counting from D. F. Malan or H. F. Verwoerd or P. W. Botha, from 1910 or from 1948. The key here is the understanding of the mystery: this beast, this powerful merciless, violent beast, was and is not and goes to perdition. . . . It has no life and no future. It comes from hell and goes to hell.[150]

On the prophecy about the fall of Rome and, by extension, the fall of the apartheid regime, he notes:

> We must remember that as John writes there is no sign whatsoever of the imminent fall of Rome. He speaks like an Old Testament prophet. The vision is so clear, God's decision so certain, that for all intents and purposes it has already happened. Rome still stands, but John already can hear and see the rumblings and ripples of the mighty earthquake that will hit the city. He knows the end of Rome is near. . . . Rome may still have power, but John knows that we are seeing the beast's final convulsions.[151]

A final example comes from his stinging words on the need for a new heaven and new earth:

> How well should we understand this, we people of the twentieth century. We saw the heavens polluted by the foul and vile smoke from the factories, made hopelessly inhabitable for the birds of the sky in the name of progress. We know about "missiles carving highways of death through the stratosphere." . . . Can the heavens ever be clean again after Hiroshima and Nagasaki? Can the heavens ever be purified of the stench of gas ovens, burned-out villages in Asia, or utterly destroyed Palestinian camps in Lebanon? And the vilest stench of all: those powerful and mighty men in top hats, sashes, and uniforms who threaten and maim, kill and destroy, and then go to prayer breakfast and call upon the name of God. . . . No, John is so right — there must be a new earth and new heaven.[152]

Though Boesak would have his own temptations and struggles with the seduction of the beast, his commentary has few rivals among those seeking to bring one's context to bear on the interpretation of Revelation.

---

150. Boesak, *Comfort and Protest*, 115-16.
151. Boesak, *Comfort and Protest*, 119.
152. Boesak, *Comfort and Protest*, 127-28.

Commentary

Prologue (1:1-8)

The first thing encountered by a hearer of Revelation is a prologue that contains the title of the book, a formal greeting that follows epistolary convention, a doxology, and two prophetic words.[1] The very first word encountered is ἀποκάλυψις (*apokalypsis,* "revelation, unveiling"). In early Christian circles a "revelation" is understood to be a revelatory word of the Spirit (cf. 1 Cor 14:6). Such a beginning suggests that all that follows is closely connected to the work of the Spirit.

The next words identify this work as a "revelation of Jesus Christ." While grammatically this Greek phrase can mean a revelation given by Jesus (a subjective genitive) or a revelation about Jesus (an objective genitive), the book's content reveals that this unveiling is both a revelation from Jesus and, at the same time, a revelation about Jesus.[2] Johannine hearers are not surprised to learn that this revelation "was given to him (Jesus Christ) by God," for in John's gospel the Son speaks only the things that the Father gives him to speak (cf. John 1:18; 8:28; 12:49-50; 14:10; 15:15; 17:8, 14). This revelation is given "to show his servants what is necessary to take place quickly," with this verb "show" often used to "designate an unveiling of the future" (Rev 4:1; 17:1; 21:9-10; 22:1, 6, 8).[3] "His servants" could refer to believers in general, but per its OT usage its occurrence here may anticipate the numerous mentions of prophets in this book and may even be evidence that the community of Revelation is a pro-

---

1. G. R. Beasley-Murray, *Revelation* (Grand Rapids: Eerdmans, 1981), 50.
2. As E.-B. Allo (*Saint Jean: L'Apocalypse* [Paris: J. Gabalda, 1921], 3) observes, "C'est une Révélation de Jésus-Christ sur Jésus-Christ." Cf. also Resseguie, *The Revelation of John,* 62.
3. G. Schneider, "Δείκνυμι, δεικνύω," *EDNT,* 1:280.

phetic community.[4] The revelation's content is further identified as "that which is necessary to take place quickly." Both the word δεῖ (*dei*, "it is necessary") and the thought that the contents of the book must take place quickly indicate something of the urgency of this message.[5]

The revelatory chain of transmission continues to include Jesus' angel and "John his servant." The introduction of the angel in Rev 1:1 is a bit odd in that the angel does not really function as a guide until Rev 17. The order of the revelation's transmission makes clear that Jesus Christ is not in a subordinate position to the angel but, as seen later, is so far superior that he is worthy of receiving worship alongside God. The verb "showed" indicates the manner of the revelation here described, carrying with it the idea of prophetic (Acts 11:28) and/or metaphoric (John 12:33; 18:32; 21:19) language, as this verb comes from the same word family as the preferred Johannine word for "sign," suggesting a meaning that has a significance that transcends a literal or surface meaning.[6]

This revelation is entrusted to "his servant John," a well-known prophetic figure in the Johannine community, possibly to be identified with John the Elder, likely author of other Johannine documents. It is this John "who has borne witness . . . to whatsoever he saw." The significance of John's bearing witness is clear from the dominance of the idea in John's gospel, its prominence in Revelation, where one's witness is intimately connected to one's identity as a believer, and its close relationship to the witness or testimony of Jesus, the content of those things John saw. The content of this revelation is described as "the word of God and the witness of Jesus." The phrase "the word of God" occurs at a number of places in Revelation (1:2, 9; 6:9; 19:13; 20:4; cf. also 17:17 and 19:9, where the plural "words" occurs). Reminiscent of numerous OT texts where a prophetic call is being recounted (Hos 1:1; Joel 1:1; Jer 1:2, 4, 11), it prepares the way for v. 3, where the book is referred to as "the words of this prophecy." For Johannine hearers, the phrase may also point to Jesus, who is known as the Word of God in John's gospel (1:1-18) and appears to be the one named "the Word of God" in Rev 19:13. The christological inference of the first phrase is made explicit in the second, "the witness of Jesus," making clear that the content of the Revelation is not twofold ("the word of God and the witness of Jesus"); rather, these two phrases refer to the same reality, the second phrase clarifying the first.[7] It is difficult not to see in this phrase, which occurs six times in Revelation (1:2, 9; 12:17; 19:10[2x]; 20:4), reference both to Jesus' life and witness as evidenced

---

4. Cf. esp. Hill, *Prophecy*, 87-93, and Smalley, *Revelation*, 27. Beale (*Revelation*, 183) argues that this points to the community's "general prophetic vocation."
5. Osborne, *Revelation*, 55.
6. Smalley, *Revelation*, 27.
7. Resseguie, *The Revelation of John*, 64.

Prologue (1:1-8)

in John's gospel and to that which follows in Revelation, assuring the hearers of the continuity between this revelation and what is already known of Jesus.

The first of seven beatitudes found in Revelation occurs in v. 3 (also in 14:13; 16:15; 19:9; 20:6; 22:7, 14). This blessing is pronounced upon all those involved in the prophetic interpretive task. Specifically, this process includes a reader who reads aloud and those who "*hear* the words of this prophecy and *keep* the things written in it." Both participles, "hearing" and "keeping," are governed by the same article, which means that "those who hear" are identical with "those who keep."[8] "The words of this prophecy" indicate that this revelation stands in the tradition of the OT prophetic literature. In the Johannine literature those who hear Jesus believe in him (John 1:37, 40; 4:42; 14:28), belong to God (8:47), have eternal life (5:24), show that they are Jesus' sheep (10:3, 8, 16, 27), and will rise from their graves (5:25, 28). In Rev 1:3 hearing the words of this prophecy entails the appropriate response to them,[9] an emphasis reinforced by the blessing pronounced upon those who keep the things written in this book. Keeping the words or commands of Jesus entails more than simple conformity to a set of principles; it includes also an identification with and incorporation of the words and commands of Jesus. Such a response to his words results in eternal life (John 8:51-55) and a sharing in divine love (John 14:15-24; 15:10, 20; 17:6, 11-15). Hearing and keeping are no passive responses on the part of the prophetic community but entail active and sustained responses. The urgency of such responses is made clear by the words "for the time is near," a second reference in these first three verses to the fact that the things described in this book are soon to take place.

The prologue gives way to the formal opening of this circular letter in verses 4-5a, where the standard A (author) to B (recipients) greeting found in a variety of letters in Greco-Roman antiquity occurs. John, named for a second time, is now identified as the author. The addressees are the seven churches in Asia. The number seven is not exclusive but inclusive, for it is a number of completion in Revelation.[10] John is thus addressing all the (Johannine) churches in Asia.[11] The pronouncement of grace comes with the knowledge that the Logos is the one full of grace and that, out of his fullness, "we have all received one grace after another" (John 1:14, 16). Consequently, the grace conveyed in this greeting ultimately comes from Jesus Christ (John 1:17). On three occasions in

---

8. On the relationship of hearing and doing (obeying) in the OT and in a Pentecostal hermeneutic, cf. L. R. Martin, *The Unheard Voice of God: A Pentecostal Hearing of the Book of Judges* (JPTS 32; Blandford Forum, UK: Deo Publishing, 2008), 61-79.

9. Smalley, *Revelation*, 31.

10. Beale, *The Book of Revelation*, 186-87.

11. Simoens, *Apocalypse de Jean*, 16.

Prologue (1:1-8)

John's gospel, Jesus himself speaks peace to his disciples: in John 14:27, when the disciples face the prospect of his departure, and after the resurrection both to the disciples (20:19) and later to Thomas (20:26). This same peace is now spoken to the seven churches, who may also share with the disciples in John's gospel a "troubled" context.

The gifts of grace and peace have a threefold origin, coming from "the one who is, who was, and is coming," the seven Spirits, and Jesus Christ. This second mention of God underscores that there is no time at which God does not exist. Present, past, and future converge in his presence and being. The grace and peace that come from him have no limits in time. As with the seven churches, so reference to the seven Spirits implies completion, the fullness of the Spirit in the presence of the one who sits on the throne.[12] Though sometimes taken to be angelic beings,[13] it appears that the "seven Spirits" refer to the Spirit himself. The intertext that converges with John's experience here is likely Zech 4:2, where the seven-branched lampstand stands in the holy place in the temple.[14] The description "the one who sits on the throne" affirms God's sovereignty over all creation, and his throne is viewed in contrast to the thrones of others. The close proximity of the seven Spirits to the one who sits on the throne implies their nearness to God and the fact that, when they act, it is God himself who acts. This grace and peace thus come from the throne of God by means of the seven Spirits before the throne. These gifts also come from Jesus Christ, who is "the faithful witness," a phrase that anticipates the connection between witness and death that the second description conveys. Jesus is also called "the firstborn of the dead," making clear the connection between Jesus' faithful witness and death, but at the same time underscoring that, though he experienced death, he is no longer dead. Jesus is also called "the ruler of the kings of the earth," which indicates that this revelation of Jesus Christ makes known things about him not yet fully appreciated. In John's gospel, Jesus is known to be the King of Israel (John 1:49), for a true Israelite declares him so (1:47). In Revelation, this reign now extends over all kings of the earth, a statement that would convey a sense of assurance in the face of the kings of the earth, often experienced in opposition to God and his kingdom, serving as a subtle indication of the later positive role of the kings of the earth in the New Jerusalem (Rev 21:24).

Reflection upon the extraordinary nature of Jesus Christ explodes into a spontaneous doxology of praise focusing upon three aspects of his redemptive

---

12. Resseguie, *The Revelation of John*, 66.
13. Aune, *Revelation 1-5*, 34-35.
14. Cf. the helpful discussion in Bauckham, *The Climax of Prophecy*, 162-66.

work (vv. 5b-6).[15] He is "the one who loves us." The nature of this love for the community is reflected in John's gospel. It is complete and ultimate — Jesus "loved his own until the end" (13:1). It is sacrificial; the Father (17:23) sent his Son into the world (3:16). Jesus' love is also made known in 1 John 3:16, "In this we have known love, because that one laid down his life on our behalf." Mention of "the one who loves us" continues the thought of Jesus' death from v. 5 and anticipates the next description as he "who loosed[16] us from our sins by his blood." It is well known within the community that Jesus is the one who sets free from sin, for he is the "Lamb of God who takes away the sin of the world" (John 1:29). This implicit paschal imagery points in the direction of the efficacious power of Jesus' blood noted later in John's gospel (6:53-56; 19:34), and made explicit in 1 John 1:7–2:2 and 5:6-7. The statement that Jesus loves us and destroyed our sins also prepares for the paschal imagery in Rev 5:6. The idea that Jesus destroyed sin is in continuity with 1 John 3:8, "The Son of God was manifested in order to destroy the works of the devil" (cf. 1 John 3:4-10). Jesus is also said to have "made us a kingdom, priests to God and his Father" (Rev 1:6). This kingdom is identified as "priests to God," indicating that they are set apart for service unto him. As the book unfolds, there is a clear connection between their service to God, the effects of the blood of Jesus, and reigning with God (cf. esp. 5:9-10 and 20:6). By placing the object of the doxology first in the Greek sentence, emphasis is placed upon the worthiness of this one to receive praise, before praise is even given. It is to the one who has accomplished all these spectacular things that glory and honor are given eternally. In this first occasion of worship in Revelation, John leads the way in giving glory and honor to Jesus. The unlimited praise "for ever and ever" matches the unlimited worthiness of Jesus. The prayer "amen," or "so let it be," concludes the doxology.

At this point, two prophetic utterances explode upon the scene.[17] These words continue the worship of God and contribute toward the development of two themes revealed in the first six verses. The first prophetic utterance consists

---

15. Beale, *The Book of Revelation*, 191.

16. There is some question as to the original reading at this point in the manuscript tradition; λύσαντι (*lysanti*, "who loosed" or "who destroyed") is supported by the bulk of the best manuscripts. The other option, λούσαντι (*lousanti*, "who washed") would fit well with the idea of the washing away uncleanness (sin) found in John 13:10, while the former would fit well with the fact that in Revelation a variety of things are loosed (Rev 5:2; 9:14, 15; 20:3, 7).

17. The placement of these prophetic words within a context of worship in the prologue may indicate something of the way in which prophecy functioned within community gatherings. From these verses it would appear likely that prophetic utterances came forth in moments when the community was engaged in times of spontaneous praise.

of words about the resurrected Jesus, while the second prophetic utterance consists of the words of God.

In v. 7 sacred texts, sacred teaching, and the experience of the Spirit converge. The "faithful witness," "the firstborn of the dead," "the ruler of all the kings of the earth" will "come with the clouds." Within the Johannine trajectory something new is revealed, for while the promise of Jesus' return is part of the Johannine tradition, "coming with the clouds" is not. At his appearing "every eye will behold him — even those who have pierced him." Such language suggests that those responsible for Jesus' death will look upon him (John 19:37), extending beyond the cross to a different kind of beholding. Here, this appearance is the moment of his vindication, in accord with the oracle from Zech 12:10-12, "all the tribes of the earth will mourn because of him." It is the mourning of lost opportunity, of opposing this returning one. The conclusion of this first prophetic word is indicated by the addition of John's own "yes" and "amen."

The second prophetic utterance begins with the words ἐγώ εἰμι (*egō eimi*, "I Am"), which are often on the lips of Jesus in John's gospel, where they convey the idea of identification with Yahweh.[18] In Rev 1:8 the predicate to the "I Am" statement is "Alpha and Omega." But here, this "I Am" is not in reference to Jesus but to the Lord God. In a move reminiscent of 1 John, a statement normally associated with Jesus (in John's gospel) is reappropriated with reference to God. This identification indicates that God is the Beginning and the Ending, the First and the Last — he is the all in all. The eternality of God is underscored once again by his identification as "the one who is, and was, and is coming." The last words of this prophetic utterance, and the prologue as a whole, further identify God as ὁ παντοκράτωρ (*ho pantokratōr*, "the All Powerful One"), an identification that will act as a refrain throughout the rest of the Apocalypse (4:8; 11:17; 15:3; 16:7, 14; 19:6, 15; 21:22). This claim places an exclamation point as to God's sovereignty, power, and unrivaled status.[19]

---

18. Cf. the very helpful piece by D. Ball, *"I Am" in John's Gospel: Literary Function, Background, and Theological Implications* (JSNTS 124; Sheffield: JSOT Press, 1996).

19. Osborne, *Revelation*, 72.

"In the Spirit on the Lord's Day" (1:9–3:22)

The first major section of Revelation consists of 1:9–3:22, the onset indicated by the first "in the Spirit" phrase (1:10). This section is divided into two major parts; the inaugural vision of Jesus (1:9-20) and his seven prophetic messages to the seven churches of Asia (2:1–3:22). This section is held together by (1) the resurrected Jesus, whom John sees, speaking prophetically to the seven churches and (2) an element from the inaugural vision of Jesus being incorporated into each of the seven prophetic messages.

The Inaugural Vision of Jesus (1:9-20)

In this inaugural vision of Jesus, the hearers learn of John's geographic and spiritual locations, his initial commissioning for his prophetic task, the stunning description of the resurrected Jesus, and pneumatic discernment.

For a third time the author identifies himself as John, his name made emphatic by the personal pronoun ἐγώ (*egō*, "I"). In the three verses that follow, the hearers learn several things about John. First, he is their "brother." While the preponderance of occurrences of this term in John's gospel refers to a physical relationship, by the time of John 21:23 the term appears to have taken on a spiritual connotation, its dominant meaning in 1 John and 3 John. While the term "brother" retains this spiritually intimate meaning in Revelation, it shows signs of taking on the added meaning of prophet.

Second, John is their "participant" or "sharer." The idea of fellowship, significant within the Johannine community (1 John 1:3, 6-7; 2 John 11), is not far from the thought expressed.[1] John is a participant in tribulation, a bittersweet reality, for although it entails suffering, it is not suffering without reward. Jesus reminds the disciples that, though they suffer tribulation in this world, they will rejoice, as surely as a woman who rejoices at the sight of her child after suffering the tribulation of childbirth (John 16:21). In the midst of such tribulation Johannine hearers are comforted by the fact that Jesus has overcome the world (John 16:33). No doubt the hearers of Revelation understand John to share with them in this bittersweet experience. As the book will reveal, such tribulation is known all too well by the hearers (Rev 2:9-10; 7:14). John also is a participant in the kingdom, into which Jesus has made the believers (1:6). Additionally, he is a participant with them in "faithful endurance." Such steadfastness is an absolutely essential quality for those who seek to be faithful witnesses to Jesus

---

1. Smalley, *Revelation*, 49.

in Revelation. Each of the things in which John is a participant with the community are said to be "in Jesus," and each of them are connected to Jesus in a special way.[2] For he has overcome the world, made them into a kingdom, and has himself been a faithful witness.

John's geographic location on the island called Patmos is revealed, as is the reason for his location. Patmos is a ten-by-six-mile island located about thirty-six miles off the coast of Asia (Minor) in the Aegean Sea. It was near a group of islands where, according to Tacitus (*Annals* 4.30), political prisoners were regularly exiled. If John was indeed on Patmos because of political banishment, it might reveal something of his social status, as only nobility and priests were afforded the luxury of exile. John's location on Patmos was owing to "the word of God and the testimony of Jesus." The phrase could be taken to mean that John had gone to Patmos to engage in missionary activity there or that he had been exiled there owing to his "Christian" identity, which fits with the theme of suffering and persecution in the book. It is also possible to take the phrase "on account of the word of God and the testimony of Jesus" as indicating that John was on Patmos for the purpose of witnessing to all he would see (namely, "the word of God and the testimony of Jesus").[3] At any rate, his location there is clearly tied to his activity as witness.

Previously, the hearers are told, "I was on an island called Patmos." In v. 10 they hear, "I was in the Spirit on the Lord's Day." While the identical construction with which these statements open clearly connects John's geographic location with his spiritual location, it also serves to contrast these two locations. Although John may be on an island, he is at the same time "in the Spirit."

The connection between the seven Spirits before the throne and John's being "in the Spirit" would not be lost on the hearers. Because the seven Spirits are in such close proximity to the throne, we understand that, when they act, it is God himself who acts. Since this revelation of Jesus Christ is given by God, it should come as no surprise that the Spirit is so crucially involved. It also reveals the ways in which the work attributed to the Spirit in Revelation is at the same time the work of God. As noted, the phrase "in the Spirit" is an important one, for it occurs four times in very significant locations. In fact, by means of this phrase we see the book's structure, suggesting that the Spirit is the means by which the revelation of Jesus Christ takes place. It is in this state that John sees things, hears things, tastes things, touches things, and interprets things. "In the Spirit" there are moments of convergence where all that John is, is drawn upon as new and constructive dimensions of present and future reality are experi-

---

2. Smalley, *Revelation*, 50.
3. Smalley, *Revelation*, 51.

enced. The community would likely understand being "in the Spirit" as being intimately connected to prophetic activity (i.e., the way in which one receives and makes known prophetic visions, messages, and words). It seems not to be going too far to say that the community would likely see their own participation in the discerning process as being "in the Spirit" as well.

The only indication of when John is initially "in the Spirit" is conveyed by the phrase "on the Lord's Day." In a book known for its pregnant imagery, it is possible that more is being given than a detail about the day of the week on which John experiences the revelation. John may be giving his writing an eschatological date.[4] On this view, the phrase "on the Lord's Day" might very well cause the hearers to think of the OT idea of יום יהוה (*yom Yahweh*, "the Day of the Lord/Yahweh"). However, the hearer is not likely to take this simply as a reference to the OT "Day of the Lord," but that day as the Lord's Day when Jesus himself will appear to resurrect the righteous dead. This intertextual understanding of the phrase may also explain why John does not simply utilize the OT language for *yom Yahweh*, for it is that day and more! Not only is this reading of "the Lord's Day" consistent with the rich symbolism of the document, but it also dovetails nicely with the eschatological context in which Rev 1:10 is located, namely, between the prophetic word by Jesus about his return (v. 7) and the vision of the resurrected Jesus (vv. 12-20). The Lord's Day relativizes all other days. The hearers thus stand with John on the verge of the day to which all of history points, the Lord's Day.

While he is in the Spirit on this day, John hears "behind him a great voice as a trumpet." In this verse John, who hears a great many things in Revelation, hears the words of this prophecy for the first time himself. Mention of a great voice introduces an idea that follows often in the book. Whenever mention is made in Revelation of a trumpet (4:1; 8:2, 6, 13; 9:14) or the sounding of a trumpet (8:6-8, 10, 12-13; 9:1, 13; 10:7; 11:15), the sound comes from God either directly or indirectly. Many of the sounds John describes in the book are the loudest human-made or natural sounds possible in the first century CE. The effect of such intensity of sound should not be ignored or minimized.[5] In these sounds, the initial words of Jesus in Revelation, John receives a commissioning for his prophetic task. His commission is twofold: to write and to send. The hearing of this command for John to write what he sees in a book is doubly comforting for the hearers, who are reaping the fruit of John's faithful witness as they hear this book read. The hearers also understand that "the words of the book of this

---

4. Bacchiocchi, *Sabbath*, 111-31.
5. On the trumpet, cf. R. Skaggs and P. Benham, *Revelation* (PCS; Blandford Forum, UK: Deo Publishing, 2009), 27.

prophecy" is a book written at divine direction. What John sees, he writes, something he claims as early as 1:2. Near the end of the account of this inaugural vision of Jesus, John will again be instructed to write (v. 19). In addition, John is commissioned to send the book to the seven churches. Although not identified as the seven churches of Asia, as in v. 4, the seven churches are here individually named. They are the churches in Ephesus, Smyrna, Pergamum, Thyatira, Sardis, Philadelphia, and Laodicea. These cities are mentioned in a clockwise fashion, beginning in the southwest with Ephesus and ending in the southeast with Laodicea,[6] perhaps conforming to a circular ancient postal route.[7] Clearly, all the Johannine churches are the intended audience of this book.

With the onset of v. 12 the hearers are introduced to what will be a recurring phenomenon within the book: John hears something, but what he sees has changed (before his eyes), not unlike psychedelic imagery, where one form morphs into another before one's eyes. On this occasion John turns to "see" the voice that was speaking with him, a reference that may very well underscore the significance of the commission that comes from this voice in 1:10-11.[8] Perhaps the hearers would be reminded of the way in which Mary Magdalene turns to see the resurrected Jesus in John 20:14, as the same Greek verb occurs in both contexts.[9] John says, "And I turned to see. . . . And turning I saw." What he sees, however, is not a voice but "seven golden lampstands." John's focus goes immediately to the midst of the lampstands.

In the stunning vision of Jesus that follows, elements from a variety of OT texts converge in new and creative ways, giving John a glimpse of one who combines numerous characteristics of God, the Son of Man, and his servants. From Zechariah we see lampstands (4:2); from Daniel, characteristics of "one like the Son of Man" (7:13), "the Ancient of Days" (7:9), the fiery furnace (3:6), and a man dressed in linen with a gold belt around his waist (10:4-6); from Ezekiel, elements from the wheel within a wheel (1:16) and the man in linen (9:11); from Isaiah, a mouth like a sharpened sword (49:2); and from Judges, words about the face of the Lord (6:22). Yet none of these details on their own, nor simply an accounting of them from their OT texts, does justice to the vision.[10] Such a convergence of elements and details indicates that the revelation of Jesus Christ continues in astounding fashion as he is seen and experienced as never before. His being identified with enigmatic figures, as well as with God himself, indicates that, in Jesus, there is a culmination of God's purposes and

---

6. Smalley, *Revelation*, 52.
7. Osborne, *Revelation*, 85.
8. Osborne, *Revelation*, 86.
9. Smalley, *Revelation*, 52.
10. Cf. Osborne, *Revelation*, 89.

The Inaugural Vision of Jesus (1:9-20)

activities. As Son of Man, the promise of Jesus' return rings in the ears of the hearers from v. 7. As one attired in the robe and sash, with eyes that are ablaze, feet like glowing brass, and a voice of many waters, he is securely in control of the future. With head and hair white like wool, he is intimately identified with the Ancient of Days. With the stars in his hands and a mouth sharp as a double-edged sword, he too speaks and acts prophetically. And the brilliance of his face — it is like the sun, shining with all its power, like that of God's face. Such brightness, such radiance is almost blinding, impossible to comprehend.

John's response when he saw this figure was to fall "at his feet as though dead." Such a response cannot be unexpected, given this encounter with the resurrected Jesus, revealed in all his glory. It also sets a precedent of sorts for prostration as an element common in contexts of worship in Revelation (4:10; 5:8, 14; 7:11; 11:16; 19:4; 22:8). Such a response would appear to be an involuntary reflex by John, who is clearly overwhelmed by the glory of Jesus.

John's response is met by Jesus' own response, a combination of touching and speaking. That Jesus places his right hand, which has the seven stars in it, upon John suggests that this touch is not a mere sign of comfort. Such a description suggests that this act has something to do with prophetic communication. This action is accompanied by the words of the one who has a sharp two-edged sword in his mouth and conveys the sound of many waters when he speaks. He utters words that are both recognizable and, at the same time, continue to reveal aspects of Jesus' identity not yet known. His words "fear not, I Am" remind us of Jesus' words in John's gospel to the fearful disciples who had just seen Jesus walk to them on the water (6:19-20). On that occasion Jesus says, "I Am, fear not." On this occasion, the command "fear not" is followed by the predicate use of "I Am." In words reminiscent of the prophetic words of God in 1:8, Jesus says "I Am the First and the Last" in 1:17. His appropriation of language synonymous in meaning to the words of God confirms what the vision has implied: a deep and intimate identification between God and Jesus. As with God, Jesus himself embraces beginning and end. There is nothing that lies outside him and his influence or power. This penetrating speech continues in v. 18, where Jesus identifies himself as "the Living One." For Johannine hearers, such a statement is not surprising, for "in him was life" (John 1:4), and he is "the Way, the Truth, and the Life" (14:6). In this passage (Rev 1:18), Jesus' emphasis appears to be upon his being continually alive, as the present participle "the Living One" implies. This understanding is confirmed by the next words of Jesus, who says, "I was dead, and behold I am living forever and ever." The grammar makes clear the primary point. Jesus had been dead at one point, but he is now alive forever. Such a statement expands the previous description of Jesus as the firstborn of the dead, which also implies that he *was* dead, but dead no longer. Attention to his present state is underscored by "behold." Just as God is the one "who is, who was, and who is coming," so Jesus is "the First and the Last" and "is living forever more." His past experience with death and continuous experience with life have made him a captor of and victor over death and its companion Hades (cf. Rev 6:8; 20:13-14). This mastery is conveyed by the imagery of Jesus having "the keys of Death and Hades."[11] The one who holds the keys controls the door, determining who goes in and who goes out. The not so subtle message is simply that there is no need to fear Death and Hades because Jesus holds the keys! His death and continual life have given him possession of these keys.[12] The one who is seen in all his glory is first and last, was dead and lives forever, has dominion over Death and Hades.[13] What an extraordinary figure he is!

At the beginning of this inaugural vision (v. 11) and again near the end of this vision, John is commanded to write what he has seen. These commands serve to function as borders or boundaries (an inclusio) around this vision of Jesus. By this means a close connection is made between the authority of John's commission and the authority of the one who commissions. The use of the term "therefore" serves to underscore that John is commanded to write owing to his experience of the resurrected Jesus. Here he is specifically instructed to write "what he has seen, and what is, and what is about to happen after these things." The urgency with which the book begins, with regard to things that must take place quickly or soon (vv. 1-3), thus reappears in v. 18. There are present and future realities that John will see ("after these things"), about which he must write.

In this vein, John and his hearers receive their first overt instruction about pneumatic interpretation, as Jesus himself on this occasion offers an explanation of "the mystery of the seven stars . . . and the seven golden lampstands." Mention of the word "mystery" alerts us that at least these details in the vision of Jesus call for interpretation that is available only by means of divine (Jesus' own) explanation. Such an occurrence conveys the reality that writing (and reading, hearing, and keeping!) "in the Spirit" is facilitated by the intervention of God himself. The seven stars in his right hand, which has been placed upon John, are the seven "angels" or "messengers" of the seven churches. On this understanding, these seven stars in his hand are the means by which he communicates with the churches. In some ways, such an understanding minimizes the importance of the debate that seeks to determine whether these "messengers" are human messengers or angelic beings. While either interpretation can do justice to the text, given the prominent role of angels in the rest of Revelation and the lack of

---

11. Beale, *The Book of Revelation*, 214-15.
12. Osborne, *Revelation*, 96.
13. Smalley, *Revelation*, 56.

a human referent for this term within the book, it would appear that "angels" is the best translation/interpretation here.[14] Jesus also makes known to John the meaning of the seven lampstands in the midst of which he is standing. They are the seven churches, already mentioned twice before. Jesus' presence in the middle of these lampstands, which stand for all churches, underscores the vital relationship that exists between Jesus and the churches. As will become clear, it is his presence that determines whether or not the church is a church.

The Seven Prophetic Messages to the Seven Churches of Asia (2:1–3:22)

Though many translations and commentators treat chapters 2 and 3 as distinct from chapter 1, there is no break in thought or sequence in the Greek text of Revelation. The things described in the next two chapters are experienced by John in a position of prostration, with the right hand of Jesus upon him the entire time, the same right hand in which he holds the seven stars that have just been identified as the seven messengers of the seven churches.

Though each of the prophetic messages is distinct in terms of content and detail, they share a similar structure and for the most part comprise the same elements.[15] Each of the messages begins with the command, "To the angel of the church in . . . write." Each of the prophetic messages contains a description of Jesus taken from the inaugural vision. Each contains words of Jesus that reveal his intimate knowledge of the church being addressed, often with the phrase "I know your works." Five of the prophetic messages contain a call for repentance. Each of them contains a promise to those who overcome or are victorious. Each includes the refrain, "The one who has an ear, let him or her hear what the Spirit says to the churches," which stands next to last in the first three prophetic messages, and last in the remaining four messages.

To the Angel of the Church in Ephesus (2:1-7)

Without a break in the Greek text, the first of seven additional commands to write occurs in 2:1, where the angel of (and in turn) the church in Ephesus is addressed. While it is likely that the appearance of "angel" or "messenger" refers to an angelic messenger, owing to the fact that an individual "human" messenger would no doubt deliver the book to the individual congregations,

---

14. Osborne, *Revelation*, 99.
15. Simoens, *Apocalypse de Jean*, 28-30.

perhaps the hearers would not be overly preoccupied with the meaning of the term. That the angel of the church at Ephesus is addressed first is no surprise, given the somewhat circular order of the churches to be addressed (1:11), the close proximity of Ephesus to Patmos, and Ephesus being known as the place of first landing in Asia.[16] The address of Ephesus first might even reflect its standing among the other churches in the community.[17]

It is not altogether clear how important knowledge of the ancient city of Ephesus is for the proper interpretation of the prophetic messages. Despite numerous attempts to provide a historical backdrop against which to read chapters 2 and 3,[18] in the end precious little is known about the churches themselves, with the most reliable information coming directly from the text itself.[19] While it is quite likely that residents of a particular location would pick up on subtleties in the text about the city in which they live, it is clear that all the hearers are the intended audience, many of whom would not be in the same interpretive position.

What would the hearers think of when encountering the name Ephesus? Perhaps they would think of one of the great cities of the Roman world, which had a population of around 250,000 inhabitants. Perhaps they would think of a leading religious center that was home to one of the seven wonders of the ancient world, the Temple of Artemis, "the Mistress of Wild Animals," whose image included various fertility symbols, such as a chest that was covered with breasts.[20] Perhaps they would think of a center of commerce or think of the leading city in the province.[21]

Whatever the hearers may think about Ephesus, they soon discover what Jesus thinks. With the description of Jesus as "the one who holds the seven stars in his right hand, the one who stands in the midst of the seven lampstands," they are introduced to the use of characteristics of Jesus in the inaugural vision in each of the prophetic messages, providing a link to this vision while conveying other subtle details to the hearers. For example, though subtle, the shift in vo-

---

16. Ramsay, *The Seven Letters to the Seven Churches of Asia and Their Place in the Plan of the Apocalypse*, 227-28.

17. Smalley, *Revelation*, 59.

18. Cf. esp. the work of Ramsay, *The Seven Letters to the Seven Churches of Asia and Their Place in the Plan of the Apocalypse*, and Hemer, *The Letters to the Seven Churches of Asia in Their Local Settings*.

19. Cf. the work of Moyise, *The Old Testament in the Book of Revelation*, 24-44, and Koester, *Revelation and the End of All Things*, 41-72.

20. For an image of the Ephesian Artemis, cf. *National Archaeological Museum of Naples* (ed. S. DeCaro; Naples: Electa Napoli, 1999), 30.

21. C. J. Hemer, "Seven Cities of Asia Minor," in *Major Cities of the Biblical World* (ed. R. K. Harrison; Nashville: Nelson, 1985), 236.

cabulary from Jesus "having . . . seven stars" in 1:16 to "holding seven stars" in 2:1 is noteworthy. In Revelation the term "holding" implies something firmly in one's grasp (2:1; 7:1; 20:2) or a strong attachment to a teaching or person (2:13-15, 25; 3:11), emphasizing that the seven stars, the seven messengers, are firmly in the hand of Jesus and, consequently, at his full disposal. Similarly, in 2:1 Jesus is said to be "walking" in the midst of the lampstands instead of merely being in their midst (1:13), which conveys both the notion of intimate relationship between Jesus and the churches (3:4; 21:24) and the idea of activity on Jesus' part. The one who is in the midst of the churches is the one who knows the churches and is active within them.

In v. 2, in the phrase "I know your works," the hearers are introduced to a most significant term in Revelation, "works." In this book the word can be used of good (2:2, 5, 19, 26; 3:1, 8, 15), bad (2:6), or incomplete (3:2) works. There are works for which repentance should be, but is not always, offered (2:22; 9:20; 16:11). Some works are an extension of one's witness beyond death (14:13). Other works are the direct actions of God (15:3). On several occasions, works are the basis of one's (future) judgment (18:6; 20:12-13) and/or one's reward (2:23; 22:12). Clearly, the idea of works is an integrative one that includes one's activity or actions and that carries a sign-like quality revealing something about one's relationship with God and/or Jesus.[22]

"I know your works" introduces the hearers to the content of the bulk of this communiqué (vv. 2-6), for in this section several dimensions of Jesus' knowledge of this particular church are revealed. Specifically, the church is commended for its "works" (vv. 5-6), "labor" (v. 2), and "patient endurance" (v. 3). Apparently, each of these qualities is to be understood as related to the church's resistance of "evil ones," manifested in the form of false apostles and teachers, an emphasis made clear in that the content of this prophetic message begins and ends with reference to such individuals, in the form of the "evil ones"/"false apostles" (2:2) and the Nicolaitians (2:6). One important dimension of the church's commendation is that they "are not able to bear/support evil ones." But while they are not able to support evil ones, they do "support/bear on account of my name" (2:3).[23]

Their lack of support for such evil ones is illustrated initially by their "testing those who say of themselves that they are apostles." While mention of apostles in this verse might be taken as a reference to the twelve apostles, the evidence of the broader Johannine tradition would seem to subvert such an understanding, for the term "apostle" never appears in John's gospel or in

---

22. Though nuanced differently, cf. the definition offered by Osborne, *Revelation*, 113.
23. Aune, *Revelation 1–5*, 143.

1–3 John with that meaning. Its lone appearance in these documents is in John 13:16, where the term is part of a proverbial saying used alongside the verbal form πέμψαντος (*pempsantos*, "the sending one"), not as a reference to the Twelve. In that context, ἀπόστολος (*apostolos*, "apostle" or "sent one") prepares the reader of the Gospel of John for a reference to the mission of the disciples (13:20), where again one finds forms of the verb πέμπω (*pempō*, "send").[24] Often in John's gospel John the Baptist (1:6), the Son (3:17), and the disciples of Jesus (4:38) are spoken of as being or having been sent by God, using a form of the verb ἀποστέλλω (*apostellō*, "send [out]"). Similarly, a form of the verb *pempō* refers to John the Baptist (1:33), the Son (4:34), the Paraclete (14:26), and Jesus' disciples (20:21). Such usage suggests that, for the Johannine community, "sending" language has become theologically conditioned with special reference to divine mission but has stopped short of becoming technical language for the Twelve. Owing to this extensive theological background, "those who claim to be apostles" would be understood as referring to individuals who claim a special status as having been sent by God to the community. Yet, despite these individuals claiming to be apostles, Jesus declares that they are not, a verdict in agreement with the discernment of the Ephesian church, whose testing finds that they are not apostles at all but liars. Such a description would perhaps remind hearers of the way Jesus speaks of the devil in John 8:44, as a liar and the father of lies. The other occurrences of the term "test" in Revelation (2:10; 3:10) suggest that this testing is understood as quite an intense process. If the admonitions to test the S/spirit(s) found in 1 John 4:1-6 were utilized,[25] then the testing of these would-be sent ones would involve a discernment process that included the entire Ephesian church community. Since prophetic activity attributed to the Spirit must be in conformity to the Spirit confession "Jesus Christ coming in the flesh," it might be inferred that these so-called sent ones were found lacking in this regard. Since prophetic activity attributed to the Spirit was expected to exhibit continuity with the community's experience of and belief in Jesus, it appears there was a lack of such evidence on the part of the would-be apostles. The words and actions of these imposters were apparently found to be the result of the spirit of deception rather than the Spirit of Truth. It should be obvious that this testing process would imply that other sent ones are indeed sent by God to the community and would be judged accordingly.

In the face of such liars, the church at Ephesus exhibits patient endurance,

---

24. On this interpretation, cf. J. C. Thomas, *Footwashing in John 13 and the Johannine Community* (JSNTS 61; Sheffield: JSOT Press, 1991), 111.

25. Osborne, *Revelation*, 113. On this interpretation, cf. J. C. Thomas, *1 John, 2 John, 3 John* (London: T&T Clark International, 2004), 197-214.

a spiritual characteristic they share with John (1:9). Specifically, such patient endurance is exhibited in their "bearing" certain unnamed burdens "on account of my name," a phrase that introduces a very significant term in Revelation: "Jesus' name." Belief in Jesus' name leads to the authority to become children of God (John 1:12), to have eternal life (John 20:31; 1 John 5:13), and to have the forgiveness of sins (1 John 2:12). Furthermore, anything they can ask for in his name will be received (John 14:13-14, 26; 15:16; 16:23-24, 26). The hearers also know that solidarity with the name brings persecution (John 15:20-21) and that belief in his name is closely associated with loving one another (1 John 3:23). In Revelation its appearance carries a deep sense of solidarity and personal identification with Jesus, here conveyed by the hearers' bearing adversity on account of his name (2:3). They hold onto his name (2:13) as he holds the seven stars in his right hand, and they do not deny his name (3:8). To those of whom Jesus says in v. 2, "I know your ... labor," he now says "you have not labored out" (i.e., become worn out). The church in Ephesus is clearly commended for its tenacious loyalty under difficult circumstances.

Owing to such stellar praise, the hearers can hardly be prepared for the phrase they next encounter: "But I have against you that...." The change in tone and direction is indicated by the strong word of contrast "but" and by the grievance that Jesus lodges against the church in Ephesus. In these first words of rebuke by Jesus in Revelation, the church in Ephesus is told, "You have left your first love." The central significance of the rebuke is made clear by the phrase's structural location, standing at the center both of the content of the message (vv. 2-6) and of the entire message to the church at Ephesus (vv. 1-7), and being bounded on either side by Jesus' words of commendation in vv. 2-3 and v. 6. Furthermore, the rebuke begins with "first love," moves to a call to "repent" and to do "first works," and closes with words of "repentance," implying a connection between the "first love" and "first works," as well as a connection between repentance and "first works."

Standing first in the rebuke are the words "first love," indicating something of their importance in the sentence and thought. It is sometimes thought that the words "first love" would refer to the zeal of a new believer and, in this context, the waning of such zeal. However, the role and function of love within the Johannine literature, the most dominant theme within this corpus, suggest that the phrase would have a more concrete meaning here. Love is dynamic, active, and relational. It begins with God (1 John 4:7, 16b), who loved the world so much that he sent his unique Son (John 3:16; 1 John 4:9-10). Jesus' love for his own is understood to be complete and ultimate (John 13:1), leading to the laying down of his life for others (1 John 3:16). This love can even be spoken of as "perfected" or "completed" in believers (1 John 2:5; 4:12, 17-18). Such love is no abstract concept but is understood as manifest in work and truth, that is, the concrete actions of emotive, sacrificial giving to the point of giving one's life (1 John 3:16-18). Significantly, the command for believers to love one another is rooted and grounded in the fact that "he first loved us" (1 John 4:19). The words "first love" appear to stand as an amalgam of ideas fused together throughout the Johannine literature.

Given the earlier mention of Jesus' love for the hearers (1:5), the "first love" in 2:4 may have primary reference to Jesus. If so, Jesus' rebuke that they have left their first love is especially stinging in the light of his earlier praise for them, for bearing opposition on account of his name. The existence of this rebuke on the heels of such stellar praise creates a dialectic around their relationship with Jesus — they hold to his name, but they have left their first love.

Jesus next issues a command that grows out of this rebuke, as the presence of "therefore" indicates. The command to remember suggests that this rebuke takes the church in Ephesus by surprise, that they may not be aware until this moment that they have left their first love. At the least, it implies that they have forgotten this fact. The call to remembrance challenges them to recall all that their first love involved and how far they have fallen from that place. Perhaps the appearance of the word "fallen" would remind readers that, while John fell at Jesus' feet as though dead, they have fallen away from him. The exact meaning of their "fallen" situation is quickly revealed in the double command to "repent and do your first works." Though the command to repent might be a bit of a surprise to Johannine hearers, as the word does not occur in John's gospel or 1–3 John, it is a very important theological concept in Revelation. The majority of the term's occurrences appear with reference to the seven churches in the seven prophetic messages (2:5[2x], 16, 21-22; 3:3, 19), while four times the word appears with reference to those who refuse to repent of the "works of their hands" (9:20-21; 16:9, 11), despite the gracious judgments of God. Here the command to repent calls for a turning away from the action that Jesus judges, namely, leaving their first love. There is an explicit connection between repenting and doing "first works," which must involve love.

Within the Johannine community, there could hardly be any misunderstanding about what first works requires: love for one another. This is, after all, the new command that Jesus gives to his disciples (John 13:34), the criterion by which all will know that "you are my disciples" (13:35), and the way in which we know that we love God and Jesus (1 John 4:7–5:5). It appears, then, that, while the hearers in Ephesus have been extraordinarily resilient in opposing "evil ones," they have left their first love, Jesus, by their lack of love for one another.[26]

---

26. Fee, *Revelation*, 27.

Repentance for leaving the first love necessarily entails the first works of loving one another, while loving one another is the fruit that they have truly repented.

The absolute necessity of repentance is underscored by a veiled threat contained in Jesus' next words, "If not, I will come to you," the first of seven places in Revelation where Jesus announces his imminent "coming" (2:5, 16; 3:11; 16:15; 22:7, 12, 20). Owing to the mourning generated by Jesus' appearance described in 1:7, it would come as no surprise that Jesus' first words about his coming have an ominous tone. While the prophetic words of 1:7 rather clearly speak of Jesus' eschatological return, in 2:5 they appear to refer to his ongoing activity. Rather than taking these ideas as referring to wholly distinct activities of Jesus, the hearers would likely see a great deal of continuity between them, while holding them in some tension.[27] We should not see the eschatological coming of Jesus in too great a tension with his ongoing activity, for there appears to be a certain merging of these ideas in Revelation. The Jesus who is coming in eschatological glory (1:7) comes even now to the seven churches (2:5). Consequently, Jesus' ongoing activity would be seen as eschatological activity, an understanding not far removed from the eschatological emphases of John's gospel.

Jesus' specific threat to the church at Ephesus, should it refuse to repent, is "I will remove your lampstand from its place," the devastating implication being that the lampstand would be extinguished; that is, the church at Ephesus would cease to exist.[28] The lampstand would be removed from its place by the one who walks among the lampstands. If leaving the first love refers to Jesus, it is not surprising that such action would ultimately result in the destruction of the church by the one abandoned, Jesus. The seriousness of the situation is made clear in that a call for repentance occurs at the beginning, middle, and conclusion of v. 5, an emphasis that alerts the hearers as to the need for repentance on behalf of this church, while indicating that this issue is a major one in Revelation.

The prophetic words of Jesus in v. 6 reveal that the content of the message is coming to a close and is connected with what precedes it in at least two ways. Most immediately, the words of v. 6, "But you have ... ," stand in contrast to the words of v. 4, "But I have. . . ." The words of rebuke in v. 4 are followed by words of encouragement in v. 6, indicating that all is not lost. Earlier such evil ones were identified as "those who claim to be apostles but are not." Here they are identified as the Nicolaitans. The chiastic balance of these examples in vv. 2 and 6 implies that both "those who claim to be apostles" and "the Nicolaitans" are to

---

27. Osborne, *Revelation*, 118.
28. Aune, *Revelation 1–5*, 147.

be identified as "evil ones." What might be somewhat surprising is the positive use of the word "hate" on this occasion, for in the Johannine literature the term rarely has a positive meaning, often appearing to describe the world's hatred of the Father (John 15:23-24), Jesus (John 3:20; 7:7; 15:18, 23-25), and his followers (John 15:18-19; 17:14; 1 John 3:13), and in its association with the Elder's rebuke, it is directed to one who hates one's brother (1 John 2:9, 11; 3:15; 4:20). The lone positive use of the term is found in John 12:25, where Jesus says, "The one who loves his life will lose it, and the one who hates his life in this world will guard it unto eternal life." In Rev 2:6 the Ephesian believers are praised for hating the "works of the Nicolaitans." Furthermore, they learn that Jesus himself "hates" such works. Perhaps in such shocking language the hearers would discern a distinction between their own works, which Jesus knows (and praises), and the works of the Nicolaitans, which Jesus (apparently knows and) hates. While little is known about the Nicolaitans outside Revelation, a few additional details are revealed in 2:14-15.[29] At this point it is enough to know that the church in Ephesus stands in solidarity with Jesus against their adversaries.

Jesus' first prophetic message reaches its conclusion in v. 7, where two distinct components of the seven prophetic messages occur for the first time in Revelation. The first is a call to discerning obedience, "The one who has an ear, let that one hear what the Spirit is saying to the churches," a phrase that appears seven times in chapters 2-3. It is anything but perfunctory, as a number of ideas converge in this rich theological refrain. This invitation suggests that the interpretive, discerning process to which they are called is not only a christological endeavor but is also a pneumatological one. While the refrain places emphasis upon what the Spirit is saying, it is clear that these words are the prophetically spoken words of Jesus. Thus, it is clear that the words the Spirit is saying are coterminous with the words prophetically spoken by Jesus. Such a phenomenon reminds us of the relationship between Jesus and the Spirit of Truth in John's gospel. It also indicates that the relationship between Jesus and the Spirit is an especially close one in Revelation. At this point it is sufficient to note that Jesus and the Spirit speak with one voice.[30] The hearers cannot help but remember that the Spirit who is speaking now in the prophetically spoken

---

29. One of the only other occurrences of the word "hate" in Revelation is in 17:16, where it describes the eventual hatred of the Great Whore by the Beast and the Ten Horns. Such a linguistic connection might imply a religiotheological connection between the Great Whore and the Nicolaitans.

30. It might be worth noting that the phrase "The one who has an ear to hear, let that one hear" occurs often in the sayings of Jesus in several Synoptic texts (cf. Matt 11:15; 13:9, 43; Mark 4:9, 23; Luke 8:8; 14:35). Such evidence, if known by the hearers, would underscore the fact that these are indeed Jesus' words. Cf. Aune, *Revelation 1-5*, 155.

The Seven Prophetic Messages to the Seven Churches of Asia (2:1–3:22)

words of Jesus is the same Spirit who is before the one who sits on the throne (1:4), the same Spirit who makes possible John's revelatory experience (1:10). This understanding may even suggest that these words of Jesus, coterminous with the Spirit's words, are also directly connected with the one who sits on the throne. For a third time in Revelation the term "hear" appears, having occurred in the beatitude near the book's beginning (1:3) and in the description of John's initial revelatory encounter (1:10), the former occurrence being closely connected to the idea of "keeping" (i.e., obeying) the words of this prophecy. As the book unfolds, it becomes obvious that the call to "hear" is a call to obedience (cf. esp. 3:3). The hearing called for here is a specifically pneumatic activity. Owing to John's being "in the Spirit" when he sees (and writes!), to these words being the prophetically spoken words of Jesus, and to John and his hearers already having received divine interpretive assistance from Jesus himself, it appears that the entire process from first encounter to discerning obedience is a pneumatic experience. In this activity, the hearers stand in solidarity with John, Jesus, and the Spirit. If John's role is to "write in the Spirit," the role of others in this prophetic community is to "hear in the Spirit." If part of the discerning obedience called for in Revelation is one of the ways in which the hearers "keep the words of this prophecy," then the first concrete call for such obedience involves continued "hard labor," "patient endurance," and "bearing the name of Jesus." It also involves repentance for any abandonment of one's first love (Jesus) and a doing of "first works" (loving one another). There is more to keeping the words of this prophecy than having knowledge of inside information on the unfolding of history. It involves discerning obedience.

The conclusion of this first prophetic message is marked by a second component characteristic of each of the seven prophetic messages: a promise for the one who overcomes. The idea of overcoming is informed by Jesus himself stating, in John's gospel, "I have overcome the world," a victory over both the world that hates him (15:18–16:4) and its ruler, who is already being judged (16:11). Through Jesus (1 John 5:5), believers also overcome the evil one (1 John 2:13-14) and the world (1 John 4:4; 5:4). In keeping with John's gospel, in Revelation the word describes the activity of Jesus as Lion (5:5) and Lamb (17:14), as well as the rider on the white horse that Jesus unleashes with the opening of the first seal (6:2). While "overcoming" is used even of the activity of the beast against the saints (11:7; 13:7), the vast preponderance of its occurrences is in contexts used to describe believers in Revelation. Early in the book the term appears in the context of promises to those who overcome (2:7, 11, 17, 26-28; 3:5, 12, 21). But as Revelation unfolds, the saints' overcoming is spoken of in the past tense, as an accomplished reality (12:11; 15:2). This combination of promise and fulfillment culminates in the term's final occurrence in the eschatological promise of 21:7.

The first of the seven promises made in Rev 2–3 reveals that they are eschatological in nature. Jesus' words "I will give . . ." make it clear that he is the giver of these promises. Here he will give those who overcome something to eat, an idea common in John's gospel, where Jesus gives a variety of things to be eaten, including himself (cf. esp. John 6)![31] The promise to eat of the tree of life would take the hearers to the beginning of the biblical canon, where the paradise of God includes a tree of life (Gen 2:9). The fruit of this tree, when eaten, enables one to live forever (3:22). However, as a result of the disobedience of Adam and Eve, God denies access to the tree by barring entry into his garden (3:23-24). Jesus' promise carries with it concrete evidence of the reversal of the curse found in Genesis, for access to the tree of life is no longer denied but granted, indicating that access to this tree means access to eternal life. This promise comes from Jesus, "the one who lives," "who was dead and is living forevermore" (1:18), the one identified as life (John 1:4; 14:6), even eternal life (1 John 1:2). Although God barred access to the tree of life owing to disobedience, access is granted by Jesus, owing to the overcomers' obedience. Mention of the location of the tree of life as in the paradise (or garden) of God reminds readers of the idyllic environment of creation described in Genesis while drawing upon the eschatological associations paradise comes to have in the Hebrew Bible (Isa 51:3; Ezek 28:13; 31:8-9),[32] anticipating the idea of paradise fulfilled in the city of the New Jerusalem. With these words, the first prophetic message of Jesus to the seven churches comes to a close.

To the Angel of the Church in Smyrna (2:8-11)

Without delay, Jesus instructs John to write to the angel of the church at Smyrna. Encountering the name Smyrna, a city located some forty miles north of Ephesus, perhaps the hearers think of its history of destruction (ca. 600 BCE) and rebuilding (ca. 300 BCE). Perhaps they think of its oft-depicted crown-like acropolis, located on a hill more than 500 feet high, or that Smyrna rivaled Ephesus as Asia's "first city."[33]

However the hearers regarded Smyrna, they quickly hear Jesus' assessment. Again, Jesus identifies himself by means of elements familiar from John's stunning inaugural vision. The words "the First and the Last" (1:17) underscore

---

31. On this theme, cf. esp. J. S. Webster, *Ingesting Jesus: Eating and Drinking in the Gospel of John* (Atlanta: SBL, 2003), 149-50.

32. Aune, *Revelation 1–5*, 152.

33. Cf. Hemer, "Seven Cities of Asia Minor," 239-40, and Murphy, *Fallen Is Babylon*, 118-19.

Jesus' intimate identification with God — nothing lies outside his influence;[34] this is the first of several contrasts found in Rev 2–3.[35] As before, the identification of Jesus as "first and last" is followed by reference to his death and life, described as a past event. Whereas 1:18 highlights the reality of Jesus' continuing life, here the point at which Jesus became alive is underscored — his resurrection from the dead.

The one outside of whose influence nothing lies knows the Smyrnean believers well. Specifically, he knows of their "tribulation, poverty . . . and the blasphemy of those who claim to be Jews but are not." They would likely remember the transitory nature of tribulation, for Jesus himself has assured his disciples that, though they are certain to experience tribulation in this world (John 16:33), joy is sure to follow (16:21). Knowledge that John the prophet is himself their brother in tribulation would encourage the hearers that tribulation is shared by the servant chosen to testify of this extraordinary revelation (Rev 1:9).

Not only does Jesus know of their tribulation, he also knows of their poverty. Though Smyrna was a prosperous city, the members of the church are poor. It is not altogether clear whether their poverty is owing to their faithful witness, but given the extent of the persecution of which Jesus speaks, such is a distinct possibility. Instead of a rebuke, Jesus offers a prophetic insight into their situation. Despite their poverty, they are rich. Unlike other mentions of riches or being rich in Revelation (cf. 3:17-18; 6:15; 13:16; 18:3, 15, 19), here being rich is clearly positive. Perhaps such juxtaposition reveals that "spiritual," rather than material, riches are here described.[36] The identity of these riches may be that there is no rebuke of the church at Smyrna and that they have endured great hardship for their faith — riches that enable their faithful obedience.

A third aspect of Jesus' knowledge of the church at Smyrna concerns "the blasphemy of those who say that they are Jews and are not but are a synagogue of Satan." This charge of blasphemy conveys the ideas of accusation and contempt for the church at Smyrna. This blasphemy comes from "those who say that they are Jews but are not," a phrase that would remind readers of a similar construction in 2:2, where reference is made to "those who claim to be apostles and are not." While the latter were tested and found to be liars by the church at Ephesus, nothing suggests that the former were tested and found not to be Jews by the church at Smyrna. Rather, Jesus' prophetic insight reveals a reality not previously known. Despite arguments to the contrary, it appears that these

---

34. Resseguie, *The Revelation of John*, 88.
35. Note the contrasts "first and last," "was dead and became alive," "poverty and rich," "claim to be Jews but are not," "those faithful to death receive a crown of life." Murphy, *Fallen Is Babylon*, 120.
36. Osborne, *Revelation*, 130.

individuals would be identified with part or all of the Jewish community in Smyrna.[37] Jesus' prophetic insight reveals that, despite these individuals' outward appearance as Jews, in reality they are not. Although they may be ethnic Jews, they are not Jews spiritually — not the legitimate heirs of Israel. These stinging words[38] give way to even more stinging words when Jesus calls these individuals "a synagogue of Satan." This first mention of Satan in Revelation may very well remind the hearers of Jesus' words about his Jewish opponents in John's gospel (8:44), whom he calls children of their father the devil, owing to their behavior. These words carry the scathing indictment that their synagogue, a gathering place for the people of God, has been turned into a place of the adversary of God's people.[39] Thus, the accusations brought against the church in Smyrna actually have a satanic origin, as the phrase "synagogue of Satan" introduces the primary adversary of God and his people in Revelation (cf. esp. 2:13, 24; 3:9; 12:9).[40] Fittingly, Satan's first mention comes in the context of accusations brought against the church. Despite these scathing words, the hearers appear to have a clear appreciation for their Jewish heritage, as its presumed familiarity with the OT and the grounding of certain "Christian" details in Jewish roots make clear. The words of 2:9 make it clear that there is tension between some of the churches of Revelation and the broader Jewish community, a tension that appears to revolve around the issue of identity of God's people.

Instead of a call for repentance in v. 10, words of warning are bounded on either side by words of instruction. Jesus knows the current situation of the church at Smyrna, as well as its future. The words "do not fear" remind us of Jesus' words in John's gospel to fearful disciples who had just seen him walk on the water (6:19-20) and of the words of the resurrected Jesus in Rev 1:17. Just as these individuals should take courage from Jesus' being with them, so should the church at Smyrna, who hears these words in advance of the circumstance that might otherwise produce fear, specifically, "that which they are about to suffer." Both the immediacy of the suffering ("about to") and its severity ("to suffer") are here conveyed. Perhaps this term would also bring to mind Jesus' own suffering, explicitly identified with the Passover in John's gospel and alluded to in the reference to "the Lamb who looked as if he had been slain" in Rev 5:6.

This warning begins with a formula of revelation, which describes the

---

37. Cf. esp. P. L. Mayo, *"Those Who Call Themselves Jews": The Church and Judaism in the Apocalypse of John* (PTMS; Eugene OR: Pickwick Publications, 2006), 51-76.

38. Indeed, it appears that many NT documents share the idea that Christians are the legitimate heirs to Israel, not the non-Christian Jewish community.

39. R. H. Gause, *Revelation: God's Stamp of Sovereignty on History* (Cleveland, TN: Pathway Press, 1983), 53, and Mayo, "Those Who Call Themselves Jews," 71-73.

40. As the name implies. Cf. Osborne, *Revelation*, 132.

church in such a way so as to reveal something about its situation, mission, or destiny.⁴¹ The fact that μέλλει (*mellei,* "about to") reappears so quickly in v. 10b after its mention in v. 10a and is the first word to follow "Behold" demonstrates the connection between the warning that follows and the words found in the previous sentence. Specifically, "The devil is about to cast some of you into prison in order that you might have be tested and have tribulation for ten days." This first mention of the devil in Revelation is quite appropriate in this context, which has just mentioned the slander of blasphemy, as the devil is described by Jesus in John's gospel as the "father of lies" (8:44). It is also appropriate, given that the devil put it into Judas's heart that he should betray Jesus (13:2). The fact that the devil is about to cast some of them into prison may also bring to mind that John (the Baptist) had been cast into prison before them (3:24). In the number 10, the hearers encounter for the first time a number that will always have negative connotations in Revelation. Yet, despite the ominous foreboding such a number might bring, the church at Smyrna would likely be encouraged by several facts. If John is on Patmos owing to exile, his role as their "brother in tribulation" (1:9) would take on even greater significance and encourage them all the more. Describing this tribulation as lasting ten days indicates that it is of a limited duration. Mention of the church being tested for ten days may well remind the hearers of Dan 1:12, 14, where the four young Israelite men refuse the food of the Babylonians and propose that they be tested for ten days.⁴² Such an intertext from Daniel might serve to encourage the church at Smyrna to turn what, on the surface, could be interpreted as a passively experienced persecution into active witness, with the anticipation of God's intervention on their behalf.

The second admonition, "Continue to be faithful unto death," serves to balance the first. Reminiscent of Jesus' words to Thomas, "Do not continue to be unfaithful but (be) faithful" (John 20:27), such language would not be lost on the hearers. Already in Revelation Jesus has been identified as "the faithful witness" (1:5), a title clearly connected with his witness unto death. The faithfulness called for, like the faithfulness of Jesus, is a "faithfulness unto death." Clearly, the faithfulness called for could very well entail a witness that results in the death of some of those in the church at Smyrna. But the hearers would not be unaware that such a call comes from "the one who was dead and came to life" (2:8), "the one who holds the keys to Death and Hades" (1:18). Consequently, it is this one who promises to give those who exhibit such faithfulness "the crown

---

41. Cf. the discussion of M. de Goedt, "Un schème de révélation dans le quatrième évangile," *NTS* 8 (1961-62): 142-50.

42. Note esp. Dan 1:14; Prigent, *L'Apocalypse de Saint Jean,* 128-29.

of life." In yet another contrast, the one faithful to death is given a crown of life. The crown imagery clearly indicates a reward for the successful completion of a difficult challenge. It is not surprising that the one who is alive can give such a crown, for the gift and the giver are coterminous.

The refrain "the one who has an ear to hear let that one hear" appears for a second time. How would the hearers respond to this pneumatic call for discerning obedience? Specifically, this response would involve a conscious reflection upon (1) their being deemed rich by the resurrected Jesus, despite their physical poverty; (2) their refusal to fear in the face of suffering; and (3) their faithfulness even unto death. Once again, keeping the words of this prophecy necessitates complete and utter faith in and faithfulness to "the one who is the First and the Last, who was dead and came to life."

The prophetic message to the church at Smyrna also concludes with an eschatological promise to those who overcome. As might be expected from the description of Jesus (v. 8) and the promise of "the crown of life" by Jesus (v. 10), those who overcome are assured that they will not be harmed at all by the "second death," an appropriate gift from the one who was dead and came to life.

To the Angel of the Church in Pergamum (2:12-17)

Jesus next instructs John to write to the angel of the church at Pergamum, a church located forty-five miles north of Smyrna. Perhaps the hearers think of its imposing location on a thousand-foot-high cone-shaped mountain, a city whose name means "citadel." Or perhaps they think of Pergamum as an administrative center for Roman justice, signified by the sword. Perhaps they think of the city's fame as a religious center, with its enormous sculptured altar dedicated to Zeus and the other religious sites built for Athena, Dionysus, or their most characteristic god, Asklepios, whose image was a snake, which drew numerous religious pilgrims in search of healing. Or perhaps they thought of Pergamum's having the first officially sanctioned temple dedicated (in 29 CE) to "divine Augustus and the goddess Roma" (Tacitus, *Annals* 3.37).[43]

But now the hearers find out what Jesus thinks of the church in Pergamum. Again Jesus identifies himself by means of elements familiar from the inaugural vision of himself, which would bring to mind that stunning event. Here, he calls himself "the one who has a double-edged sword." Earlier, a double-edged sword came out of his mouth (1:16), highlighting Jesus' pro-

---

43. Cf. Hemer, "Seven Cities of Asia Minor," 241-42, and R. H. Mounce, *The Book of Revelation* (NICNT; Grand Rapids: Eerdmans, 1977), 95-96.

phetic speech. While reference to his mouth is omitted in 2:12, it might cause more attention to be focused upon the dangerous nature of this instrument.

As before, "I know" introduces the hearers to the bulk of the content of the prophetic message (vv. 13-17), with the word "live" standing at both the beginning and the end of v. 13. Here attention is focused upon the church's location. Specifically, Jesus knows where the church lives, "where the throne of Satan is." Only in 2:13 does the verb "live" denote a specific location. This statement would assure that Jesus knows the church in Pergamum lives in the same place where Satan's throne is located. That his throne is located in Pergamum, described by the articular construction "where the throne of Satan is,"[44] may indicate that Satan's presence may be felt more intensely there because it is the center of his activity. Why would Pergamum merit such a description? Perhaps it is owing to a variety of idolatrous associations found within the city. This combination of ideas may uniquely qualify Pergamum for such a description over against the other cities addressed in these opening chapters. Mention of Satan's throne also indicates that Satan is in direct contrast and conflict with the one who sits on the throne. However, since the designation "the one who sits on the throne" is used on numerous occasions in Revelation with reference to God, it leaves no doubt as to his sovereignty.

Despite living where Satan's throne is located, the church at Pergamum is commended by the resurrected Jesus for two specific things. First, "you are holding to my name." Such an expression indicates a firm grasp or strong attachment (2:1), reminiscent of the patient endurance of the church at Ephesus, who bore a number of things on account of Jesus' name (2:3). They have a deep sense of solidarity and personal identification with Jesus. Second, the church is told, "You did not deny my faith." Positively, the one who does not deny is in company with John (the Baptist) (John 1:20). Negatively, the language of denial recalls Peter's denial of Jesus (13:38; 18:25) and the activity of the antichrists (1 John 2:22-23). The church at Pergamum clearly exhibits the kind of witness characteristic of John. While "my faith" might be taken to mean "faith in me,"[45] the meaning of the preceding construction, "you are holding to my name," suggests that "my faith" would have a similar meaning. The lone occurrence of "faith" in John's gospel and 1–3 John (1 John 5:4-5) reads, "And this is the overcomer who has overcome the world, our faith. Who is the one who overcomes the world except the one who believes that Jesus is the Son of God?" Here "our faith" is closely connected to overcoming the world and belief in, rather than a denial of, Jesus. The broader context of Rev 2:13 also argues for this meaning, as it focuses upon

---

44. Aune, *Revelation 1–5*, 182.
45. So Prigent, *L'Apocalypse de Saint Jean*, 132, and Beasley-Murray, *Revelation*, 84.

faithfulness. It would therefore seem that the phrase "my faith" suggests something of the church's solidarity with the faithfulness of Jesus; that is, their own faithful actions meant that they did not deny the faithfulness of Jesus.

Such an interpretation fits well with the phrase that follows — "even in the days of Antipas, my faithful witness, who was killed among you, where Satan lives." It is sometimes argued that, since Antipas is the only person named as a martyr to this point, no one else had been put to death in the community. Such an interpretation misses the point of the text, however, for Antipas is cited as an example of one who held onto Jesus' name and did not deny his faith. Mention of Antipas makes clear that the possibility of being put to death owing to one's faithfulness, described in the previous message, has become a reality in this message. In this verse Antipas, "my faithful witness," stands in extremely close solidarity with Jesus, "the faithful witness." As with the description of Jesus (1:5), so here the words about Antipas are followed up by reference to the death of the faithful witness. Antipas's death is situated in two locations. It is placed both among the community ("among you"), underscoring the intimate relationship between Antipas and the church in Pergamum, and in the place "where Satan lives," which indicates the close connection between where Satan lives and the deadly persecution of the church. Earlier in v. 13, mention of Satan's throne underscored his power in Pergamum. Now, the hearers learn that they live where he lives. The end of the first portion of the message's content is revealed by the reappearance of the word "lives," which forms an inclusio around this verse.

The next portion of the message is marked by the words of rebuke, "But I have a little against you." This "a little" suggests that the rebuke to follow will not be as severe as the one to the church in Ephesus. Jesus' words of rebuke reveal that some among them are holding to the teaching of Balaam and the teaching of the Nicolaitans. In each of these condemnations the same verb is used as appears earlier to describe their holding to Jesus' name. The contrast here is between those who "hold to my name" in 2:13 and those who "are holding to the teaching of Balaam . . . and the Nicolaitans."

Although the teaching of the Nicolaitans continues to be cloaked in ambiguity, the teaching of Balaam is identified more fully. The name Balaam is apparently assigned by Jesus to a teacher within the community, perhaps an acknowledgment of his "prophetic" status. The name would bring to mind the story of Balaam in Num 22–24. There, Balaam is called upon by Balak, the king of Moab, to curse the Israelites, who are traveling to Canaan. Intervening divine encounters, however, result in Balaam blessing Israel three times instead. Following his faithful prophesying, the Israelites enter into sexual immorality and apparently eating food sacrificed to idols (Num 25:1-2), with Balaam's counsel blamed for these activities (31:16). Jesus' words in Rev 2:14 focus upon Balaam's culpability by his teaching Balak "to place a stumbling block" before the sons of Israel to eat food sacrificed to idols and "to commit sexual immorality." In John's gospel "stumbling block" terminology occurs in contexts that describe the refusal of disciples to remain with Jesus (John 6:61-66) and as a warning not to leave (16:1). Here it serves to register the level of threat such teaching poses to the church. The specifics of the stumbling block placed before Israel, "eating food sacrificed to idols" and "committing sexual immorality," introduce these major themes in Revelation.

Eating food sacrificed to idols brings up the theme of idolatry. But what exactly would this practice mean to the hearers? The Numbers text indicates that such activity occurred in the context of offering sacrifices to idols, but food sacrificed to idols was widely available in a variety of contexts in first-century Asia. In Pergamum, with its many religious centers, there would be public feasts, where food earlier sacrificed to idols would be distributed to the populace, civic and religious banquets that would often include the symbolic presence of a particular deity and, consequently, an offering to him or her, and the availability in the local market of surplus meat earlier sacrificed to a particular deity. The temptation to participate in one or more of these activities would be strong for believers seeking to make their way within the social and commercial life of Pergamum. The language of Revelation appears to be a bit more rigid on this issue than one finds in the Pauline admonition of 1 Cor 10:25-30.

The other primary activity associated with the teaching of Balaam is sexual immorality. The Numbers text suggests the reference to "sexual immorality" is literal, which seems to be its primary meaning there. Clearly, however, this imagery functions metaphorically at a number of places in the OT and Revelation to denote religious infidelity. The reference to sexual immorality likely conveys both ideas here: a lax attitude toward issues of sexual purity and an unfaithfulness with regard to commitment to Jesus. Perhaps the intertext that results in v. 14, where, despite Balaam's faithful prophesying, he is remembered only for his leading the children of Israel astray, would convey a warning that, despite any prophetic activity that comes from their own "Balaam," in the end all that will be remembered is his own involvement in leading "Israel" astray.

For a second time, the Nicolaitans are mentioned by Jesus in the charge "you also have some who are holding to the teaching of the Nicolaitans as well." From their previous mention, the Nicolaitans are clearly viewed in an antagonistic position to Jesus and his followers. Yet, unless they are to be identified with the teaching and practices of Balaam, a grammatical possibility, they continue to be largely unknown.[46] If so, there would be an emphasis upon their

---

46. Cf. Mounce, *The Book of Revelation*, 98.

"prophetic" claims, as well as advocating an accommodating view toward the surrounding pagan society.

The words of rebuke are followed by a call to repentance on the part of the church. Such repentance would involve a repudiation of the teaching of Balaam and of the Nicolaitans, which Jesus himself repudiates. As before (2:5b), failure to repent will be met by an eschatological fate — "I will come to you quickly." Here the warning is directed to those who continue to hold to the teaching of Balaam and the Nicolaitans, as Jesus uses the words "I will make war with them," not "with you." The occurrence of war language at this point introduces a major theme within Revelation, involving frequent appearances of both the verb form and the noun form. While an immediate visit by Jesus in judgment is not ruled out altogether, such significant occurrences of this terminology in eschatological contexts further supports the eschatological nature of the judgment spoken of to the church at Pergamum. The instrument of war on this occasion is the same instrument described at the beginning of this prophetic message: "the sword of my mouth." There is an obvious reference to the prophetic mouth of Jesus, which is able to speak and to bring judgment. The convergence of this sword and that of the angel of the Lord in the Balaam story would underscore that such a fate awaits any prophetic figures who mislead God's people as had Balaam. Unlike the prophetic message to the church in Ephesus (2:6), this call for repentance is not softened in any way. It stands without final words of commendation.

For a third time in the book, Jesus' prophetic message concludes with a call to discerning obedience. What is the Spirit saying to (all) the churches through this prophetic message? Clearly, the churches are to keep the words of this prophecy by holding on to Jesus' name, even in the face of Satan's rule, even in the face of death, and by repenting of any identification with the teaching of Balaam or the Nicolaitans. The lines of demarcation between the church and the world must be clear.

The eschatological promise made to those who overcome includes two items. Initially, Jesus promises to give such a one "the hidden manna." Mention of manna would bring to mind the gracious gift of God to Israel in the wilderness, an ongoing provision until Israel left the wilderness (Exod 16; Josh 5:12). Jesus' promise of hidden manna would remind readers of the miraculous nature of the divinely preserved manna, while pointing forward to its eschatological nature. Here there is a close connection between the manna in the wilderness that God gave (John 6:31, 49) and the bread from heaven that is given by, and is, Jesus (6:29, 33, 35, 50-51) — if one eats his flesh and drinks his blood, such a one has eternal life (6:53-58). If a subtle hint exists that Jesus gives of himself in giving the overcomer to eat of the tree of life in Rev 2:7, the hint is less subtle in

The Seven Prophetic Messages to the Seven Churches of Asia (2:1–3:22)

2:17. In contrast to those who eat food sacrificed to idols, those who overcome are promised supernatural provision of an eschatological nature.

Jesus also promises to give the overcomer "a white stone and upon the stone a new name written thiat no one knows but the one who receives it." The color of the stone indicates a high degree of solidarity with Jesus, whose head and hair are earlier described as white as wool and snow, and with any number of other white objects.[47] The significance of the stone is clearly connected to that which is written upon it, "a new name." While it is possible that the new name is the overcomer's (John 1:42), it is more likely that these ambiguous words refer to Jesus' new name.[48] This initial occurrence of the word "new" in the book introduces the hearers to a universe of "new" things in Revelation.[49] It makes sense that those who hold to Jesus' name (2:13) are those promised his name as an eschatological reality (2:17). The recipient of such a stone stands in continuity with Jesus and his future.

To the Angel of the Church in Thyatira (2:18-29)

Jesus instructs John next to write to the angel of the church in Thyatira, a city located some forty miles southeast of Pergamum. When encountering the name, the hearers perhaps think of a former military outpost located in the broad and fertile Lycus valley, or of the image found on its coins of a warrior with an ax ready to smash his enemies. Perhaps they think of the numerous well-known industries and professional trade guilds located there, or maybe they think that, since it is the fourth church addressed, its message is the central and, conceivably, the most important one.[50] That this is the longest of the seven letters would be corroborating evidence of its importance.

Whatever the hearers think of with regard to Thyatira, they soon find out what Jesus thinks. Jesus first introduces himself by a title not found in the

---

47. Murphy (*Fallen Is Babylon*, 133) notes, "The whiteness of the stone fits well with the use of white in the rest of Revelation. White appears twenty-one times in Revelation, symbolizing purity, that is, fitness for entering the heavenly world where God is enthroned, and readiness for being part of the new Jerusalem. It represents victory over evil and the joy of communion with God and Christ. The color white figures in the vision of Christ (1:14 [three times]), the white garments of the saved (3:4, 5, 18; 6:11; 7:9, 13, 14), Christ's white horse for the final battle (19:11), the garb of the heavenly army (19:14 [twice]), and the great white throne on which God sits at the end of time (20:11)."

48. Beale, *The Book of Revelation*, 254-56.

49. Wall, *Revelation*, 76.

50. Charles, *The Revelation of St. John*, 1:67-68, and Murphy, *Fallen Is Babylon*, 133.

inaugural vision: the Son of God. Though a departure from his established convention, this title is familiar from other places in the Johannine tradition (John 1:18, 34, 49; 3:16-18, 35; 5:25; 10:36; 11:4, 27; 19:7; 20:31; 1 John 1:3, 7; 2:22-24; 3:8, 23; 4:9-10, 14-15; 5:5, 9-13, 20; 2 John 3, 9). Through this title, Jesus underscores his intimate relationship to "the one who sits on the throne," making its connection to Daniel's Ancient of Days even more explicit! This only occurrence of the title in Revelation fits nicely with other statements about the relationship between the Father and the Son in the book (Rev 1:6; 2:28; 3:5, 21; 14:1). Its appearance along with the words "my Father" (2:28) forms an inclusio around the message to this church.

Jesus next describes himself with elements taken from the inaugural vision, "the one who has his eyes as flaming fire and his feet as glowing brass." His flaming eyes bring to mind his penetrating prophetic vision; the mention of his feet points to Jesus' strength and stability. We are thus reminded of the earlier stunning vision of Jesus.

For a second time, Jesus' "I know" statement makes reference to "your works" (2:2). In fact, v. 19 begins and ends with reference to their works. This is the most comprehensive list of works to be found in any of the seven prophetic messages. The church is commended for their love, faith, service, and patient endurance. Love language has appeared in the letter's greeting, where reference is made to Jesus' love for the Johannine believers, and in Jesus' rebuke of the church in Ephesus (2:4), which left its first love. This commendation of the church at Thyatira indicates that it is in solidarity with Jesus, who loved them, and exemplifies the characteristic identified by Jesus as most essential in Johannine discipleship (John 13:35). The church at Thyatira is also commended for its faith, a term very closely associated with the idea of faithfulness[51] and the idea of faithful witness — being intimately connected with patient endurance and overcoming. The church in Thyatira thus identifies with Jesus, who is love, and with the kind of faith(fulness) that he too possesses (2:13) and has demonstrated as a faithful witness.

Jesus also commends the church for its service. In John's gospel, the verbal form of the term is closely associated with Jesus' death (John 12:2, 26). Would-be disciples are instructed that they must follow him in death. For "the one who loves his life will lose it, and the one who hates his life in this world will keep it unto eternal life" (John 12:25).[52] The appearance of this term in Rev 2:19, alongside "love" and "patient endurance," would be in keeping with this emphasis. Διακονία (*diakonia*, "service") is one of several Greek terms used to

---

51. Prigent, *L'Apocalypse de Saint Jean*, 139.
52. A. Weiser, "Διακονέω," *EDNT*, 1:304

denote service of one kind or another and is semantically related to the term δοῦλος (*doulos*, "servant"), which regularly appears in Revelation, sometimes with the meaning "prophet." It may very well be that the term "service" would on this occasion convey both the idea of loving service,[53] manifested in one's faithfulness unto death, and the service of prophetic vocation, which is intricately connected to the former. The church is also commended for its "faithful endurance," which draws together the experience of John (1:9), the church at Ephesus (2:2-3), the church of Thyatira, and Jesus (3:10). This defining work for the saints in Revelation reveals something of the steadfastness of this church's life and witness for Jesus.

The commendation concludes with an affirmation of the progressive nature of the church's works: "and your last works are more than your first ones." In contrast to the church in Ephesus, the church in Thyatira is ever increasing in works. Perhaps such praise is an indication that the church brought forth more fruit as a result of their remaining in Jesus (John 15:2).

Despite such stellar praise, the words "but I have against you" indicate that words of rebuke are to follow. Jesus' rebuke focuses upon a particular self-proclaimed prophetic figure and those who align themselves with her. The church at Thyatira "tolerates the woman Jezebel, who says of herself that she is a prophetess." The word "tolerate" does not necessarily convey the idea of active participation, but rather of permitting something or someone to continue, reminiscent of the words of the chief priests and Pharisees about Jesus: "If we leave him alone (tolerate him), all will believe in him" (John 11:48). Though toleration of the false prophetess may be the extent of the church's inappropriate activity, such toleration has eternal consequences. The name Jezebel appears to have been assigned to this woman by Jesus himself, as the one whose eyes of fire have penetrating prophetic insight. The significance of this name would in itself indicate why toleration of such a person is inappropriate, for the name brings to mind one of the archenemies of Israel: the wife of Ahab, the opponent of the prophet Elijah. Ahab's marriage to Jezebel, daughter of Ethbaal, king of the Sidonians, resulted in his adopting Baal worship, going so far as to erect an altar and temple for Baal in Samaria (1 Kgs 16:31-32). Jezebel's impact is not confined to offering sacrifices to foreign gods (and eating such meat?); she is later remembered (2 Kgs 9:22) as promoting "sexual immoralities" and "sorceries." Jesus' naming this woman Jezebel would alert the church to her true identity, suggesting that its discernment with regard to this figure was lacking.

The hearers next learn of the self-claims this Jezebel makes. The language, reminiscent of that found in 2:2 and 2:9, reminds us that one's self-claims are not

---

53. For this dimension of the term, cf. H. Beyer, "Διακονία," *TDNT* 2:87.

always in keeping with Jesus' own penetrating insight. The problem here is not that the claims come from a woman, for it is likely that women were numbered among the prophets in this prophetic community. Rather, the problem is with her activity and lifestyle. Jezebel "teaches and deceives my servants to commit sexual immorality and to eat food sacrificed to idols." It is significant that Jezebel teaches, for within the Johannine tradition, "teaching" is the exclusive domain of Jesus (John 1:38, 49; 3:2; 4:31; 6:25, 59; 7:14, 28, 35; 8:20; 9:2; 11:8, 28; 13:13-14; 18:20; 20:16; 2 John 9), the Father (John 6:45; 8:28), and the Paraclete/Chrisma (John 14:26; 1 John 2:22). Outside of one reference to John (the Baptist) as "Rabbi," there are no positive examples of human teachers to be found in the Johannine literature.[54] Rather, this Jezebel stands in line with the antichrists and deceivers (1 John 2:22), Balaam (Rev 2:14), and the Nicolaitans (2:15) in her attempts to teach. She also "deceives." In the Johannine world deception is the exclusive domain of the community's opponents (1 John 1:8; 2:26; 3:7; 4:6; 2 John 7). This deception is so dangerous that even Jesus' servants, the prophets, are susceptible to Jezebel's teaching. This remarkable idea, that servants/prophets of God could be deceived to take the side of Jezebel instead of Elijah, suggests that the Mount Carmel events function as an implicit warning. Jezebel advocates sexual immorality and eating food sacrificed to idols, the very activities promoted by "Balaam." Given Thyatira's dependence upon professional trade guilds and industries, where commercial activities inevitably led to participation in banquets honoring the gods, such temptations to accommodate were very real indeed. Neither can it be ruled out that such accommodation led to immoral sexual activities.

Earlier, Thyatira compared favorably with Ephesus, owing to its persistence in love and its last works being more than the first. Now, the comparison is unfavorable, as the church in Ephesus was able to discern that those who claimed to be apostles were in reality liars, while Thyatira could not discern that the woman who claimed to be a prophetess was in actuality a Jezebel.

While the church tolerates its Jezebel, giving her room to operate, Jesus gives her time "in order that she might repent." Perhaps this opportunity came via the prophetic words of Jesus in the context of community worship, or in a confrontation with a prophetic figure,[55] or even with John himself. Initially, this statement might be taken as a call to repentance consistent with other calls for repentance found earlier (2:5, 16). But despite the time and opportunity given by Jesus for her to repent, "she does not desire to repent of her sexual immorality."[56]

---

54. Cf. the negative attribution of the title "teacher of Israel" to Nicodemus in John 3:10.
55. Osborne, *Revelation*, 158.
56. Perhaps she saw no need to repent, as Murphy (*Fallen Is Babylon*, 137) notes.

Her teaching "my servants" (to commit sexual immorality) grows out of her own identity (and practice of sexual immorality). For this identity and activity she has no intention of repenting. She is the first example of obstinate disobedience.

The next portion of this prophetic message (vv. 22-25) conveys Jesus' intentions for the woman, her lovers, her children, and the rest of those in Thyatira. These verses are marked out as standing together, as forms of the word "cast" occur near the beginning and the end of this section.

As for the obstinate, sexually immoral Jezebel, Jesus says, "I will cast her upon a bed." Such a graphic phrase could be taken to mean, "I will place her upon a bed," a usual place for a sexually immoral person. This phrase, however, could be an idiom meaning "I will cast her upon a sick bed,"[57] suggesting that Jezebel will suffer physically for her obstinate disobedience.[58]

Not only will this woman be cast onto a sick bed, but "those who commit adultery with her (will be cast) into great tribulation if they do not repent of her works." The language of sexual immorality gives way to the related language of adultery. This shift conveys both the idea of participation in illicit sexual activities, as well as the idea of unfaithfulness on the part of the ones who commit adultery. Like Jezebel, those who commit adultery with her will be cast into great tribulation. Unlike those who share in tribulation owing to their faithful witness to Jesus — John (1:9) and the church at Symrna (2:9-10), where the suffering comes at the hands of Satan — the suffering that awaits those who commit adultery with Jezebel comes from the hand of Jesus. The language of "great tribulation" may also indicate something of the eschatological nature of such a judgment, a judgment that is imminent. But they need not share Jezebel's fate, provided they repent of her works, works that stand in strong contrast to the works commended by Jesus in v. 19, which should be emulated. The choice between these works is stark and makes all the difference. The repentance here called for would doubtless involve a repudiation of all the activities that would compromise their faithful witness — absolute faithfulness to Jesus, the faithful witness, is required.

As for her children, Jesus says, "I will kill in death/with a plague." This phrase could be taken to mean "I will surely kill," indicating the certainty of the promised death, or it could be translated "I will kill with a plague," as appears to be the phrase's meaning in Rev 6:8.[59] At one level both meanings would register, for none of the hearers would doubt the certainty of the fulfillment of

---

57. Cf. F. G. Untergassmair, "Κλίνη," *EDNT*, 2:300.
58. On the relationship between sin and illness in the Johannine literature, esp. John 5.14; cf. J. C. Thomas, *The Devil, Disease, and Deliverance: Origins of Illness in New Testament Thought* (Cleveland, TN: CPT Press, 2010), 80-120.
59. Aune, *Revelation 1–5*, 198.

such words, nor would the idea that Jezebel's children might suffer death owing to a plague be out of keeping with the sickness with which their mother is to be struck. Who are the children of this Jezebel? Here "children" likely functions metaphorically, if not literally. If those who commit adultery with Jezebel are unfaithful members of the Johannine community, then it would appear that her children are likely those born of her sexual immorality.[60] Such ones would undoubtedly bear her characteristics with regard to sexual immorality and eating food sacrificed to idols, and would perhaps be those who would continue her works. Given their fate, they seem to be wholly identified with their mother. The severity of the punishment would no doubt remind hearers of the story of Jezebel in the OT, specifically the slaughter of Ahab's children (his seventy sons, 2 Kgs 10:1-11), a powerful reminder of the certainty of the fate prophesied.[61] As Elijah's words had come to pass, how much more the words of Jesus!

The resurrected Jesus next addresses all the churches at once: "And all the churches will know that I Am the one who searches minds and hearts, and I will give to you each according to your works." This sentence indicates that events in Thyatira have significance for all the churches everywhere and that his actions at Thyatira have a testamentary nature for all.[62] It reinforces the idea that Revelation is one circular letter, the contents of which are important to all its hearers. The use of the ἐγώ εἰμι (*egō eimi,* "I Am") formula lays claim to Jesus' intimate identity with the Father (1:8). This emphasis is reinforced in that Jesus further identifies himself as "the one who searches minds and hearts," similar to constructions used to describe the activity of God at various places in the OT (Ps 7:10[9]; Jer 11:20; 17:10; 20:12). The introduction of Jesus in 2:18 as the one whose eyes are as fire makes clear the basis of his ability to search the inner recesses of individuals and churches. Jesus' promise to "give to you each according to your works" heightens the level of awareness regarding with which set of works the hearers will align themselves. The use of emphatic second person plural language further underscores that such words occur in direct address. Significantly, the words of Jesus are located midway through this prophetic message, which is located midway through the seven prophetic messages, indicating that they are not only directed to the church at Thyatira but are also explicitly directed to all the churches of Revelation. These words serve as a summary of Jesus' activity among the lampstands: searching minds and hearts, giving according to one's works. The statement may indeed be the theological zenith of the seven prophetic messages.

60. Smalley, *Revelation,* 75.
61. Beale, *The Book of Revelation,* 263-64.
62. Smalley, *Revelation,* 75.

Attention is now focused upon "the rest of you in Thyatira," quickly identified by Jesus as "those who do not have this teaching." Unlike those who hold to the teaching of Balaam and/or the Nicolaitans, the rest in Thyatira do not have the teaching of Jezebel. The fault of the church at Thyatira is toleration of Jezebel, not active participation with her. "Not having this teaching" means that they do not "know the deep things of Satan." Although the latter are viewed as synonymous with "this teaching" of Jezebel, it is not clear what the "deep things of Satan" are. Perhaps Jesus' prophetic words imply that, though they may make claims to know the "deep things of God," in reality they are holding on to the "deep things of Satan." But the words that follow, "as they say," tend to subvert this meaning, for normally, when certain false claims are being made by opponents in Revelation, one encounters something like the phrase "who say that they are." What one might expect here, then, is something like "who say that they know the deep things of God, but they do not. Rather, they know the deep things of Satan." Thus, it appears that Jezebel and her associates indeed claimed to know the "deep things of Satan." What would such a claim entail? Apparently, such deep things were not known by everyone but only by those who identified with Jezebel. These words might be related to Jezebel's attitude and teaching toward eating food sacrificed to idols and sexual immorality. Perhaps knowledge of Satan's deep things was believed to enable believers to participate in commercial and social activities with impunity — nullifying Satan's powers or at the least allowing believers to avoid areas and actions where they would be most vulnerable. While it is impossible to know exactly what such knowledge entails, it would not be lost on the hearers that, just as the churches in Smyrna and Pergamum have to contend with Satan, so does the church in Thyatira. As such, Jesus sees Jezebel and those who stand with her as in association with Satan's work elsewhere — his synagogue and his throne.

This portion of the message (vv. 22-25) draws to a close with Jesus' words that he will not cast another burden upon the rest of those in Thyatira. A word play in the Greek text suggests a direct connection between the activity of the hearers in Thyatira and Jesus' subsequent action. Since the rest of the Thyatirans do not know the βαθέα (*bathea*, "deep things"), Jesus will not βάλλω (*ballō*, "cast") another βάρος (*baros*, "burden") upon them. Interestingly, this convergence of ideas and words occurs elsewhere — in Acts 15:28-29, where a decision was reached regarding appropriate Gentile Christian behavior in order to promote table fellowship with Jewish Christians. The agreement was to abstain from "food sacrificed to idols, blood, strangled food, and sexual immorality." The convergence of the words "burden," "food sacrificed to idols," and "sexual immorality" in both passages is striking, perhaps even being an indication of the way the community was to discern their relationship with their culture, especially with regard to these two issues. Such would confirm the nonaccommodating approach advocated in Revelation.

The final words of vv. 22-25 are a call for specific action — "In any case, that which you have, hold until I come." While not having the teaching of Jezebel, the people in the church do have love, faith(fulness), service, and patient endurance (2:19). Since their last works are more than their first, these words call for the church to continue with such works until Jesus comes. Perhaps the command "hold" would convey the promise of divine assistance, as this word is found as part of the divine title "All Powerful One."[63] Such language, reminiscent of Jesus' earlier call for faithfulness unto death (2:10) and his promises to come to two of the churches in judgment (2:5, 16), implies the same kind of faithfulness here, as well as pointing to his eschatological advent more clearly than in the other messages.

For the first time the promise to the overcomers precedes the call for discerning obedience, a change in order that will be followed in the next three messages as well. Perhaps such an inversion underscores the significance of discerning obedience by focusing attention on this dimension rather than the promise of rewards.[64] This inversion also serves to divide this series of seven into subgroups of three and four, which differs from subsequent divisions of the sevens into groups of four and three.[65]

Here, the one who overcomes is "the one who keeps my works until the end." The language of keeping is familiar from its earlier occurrence (1:3), where an active and sustained response is called for. Now, the idea of keeping is combined with the theme of works, the sixth and final occurrence of this term in this message. Jesus commends the church for both the quantity and quality of their works (2:19), makes clear that works are the basis of the future judgment (2:23), and now identifies these works as his own works. The words "until the end" are reminiscent of the way Jesus' love is described in John's gospel, "He loved his own until the end" (13:1). These words, which can be translated as "until the end" or "completely," likely mean both, here in John,[66] as well as in Revelation. The church is thus praised for both past and present faithfulness, while being encouraged to continue such faithful activity until completion.

To such a one, Jesus says, "I will give to him authority over the nations," as he is "the ruler of all the kings of the earth" (1:5). That the overcomers will

---

63. Simoens, *Apocalypse de Jean*, 33.
64. Murphy, *Fallen Is Babylon*, 142.
65. Bauckham, *The Climax of Prophecy*, 10.
66. Thomas, *Footwashing in John 13 and the Johannine Community*, 81-82.

share in Jesus' rule becomes even clearer as his words of promise continue, for they echo those found in Ps 2:8-9, widely regarded as a messianic psalm. This authority is to be exerted with power, for "he will rule (shepherd) them with a rod of iron, as he breaks the clay vessels." At first, the appearance of the word ποιμαίνω (*poimainō*, "rule" or "shepherd") in the same context as the breaking of vessels to bits might be deemed as a bit unexpected, if not inappropriate. The activity of smashing pottery to pieces does not seem to fit the meaning often attributed to "shepherd"! The shepherd's duties, however, included protection of the sheep, which might involve the use of his rod as a weapon. Just as Jesus' rule is spoken of as firm, so is that shared by those who overcome; it will be firm but sure.[67] Jesus also makes clear that his giving of authority is based upon what he has received from the Father. The underlying Greek construction results in a meaning something like, "I give . . . as even I received." After all, Jesus' Father is the one who gave him authority over all flesh (John 17:2) and is the one who sits on *the* throne (Rev 1:4), a throne he will share with his Son (3:21). In addition, Jesus will give to the one who overcomes "the morning star." There is more to this promise than that Jesus will give them Venus, for he is the one who holds the seven stars in his right hand (even as he speaks these words!). Earlier promises have implied a giving of Jesus himself to those who overcome (2:7, 17).[68] Here, the promise is more explicit, as the identity of overcomer with Jesus appears more extensive.[69]

For a fourth time, Jesus' prophetic message concludes with a call to discerning obedience. Here, the call is heightened in that it follows, rather than precedes, the promise to the overcomer, and in that previously (v. 23) Jesus makes clear that this message is indeed to all the churches. What is the Spirit saying to all the churches through this prophetic message? Quite obviously, keeping the words of this prophecy is intimately connected to holding to what they have and keeping Jesus' works until completion. Their love, faith(fulness), (prophetic) service, and patient endurance must continue, even as Jezebel, her lovers, and her children meet their appointed judgments. The line of demarcation between the church and the surrounding (commercial and social) world is clearly drawn by Jesus. There is to be no toleration, even of self-proclaimed prophetic figures who advocate a theology of accommodation by means of the "deep things" of Satan.

---

67. Skaggs and Benham, *Revelation*, 44.
68. Aune, *Revelation 1–5*, 212, and Fee, *Revelation*, 44.
69. If the message to the church in Pergamum is still in the ears of the hearers, perhaps they would see both the star and the scepter as issuing out of Balaam's prophecy in Num 24:17. Cf. Murphy, *Fallen Is Babylon*, 141.

To the Angel of the Church in Sardis (3:1-6)

Jesus next instructs John to write to the angel of the church in Sardis, located some thirty miles southeast of Thyatira. What would the hearers think of when they heard the name Sardis? Perhaps they would think of the prosperous city located on the famous highway that ran all the way from ancient Susa through Asia (Minor). Or perhaps they would think of the natural citadel where Sardis was originally located, with rocks that go up some 1,500 feet. Perhaps they would think of the way the city dominated the rich Hermus valley from its location. Or perhaps they would think of Roman life reflected in its theater, stadium, and exceptionally large, though never completed, temple dedicated to Artemis. Or maybe the image of the deified empress Livia, found on coins struck in Sardis. Or perhaps they knew of this impregnable city falling twice — to Cyrus and to Antiochus the Great — owing to a lack of vigilance on the part of its inhabitants.[70]

The hearers now learn what Jesus thinks of the church in Sardis. He first identifies himself as "the one who has the seven Spirits of God and the seven stars." While not part of the inaugural vision, "the seven Spirits of God" have been encountered in the document's prologue, located "before his (God's) throne" (1:4), indicating something of the Spirit's very close association with God. The words of the Spirit are coterminous with the words of the resurrected Jesus, as is made clear by the repeated calls for pneumatic discernment. The intimate connection between Jesus and the Spirit is now made even clearer with the phrase "the one who has the seven Spirits of God," which makes explicit the close association between God and the Spirit; it may be a hint that Jesus now shares the throne with God,[71] and as a result he "has" the seven Spirits of God. Such an association further underscores his ability to "search hearts and minds" of men and women.

Jesus' words about "having the seven stars" remind us of these stars' location, namely, in Jesus' right hand, still upon John as Jesus prophetically speaks, conveying the idea that these messengers are firmly under his control and speak truthfully. The one who has the seven stars in his control, earlier threatened to remove the lampstand from the church in Ephesus (2:5), if the church does not repent. This message to Sardis begins (3:1) and ends (3:5) with reference to angels. In both occurrences, there appears to be an emphasis upon the truthfulness of Jesus' words to the church at Sardis, and in turn to all the churches of Revelation.

---

70. Caird, *The Revelation of Saint John*, 47-48, and Mounce, *The Book of Revelation*, 109.
71. Adela Yarbro Collins, *The Apocalypse* (NTM 22; Collegeville, MN: Michael Glazier Press, 1979), 24.

The Seven Prophetic Messages to the Seven Churches of Asia (2:1–3:22)

Jesus' next words are the familiar, "I know your works." It is no surprise that "the one who has the seven Spirits of God and the seven angels" would know the works of this church. Significantly, there are no words of affirmation offered, as there are in the other messages; rather, there are simply words of rebuke, making this message the most severe judgment among the seven messages.[72] "You have a name that you are alive, and you are dead." Emphasis is placed upon the word "name," which stands first in the Greek sentence, perhaps an implicit contrast between the significance of Jesus' name, for which the church in Ephesus bore many things (2:3), to which the church in Pergamum held firmly even to the point of death (2:13), which they are promised if they overcome (2:17), and the fact that here, it is the church that has a name. There is a further contrast between Jesus, who was dead and is alive (1:18), and the church that has a name that they are alive, but they are in fact dead (3:1). Obviously, Jesus is uniquely qualified to judge those who are alive and those who are dead because he was dead but is now alive (2:8)! The contrast between the church's name and the reality of its true identity would bring to mind Jesus' prophetic insight in other situations in the seven prophetic messages where the claims of the churches do not match the reality (2:3, 9, 20).[73] Perhaps this "death" refers to some sort of spiritual death, an idea found elsewhere in the Johannine literature. First John 3:14 reads, "We know that we have passed out of death into life, because we love the brothers; the one who does not love remains in death." A similar contrast between life and death also occurs in 1 John 5:16, which may echo John 8:24. The fact that there is a "sin unto death" (1 John 5:16) and a "second death" (Rev 2:11; cf. also 20:6, 14; 21:8) would make Jesus' statement here all the more ominous.

Even though dead, they are to "wake up and strengthen that which remains, which is about to die." Jesus' words convey the idea of wakefulness and watchfulness, combining the idea of vigilance with eschatological expectation. This idea is paired with "strengthen," which combines the idea of "strengthening" in the light of the return of Jesus (cf. Jas 5:8). Such strong language is in order, for the rest of the things that remain are on the verge of death. The hyperbolic language of v. 1 thus gives way to the more precise language of v. 2, revealing that the situation is very desperate indeed. The little that they have is near death. "For I have not found your works fulfilled before my God." The one who knows their works has not found them to be complete. As the temple of Artemis has not been completed, neither have the works of the church. The

---

72. As Prigent (*L'Apocalypse de Saint Jean,* 147) notes, "C'est sans doute le jugement le plus sévère des sept Lettres."
73. Resseguie, *The Revelation of John,* 95.

word "fulfilled" often occurs in the Johannine literature to designate the fulfillment of Scripture (John 12:38; 13:18; 15:25; 17:12; 19:24, 36), Jesus' word (18:9, 32), or joy that has been made complete (John 3:29; 15:11; 16:24; 17:13; 1 John 1:4; 2 John 12). Here it indicates that their works have stopped short of completion, standing in contrast to the church in Thyatira, whose last works were more than their first (2:19). The works of the church in Sardis, which are incomplete before God, stand in contrast to the seven Spirits, which are complete (seven) before the one who sits on the throne. The resurrected Jesus, who has the seven Spirits of God, now makes reference to God as "my God," further developing the tight association between them.

In the light of this dreadful situation, the resurrected Jesus "therefore" calls for specific action from the church at Sardis. They are called upon to "remember" (3:3; see also 2:5) what they received. Perhaps two things would stand out. Jesus' words to "receive the Holy Spirit" (John 20:22), which are reinforced by the Elder's words of 1 John 2:27, and "the command received from the Father" to love one another (2 John 4). The call is thus of fundamental importance, as both the emphasis upon the Spirit and the love command are central in Johannine thought. They are also to remember what they have heard. Owing to the extremely close connection between hearing and belief in John's gospel, we can take this admonition as a call back to belief, another fundamental element in Johannine thought. As Jesus' words unfold, he instructs them to "keep" those things they received and heard, and to repent for their incomplete works before God. In John's gospel keeping the words or commands of Jesus includes an identification with and incorporation of those words and commands. Such a response to his words results in eternal life (John 8:51-55) and a sharing in the kind of love characteristic of the Father and the Son (John 14:15-24; 15:10, 20; 17:6, 11-15). Therefore, the command to "keep" underscores two of the basic components of Johannine thought: eternal life and love. This emphasis is all the more significant, since these words are spoken to those who are dead or who are about to die. Not only are they to keep, they are also to repent. The call for repentance is the culmination of a series of five imperative verbs beginning in v. 2. Such a direct call would involve the activity of being awakened, the strengthening of what remains, remembering things received and heard, as well as keeping those things. Thus, concrete action is envisioned in this call.

In the words "therefore, if you do not wake up, I will come as a thief, and you will not know the hour when I come upon you," Jesus makes clear the consequence of failing to comply with his commands. Here, failure to repent is met with the threat "I will come as a thief." On this occasion it appears that reference is being made to Jesus' eschatological return, as "thief" imagery is frequently found in early Christian eschatological discourse (Matt 24:43; Luke

12:39; 1 Thess 5:2; 2 Pet 3:10). Although it might be thought odd that Jesus would identify his coming with a thief, given its meanings in John's gospel (10:1, 8, 10; 12:6), such language conveys the suddenness of an event, for a thief, as opposed to a robber, takes the victim by surprise;[74] as Jesus' next words reveal: "And you will not know what hour I will come upon you." The threat/promise of Jesus' return to the church in Sardis is not conditional, predicated by whether or not they repent. The emphasis here is upon the certainty and suddenness of his coming to them in judgment, as well as upon their unpreparedness for it, and consequently their being unaware of its timing. The only conditional aspect of his words is whether or not they will be prepared for and aware of his coming. Perhaps the hearers would think of the way in which Cyrus and Antiochus the Great came upon Sardis unawares.[75] The "hour" of which the resurrected Jesus speaks would remind them of its soteriological significance in John's gospel (John 2:4; 7:30; 8:20; 12:23, 31-32; 13:1; 17:1). Its occurrences in Revelation, however, carry with them eschatological significance.[76]

In v. 4, instead of the words "but I have," we see "but you have." Such a change in personal pronouns prepares for a change of content. Normally, the churches hear words of rebuke at this point, after having heard words of commendation. Earlier (2:14), Jesus told the church at Pergamum that he had against them "a little" or "a few" things. Now he tells the church in Sardis, "But you have ὀλίγα (*oliga*, "a little" or "a few") names." The contrast would be apparent. Whilst there was much to praise about the former, and little to criticize, there is little to praise and much to criticize in Sardis. Earlier (3:2), Jesus had said, "You have a name that you are alive, but you are dead," indicating that the church's name did not match its spiritual reality. In v. 4 the name is the reality, with reference made simply to "a few names in Sardis." These names are described by means of their clothing — they have not "stained their clothes, and they walk with me in white." Mention of stained or defiled garment imagery reminds us of Zech 3:3-5, where Joshua the high priest stands in filthy garments before the face of the angel of the Lord. The replacement of filthy garments by clean ones is described by the Lord as follows: "Behold, I have taken away your iniquities" (Zech 3:4).[77] Such defilement indicates one's estrangement from God and Jesus. In 3:1-6 perhaps spiritual slumber, weakness, and incomplete works are part of such defilement. There are a few names in Sardis who have avoided such contamination. Jesus also describes them actively as those who "walk

---

74. Collins, *The Apocalypse*, 24.
75. Sweet, *Revelation*, 99.
76. Cf. H. Giesen, "Ὥρα," *EDNT*, 3:507-8.
77. Smalley, *Revelation*, 84.

with me in white, because they are worthy." Walking is a familiar metaphor in the Johannine literature. Walking with Jesus (John 6:66), walking in the truth (2 John 4; 3 John 3-4), and walking in the light (1 John 1:6-7) all seem to refer to the same spiritual reality, conveying the idea of fellowship with and/or being with Jesus.[78] The words "they will walk with me in white" further underscores the idea of their identity with Jesus, for as is already known, white is a color intimately connected with Jesus (Rev 1:14). The fact that they appear in white anticipates the eschatological reality that awaits those who overcome (3:5). The phrase "because they are worthy" is typically Johannine in that it is capable of a double meaning. The phrase could mean that they will walk with Jesus in white because they have proven themselves worthy of such a close association. Or the phrase could imply that these individuals (these "few names") in Sardis are worthy to wear white because of their close association with Jesus. Such Johannine ambiguity invites reflection upon the integral connection between the two ideas, which involves a symbiotic relationship between them rather than a purely causal one, making explicit the connection between being in white and being worthy.[79]

Next, three eschatological promises are made; one with reference to the overcomer's clothing, two with reference to the overcomer's name. "Thus, the one who overcomes will be clothed in white garments." The appearance of the term "thus" indicates that this first promise is closely connected to the description of the rest in Sardis, which precedes this statement.[80] This explicit connection is overt evidence that those who presently walk with Jesus in white anticipate this eschatological reward and, in good Johannine fashion, already experience it to a certain degree. White clothing as a theological reality in Revelation indicates that the wearer has an intimate association with Jesus by proving to be a faithful witness and thus experiencing this eschatological reward.

While this church's name does not match its spiritual reality (3:1), there are those in Sardis whose names *are* the spiritual reality (3:4). To such ones as these the second and third promises are directed, one negative and one positive. The second eschatological promise, "I will never erase his name out of the book of life," introduces book imagery, important in Revelation. Such language appears grounded in the language of Exod 32:31-33:[81]

78. Cf. the discussion in Thomas, *1 John, 2 John, 3 John*, 23-24, 75-76.
79. Smalley, *Revelation*, 85. The only other occurrence of the word ἄξιος (*axios*, "worthy") with reference to believers is found in 16:6, where it appears to have the meaning of "fitting," "appropriate," or "proper."
80. Aune, *Revelation 1–5*, 223.
81. Smalley, *Revelation*, 86.

So Moses went back to the Lord and said, "Oh, what a great sin these people have committed! They have made themselves gods of gold. But now, please forgive their sin — but if not, then blot me out of the book you have written." The LORD replied to Moses, "Whoever has sinned against me I will blot out of my book." (NIV)

From this text the hearers would know that there is a book in which God has written names and that God can expunge names from it, owing to sinful activity on the part of those whose names appear in the book. In Rev 3:5 it is the resurrected Jesus who has the authority to take such an action. We hear that the name of the one who overcomes will never be erased, which suggests that they have not defiled their garments and that they have continued to walk with Jesus in white. Absence of sin is also implied. The book in which these names appear is the book of life, which contains only the names of those who are alive. Clearly, the names of those who are dead would not be written there or would be erased.[82] The one who is alive, who is Life, is the one who has authority to expunge names from the book of life. For this book belongs to him.[83]

The third eschatological promise, "And I will confess his name before my Father and before his angels," would be both familiar and startling, as "confession" language is found at various places in the Johannine literature (John 1:20; 9:22; 12:42; 1 John 1:9; 2:23; 4:2-3, 15; 2 John 7). With one exception (1 John 1:9), every occurrence of the word is related to the confession of Jesus. Here, however, it is Jesus who confesses, and it is the name of the one who overcomes that is confessed! The power of this promise indicates something of the faithfulness Jesus feels toward those who have been faithful to him. They have been faithful to confess in the face of excommunication, persecution, even death. His faithfulness to confess such ones would not be less than theirs. Incredibly, his confession takes place before the ultimate authority, "my Father." The church apparently has a desire for a name that they are alive, but Jesus reminds them that the only name they should worry about is the name of the one before whom he confesses their name. Jesus' reference to "my Father" balances his claim about "my God," with which this message began. Likewise, his reference to confession of the name "before his angels" in v. 5 balances his claim to have "the seven stars" in v. 1. Mention of "his angels" at this point reminds hearers both of the location of this confession, heaven, and its veracity, as the angels are witnesses to it.

---

82. As M. Kiddle (*The Revelation of St. John* [New York: Harper, 1941], 47) notes, "This promise . . . is made with a backward glance at the atrophied members of the church at Sardis."

83. Cf. the discussion by H. Balz, "Βιβλίον," *EDNT*, 1:217-18.

This message closes with the now-familiar call for discerning obedience. What is the Spirit saying to those who have ears to hear? Perhaps part of the answer is found in the many imperatives that come from Jesus in this message. Thus, the churches should wake up, strengthen what is about to die, and bring their works to completion before God. They are to remember what they have received and heard, faithfully keep all those things, and repent for their spiritual death. They must keep their garments pure, maintaining uninterrupted fellowship with Jesus.

To the Angel of the Church in Philadelphia (3:7-13)

Jesus next instructs John to write to the angel of the church in Philadelphia, located some thirty miles south-southeast from Sardis. What would the hearers think of when they encountered the name Philadelphia? Perhaps they would think of its founder, Attalus II, whose love for his brother, Eumenes II, gave rise to the city's name. Or perhaps they would think of its strategic location at the junction of routes leading to Mysia, Lydia, and Phrygia, making it the gateway to the east. Maybe they would think of its location on rich, volcanic soil, remembering that it frequently experienced earthquakes. Perhaps they would think of the fact that, on at least two occasions, the city changed its name: once to Neocaesarea as a sign of gratitude to Tiberius for the aid received after a devastating earthquake in 17 CE, and again when it adopted the family name of Emperor Vespasian, changing its name to Philadelphia Flavia. Or perhaps they would think of the city's economic prosperity and its many religious temples and festivals.[84]

Whatever those who hear this prophetic message think, they now hear Jesus' opinion of the church there. Again, the resurrected Jesus first identifies himself by words not contained in the inaugural vision. On this occasion, he identifies himself as "the Holy One, the True One." "The Holy One" would be familiar to Johannine hearers, as Jesus is called "the Holy One of God" by Peter (John 6:69; cf. also 1 John 2:20), refers to himself as the one whom the Father has sanctified (John 10:36), and says that he sanctifies himself (17:19). Since such holiness and/or sanctification rather clearly comes from God, it is no surprise that God is himself also called "Holy Father" by Jesus in prayer (John 17:11). That such holiness and/or sanctification is to extend to the followers of Jesus is revealed in his prayer that they be sanctified in the truth (John 17:17,

---

84. Cf. Mounce, *The Book of Revelation*, 114-15; Hemer, "Seven Cities of Asia Minor," 245; and Koester, *Revelation and the End of All Things*, 65.

The Seven Prophetic Messages to the Seven Churches of Asia (2:1–3:22)

19) and in the admonition in 1 John for believers to purify themselves, just as Jesus is pure (1 John 3:3).[85]

Jesus also identifies himself as "the True One." Such a designation taps into an extremely rich and deep Johannine theological reality. Not only is Jesus "full of truth" (John 1:14), but he is also identified as "the truth" (John 14:6). Truth is thus christologically conditioned and defined. Such a rich theological concept would color the way that the phrase "the True One" would be understood. Here, the term "true" takes on the distinct nuance of true as opposed to false, genuine or real as opposed to fake or unreal, authentic as opposed to inauthentic. In John's gospel Jesus is the true light (1:9; cf. also 1 John 2:8), the true bread from heaven (6:32), the true vine (15:1), the one whose judgment is true (8:16). As with "the Holy One," this term is also shared by God (John 17:3; cf. also 1 John 5:20). Such an understanding of Jesus as "the True One" converges nicely with the picture of Jesus that continues to emerge as Revelation unfolds. Specifically, it reinforces the reality that Jesus has no rivals on this earth, for he is "the ruler of the kings of the earth." It also places Jesus and his words in contrast to a variety of others encountered in the preceding messages who have proven to be liars.

Jesus next identifies himself as "the one who has the key of David, the one who opens and no one can close, who closes and no one can open." The intertext that results in this passage for the hearers is a combination of images that emerges from Isa 22:22, the inaugural vision of the resurrected Jesus (Rev 1:18), and John's gospel (10:7). "The key of David" clearly reflects imagery found in Isa 22:22, where the glory and authority of David's throne are transferred to Eliakim. The text reads, "I will place on his shoulder the key to the house of David; what he opens no one can shut, and what he shuts no one can open." The use of such imagery reveals that Jesus is making certain messianic claims for himself and claims about who is part of his messianic kingdom and who is not. For the one who possesses David's key determines who enters and who is denied entry. "The key of David" imagery also brings to mind a detail found within the inaugural vision of Jesus, where he says, "I have the keys of Death and Hades" (1:18). There, Jesus is depicted as having complete mastery over Death and Hades, indicating that there is no need for the believer to fear these foes, for Jesus holds the keys. He opens and closes death's door, he provides the way to life! In John's gospel Jesus identifies himself as "the door of the sheep," the door through whom anyone who enters will be saved, will have life, and have it in superabundance (John 10:7-10).[86]

---

85. J. C. Thomas, *He Loved Them until the End: The Farewell Materials in the Gospel according to John* (Pune, India: Fountain Press, 2003), 59-61, and Thomas, *1 John, 2 John, 3 John*, 152-53.
86. Collins, *The Apocalypse*, 27.

"In the Spirit on the Lord's Day" (1:9–3:22)

The content of the message begins "I know your works." Before these works are enumerated, however, a parenthetical statement breaks into the message: "Behold, I have placed before you an opened door, which no one is able to shut." These words would be understood in relationship with Jesus' messianic claims, including his ability to make alive, to open the door to life, for he is the door. The perfect tense forms of the verbs "I have placed" and "having been opened" imply that this opened door was placed before them at some point in the past and remains open before them even now. This opened door likely refers to the point at which they heard the witness of Jesus Christ and responded in faith to him.[87] Perhaps there is even a subtle hint that this church is to play a role in the conversion of those around them. Following the parenthetical statement, Jesus now enumerates the church's works, "You have little power, and you have kept my word and have not denied my name." Although the phrase "you have little power" might convey the idea of poverty, such is not its normal Johannine meaning, where often this language is associated with the ability or inability to do or accomplish something. Here, it is interesting that, despite the church's little δύναμις (*dynamis*, "power"), no one "is able" or "has the power" to shut the door that Jesus has placed before them. Their little power thus does not make them vulnerable to those who would wish to counteract Jesus' salvific activity on their behalf. Though they have little power, still they have demonstrated an extraordinary commitment to Jesus, having kept his word, having not denied his name. In Johannine thought there is an extremely tight interplay among keeping Jesus' word or commands, eternal life (8:51), loving Jesus and being loved by the Father (14:15, 23-24; 15:10; 1 John 2:3-4; 5:3), mutual indwelling (1 John 3:22-24), and walking as Jesus walks (1 John 2:6). The beatitude, with which Revelation begins, focuses on keeping the things written in this book (1:3). Such a matrix of thought indicates that Jesus' words in Rev 3:8 reveal something about the intimate relationship shared by the church in Philadelphia and Jesus. These words of affirmation are followed by "they have not denied my name." The church at Philadelphia exhibits the kind of witness characteristic of John (the Baptist), the patient endurance of the church at Ephesus, which bore a number of things on account of Jesus' name (2:3), and the church at Pergamum, which firmly holds on to his name (2:13) and are even promised his new name (2:17). These earlier associations, as well as the rich Johannine understanding of Jesus' name, suggest that the church in Philadelphia has a deep sense of solidarity and personal identification with Jesus, even at the risk of personal vulnerability.

The next verse is composed of two sentences, each of which begins with

---

87. Smalley, *Revelation*, 89.

"behold," with the second occurrence of this term picking up on the previous one. Verse 9 may offer an implicit commentary on the previous verse, providing the context for understanding the phrases "having kept my word" and "not having denied my name." That is, a connection likely exists between the adversities experienced by the church and the "synagogue of Satan" mentioned in v. 9. Such a connection would not come as a complete surprise, owing to this same connection previously in the message to the church in Smyrna.

Jesus' mention of the "synagogue of Satan" gives way to a description reminiscent of its description above (2:9), for the phrase "they say that they are Jews" reappears here as well. Previously, this "synagogue of Satan" refers to some or all of the Jewish community in Smyrna. Here, it appears that at least some of the Jewish community in Philadelphia is in view. As before, Jesus' prophetic insight reveals that, although these individuals may be ethnic Jews, they are not Jews spiritually; that is, they are not the legitimate heirs of Israel.[88] On this occasion, however, his language escalates as he charges, "But they are lying." Such language would remind hearers of the would-be apostles who were found to be liars by the church in Ephesus (2:2). It also provides part of the rationale for why this synagogue is called a synagogue of Satan; through its lying activity, this synagogue exhibits one of the characteristics of the devil, who is a liar and the father of lies (John 8:44).

After the second "behold" in v. 9, a most remarkable statement occurs: "Behold I will make them, in order that they might come and worship before your feet and know that I have loved you." Once again, Jesus' words to this church echo the words of Isaiah, whose prophecies envision a time when the kings of the nations and the wealth of land and sea will come to Jerusalem (Isa 60:1-22), when those from afar will come to worship and serve Israel because God is with them (45:14), when the Holy One of Israel will declare, "I have loved you" (43:3-4). This matrix of passages clearly anticipates a time of vindication for Israel. In a stark reversal of fortunes, this "synagogue of Satan, who claim to be Jews but are not," will not receive the long-awaited vindication before the Gentiles but will themselves be required by Jesus to take the role of the Gentiles in the vindication of the church.[89] These ethnic Jews have forfeited their inheritance, while the church in Philadelphia receives the heritage of Israel.[90] The church will inherit these eschatological promises and vindication before the very ones who have caused them such distress.[91] Perhaps there is

---

88. Murphy (*Fallen Is Babylon*, 154) notes, "For the author, who is himself Jewish, the definition of 'Jew' has changed."

89. Smalley, *Revelation*, 90-91, and Mayo, *"Those Who Call Themselves Jews,"* 70.

90. Prigent, *L'Apocalypse de Saint Jean*, 156.

91. Cf. Beale, *The Book of Revelation*, 288.

some connection here to the kind of vindication Jesus himself receives when he comes with the clouds, when every eye will see him, even those who have pierced him (Rev 1:7). The words "and they will bow down or worship before your feet" introduce the significant theme of worship, around which the lines of demarcation are drawn in the book. While it is possible to take this term to mean "to bow down" as in Isa 45:14, owing to its meaning elsewhere in Revelation (and John's gospel: 4:20-24; 9:38; 12:20), it seems likely that it points in the direction of its fuller meaning in 3:9. While the word would be taken to mean vindication in some sense, perhaps it also points in the direction of the worship of Jesus, in that Jesus stands behind this church.[92]

The words "and they will know that I have loved you" not only echo the words of the Holy One of Israel but also come from "the Holy One," a title by which Jesus earlier identified himself. This phrase also hearkens back to the prologue, where John described Jesus as "the one who loved us and loosed us from our sins and made us a kingdom, priests to God and his Father." For the "synagogue of Satan" to know that Jesus has loved the church would entail an acknowledgment that the church is indeed the kingdom of the Father and priests dedicated to his service, further underscoring the inversion motif found here, where the promises made to Israel are fulfilled in the church.

The main idea of v. 10 is conveyed by means of its structure around two primary and interrelated parts: "Because you have kept my word . . . even I will keep you." Something of the quality of the believers' commitment to Jesus and his word by the church in Philadelphia is indicated by there being no rebuke of the church to this point. Here, the phrase Jesus uses is modified slightly from 3:8, "You have kept my word of patient endurance," indicating a deep connection between "keeping my word" and "patient endurance," exhibited earlier (1:9; 2:2-3, 19). Such an expression indicates that the faithfulness of the church in Philadelphia is beyond doubt, in keeping with that of the resurrected Jesus, who is speaking.[93] Jesus therefore says, "Even I will keep you from [ἐκ (*ek*, 'from' or 'out of')] the hour of testing that is about to come upon the whole inhabited world to test the inhabitants of the earth," eschatological words familiar to Johannine hearers from Jesus' words in John's gospel:

> I have given them your word, and the world has hated them, because they are not of the world, just as I am not of the world. I do not ask in order that

---

92. J. M. Nützel, "Προσκυνέω," *EDNT*, 3:175.

93. Sweet (*Revelation*, 104) is close to this idea when he observes that the word of my patient endurance has reference not merely "to Jesus' sayings, but his whole self-revelation, characterized as *endurance*."

you take them out of the world, but in order that you keep them from [*ek*] the evil one. (John 17:14-15)

Significantly, these words follow Jesus' description of the disciples as having kept God's word (17:6).

One of the important aspects of this verse is the introduction to the idea of the hour of testing that is to come upon the whole earth. The ominous combination of the words "hour" and "testing" would indicate something of the extraordinary importance of this impending event. Perhaps the relationship between "hour" and suddenness would still be in the hearers' minds from the warning of Jesus in 3:3 that he comes as a thief and that no one knows the hour he comes. The idea of testing can carry with it both positive and negative connotations in Johannine thought. It can be the activity of Jesus (John 6:6) and his church (Rev 2:2), or that of the devil (Rev 2:10). While the identity of the one who brings this hour of testing might not be clear, it is clear that Jesus has the power to keep the hearers from it. The scope of the testing might indicate something of its origin. The hour of testing is about to come upon the "whole inhabited world," a phrase that appears three times in Revelation, where it refers to God's opponents and/or those who do not believe (12:9; 16:14).[94] This phrase indicates that, with the exception of those whom Jesus will keep from it, this hour of testing will be experienced by all of the world's inhabitants. The scope of this hour of testing is made clearer by the words "to test those who live upon the earth," offering implicit evidence that this testing comes from God and is directed to those who are his opponents and/or fail to believe. This hour of testing will come upon these inhabitants, not upon those who, like the church in Philadelphia, have kept Jesus' word of patient endurance. Reference to this ominous hour of testing, the arrival of which is imminent, could not help but heighten the dramatic tension. For while its content and nature are not yet known, the certainty of its arrival is!

The content of the message comes to a close with Jesus' words in v. 11, "I come quickly; hold on to what you have in order that no one may take away your crown." Here, Jesus' words have primary reference to his eschatological return, being the clearest of his promises so far to return, following up nicely on 3:3. Coming on the heels of the words about the hour of testing (v. 10), these suggest a somewhat close connection between this hour of testing and Jesus' return. Previously, mention of Jesus' return has come as part of a warning to some of the churches in need of repentance (2:5, 16; 3:3). Here, Jesus' words are not part of a call to repentance but do constitute a warning. For they precede

---

94. H. Balz, "Οἰκουμένη," *EDNT*, 2:504.

the admonition to "hold on to what you have." The occurrence of the verb "hold on" or "grasp" calls to mind its earlier appearances in Revelation (2:1, 13-15). But the nearest parallel to 3:11 is Jesus' admonition to the church in Thyatira to "hold what you have until I come" (2:25). Although the church in Philadelphia has little power, they have kept Jesus' word of patient endurance and have not denied his name, despite opposition from a "synagogue of Satan." Neither have they been rebuked by Jesus or called to repentance. The reason for this call for continued vigilance is "in order that no one take away your crown." This crown, likely to be identified with "the crown of life" promised to those who are faithful unto death (2:10), is a reward for the successful completion of a very difficult task. This statement suggests that the church has already completed its task and been rewarded for its faithfulness. Yet, despite already having been rewarded for completing its task, it is still possible for it to have its crown (of life) taken away from it.[95] Although the believers in Philadelphia will be kept from the hour of testing, they will still face opposition and persecution capable of causing them to forfeit their crown. Vigilance is called for, even in the best of circumstances.

The first of Jesus' eschatological promises is "I will make him a pillar in the temple of my God, and I will never cast him out," an especially powerful promise to the church in Philadelphia, making abundantly clear that those in the church, not those in the "synagogue of Satan," are the true Jews. It also underscores the promise of vindication Jesus makes earlier to this church (3:9). In addition, the imagery of being a pillar in the temple conveys the idea of stability and permanence to the hearers.[96] This imagery, combined with the promise "I will never cast him out," would be especially significant to those who live in an area so often destabilized by earthquakes. But the primary meaning of the imagery "a pillar in the temple of my God" concerns the overcomer's permanent location in God's presence. The promise that the overcomer will never be cast out underscores this point. The one who overcomes is promised a permanent place in God's presence, with no fear of being removed from that presence.

In the second set of promises Jesus says, "And I will write upon him the name of my God and the name of the city of my God, the New Jerusalem coming down out of heaven from my God, and my new name." The writing of these names rather clearly indicates the idea of solidarity with, even possession by, those whose names are written upon the item or person. The overcomer is thus promised absolute identity and solidarity with God, his city, and Jesus, his Son. The inscription of God's name upon the overcomer might also remind hearers that, in the Torah, the priest of God was instructed to wear a gold plate inscribed

---

95. Mounce, *The Book of Revelation*, 155.
96. Resseguie, *The Revelation of John*, 99.

with the words "Holy to the Lord" attached to the turban. This name was to be worn upon the forehead in order that the people might be accepted before the Lord (Exod 28:36-38). It would not be lost on the hearers that Jesus has made these Johannine believers priests unto God (Rev 1:6), for they have just learned that the one who overcomes will be a pillar in God's temple.

Jesus also promises to write the name of God's city upon the overcomer. Without question, the imagery would identify such an individual as a member or citizen of that city. That this belongs to God would further underscore the identity of the overcomer with God. The hearers are introduced for the first time to the "New Jerusalem" (also 21:2, 10). On each occasion it is described as "coming down out of heaven from God." The repetition of this phrase, each time with a present participle being used, implies that this "coming down out of heaven from God" is a permanent characteristic of this city.[97] It is always coming down out of heaven from God! It is an eschatological promise of immediate and direct access to God. Its mention comes closely on the heels of the promise that the overcomer will be made a pillar in the temple of God. Jerusalem was God's chosen site for his temple. But the name New Jerusalem conveys a certain degree of discontinuity as well. For this Jerusalem is characterized both by its newness and by its quality as permanently coming down from heaven from God. Its mention here also creates a certain anticipation and expectancy. Mention of the New Jerusalem may also bring to mind how this message began with reference to Jesus' possession of the key of David. It would only be fitting that the one who holds that key has authority to write its name upon the one who overcomes. Jesus' promise to write this name upon the one who overcomes indicates that the future of this city and the future of the one who overcomes are coterminous.

Finally, Jesus promises to write "my new name" on the one who overcomes. This promise would be reminiscent of the promise for vindication, made to Israel, involving a new name that comes from the mouth of the Lord (Isa 62:2), as well as the promise to the church in Pergamum of a white stone with a new name written upon it (2:17). Furthermore, it is indeed fitting that those in Philadelphia who "have not denied my name" (3:8) are those who will receive "my new name" (3:12). The writing of Jesus' new name upon the one who overcomes makes complete the intimate connection between the resurrected Jesus and the one who overcomes.

This message closes with the familiar call for discerning obedience, as do all the messages. What is the Spirit saying to those who have ears to hear?

---

97. Caird (*The Revelation of Saint John,* 55) describes this construction as an "iterative present, denoting a permanent attribute of the new Jerusalem."

Primarily, the hearers are to continue holding on to what they have, keeping Jesus' word of patient endurance and not denying his name, even in the face of persecution. Continued vigilance is important lest the crown (of life) that they already possess be taken away by someone or something. By continuing to keep these things, those in the church in Philadelphia will be kept from the hour of testing. They will receive the promises of a permanent location in the presence of God and of full identification with him by bearing the names of God, his city, and his Son.

To the Angel of the Church in Laodicea (3:14-22)

Jesus next instructs John to write to the angel of the church in Laodicea, located some forty miles to the southeast of Philadelphia. What would Laodicea bring to mind to ancient hearers? Perhaps they would think of a major commercial center located at the intersection of the road that runs through Pergamum, Thyatira, and Philadelphia and another road that leads west all the way to Ephesus. Or perhaps they would think of its bank and medical school. Perhaps they would think of the black wool for which Laodicea was famous. Or perhaps they would think of the city's rebuilding after a deadly earthquake in 60 CE, without imperial aid, on which occasion a stadium and other large civic buildings were donated by Laodicean benefactors. Perhaps they would think of the aqueduct system by which the city received much of its water supply. Or perhaps the hearers would understand that this is the seventh and final church to be addressed by the resurrected Jesus and anticipate its climactic significance.

But now the hearers will learn Jesus' knowledge of the church in Laodicea. Jesus identifies himself by three titles, the first being "the Amen." The use of "Amen" as a title or proper name is most unusual, used in this way only here in the whole of the NT.[98] Perhaps it would bring to mind that God himself is once referred to as "God, the Amen" (Isa 65:16). Part of the significance in Jesus' use of the title, then, is his appropriation of yet another title and/or name that otherwise is reserved for God.[99] The term also has well-known liturgical significance, with the double "amen, amen" being used by Jesus in John's gospel as part of an oath formula to introduce a variety of important utterances, indicating the reliability and trustworthiness of the words that follow. The previous liturgical uses of the term in Revelation (1:6-7) also have clear christological connections.

---

98. Smalley, *Revelation*, 96.
99. Aune, *Revelation 1–5*, 255.

The resurrected Jesus next identifies himself as "the faithful and true witness," familiar words that hearken back to Jesus' identification as "the faithful witness" (1:5) and as "the True One" (3:7). The convergence of these ideas in 3:14 once more draws attention to the place of faithful witness, with Jesus again serving as the model after which believers are to pattern themselves. His faithful and true witness entails suffering and death, as well as being raised from the dead. Perhaps the mere appearance of this title already raises the question of the faithful witness, or lack thereof, of the church in Laodicea.[100] His trustworthiness and identification with and as the truth underscore the authenticity of his words to the church in Laodicea (as well as all the churches). As the "faithful and true witness," his words are amplified in this last of the seven prophetic messages.

Finally, he identifies himself as "ἡ ἀρχή [hē archē, "the origin"] of the creation of God," perhaps reminding hearers of his identity in John's gospel as λόγος (logos, "Word"), whose role in creation is central. The fact that in John 1:1 the Word was ἐν ἀρχῇ (en archē, "in beginning"), before creation, might go some way toward contributing to this identification as "the Origin of God's creation" here in Rev 3:14.[101] It is also possible that the hearers would discern in this phrase an echo of Rev 1:5, where Jesus is identified by John with a related term, "ὁ ἄρχων [ho archōn, "the ruler"] of the kings of the earth."[102] Jesus' self-designation as "the Origin of God's creation" alerts the hearers to God's creation figuring prominently in the remainder of the book.

"I know your works" both introduces the content of the message and prepares for the contrast between Jesus' knowledge and the Laodicean church's lack of knowledge.[103] No words of praise or commendation are offered, making this church the object of Jesus' severest judgment among the seven prophetic messages.[104] "You are neither hot nor cold. Would that you were either hot or cold. So because you are lukewarm and neither cold nor hot, I am about to spit you out of my mouth." The characteristics conveyed by the terms "hot" and "cold" are deemed positively by Jesus, for they stand in contrast, not to one another, but to the state of being "lukewarm." The dining context in which they occur would likely bring to mind the common practice of using both hot and cold drinks with a meal and on other occasions, with both hot and cold water

---

100. Collins, *The Apocalypse*, 30.

101. Although it is possible to translate this phrase "the beginning of God's creation," implying that Jesus was the first thing created, such an idea is at odds with the rest of Johannine thought, which goes to great lengths to demonstrate that Jesus was not "created" by God.

102. On this possibility, cf. Murphy, *Fallen Is Babylon*, 160.

103. Murphy, *Fallen Is Baylon*, 162.

104. Prigent, *L'Apocalypse de Saint Jean*, 164.

often being available to be added to wine and other beverages.[105] Jesus' graphic description of spitting out the lukewarm substance was an action repeated at banquets in antiquity when a diner was not pleased with the taste of something served. Lukewarm water or beverages were less distinctive than their hot and cold counterparts and could even be used to induce vomiting! Here, the "lukewarm" imagery would likely convey the idea of reflecting the temperature of the environment; it requires no work but results from the accommodation of the substance to its surroundings. Jesus' message to the church is that its works reflect accommodation to its environment and the loss of its distinctive "Christian" temperature — its own "faithful witness" is now indistinguishable from its surroundings. As such, these works will be spit out of Jesus' mouth because they are so unpalatable, perhaps suggesting that their works cause Jesus to become sick to his stomach and to vomit them out![106] Jesus will return to dining imagery near the end of this message (v. 20).[107]

Jesus' words in v. 17 suggest that their sickening works are directly connected to their claims, namely, "I am rich and I have become rich, and I have need of nothing." Perhaps this attitude echoes Ephraim's similar claim (Hos 12:8), which God himself subverts. The triple emphasis of Rev 3:17 underscores the confident self-assessment of the church with regard to its riches and independence. The previous inversion of poverty and riches in the message to the church at Smyrna suggests that the emphasis of 3:17 means the church in Laodicea was rich financially and materially and understood itself to be rich spiritually as well, having need of nothing. An accommodating attitude to their environment may have led to their financial stability, as well as their prosperous spiritual self-assessment. Their claims, however, could not be further from the truth. For Jesus knows (v. 15) what they do not (v. 17), "that you are miserable and pitiable and poor and blind and naked." This complex predicate, with

---

105. On this whole matter, cf. the extremely insightful work of Craig R. Koester, "The Message to Laodicea and the Problem of Its Local Context: A Study of the Imagery in Rev 3:14-22," *NTS* 49 (2003): 407-24. These comments are heavily indebted to his fine analysis.

106. Aune, *Revelation 1–5*, 258.

107. The oft-repeated line of interpretation that posits that the "hot," "cold," and "lukewarm" language draws upon the fact that Hierapolis was known for its "hot" water, Colossae for its "cold" water, and Laodicea for its "lukewarm" water (brought via an aqueduct) does not quite fit the evidence. This interpretation ignores the dining context, does not take into account the fact that Strabo (*Geography*, 13.4.14) declared the water in Laodicea to be fine for drinking, nor does it pay sufficient attention to the fact that several of these seven cities had at least a portion of their water needs supplied by aqueducts. There were three aqueducts in Ephesus, two in Smyrna, and one each in Pergamum and Sardis. Unfortunately, such a line of interpretation has concealed, rather than revealed, the meaning of the text. On all this, cf. Koester, "The Message to Laodicea and the Problem of Its Local Context," 407-24.

each adjective connected by "and," underscores the deplorable condition of the church.[108] As the resurrected Jesus relentlessly piles term upon term, the weight of their desperate situation becomes heavier and heavier. In reality, the church is a miserable entity, something to be pitied because of its dreadful condition. While the first two terms in this list of five are general descriptions, the last three describe concrete characteristics of the church in Laodicea and serve as the basis of Jesus' words that follow (v. 18). In contrast to their claims to be rich, they are actually poor. Jesus' statement here is the reverse of his words to the church in Smyrna (2:9). Clearly their poverty is a spiritual poverty that is in some way connected to their lukewarm nature — the result of accommodation to their surroundings. They are also spiritually blind, a condition that is the result of one's location in spiritual darkness and is a sign that one remains in sin (John 9:1-41; 1 John 2:11). A more damning Johannine indictment of a church is difficult to imagine. The church is also described as spiritually naked. Wealth in antiquity was often measured in part by one's wardrobe. It is thus quite unexpected that a church that considers itself wealthy would be declared naked. Peter's action in John's gospel, where he clothes himself before jumping into the water to swim to Jesus because he was naked (John 21:7), suggests that there is something inappropriate about the naked condition. Here Jesus' charge clearly indicates that the church in Laodicea is in an exposed and humiliating position.

These final three descriptions of the church's deplorable condition in v. 17 become the basis of Jesus' admonition to those in Laodicea in v. 18. He says, "I advise you to buy from me. . . ." Perhaps Jesus' words would remind hearers of this term's earlier appearance in the Johannine literature, where Caiaphas's advising the Jews that it would be expedient if one man died for the people (John 18:14) proves discerning.[109] The occurrence of the emphatic personal pronouns "you" and "me" may heighten the contrast between the need of the Laodiceans and the resources of Jesus. There is also the interesting phenomenon of Jesus advising those who are spiritually poor to "buy" certain needed things from him. Clearly, his counsel assumes that the Laodiceans must learn to purchase, not out of their material wealth, but in keeping with the admonition found in Isa 55:1-3, where those without money are invited to "come and buy" in order that their souls may live. In this Isaianic text, such purchases are synonymous with listening to the Lord and following his ways. The church is advised to buy gold, white garments, and eyesalve. The mention of "gold refined in fire" would no doubt cause the hearers to pause, since if they are rich, they would possess some gold already. But just as the imagery of riches has more than one mean-

---

108. Aune, *Revelation 1-5*, 259.
109. Osborne, *Revelation*, 208.

ing, so does the imagery of gold. That Jesus has gold is clear from the golden girdle that he wears (1:13) and from the seven golden lampstands, in the midst of which he walks (1:12, 20; 2:1). But he reveals more about this gold when he describes it as "fired by fire," with both the noun and the verb coming from the same root word. Normally such language would convey the idea of the removal of impurities from a substance by refining it in fire so that it comes out pure. In this context it is difficult not to see here a reference to the fire of suffering that opposition and/or persecution brings to the community. Perhaps these words of Jesus are a call to reject their accommodating disposition to their surroundings that has resulted in their lukewarm condition. Purchasing gold fired by the fire of suffering owing to one's faithful witness results in true riches.[110] Ironically, the acquisition of this gold might very well involve the relinquishment of the gold they currently possess.

Jesus also advises the church to purchase "white garments," an appropriate instruction coming from Jesus, for white is intimately connected with him (1:14) and those who walk with him (3:4). Jesus' admonition is an implicit call to those in Laodicea to be dressed like their resurrected Lord. There are already some who walk in white with Jesus, which underscores the meaning of "white garments" as not simply an eschatological promise but a present possibility. The purchase of these garments would be made in precisely the same way as the purchase of gold from Jesus — namely, by hearing his word and following his commands. The purpose of such garments is "in order that you might be clothed and the shame of your nakedness might not be manifested." In this context the imagery of white garments is clearly connected to the reversal of their spiritual lukewarm state of nakedness — a reference that their works leave much to be desired. Reference to the shame of nakedness might well remind Johannine hearers of the possibility of being ashamed at Jesus' parousia (1 John 2:28), where the ideas of being ashamed and being put to shame are both present.[111] Here, then, the shame or disgrace of their nakedness refers to the lukewarm and sickening state of their works. Such a purchase will ensure that they do not have to face Jesus at his coming in disgrace; instead, they can be clothed like him and can resemble him in appearance.

Third, Jesus advises the church to buy "salve to anoint your eyes." The powder used for eyesalve produced in nearby Phyrgia is perhaps in mind, but there is a deeper meaning to be discerned. First, there is a remarkable similarity between ἐγχρίω (*enchriō*, "anoint"), the word used here to describe the anointing of the eyes, and ἐπιχρίω (*epichriō*, "anoint"), the word used in John 9:6

---

110. Beale, *The Book of Revelation*, 305.
111. Thomas, *1 John, 2 John, 3 John*, 144-45.

to describe Jesus' anointing the eyes of the man born blind. The result in both John's gospel and Revelation is the receiving of sight.[112] Second, there is a similarity between this anointing and the anointing that all believers have received from the Holy One (1 John 2:20) — the former allowing one to receive spiritual sight, the latter enabling one to know all things (1 John 2:27). The purpose of the anointing described by Jesus in Rev 3:18 is that "you might see," resulting in a move from darkness to the light. The fact that the remedy for blindness stands last in the series of remedies may suggest that spiritual blindness is the church's major problem. Jesus has the remedy for their deficiencies and can transform their works from those that are nauseating to those that are worthy of their Lord.

Listening to the last of the seven prophetic messages would likely heighten the dramatic effect of Jesus' words, perhaps causing the hearers to take these final words not simply as the conclusion of this message but as the conclusion of all the messages. If so, this blurring of the lines begins with the end of v. 18 and the beginning of v. 19.

Jesus next says, "Those whom I love, I rebuke/convict and discipline." The emphatic personal pronoun "I" underscores that Jesus is in a position to rebuke and discipline. Mention of Jesus' love for them (1:5; 3:9) comes as a welcome sign of encouragement in a message that has contained no affirmation for the church, suggesting that, despite their sickening condition, Jesus still loves them and, consequently, speaks these words to them. For those he loves he "rebukes" and "disciplines." The word translated "rebuke" can also carry the idea of "convict" or "prove wrong" (John 16:8-11). The word παιδεύω (*paideuō*, "discipline") is closely related to παιδία (*paidia*, "children"), which often appears in 1 John as a term of endearment for the believers. Even words that convey rebuke and discipline may also carry a hopeful expectation that such conviction and discipline will be met with an appropriate response. The words "therefore, be zealous and repent!" are reminiscent of the disciples' remembrance of Ps 69:9 with reference to Jesus' death, "Zeal for your house will destroy me," a quote that indicates his zeal for God's house will ultimately lead to his own death. Here the message is that there is no substitute for a zealous commitment to Jesus, even if that commitment leads to the loss of one's life! This word of challenge would function as a word of encouragement to those churches that have and continue to demonstrate such a zealous commitment in their faithful witness. Jesus' call to repentance is not surprising, given the church's deplorable condition. The concrete elements of this repentance would no doubt include the

---

112. The fact that a form of βλέπω (*blepō*, "I see") occurs in both passages makes this connection all the stronger.

buying of gold, white garments, and eyesalve and a rejection of the environment that leads to a lukewarm nature. They are to be zealous, moving from a state of being lukewarm to being hot or cold. The intensity of this call to repentance is heightened in importance in that it is the final call for repentance to be found in the seven prophetic messages.

The words in v. 20 are a conclusion to the content of this message, as well as a fitting conclusion to the seven prophetic messages as a whole. Jesus' first words, "Behold, I stand at the door and I knock," reveal that, despite the sickening condition of the church in Laodicea, he is still present and active. The perfect tense verb "I stand" indicates that Jesus has taken up a position outside the door of the church and remains there. The present tense verb "I knock" reveals that he is continuously knocking, seeking entry.[113] Ironically, Jesus, who himself is the door, stands before the door of the church, an image suggesting that the church is not in fellowship with him, despite his continued entreaties. Jesus' next words confirm this lack of fellowship: "If anyone hears my voice and opens the door, I will enter in to it, and I will dine with him, and he with me." "Hearing my voice" is a familiar theme in Johannine circles, echoing numerous words of Jesus in John's gospel. Hearing the voice of Jesus includes an eschatological dimension (John 5:24-28), is closely associated with identity and discernment (10:3-5, 16, 27), and culminates with Jesus' climatic response to Pilate, "Each one who is of the truth hears my voice" (18:37). Such rich imagery indicates that the activity of hearing Jesus' voice reveals whether or not they know him and are identified as his sheep. This image thus pushes the hearers to discern their own status before, and relationship with, the resurrected Jesus. Though Jesus has the power to open this door (Rev. 3:7), this door will not be opened by him.[114] Rather, it must be opened by the church(es).[115] Unless the church is active in its response to Jesus' entreaty, it will not share a meal with him, for it is not in fellowship with him.[116] Its lukewarm condition must give way to an active response. The result of a positive response, the opening of the closed door, is the fellowship of a meal between Jesus and his church. Jesus has already hinted about an eschatological fellowship meal (2:7, 17). The appearance of the verb δειπνήσω (*deipnēsō*, "I will eat") might well remind readers that δεῖπνον (*deipnon*, "dinner") occurs in four places in John's gospel (12:2; 13:2, 4; 21:20), each of which has sacramental overtones, suggesting that Jesus' words in Rev 3:20 might be taken as a subtle reference to the Eucharist, as a sign of the

---

113. Smalley, *Revelation*, 101.

114. Mounce (*The Book of Revelation*, 129) insightfully observes, "In an act of unbelievable condescension he requests permission to enter and reestablish fellowship."

115. Osborne, *Revelation*, 213.

116. Resseguie, *The Revelation of John*, 102.

fellowship to be enjoyed by Jesus and the church.[117] The intimacy of this meal is made clear by the phrase "I with him and he with me."

For a seventh time, an eschatological promise is made to the one who overcomes. Jesus promises, "I will give to him to sit with me on my throne, even as I have overcome and I have sat with my Father on his throne." To be promised to sit on Jesus' throne with Jesus, the ruler of the kings of the earth (1:5), is almost beyond comprehension! Since Jesus is proclaimed to be "the ruler of the kings of the earth," the hearers would not be completely surprised that he here reveals that he has a throne. The throne is Jesus' to give, since he himself is one who has overcome. The mention of Jesus' overcoming would remind hearers of words of his to the disciples in John's gospel: "In this world you have tribulation; but be courageous, I have overcome the world" (16:33). Jesus' overcoming activity is developed further in 1 John 5:4-5, where there is an extremely tight connection between Jesus' overcoming and the believer's overcoming. In Rev 3:21 this connection becomes even clearer, for Jesus' overcoming work is the explicit model for the believer's overcoming work.[118] "The one who overcomes will sit . . . even as I have overcome and sat." The word ἐνίκησα (*enikēsa*, "I overcame"), an aorist tense verb, indicates that Jesus has a specific past event in mind. While the hearers would doubtless look upon Jesus' entire life as representing his overcoming work, this victory is intimately connected to his death and resurrection. The overcoming work of Jesus as faithful and true witness is thus inextricably bound to his place on the throne and his ability to give to others the right to sit on his throne. Jesus' faithful witness would stand in stark contrast to the lukewarm witness of the church in Laodicea. The conclusion of v. 21 continues to develop the close identification between Jesus and God. The one who sits on the throne is God, Jesus' Father. That the overcomers would share the throne reinforces the idea that they share a variety of attributes, while suggesting that their identities are mysteriously interconnected. If the one who overcomes is promised to sit on Jesus' throne with him, and Jesus sits on the throne of his Father, then by implication, the one who overcomes will participate in the activity of God and at some level share in his identity. Such an implication, though stupendous, is not out of keeping with the promises that the one who overcomes will be a pillar in God's temple, will have authority over the nations, and have God's name, the name of God's city, and Jesus' name written upon him or her. In some ways this promise is a fitting conclusion to the seven messages, for it appears to be the comprehensive promise to the one who overcomes. The emphasis placed upon the throne(s) continues to develop

---

117. Smalley, *Revelation*, 102.
118. Prigent, *L'Apocalypse de Saint Jean*, 168.

a theme that becomes dominant in the rest of the book,[119] providing the perfect transition to the next major section of Revelation.

The seven prophetic messages end with the familiar call to discerning obedience. At one level, this call is specific to the church in Laodicea. But owing to its strategic location as the final church addressed, and given that the horizons of this message and all the messages begin to merge from about v. 19 onward, the hearers from all churches would have reason to pause and reflect upon the words of Jesus in this entire section of the book. What response should be given to the words of the resurrected Jesus, which are spoken by the Spirit? How can the hearers keep the words of this prophecy? With regard to the message to the church at Laodicea, it is clear. The faithful witness of the church must remain active and not become diluted through accommodation to its environment. Whatever the costs, it must be hot or cold, not lukewarm. Jesus, the true and faithful witness, has all the provisions to enable believers to see spiritually with eyes that he has healed, to appear with him in white garments, and to possess the gold that has been tried by the fire of persecution. Jesus' entreaties are to be met with an active response. It involves a demonstration of zeal for him and his cause, as well as repentance. One theme stands out above all others: that of faithful witness. Jesus and the Spirit continually and consistently call for faithful witness from the churches. Such faithful witness is to be given in the face of persecution that could result in death, the teaching and presence of false prophets and apostles, and the temptation to accommodate their witness to the surrounding religious and commercial environment. Faithful and true witness is the appropriate response to the faithful and true witness himself, Jesus Christ.

---

119. D. Sanger ("Θρόνος," *EDNT*, 2:156) notes that, of the some sixty occurrences of the word θρόνος (thronos, "throne") in the NT, three-fourths appear in Revelation.

"In the Spirit in Heaven" (4:1–16:21)

The second and largest section of the body of Revelation (4:1–16:21) includes the inaugural vision of heaven (4:1–5:14), the opening of the book sealed with seven seals (6:1–8:5), the seven angels with the seven trumpets (8:6–11:19), the struggle of God's people in cosmic perspective (12:1–14:20), and the seven angels with the seven bowls of plagues (15:1–16:21). In this section, the hearers encounter the second occurrence of the phrase ἐν πνεύματι (*en pneumati*, "in the Spirit"), indicating the beginning of a new section of Revelation. As noted in the introduction, not only is this section of Revelation connected to what precedes and follows it, but also it stands together as a distinct section by means of a variety of literary markers.

The Inaugural Vision of Heaven, the One Who Sits on the Throne, the Lamb, and the Scroll Sealed with Seven Seals (4:1–5:14)

The transition from the first major section of the book to the second major section is indicated in two ways. For the first time since Jesus began speaking (1:17), the hearers again encounter John's voice. The phrase "after these things I saw" signals the conclusion of the seven prophetic messages to the seven churches. Earlier John saw the risen Jesus (1:12-20). In 4:1 John saw "a door that had been opened in heaven." Mention of the opened door would remind readers of another open door that Jesus himself had placed before the church in Philadelphia (3:8). This door also represents access to God.[1] Grammatically, the form of the verb "which had been opened" is a divine passive, indicating that the door had been opened by God, or in this case, Jesus,[2] who is in possession of the "key of David." The perfect tense suggests that the door had been opened and remains open for John and perhaps others (in the prophetic community) as well. For not only does John make his way through this opened door, but the hearers also accompany him on his journey and are called upon to discern what they experience as they engage in pneumatic interpretation. There is also an explicit contrast between Jesus standing at and knocking on the door of the church in Laodicea, asking the church to open the door, and the door that Jesus has opened in heaven.[3]

"And the first voice, which I heard as a trumpet, was speaking with me,

---

1. Collins, *The Apocalypse*, 34.
2. Smalley, *Revelation*, 113.
3. Koester, *Revelation and the End of All Things*, 71.

saying, 'Come up here, and I will show you that which is necessary to take place after these things.'" Such language reveals that the one who was speaking, Jesus,[4] continues to speak to John. The phrase "the first voice, which I heard as a trumpet," hearkens back to John's initial prophetic encounter with Jesus (1:10). The fact that the first voice speaking with John now speaks to him again underscores the continuity between Jesus' words in Rev 1–3 and his words in 4:1. The words "Come up here," an invitation to enter into heaven through the opened door, would likely bring to mind certain OT prophetic figures who were also given visions of heaven. Though differences exist between the visions of heaven that Isaiah and Ezekiel received and the one John receives, they and John see the same God.[5] Jesus' promise to show John that which is necessary to take place, familiar language at this point (1:1), indicates that what follows is not disconnected from that which precedes. This language carries with it the idea of divine sovereignty, as "it is necessary" for these things to take place. The introductory nature of 4:1 is also indicated by this verse beginning and ending with the words "after these things."

"Immediately I was in the Spirit." Since there is no hint that John was no longer "in the Spirit," the appearance here of this phrase would convey a sense of continuity between John's experience in chapters 1–3 and his experience in chapter 4 and following.[6] Owing to its previous occurrence, additional prophetic words from or about Jesus in what follows are likely expected. This phrase is central to the book's structure, being the means by which the revelation is given. Here, the phrase "in the Spirit" follows the words of Jesus, while in 1:9-10 the words of Jesus follow this phrase. In the former, being "in the Spirit" leads to the revelation of Jesus' words, while in the latter the words of Jesus lead to John's being "in the Spirit." Such an inversion reinforces the emerging picture of the relationship between Jesus and the Spirit in Revelation, whose words and activities seem to be coterminous. There appears to be a connection between certain geographic locations and being "in the Spirit." In chapter 1, John was on the island of Patmos when "in the Spirit" (1:9-10); in 4:2, John is in heaven.

"And behold, a throne stood in heaven, and upon the throne one was seated." This statement indicates a change in John's geographic location; he is now in heaven, while continuing the throne emphasis that has been building, introduced very early in the book (1:4). But Jesus' promise that the overcomer will "sit on my throne, even as I . . . have sat on my Father's throne," is no doubt still in the hearers' minds. They would thus not be completely surprised that

---

4. Osborne, *Revelation*, 224.
5. Kiddle, *The Revelation of St. John*, 67.
6. Smalley, *Revelation*, 114.

there is a throne in heaven, or that there is one who sits on this throne! Unlike with the descriptions of God in Isaiah and Ezekiel, however, John is reticent about describing concretely "the one who sits on the throne." Rather, John's description takes the form of beautiful translucent objects and colors that convey theological truths.[7] For "the one who sits on the throne" was in appearance as the stones jasper and sardius (a variety of cornelian), while a rainbow encircled the throne in appearance as emerald. These particular colors are also found together on the sacred breastpiece worn by the high priest (Exod 28:17-21), with twelve different stones being sewn on this garment, with the name of one of the twelve tribes engraved on each one. Significantly, jasper is the final stone of the twelve, while the first row of three stones begins with sardius. These two colors, representing the whole of Israel in inverse order, would point to the close connection between the one who sits on the throne and his people. This detail perhaps suggests why these particular colors are present on the high priest's breastpiece in the first place, for they are tied to the identity of God. Thus, the presence of God is first conveyed to John and his hearers by means of these theologically significant stones. In addition, there is a rainbow, in appearance as emerald, encircling the throne. It is very difficult not to see here a reference to the sign of God's covenant with Noah not to destroy the earth by a flood again (Gen 9:8-17).[8] Standing as it does in this inaugural vision of God in heaven, this sign would serve as a constant reminder throughout Revelation that, despite the divine judgment poured out upon the world, God's mercy is not forgotten.[9] This detail would underscore God's faithfulness to his creation.[10] The rainbow that here appears as encircling the throne in Rev 4–5 anticipates the circle that encompasses the whole universe. The rainbow's emerald color would remind readers of God's identity, as this color too is found on the high priest's breastpiece, appearing as the first stone in the second line of twelve stones. These theologically significant objects and translucent colors give the hearers their first glimpse of the one who sits on the throne.

"And encircling the throne were twenty-four thrones, and upon the thrones were sitting twenty-four elders clothed in white garments, and upon their heads were golden crowns." With these words the unbelievable promise of the resurrected Jesus to the one who overcomes (3:21) is fulfilled before John's eyes (and the hearers' ears). The detailed description of those who sit on these

---

7. Smalley, *Revelation*, 115; Osborne, *Revelation*, 226.

8. Smalley, *Revelation*, 115.

9. As Caird (*The Revelation of Saint John*, 63) observes, "The rainbow . . . tells us that there is no triumph for God's sovereignty at the expense of his mercy, and it warns us not to interpret the visions of disaster that follow as though God had forgotten his promise to Noah."

10. Bauckham, *The Climax of Prophecy*, 254, and Wall, *Revelation*, 92.

thrones indicates at almost every point the connection between the twenty-four who sit on the thrones and the promises to those who overcome.[11] Significantly, those who sit on these thrones are described as elders. Within early Christian communities, elders, or *the* elder, are leaders who in some way represent the entire community or church. Owing to the unique position of *the* elder in 2 and 3 John, the exemplary and representative nature of the term would be all the more striking. A number of ideas converge at this point. The number itself invites reflection on its biblical significance. The prominence of the number 12 in the OT may indicate that here there is a doubling of that number, indicating that the theologically significant number 12 is here part of a fuller number still. It is very difficult not to see in this number some kind of combination of the theological significance of the number 12 in both the OT and the Johannine tradition. One of the things the number 24 would suggest is that there is a profound relationship between these twenty-four elders and those represented by the twelve tribes and the twelve apostles, the whole certainly being greater than the sum of its parts. Perhaps this comprehensive number refers to the role of believers as priests to God (1:6). The division of the priesthood into twenty-four courses would be common knowledge (1 Chr 24:4-6),[12] while the elders will exhibit various priestly functions as the book unfolds. The identity of the twenty-four elders is further confirmed by the description of their white garments and golden crowns. Their appearance in white garments fulfills the eschatological promise given by Jesus (3:5). Their appearance in white mirrors Jesus' appearance, just as their faithful witness is patterned on his faithful witness. The golden crowns on their heads also appear to indicate fulfillment of the resurrected Jesus' promise that the one who is faithful unto death will be given a crown of life (2:10). That the crown is now described as golden indicates something about the way in which the fulfillment of eschatological promises is even greater than anticipated. The "white garments" and "golden crowns" the elders possess demonstrate that the promises to the one who overcomes are based upon heavenly realties.[13] It indicates something of the eschatological interplay between present and future realities that "crowns" have already been received by the church in Philadelphia (3:11). Owing to the convergence in 4:4 of ideas found in 2:10, 3:5, and 3:21, it is clear that these standing nearest the throne are those who have been faithful witnesses, like their Lord. If a rainbow

---

11. On the identity of the elders, cf. the helpful piece by L. W. Hurtado, "Revelation 4–5 in the Light of Jewish Apocalyptic Analogies," *JSNT* 25 (1985): 105-24, esp. 111-16. Cf. also Fee, *Revelation*, 69.

12. Simoens, *Apocalypse de Jean*, 43.

13. Hurtado, "Revelation 4–5 in the Light of Jewish Apocalyptic Analogies," 114.

of mercy encircles the throne, those who have experienced God's mercy themselves next encircle it.

Three additional things about the throne are revealed in vv. 5-6a, the grammar indicating that they are to be understood together. First, "lightnings, sounds, and thunders" come forth from the throne. There is no mistaking the significance of such language, for it is standard theophany vocabulary indicating the presence and activity of God (cf. Exod 19:16; Ezek 1:13; Ps 77:18; Dan 7:9). Here, these theophanic elements reveal the awesome presence and power of God proceeding directly from his throne, some of the loudest and most impressive phenomena known within the first century. The present tense verb "coming out/from" indicates their ongoing nature.[14] Such language also conveys the idea that God is not some distant passive deity but is active in creation and human history. Significantly, these theophanic elements will appear at the conclusion of the opening of the seventh seal, the blasting of the seventh trumpet, and the pouring out of the seventh bowl of plagues, indicating that these activities come from the same God who is here depicted.[15] Their growing intensity conveys a sense of progression and completion of the divine judgments.

Next comes the mention that "seven torches of fire are burning before the throne, which are the seven Spirits of God," calling to mind the seven lamps standing in the temple's holy place (Exod 25:31-40; 40:4, 24-25) and standing on Zechariah's golden lampstand (Zech 4:1-14).[16] This convergence suggests that what John sees is the heavenly reality to which other texts and visions point. This statement makes clear that "the seven Spirits before the throne" described by John in the prologue (Rev. 1:4) are indeed to be understood as "the seven Spirits of God," as Jesus has implied (3:1). Their close proximity to God underscores that, when they act, he acts. The reappearance of the "seven Spirits" language at this point, after the numerous references to the Spirit in chapters 2-3, underscores that the seven Spirits of God and the Spirit are indeed identical.[17] The Spirit is in close proximity and relationship to God (1:4; 3:1; 4:5), which is the means by which this revelation is experienced (1:10; 4:2), and the Spirit shares an intimate relationship with Jesus, speaking with one voice (Rev 2–3). After such emphasis upon Jesus' relationship with the Spirit, the mention of "the seven Spirits of God" before the throne reminds readers that the Spirit's identity cannot be understood apart from his intimate relationship with God. This is to say, the seven Spirits of God that Jesus "has" are indeed the seven Spirits *of God*.

---

14. Aune, *Revelation 1–5*, 294-95.
15. Beale, *The Book of Revelation*, 326; Osborne, *Revelation*, 232.
16. Bauckham, *The Climax of Prophecy*, 162-63.
17. Simoens, *Apocalypse de Jean*, 44.

The hearers learn that "before the throne is as a glass sea like crystal," which represents an enigma, for in the biblical tradition, the sea often has negative associations.[18] Here in John's vision of heaven the glassy crystal appearance of this sea is designed for reflection. In this context the sea would reflect the lightning and other visual theophanic qualities of the throne.[19] In other words, this glassy crystal sea is designed to reflect the glory of God. This characteristic of the sea may also go some way toward explaining its presence here in heaven, despite its otherwise negative connotations. Perhaps the hearers discern in this somewhat mixed image the theological truth that even those objects that have negative associations somehow reflect the glory of God.[20]

"And in the midst of the throne and around the throne were four living beings full of eyes in front and in back." Like the twenty-four elders, these beings are also described as being around or encircling the throne. They are said to be located in the very middle of the throne, conveying the sense of extraordinarily close proximity to, and dynamic movement in and around, the throne.[21] While the term "living beings" is sometimes rendered as "beasts," such a translation is misleading, for it is not at all related to the word "beast." Though the translation "living beings" is technically accurate, perhaps a better contextual translation would be "living creatures."[22] These living creatures are connected to creation, but they appear in heaven. While these four living creatures might bring to mind similar creatures described by Ezekiel (1:4-28), unlike those creatures, John sees creatures "full of eyes in front and in back," indicating that these living creatures possess complete and comprehensive vision with which to see all the magnificence, omnipotence, and holiness of the one who sits on the throne.[23] The comprehensive nature of their vision underscores their qualification to praise God as "the All Powerful One."

This initial description gives way to an enumeration of the living creatures and a more extensive physical description. For the first time in the book, an enumerated series is encountered in which the items in the series are numbered

---

18. Caird, *The Revelation of Saint John*, 65.

19. Schüssler Fiorenza, *Revelation: Vision of a Just World*, 59. It should also be noted that the grammatical construction of vv. 5-6a makes clear that these sentences stand together.

20. I am indebted to my colleague L. R. Martin for this insight.

21. The attempt to understand the phrase "in the midst and around the throne" as having reference to the design of the throne fails to convince, owing in part to the dynamism of the passage. On this view the four living creatures are an integral part of the throne, its back and legs, just as the cherubim are part of the mercy seat on the ark of the covenant owing to their location on or in it. For this proposal, cf. R. G. Hall, "Living Creatures in the Midst of the Throne: Another Look at Revelation 4:6," *NTS* 36 (1990): 609-13.

22. Simoens, *Apocalypse de Jean*, 45.

23. Resseguie, *The Revelation of John*, 111.

in order. Here the enumeration appears simply to draw specific attention to the individual objects in the series. The first living creature is in appearance as a lion, the second as an ox, the third has the face of a man, and the fourth as a flying eagle.[24] Both the number 4[25] and the individual physical forms of the living creatures suggest that they are representatives of the different realms of creation.[26] There are the ferocious and terrifying lion, the domesticated ox, the human being, and the eagle, whose domain is the heavens.[27] These four creatures seem to have a representative function for all of creation. But things do not revolve around humankind; rather, here humanity is simply a part of this heavenly vision. God is central.[28] As in the vision of Isaiah, the four living creatures, like the seraphim (Isa 6:2), have six wings. Such imagery reinforces the sense of awe and holiness of this scene in Revelation. Earlier, they are "full of eyes in front and in back," while in v. 8 they are "full of eyes all around and within." Perhaps this change in description suggests some connection between their being "full of eyes all around and within" and their location "in the midst of and all around the throne." "And they do not cease day and night saying...." Very literally, "and they have no rest from saying." Their praise is an ongoing, never-ending activity. They are creatures designed to praise God, and when they do this unceasingly, the reason for their existence is fulfilled. At this point, the first of numerous hymns occurs in Revelation,[29] hymns that underscore the theological importance of worship in the book, while conveying numerous theological truths.[30]

The opening words of this hymn are "Holy, holy, holy." This triple declaration of the Lord's holiness echoes the words of the seraphim in Isa 6:3, focusing attention upon the absolute holiness of the one who sits on the throne. Such

---

24. Irenaeus (*Adversus Haereses*, in *The Apostolic Fathers: Justin Martyr and Irenaeus* [ed. Alexander Roberts and J. Donaldson; rev. A. Cleveland Cox; Ante-Nicene Fathers 1; Peabody, MA: Hendrickson, 1984], 3.11.8) appears to be the first to equate the four living creatures with the four Evangelists (Matthew/lion, Mark/ox, Luke/man, and John/eagle), an identification that has proven to be very popular in the history of the church.

25. As Bauckham (*Climax of Prophecy*, 30-32) points out, the number 4 is the number of the created world in Revelation. For example, the earth has four corners (7:1; 20:8), four winds (7:1), and can be divided into four divisions (5:13; 8:7-12; 14:7; 16:2-9).

26. Fee, *Revelation*, 72-73.

27. B. M. Metzger (*Breaking the Code* [Nashville: Abingdon, 1993], 50) describes the four living creatures as follows: "These symbolize, respectively, what is the noblest, strongest, wisest, and swiftest in creation."

28. Koester, *Revelation and the End of All Things*, 72.

29. Hymns appear in the Apocalypse in 4:8, 11; 5:9b-14; 7:10-12; 11:15-18; 12:10-12; 13:4; 15:3-4; 16:5-7; 18:20; 19:1-8.

30. Cf. R. Morton, "Glory to God and the Lamb: John's Use of Jewish and Hellenistic/Roman Themes in Formatting His Theology in Revelation 4–5," *JSNT* 83 (2001): 89-109.

words of praise are consistent with those of Jesus, who has called God "Holy Father" (John 17:11). This triple declaration also reminds readers that Jesus has earlier identified himself as "the Holy One" in Revelation (3:7), suggesting that, even here, thoughts of Jesus are never far away. The words that follow echo the words of God, spoken in 1:8. The four living creatures' accurate knowledge of God inevitably leads to true worship.[31] He is "Lord, God, the All Powerful One, the one who was, the one who is, and the one who is coming." The four living creatures praise God because, as the All Powerful One, he has no rivals. He is praised because in him the past, present, and future converge; there is no place or time in which he does not exist. This opening volley of praise sets the stage for what follows. The four living creatures praise him for who he is: holy, Lord, God, all powerful, eternal/never ending.

"Whenever the living creatures give glory and honor and thanks to the one who sits on the throne, the one who lives forever and ever, the twenty-four elders fall before the one who sits upon the throne, and they worship the one who lives forever and ever, and they cast their crowns before the throne," indicating that the four living creatures never stop offering praise to God. The rendering of "glory and honor and thanks" is also related to the words of praise recorded in the previous verse — whenever they sing this hymn, they are giving "glory and honor and thanks." In John's gospel, glory is associated with God and his Son, Jesus, belonging to the realm of God as it precedes the creation of the world (John 17:5). It is especially reflected in the incarnation of Jesus (1:14) and is manifested at numerous points in his ministry (2:11; 11:4, 40). Above all, one should seek the glory of God (7:18; 8:50-54), in contrast to those who love the glory of other people more than the glory of God (12:43). It would not surprise John that glory is the first element in this trilogy of praise. Honor, the second element, is also intricately connected to God in Revelation (4:9). Thanks is also closely associated with God in Revelation, though not mentioned as often. The clear object of this praise is the one who sits on the throne. Here the emphasis that he is the one who lives forever and ever is made clear by the twofold description in vv. 9-10 of this one sitting upon the throne. Such emphatic language follows up nicely on this one having been described three times previously in the book as "the one who was and the one who is and the one who is coming." Together these descriptions underscore the eternality of the one who sits on the throne;[32] his existence never comes to an end.[33] If his existence never comes to an end, therefore neither does his reign.[34]

---

31. Bauckham, *The Theology of the Book of Revelation*, 32.
32. Smalley, *Revelation*, 123.
33. Beale, *The Book of Revelation*, 333.
34. Osborne, *Revelation*, 239.

Whenever the four living creatures worship, which they continually do, the twenty-four elders follow their lead by doing three things. First, they leave their thrones and "fall before the one who sits on the throne." Like John, who falls at the feet of Jesus (1:17), so the twenty-four elders fall before the one who sits on the throne. Since John's prostration before Jesus appears to be an involuntary response by John, overwhelmed by the glory of Jesus, a similar response on the elders' part may be assumed. Such a response would not be wholly unexpected, given the extraordinarily awesome description of the one who sits on the throne. The similarity of the responses of John and the elders may also encourage the connection between those who overcome and the elders. Second, the elders "worship the one who lives forever and ever." In this first clear reference to the worship of God, the hearers are reminded that the worship of God is absolutely fundamental and necessary. Given that this worship is rendered to one who lives forever and ever, it becomes clear that such worship is to be restricted to such a one. Third, the twenty-four elders "cast their crowns before the throne," indicating that, despite their receiving of rewards owing to their faithful, overcoming witness, they do not celebrate their own accomplishments or reign but those of the one who sits on the throne.[35] This activity makes clear that these rewards are gifts of God, who has made all possible; despite their wearing of golden crowns, they recognize that there is only one authority, the throne of God.[36]

The twenty-four elders also worship with a hymn.

> You are worthy, our Lord and God,
> to receive the glory and the honor and the power,
> because you created all things
>   and on account of your will they are
>   and they have been created.

The hymn's first word in Greek, "worthy," has already appeared in 3:4, which mentions those in Sardis who are worthy to walk with Jesus. This commercial term was used in the context of weights and balances to determine whether something was equal or adequate.[37] In Revelation, one is deemed worthy to receive something or to do something owing to who one is or what one has done. The addition of the pronoun "our" indicates something of the personal nature of the relationship between the elders and God.[38] In this con-

---

35. Koester, *Revelation and the End of All Things*, 74-75.
36. Smalley, *Revelation*, 124,
37. Trummer, "Ἄξιος," *EDNT*, 1:113.
38. Resseguie, *The Revelation of John*, 113.

text, "our Lord and God" is worthy "to receive the glory and the honor and the power." This hymn of the elders (v. 11) includes a trilogy of praise. While they join in ascribing glory and honor to our Lord God, their hymn uses the definite article with each element of praise, perhaps underscoring the fact that God, like no other, is worthy of "the" glory and "the" honor and "the" power. Instead of thanks, the elders' trilogy contains reference to power, as power is closely associated with God's creative activity. "Our Lord and God" is deemed worthy of such worship owing to his role as creator.

These statements take on a chiastic structure where the first part of the statement is mirrored by the final portion.[39] It could be set out as follows:

You created all things
 and on account of your will they are
and they have been created.

The statements begin and end with reference to God's creative activity, using forms of the word "create" at both the beginning and the end. The middle statement then becomes the focal point. Despite this strong affirmation of God as creator, thoughts of Jesus are never far from mind, as a very similar statement is made about the Logos in John 1:2-3. Here "our Lord and God" has created all. His work as creator is connected to the core of his being, for it is on account of his will that they are. For Johannine hearers, God's creative activity and will cannot properly be understood without the understanding that God does not will that any be lost (John 6:38-40). The divine passive rendered "they have been created" conveys something of God's active agency in creation, balancing the active voice statement with which this chiastic section begins. Thus, despite any marring of his creation that may have taken place, God is still praised for his creative activity by the twenty-four elders.

John now sees something new, for "in the right hand of the one who sits on the throne is a book with writing on the inside and outside sealed with seven seals." This scroll is in the *right* hand of the one who sits on the throne, which emphasizes the power of this one who created all things, the right hand being regarded as the hand of power.[40] While the identity of the scroll is much debated, its significance at this point is conveyed by its location and physical description. Normally a scroll would have writing on the inside only, protecting what is written from becoming worn by frequent handling. This scroll, like the one given to Ezekiel by God, has writing on both the inside and the outside,

---

39. Osborne, *Revelation*, 242.
40. Resseguie, *The Revelation of John*, 115.

suggesting that its contents can barely be contained. Seals upon a legal document were often placed there by witnesses, who would stand ready to testify to the authenticity and trustworthiness of its contents. The fact that seven seals are affixed to this scroll suggests that the one who sits upon the throne himself, and/or the seven Spirits located before his throne, is the one who validates the scroll's contents. The seven seals affixed to this scroll also indicate that its contents have been made completely inaccessible to anyone whom God does not authorize to open it.

Next John says, "And I saw a mighty angel preaching with a great voice." This mighty angel's great voice is apparently strong enough to be heard by all creation;[41] its intensity is in keeping with the other extraordinarily loud sounds described to this point. Significantly, the angel's activity is described by the word "preaching."[42] Such a detail implies that this angel's activity is not simply an invitation to anyone who might be worthy to open the scroll but carries with it implicit proclamation, suggesting there is indeed one who is worthy to open the scroll. Such a meaning is made more likely in that this is the only appearance of this term in the whole of the Johannine literature.[43] The mighty angel's proclamation, "Who is worthy to open the book and to loose its seals?" reminds hearers of the one who sits on the throne, who himself has been praised as worthy. Here, as there, the term "worthy" conveys the idea of one who is adequate or equal to the task. This question implies a call for one who is qualified for such a task. Given that the one who sits on the throne is deemed worthy (4:11), that the book is in his right hand, and that the book has been sealed by him or his seven Spirits, only one who shares such worthiness would be worthy (and authorized!) to open the scroll and loose the seals with which God has sealed and authorized its contents. The mighty angel's preaching is concerned with a uniquely qualified one indeed![44]

But alas, no one in all of creation, "in the heaven or upon the earth or under the earth," was able — very literally "had the power" — "to open the book or to see it." This three-tiered description of those unable to open the book adds to the heightened drama experienced. Since the one who sits on the throne is ascribed "power" owing to his creative activity (4:11), it would not surprise that the one deemed worthy would also require power (5:3). The shift from the phrase "loosing the seals" in v. 2 to the phrase "or to see it" in vv. 3-4 would

---

41. Mounce, *The Book of Revelation*, 143.

42. Smalley, *Revelation*, 129

43. E. Lohse (*Die Offenbarung des Johannes* [NTD; Göttingen: Vandenhoeck & Ruprecht, 1960], 38) goes so far as to call κηρύσσω (*kēryssō*, "preach") "the decisive key word of the entire vision."

44. Kiddle, *The Revelation of St. John*, 97, and Aune, *Revelation 1-5*, 347-48.

perhaps link the one worthy to see this book with the things that John himself is commissioned to see (1:11). This disappointing turn of events proves to be quite traumatic for John, who says, "And I wept much," the Greek imperfect tense suggesting a translation like, "I wept and wept much." This verb[45] brings to mind the weeping that accompanies the death of Lazarus (John 11:31, 33) and Jesus (20:11, 13, 15). John's continuous weeping (Rev 5:4) indicates that he is distraught in that "no one was found worthy to open the book or see it." This divine passive, "was found," perhaps implies that God himself could find no one worthy for this essential task. The incredible dramatic tension of the scene, where everything seems to be moving to this point, is thus frustrated in that no one in all of creation is found worthy to open the book. If the divine will can be frustrated in the very throne room of God, what are the implications for those on earth who are called to faithful witness in the face of powerful opponents? John may well fear that his prophetic task is being frustrated. Such a devastating disappointment is not simply personal regret,[46] but the frustration of John's prophetic call and vocation.

At this point, one of the elders speaks to John, instructing him to "stop weeping," a present tense prohibition used to stop an action already in progress. This construction sits well with v. 4.[47] More than comfort is being offered to John, for these words reveal that all is not lost. The divine will is not frustrated. John's prophetic mission is to be completed. "Behold, the Lion of the Tribe of Judah has overcome, the Root of David, to open the book and loose its seals." Here emphasis is placed upon "has overcome,"[48] as it stands immediately after "behold" in the Greek sentence. This familiar "overcoming" terminology now appears on the lips of a representative of those who have themselves overcome.[49] Perhaps the most important association this terminology would evoke is Jesus' self-identification as one who has overcome (3:21) and sits on the throne with his Father.[50] The elder identifies the one who has overcome as "the Lion of the Tribe of Judah" and "the Root of David," two most significant titles, in which a number of OT messianic ideas converge.[51] The first message is connected to the patriarchal blessing spoken in Gen 49:8-12, with its image of the lion, a

---

45. H. Balz, "Κλαίω," *EDNT*, 2:293.
46. Smalley, *Revelation*, 130.
47. Aune, *Revelation 1-5*, 322.
48. Osborne, *Revelation*, 253.
49. Allo notes (*Saint Jean: L'Apocalypse*, 62) that the intervention of one of the elders with John shows very well the special rapport between these personages and humanity.
50. L. L. Johns, *The Lamb Christology of the Apocalypse of John: An Investigation into Its Origins and Rhetorical Force* (WUNT 2.167; Tübingen: Mohr Siebeck, 2003), 178-79.
51. G. E. Ladd, *A Commentary on the Revelation of John* (Grand Rapids: Eerdmans, 1972), 83.

ferocious, destructive, and irresistibly strong figure.[52] In the Torah, Judah is "a lion's whelp," who stoops and crouches as a lion (49:9). It is also said of Judah that the scepter in his hand and that the ruler's staff between his feet will not depart from this tribe until Shiloh comes, to whom all people will be obedient (49:10). The resurrected Jesus is already identified as "the one who has the key of David" (Rev 3:7), who determines entry to and exclusion from his kingdom. This title also draws upon Isa 11:1-10, which speaks of the shoot that will come from the root of Jesse. Significantly, in describing this individual as one upon whom the Spirit will rest, there appears to be a sevenfold emphasis:

> And the Spirit of the LORD will rest upon him, the spirit of wisdom and understanding, the spirit of counsel and might, the spirit of knowledge and the fear of the LORD. (11:2)

This root of Jesse will smite the earth with the word (LXX) of his mouth (Isa 11:4), will usher in eschatological peace (11:6-8), and will be a sign to the nations, who will seek him (11:10). It would thus come as no surprise that the Lion of the Tribe of Judah, the Root of David, "has overcome . . . to open the book and its seven seals."[53]

For a third time the phrase "and I saw" occurs. The object John sees is "in the midst of the throne and the four living creatures and in the midst of the elders." This somewhat surrealistic description suggests that the object John now describes is closer to the throne than any of those previously mentioned. In the inaugural vision of Jesus, John heard a voice like a trumpet, but when he turned to "see" the voice, he saw seven golden lampstands and one like a Son of Man in their midst (Rev 1:12-13). On this occasion, John hears about the Lion of the Tribe of Judah, the Root of David, but what he sees is "a Lamb standing, as if slaughtered." This psychedelic-like morphing of one form into another is both unexpected and meaningful. While it is possible to replace all previous OT lion imagery with slaughtered Lamb imagery,[54] it appears that each of these images interprets and clarifies the other.[55] The Lamb is, at the same time, the Lion.[56] He does not stop being the Lion, owing to the appearance of Lamb imagery. The Lion in 5:5 cannot be fully understood without the vision of the slaughtered

---

52. Bauckham, *The Climax of Prophecy*, 182.
53. Cf. G. Schimanowski, *Die himmlische Liturgie in der Apokalypse des Johannes: Die frühjüdischen Traditionen in Offenbarung 4–5 unter Einschluß der Hekhalotliteratur* (WUNT 2.154; Tübingen: Mohr Siebeck, 2002), 197-204.
54. So Caird, *The Revelation of Saint John*, 74.
55. Michaels, *Revelation*, 95.
56. Murphy, *Fallen Is Babylon*, 193.

Lamb. Such dialectical imagery means that the Lion cannot be thought of any longer without the slaughtered Lamb.

The image of the slaughtered Lamb is pregnant with meaning, as a number of associations converge here.[57] Readers certainly know about the Passover lamb of the exodus story. The verb "slaughter" also brings to mind Isa 53:7, where the same root word describes the suffering servant "as a lamb led to the slaughter." The significance of Jesus as the paschal lamb in John's gospel would also be well known (John 1:29),[58] as would the emphasis in John's gospel on Passover imagery, concluding with Jesus' death at the time the Passover lambs are slain (19:31). The occurrence of the perfect passive participle "slaughtered" would also point to Jesus' death as a one-time event, the effects of which are still felt.[59] The description of the slaughtered Lamb as standing may be an oblique reference to the resurrection of this slaughtered Lamb,[60] reminding hearers of Jesus' earlier claims about his death and resurrection (Rev 1:18; 2:8).[61]

This Lamb, which will become one of the dominant figures in Revelation with reference to Jesus, is described as having seven horns. Not only is he the first animal in Revelation described as having horns,[62] clearly a reference to his power, but as having *seven* horns, an indication that his power is complete. This provides a point of real continuity between the image of the Lion and that of the Lamb. John sees that the Lamb also has seven eyes. This image would convey the idea that the slaughtered Lamb has perfect vision and, consequently, perfect knowledge, for he sees all; this endowment is consistent with Jesus' numerous "I know" statements found in the seven prophetic messages in Rev 2–3.[63] Remarkably, the seven eyes are identified as "the seven Spirits of God sent out into all the earth," implying that the Lamb possesses the fullness or completeness of the Spirit.[64] By this image the intimate relationship between Jesus and the Spirit continues to develop. Here, the seven Spirits of God are identified as the Lamb's seven eyes. In Revelation the eyes of Yahweh, as depicted in Zech 4:10, are also depicted as the eyes of the Lamb.[65] These seven Spirits of God,

---

57. Cf. N. Hillyer, "'The Lamb' in the Apocalypse," *EQ* 39 (1967): 228-36.

58. Though John's Gospel and Revelation use different words for lamb, ἀμνός (*amnos*, "lamb") and ἀρνίον (*arnion*, "lamb" or "sheep") respectively, the words appear to be theological equivalents. Cf. Prigent, *L'Apocalypse de Saint Jean*, 191.

59. Smalley, *Revelation*, 132.

60. Aune, *Revelation 1–5*, 352.

61. Prigent (*L'Apocalypse de Saint Jean*, 192) notes that in these images we have the equivalent of Christological propositions.

62. Prigent, *L'Apocalypse de Saint Jean*, 193.

63. Metzger, *Breaking the Code*, 53.

64. Prigent, *L'Apocalypse de Saint Jean*, 193.

65. Bauckham, *The Climax of Prophecy*, 164.

these seven eyes of the Lamb, go out into all the earth.[66] The Lamb has perfect knowledge and vision, reminding readers of Jesus' words with regard to the Paraclete, who will convict the world concerning sin and righteousness and judgment (John 16:8-11). Thus, there is a very active dimension to the activity of the seven Spirits of God. A very tight connection also exists between the activity of the seven Spirits of God and the prophetic witness of the church — the Spirit is the one who inspires the faithful witness of all those who are part of this prophetic community.[67]

The juxtaposing of the contrasting images of the Lion of the Tribe of Judah, the Root of David, and the slaughtered Lamb reveals that the symbol of conquest is the symbol of sacrificial death.[68] This collocation of images makes clear to John and his hearers that their own "faithful witness" and "overcoming" are intimately connected with the sacrificial death of Jesus — and may even necessitate their own death.[69] Such a realization would make all the clearer Jesus' words to the church in Smyrna (2:10) "to be faithful unto death."

Verse 7 describes one of the most significant events in the book, one that triggers the most incredible acts of worship contained within Revelation. The Lamb, who is the Lion and the Root, "went and took (it) out of the right hand of the one who sits upon the throne." The occurrence of the perfect tense "took" indicates that the results of this past action continue to be felt into the present. This act indicates the unique worthiness of the Lamb, as no one in all creation is qualified to take the book but he. This act could be seen as the central moment in salvation history,[70] for the one who takes the book from the one who sits on the throne is the one who has been slain but is now alive. It is exceedingly difficult not to see in this image a symbol of the obedient death of the Lamb.[71] Instantaneous worship immediately results, indicating the significance of the Lamb's actions.[72]

As soon as the Lamb takes the book, he too becomes an object of worship,[73] making clear the connection between the Lamb's taking the book and the subsequent worship of him. It is truly remarkable in a book that underscores the importance of true worship given to God alone that here another figure receives the worship that God receives,[74] indicating simply

---

66. Resseguie, *The Revelation of John*, 120.
67. Bauckham, *The Climax of Prophecy*, 165-66.
68. Bauckham, *The Climax of Prophecy*, 179-85.
69. Johns, *The Lamb Christology of the Apocalypse of John*, 175-80.
70. Prigent, *L'Apocalypse de Saint Jean*, 194.
71. Kiddle, *The Revelation of St. John*, 102.
72. Aune, *Revelation 1-5*, 355.
73. Michaels, *Revelation*, 95.
74. Bauckham, *The Climax of Prophecy*, 133-38.

that the Lamb shares in divine worship. The nature of this worship consists of four activities. First, the four living creatures and the twenty-four elders fall down before the Lamb. Second, each of them had "harps" or "lyres." Only the elders are likely to possess such instruments, as the masculine phrase "each one having" clearly goes with the elders (in the masculine gender in Greek) and would not include the four living creatures (in the Greek neuter gender).[75] Harps often appear in worship contexts in the OT (Pss 33:2; 98:5; 147:7). In Revelation the harps are found exclusively in heaven and are always connected with singing (5:8-9; 14:2; 15:2). Third, each of the twenty-four elders also has "golden bowls full of incense." These priestly functions would be further evidence of the connection between the twenty-four elders and their counterparts on earth.[76] This description envisions the burning incense that goes up before God in his temple and is a sweet smell to him. Just as the hearers are earlier told of the meaning of the seven eyes of the Lamb, so here they are told the meaning of the "bowls full of incense" — they are "the prayers of the saints" (5:8). This image indicates that the relationship between the twenty-four elders and the "saints" is an especially close one. It would underscore that, rather than being a burden to God, the prayers of the saints are an aroma pleasing to him. This image makes clear that there is a connection between the worship of those on earth and those in heaven![77] The prayers of the saints are reflected in the activity around the throne of God himself. If the prayers of the saints on earth enable them to participate in heavenly worship, surely the same would be true of other forms of worship. Here for the first time in the book the term ἅγιοι (*hagioi*, "saints") appears. The term would suggest their special relationship to Jesus and God, since both have earlier been called ἅγιος (*hagios*, "holy" — 3:7; 4:8). In Revelation the word becomes the term of choice for believers.[78]

Fourth, "and they sang a new song." In the OT new songs are frequently the response of God's people to new acts of salvation (Pss 33:3; 40:3; 96:1; 98:1; 144:9; 149:1; Isa 42:10). This is the first time in Revelation that specific lyrics are identified as a "song," a point perhaps emphasized by the use here of the cognate accusative construction "they sang a song," where the verb and the direct object noun come from the same root. The appropriateness of their singing a new song is clear, for no other action in all of history parallels these things described in Rev 5.

---

75. Beale, *The Book of Revelation*, 357.
76. J. D. Charles, "The Apocalyptic Tribute to the Lamb (Rev 5:1-14)," *JETS* 34 (1991): 470.
77. Metzger, *Breaking the Code*, 53.
78. Murphy, *Fallen Is Babylon*, 196.

> You are worthy to take the book
>   and to open its seals,
> because you were slaughtered, and you purchased for God in your blood
>   out of every tribe and tongue and people and nation
> and you made them for our God a kingdom and priests,
>   and they will reign upon the earth.

This song begins with words identical to those that began the previous hymn (4:11), a detail that underscores the fact that the Lamb is worshipped in the same way God is![79] The Greek sentence begins with "worthy," which makes this parallel all the more obvious. As God before him, the Lamb is now declared to be qualified for a specific task. The unique worthiness of the Lamb now becomes the basis of this new song sung to him — he is worthy to take the book and to open its seals!

The qualifications for this worthiness are set out in the next three stanzas: because "he was slaughtered," "he purchased," and "he made." The first stanza consists of only one word in the Greek text, which dramatically underscores the crucial significance of the sacrificial death of the Lamb. The next stanza focuses upon the second qualification lifted up in this new song: "and you purchased for God in your blood out of every tribe and tongue and people and nation." The term "purchase," though carrying a commercial meaning in its occurrences in John's gospel (4:8; 6:5; 13:29), takes on a decidedly theological meaning in Revelation. Its only other appearance to this point in Revelation is found in Jesus' words to the church in Laodicea to purchase gold, white garments, and salve from him (Rev 3:18). In 5:9 the term describes the purchase of individuals for God. The language implies ownership of those purchased, placing a great deal of emphasis upon the price of the purchase, namely, "your blood." Mention of the blood of Jesus obviously is connected to the discussion of the slaughtered Lamb in the previous verses, indicating that the sacrificial death of the Lamb makes possible such a purchase. The other aspect of this purchase is its universal quality, for individuals are purchased for God from "every tribe and tongue and people and nation."[80] The occurrence of this fourfold designation underscores the universality of those purchased in the Lamb's blood for God. They are not restricted to any particular ethnic, national, or linguistic group; the redemptive work of the Lamb knows no such limits. The song's final stanza is devoted to the third qualification of the Lamb to take the book and open its seals: "and he made them to our God a kingdom

---

79. Sweet, *Revelation*, 130.
80. Cf. Bauckham, *The Climax of Prophecy*, 326-37.

and priests, and they will reign upon the earth." Reiterating John's words about Jesus in the prologue, this activity is closely associated with his blood. Here, it becomes clear that such a kingdom and such priests come from all groupings of humankind. Those in this kingdom "will reign upon the earth." The song's emphasis upon reigning on the earth might remind hearers of (1) the earlier promise to the one who overcomes to wear crowns and sit upon thrones, (2) the twenty-four elders, and (3), to the overcomers in the church in Thyatira, Jesus' promise to give authority over the nations, which they will rule with a rod of iron (2:25-27).

For a fourth time the words "and I saw" occur. Here, what John sees leads him to what he hears; what John encounters, he encounters both visually and audibly. What he hears is "the voice of many angels," who encircle the throne. Previously, the focus upon the throne moved from the outside in: from the twenty-four elders who encircle the throne, to the four living creatures who seem to dart in and around the throne, to the Lamb, who is in the midst of, even on, the throne. With the introduction of the angels, the focus moves further out to a larger circle. These angels speak with one voice, though their number is exceedingly great. These angels are the first objects to be described by the word "number," the description of their number given in an almost poetic fashion: "tens of thousands of tens of thousands, and thousands of thousands." Such staggering numbers indicate that the heavens are literally filled with angelic beings around the throne, the living creatures, and the twenty-four elders, leaving the impression that no creature in heaven is *not* preoccupied with worship of the Lamb. The words that come from the angels echo those of the twenty-four elders (4:11). As in the worship of God, so the first words of the angels declare, "Worthy is the Lamb, who was slaughtered," as they build upon and reiterate the words of the new song (5:9-10); the Lamb is worthy precisely because he was slaughtered. In 5:12 he is declared worthy to receive worship in a sevenfold way. As God was deemed worthy to receive a trilogy of praise (4:11), even more so the Lamb is deemed worthy to receive sevenfold praise, which includes the trilogy of praise rendered to God in inverse order.[81] Significantly, the sevenfold doxology begins with the element with which the trilogy of praise of God concludes: "the power." This occurrence provides a point of continuity between God and the Lamb, while underscoring "the power" of the one who has overcome by his own blood to be worthy to take the book and open its seals. The attribution of "wealth" to the Lamb would remind readers of the wealth of the church in Smyrna, despite their poverty and tribulation (2:9), and of the poverty and wretchedness of

---

81. Resseguie, *The Revelation of John*, 122.

The Inaugural Vision of Heaven (4:1–5:14)

the church in Laodicea, despite their claims to be rich (3:17). The attribution of "wisdom" to the Lamb will later be seen as a quality shared by God (7:12) and essential for pneumatic interpretation on the part of the hearers (13:18; 17:9). The fourth element, "strength," will be intimately associated with God (7:12; 18:8), as well as his angels (5:2; 10:1; 18:2, 21) and worshippers (19:6). The fifth element, "honor," appears as the second element in the trilogy of praise rendered to God in Rev 4:9. Again, the Lamb receives that which is intricately connected to God in Revelation (4:9, 11). The sixth element is the theologically rich "glory," part of the trilogy of praise rendered to God by the four living creatures (4:9). Its intricate connection with God in Revelation (4:11; 5:13), as well as its deep association with Jesus in John's gospel, makes its occurrence here all the more significant. Not only does the close relationship between God and the Lamb continue to develop, but there is also the implicit answer to Jesus' prayer for the Father to glorify him consistent with the glory he shared before the world began (John 17:5). The seventh and final element in this angelic chorus of praise is "blessing," which is also intimately connected with God in Revelation (5:13; 7:12). The implication of this deafening chorus is clear: the Lamb is worthy to receive praise that is worthy of God himself. It is impossible to imagine a more complete heavenly song of praise than this. And yet. . . .

Unbelievably, the throng of worshippers expands beyond the boundaries of heaven to include the entire universe. "Every creature" reminds hearers of the twenty-four elders' song (4:11), which underscores God's creative activity and will. The inclusive nature of this group is made clear: "And every creature that is in heaven and upon the earth and under the earth and upon the sea and all the things in them." Here, the phenomenon of fourfold divisions to refer to the created order in Revelation is introduced.[82] The phrase "and all the things in them" serves as an inclusio with "every creature," surrounding the fourfold division of creation. All the things God created (4:11) are included in this grouping. Astoundingly, these words of praise are directed to the one who sits on the throne *and* to the Lamb.

> To the one who sits on the throne and to the Lamb
> be the blessing and the honor and the glory and the might
> for ever and ever.

The Lamb, who earlier received praise in his own right, now joins the one who sits on the throne as the object of praise. The Lamb does not replace the

---

82. Bauckham, *The Climax of Prophecy*, 31.

one who sits on the throne[83] but is inextricably joined to him as the object of universal worship.[84] The praise rendered by the fourfold division comes in a fourfold doxology, each individual component being a provocative integration of doxological elements that have been used to describe God and/or the Lamb. Beginning with "the blessing," the last element of the sevenfold angelic doxology directed to the Lamb (5:12), the ascription of this element to both God and the Lamb makes clear that the Lamb is not in a superior position to the one who sits on the throne but is worshipped along with him. The ascription of "honor and glory," previously rendered to the Lamb by the angelic chorus (5:12) and to God by the four living creatures as "glory and honor" (4:9), here emphasizes their shared worship. The final doxological element — "might," or "power" — has appeared with reference to the Lamb (1:6), as well as on the lips of the four living creatures in the title "the Almighty One" or "the All Powerful One," referring to the one who sits on the throne (4:8). Fittingly, the praise rendered by every creature in the universe is intended to last for every moment of existence, "for ever and ever."

The last word of praise — "Amen" — comes from the four living creatures, who spoke the first words of praise in this scene (4:8). Not only does the utterance of the "Amen" have good liturgical precedence in Revelation (1:6-7), but it is also closely associated with Jesus in each of those contexts and even becomes a title by which Jesus identifies himself (3:14). Upon hearing the "Amen," the twenty-four elders fall down yet again. It is altogether fitting that the words with which this section concludes are "and they worshipped"!

The Opening of the Scroll Sealed with Seven Seals (6:1–8:5)

The second section of this largest portion of the book (4:1–16:21) is primarily devoted to the opening of the seven seals by the Lamb, in which three things will stand out. First, the opening of each enumerated seal is accompanied by eschatologically and theologically significant events (6:1-17). Second, the first of several interludes found throughout the book occurs here, separating the opening of the sixth and seventh seals (7:1-17). Third, the opening of the seventh seal (8:1-5) is intimately connected to the seven angels with seven trumpets, which immediately follows (8:6–11:19).

---

83. Koester, *Revelation and the End of All Things*, 80.
84. Michaels, *Revelation*, 97. Kiddle (*The Revelation of St. John*, 105) notes, "Nowhere else in the New Testament is Christ adored on such absolutely equal terms with the Godhead."

The Opening of the First Six Seals (6:1-17)

Attention is now focused upon the opening of the seven seals by the Lamb. The seals fall into a four-three pattern, where the first four stand together, while the fifth, sixth, and seventh seals stand on their own to a certain extent. There is clearly a tight connection between the actions of the Lamb in chapter 5 and his actions here. Sometimes this connection is not fully appreciated, as the opening of the seals is accompanied by suffering and death inflicted upon the world. Some contemporary readers are tempted to believe that such activity is not appropriate for the slaughtered Lamb, who has just received such universal worship. However, there is a very tight connection between the events of chapters 5 and 6, for the eschatological events that accompany the opening of the seals are under the control of God, and the Lamb is the one worthy to open them.

The scene opens with the familiar "I saw." The words "when the Lamb opened one of the seven seals" indicate that the long-awaited action of the Lamb is now underway. Somewhat unexpectedly, John immediately describes not what he sees but what he hears, for one of the four living creatures was speaking with a voice like thunder. The appearance of one of the four living creatures reminds readers of the creatures' strategic location in and around the throne. The creature's voice as thunder suggests a close association between this living creature and the throne of God, where thunder was one of the theophanic elements to come from it (4:5). Such an indicator suggests that, when the living creature speaks, he speaks for the one who sits on the throne.[85] Mention of the living creatures points to the continuity that exists between those who worship in chapters 4–5 and those who act in chapter 6.[86] The utterance of this thunderous voice is the enigmatic command "come" or "go."

Once again the words "I saw" appear, followed by "and behold." John next sees "a white horse, and the one sitting upon it having a bow, and there was given to him a crown, and he went out overcoming, even in order that he might overcome." The horse was a powerful figure, often used to dominate those on foot. This particular horse is reminiscent of those mentioned in Zech 1:8 and 6:2-6, sent by the Lord to patrol the earth. The appearance of this horse and rider as the first seal is opened creates an extraordinary expectancy, heightened by the fact that this horse and rider resemble to an astonishing degree the emerging picture of Jesus and his followers in Revelation. The color of the horse, white, is one that has been intimately associated with Jesus and his followers to this point in the book (1:14; 2:17; 3:4-5, 18; 4:4). The appearance

---

85. Beale, *The Book of Revelation*, 374.
86. Wall, *Revelation*, 109.

of the white horse would thus at least give the hearers pause as to whether this rider is somehow connected with Jesus. Not only is Jesus involved in the giving of crowns (2:10), but the retaining (3:11), wearing (4:4), and casting down (4:10) of crowns are all characteristic of his followers. The connection between the giving of the crown to the rider and his overcoming activity is reminiscent of Jesus having overcome and being given the right to sit on the throne with God (3:21). Throughout the book, there has been an emphasis placed upon the need for Jesus' followers to overcome (2:7, 11, 17, 26-28; 3:5, 12, 21) and upon Jesus' own overcoming (3:21; 5:5). Thus, the emphatic statement that this rider goes out "overcoming in order that he might overcome" would not surprise the hearers. Furthermore, it would not be all that surprising that Jesus, earlier portrayed as one like the Son of Man, the Lion of the Tribe of Judah, and the slaughtered Lamb, could now be portrayed as the rider on a white horse. Minimally, this imagery (v. 2) would convey the idea that, wherever this horse and rider go, Jesus himself goes.[87] His bow indicates that he is not unarmed; rather, he is an offensive force (Isa 21:17; Jer 50:29; 51:3). The last words of this verse indicate that this white horse and its rider actually go out to accomplish the assigned task.

Immediately, the slaughtered Lamb opens the second seal. The enumeration of this "second" seal in a set of seven is a new development in Revelation and will be followed consistently throughout the book with regard to the seals, trumpets, and bowls in this section (4:1–16:21). The opening of the second seal, like that of the first, is accompanied by a sound, with John reporting, "I heard the second living creature saying. . . ." Although the identity of this living creature is not clear, one of those intimately connected with the throne is active here. This one too gives the identical command "come" or "go." Then, "and another red horse went out." In v. 4 the activity of going out precedes the rest of the description of the horse and rider. The word "another" could possibly be an indication that the first horse is separate from those that follow,[88] suggesting that the white horse and rider are closely associated with Jesus. Yet, there is little need to drive too deep a wedge between any of these four horses and riders, for all four are sent from heaven[89] from those very near the throne — one might say, from God himself. The color of the second horse, red, also reveals something of its mission and identity. Red is the appropriate color for this horse and rider, for he takes peace from the earth, encourages slaughter, and bears

---

87. The identification of Jesus with the white horse and its rider has a long and rich history in early Christian interpretation of Revelation, beginning with Victorinus. Cf. Kovacs and Rowland, *Revelation*, 78-80.

88. Aune (*Revelation 6–16*, 395) mentions this possibility.

89. J. C. Poirier, "The First Rider: A Response to Michael Bachmann," *NTS* 45 (1999): 257.

a great sword. The activity and function of the rider are given in a chiastically structured statement.

> There was given to him to take peace from the earth
>   in order that they might even slaughter one another
> and there was given to him a great sword. (Rev 6:4)

The divine passive "there was given" stands in both the first and third lines, revealing that the ability to take peace from the world is accomplished by means of the great sword with which the rider is entrusted. The purpose of this gift is made clear in the purpose clause standing in the middle of this chiastic statement: "in order that they might slaughter one another." The color of the horse thus makes perfect sense, for wherever he goes, blood will be spilt. The occurrence of "they might slaughter" might be a bit surprising, as the term has earlier been exclusively associated with the slaughtered Lamb. Here, the slaughtered Lamb opens the seal that occasions the emergence of this horse and its rider. Would such a linguistic connection suggest some relationship between the slaughter of the Lamb and the slaughter of one another by those upon the earth? Have the slaughterers now become the slaughtered?

The words "and when he opened the third seal" convey the ongoing activity of the Lamb. The opening of this seal is accompanied by the voice of one of the four living creatures, whose word is identical to that of the first two: "come" or "go." John next sees "a black horse, and the one who sits upon him having a scale in his hand." The black horse's color is clearly an ominous sign, as within the Johannine community darkness takes on spiritual overtones. The scale, an instrument of commerce, in his hand indicates that the domain of his mission is commercial. For the first time, the emergence of one of these horses and riders is accompanied by another voice, also associated with the four living creatures. This voice, however, is heard coming from the midst of the four living creatures! Only two entities have been located in the midst of the four living creatures: the throne of God and the slaughtered Lamb. If the four living creatures earlier speak for God, owing to their close proximity around the throne, this voice makes clear that God[90] and/or the Lamb is speaking more directly,[91] giving the horse and its rider a specific directive. The voice describes famine-like conditions with the words, "A quart of wheat for a denarius, and three quarts of barley for a denarius." Since this amount of grain was a meager ration for a cavalryman and his horse, or barely

---

90. Sweet, *Revelation*, 140.
91. Smalley, *Revelation*, 153.

enough for an individual and a domestic animal, it is clear that basic necessities are in view.[92] As a denarius was the usual daily wage, the implications of the situation are easy to see. These prices, ten to twelve times higher than normal,[93] reveal a siege-like economy.[94] The description of these famine-like conditions is followed by the prohibition, "And do not harm the oil or wine." It is possible to take this prohibition as a sign that, despite the famine, the rich are not denied their accustomed luxuries, in this case, oil and wine. While landowners could make more money from olive groves and wine vineyards than from wheat, and were sometimes tempted to develop the former as opposed to growing the latter,[95] oil and wine are not luxuries limited to the rich but commodities utilized by all.[96] Their mention here seems to have more to do with the olive tree and the vine not being as susceptible to drought, because their roots go deeper than do those of wheat and barley.[97] The divine command thus connotes a limitation to the famine. Though severe, it is not severe enough to affect olive trees or grape vineyards.[98]

At the opening of the fourth seal, "I heard a voice of the fourth living creature, saying. . . ." In one sense the mention of the fourth living creature conveys a sense of anticipation in that there are only four living creatures, but seven seals to be opened. Although three other seals remain to be opened, at one level there is a kind of finality with the reference made to the voice of the fourth living creature. As with the first three living creatures, the fourth one also says "come" or "go."

The words "and I saw, and behold a horse" indicate a new element in the vision. The color of the fourth horse, "pale" or "yellowish green," is the color of sickness and death,[99] the color of a corpse! This color indicates that the fourth horse's arrival is even more ominous than the one that preceded it. Unlike the other riders, the one who sits on this horse is given a name[100] and has a companion: "His name is Death, and Hades follows along with him." For a second time death is personified, and on both occasions Death is linked to Hades.[101] The imagery of Death being followed along with Hades produces a gruesome

---

92. Aune, *Revelation 6–16*, 397.
93. This observation is based upon remarks about normal prices by Cicero, *Verr.* 3.81.
94. Wall, *Revelation*, 110.
95. Collins, *The Apocalypse*, 46.
96. Aune, *Revelation 6–16*, 398.
97. Mounce, *The Book of Revelation*, 155.
98. Resseguie, *The Revelation of John*, 128.
99. Smalley, *Revelation*, 155,
100. Beale, *The Book of Revelation*, 382.
101. Aune, *Revelation 6–16*, 401.

picture, where all the victims of Death are quickly captured by Hades.[102] Here, Death and Hades are divinely given "authority over one-fourth of the earth to kill with sword and with famine and with death and by means of the beasts of the earth." But even the devastation described with the opening of the fourth seal is not without its limits, for only one-fourth of the earth is affected.

The first set of four seals within the seven is now completed. The revelation that one-fourth of the earth would be killed brings to mind Jesus' warning to the children of Jezebel, that they too would be killed if repentance was not forthcoming (2:23). This warning, similar to that envisioned in Jer 15:2, is the direct result of God's patience having run out with those in question.[103] It appears that these four elements are a culmination of the effects that accompany the opening of the first four seals. The mention of the sword may even remind hearers that Jesus has a double-edged sword coming from his mouth (1:16). Is it possible that such a detail might suggest to John and his hearers that the Lamb, who opened this seal, is present in its effects as well?

While the phrase "and when he opened the fifth seal" sounds identical to the previous four, there is one modification in the Greek text; namely, the number precedes the word "seal." This slight modification anticipates the distinction that follows, as John does not hear one of the four living creatures say, "come" or "go," nor does he see a horse and its rider. Rather, "I saw under the altar the souls of those who had been slaughtered on account of the word of God and the witness that they had." This initial encounter with an altar in Revelation unleashes a variety of associations, for the altar is a very important article in God's house, coming to represent his very presence. Here sacrifices are offered, with the blood of the sacrifices running down from the top and sides of the altar, collecting under it. The location of these "souls" indicates that they are sacrifices offered to God[104] and indicates their extraordinarily close proximity to him. The location of these dead believers would not be a complete surprise (cf. John 14:2-3; 17:24). Here the word ψυχαί (*psychai*, "souls") means more than disembodied spirits, for the word often means "life," that may be laid down on behalf of another individual (John 10:11, 15, 17; 13:37-38; 15:13; 1 John 3:16). Such a meaning fits well with its use in Rev 6:9, for these "souls," or "lives," have

---

102. This scene is captured well in Albrecht Dürer's *The Four Horsemen of the Apocalypse*, where Hades' gaping mouth quickly swallows Death's victims. Cf. van der Meer, *Apocalypse*, 289. The image generated by Rev 6:8 leads Kiddle (*The Revelation of St. John*, 118) to observe, "The sufferer does not find peace as his tortured heart stops beating; he must wait the final judgment in the cheerless underworld of the dead, full of unknown terrors."

103. Poirier ("The First Rider: A Response to M. Bachmann," 260) goes so far as to say of this verse, "Rev 6:1-8 seems to be Jer 15:2 in apocalyptic dress."

104. Collins, *The Apocalypse*, 47.

indeed been laid down on behalf of another. The word "slaughtered" points to their intimate connection with Jesus. They have suffered the same fate as the Lamb[105] and, no doubt, bear the same marks as he, looking as though they have been slaughtered! Earlier the connection between the blood of the slaughtered Lamb and those purchased from every tribe and tongue and people and nation (5:9) was seen. Now the connection between those slaughtered souls who are under the altar and their identification with Jesus is revealed. These souls have been slaughtered on account of the Word of God and the witness that they have. Such language brings to mind John (1:2, 9), Jesus (1:5; 3:14), and Antipas (2:13). Clearly, these souls under the altar have been slaughtered owing to their identification with Jesus, his witness, and his message.[106] Such deaths, however, are not viewed simply as random acts of violence, for they are sacrifices actively offered to God through intentional participation in the witness of Jesus. Their complete solidarity with Jesus could not be more explicit.[107]

These slaughtered souls under the altar "cried out with a great voice, 'How long, O Master, the Holy and True One, will you not judge and avenge our blood on those who dwell upon the earth?'" This fourth loud voice (1:10; 5:2, 12) comes from the souls crying out in unison. Their words stand in clear continuity with a number of the voices in the Psalms that ask the same question, "How long, O LORD?" (13:1-2; 74:10; 79:5; 82:2; 89:46; 90:13; 94:3). Their cry most parallels Ps 79(78), where similar terminology is found. It is not altogether clear whether this prayer is directed to God or to Jesus. The term δεσπότης (*despotēs*, "Master" or "Lord") is used some seventeen times for God in the LXX,[108] and it would fit the context well here, for in Revelation God is normally the one who judges. The adjectives "holy" and "true," however, have previously been used by the resurrected Jesus with reference to himself (3:7). The Lamb is the one who opens the seals and is in some way identified with the first rider, and he will be identified with wrath later in this passage, all of which suggests that the term "Master" or "Lord" may here refer to Jesus. Such ambiguity might suggest that

---

105. Smalley, *Revelation*, 157.

106. S. Pattemore, *The People of God in the Apocalypse: Discourse, Structure, and Exegesis* (SNTSMS 128; Cambridge: Cambridge University Press, 2004), 79.

107. Two details might lead Johannine hearers to conclude that OT believers might be among the souls under the altar. First, in 1 John 3:12 reference is made to Cain, who slaughtered his brother. Second, in Rev 6:9 one would normally expect "on account of the witness of Jesus" instead of "on account of the witness that they had." Perhaps this less overtly Christological reference would give John and his hearers pause at this point. Cf. A. Feuillet, "Les martyrs de l'humanité et l'Agneau égorgé: Une interprétation nouvelle de la prière des Égorgé en *Ap* 6:9-11," *NRT* 99 (1977): 189-207, and Pattemore, *The People of God in the Apocalypse*, 78-79.

108. Aune, *Revelation 6–16*, 407.

the thought is primarily of God in this verse and secondarily of Jesus.[109] The cry of the slaughtered souls, "How long . . . will you not judge and avenge our blood on the inhabitants upon the earth?" focuses upon the divine delay in the dispensing of justice and vindication. Owing to the souls' close proximity to God and the certainty of God's judgment in the OT, the delay in its arrival is all the more difficult to understand. Accompanying this cry is another one: to avenge their blood. The term ἐκδικέω (*ekdikeō*, "avenge"), which comes from the root word for "justice,"[110] conveys the idea of vindication. Such vindication is not simply a matter of the reputation of God's people but of God himself![111] The introduction of the words "our blood" further underscores the identification between the slaughtered Lamb (5:6, 12) and his slaughtered followers — the faithful witness to which they are called, patterned on Jesus' own faithfulness unto death. The phrase "the inhabitants upon the earth" reveals a basic division in the ranks of humanity.[112] Such a visceral prayer reveals something of the depth of the pain and anguish of these souls. While such strong language has struck some commentators as being unchristian and/or unworthy of the love ethic found in the NT, such reactions may well have more to do with the context of contemporary readers than the content of the text. Perhaps the testimony of readers of Revelation from outside the context of comfort and affluence would go some way toward enabling a more authentic and robust hearing of this verse.[113]

Apparently, "the holy and true Master" himself offers a twofold response to their prayer. First, "there was given to each of them a white robe," with the divine passive, "there was given," indicating the divine origin of the gift. This gift reveals that their identification with Jesus is an intimate one, as white is the color closely associated with Jesus in Revelation (1:14), and those who follow him are promised white garments in which they will walk with him (3:4-5, cf. also 3:18). Such white garments are already worn by the twenty-four elders

---

109. Pattemore (*The People of God in the Apocalypse*, 83) notes, "It may well be that John is deliberately creating an overlap of reference as part of his narrative christology."

110. Murphy, *Fallen Is Babylon*, 210.

111. Cf. the remarks of Beale, *The Book of Revelation*, 392.

112. Pattemore, *The People of God in the Apocalypse*, 85.

113. As Boesak (*Comfort and Protest*, 72) notes, "People who do not know what oppression and suffering is react strangely to the language of the Bible. . . . The oppressed do not see any dichotomy between God's love and God's justice." To this comment might be added the observations of Schüssler Fiorenza (*Revelation: Vision of a Just World*, 64), "Exegetes, who generally do not suffer unbearable oppression and are not tormented by God's apparent toleration of injustice, tend to label this outcry for justice as unchristian and contrary to the preaching of the Gospel. One can adjudicate the central quest of Revelation in theological terms, however, only if one comprehends the anguish that fuels this outcry for justice and vindication, for divine revenge and restitution for so many lives taken, and for so much blood unnecessarily shed."

seated around the throne (4:4), indicating that the promises made to those who overcome are being fulfilled before their very eyes or ears. These elders come to represent all those who have been faithful even unto death, not having soiled their garments. They are faithful witnesses like their Lord. Second, "it was said to them that they should wait a little time more, until they might be full, both their fellow servants and their brothers who are about to be killed even as they." Another divine passive, "it was said," reveals that this response comes from the one addressed by the souls. The words "they should wait" introduces the theme of delay. Despite the desires of the "souls under that altar," their cry for judgment and vindication is met with instruction to wait a little while longer. The souls are to wait "until they are full" or "complete," indicating that justice and vindication would be premature, since others must first join these "under the altar." These souls will be "full" or "complete" only when others who have also been slaughtered join them. The ones whom the souls await are "their fellow servants and their brothers who are about to be killed, even as they." These terms are closely associated with prophetic vocation in Revelation, used previously to describe John as a servant of God (1:1) and a brother of the hearers (1:9). This warning is made explicit in that those who will join the "souls under the altar" are those "who are about to be killed, even as they." The same fate awaits these fellow servants and brothers that met these souls. They will be slaughtered even as these souls had been, even as the Lamb whom they follow. Thus, as these souls wait, their earlier cry would be understood to expand to include the prayer for justice and vindication both for them and for those who will complete them. And John and his hearers wait as well.

The opening of the sixth seal parallels the opening of the first seal, "and I saw when he opened the sixth seal," and may serve as an inclusio, indicating that these first six seals stand together. The description of the sixth seal is nearly twice as long as that devoted to the opening of the fifth seal. There is also a sense of finality conveyed in the opening of this sixth seal, for within it are two nonenumerated sets of sevens. The first set of seven describes the cosmic upheavals that accompany the opening of the sixth seal, while the second set describes the human reactions to these cosmic events.[114]

John first sees the eruption of seven cosmic events, which suggests a cosmic collapse. These elements include those that appear in a variety of OT texts. The cosmic upheaval revealed in vv. 12-14 begins with reference to a great earthquake, bringing to mind the many references to earthquakes found in OT eschatological contexts (Isa 13:13; Joel 2:10; Hag. 2:6). This great earthquake would serve as a sign of the beginning of the end. Next, the sun becomes black

---

114. Aune, *Revelation 6-16*, 391.

as sackcloth (Isa 50:3), a cloth especially suitable for mourning, while the whole moon becomes as blood (Joel 2:31). Not only so, but "the stars of heaven fell upon the earth as a fig tree casts its fruit when shaken by a great wind" (Isa 34:4). No sooner do they fall than the heaven itself vanishes as a scroll vanishes when it is rolled up (Isa 34:4). Finally, "every mountain and island was removed from their places" (Jer 4:24). It conveys a sense of finality that seven elements are included in these cosmic upheavals. From these words, it is impossible to imagine that all of creation itself is not being destroyed.[115] That so many of these elements are associated with the promised eschatological activity of God in the OT, many of which signal "the Day of the Lord," would leave no doubt that God himself is present in these events. The theme of shaking, removing, even vanishing is clearly at the heart of the activities that accompany the opening of this seal; the earth, the stars, heaven, mountains, and islands all feel the effects. Mention of the sun turning black as sackcloth would bring to mind the third horse and his mission. The moon appearing as blood would remind hearers of the blood of the Lamb and the souls under the altar. The falling of the stars "to the earth" might be seen in connection with the cry for vindication of the souls under the altar that their blood be avenged upon "the inhabitants upon the earth." Perhaps the mention of the removal of every mountain and island from their places is a tacit reminder that even the island of Patmos, where John is located, will at some point be removed from its place.

The human reaction to these cosmic events is united and complete, for seven distinct classes of human society respond in unison. The number 7 indicates that humanity in its entirety is here represented, while the groups span the range of humankind from kings to slaves and free persons. The first group, "the kings of the earth," includes those over whom Jesus has already been said to be ruler (1:5). Joining them are "the great men" and "the generals." The rich and the strong are also part of this vast society of individuals, as are every slave and every free person. These last two groups stand in special relationship to one another, as the word πᾶς (*pas*, "each" or "every") governs them both in the Greek text, similar to the way in which mountain and island stand together in 6:14. These seven classes of humanity join together hiding themselves "in the caves and in the rocks of the mountains," an eschatological activity anticipated in Isaiah (2:10, 19, 21). They also call upon the mountains and the rocks in which they are hiding, saying:

> Fall upon us and hide us from the face of the one who sits on the throne and from the wrath of the Lamb, because the great day of their wrath has come, and who is able to stand?

---

115. Resseguie, *The Revelation of John*, 131.

These words indicate that, despite the staggering activities that accompany the opening of the seals, a portion of humankind survives. Perhaps the hearers would assume this number to be three-fourths, based upon 6:8. Clearly these individuals consider themselves helpless in the face of their adversaries. The events that accompany the opening of the seals are no doubt viewed as the reason that they hide themselves and call out to the rocks and mountains to hide them. Ultimately, however, they consider God and the Lamb to be responsible for these calamities and consequently desire to be hidden from them. Humanity's description of both God and the Lamb might strike the hearers as a bit odd, for to this point there is no description of the face of the one who sits on the throne, in keeping with OT thought (Exod 33:20). Perhaps in these events his face is being revealed. If so, it is the Day of the Lord! The words "the wrath of the Lamb" are also surprising, but they remove all doubt as to the Lamb's involvement with the events that accompany the opening of the seals. While such a description might not seem quite appropriate for one earlier identified as slaughtered, it does fit well with the Lamb's activity in chapter 6. It is significant that the first mention in Revelation of the word "wrath" appears in association with the Lamb,[116] for in its other occurrences, it is used in association with God (6:17; 11:18; 14:10; 16:19; 19:15). This attribution might also bring some clarity to the identity of the rider on the white horse. If that rider is identified as the Lamb, reference to his wrath in v. 16 would form an inclusio with the reference in v. 2. Not only is the ongoing activity of the Lamb chronicled with the opening of each seal, but his overall involvement is also underscored by his presence at the beginning and end of this section devoted to the opening of the first six seals. Appropriately enough, this eschatological moment is identified as "the great day of their wrath."[117] Perhaps the discerning Johannine reader would remember that, instead of receiving eternal life, the one who does not obey the Son incurs the wrath of God (John 3:36). The theme of the Day of the Lord continues with humanity's last question, "And who is able to stand?" calling to mind the prophecies of Nahum (1:6) and Malachi (3:2). In fact it is the Day of the Lord; who is able to stand?

The Interlude of the 144,000 and the Great Multitude (7:1-17)

Surprisingly, the next words encountered are not "And I saw when he opened the seventh seal" but rather, "And after this I saw," indicating that the seventh

---

116. Osborne, *Revelation*, 296.
117. Smalley, *Revelation*, 170.

seal is not to be opened quite yet, which delays the end of all things.[118] John describes "four angels standing upon the four corners of the earth, grasping the four winds of the earth in order that the wind might not blow upon the earth nor upon the sea nor upon any tree." The appearance of the four angels indicates that God continues to be active, for these angels have control over various portions of nature. The emphasis upon the number 4 points to God's complete control over the earth, as the four corners of the earth suggest the world in its entirety.[119] The four winds, a traditional sign of God's destructive power in the OT (Jer 49:36; cf. also 4:11-12; 51:1-2; Ezek 5:12),[120] might remind readers of the four riders described previously in the opening of the first four seals, who bring various degrees of destruction upon the earth. Such an association is all the more likely, given the close connection between the four chariots of horses and the four winds of heaven described in Zech 6:5 (cf. Rev 6:2).[121] The purpose of the angels' restraining activity is to keep these winds from prematurely bringing destruction upon the earth, sea, and trees. The scope of the winds' potential activity is conveyed not only by "the earth" and "the sea," which denote the major components of the world, but also by "any tree," which represents those things most vulnerable to the destructive force of the wind.[122]

Immediately John recounts seeing yet another event. "And I saw another angel coming down from the rising of the sun, having a seal of the living God. And he cried with a great voice to the four angels, to those to whom had been given to harm the earth and sea, saying. . . ." This other angel comes from the realm of God, "from the rising of the sun" or "from the east of the sun," and possesses a "seal of the living God." This seal likely refers to a signet ring, commonly used in antiquity by kings and their designees to seal or mark their personal property.[123] Since this seal belongs to "the living God," it could not help but bring to mind the book, sealed with seven seals, that was in the hand of the one who sits on the throne in 5:1. What was inferred there becomes clearer here: the seven seals are indeed the seals of God. The significance of this seal is underscored by reference to "the living God," a title that contrasts the true and living God with the idolatry of the false gods (2 Kgs 19:4, 16).[124] Also, God has earlier been called "the one who lives forever and ever" (Rev 4:9-10). This angel is thus God's authorized agent, acting on his behalf, who now cries out with

---

118. Resseguie, *The Revelation of John*, 135.
119. Pattemore, *The People of God in the Apocalypse*, 125.
120. Smalley, *Revelation*, 181.
121. Caird, *The Revelation of Saint John*, 94, and Allo, *Saint Jean: L'Apocalypse*, 91.
122. Sweet, *Revelation*, 147.
123. Metzger, *Breaking the Code*, 60.
124. Mounce, *The Book of Revelation*, 167.

"In the Spirit in Heaven" (4:1–16:21)

a great voice, speaking for God. The subjects of his words are the four angels mentioned previously. In v. 1 it was implied that these angels held back the four winds from harming the earth, sea, and trees, the divine passive "was given" indicating that their authority comes from God.

This angel next addresses the other four, "Do not harm the earth nor the sea nor the trees, until we seal the servants of our God upon their foreheads." The prohibition against harming follows naturally, since these angels have the authority and apparently have been commissioned to do so. But the prohibition postpones rather than prohibits the work of harming. The destructive work of the four angels is to be delayed until the time "we can seal the servants of our God upon their foreheads." The first person plural verb "we seal" reveals that this other angel is to be joined by the four angels who at present are at the four corners of the earth, suggesting that this other angel has some degree of authority over the four. Clearly, "the servants of God" are to be sealed with the seal of the living God. The mention of sealing would generate a convergence of ideas drawn from the biblical tradition, beginning with Gen 4:15, where God places a mark upon Cain in order that no one would take his life, and including Exod 12, where the blood of the Passover lamb is placed upon the doorposts of the Israelites, sparing the lives of their firstborn, and Ezek 9:1-11, where a mark is placed upon the foreheads of those who "sigh and groan" over the sin of the city, and as a result their lives are spared.[125] Mention of the seal of the living God would no doubt refer to God's signet ring. In appearance, a signet ring would have on its topside raised letters or a symbol that, when pressed upon a soft surface, would leave its impression on that object. God's signet ring would likely be thought of as bearing his name, leaving its imprint upon any so sealed. In John's gospel this verb indicates authentication of the witness of Jesus by the one who believes (John 3:33), and of the person of Jesus by God the Father (6:27). This seal and sealing stand in the context of, and in contrast to, the seven seals and their unsealing by the slaughtered Lamb. The fact that this verb occurs five times and the noun form once in a span of seven verses highlights the importance of this activity.[126] Those to be sealed are identified as "the servants of our God," a designation that has prophetic associations in Revelation (cf. 1:1; 2:20).[127] These servants of God are to be sealed upon their "foreheads." This term appears only in Revelation in the whole of the NT, always designating a place where a seal (7:3; 9:4), mark (13:16; 14:9; 20:4), or name (14:1;

---

125. Already with Origen, the similarities between these passages has been noted; cf. Allo, *Saint Jean: L'Apocalypse*, 91.

126. Resseguie, *The Revelation of John*, 136.

127. Kiddle, *The Revelation of St. John*, 134, and Caird, *The Revelation of Saint John*, 95.

17:5; 22:4) is placed.[128] Perhaps the seal is placed upon the forehead because it is the most visible place on the face, immediately indicating that these individuals belong to God. The purpose of this sealing is also for protection, the implication being that these servants of God would be protected from the harm about to be unleashed by the four angels.

John does not see the sealing of the servants of God, but he hears a message: "And I heard the number of those sealed, 144,000, sealed out of every tribe of the sons of Israel." John does not say how he hears this number, but clearly the number sealed is the result of the activity of these angels. As the following verses make clear, this number is a perfect square number, being the sum of 12,000 from each of the twelve tribes of Israel.[129] Perhaps the hearers are reminded of Num 31, where Moses takes 12,000 men, 1,000 from each of the twelve tribes of Israel, into battle with Midian. If so, that such a force is here squared would suggest that it is a perfect force in number, and that the whole is represented by each of its parts. This number suggests perfection and completion; not one member is excluded.

The first hint as to the identity of the 144,000 is found in the phrase "the servants of our God" (v. 3), which, earlier in Revelation, is used with reference to John, underscoring his prophetic identity, here suggesting some connection between these "servants of God" and these "sons of Israel" (v. 4). Related to this thought is the presence in the cities where the churches are located of those who claim to be Jews but are not (2:9; 3:9). According to Jesus, those who identify with and believe in him are those who may lay claim to being God's people. Though never called Jews in the book, Johannine believers appear to have a close affinity with the name Israel, for in John's gospel Israel is closely identified with Jesus and his followers. There, John comes baptizing that the Messiah might be revealed to Israel (John 1:31), a witness that results in the declaration by "the true Israelite," Nathaniel (1:47), that Jesus is "the King of Israel" (1:49). Though Nicodemus, the "teacher of Israel," does not understand Jesus' teaching about "birth from above" (3:10), Jesus is declared to be "the King of Israel" by those who receive him in Jerusalem (12:13). Clearly, Jesus and those who believe in him are identified with Israel. The initial occurrence of the phrase "sons of Israel" in Revelation also implies some identification between this title and the Johannine believers (Rev 2:14). It thus appears likely that the mention of "the tribes of the sons of Israel" refers to Johannine believers. Such language continues to make explicit the connection between Jesus, the Lion of the Tribe of Judah, the one who has the key of David, his redemptive work, and the heritage

---

128. P. Lampe, "Μέτωπον," *EDNT*, 2:421-22.
129. Bauckham, *The Climax of Prophecy*, 218.

of Israel. Here, the heritage of Israel is most important, but as will be seen, it is Israel in its transformed state. Something more of this "transformed" role of the heritage of Israel is revealed as the hearers encounter the list of the twelve tribes in vv. 5-8.[130]

The list of tribes found in 7:5-8 begins with reference to 12,000 that are sealed from the tribe of Judah. Judah as the first tribe listed would make perfect sense, though not normally the first tribe in most lists. Judah is, after all, the tribe from which the Messiah is prophesied to come, the tribe of David from which come all but one of the kings of Israel and Judah.[131] It is the tribe identified with Jesus, who has the key of David and is the Lion of the Tribe of Judah. The participle "who were sealed" reaffirms the purpose of this activity, reminding readers that these are identified as belonging to God and being protected by him. The hearers next encounter 12,000 from the tribe of Reuben. Often Reuben appears first in listings of the twelve tribes, because he was Jacob's firstborn. Though he here stands in a subordinate position, the tribe of Jacob's firstborn son is still important in this transformed Israel. Surprisingly, the next 12,000 sealed are not from the tribe of Simeon, Jacob's secondborn, but Gad, the son of a handmaid. In fact, the next three groups of 12,000 come from tribes whose heads were born, not from Leah or Rachel, but from Zilpah and Bilhah, their respective handmaids. The tribes of Gad and Asher trace their origin to Jacob through Zilpah, Leah's handmaid, who bore children from Jacob for her mistress. The same phenomenon is true of the next tribe, Naphtali, whose origin is traced to Jacob through Bilhah, Rachel's handmaid.[132] This unusual placement conveys a sense of inversion, where less important tribes find themselves elevated in this group. Often the tribes that come from the handmaids are listed last, or near last, and their treatment and status sometimes even border on second-class status. It becomes clear that these "tribes of the sons of Israel" come from an Israel that has been transformed, not only in its messianic quality, but in its egalitarian nature. The next group comes not from Dan, the other head from the handmaid Bilhah, but from the tribe of Manasseh. This surprising displacement might imply that Dan's propensity toward idolatry has resulted in a forfeiture of his place among the tribes (Judg 18:30-31; 1 Kgs 12:25-33). That Manasseh is a grandson of Jacob may say something about the extent of this new and transformed Israel. Mention of Manasseh could not help but remind the hearers of Joseph, his father, whose prophetic nature was well known from the OT. Instead of Ephraim, the next

---

130. Smalley, *Revelation*, 187.

131. Smalley, *Revelation*, 187.

132. C. R. Smith, "The Portrayal of the Church as the New Israel in the Names and Order of the Tribes in Revelation 7:5-8," *JSNT* 39 (1990): 113.

12,000 sealed come from the tribe of Simeon. The omission of Ephraim in some ways fits well with the omission of Dan, as Ephraim was also given to idolatrous activity. Oddly enough, the mention of Manasseh where Dan is expected and its implicit reference to Ephraim, which is also omitted, places Manasseh in a most strategic position. As with Reuben, mention of 12,000 sealed from Simeon reminds the hearers of the importance of the heritage of Israel, as do the next three groups of 12,000, coming from tribes traditionally given places of importance: Levi, Issachar, and Zebulun. While often omitted from lists of tribes, the mention of Levi is most fitting in Rev 7:7, as Levi's presence would underscore the priestly theme that has been developing as the book unfolds, reinforcing the identification of the Johannine believers as priests to God (1:6; 5:10),[133] which provides yet another point of contact between these "sons of Israel" and the Johannine "servants of God." The eleventh group comes from the tribe of Joseph. Normally when Manasseh appears in a list, Joseph is absent, in favor of his other son, Ephraim. Joseph's mention reminds hearers of his prophetic activities and in turn the prophetic vocation of the community. Significantly, Joseph's appearance here stands in chiastic parallel to Reuben, who was the one brother who did not wish to kill Joseph, thereby preserving his life. The final group comes from the tribe of Benjamin, the last son of Jacob. Mention of Benjamin last forms an inclusio with Judah, as these two tribes are the only ones from which the kings of Israel and Judah arose, emphasizing the messianic nature of the list yet again. This inclusio might also be an implicit acknowledgment of the place of the nation of Judah, which was composed of Judah and Benjamin, in this transformed Israel. The participle "who were sealed," which last appeared with the mention of the Tribe of Judah, reappears here, again forming an inclusio around the tribes and reinforcing the purpose of this sealing.[134] These 144,000 belong to God, bearing his seal, being protected by him.

What might be said about the identity of this group of 144,000, these sealed from "the tribes of the sons of Israel"? There is a strong connection between the Johannine community and the 144,000, with no evidence suggesting that this number is disconnected from the churches described in Rev 2–3. It is obvious that the 144,000 is a messianic group. Clearly, this group functions as the heirs to what God has done through Israel, owing to the presence of the historically important tribes. This group is also marked in part by its priestly identity. Their prophetic characteristics are also clear, a calling in which the church participates. Finally, this group is clearly marked out as belonging to God and protected by him.

---

133. Smalley, *Revelation*, 189.
134. Smalley, *Revelation*, 189, and Resseguie, *The Revelation of John*, 137.

Owing to the way in which things heard sometimes morph into things seen in Revelation, John's words "after these things I saw . . ." suggest the possibility that the description that follows may indeed be related at a profound theological level to that which precedes.

"Behold" directs attention to "a great crowd," the first crowd to be mentioned in the book. This crowd stands in contrast to the previous group, for while that group had a number, this crowd no one can "number." This crowd is innumerable, which would be all the more astounding in that the number of Christians within the Johannine community would not likely be very large.[135] The sheer magnitude of this innumerable crowd could not help but be an extraordinary encouragement as they face what must seem to be insurmountable odds. While the previous group was composed "out of each tribe of the sons of Israel," this crowd is composed "out of all nations and tribes and peoples and tongues." These four components point to the universal nature of this crowd (cf. 5:9). The contrast between these groups is conveyed by the move from a somewhat nationalistic group focused upon Israel to a more inclusive and universalistic crowd. The statement that this group is "standing before the throne and before the Lamb" directly answers the question with which chapter 6 closes, "Who is able to stand" before the one who sits on the throne and the Lamb? The answer? This innumerable crowd drawn from every nation, tribe, people, and tongue.[136] In contrast to those who fear the revelation of the face of the one who sits upon the throne and the wrath of the Lamb, this crowd shares intimate fellowship with God and the Lamb and stands in very close proximity to them. Rather than hiding from the divine presence, those in this crowd participate in it in a threefold fashion. They are clothed in "white robes," attire that suggests this crowd has proven faithful in its witness to Jesus, pointing to a direct connection between the souls under the altar mentioned in 6:9-11 and the crowd mentioned here (7:9). That they have "palm branches in their hands" reminds readers of Jesus' triumphal entry into Jerusalem (John 12:13).[137] In Rev 7:9 the appearance of palm branches would be a sign of the victory of the Lamb and the identification of this innumerable crowd with their King. As their attire and activity reveal, they too have overcome. The crowd also participates in the divine presence by crying out with a great voice, "Salvation to our God, who sits upon the throne, and to the Lamb!" This hymn-like confession conveys a sense of finality, focusing upon salvation in its most comprehensive, eschatological sense.[138] For Johan-

---

135. Aune, *Revelation 6-16*, 467.
136. Resseguie, *The Revelation of John*, 138.
137. Fee, *Revelation*, 111.
138. Schüssler Fiorenza, *Revelation: Vision of a Just World*, 68.

nine hearers this "salvation" is likely to have a comprehensive meaning,[139] being informed by Jesus' words that "salvation is of the Jews" (John 4:22) and by the declaration of the Samaritan believers that Jesus is "truly the Savior of the world" (4:42). The trajectory present in these words of Jesus in John 4 is, interestingly enough, present in the movement of Rev 7. Just as the statement that "salvation is of the Jews" precedes the affirmation that Jesus is "the Savior of the world," so the sealing of the 144,000 precedes the innumerable crowd, the implicit implication being that a necessary connection exists between the mission of the 144,000 from the transformed Israel and the universal, eschatological people of God present in 7:9. This parallel helps to define these two groups and their relationship to one another. In both John 4 and Rev 7 it appears that universal salvation grows out of Israel and its strategic salvific role.

"All the angels standing around the throne and the elders and the four living creatures — and they fell before the throne upon their faces and worshipped God." All the angels would include the thousands of thousands and ten thousands of ten thousands of angels mentioned in 5:11-12. The act of prostration before the throne brings to mind John's response to the resurrected Jesus (1:17) and the constant reaction of the twenty-four elders (4:10; 5:8, 14). In addition, the angels "worshipped God," saying, "Amen, the blessing and the glory and the wisdom and the thanksgiving and the honor and the power and the strength to our God forever and forever; amen." The doxology begins and ends with "amen," underscoring its liturgical character, calling to mind the earlier appearances of the term and its christological associations (1:6-7; 3:14; 5:14). The doxology takes a sevenfold form, indicating the completeness of this act of worship. Except for the substitution of "the thanksgiving" for "riches," the individual elements of this doxology are the same as the one offered by the angels to the Lamb (5:12).[140] Appropriately enough, "thanksgiving" has earlier been rendered to the one who sits on the throne by the four living creatures (4:9). The repetition of these elements again underscores the way in which both God and the Lamb share in the worship rendered by various groups in Revelation. Each of the elements in the doxology are articular in form, paralleling the fourfold doxology rendered to the one who sits upon the throne and the Lamb by every creature in all of creation (5:13), further heightening the meaning of each element in the doxology.[141]

Next, John says, "One of the elders answered, saying to me, 'These who are clothed in white robes, who are they, and from whence did they come?'" This

---

139. Pattemore, *The People of God in the Apocalypse*, 146.
140. Prigent, *L'Apocalypse de Saint Jean*, 224.
141. Mounce, *The Book of Revelation*, 172.

question suggests there is more to be revealed about the identity of this crowd than their attire. Sometimes the prophet or seer is asked certain questions by God and/or his agent; the occurrence here underscores John's prophetic identity. His response, "Sir, you know," is similar to that of other prophetic figures (Ezek 37:3),[142] an acknowledgment of the limits of his knowledge, and may suggest that John expects additional revelation to come from this elder. In fact, the identity of those dressed in white is made clear by the elder's words, "These are the ones coming out of the great tribulation, and they have washed their robes and made them white in the blood of the Lamb."

The first thing revealed is the origin of this innumerable crowd, "coming out of the great tribulation." Though the present tense participle, "coming," will be governed by two aorist verbs that follow and thus translated as a past tense, its initial impact likely suggests that this crowd is coming out of the great tribulation before John's eyes. In Revelation, tribulation is regarded as a necessary part of the believer's life (cf. John 16:21, 33; Rev 1:9; 2:9-10; 3:19). It would appear that there is some continuity between tribulation already experienced by believers and "the great tribulation," out of which this innumerable crowd comes. The words "tribulation" and "great" are both accompanied by the definite article, indicating that a particular ordeal is here in mind,[143] one unlike other times of tribulation in terms of intensity and duration. Such language reminds hearers of the tribulation unlike all other tribulations, of which Daniel speaks (Dan. 12:1-2).[144] Significantly, this tribulation also speaks of the complete deliverance of the people of God. "The great tribulation" is defined in the rest of v. 14 in terms of the activity of the crowd: "And they washed their robes and made them white in the blood of the Lamb." Whatever they experienced in "the great tribulation," this innumerable crowd did not experience it passively, for they actively participated in the receiving of robes by washing them and making them white. Perhaps this statement would generate reflection on the ways the resurrected Jesus continually speaks to the seven churches about their works and the implicit relationship between them and the believers' ability to overcome, or it would remind them of the way in which believers are called upon to offer an active, faithful witness to Jesus. Their robes, made white in the blood of the Lamb, make clear the connection between their own faithful witness and the faithful witness of the Lamb, whose blood stands at the center of redemptive history. They know that confession of sin is met with cleansing and forgiveness from that sin, accomplished by the blood of Jesus (1 John 1:7, 9),

---

142. Murphy, *Fallen Is Babylon*, 226.
143. Murphy, *Fallen Is Babylon*, 226.
144. Beale, *The Book of Revelation*, 433.

and that his blood looses from sin (Rev 1:5) and purchases for God out of "every tribe and tongue and people and nation" (5:9). This crowd, comprising those from all nations and tribes and peoples and tongues, has washed its robes and made them white in the blood of the Lamb, indicating that they have confessed their sin and stand in solidarity with Jesus. Given that the "souls under the altar" were slaughtered and their blood shed "on account of the Word of God and the witness that they have" (6:9-11), perhaps they would suspect that this crowd's solidarity with Jesus' blood might entail their own slaughter and shed blood.

The words continue to take the form of eschatological promises, revealing continuity between the seven prophetic messages, the phrase "on account of this" (7:15) making this connection clear. The statement "they are before the throne of God" picks up on v. 9, explaining why they are before God's throne — for they have come out of "the great tribulation." The present tense verb "are" reemphasizes their intimate relationship with God exemplified by their close proximity to him. Here, the promises shift from present tense to future tense verbs, focusing upon the final realization of these eschatological promises. The words "they will serve him day and night in his temple" call to mind the eschatological promise made to those in Philadelphia (3:12) that they will be "pillars in the temple of my God," never departing from the divine presence. In 7:15 the promise of being in the permanent presence of God again focuses upon the temple as the place of the divine presence, moving from the somewhat passive image of "pillar" to the more active image of "serving." The term λατρεύουσιν (*latreuousin,* "they will serve") would not be surprising, owing to their own priestly identity (1:6; 5:10). This democratic word fits well with the idea that those who "serve" God come from "all nations and tribes and peoples and tongues."[145] In serving God "day and night," this crowd stands with the four living creatures, who "day and night" never cease to sing to the one who sits on the throne. For such ones "the one who sits on the throne will tabernacle over them." The verb σκηνώσει (*skēnōsei,* "will tabernacle") unleashes a variety of significant theological ideas, calling to mind the OT tabernacle as the place of God's dwelling among his people,[146] which gives way to the incarnation, "and the Word became flesh and tabernacled among us" (John 1:14).[147] Here the language underscores that God will offer protection by the shelter of his divine presence.

"They will not hunger anymore, nor will they thirst anymore, nor will the

---

145. Pattemore, *The People of God in the Apocalypse,* 155.

146. J. A. Draper ("The Heavenly Feast of Tabernacles: Revelation 7:1-17," *JSNT* 19 (1983): 133-47) goes so far as to suggest that the feast of Tabernacles underlies and informs this entire section.

147. Osborne, *Revelation,* 329.

sun beat upon them, nor any scorching heat." This promise of food, drink, and shelter is more than the basic concerns of humankind; here they have eschatological and salvific import. As the Bread of Life, Jesus says, "The one who comes to me will never hunger, and the one who believes in me will never thirst" (John 6:35). He speaks words about quenching the thirst of those who come to him (4:13-15; 6:35), for out of his belly flow rivers of living water (7:37-39). Joined to these promises is the promise of shelter. Protection from the destructive effects of the sun and scorching heat is singled out. These promises guarantee that all their "physical" needs are to be met. Such promises are also closely connected to the Lamb, a connection made explicit by the words of Rev. 7:17, "For the Lamb in the midst of the throne will shepherd them and guide them unto wells of living water." The Lamb is at the very center of God's throne and activity, having been given authority to sit upon his Father's throne (3:21) and being located in its midst (5:6). Reference to "the Lamb . . . who will shepherd them" reminds hearers that this slaughtered Lamb is the Lion of the Tribe of Judah, who has the key of David. He is the one who gives those who overcome the authority to rule over the nations with an iron rod (2:27). But perhaps most significant, he is the Good Shepherd, who loves his sheep so much that he lays down his life for them (John 10:1-21). It is this same slaughtered Lamb who will shepherd the innumerable crowd. Chief among his activities will be to "guide them unto wells of living water."[148] This potent description calls to mind both the guiding activity of the Spirit of Truth (John 16:13) and the emphasis placed upon wells of living water in John's gospel (4:14; 7:38), again reminding hearers of the intimate relationship that exists between Jesus and the Spirit in Revelation. The final promise echoes the words of Isaiah (25:8), "And God will wipe away each tear from their eyes." This comforting act appears to be in response to tears of death. Not only does Isaiah make this connection, but also in John's gospel Jesus weeps at the tomb of Lazarus (John 11:35). In response to whatever the innumerable crowd has endured in the great tribulation, including death, God will wipe away each tear. Such comfort, offered in this context of death, is a fitting conclusion to the interlude that is chapter 7.

How would the extraordinary images contained in this chapter impact John and his hearers? Taken together, these two images appear to be distinct but related representations of God's people. Furthermore, it seems that these images appear before and after "the great tribulation." Both images offer encouragement, for the messianic "tribes of the sons of Israel" are sealed by God before the four angels unleash the four winds of the earth, while the innumerable crowd comes forth from the great tribulation clothed in white robes, standing

---

148. Smalley, *Revelation*, 201.

before the throne. Furthermore, these two images are related to one another, for that which is heard gives way to that which is seen. While numerous questions remain, there is little doubt for the hearers that the 144,000 from the tribes of the sons of Israel are transformed before their very eyes into a universal innumerable crowd that stands before the throne having come out of the great tribulation. Many of these promises will reappear near the book's conclusion, indicating this particular image may be regarded as a prolepsis of the end.[149] Both these images give a great deal of encouragement that, despite the horrific effects of the opening of the seven seals, God's people are not forgotten. In fact, they stand before his very presence!

The Opening of the Seventh Seal and the Golden Altar (8:1-5)

"And when he opened the seventh seal. . . ." John and his hearers would likely expect that, with the opening of the seventh seal, the end of all things has been reached, for the beatific image with which chapter 7 closes strongly implies that the end is very near indeed. Yet, when the seventh seal is opened, "there was silence in heaven as a half hour." Such silence is striking, since the heavens have virtually been teeming with the sounds of praise from all creation! The replacement of such thunderous sounds of praise by silence would have a stunning effect.[150] Such silence reminds readers of the prophetic call for silence before the presence of God (Hab 2:20), especially as he is roused to action (Zech 2:13).[151] This silence might also call to mind the words of Zephaniah (1:7), "Be silent before the Lord GOD, for the Day of the LORD is near." At various places in Revelation things heard are paired with things seen, generating dialectical images that are theologically potent. Could it be that this silence will give way to something seen in ways similar to earlier occurrences of this phenomenon? The significance of the duration of the silence, "as a half hour," is not altogether clear. This is the first such temporal indicator to appear in the book. While it possibly refers to a specific period of time that is not obvious to modern readers,[152] its significance may not be so very different from that for modern hearers. Perhaps the impact of this short, impressive break can best be gauged

---

149. Murphy, *Fallen Is Babylon*, 228.
150. Gause (*Revelation*, 127) notes, "When God holds in suspension the chief function of all his creatures, the glorifying of his name, it can only mean one thing. God is about to do something awesome."
151. Murphy, *Fallen Is Babylon*, 231.
152. For example, Bauckham (*The Climax of Prophecy*, 83) argues that "a half hour" is the amount of time it would take to offer incense at the morning ritual in the temple in Jerusalem.

in real time. Although it is the shortest of the temporal indicators to appear in the book, if the reader of Revelation (1:3) stopped reading for about half an hour at this point, the extent of the delay and the significance of the silence would become all the more real.

"I saw the seven angels who were standing before God, and seven trumpets were given to them." In ways not unlike the Lamb and the Lion, and the innumerable crowd and the 144,000 from the tribes of the sons of Israel, the silence and the seven angels with seven trumpets seem to stand in opposition to one another, with silence being the absence of sound, while the seven trumpets represent one of the loudest human-made sounds. On this view, the silence morphs into the seven angels and indicates rather explicitly that, when the seventh seal is opened by the Lamb, the half-hour silence and the seven angels with the seven trumpets are the result. Both the silence and the seven angels frustrate the expectation of the imminence of the end. Knowledge of the opening of the seven seals would suggest that the activity of each of the seven angels will be recounted before the description of the end is offered. The emergence of the seven angels instead of the four angels who hold back the four winds is a bit surprising, as the activity of the latter had appeared to be imminent in 7:1-3.[153] Yet, instead of four angels, there are seven. Their number implies perfection, indicating that what they do is complete and full. The appearance of the definite article in describing "the seven angels" indicates that, although this is their first mention in the book, they are apparently known to the hearers.[154] The angels are in very close proximity to God — standing before him, indicating their willingness to serve him and their direct access to him. These seven angels are given seven trumpets. The passive voice verb "were given" used to describe the gift of the seven trumpets reveals their origin: they are divine gifts, coming from God himself. Whatever use is made of the trumpets by the angels is in accordance with God's own will and desires.[155] Twice to this point the word "trumpet" has been used with reference to the voice of Jesus (1:10; 4:1). Such a christological and prophetic association would make reference to the trumpets in 8:2 all the more significant. More of a signal instrument than a musical one, being capable of only a few notes,[156] its various OT uses reveal the trumpet to be the instrument par excellence that signals the grand moments of Israelite history and life.[157] Their mention here would indicate that John and his hearers are on the verge of witnessing additional significant acts of God.

153. Ladd, *Revelation*, 124.
154. Aune, *Revelation 6–16*, 509, and Smalley, *Revelation*, 213.
155. Resseguie, *The Revelation of John*, 142.
156. H. Lichtenberger, "Σάλπιγξ," *EDNT*, 3:226.
157. Prigent, *L'Apocalypse de Saint Jean*, 230.

Another angel appears, who "came and stood at (or over) the altar, having a golden censer, and there was given to him much incense, in order that he might place (it) with the prayers of all the saints upon the golden altar before the throne." In the only other place where incense and prayers have been mentioned together, the incense is identified as "the prayers of the saints" (5:8), and as such, the prayers of the saints frame the recounting of the opening of the seven seals, suggesting a very tight connection between the prayers offered and the activity of God in the seals.[158] In 6:9-11 "the souls under the altar" cry out to God for justice and vindication. The response described in 6:11 makes it clear that their cries were heard by God, suggesting that in Rev 8:3 a divine response would come on this occasion as well.[159] The censer mentioned appears to be a ladle-shaped object, its composition of gold indicating that it is worthy of its purpose.[160] "Much incense" was given to this angel, which prepares for its being offered with the prayers of *all* the saints.[161] In 6:10 it is the cries of those who had been slaughtered that are heard; here it is the prayers of *all* the saints. The broadening of the scope of the prayers offered has increased to include not only those who have been martyred but also those who are alive.[162] Such a move would indicate that their prayers are not perfunctory but actually make their way to the very presence of God and are even now before him. That the incense appears to be offered along with the prayers of the saints underscores the pleasing, fragrant nature of the prayers that can be seen to rise visibly before the Lord. Being placed upon the golden altar before the throne not only reveals that these prayers will be heard by God but also suggests that there is something sacrificial about them.[163] This imagery further suggests that the incense and prayers kindle and sustain the fire of the altar.[164]

"And the smoke of the incense with the prayers of the saints arose out of the hand of the angel before God." While the content of the prayers is not revealed, they would likely be understood as standing in some continuity with those offered in 5:8 and 6:9-11. That the smoke arises "before God" and "before the altar" encourages readers regarding the certainty that their prayers are received by God himself.

"And the angel took the censer and filled it with (out of) the fire of the

---

158. Murphy, *Fallen Is Babylon*, 234.
159. Beale, *The Book of Revelation*, 454-55.
160. On the previous use of gold in the Apocalypse, cf. 1:12, 13, 20; 2:1; 4:4; 5:8.
161. Smalley (*Revelation*, 215) notes that the vast amount of incense is for the vast amount of prayers.
162. Michaels, *Revelation*, 118.
163. Mounce, *The Book of Revelation*, 182.
164. Schüssler Fiorenza, *Revelation: Vision of a Just World*, 71.

altar and cast it upon the earth." The same angel performs the double action of placing the incense and prayers of the saints upon the golden altar and casting fire from the altar upon the earth.[165] He uses the same censer[166] and places them upon the same altar. Clearly, there is an intimate relationship between the prayers of the saints and the latter activity of the angel who casts down fire upon the earth, an activity fueled by the prayers of the saints.[167] The interesting construction "out of the fire of the altar" makes explicit the connection between the prayers and the fire.[168] Fire falling from heaven would be an especially familiar OT image of judgment (Gen 19:24; 2 Kgs 1:10, 12, 14; Job 1:16; Ps 11:6). The story of Elijah's encounter with the prophets of Baal (1 Kgs 18:36-40) is of special relevance,[169] as is the description of the man dressed in linen in Ezek 10:2-8, who is instructed to fill his hands with burning coals from between the cherubim and scatter them over the city in judgment of the guilt of the house of Israel and Judah, an act he performs after he has placed a mark upon the foreheads of those who sigh and groan over all the abominations that have been committed (9:4).[170] The angel casting fire from the altar "upon the earth" is evidence that the prohibition against harming the earth (Rev 7:3) is no longer in effect. It may even suggest that the four winds held back by the four angels in 7:1 are somehow to be identified with the action of the angel here in 8:5. In any event, the silence with which this section begins (8:1) gives way to the unleashing of additional judgments of God portended in the pregnant imagery of fire being cast down from heaven. That the initiation of this judgment comes from God is further emphasized by the reappearance of the theophanic elements the hearers first encountered in the heavenly throne-room scene in 4:5, which conveys a sense of continuity between the God who is active in creation and human history (4:1) and the God who is active in judgment (8:5). The inverted order of the original list, which moves from thunder to sounds (voices) to lightning, suggests that, on this occasion, the idea of lightning is being underscored. It may be significant that lightning comes forth from the coals of fire located in the midst of the four living creatures described in Ezek 1:13, providing yet another point of continuity between this passage and that prophetic writing.[171] The introduction of earthquake, an additional theophanic element, indicates

---

165. Allo, *Saint Jean: L'Apocalypse*, 104.
166. Murphy, *Fallen Is Babylon*, 234-35.
167. Resseguie, *The Revelation of John*, 143.
168. On the nature of this relationship Michaels (*Revelation*, 118) states, "Prayer is the engine driving the plan of God toward completion."
169. Wall, *Revelation*, 123.
170. Bauckham, *The Climax of Prophecy*, 82.
171. Bauckham, *The Climax of Prophecy*, 82.

an intensification of God's presence and introduces the idea of judgment. The addition of earthquakes would be especially significant, as it was perhaps the most feared natural disaster in antiquity and was not infrequent in Asia Minor. The theophanic elements occur at a strategic location in Revelation, at the conclusion of the opening of the seven seals and at the beginning of the sounding of the seven trumpets, revealing something of the book's structural significance.

Seven Angels with Seven Trumpets (8:6–11:19)

"And the seven angels who have the seven trumpets prepared them in order that they might trumpet." The activity of this other angel is framed by reference to the seven angels, suggesting a tight interplay between their activities. The casting of fire from the altar upon the earth is directly related to the prayers of the saints. Reference to the seven angels preparing the trumpets is therefore more than a dramatic pause, for it envelops and links the previous section with what follows.[172] Significantly, the noun "trumpets" derives from the verb "sound/play." It might more appropriately be translated "to trumpet," bringing out this connection, suggesting the translation, "And the seven angels who have the seven trumpets prepared them in order that they might trumpet."

The Sounding of the First Six Trumpets (8:6–9:21)

At long last, the activity of the seven angels commences. "And the first one trumpeted," with the result that "there was hail and fire mixed with blood, and it was cast upon the earth." The imagery of hail and fire mixed with blood is pregnant with meaning, as each of these elements appears in the plagues God sent upon Egypt (Exod 7:20-21; 9:22-26). Such connections perhaps suggest that, just as God sent plagues upon the enemies of his people, so he is about to act in the present. If these elements raise the exodus motif, then it is likely that the purpose of such divine intervention would be to bring their enemies to repentance. This first reference to hail in Revelation points to the activity of God. Reference to fire brings to mind the fire from the altar that was cast upon the earth by the other angel. Just as that fire was cast upon the earth (8:5), so too this fire (with the other elements) is said to be "cast upon the earth," the passive voice underscoring that this is God's activity. The tight connection between the cry of the souls under the altar for God to "avenge (or vindicate) their blood"

---

172. Murphy, *Fallen Is Babylon*, 235.

(6:10) and the moon turning to blood with the opening of the next seal (6:12), would also likely inform this phrase, reminding readers of the relationship between this judgment of God and the witness of the saints. When these elements are cast upon the earth, "a third of the earth was burned up, and a third of the trees were burned up, and all the green grass was burned up." While this judgment is quite devastating, it is not final or complete. More intensive than the judgments that accompany the opening of the seals, in which one-fourth of the earth's population is killed (6:8),[173] it reveals that the judgments of the seals, which seemed so final, were simply a first step in God's judgment. The increase in the severity of the judgments would suggest that these judgment cycles are not merely repetitious but are moving along in a somewhat linear fashion. That a third of the earth is affected, rather than the whole of the earth, would clearly convey the idea that, while judgment is certain, there may yet be room for repentance. There may even be a hopeful inversion of Zech 13:8-9, where one-third survived,[174] revealing that, while the judgments that await the inhabitants of the earth are indeed terrifying, they could, almost inconceivably, be worse. The devouring of pastures and trees by the flame would also perhaps call to mind Joel's prophecy (1:19-20) indicating the arrival of the Day of the Lord.

"And the second angel trumpeted; and something like a great mountain burning with fire was cast into the sea."[175] This overwhelming image provides continuity with the fire from the altar, as the passive voice "was cast" indicates its divine origin. The consequences of the fiery mountain being cast into the sea are as devastating as the first, for "a third of the sea became blood, and a third of the creatures having life in the sea died, and a third of the ships were destroyed." This judgment is also reminiscent of the plagues that befell Egypt, where the water of the Nile turns to blood, causing the death of all the fish (Exod 7:20-21). The appearance of blood points to the connection between these judgments and the witness of the saints. Again, the extent of the destruction, though severe, is limited to a third. While the first judgment points to the death of a third of the inhabitants of the earth, the second points to the death of a third of the creatures that have life in the sea. Not only is the loss of life of the living creatures in the sea described, but there is considerable economic loss as well, for a third of the ships that sail the sea are destroyed. Something of the nature of the destruction that ensues is conveyed by the occurrence of the compound verb διεφθάρησαν (*diephtharēsan*, "were destroyed").[176]

---

173. Metzger, *Breaking the Code*, 64.
174. Resseguie, *The Revelation of John*, 145.
175. Michaels (*Revelation*, 122) suggests that it is as if the whole of Mt. Sinai were on fire.
176. A. Sand, "Διαφθείρω," *EDNT*, 1:316.

The remaining angels with trumpets follow in rapid-fire succession. "And the third angel trumpeted, and a great star burning like a torch fell out of heaven." The blasting of the third trumpet is also in continuity with the casting upon the earth of the fire from the altar, as the great star is burning like a torch. The falling of a great star is a remarkable enough occurrence. On its own, it would no doubt be taken as a sign from God, but the words "out of heaven" make this conclusion all the clearer. The previous occurrence of the word "torch" comes in reference to the seven torches before the throne in 4:5, further underscoring the connection of this star to God. This star "fell upon a third of the rivers and upon the fountains of water." The object of this star appears to be sources of drinking water. "And the name of the star is called Apsinth," a revelation that may be a case where the hearers' pneumatic interpretation is aided by direct divine instruction, as there is no evidence of a star being called by this name in antiquity.[177] The word "apsinth" appears to come from the plant by this name, which is quite bitter to the taste. This etymology explains why the term is often translated "wormwood."[178] Its potency is great; it can still be tasted when one ounce has been diluted in 524 gallons of water![179] "And a third of the waters became wormwood (or bitter), and many men died from the water because they had been made bitter." The bitterness of this star far exceeds the bitterness of the Apsinth plant, for the bitterness of this star is lethal, while that of the plant was not considered so.[180] The star's name may also encourage the hearers to discern the way in which these events intersect with Jeremiah's prophecy regarding his idolatrous people and their adulterous shepherds, the prophets. So upset is God that he vows to feed his people (Jer 9:15) and their prophets (Jer 23:15) with wormwood and give them poisonous water to drink. The poisoning of the rivers and fountains of water is an inversion of the events at Marah, where God makes the bitter water sweet (Exod 15:25). Intriguingly, the words "star," "fountains," and "rivers" are all terms that have a special relationship to Jesus (cf. Rev 2:28; John 4:14; 7:38, respectively). The contrast between the use of these objects in association with Jesus and here in this passage is striking.

When the fourth angel trumpeted, "a third of the sun and a third of the moon and a third of the stars were struck." Once again a third of the objects are affected.[181] The term ἐπλήγη (*eplēgē*, "were struck") carries with it the idea

---

177. Aune, *Revelation 6–16*, 521.
178. Smalley, *Revelation*, 222.
179. Aune, *Revelation 6–16*, 522.
180. Contra Beale, *The Book of Revelation*, 479.
181. Sweet, *Revelation*, 164.

of being struck with force,[182] introducing a term whose cognate πληγή (*plēgē*, "plague") is significant in Revelation. The force of this blow is so strong "that a third of them were made dark, and the day was not allowed to shine for a third of it, and the night as well." Again the imagery of the exodus looms, for the events of 8:12 are reminiscent of the plague of darkness that fell upon Egypt (Exod 10:21-23), bringing to mind that the same God active in the exodus is once again active in the face of stubborn unbelief. Perhaps the relationship between darkness and the Day of the Lord would be discerned as well (Amos 5:18). With the blasting of this fourth trumpet, all four spheres of God's creation (earth, sea, fresh water, and heavens) have been affected.[183]

A break occurs after the fourth angel sounds his trumpet, which is marked by language now long familiar, "And I saw, and I heard. . . ." Unlike previous occurrences, there is an inversion of the normal order of hearing and then seeing. John heard "an eagle flying in the middle of the sky (or heavens), saying with a great voice. . . ." The words translated "an eagle" literally mean "one eagle." While εἷς, ἑνός (*heis, henos*, "one" or "an") could function as an indefinite article,[184] it might very well remind hearers of any number of things for which "one" is used to distinguish between similar beings, such as "one of the living creatures" or "one of the elders." This designation might remind readers of "one of the living creatures" encountered earlier (Rev 4:7), described as "flying like an eagle" and as being involved in some of the events that accompany the opening of one of the seals in Rev 6. The location of this eagle, "in the middle of the sky" or "heaven," is at the highest point reached by the sun in the sky, its zenith.[185] The flying activity of the eagle could thus hardly be missed, nor his words unheard, for they are spoken with a great voice (1:10; 5:2, 12; 6:10; 7:2, 10). His proclamation is introduced by a triple woe, followed by an urgent warning, "Woe, woe, woe to the inhabitants upon the earth at the rest of the sounds of the trumpets of the three angels that are about to trumpet." The woe, well known from the OT prophetic literature as a divine warning and/or threat (Hos 7:13; Isa 1:4; 10:5; Jer 23:1; Ezek 24:6; and the sixfold woe in Isa 5:8-22),[186] appears here in a threefold form, indicating something of its magnitude. That these woes are directed to "the inhabitants of the earth" reminds hearers of the cry of the souls under the altar that their blood be avenged upon "the inhabitants of the earth" (6:10). As these woes are clearly directed to those who stand in opposition to God and his people, perhaps John and his hearers would recall that the 144,000 have been

---

182. Smalley, *Revelation*, 223.
183. Michaels, *Revelation*, 121.
184. Smalley, *Revelation*, 224-25.
185. W. Radl, "Μεσουράνημα," *EDNT*, 2:412.
186. H. Balz, "Οὐαί," *EDNT*, 2:540.

sealed for protection by God's angels. Despite the woes awaiting "the inhabitants of the earth," those of "the tribes of the sons of Israel" will be protected. The three woes are explicitly tied to the remaining trumpets and the three angels about to trumpet them, suggesting that the blasting of these three trumpets will be accompanied by events even worse than the first four! Something of the imminence of these blasts is conveyed by "which are about," a Greek term that has appeared throughout Revelation to designate things on the verge of taking place (1:19; 2:10; 3:2, 10, 16; 6:11).

"And I saw a star fallen out of heaven unto the earth, and a key of the shaft of the Abyss was given to him." Mention of a star falling to earth is reminiscent of the blasting of the third trumpet, where a great star, burning as a torch, fell upon a third of the rivers and fountains of water (8:10-11). Reference to the star's fallenness indicates that the star has its origin in heaven. The warning given to the inhabitants upon the earth (8:13) suggests that the falling of this star has repercussions for the earth's inhabitants. Unlike the star of 8:10, this star bears personal characteristics, for there was given to him "the key of the shaft of the Abyss," the divine passive "was given" indicating the activity of God.[187] The articular phrase "the shaft of the Abyss" suggests that the Abyss is a familiar place. The shaft, mentioned four times in 9:1-2, is the place of access to the Abyss. Earlier in the book Jesus claims to have the key of Death and Hades (1:18), as well as the key of David (3:7), indicating his mastery over the former and authority to act on behalf of the latter. Owing to the widespread perception that the Abyss is the realm of the dead (Hades) and the place of punishment (Gehenna),[188] perhaps a connection would be discerned between the authority of this star and that of the resurrected Jesus. While the divine passive implies that the key is given to the star by God,[189] the activity of Jesus would not be far from the hearers' minds.

When the shaft was opened, "smoke arose out of the shaft as smoke from a great furnace, and the sun and the air were darkened by the smoke of the shaft." Smoke pouring forth from a great furnace would heighten the ominous sense of expectancy, as the darkness here mentioned would bring to mind the ninth plague of darkness inflicted upon the Egyptians during the period of the exodus. "And out of the smoke came locusts upon the earth, and authority was given to them as the scorpions of the earth have authority." It is not clear whether the locusts come out of the smoke or the smoke resolves itself into locusts. Their emergence upon the earth would be a terrifying sight, for their

---

187. Osborne, *Revelation*, 362.
188. O. Böcher, "Ἄβυσσος," *EDNT*, 1:4.
189. Resseguie, *The Revelation of John*, 146.

destructive power was well known. Not only could locusts "travel in columns several feet deep, and up to four miles in length, stripping the earth of all its vegetation,"[190] but they also were widely regarded in the OT as a sign of God's judgment (Deut 28:42; 1 Kgs 8:37; Ps 78:46). An infestation of locusts was the eighth plague sent upon Egypt during the period of the exodus (Exod 10:4-20). These locusts receive divine authority, revealed in the use of the divine passive "was given," a statement reminiscent of 6:8, where Death and Hades are given authority over a fourth of the earth to kill those who reside therein. The locusts' authority is like the authority of the scorpions of the earth, who could dominate in the insect and animal world by using their poisonous stingers. Although nonlethal in humans, the sting of a scorpion was an extraordinarily painful torment. The authority of the scorpions, which the locusts are given, is their ability to terrorize humankind owing to the fear of being stung.

"It was said to them in order that they should not harm the grass of the earth nor any green thing nor any tree, except those men who did not have the seal of God upon their foreheads." The divine passive "it was said" makes clear that this command comes from God. The prohibition reveals a most unusual characteristic about these locusts. Locusts were feared precisely because they strip bare all manner of green vegetation lying in their path. Here they are prohibited from devouring green vegetation! This prohibition would remind hearers of the similar prohibition in chapter 7. The prohibition against harming anything except for humans who do not have the seal of God upon their foreheads would explain the purpose of the sealing of the 144,000 (7:3-8). These individuals bear the seal of the living God in order that they might be protected from the judgments that accompany the opening of the seventh seal, that is, the blasting of the seven trumpets by the seven angels. Just as God protected Israel from the plagues directed against Egypt, so God protects those who have his seal upon their foreheads, the transformed Israel, from this judgment.

Authority was given "that they might not kill them, but that they might be tormented five months, and their torment will be as torment of a scorpion when it has stung a man." Like Death and Hades, the locusts are given authority. Unlike them, the locusts are not given authority to kill. Rather, the locusts' authority is to torment those who do not have the seal of God upon their foreheads. The verb "might be tormented," together with its cognate "torment," appears a total of three times in this verse alone. These words convey the idea of intense bodily pain, so intense that this language is often used to describe eschatological torment.[191] The torment that these locusts are to inflict is lim-

---

190. Smalley, *Revelation*, 228.
191. W. Stenger, "Βασανίζω," *EDNT*, 1:200.

ited in nature, for the humans in question are to be tormented for a period of "five months."[192] While the significance of "five months" might be connected to the use of 5 as a round number meaning "a few" (Lev 26:8; 1 Cor 14:19),[193] it also might be explained by noting that five months is the normal life cycle of a locust. Thus, unlike typical locusts, which do not normally afflict a particular place for more than a few days, the torment of these locusts is prolonged while being just as concentrated. The nature of the torment is likened to that of a scorpion sting, a detail that reveals something of the intensity of the torment and explains why the locusts' authority had earlier been likened to that of the scorpions of the earth. The agony caused by these stings is so great that

> in those days men will seek death, and they will not find it,
> and they will desire to die, and death flees from them.

This poetic couplet[194] stands in parallel to a certain degree with the content of 6:16, a parallel reinforcing that those described in 9:6 stand in solidarity with those who fear close contact with God and the Lamb. Ironically, in contrast to the way in which Death pursues and kills one-fourth of humanity when the fourth seal is unsealed (6:8), here Death cannot be found. In fact, Death flees (keeps on fleeing)[195] from those who desire it! Given the control that the resurrected Jesus has over Death in Revelation (1:18; 2:11; 6:8), it would seem that Death cannot be found by those who seek it because the one who controls Death will not allow it to be found. The torment is thus made all the more painful, as not even Death can save those afflicted from it. Perhaps one of the implications of no lives being lost during this judgment might be that humanity is being given a specific period of time in which to repent, just as had the false prophetess Jezebel (2:21).

The locusts are said to look like "horses prepared for battle," a description conveying something of the size and power of these creatures, while bringing to mind a similar description of locusts found in Joel, where such creatures have a special association with the Day of the Lord (Joel 1:4-7; 2:1-11). Upon their heads are crowns as of gold. The exclusively positive connotations of the word στέφανος (*stephanos*, "crown") to this point (Rev 2:10; 3:11; 4:4, 10; 6:2) suggest that its appearance here would be taken in a positive rather than a negative fashion. Rather than being a parody of the Lamb,[196] the golden crowns indicate

---

192. Resseguie, *The Revelation of John*, 147.
193. Aune, *Revelation 6–16*, 530.
194. Wall, *Revelation*, 129.
195. So Osborne, *Revelation*, 369.
196. So Sweet, *Revelation*, 169.

that these locusts have the power and authority to accomplish their (divinely authorized) task. The locusts are said to have "faces as the faces of men," a detail perhaps indicating intelligence;[197] it would remind readers of the description of the third living creature around the throne of God (Rev 4:7), underscoring the idea that even these hideous locusts are divinely commissioned. The hair of these locusts is "like the hair of women." This image would likely convey a sense of vitality, as it does with Samson (Judg 16:13-22) and Absalom (2 Sam 14:25-26).[198] The teeth of these locusts are like the teeth of lions, bringing the ferocious nature of these locusts into sharper focus, conveying a sense of dread and fear, while reminding hearers of the first living creature described (Rev 4:7). This association with the four living creatures again underscores the divine nature of these locusts' commission. The phrase "and they have breastplates as iron breastplates" suggests that the scales normally found on the chests of locusts are very strong indeed, being like iron breastplates; they are virtually indestructible.[199] "And the voice of their wings is as the voice of many chariots of horses running into war." This thunderous voice carries with it the familiar sounds of war, one that these locusts are well equipped to carry out. "And they have tails as scorpions, and stingers, and in their tails their authority to harm men for five months." The things implied in 9:5 are made explicit here. Unlike the locusts in Prov. 30:27, these locusts have a king over them. If locusts that have no king manage to maintain rank as they march, these insidious locusts are even more organized! Their king is identified as "the angel of the Abyss." This angel is named in a rather striking way, for his name is given in both Hebrew and Greek (cf. John 5:2; 19:13, 17, 20). The Hebrew name is given (in Greek transliteration) as Ἀβαδδών (*Abaddōn*, "Destruction"), a term familiar from its somewhat frequent appearance in the Writings, where it often is closely associated with Death (Job 26:6; 28:22; 31:12; Prov. 15:11; Ps 88:11). There, it is the name of a place, never the name of an angel. Its appearance in Rev 9:11 as a proper name for the angel of the Abyss, however, would fit well with the context and would serve to personify Destruction. The Greek name, Destroyer, is more than a mere translation, carrying a deeper significance. It is clear that God himself is responsible for the angel who unlocks the Abyss and, in turn, the emergence of these locusts. Given previous exodus associations, mention of this Destroyer would perhaps bring to mind the Destroyer found in the exodus story,[200] who is also under divine commission and leaves those with God's mark unharmed.

---

197. Prigent, *L'Apocalypse de Saint Jean*, 243.
198. Smalley, *Revelation*, 232.
199. Mounce, *The Book of Revelation*, 197.
200. Beale, *The Book of Revelation*, 504.

A different word is used here than the one in Exod 12:23, perhaps, at this point in Revelation, in accord with the Destroyer's not bringing death but organizing excruciating suffering. The emphasis conveyed by the name being given in both Hebrew and Greek further underscores the dreadful nature of these locusts.

The conclusion of these events is signaled in v. 12, where the fifth trumpet is identified with the first of the three remaining woes of which the eagle has spoken in 8:13: "The first woe has departed; behold, two woes are still coming after these things." This explicit connection between the fifth trumpet and the first of the three woes makes the ominous nature of the final two trumpets all the clearer. For the events of the fifth trumpet are by far the worst in this series and are the most extensively described. The warning that two woes are still to come prepares for the blasting of the next two trumpets.

"And I heard one voice out of the four horns of the altar of gold before God." Since other references to the altar are all closely associated with the prayers of the saints (6:9; 8:3), the directives of this voice may be related to the previously mentioned prayers. The close proximity of the altar to God suggests that this is the voice of God, directly or indirectly; the voice is one of divine authorization,[201] and the four horns convey the image of divine strength.[202] The redundancy of the words "saying to the sixth angel, the one who has the trumpet," makes the identity of this angel very clear, heightening the sense of dramatic tension. This sixth angel is directed to "loose the four angels who have been bound at the great Euphrates River." Mention of these four angels would remind hearers of the four angels in 7:1. The articular construction suggests a familiarity with them, perhaps implying that these two groups would be identified as the same.[203] The perfect passive participle "who have been bound" implies that they have been bound by God at some point in the past and remain bound even now. In the Johannine literature, this verb is used to describe the binding of Lazarus (John 11:44) and Jesus (19:40) as part of their respective burials, as well as the binding of Jesus during his arrest (18:12, 24). Binding also occurs in conjunction with loosing (John 11:44; Rev 9:14; 20:2, 7), indicating that the binding in question is for a specific purpose. The location of these four angels at the great Euphrates River would strike an ominous note, as it is one of the historical boundaries for Israel (Gen 15:18; Josh 1:4) and the location of some of Rome's most feared enemies, the Parthians.

These angels were indeed released, with the divine passive "were loosed" standing in the place of emphasis. These are those "who had been prepared for

---

201. Smalley, *Revelation*, 235.
202. Kiddle, *The Revelation of St. John*, 161.
203. Murphy, *Fallen Is Babylon*, 146.

the hour and day and month and year." As others before them (8:6; 9:7), these four angels had been prepared for this very moment. To this point the verb "prepare" is used to designate something or someone prepared by God (9:15) and/or prepared to accomplish his purpose (8:6; 9:7). The extent of their preparation goes to the exact moment they are to carry out their mission, pointing to the exact hour, day, month, and year. This unique formulation is paralleled to a certain extent by Num 1:1 and Zech 1:7 (cf. also Hag 1:15), where day, month, and year are cited with reference to the coming of the word of the Lord. The passive participle "those prepared" and this peculiar means of temporal calculation combine to convey the extent of God's involvement in the activity of these angels. The reason for their divine commission is revealed by a purpose clause, "in order that they might kill a third of all men." In continuity with the first four trumpets, a third of the objects concerned are affected, but for the first time human beings are killed. The escalation in the numbers of those who are killed from when the fourth seal is opened (one-fourth) to the blasting of the sixth trumpet (one-third) fits well with the intensification of judgment expected in the second and third woes (8:13), while contributing to the sense of accelerated movement toward the end.

It appears that these four angels morph into an unbelievably large force — "the number of the soldiers of horses (cavalry)." The astronomical number "twice ten thousand times ten thousand," is reminiscent of the angels described in 5:11. Significantly, this number appears in Ps 68:17 with reference to the chariots that accompany the Lord as he comes to his Holy Place from Sinai. Such similarity implies that the army in Rev 9:16 comes from the Lord, just has had the chariots in Ps 68. The enormity of this number indicates its supernatural nature,[204] a force 200,000,000 strong, which cannot conceivably be resisted.[205] It will accomplish God's purpose. John's words "I heard their number" is reminiscent of 7:4, where John heard the 144,000 numbered but then sees an innumerable crowd.

What John heard again gives way to what he saw: "And I saw horses in the vision and those sitting upon them as. . . ." Here, John makes explicit reference to "the vision" for the only time in Revelation. When John actually describes the appearance of horse and rider, it is as though they converge into one entity,[206] for the ascription of breastplates that appear fiery, hyacinth-like, and sulfurous does not distinguish between them in any way. One focus is upon the breastplates, which appear somewhat hazy, while reflecting elements

---

204. Prigent, *L'Apocalypse de Saint Jean*, 246.
205. Gause, *Revelation*, 142.
206. Beasley-Murray, *Revelation*, 165.

capable of destruction. This is the case with the elements "fiery" and "sulfurous," and may also be the case with "hyacinth-like," which appears to refer to a gem that generates a dark-blue or a dark-red, bordering on a black luster,[207] perhaps resembling the appearance of smoke. The true objects of focus, though, are the horses, which are well protected by their breastplates and well armed. Something of the offensive nature of this army is revealed by the words "and the heads of the horses were as the heads of lions, and out of their mouths came fire and smoke and sulfur." The description of their heads would remind readers of the description of the locusts' teeth as lions' teeth in 9:8, as well as the physical appearance of the first living creature in 4:7. By this image, both the ferocious nature of this army and its divine commission are conveyed. Out of the mouth of these lion-like heads come ominously destructive elements, which bear a striking resemblance to the appearance of this army's breastplates: fire, smoke, and sulfur. The cumulative nature of this army's activities is revealed by the way some form of fire appears with the sounding of the first four trumpets, smoke with the fifth, and sulfur with the sixth. A clarifying remark follows: "From these three plagues a third of men were killed, out of the fire and the smoke and the sulfur that were coming out of their mouths." Significantly, these destructive elements are called "plagues," the first attribution of this word to a judgment in Revelation. Such language would call to mind the ten exodus plagues directed toward Egypt. These three plagues are explicitly identified as those elements responsible for the killing of a third of humankind, suggesting that these plagues represent eschatological judgments inflicted in advance of the end. Not only "the authority of the horses is in their mouths," but this authority is also "in their tails, for their tails are like serpents, having heads and with which they harm." Serpent imagery used for the tail of an animal may not be so unusual, but these "serpents" have heads with which to harm their victims. Their ability to inflict harm is doubly impressive, as they possess heads on either part of their torsos. Perhaps such fearful images would also bring to mind Ps 91:13, where the lion and serpent pose no danger to those who dwell in the shelter of the Most High.[208]

"The rest of the men, those who were not killed by these plagues, did not repent of the works of their hands, in order that they not worship the demons and the idols of gold and silver and bronze and stone and wood, which are not able to see nor hear nor walk." It now becomes clear that these plagues were designed to give humankind an opportunity for repentance.[209] The death of a

---

207. J. H. Thayer, *A Greek-English Lexicon of the New Testament* (Grand Rapids: Zondervan, 1975), 633.
208. Sweet, *Revelation*, 173.
209. Osborne, *Revelation*, 385, and Resseguie, *The Revelation of John*, 149.

third of humanity, following on the death of a fourth of humanity (6:8), is thus now seen as a gracious restraint that affords an opportunity for those who survive to repent. In this refusal to repent, the hearers are confronted with those who have seen the arm of God himself revealed and yet choose not to repent! This failure to repent would remind hearers of Pharaoh's repeated failure to repent at the conclusion of each plague. Specifically, the rest of humanity is said not to repent of "the works of their hands." Here, there is a close connection between "the works of their hands" and the worship of demons and idols. The mention of demons at this point might come as a bit of a surprise, as there appears to be little to no interest in demons or the demonic in the Johannine literature, with no exorcisms described in John's gospel — only that Jesus is accused of being demon-possessed (John 7:20; 8:48-49, 52; 10:20-21) — and no mention of demons in 1–3 John. The appearance of demons here in 9:20 suggests some relationship between their worship and idolatry. While this mention might indicate that the worship of demons is to be equated with the worship of idols, the rest of the verse suggests otherwise, indicating that the relationship between demons and idols is that the former inspires the worship of the latter. For the first time in Revelation the word "worship" appears in connection with one other than God and/or his people (3:9; 4:10; 5:14; 7:11), thus introducing the theme of false worship into the book. The description of the idols, which sits nicely with the phrase "the works of their hands," could not help but evoke the biting words of numerous OT writers with regard to the foolishness and futility of idolatry (Isa 40:18-20; 41:6-7; 44:9-20; Jer 10; Ps 115:3-8).[210] Despite their composition, whether of gold, silver, bronze, stone, or wood, they are unable to act, to see or hear or walk. Yet, these impotent idols and the demons that inspire their worship are tenaciously grasped by those who, ironically enough, have seen firsthand the activity of "the living God" in the form of the plagues and judgments wrought upon the earth and its inhabitants!

"Neither did they repent of their murders, nor their sorcery, nor their sexual immorality, nor their thefts." Each of these activities is specifically condemned in the Torah (Exod 20:13; 22:18; 20:14, 15, respectively) and may have other specific associations within the Johannine literature. Johannine hearers would likely regard those who commit murder as children of the devil, who "was a man killer from the beginning" (John 8:44). This group might be thought to include those responsible for the death of Antipas (2:13). Sorcery[211] will be-

---

210. Murphy, *Fallen Is Babylon*, 249.

211. Here the term for "potions" appears, instead of the normal word for "magic," perhaps indicating that even the paraphernalia used with sorcery is condemned; so Osborne, *Revelation*, 387.

come closely associated with the activity of Babylon, who deceived the nations by her sorcery (18:23). Sexual immorality would recall the teaching of Balaam (2:14), as well as the activity and teaching of Jezebel and her followers (2:20). Although Jesus earlier says, "I come as a thief!" (3:3), it is clear that those who have committed theft in 9:21 are viewed, not like Jesus, but as those who enter the sheepfold illegally (John 10:1), to kill, steal, and destroy (10:10). Even more ominously, such language would be reminiscent of Judas (John 12:6), the archetype of one who refuses to repent. The refusal of the rest of humankind to repent of such activities thus reveals something of the level of their obstinate refusal to respond to the hand of God. Such a response could not help but leave the hearers with a sense of bewilderment, that the people of the world could be so adamant in their refusal of God and his work. Or perhaps it is that they are so blind that they cannot see the hand of God in the activities associated with the sixth trumpet.[212]

The Interlude of the Little Scroll and the Two Witnesses (10:1–11:14)

"And I saw another mighty angel coming down out of heaven." The beginning of this sentence — "and I saw" — alerts hearers to a new dimension of the vision being introduced, directing attention to a different object than the expected conclusion of the second woe and blasting of the seventh trumpet. Mention of "another mighty angel" reminds readers of a mighty angel in heaven (5:2) who preaches, "Who is worthy to open the book and loose its seals?" This angel is also originally located in heaven. But as he descends, the attention is directed back to earth. This mighty angel is described in terms unlike any other angel in the book, indicating something of his unique importance and function.[213] Like Jesus, who "comes with the clouds" (1:7), this mighty angel is "clothed with the cloud." Like God, whose throne is surrounded by a rainbow (4:3), this mighty angel has "the rainbow around his head." Since "the rainbow" here in 10:1 is articular, it almost certainly points back to the rainbow mentioned in 4:3. Like Jesus, whose "countenance is as the sun shining in its power" (1:16), the mighty angel's "face is as the sun." Like Jesus, whose "feet are like bronze glowing in a furnace" (1:15), the feet of this mighty angel are "as pillars of fire." Like the one who sits on the throne (5:1) and the Lamb (5:7), this mighty angel too has a

---

212. Collins (*The Apocalypse*, 63) concludes, "Verses 20-21 express the prophet's conviction that the people of his day were so alienated from the creator that no crisis could move them to repentance. Events in which the faithful would see divine providence and justice are simply acts of blind fate to others."

213. Bauckham, *The Climax of Prophecy*, 253.

book in his hand. Perhaps this angel is a manifestation of the risen Christ, now appearing in angelic form. Or perhaps this angel is a Christophany on the order of the appearance of "the angel of the Lord" found in the OT.[214] Or perhaps, owing to the remarkable convergence of the divine characteristics of both God and Jesus, and the intimate connection that exists between Jesus and the Spirit in Johannine thought, this angel *is* the Spirit.[215] It is likely, however, that the hearers would not long hold to any one of these options. For it is clear that this mighty angel is identified as "another mighty angel," underscoring his similarities in some respects to the previous "mighty angel." Furthermore, there is a remarkable consistency with which Revelation keeps the lines of demarcation between Jesus and angels clear.[216] What would these (divine) characteristics convey? It would seem that John and his hearers would see in this mighty angel a being intimately associated with God and Jesus, one authorized to act on behalf of and in accordance with the divine will, representing the divine presence and glory.[217]

This mighty angel has "in his hand an opened book." The perfect passive participle "opened" describing this book indicates that it had been opened at some point in the past and remains open even now. Mention of an opened book suggests the possibility that it is the same book that was taken from the hand of God by the Lamb, who subsequently opened its seals. If so, the book sealed with seven seals has been opened, having made its way from God to the Lamb to the mighty angel to John (1:1). On this view, the events described in chapters 6–9 are those that accompany the opening of the seals, not the revelation of the book's contents. Only when the book has been opened are its contents accessible to John and his hearers. While the word "little book" occurs here, rather than "book," as found in chapter 5, and might suggest that the little book of 10:2 is different from the book of 5:1, such a conclusion would be premature. For both these terms are diminutives, indicating that the force of "little" is relative. The angel's later instruction (10:8) indicates that these two terms function as synonyms in Revelation, for "book" appears there with reference to the angel's book.[218] John and his hearers are finally encountering the opened book! The location of the angel's feet — "he placed his right foot upon the sea, and the left

---

214. For example, Gen 16:10; 22:11-18; 24:7; 31:11-13; Exod 3:2-12; 14:19; Judg 2:1; 6:22; 13:20-22. For an extensive argument favoring this interpretation, cf. Beale, *The Book of Revelation*, 522-26.

215. For this fascinating interpretation, cf. Waddell, *The Spirit of the Book of Revelation*, 159-63.

216. Bauckham, *The Climax of Prophecy*, 118-49.

217. Gause, *Revelation*, 145

218. Cf. the very helpful discussion of the book's identity by Bauckham, *The Climax of Prophecy*, 243-57.

upon the earth" — indicates the scope and the authority of this mighty angel's universal mission and message, as he stands upon the two major components of earthly creation (Gen 1:10).[219] The activity of his feet is described first, which encourages the hearers to take earth as their vantage point for viewing this enormous figure.

"He cried out with a great voice as a lion roaring." The association of the angel's voice with that of a lion would remind readers of OT descriptions of God's voice (Hos 11:10; and esp. Amos 3:8), and be yet another way in which this mighty angel brings to mind Jesus, the Lion of the Tribe of Judah (5:5). Interestingly, the words of this angel are not recorded. Rather, "And when he spoke, the seven thunders spoke their own voices." This is the first (and only) time in Revelation when the words of an angel are not recorded.[220] There appears to be some connection between the crying out by the mighty angel and the seven thunders that follow. The sounding of the voices of thunder clearly conveys extraordinarily loud sounds, as thunder was one of the strongest natural sounds encountered in antiquity. Mention of the seven thunders would almost certainly be taken as the introduction of yet another series of sevens, like the seven seals and seven trumpets, as this seven is introduced near the end of the sequence of the seven trumpets and appears to be of heavenly origin. This articular construction — *the* seven thunders" — suggests familiarity with this group, reminding readers of the voice of God as reflected in Ps 29, where the voice of the Lord is mentioned seven times, with its initial description likening it to thunder.[221] The equation of thunder with God's voice would also be familiar to Johannine hearers (John 12:29). Neither would the significance of the role of thunder in the strategically located theophanic displays in Revelation be lost on the hearers (Rev 4:5; 8:5; 11:19; 16:18), two of which they have already encountered. Thus, the seven thunders might very well generate an expectancy for yet another series of sevens of even greater intensity.

"And when the seven trumpets spoke, I was about to write." In keeping with Jesus' command (1:11, 19), John prepares to write down those things that he witnesses. However, John says, "I heard a voice out of heaven saying, 'Seal up the words of the seven thunders, and do not write them.'" This heavenly prohibition would be astonishing, standing at odds with Jesus' previous commands (1:11, 19).[222] The heavenly origin of this voice suggests that it is that of either Jesus or God. Positively, John is commanded to "seal" the words of the

---

219. Resseguie, *The Revelation of John*, 153.
220. Aune, *Revelation 6–16*, 559.
221. Sweet, *Revelation*, 178.
222. Mounce, *The Book of Revelation*, 209.

seven thunders, a command standing in sharp contrast to the presence of the unsealed book in the mighty angel's hand! The second part of the prohibition indicates that John is to conceal these words by not writing them down, the aorist subjunctive prohibition conveying that John is forbidden to take a course of action he has not yet commenced.[223] While the words of the seven thunders do not become part of John's book, they are part of John's experience and do not seem to be invalidated or suspended. What then is their significance? If they represent yet another series of God's judgments, in line with the seven seals and seven trumpets,[224] it is probable that this series would bring with it an increase in intensity of the judgments to be experienced. Thus, whereas the opening of the seven seals saw the death of a fourth of humankind and the blasting of the seven trumpets saw the death of a third, would the words spoken by the seven thunders not involve the death of a half of humankind?[225] If so, the command to omit these words would serve to hasten the pace of the move toward the end, shortening any delay.[226] It moves the hearers toward an acknowledgment that the second woe has passed and increases expectation for the blasting of the seventh (and final) trumpet.

The words "the angel, the one whom I saw standing upon the sea and upon the earth" draw specific attention to the posture of the mighty angel. This gigantic figure now raises "his right hand into the heavens and swears" an oath. The only concrete analogy for such an incredible sight would be the Colossus of Rhodes, one of the Seven Wonders of the ancient world, which stood about 105 feet tall on the promontory overlooking the harbor of Rhodes. Destroyed by an earthquake in 224 BCE, the ruins of the Colossus were well known.[227] Yet, even this incredible analogy is dwarfed by the stature of this mighty angel, whose cosmic posture connects the heavens with land and sea.[228] This mighty angel "swore by the one who lives forever and ever, who created the heaven and the things in them and the earth and the things in it and the sea and the things in it." The mention of "the one who lives forever and ever" along with "the one who created" carries the hearers back to the throne-room scene (Rev 4), where the former is twice used with reference to the one who sits on the throne. The designation "the living God" also appears in 7:2 with reference to his seal. Likewise, the reference to God as creator occurs twice in 4:11, where in a chiastic song of praise God receives the worship of the four living

---

223. Aune, *Revelation 6–16*, 549.
224. Skaggs and Benham, *Revelation*, 108.
225. A. M. Farrer, *The Revelation of St. John the Divine* (Oxford: Clarendon, 1964), 125.
226. Resseguie, *The Revelation of John*, 154.
227. Aune, *Revelation 6–16*, 556–57.
228. Bauckham, *The Climax of Prophecy*, 253.

creatures for his strategic role in the creation of all things. On this occasion, the comprehensive nature of God's creative activity is further underscored, not only by the threefold mention of heaven, earth, and sea, but also by the explicit mention of "the things that are in it," which follows each division of creation. The incredible statement "there is no more time" would have a startling effect. After all, the words of the seven thunders had just been sealed in order to avoid further delay. At one level, these words would convey the idea that the end itself is soon to be experienced and may be taken as a response of sorts to the cries of the souls under the altar in 6:9-11.

A bit more time remains, however, as the mighty angel continues his message, "But in the days of the voice of the seventh angel, when he is about to (sound his) trumpet, the mystery of God will be fulfilled, as he preached to his servants the prophets." The first word is the strong word of contrast "but," leading to a translation something like, "There is no more time, but . . . ," meaning that, although time has run out, "the days of the voice of the seventh angel" remain. Significantly, explicit mention is made that he "is about to trumpet." The blasting of the seventh trumpet is thus closely associated with there being no more time. Furthermore, in the days when the seventh trumpet sounds, "The mystery of God will have been completed." Previously, the word "mystery" refers to something in need of interpretation (Rev 1:20). The occurrence of "the mystery of God" in 10:7 would indicate that something else is in need of (divine) explanation. The aorist passive "has been completed" appears here with reference to the future, conveying an additional sense of certainty with regard to the completion of the mystery of God.[229] The occurrence of this term reminds hearers of Jesus' desire to complete the work of his Father (John 4:34; 5:36; 17:4) and of Jesus' last words on the cross, "It is completed" (19:30). The implications with regard to the relationship between Jesus' death and the completion of the mystery of God in Revelation are not difficult to see. Neither would Johannine hearers be unaware that the love of God can be completed in the lives of believers (1 John 2:5; 4:12, 17-18). The convergence of these ideas may indicate the way in which the mystery of God will be completed. Another aspect of this mystery is that God preached it to his servants the prophets. The occurrence of the word εὐηγγέλισεν (*euēngelisen*, "preached [the good news]") to describe God's revelation of this mystery to his servants further underscores the connection between this mystery and the life and death of Jesus. Significantly, the term κηρύσσοντα (*kēryssonta*, "proclaiming") is used of the mighty angel's proclamation in 5:2, while the mighty angel of chapter 10 uses the word *euēngelisen* to describe God's making known this mystery. Both mighty angels are connected

---

229. Smalley, *Revelation*, 265.

in one way or another with terms associated with gospel proclamation! Who are these servants, these prophets? Rather clearly this statement would refer to OT prophets, the words of Amos 3:7 almost certainly coming to mind. But it is also likely that Christian prophets would be included as the recipients of this preaching, as many of the occurrences of servants (1:1; 2:20; 7:3; 11:18; 22:6) and prophets (10:11; 11:3, 10, 18; 16:6; 18:20, 24; 22:6, 9) in Revelation appear to refer to Christian prophets. A very similar phrase appears in 11:18, where servants and prophets are again connected; it at least includes Christian prophets. John is himself engaged in just such an experience in writing down the words of this prophecy and finds himself among certain other "brothers the prophets" (22:9). Thus, the "mystery of God" has been revealed to God's servants the prophets, a revelatory process that includes John and his community.

"Go, take the opened book in the hand of the angel who was standing upon the sea and upon the earth." As in v. 4, this voice is the voice of either God or Jesus. Earlier, this divine voice prohibits writing down the words of the seven thunders. Now it commands John to take the opened book in the hand of the mighty angel. The episode takes the form of a prophetic commissioning as John is directed to come and take the open scroll, bringing to mind Ezekiel's prophetic commission (cf. esp. Ezek 2:8–3:2). The command "go" may carry with it additional theological weight, as the term often appears in John's gospel in close association with the mission of Jesus, while the command "take" is defined in large part by its appearance in describing the activities of the Lamb in taking the book in Rev 5. Such a twofold command suggests that John is no passive instrument in prophetic communication but is called to active participation in this prophetic call.

Interestingly, John does not "take" the book from the gigantic figure but rather says, "And I went to the angel, asking him to give to me the little book." No sooner does John obey the heavenly voice than he receives a command from the mighty angel, "Take and eat it, and your stomach will be bitter, but in your mouth it will be sweet as honey." The words of the mighty angel show remarkable similarities to Ezekiel's words, indicating that indeed John is receiving a(nother) prophetic commission. While the word κατάφαγε (*kataphage*, "eat") can be translated simply "eat," in this context, as in the Johannine literature as a whole (John 2:17; Rev 11:5; 12:4; 20:9), the term has the stronger connotation of "devour" or "consume."[230] Clearly, the image conveys the idea that John is to devour the book by ingesting it, and in so doing the content of the book will become a part of him. There is a direct relationship between the contents of this book and John's prophetic ministry. While the imagery that the book would

---

230. Mounce, *The Book of Revelation*, 214 n. 37.

be bitter to the mouth of John but sweet as honey in his mouth might remind readers that the word of the Lord is sweet as honey to the taste (Ps 119:103) and that the prophetic message can sometimes be a bitter one, as with the case of Ezekiel,[231] it appears that this imagery points to specific dimensions of the little book's content. The activity of God and his agents could sometimes involve bitterness, for many people were described as having died in 8:10-11 owing to the fact that a third of the rivers and fountains of water had been made bitter by the star that had fallen upon them. Though the hearers could not likely discern the full meaning of this bitter and sweet imagery at this point, the meaning will become clear by the conclusion of this section of the book. By way of preview, it appears that the reason the book is bitter to John's stomach while sweet as honey to his mouth is very much related to the implications of the book's contents for John and his hearers. Specifically, it will be made clear that their prophetic witness will result in death, though they will receive divine protection until their witness is complete (cf. esp. 11:7). That the mighty angel mentions bitterness before sweetness might well alert them to the dangerous nature of their activities as faithful witnesses. When John devours the book, it will devour him; it will indeed be both bitter and sweet.

Faithful to this prophetic call, John actively takes the little book out of the hand of the angel and devours it. Inverting the words of the angel, John first notes that the book was as sweet as honey in his mouth and then that his stomach was made bitter when it had been consumed, alerting the hearers that in the prophetic words to follow, they will first encounter their sweetness, the promise of divine protection, and then their bitterness, the call to martyrdom.[232] Perhaps it would be remembered that Daniel's own prophetic encounter left him physically ill (Dan 10:8-17). Nowhere in Revelation does John more fully enter into this visionary drama than here. It is significant that his actions here are similar to those of the Lamb in chapter 5, who also takes the book. Such similarities convey a sense of identification with the Lamb and John's own participation in the salvific activity of the Lamb. It may even imply that John, too, will follow in the way of martyrdom.[233]

John again receives divine instruction, which contains an explicit prophetic call, "And they say to me, 'It is necessary for you to prophesy again to many people and nations and tongues and kings.'" While the words "they say to me" might be surprising, it is likely that the indefinite plural "they say" would be understood as an idiomatic substitute for the passive, found in both Hebrew

---

231. Wall, *Revelation*, 139-40.
232. Koester, *Revelation and the End of All Things*, 104.
233. Smalley, *Revelation*, 266-67.

and Aramaic, resulting in a translation something like "I was told."[234] The first word spoken to John in the Greek text means "it is necessary," conveying the idea of divine compulsion or necessity,[235] which has appeared twice previously with reference to those things that must take place (1:1; 4:1). Its reappearance here would imply that John is to be a very real part of those things that are to take place. It is necessary for John to prophesy again. It is difficult to ignore the implication that John's previous prophesying, recording the things he has seen and heard, is coming to an end and is to give way to another round of prophesying.[236] This commission to prophesy again, along with John's devouring of the open book, suggests that his future prophetic activity will take on a more intense and personal dimension, if such is possible! This verse indicates that John is now to prophesy, not just to the church, but ἐπί (*epi*, "to" or "about") "many peoples and nations and tongues and kings." While it is possible to translate *epi* as "against," reminiscent of Ezekiel's prophesying against the nations,[237] John's prophetic mandate is to prophesy to all nations by bearing faithful witness to the Lamb. The translation "to" is thus the likely meaning in this context.[238] The fourfold phrase "many peoples and nations and tongues and kings" is reminiscent of the fourfold formulas that have previously occurred in 5:9 and 7:9. The list found in 10:11, however, differs in two ways. First, the word "kings" appears here in the place of "tribes," perhaps preparing the hearers for the emphasis upon kings that follows in chapters 16–21. Second, while the first two lists occur in contexts where they testify to the universality of the people of God, here the list describes the nations, as it will from this point on in Revelation.[239] Such philological links suggest that not simply will individuals from these groups experience salvation, but they also might become witnesses to the groups from which they come.[240] John is thus commissioned to prophesy yet again, this time on the world stage.

"And there was given to me a reed as a rod, saying, 'Rise and measure the temple of God and the altar and the worshippers in it.'" Such a close connection between John's prophetic commission and the prophetic task given suggests that the activity described in the following chapter in some way functions as the accomplishment of that commission.[241] The commission's divine origin is

---

234. Aune, *Revelation 6–16*, 573.
235. Smalley, *Revelation*, 249.
236. Collins, *The Apocalypse*, 65.
237. Beale, *The Book of Revelation*, 554-55.
238. D. E. Holwerda, "The Church and the Little Scroll (Revelation 10,11)," *CTJ* 34 (1999): 154.
239. Bauckham, *The Climax of Prophecy*, 265.
240. Koester, *Revelation and the End of All Things*, 103.
241. Prigent, *L'Apocalypse de Saint Jean*, 260.

indicated by the divine passive "there was given." John's instrument is a "reed." Symbolic prophetic acts are well known in the OT, with the act of measuring not unusual (2 Sam 8:2; 2 Kgs 21:13; Isa 28:16-17; 34:11; Jer 31:38-40; Ezek 40–48; Lam 2:8; Amos 7:7-9; Mic 2:5; Zech 1:16; 2:1-2). The significance of John's measuring is different from any of its predecessors, however, for here John is instructed to measure certain things but not to measure others. What would the command to "measure the temple of God and the altar and those who worship in it" mean? While the temple, altar, and worshippers could refer to a current or future temple complex, upon closer inspection such an interpretive option does not appear to be likely. When the term ναός (*naos,* "temple" or "sanctuary") appears in the Johannine literature, it does not normally refer to the literal temple complex. Rather, ἱερόν (*hieron,* "temple") is the term of choice for the temple complex in John's gospel (2:14-15; 5:14; 7:14, 28; 8:20, 59; 10:23; 11:56; 18:20). In fact, *naos* appears only three times in John's gospel, each time with reference to the temple of Jesus' body (2:19-21). Such a theologically significant understanding of this term would suggest that the temple here in view is not a literal temple complex but one that is filled with theological significance. This understanding would be confirmed by the term's earlier appearance, where the resurrected Jesus promises the one who overcomes that Jesus will make him "a pillar in the temple of my God" (Rev 3:12), implying that such a one has a permanent place in God's presence. Its other occurrence refers to God's heavenly temple, where those who have come out of the great tribulation serve him day and night (7:15). Given these indicators, it appears likely that mention of the temple in 11:1 refers to God's temple in heaven, with which believers are intimately connected.

Mention of the second component to be measured, "the altar," points in this same direction, as previously this term refers to the heavenly altar (6:9; 8:3; 9:13). As with the temple imagery, so the altar imagery is intimately connected to believers to this point in the book, including the "souls under the altar" (6:9) and the relationship between altar and "the prayers of the saints" (8:3), which appear to be related to the judgments of God released from the altar (9:14). The heavenly altar is in the very presence of God, which confirms the same message that the temple imagery conveys. The third component to be measured also points in this direction. Johannine hearers would be aware that true worshippers are those who worship the Father in Spirit and in truth (John 4:23), which is not tied to a particular geographic location (4:20-24). In Revelation the twenty-four elders, who bear a striking resemblance to those who overcome, are always falling down and worshipping in heaven (Rev 4:10; 5:14; 7:11; 11:16). In addition, Jesus has made those who believe in him into priests to our God (1:6; 5:10), at least some of them understood to be serving God in heaven (5:10). Thus, it is likely that these items refer to the believing community in the very presence of God.

"And the court outside the temple leave out (cast outside) and do not measure it, because it has been given to the nations, and they will trample the holy city for forty-two months." It is likely that, given the previous associations between the temple and the believing community, the shift in focus to the "outer court of the temple" would carry with it some of its previous associations. For "the outer court of the temple" is still part of the temple, and if the temple is closely associated with the believing community in the very presence of God, so the outer court of the temple would also carry some of those positive connotations. In John's gospel, the term "courtyard" is identified both with the safety of the sheepfold (10:1, 16) and as a place of vulnerability, as Peter discovers in the court of the high priest (18:15). The phrase "cast outside" underscores the idea of vulnerability, if not outright abandonment! Being cast out into a world of vulnerability, however, would not leave them without hope. For as the formerly blind man in John's gospel discovers, Jesus himself is waiting there for those who believe in and worship him (John 9:34-38). The reason the outer court is not to be measured becomes clear in the next phrase: "it has been given to the nations." Significantly, the same divine passive that appeared in 11:1 to make clear the divine origin of John's prophetic task reappears here to make clear the divine origin of the giving of the outer court of the temple to the nations. Such a divine act will result in the trampling of the holy city for forty-two months. If this image of trampling draws a convergence of ideas from Zech (LXX) 12:3 and Dan 8:11-14,[242] it would add to the ominous nature of what is being described. It appears that "the outer court of the temple" and "the holy city" are identical in this verse. The linkage between the people of God as temple, altar, worshippers, outer court of the temple, and holy city thus reveals the meaning of these images in 11:1-2. The time of the holy city's vulnerability is of limited duration, forty-two months. This reference to a limited period of time would likely bring to mind Daniel's "time, times, and half a time" (Dan 7:25; 12:7), which designates a period of unprecedented trauma and persecution for the people of God.

From the foregoing it appears here that reference is made to the people of God marked out as being in his very presence, with the implicit promise of protection.[243] It is clear, however, that the people of God are still subject to vulnerability, owing to the response of the nations to them. The protection and

---

242. Waddell, *The Spirit of the Book of Revelation*, 169-70.

243. Though measuring never means protection in the OT texts where measuring is described. On this point, cf. M. Jauhiainen, "The Measuring of the Sanctuary Reconsidered (Rev 11:1-2)," *Biblica* 83 (2002): 507-26.

vulnerability of the people of God thus coexist in a way remarkably reminiscent of the picture of God's people in chapter 7, where the 144,000 are sealed by God for protection against the impending divine judgments, while the universal, innumerable crowd is identified as coming out of the great tribulation! This combination of protection and vulnerability for the people of God in 11:1-2 results in a certain merging of the people of God in their heavenly and earthly manifestations. The hearers now are therefore very near the theological heart of Revelation, for the images of 11:1-2 appear to reveal something of the content of the opened book that John has devoured, which makes more explicit the nature of Christian prophetic witness.

Significantly, John is nowhere described as carrying out this prophetic task. This unresolved tension may suggest that what follows is in some way connected to or a fulfillment of John's prophetic task. Without any break the divine voice continues to speak, "And I will give to my two witnesses, and they will prophesy 1,260 days being clothed in sackcloth." The first person pronoun in "I will give to my two witnesses" indicates the close connection between the prophetic activity to follow and the divine speaker. God, and or Jesus, is the initiator of prophetic witness.[244] The two witnesses are described as the recipients of the divine gift. While interpretive history is full of attempts to identify these two witnesses,[245] their number is in accord with the Torah stipulations with regard to the minimal number of witnesses needed to validate a truth claim (Num 35:30; Deut 17:6; 19:15).[246] Their identification as witnesses would remind hearers of the other witnesses encountered to this point in the book: John (Rev 1:2), Jesus (1:5),[247] and Antipas (2:13). They are called "my" witnesses, which makes clear that their prophetic activity belongs to God. Their activity, described as prophesying, indicates that the activity of witnessing and prophesying are synonymous. It is prophetic witness. Previously, prophetic language has been used with reference to "the words of this prophecy," to which John gives careful witness (1:3), and the commission John receives to "prophesy again" (10:11). The duration of their prophetic activity is the same length of time that "the outer court of the temple," "the holy city," will be trampled by the nations (11:2). However, instead of forty-two months, it is here described as 1,260 days. While this may be no more than literary variation,[248] such a conclusion might be a bit premature. For while both designations, forty-two months and 1,260 days, are used but twice each in the book, the former is found in contexts de-

---

244. Gause, *Revelation*, 151.
245. On this, cf. the discussion by Kovacs and Rowland, *Revelation*, 126-30.
246. Resseguie, *The Revelation of John*, 162.
247. Osborne, *Revelation*, 419-20.
248. Smalley, *Revelation*, 276.

"In the Spirit in Heaven" (4:1–16:21)

scribing opposition to God (13:5) or his people (11:2), while the latter is found in contexts describing the activity of God's people (11:2) or their divine protection (12:6).[249] Perhaps these designations suggest that the same period of time looks different, depending upon one's perspective, whether the perspective of God or that of his opponents. In any case, the trampling of God's people by the nations will not be experienced passively but will be met with active prophesying.[250] The attire of these two witnesses might well remind hearers that in the OT sackcloth was a sign of mourning (Isa 22:12; Jer 4:8; Jonah 3:6-8), suggesting that their message is closely related to the mourning that results from divine judgment, while holding out the hope that those who hear their prophetic message might respond with repentance.[251]

Just as in the inaugural vision of Jesus, where the hearers encounter an incredible convergence of intertexts from a variety of OT locations, so they would detect in the description of these two prophetic witnesses a similar intertextual convergence.[252] There are olive trees and lampstands from Zechariah, the ability to bring forth fire and close the heavens like Elijah, the ability to turn water into blood and bring other plagues like Moses, and incredibly a death, resurrection, and ascension like that of Jesus. "These are the two olive trees and the two lampstands that are before the Lord of the earth." Significantly, both "the two olive trees" and "the two lampstands" are articular constructions, suggesting that they are well-known entities to the hearers.[253] The mention of these items would remind readers of Zech 4, where two olive trees stand on either side of the central lampstand, which has seven lamps on it. There, two branches of the two olive trees are connected to golden pipes, through which the oil is poured out. Both the word of the Lord spoken to Zerubbabel, "Not by might, nor by power, but by my Spirit, says the LORD of Hosts" (Zech 4:6), and the identification of these two olive branches as "the two anointed who stand before the face of the whole earth" in 4:14 would clearly assist readers in discerning that these two prophetic witnesses are Spirit-anointed prophets. This identity is underscored when these witnesses are described as the two lampstands (Rev 11:4). Other dimensions of the meaning of the lampstands would also be present. Earlier, the resurrected Jesus identifies the seven golden lampstands, in the midst of which he stands, as the seven churches (1:20), while in the inaugural vision of heaven, seven lampstands of fire are located before

---

249. Bauckham makes a similar point, referring to the forty-two months as "the Beast's time" and the 1,260 days as "the church's time" (*The Climax of Prophecy*, 402).
250. Resseguie, *The Revelation of John*, 162.
251. Cf. esp. Waddell, *The Spirit of the Book of Revelation*, 173.
252. Koester, *Revelation and the End of All Things*, 108.
253. Allo, *Saint Jean: L'Apocalypse*, 132.

the throne, which are the seven Spirits of God (4:5). Such previous associations indicate that, in the description of the two prophetic witnesses in 11:4, there is a convergence of the churches, the Spirit, and these witnesses. In these two prophetic witnesses, there thus appears to be a convergence of the activity of Jesus, the prophetic ministry of the Holy Spirit, and the ongoing witness of the churches. We thus have reference to the prophetic, Spirit-inspired ministry of the church itself.[254] The witnesses' location, "standing before the Lord of the earth," underscores their close proximity to God, being in the same location as the Spirit, indicating that the actions and words of these witnesses are to be closely identified with the actions and words of God himself. Just as the words of the resurrected Jesus are coterminous with those of the Spirit, so are the words and deeds of these witnesses.[255]

"If anyone desires to harm them, fire comes out of their mouth and consumes their enemies." The construction "if anyone desires to harm" is known in Greek grammar as a first class conditional clause, which emphasizes the reality of this condition,[256] underscoring the certainty that there will be those who desire to harm these two witnesses. The certainty of this potential opposition, however, will be met with the certainty of the witnesses' divine protection. These words remind us of Yahweh's words to Jeremiah, "I will make my words in your mouth a fire and these people the wood, and it will consume them" (Jer 5:14); of Elijah, who called down fire from heaven against the messengers of Ahaziah (2 Kgs 1:10);[257] of the major role fire plays in some of the judgments that accompany the trumpet blasts (Rev 8:6-11); and perhaps of the power ascribed to the mouth of the resurrected Jesus, the double-edged sword (1:16), with which he makes war (2:16).[258] Fire (11:5) is described as coming from the mouth, not mouths, of these two witnesses, which underscores their working in unison and their not being able to be identified separately from one another. The emerging description of these two prophetic witnesses suggests that they be understood as prophetic identical twins.[259] "And if any desire to harm them, in this manner it is necessary for them to die." The idea of divine necessity reiterates the fact that their protection is of divine origin.

---

254. Beale, *The Book of Revelation*, 573.

255. Waddell (*The Spirit of the Book of Revelation*, 176-77) aptly concludes, "As a priesthood of all believers, the church offers worship to God, but as a prophethood of all believers, the church bears the witness of God to the world."

256. Aune, *Revelation 6–16*, 613.

257. Beasley-Murray, *Revelation*, 184.

258. Sweet, *Revelation*, 185.

259. C. H. Giblin, "Revelation 11:1-13: Its Form, Function, and Textual Integration," *NTS* 30 (1984): 442.

The two prophetic witnesses also have prophetic authority in keeping with the authority exercised by some of Israel's most famous prophetic figures. Like Elijah, who caused a drought (1 Kgs 17:1), and Jesus, who shuts and no one can open (Rev 3:7), "these have the authority to shut the heaven in order that no rain would fall during the days of their prophecy." This extraordinary authority is present during the entire period of their prophetic witness. Their witness thus appears to take place during the entire time the nations trample the Holy Place (Rev 11:2). Like Moses, who struck the water in Egypt, causing it to turn into blood (Exod 7:17), and caused all kinds of plagues to fall upon Egypt (1 Sam 4:8), these prophetic witnesses "have authority over the waters to turn them into blood and to strike the earth with every plague as often as they desire." These two prophetic witnesses, who stand in continuity with the prophetic witness of the churches, are endowed with prophetic powers that appear to be the accumulation of all the prophets who have preceded them. In them, the prophetic anointing by the Spirit seems to be complete.

But the two witnesses' impenetrable invincibility has its limits. "And when they completed their witness, the beast, the one who comes up out of the Abyss, will make war against them and will overcome them and will kill them." Although their prophetic witness comes to an end, it does not end until their witness has been fully offered, has been completed. The witness and activity of the two witnesses mirrors that of Jesus, who completes the work of his Father on the cross, saying, "It is completed."[260] This similarity would be all the more significant in that Jesus' faithful witness is tied so closely to his own death in Revelation. The end of their prophetic witness thus does not come prematurely, but only when it has been completed. While this is the first mention of "the beast" in Revelation, the articular construction indicates that he is a well-known figure.[261] Perhaps this familiarity is based upon the resemblance this figure bears to the terrible, dreadful, exceedingly strong fourth beast of Dan 7:7-23, who made war with the saints and overcame them (7:21).[262] The modifying phrase "the one coming up out of the Abyss" indicates the place from which the beast comes, not the moment of his ascent from the Abyss.[263] The beast's activity is described in threefold form, with each verb appearing in the future tense, perhaps pointing to the beast's opposition to the one who stands behind their witness, as it "makes war against them and overcomes them and kills them." Significantly, when war imagery has previously appeared in Revelation,

---

260. Wall, *Revelation*, 145.
261. Resseguie, *The Revelation of John*, 163.
262. Prigent, *L'Apocalypse de Saint Jean*, 273.
263. Smalley, *Revelation*, 280.

it has been in connection with other figures that also come up out of the Abyss (Rev 9:7, 9). Yet, the hearers know of one capable of making war with the sword of his mouth (2:16). In 11:7 the making of war against the two witnesses by the beast is clarified by the second phrase in this trilogy, "and he will overcome them." Nowhere to this point in Revelation have the opponents of God's people been spoken of as overcoming. Only Jesus (3:21; 5:5) and those faithful to him (2:7, 11, 17, 26-28; 3:5, 12, 21) are so identified.[264] That the beast overcomes these two witnesses threatens to subvert the understanding of overcoming. The third part of the trilogy makes even clearer the nature of the beast's warring: "and he will kill them." This statement would remind hearers yet again of "my faithful witness Antipas," who was killed in Pergamum owing to his allegiance to Jesus. Although their witness is complete before their death, their death is intimately connected to their witness.

"And their body upon the streets of the great city lies." Proper burial was a right recognized nearly universally in antiquity. Its denial indicates an absolute disregard for decency and would convey utter disrespect and hatred for those so affected.[265] Here, it is an indication of the beast's hatred for and opposition to Jesus and his witnesses. Their corpses are spoken of in the singular ("their body"), reinforcing the singularly of their witness.[266] The location where these dreadful events take place is conveyed in almost kaleidoscopic[267] or psychedelic fashion, for the description of this great city changes before the eyes and ears of the hearers with each new detail. While the great city could be thought of as any great city of antiquity, in Revelation this designation will come to be identified more and more with Babylon (16:19; 17:18; 18:10, 16, 18-19, 21). If initially puzzled by mention of the great city, the hearers find immediate divine assistance offered for its interpretation in the words, "which is called pneumatically Sodom and Egypt, where also their Lord was crucified." The Greek text makes explicit the nature of this interpretative assistance. While the term πνευματικῶς (*pneumatikōs*, "pneumatically") is often translated "figuratively, metaphorically, symbolically," or even "spiritually," none of these translations are adequate, as they fail to bring out that this identification comes by means of the Spirit.[268]

---

264. The lone exception is the rider on the white horse in 6:2, who, as noted, bears a striking resemblance to Jesus.

265. Beasley-Murray, *Revelation*, 186.

266. Osborne, *Revelation*, 426 n. 9.

267. Koester, *Revelation and the End of All Things*, 110.

268. Waddell (*The Spirit of the Book of Revelation*, 183) notes, "In the center of the Apocalypse, John places the story of the two witnesses, and in the center of this brief narrative, John describes the spiritual insight of the church discerning the reality of the great city.... Like John, who was in the Spirit when he saw his visions, the church must also see Spiritually."

This city is called Sodom, in that it is a place of moral degradation,[269] one so filled with vice that normal standards of hospitality and decency are turned upside down, as the refusal of burial for the two witnesses indicates. It is also called Egypt, in that it too is a place of tyranny,[270] associated with slavery and oppression, as the making of war by the beast upon the two witnesses indicates. This great city is also "the place where their Lord was crucified." Though this phrase could be taken as a reference to the literal Jerusalem, such an interpretive conclusion appears to be a bit premature.[271] This reference is a clear indication that the two witnesses experienced the same fate as Jesus, perhaps suggesting that any city in which his faithful witnesses die is the same city in which he was crucified. The fact that Jesus is here called Lord for the first time in Revelation underscores this identification.[272] Just as this great city is the place where their Lord was crucified, so the great city will also be identified as the place in which "the blood of the prophets and the saints is found and of all those who have been slain upon the earth" (18:24).[273]

Apparently this city morphs into a globally diverse cosmopolitan center, for "some out of the peoples and tribes and tongues and nations see their body for three and one-half days." There is a striking similarity between the constituency of this city and "the peoples and nations and tongues and kings" to which John is earlier commissioned to prophesy (10:11), providing yet another link between the prophetic witness of these two witnesses and that of John. Individuals from all over the world see their body in the streets, which indicates something of the complete and absolute extent of their humiliation. But their humiliation has its limits, for their body will be exposed for only three and a half days. Perhaps more important, this period of time could not help but remind hearers of the length of time of Jesus' own death,[274] making clear that this time of humiliation is drawing to a close. The reason for the location of the witnesses' body in the streets of the great city is revealed in v. 9: for those who see them "would not allow their bodies (plural) to be placed into a tomb."

"The ones who dwell upon the earth will rejoice over them and will celebrate and will send gifts to one another, because of these two prophets who tormented the ones who dwell upon the earth." The chiastic structure of this verse places emphasis upon "the ones who dwell upon the earth," a phrase that identifies them as the opponents of God and his people (3:10; 6:10; 8:13). The ac-

---

269. Metzger, *Breaking the Code*, 70.
270. Caird, *The Revelation of Saint John*, 138.
271. Resseguie, *The Revelation of John*, 164.
272. Pattemore, *The People of God in the Apocalypse*, 164.
273. Kiddle, *The Revelation of St. John*, 185-86.
274. Bauckham, *The Climax of Prophecy*, 280.

tivities of these individuals are described in triple form. First, these individuals "will rejoice over them," perhaps a reminder of Jesus' words in John's gospel that, upon his departure, while his disciples mourn, "the world will rejoice" (John 16:20). The phrase "over them" makes clear that this rejoicing, like the denial of burial, will be at the expense of these witnesses. The second activity described, "and they will celebrate," underscores the disgraceful nature of their response. The third component in this trilogy of disgrace is that those who dwell upon the earth will be so overjoyed at the death of these two witnesses that they will actually mark this event as a festival, complete with the exchanging of gifts![275] All this rejoicing is owing to the death of "these two prophets who tormented those who dwell upon the earth." Though the prophetic nature of their witness has been inferred, here for the first time these two witnesses are called "prophets," confirming that their activity is Spirit-inspired prophetic witness. Their prophetic activity, like that of certain judgments before them (9:5), involved tormenting those to whom they prophesied, which likely refers to the whole of their prophetic activity.

After the three and a half days, "a Spirit of life out of God entered in them, and they stood upon their feet, and great fear fell upon those beholding them." Significantly, the Spirit who now enters the two prophets is the same Spirit who has inspired their prophetic activity. If the beast's opposition lasts beyond their life, so does the activity of the Spirit, in and through them. There thus is continuity with what has preceded in that this same Spirit, who stands before the throne, who speaks the words that Jesus speaks, in whom John experiences the visions of this book, who inspires prophetic witness, now enters into these two prophets. The Spirit's relationship to God is expressed in still another way: he is the Spirit "out of" God, having his origin in God, an idea familiar from John's gospel (John 14:17). Such language could hardly help but remind readers of Ezek 37:5 (LXX), where the identical phrase, "spirit of life," also occurs. Consequently, this Spirit, who has his origin in God, is now intimately connected with the activity of the resurrection of these two prophets. The certainty of the witnesses' resurrection is underscored by the words "they stood upon their feet," again identical to words that occur in Ezekiel (37:10). This extraordinary sight, the divine vindication and resurrection of the two prophets who experienced total and absolute humiliation, results in great fear falling upon those who behold this. What does such fear convey? Significantly, a similar fear was experienced by those who beheld Jesus walking on the water in John's gospel (6:19). The participle "those beholding" comes from a verb that in John's gospel is often associated with divine signs or activity (2:23; 4:19; 6:2, 19, 40; 12:45; 14:19;

---

275. Wall, *Revelation*, 147.

17:24; 20:14). That such a verbal form appears at this point in Revelation (11:11) suggests that this fear is experienced more positively. Later, there will be a clear equation drawn between those who fear God's name and those who worship him (11:18). This very equation comes to be stated more clearly as the book unfolds (14:7; 15:4; 19:5). It appears that the resurrection of these two prophets results in a reverential fear on the part of those who behold them and would not be taken in isolation from the rest of their Spirit-inspired prophetic ministry but as a further vindication of it and its completion.

"And they heard a great voice saying to them, 'Come up here.' And they went up to heaven in a cloud, and their enemies beheld them." Reminiscent of Rev 4:1, these two witnesses are themselves invited up to heaven. The similarity between these invitations would again point to the connection between John's own prophetic work and that of the two prophets. Though unidentified, this "great voice" is a heavenly voice, suggesting it is the divine voice. The invitation to "come up here" indicates that the mission of the two prophets is over and all that awaits them is the heavenly presence of God, joining the souls under the altar and the crowd coming out of the great tribulation. No sooner was the invitation voiced than they went up to heaven in a cloud. There is a striking parallel between the words of the resurrected Jesus that he will come with the clouds (1:7) and the witnesses going up in the cloud. Just as every eye will see Jesus, even those who have pierced him, so their enemies behold the two prophets being taken up into heaven! The parallel between Jesus' own experience of death, resurrection, and ascension and that of these two prophets indicates that the prophetic ministry of the church stands in direct solidarity with that of their Lord.

"And at that hour there was a great earthquake." That the great earthquake takes place at the very hour the two prophets ascend to heaven indicates a concrete connection between these events, suggesting that it is part of their vindication and their witness. When the sixth seal was loosed, a great earthquake occurs that was part of a cosmic cataclysm apparently designed to bring people to the worship of God (6:12). Instead of drawing human beings to God, however, all strata of humankind cried for the mountains and the rocks to fall upon them so that they might hide from the face of the one who sits on the throne and the wrath of the Lamb (6:16). Strikingly, whereas time has been measured in terms of 42 months, 1,260 days, and 3½ days, it is now measured in terms of one hour, an indication that time itself is speeding ahead toward the end. This great earthquake has the result that "a tenth of the city fell, and 7,000 men died in the earthquake." These two figures suggest the limited nature of this judgment, for in OT imagery one-tenth was equated with the remnant that survives God's judgment (Isa 6:13; Amos 5:3), while the number 7,000 is associated with the minority who are faithful to Yahweh (1 Kgs 19:18). In Rev 11:13 these numbers are reversed, with the remnant being identified with the majority, the 90 percent, the 63,000 who survive, with only the minority perishing.[276] "The rest were fearful and gave glory to the God of heaven." The level of fear experienced by these survivors is conveyed by the emphatic term "terrified," continuing the theme of fear introduced in v. 11. Here, fear is joined with giving glory, suggesting that the words fear, worship, giving glory, and repent function as synonyms in Revelation.[277] In this act, the rest join with others (4:9, 11; 5:12-13; 7:12) in giving glory to God. This remnant comes from the pagan world, which is made clear by the phrase "the God of heaven," a well-known Jewish expression used in communication with pagans.[278] The witness and vindication of the two prophetic witnesses thus result in the majority of those to whom they bore witness converting to the worship of the God (of Israel). This incredibly optimistic story could not help but encourage the hearers that, despite their circumstances, the conversion of the nations awaits them.[279]

Since the end of chapter 9 the hearers have expected the identification of the second woe, but the long interlude devoted to prophetic witness in 10:1–11:13 has postponed its identification. The words of 11:14, "the second woe has departed; behold the third woe comes quickly," thus serve to direct attention back to the events that accompany the blasting of the sixth trumpet, where one-third of humankind is killed by the three plagues of fire, smoke, and sulfur that issue forth from the mouths of the horses (9:13-21). But such judgments did not result in the conversion of those who survive, for "the rest of the men did not repent of the works of their hands" (9:20-21). The conversion of "the rest" awaits the completion of the witness of the two prophets. By the time the sixth trumpet is identified as the second woe, its memory has been softened by events that led to the conversion of the majority of those to whom the two prophets bore witness. Consequently, there is evidence that the woes themselves may be in the process of transformation. The announcement "behold, the third woe comes quickly" would thus fill the hearers with even greater expectancy. It is clear that the hearers would be anticipating the third and final woe, which at this point might be taken as a sign of the end itself. The hints as to the transformation of the second woe would create an expectancy that the third and final woe might be transformed in even a greater way. The words "comes quickly" would bring to mind the "I come quickly" of the resurrected Jesus, found on two earlier

---

276. Koester, *Revelation and the End of All Things*, 110-11.
277. Caird, *The Revelation of Saint John*, 140.
278. Aune, *Revelation 6–16*, 629.
279. Bauckham, *The Climax of Prophecy*, 283.

occasions both as threat (2:16) and as promise (3:11). Perhaps the hearers would perceive some connection between the soon coming of the third woe and the soon coming of Jesus himself!

The Sounding of the Seventh Trumpet (11:15-19)

At long last the seventh angel trumpeted. The blasting of this trumpet signals the advent of the third terrible woe and the end of all things. In addition, "There were great voices in heaven saying, 'The kingdom of this world has become the kingdom of our Lord and his Christ, and he will reign forever and ever.'" This radical divergence from the pattern of the previous trumpet blast indicates that the woes themselves are indeed being transformed, with the third woe transformed into the end itself, with the praise of God and the Lamb forming the scene's center. For the first and only time in Revelation, mention is made of great voices in heaven speaking,[280] which would remind hearers of the many great voices in heaven encountered previously heard in the praise of God and the Lamb (5:11-12; 7:10; 11:12). It is no surprise, then, that what comes from these great voices is yet another hymn of praise. The primary focus of this hymn is revealed by the subject of the first phrase and the verb of the second, each coming from the same Greek root, βασιλεία (*basileia*, "kingdom") and βασιλεύσει (*basileusei*, "will reign"), respectively. This emphasis might best be conveyed by the translation, "The reign of this world has become the reign of our Lord and his Christ, and he will reign forever and ever." Mention of "the kingdom of this world" would likely remind readers of Jesus' words in John's gospel, which make it clear that his kingdom is not of this world (John 18:36), a world that has its own ruler (14:30), who has already been judged (16:11). That "the kingdom of this world," which has stood in such opposition to God and the Lamb throughout Revelation, "has become the kingdom of our Lord and his Christ" conveys a sense of finality, implying a fundamental transformation of "the kingdom of this world." Specifically, those who formerly owed their allegiance to the world now identify with "our Lord and his Christ." This transformation is likely connected to the witness of the two prophets, whose life, death, resurrection, and ascension result in the conversion of the majority that survive the great earthquake.[281] Through their Spirit-anointed witness, "the kingdom of this world has become the kingdom of our Lord and his Christ."

---

280. Smalley, *Revelation*, 289.
281. M. L. Archer, "'And the Seventh Angel Trumpeted': A Literary Analysis of Revelation 11:15-19" (Th.M. thesis, Columbia Theological Seminary, 2006), ch. 4.

The nature of this transformation is conveyed by the latter kingdom's having no temporal limitations, for "he will reign forever and ever"! The verb "reign" is a third person singular. While such a construction might cause the hearers to wonder whether this verb refers to the activity of God or that of Christ, they will soon discover that Revelation emphasizes the singularity of God and Jesus. This understanding becomes apparent in a couple of different ways. They are never the subjects of a plural verb, nor are plural pronouns used with reference to them.[282] This manner of reference appears for one of the first times with reference to the phrase "and he will reign forever and ever." It appears that the Greek grammar is not sufficient to convey the theological reality of the identity of God and Jesus.

In keeping with their previous activity (4:10; 5:8, 14; 7:11) the twenty-four elders once again "fell upon their faces and worshipped God." Their appearance and activity is reminiscent of their presence and activity around the throne in chapters 4 and 5, and the similarities between their hymn found in 11:16-18 and those found in Rev 4–5 abound, suggesting that their mention serves as an inclusio of sorts.[283] Their appearance in 11:16 also brings to mind the elders' heavenly appearance in 7:11, where they join with the angels and the four living creatures in offering hymnic praise to God (7:12). From the elders comes yet another hymn of praise that, along with its predecessor (11:15), focuses almost exclusively upon the finality of God's accomplishments.

The hymn from the twenty-four elders reveals a three-part structure. The only hymn of thanksgiving in Revelation,[284] the twenty-four elders say, "We thank you, Lord, God, the All Powerful One, the one who is and the one who was, because you have taken your great power and reigned." The words of the twenty-four elders bring to mind the throne-room scene (4:8), where the four living creatures address the one who sits on the throne as "Lord, God, the All Powerful One, the one who is and the one who was and the one who comes." Such similarities provide a sense of continuity — the same God addressed in chapter 4 is now addressed as the one who rules. On this occasion, however, the threefold phrase "the one who is and the one who was and the one who comes" (1:4, 8; 4:8) stands as a twofold phrase. God is now referred to simply as "the one who is and the one who was." He is no longer "the one who comes" — for he has already come![285] The words of the hymn (v. 15) thus treat God's reign as a present reality. The reason for the elders' thanksgiving is made clear: "because

---

282. Bauckham, *The Climax of Prophecy*, 139-40.
283. Michaels, *Revelation*, 144.
284. Archer, "And the Seventh Angel Trumpeted," ch. 4.
285. Murphy, *Fallen Is Babylon*, 271.

you have taken your great power and have reigned." Familiar with God's power from 4:11 and 7:12, we now learn that God's "great power" has been taken up by him and manifested in his rule, suggesting that, with his great power, God has begun to reign in a way not yet seen.

The hymn's second stanza turns to the nations: they "were enraged, and your rage has come." The wrath of the nations is met by the wrath of God. For when the nations ὠργίσθησαν (ōrgisthēsan, "were enraged"), God's ὀργή (orgē, "rage" or "wrath") came. In Revelation this verb is used only with reference to the nations (11:18) and the dragon (12:17), while the noun is reserved for the Lamb (6:16) and/or God (6:17; 14:10; 16:19; 19:15). The nations' enragement refers to their (sometimes violent) opposition to God, exemplified in the martyrdom of the two witnesses, and the rage or wrath of God refers to the judgments inflicted upon those who oppose him, exemplified in the earthquake that results in the conversion of those who survive.

The next words of the hymn continue the thought of the second stanza, while providing the transition to the third: "and the time to judge the dead (has come)." The connection between the second stanza and this phrase is their both sharing the same verb, "has come," which is present in the previous phrase and implied in this one, while "the time to judge the dead" is a comprehensive phrase encompassing both the giving of rewards to God's servants and the destroying of those who destroy the earth. For this is a time "to give the reward to your servants the prophets and to the saints and to those who fear your name." Clearly, the giving of "the reward" is a positive activity owing to the identity of those who are to receive it. Though this is the first mention of "the reward" in Revelation, it is known in the Johannine world. Jesus speaks of the reward that awaits those who enter into the missionary harvest (John 4:36), while the Elder warns his readers not to lose that for which they have been working but to receive a full reward (2 John 8). The relationship between "work" and "reward" seems very close in Revelation, suggesting that the understanding of "reward" in 11:18 would be informed by the many places where reference has been made to works earlier in the book, especially Rev 2:23, where the resurrected Jesus promises, "I will give to each of you according to your works." As such, works and that which is given are closely associated with the one who overcomes (2:26), suggesting that in 11:18 "the reward" is a comprehensive term referring to all those things promised to those who overcome.[286] Those to be rewarded are "your servants the prophets and the saints and those who fear your name." The

---

286. Aune, *Revelation 6-16*, 644-45. Revelation studies still await the kind of careful treatment on this topic that Matthean studies have received. Cf. B. B. Charette, *The Theme of Recompense in Matthew's Gospel* (JSNTS 79; Sheffield: JSOT Press, 1992).

connection between servant and prophet is revealed not only in the phrase "to my servants the prophets" but also in John's own person, as he is both servant (1:1) and one who prophesies (10:11). These terms serve very much as synonyms in Revelation, suggesting that, on this occasion, they would be a comprehensive reference to the believing, witnessing, prophetic community to whom this book is addressed.[287] The comprehensive nature of these terms is underscored by the next words, for though they appear to stand in continuity with what precedes, there is also a certain discontinuity. While the phrase "the small and the great" refers to those on either end of the social scale, from the insignificant to the mighty,[288] unlike the words that precede them, these words appear in the accusative case rather than the dative case. This change of case indicates that the "judging of the dead" will not be exhausted by the giving of the reward to "your servants," for the change introduces yet another group of individuals to be judged. Specifically, it is time "to destroy those who destroy the earth." Significantly, "those who destroy" stands in the accusative case, suggesting that, just as the giving of the reward encompasses the insignificant to the mighty, so the destroying of those who destroy the earth will as well. The nature of this destruction is revealed in part by the play on words between the compound verb διαφθεῖραι (*diaphtheirai*, "to destroy") and the object τοὺς διαφθείροντας (*tous diaphtheirontas*, "those who destroy"), indicating that the judgment rendered would be appropriate to the crime. Such a phrase would remind hearers of the numerous OT texts (e.g., Exod 21:24; Lev 24:20; Deut 19:21; Judg 1:7; 15:11; Ps 7:14-16) where the *lex talionis* appears to be referenced.[289] The judging of the dead (genitive) thus includes both those who are worthy of the reward (dative) and those who will be destroyed (accusative).[290]

The long-awaited and long-promised end of all things now arrives. "The temple of God in heaven was opened, and his ark of the covenant was seen in the temple, and there came lightnings and voices and thunders and an earthquake and great hail." Reference to God's temple reminds hearers of its occurrence in 11:1-2, forming an inclusio, indicating that the narrative of the two prophetic witnesses is enveloped by references to the temple and consequently stand together in some way.[291] Significantly, all the activity in this verse comes from God or is made possible by him, as the divine passives "was opened" and "was seen" reveal. God's activity is further underscored in that this temple

287. Smalley, *Revelation*, 292.
288. Smalley, *Revelation*, 293.
289. Murphy, *Fallen Is Babylon*, 271.
290. I am indebted to my colleague L. R. Martin for this insight.
291. Archer, "'And the Seventh Angel Trumpeted': A Literary Analysis of Revelation 11:15-19," ch. 4.

belongs to him, noted twice, as does the ark of the covenant, conveying the idea of God's presence reminiscent of the throne-room scene of chapter 4. The eschatological significance of the opening of God's temple and the revelation of his ark of the covenant make it difficult to imagine how God's presence could be more directly described. Grammatically, the phrase "his ark of the covenant" can be rendered as placing emphasis either on "his" ark or on "his" covenant. It is not likely, however, that the hearers would worry about choosing between these distinct meanings. Here a great deal of emphasis is placed upon both the temple and the ark being God's; this broader section (4:1–11:19) begins and ends with reference to God and his covenant faithfulness. The ark is clearly a sign of such faithfulness in 11:19, just as the rainbow around the throne is a sign of his covenant in 4:3. The theophanic elements, first observed in the throne-room scene (4:5) and again in intensified form at the end of the opening of the seven seals (8:5), reappear (11:19) with ever-increasing intensity. Their appearance here conveys something of God's very presence and signals the end of the seven trumpet blasts. The theophanic elements, described in the same order as in 4:5, form an inclusio. The increasing intensity represented by the presence of great hail is yet another sign of progression throughout the book and the nearness of the end. The hearers thus find themselves in the very presence of God as the end of all things has come. And yet . . .

The Struggle of God's People in Cosmic Perspective (12:1–14:20)

. . . the book continues! The next major subsection forms an interlude of sorts, telling the story of redemptive history in cosmic perspective. Characters and themes introduced earlier reappear in this section in much greater detail. The passage begins with a "great sign in heaven" (12:1) and is followed immediately by a "great sign in heaven" (15:1). This is followed by the book's last cycle of seven, when the angel having seven bowls of plagues appears and then pours out their contents in turn (15:1–16:21). Strikingly, the story line that leaves off in 11:19 converges in 15:1 with that found in 12:1–14:20.

Signs in Heaven: The Woman Clothed with the Sun, and the Red Dragon (12:1–13:1a)

"And a great sign was seen in heaven." Johannine hearers would be aware of the significance of signs from their place of prominence in John's gospel, where they point beyond themselves to a more profound understanding of their signifi-

The Struggle of God's People in Cosmic Perspective (12:1–14:20)

cance, and come only from the hand of Jesus. The appearance of "a great sign in heaven" would remind readers of the pregnant nature of signs in John's gospel and perhaps suggest that this sign too is somehow connected to Jesus. At least two aspects of this phrase provide points of continuity with that which immediately precedes. The term translated "was seen" would bring to mind the first appearance of this specific form just one verse previous, where "the ark of his covenant in his temple" was seen (11:19). That this great sign is seen in heaven would remind hearers of this previous verse as well, for heaven is apparently the location of God's ark. The appearance of the word "sign" would perhaps remind them that the transmission of the divine revelation experienced by John is described at the beginning of the book with the word ἐσήμανεν (esēmanen, "he showed"), which carries with it the idea of indicating the meaning of prophetic (Acts 11:28) and/or metaphoric (John 12:33; 18:32; 21:19) language. Thus, when readers of Revelation finally encounter a "great sign," they are prepared for its meaning having a significance that transcends a literal or surface meaning.

John sees "a woman clothed with the sun, and the moon is under her feet, and upon her head a crown of twelve stars, and having in the womb, and she cried (out), being in travail and torment to give birth." This woman would likely be compared to the only other woman and the only other gigantic figure to appear to this point in the book. In comparison to Jezebel (Rev 2:20-23), this woman is a picture of cosmic royalty, power, and promise. In comparison to the angel who stands with one foot on the sea and one foot on the earth (10:1-2), the woman clothed with the sun dwarfs him both in size and in significance. The cosmic brilliance of this woman is indicated in that she is clothed with the sun, conveying a sense of magnificent radiance. Her location in heaven underscores her close proximity to God himself. The moon under her feet conveys a sense of majesty and dominion. Significantly, the moon, an apparent object of idolatrous worship for many in the OT (Deut 4:19; 17:3; 2 Kgs 23:5; Job 31:26; Jer 8:2), is firmly under the feet of this spectacular woman. The "crown" upon her head, which contains twelve stars, serves to underscore her extraordinary faithfulness (Rev 2:10; 3:11; 4:4, 10). While the twelve stars might represent the signs of the Zodiac,[292] they more likely stand for the twelve tribes of the sons of the reconstituted Israel (7:4-8). These tribes are extraordinarily important, as 12,000 out of each tribe are sealed at God's command. The twelve tribes are so theologically important that their names will be inscribed on the twelve gates of the New Jerusalem (21:12-13). The equation between twelve stars and the twelve tribes is made already in Gen 37:9, where in Joseph's dream the twelve stars clearly refer to the sons of Jacob, from whom the twelve

---

292. So Murphy, *Fallen Is Babylon*, 278, and Aune, *Revelation 6–16*, 681 among others.

tribes come.²⁹³ The emerging picture of this resplendent woman is thus one that ties her very closely to Israel and/or Zion.²⁹⁴

She is pregnant, crying out in pain, laboring to give birth. Her pregnancy would convey a sense of life and hope, generating a great expectancy as to the nature of the child to be born. Such a child must have a special connection to heaven, and perhaps a special connection with God himself! The agony of the childbirth would call to mind the words spoken to Eve regarding the pain of childbearing (Gen 3:16), perhaps suggesting that the child here described (Rev 12:2) is the fulfillment of the words spoken to Eve about her child of promise (Gen 3:15). These words are also reminiscent of those spoken to Israel and/or Zion in Isaiah (26:16-17; 54:1; 66:7-9) or in Micah (4:9-10). In crying out, this woman joins a number of other positive figures who also "cry out" (Rev 6:10; 7:2, 10; 10:3). In addition to her cries, she is laboring greatly to give birth. Her ordeal bears the marks of torment as she agonizes to give birth to this child; the word used here to describe her agony has already been encountered, referring to intense physical (9:5) and emotional (11:10) torment.

Alongside the great sign of the woman clothed with the sun is "another sign in heaven," although this one is not referred to as a "great" sign, perhaps suggesting its inferiority to the first sign. However, it does describe a "great" figure: "and behold a great red dragon having seven heads and ten horns and upon his heads seven diadems, and his tail swept the third of the stars of heaven and cast them upon the earth." The first sign conveys a sense of awe, the second a sense of ominous dread! We are hereby introduced to a remarkable figure. In the OT the term "dragon" refers to many of the opponents of God and his people, including Nebuchadnezzar (Jer 51:34), Pharaoh (Ezek 29:3; 32:3-16), Egypt (Ps 74:14), and Assyria and Babylon (Isa 27:1), perhaps here suggesting the archetypal enemy of God. This color would remind readers of the rider upon the red horse, who was given authority to take peace from the earth in order that individuals might slaughter one another. Ominously, this rider is given a great sword (6:4), suggesting that this dragon is a sinister figure²⁹⁵ capable of murderous activity.²⁹⁶ The magnitude of the dragon's importance is conveyed by the word "great," a term often encountered in Revelation to distinguish the importance of one thing or event from others of the same kind, as in a great sword (6:4), earthquake (6:12-13; 11:13), day of wrath (6:17), tribulation (7:14), mountain of fire (8:8), star (8:10), furnace (9:2), the Euphrates (9:14), the city

---

293. Prigent, *L'Apocalypse de Saint Jean*, 287.

294. Beale, *The Book of Revelation*, 626.

295. C. Hauret, "Ève transfigurée: De la Genèse à l'Apocalypse," *Revue d'histoire et de philosophie religieuses* 59 (1979): 330.

296. Allo, *Saint Jean: L'Apocalypse*, 159.

The Struggle of God's People in Cosmic Perspective (12:1–14:20)

(11:8), fear (11:11), and hail (11:19). The description "great red dragon" thus underscores the enormity of this dragon over against all others, its great nature made clear in that he has "seven heads and ten horns and upon his heads seven diadems." His seven heads indicate that his rule is perceived as complete and universal.[297] His ten horns, reminiscent of those of the fourth beast in Dan 7:7, would convey his extraordinary strength and power. In contrast to the woman clothed with the sun, whose crown contained twelve stars, the dragon has seven diadems. The diadem was widely recognized as the sign of royalty, especially among the Persian kings. The wearing of the seven diadems thus corresponds to the number of the dragon's heads, seven, indicating once again the complete and universal nature of the dragon's rule. Although we may think to identify the dragon's kingdoms based upon the number of his heads and horns,[298] perhaps the immediate impact of these details would focus attention upon the brief pageantry of human history that these details embody.[299]

"His tail swept the third of the stars of heaven and cast them upon the earth." These words bring to mind the dragon's cosmic nature, who, like the woman clothed with the sun, is located in heaven. The power of his tail is reminiscent of the power of the tails of the creatures that come forth during the blasting of the fifth and sixth trumpets (Rev 9:10, 19). In 12:4 the tail is clearly a sign of the dragon's great and terrible power. Going beyond the little horn of Dan 8:10, the dragon's tail of Revelation sweeps a third of the stars of heaven and casts them to the earth. The power of the great red dragon is limited in nature, however, for he does not sweep away all the stars, just a third of them. This ominous figure "stood before the woman who was about to give birth, in order that, when she gave birth, he might devour her child." We see clearly his sinister and murderous intentions, as he prepares himself to devour the child immediately upon delivery, reminding hearers of Jesus' words about the devil, who is described as a murderer from the beginning (John 8:44). The dragon would also remind hearers of the prophetic words of Gen 3:15-16 spoken to Eve with regard to the enmity she and her seed will experience with the serpent. "He will bruise your head, you will bruise his heel." The term δράκων (*drakōn*, "dragon" or "serpent"), often used in the LXX to translate "serpent," would underscore the connection with Gen 3:15-16. The intention of the great red dragon that he might "consume" or "devour" the child is amazingly similar to the actions of King Nebuchadnezzar, who "devoured" Zion, swallowing her like a "dragon"

---

297. Gause (*Revelation*, 164) makes the intriguing suggestion that, as well as designating completion, this number may hint that his kingdoms have run their course.

298. As, for example, did Joachim and countless others after him; cf. esp. Kovacs and Rowland, *Revelation*, 140-42.

299. Gause, *Revelation*, 164.

or "serpent" (Jer 51:34 [28:34 LXX]).[300] The connection between Judah and this child and Nebuchadnezzar and the dragon could thus hardly be clearer.

The words that she "bore a son, a male child, who is about to shepherd all the nations with a rod of iron" describe the rapidity of the child's birth and reveal the child as both a "son" and a "male child." To this point in the Johannine literature the term υἱός (*huios*, "son") is used exclusively for Jesus, while believers are called "children." The description of the child here as son could thus be grounds for concluding that this use of "son" is none other than Jesus, the unique Son of God. Such an identification fits nicely with the heavenly origin of this child, born of the woman clothed with the sun. While the occurrence of the term ἄρσην (*arsēn*, "male child") could be taken as unnecessary redundancy, owing to the etymological meaning of the term as something like "that which discharges sperm,"[301] its appearance here may be an additional reference to the enmity between the seed of the serpent and the seed of Eve in Gen 3:16 — in particular, this male child is the very seed who will bruise the head of the serpent. This term may also remind readers of Isa 66:7, where it is used with reference to the unrealistically quick delivery there described. This double reference to the child would quite naturally underscore his importance, placing unusual emphasis upon his birth. The further identification as the one "who is about to shepherd all nations with a rod of iron" is reminiscent of the promise of the resurrected Jesus to those who overcome in Rev 2:27; it may be an implicit continuation of the idea that this seed will bruise the head of the serpent. Despite the woman clothed with the sun experiencing the vulnerability of pregnancy, combined with the menacing presence of the great red dragon, she courageously gives birth to this son in the very face of the dragon[302] and his hostile intents. As the identity of the child becomes clearer, it slowly begins to be revealed that this woman, who bore such a striking resemblance to Eve and Israel/Zion, the mother of the Messiah, has morphed into the mother of Jesus. Such a discovery would be of special significance for Johannine hearers, owing to the strategic role the mother of Jesus plays in John's gospel. Though she is never named there, referred to simply as the mother of Jesus, she is present near the beginning of Jesus' ministry, being a catalyst in the performance of his first sign (2:1-12), and found near the gospel's end at the foot of the cross (19:25-27). It is as though, in the emerging image of the woman clothed with the sun, the promises regarding the messianic seed given to Eve, Israel, and Mary all converge.

---

300. Prigent, *L'Apocalypse de Saint Jean*, 296.

301. J. B. Bauer, "Ἄρσην," *EDNT*, 1:158.

302. J. A. Schroder, "Revelation 12: Female Figures and Figures of Evil," *Word and Witness* 15 (1995): 181.

The Struggle of God's People in Cosmic Perspective (12:1–14:20)

"And her child was snatched up to God and to his throne." The location of the events described have shifted from heaven to earth, and now the child is described as being snatched up to God and his throne. The cosmic events described in heaven in the first few verses of chapter 12 are thus not without significance upon earth. Rather, there is a symbiotic connection between the events described in the heavens and those that take place on earth. While God and his throne technically are the objects to which the child is snatched, the passive voice verb "was snatched up" indicates that God is the one who snatches up the child. The activity of God here stands in stark contrast to other negative examples of snatching in John's gospel (6:15; 10:12, 28-29). While the depiction of the snatching up of "her child" immediately after his birth might be taken to suggest Jesus is seen here simply as a passive infant Messiah, such an interpretation ultimately fails to convince. Outside of this chapter there is no interest in the infancy of Jesus in the whole of the Johannine literature. To insist that the image here described must focus exclusively on the infancy of Jesus, to the exclusion of the rest of his life and ministry, would appear to be overly restrictive. Neither is the depiction of Jesus' life and ministry as a single moment out of keeping with John's gospel. John 1:14 describes Jesus' life and ministry in precisely this way. Given the way in which the mother of Jesus frames his entire ministry in John's gospel, the reference to "her child" in Rev 12:5 might well signal Jesus' entire life and ministry in the single moment here described. The depiction of the child being snatched up to God and his throne would also bring to mind the promise of the resurrected Jesus to those who overcome, that they will sit with him on his throne, just as he has overcome and sits with the Father on his throne (3:21)! The description of the snatching up of the child would thus likely be understood to encompass the entire life, ministry, death, and resurrection of Jesus.[303] Unlike John, who was successful in devouring the book (10:9-10), and the fire from the mouths of the two witnesses, which was successful in devouring those who oppose them (11:5), the great red dragon is unsuccessful in his attempt to devour the child.

"And the woman fled into the wilderness, where she has there a place having been prepared from God, in order that there they might nourish her 1,260 days." Her activity once again indicates the close connection that exists between this woman and Israel, whose own time in the wilderness and her divine provisions would be well known. The woman clothed with the sun, who has shown remarkable similarities to Eve, Israel, and the mother of Jesus, now shows remarkable similarities to the transformed Israel, the church to which John writes. The divine activity present in the lives of Eve, Israel, and the mother

---

303. Beale, *The Book of Revelation*, 639.

of Jesus finds its fulfillment or culmination in the church. Her actions reveal that she is an active participant in the events described, not a passive observer, and indicates that the events depicted on the cosmic stage in Rev 12 are related symbiotically to those that take place on earth. Mention of the woman's flight into the wilderness immediately conveys that her time there will be one of provision and protection, especially the words "where she has there a place having been prepared from God." Throughout John's gospel, the wilderness functions as a place of witness (John 1:23), salvific healing (3:14), provision (6:31, 49), and protection (11:54).[304] The perfect participle "having been prepared" suggests that the place had been prepared by God at some point in the past for this very time, an idea found earlier in Revelation, where both locusts (9:7) and angels (9:15) have been prepared for specific tasks at specific times. In the divine preparation of this place, it becomes clear that God is active, not only in the snatching up of the male child, but also in the life of the woman. The purpose of the woman's fleeing is made clear as v. 6 concludes, "in order that there they might nourish her for 1,260 days." As Israel before her, this woman is to receive nourishment while in the wilderness. While the verb τρέφωσιν (*trephōsin*, "they might nourish") might be translated as "he might nourish" owing to the indefinite character of the construction,[305] making clear the divine origin of the nourishment, here (12:13-17), where a variety of creatures and creation itself are involved in ministering to this woman, the third person plural form of the verb in v. 6 might anticipate that which is to follow. Interestingly, this same word appears in the LXX version of 1 Kgs 18:13 to describe the divine provisions of bread and water made for Elijah.[306] Significantly, the woman will be nourished in the wilderness for 1,260 days, the exact length of time the two witnesses will prophesy before a hostile world (11:3). If there is reason to think that the woman clothed with the sun has morphed into the church at this point, this chronological detail confirms such pneumatic discernment.

"And there was war in heaven, Michael and his angels made war against the dragon." The discovery of a war in heaven is no doubt startling, in that God's sovereignty in heaven to this point has been absolutely certain. What would account for such a war? Perhaps it is the result of the male child having been snatched up to God, with the great red dragon having gone up to heaven to make war against him there, since the dragon's intentions to consume the child have been frustrated by God himself. If the hearers expect a war between the

---

304. In John 11:54 Jesus no longer walks openly among the Jews but departs for the country near the wilderness.

305. Aune, *Revelation 6–16*, 653.

306. Smalley, *Revelation*, 321.

dragon and the one who is prepared to make war on the church in Pergamum with the double-edged sword in his mouth (2:16), they are disappointed. If this war is deemed to be an attack by the dragon on the male child, the dragon, despite his cosmic strength, does not even merit the attention of the male child, but that of Michael and his angels. The mention of Michael would both draw attention to his close relationship with God, as one who stands with him and fights (Dan 10:21), and point attention toward the people of God, as Michael was widely regarded as the protector of Israel, God's people (Dan 10:13; 12:1).[307] Though Michael is not called an angel in Rev 12:7, angels are attributed to him, which indicates that he is an authoritative figure who would likely be understood as warring on behalf of God (and the male child) and on behalf of God's people. But what is the nature of this war, and how is it to be understood? Its results, described in 12:8-12, suggest that it encompasses the whole of redemptive history as one moment. Both Michael and his angels wage war upon the dragon, and "the dragon and his angels warred" as well. Yet, despite the troubling picture of a war in heaven, its outcome is never in doubt. Michael and his angels are introduced first, perhaps indicating their superior position, and when the dragon and his angels are introduced as making war, it is immediately observed that "he was not strong (enough), nor was their place found any longer in heaven." The dragon οὐκ ἴσχυσεν (*ouk ischysen*, "was not strong" or "was not mighty"), which suggests a contrast between the dragon and the Lamb (5:12) and God (7:12), to whom ἰσχύς (*ischys*, "strength" or "might") is ascribed. There is also a contrast between the dragon, who is not strong (enough), and the two ἰσχυρός (*ischyros*, "strong" or "mighty") angels encountered earlier (5:2; 10:1). Not only does the war with Michael reveal that the dragon is not strong enough to contend with him, but also that the place he and his angels formerly had in heaven has been lost, the phrase "nor was their place found any longer in heaven" suggesting that their place has all but been forgotten, owing to the war fought and lost with Michael. If the great red dragon was "another sign in heaven" (v. 3), his locale is no longer heaven, for he has no place there any longer.

"And he was cast down, the great dragon, the ancient serpent, the one called Devil and Satan, the one who deceives the whole inhabited world; he was cast down to the earth, and his angels were cast down with him." The word translated "cast down," the only indicative verb occurring in this verse, appears not once but three times. In the Greek text it occurs just before "the great dragon" and just after "the one who deceives the whole inhabited world," as an inclusio around the dragon's names, emphasizing his nature as cast down. Such language perhaps reminds readers of the words of Jesus in John 12:31,

---

307. Koester, *Revelation and the End of All Things*, 120.

"In the Spirit in Heaven" (4:1–16:21)

"Now is judgment of this world, now the ruler of this world has been cast out," and those found in 16:11, "For the ruler of this world has been judged." All these details suggest that, in the events here described, reference is being made to the implications of the salvific work of the Lamb.[308] The passive form of the verb "was cast down" indicates that the casting down of the dragon is from start to finish divine action.[309] Significantly, within this context of the dragon's humiliating defeat, his full identity is revealed, for a somewhat comprehensive listing of his names and titles occurs. Mention of the great dragon at the beginning of the list provides continuity in that the figure earlier described is identical to the one now mentioned. "The ancient serpent" would remind hearers of the Genesis story where the serpent tempts Adam and Eve (Gen 3:1-7). The correlation between the dragon's intention to devour the woman's child at birth and the enmity between the serpent and Eve's seed would be clear. From of old, he is the ancient serpent, the liar, and the murderer. He is also "called Devil and Satan, the one who deceives the whole inhabited world." The phrase "the one called" brings to mind the most recent occurrence of the word "called" (Rev 11:8), where the great city "is called pneumatically Sodom and Egypt." Perhaps these titles are pneumatically discerned as well. The devil is known as a murderer from the beginning and as one of whom it is said that lying is his native tongue (John 8:44). "The one who commits sin is of the devil, for the devil sins from the beginning" (1 John 3:8). The antipathy between the Son of God and the devil is made clear in that the former was manifested in order that he might destroy the works of the latter (1 John 3:8). In Rev 2:10 the resurrected Jesus tells the church in Smyrna, "Behold, the devil is about to cast some of you into prison in order that he might test you. Be faithful unto death, and I will give you the crown of life." In 12:9 the devil, who poses a threat to the church, and the great red dragon are found to be identical. Consequently, when the church is "faithful unto death," it too is understood to be withstanding the onslaught of the dragon. In John's gospel Satan entered Judas just before this disciple goes out into the night (John 13:27). In Revelation this sinister figure is associated with Jewish opposition to the church, the synagogue of Satan (Rev 2:9; 3:9), the powerful presence of Satan (2:13), and the ominous nature of his "deep things" (2:24). The final title in this series, "the one who deceives the whole inhabited world," reminds hearers of those who deceive themselves (John 7:47; 1 John 1:8) or others (John 7:12; 1 John 2:26; 3:7). The lone appearance of this term in Revelation to this point (Rev 2:20) refers to the false prophetess (called "Jezebel" by Jesus), who "teaches and deceives my servants to commit

---

308. Bauckham, *The Climax of Prophecy*, 186.
309. Aune, *Revelation 6–16*, 695.

The Struggle of God's People in Cosmic Perspective (12:1–14:20)

sexual immorality and to eat food sacrificed to idols." Remarkably, the verb "deceive" is used exclusively, in Johannine thought, to describe human agents who deceive themselves or others, as is the noun "deceiver" (2 John 7). While 1 John 4:6 reveals the connection between "the spirit of deception" and those who do not confess Jesus, here, for the first time, it becomes clear that the agent of deception par excellence is the great dragon. When the churches oppose deception, they oppose the great dragon himself. This impressive cacophony of titles and names could well be overwhelming. Yet, this very creature, this very opponent has been described as being cast down, and he is now described as being "cast down to the earth." Here, for the first time, the dragon is described as being present on the earth. From this point forward, he will be thought of as "cast down" whenever his names or titles appear! In addition, those over whom he exercises authority, his angels, are also cast down to earth. To stand with the dragon is to be cast down; there is no future for them with the dragon.

"And I heard a great voice in heaven saying. . . ." The most recent encounter with "great voices" in heaven, which introduce a hymn of praise and celebration (11:15), is remarkably similar to what is found in 12:10. Its words reveal that in some ways the hymn of 12:10-12 expands upon that found in 11:15: "Now have come the salvation and the power and the kingdom of our God and the authority of his Christ." There is a convergence here of significant terms, themes, and emphases found at various places to this point throughout the book, including 11:15. Like its first occurrence (7:10), the attribution of salvation to God in praise conveys a sense of finality, focusing upon salvation in its most comprehensive, eschatological sense. That the entire hymn begins (12:10) with "now" further underscores this sense of finality. Both God (4:11; 7:12; 11:17) and the Lamb (5:12) receive the attribution of power in praise in Revelation. The third element in this trilogy of praise, "the kingdom of our God," provides a direct link back to 11:15, where "the kingdom of the world has become the kingdom of our Lord." The close connection that exists between "the kingdom of God" and the Johannine believers would be explicit, for they are "a kingdom of priests" to God (1:6; 5:10). Just as in 11:15, where the words "and of his Christ" closely follow "the kingdom of the world has become the kingdom of our Lord," so here the words "the salvation and the power and the kingdom of our God" are closely followed by "and the authority of his Christ." This statement underscores the intimate relationship between God and his Christ by placing them in close proximity to one another and by making clear that the authority of his Christ is authority derived from God, for he is again described as "his Christ" and is attributed authority in relationship to salvation, power, and the kingdom.

"Because the accuser of our brothers has been cast down, the one who accuses them before our God day and night." There appears to be a close connection between the coming of salvation, power, and the kingdom of our God and the casting down of the great red dragon, for these words are introduced by the word "because."[310] Here, the great red dragon and the accuser of the brothers are the same. In contrast to the four living creatures, who praise God day and night with the hymn recorded in Rev 4:8 ("Holy, holy, holy..."), and those coming out of the great tribulation, who serve God day and night (7:15), this individual is before our God accusing the brothers day and night (12:10). Yet, his continual work of accusation has come to an end. He has been cast down from heaven; his days of accusations in heaven are over!

"And they overcame him on account of the blood of the Lamb and on account of the word of their witness, and they did not love their life unto death." The antecedent of "they" is "the brothers," making it clear that those who have overcome are the very ones whom the accuser has constantly accused before God. But whereas the accuser of the brothers has been cast down to earth, these individuals have overcome him. There could be little doubt that the individuals described in 12:11 are heirs to the promises given by the resurrected Jesus to those who overcome in Rev 2:7, 11, 17, 26-28; 3:5, 12, 21. Here, it becomes even clearer that the one with whom the seven churches contend in chapters 2 and 3 is none other than "the accuser of our brothers, the great dragon, the ancient serpent, the one called Devil and Satan, the deceiver of the whole inhabited world." Yet, this formidable foe has been overcome! The hymn attributes their having overcome to two sources, indicated by the appearance of the double "on account of," which precedes both "the blood of the Lamb" and "the word of their testimony." First, the victory of their brothers is made possible by the "blood of the Lamb" (1:5; 5:9; 7:14). The relationship between the blood of the Lamb and the kingdom of priests is clear, as is the fact that the blood of the Lamb makes the overcoming possible. His blood looses sin, purchases men and women, and makes white! There could be no overcoming without the blood of the one who himself overcame (3:21). Second, the hymn also attributes their overcoming the accuser to "the word of their testimony." Such a statement would evoke a matrix of imagery, for the hearers have previously learned of the close relationship that exists between faithful witness and Jesus (1:5; 3:14), faithful witness and death (1:5; 2:13; 3:14; 6:9; 11:9), and John's witness, the word of God and the witness of Jesus (1:2, 9). That these conquerors have overcome by the word of their testimony conveys the idea that these individuals, like their Lord, have given the ultimate faithful witness by following him in death. Their witness is inextricably bound up with him.[311] The

---

310. Smalley, *Revelation*, 326.

311. As Caird (*The Revelation of Saint John*, 157) aptly notes, "In his story theirs was already written."

last line of this stanza, "and they loved not their life unto death," makes explicit these many connections and pushes this imagery even further, for the connection between loving one's life and the laying down of life is a rich one for Johannine hearers, with Jesus as the model of love, for he is the Good Shepherd who lays down his life for his sheep (John 10:11-17), a reality acknowledged in 1 John 3:16 (cf. also the relevant John 12:25; 13:37-38; and 15:13). Structurally, the words (v. 12) confirm those that precede them (v. 11). Their overcoming is modeled in and made possible by Jesus, to whose faithful witness unto death they themselves have witnessed in their own life and death (Rev 2:10; 11:3-13). Interestingly, the term "life" is found in the singular, reminiscent of the reference to the "body" of the two witnesses in 11:8, perhaps underscoring the communal nature of their witness and overcoming.

> On account of this,
> Rejoice, heavens and those who dwell in them.
> Woe to the earth and the sea
> because the devil has come down to you
> having great anger
> knowing that he has little time.

The first words of this stanza, "on account of this," would call attention to all that has preceded in the first two stanzas. To those who dwell in the heavens there is the command "Rejoice!" The objects of this command, "the heavens and those who dwell in them," indicate a most comprehensive audience. Not only is this the only place in Revelation where the plural form "heavens" occurs, but the phrase "those who dwell in them" would also remind readers of the many groups earlier encountered in the book, numbering in the tens of thousands and beyond! Such a command brings to mind especially the throne-room scenes in chapters 4 and 5, colored by the specificity of those who follow, for example, the souls under the altar, various angelic figures, and the two witnesses, among others. Most recently, "the heavens and those who dwell in them" would include those who witnessed the casting down of the red dragon (12:7-9) and those who have overcome him (12:11). Significantly, the verb "dwell" is reserved in John's gospel for the Word (John 1:14), and in Revelation for God and those who dwell with him in heaven (Rev 7:15; 12:12; 13:6; 21:3). Conversely, the earth and the sea receive a warning that comes in the form of a woe. The woe is clearly tied to the fact that "the devil has come down to you having great anger, knowing that he has little time." Just as the command to rejoice grows out of that which precedes (vv. 10-11), so does the warning of the woe. Because he has lost his place in heaven, being cast down to the earth, the devil has come down with great anger. The emphasis of these words would hardly be missed, for in the Greek text they begin and end with a form of the verb "has." Translated very literally, "having great anger, knowing that little time he has." The last words in the hymn indicate that his anger is because "he knows that he has little time." Perhaps it is not without significance that the word καιρός (*kairos,* "time") occurs five times in Revelation with this reference standing in the middle, while the first and last references stand in inclusio fashion in the words "for the time is near" (1:3; 22:10). Clearly, the phrase "he has little time," would be understood as eschatologically conditioned, indicating that the loss of his place in heaven is the beginning of the end. The great red dragon has great anger, but he has little time.

The two story lines found in 12:1-6 and 12:7-12 converge nicely in v. 13, "And when the dragon saw that he had been cast down to the earth, he persecuted the woman who had given birth to the male child." The dragon's loss of place is clearly identified as part of the rationale for his actions, suggesting a symbiotic connection between his war in heaven and persecution of the woman on earth. The woman clothed with the sun reappears in the story in connection with the great red dragon. Upon learning that the dragon "persecuted the woman who had given birth to the male child," Johannine hearers would recall that Jesus himself was persecuted by the Jews in John's gospel (John 5:16; 15:20), as well as his prediction that, if the world "persecuted me, they will persecute you as well" (15:20). Such associations would be added confirmation that this woman now looks remarkably like the church,[312] the transformed Israel. As such, her persecution by the dragon would be very much at home with how Johannine believers understood the implications of following their Lord. The mention of "the male child" at the end of 12:13 makes all the more explicit the central role he plays in the conflict between the dragon and the woman.

"Two wings of a great eagle were given to the woman, in order that she might fly into the wilderness into her place, where she is nourished in that place a time and times and half a time from the face of the serpent." The divine passive "were given" stands first in the Greek sentence, followed by "to the woman," which underscores that her flight is accomplished by divine means. The significant role of the eagle as closely identified with God and his work (4:7; 8:13) heightens the idea of divine activity. In the OT, Israel's experience of deliverance from Egypt by the hand of God is described in similar manner (Exod 19:4; Deut 32:11-12), as is the promise of future deliverance (Isa 40:31). In this woman the experience of Israel is thus recapitulated, even as she looks increasingly like the church. Her wings are described as those of "a great eagle," which contrasts nicely the power of this divine provision with the power of

---

312. Gause, *Revelation,* 172.

the "great red dragon." The purpose of such divinely given wings is to enable her to fly to a specific place. Her flying "into the wilderness" would likely remind readers that this place in the wilderness is one prepared for her by God himself, as the words "into her place" imply. While it is possible to regard the combination of "where" and "in that place" as pleonastic,[313] such repetition would likely be taken as continued emphasis upon the place to which she flies. The word "nourish" stands between "where" and "in that place," which also supports this understanding. Given the context, it is likely that the word translated "she is nourished" would convey the idea not only of nourishment but also of protection, as in 12:6. Earlier, the period of divine protection offered to the woman was 1,260 days. Here, this period of divine protection is coterminous with Daniel's "a time and times and half a time" (Dan 7:25). Yet, while this temporal designation is in Daniel one used to describe the time given to the fourth beast to afflict the saints, in Rev 12:14 it is a temporal designation for the period of nourishment and protection offered to the woman! Thus, there is a subtle inversion present in these words, where a time of persecution is described as a time of protection. The nourishment of the woman is said to be "from the face of the serpent," which underscores the extent of this protection, for just as the woman successfully gave birth to the male child before the dragon who wished to devour him, so the woman and her witness will be protected, despite the serpent's close proximity and evil intentions.

"And the serpent cast out of his mouth after the woman water as a river, in order that he might sweep her away with the river." These words continue the cosmic imagery of the chapter underscoring the power of the serpent while making allusions to the exodus tradition. The mention of "water as a river" might bring to mind Pharaoh's order that every male Hebrew child must be cast into the river (Exod 1:22). Just as Pharaoh pursued Israel, so the serpent pursues the woman.[314] The intention of the serpent is made especially clear by means of a word play in the Greek text of Rev 12:15. The serpent cast out of his mouth a ποταμός (*potamos*, "river") so that he might make the woman a ποταμοφόρητος (*potamophorētos*, "one swept away by a river"). Such action clearly conveys the serpent's lethal intent and reveals some detail about the way in which the dragon persecuted the woman.

"The earth rendered help to the woman, and the earth opened her mouth and swallowed the river that the dragon cast out of his mouth." The words "the earth rendered help to the woman" indicate that the following actions are to be understood as the earth's intervention on her behalf in the light of the hostile

---

313. BAGD, 238.
314. Kiddle, *The Revelation of St. John*, 236.

actions of the serpent. This activity of the earth on the woman's behalf would likely call to mind the continued emphasis in Revelation on the connection between the Creator and his creation, as here the creation appears to do the bidding of the Creator. If a connection is made earlier between the water as a river and the experience of Israel at the Nile, it is possible that the earth opening her mouth there alludes to the earth's actions in the rebellion of Korah (Num 16:31-33). It is easy to see an explicit contrast between the strength of the mouth of the serpent, from which the river of water comes, and the strength of the mouth of the earth, which is able to open and drink up the entire river.

"And the dragon was enraged at the woman and departed to make war with the rest of her seed who keep the commands of God and have the witness of Jesus." The dragon's hostility toward the woman is anything but over. Yet, as might be remembered the last time the word "enraged" appeared (Rev 11:18), it had reference to the rage of the nations, which proved fruitless in the face of the rage of God himself! But instead of the dragon's rage resulting in another direct attack on the woman, he departs "to make war on the rest of her seed." This language would remind hearers of the dragon's last making of war, which proved to be extraordinarily unsuccessful, as he was not strong enough and lost his place in heaven (12:8). Also this language would remind readers that, after the prophetic witness of the two witnesses was complete, the beast made war against them and overcame them (11:7). The point could not be clearer. Just as the temple is protected for 1,260 days and the two witnesses are protected until their witness is complete, so the woman is protected from the attacks of the dragon for 1,260 days, a time and times and half a time.[315] But just as the two witnesses are overcome and killed by the beast when their witness is completed, so war will be made upon those loyal to the commands of God and have the witness of Jesus. The language "the rest of her seed" would perhaps bring to mind the male child, borne by the woman, snatched up to heaven, the fulfillment of Gen 3:15.[316] The fuller phrase indicates that there is a concrete connection between the male child and the rest of her seed, suggesting that the mother of the male child is also in some sense the mother of all believers. One wonders if for Johannine hearers such language would be understood to extend the thought of John's gospel, where "the mother of Jesus" becomes the "mother of the Beloved Disciple" (John 19:25-27). Is it possible that the words of Rev 12:17 suggest that the mother of Jesus is "the mother of all true disciples" as well? At any rate, the transformation of the woman clothed with the sun from Eve, to Israel, to Mary, to the church would now appear to be complete. The qualification of "the rest

---

315. Resseguie, *The Revelation of John*, 175-76.
316. Murphy, *Fallen Is Babylon*, 289.

The Struggle of God's People in Cosmic Perspective (12:1–14:20)

of her seed" as those "who keep the commands of God and have the witness of Jesus" expands knowledge of their identity considerably. For keeping the command(s) of the Father is intimately connected to the command to love one another (John 13:34; 14:15, 21, 31; 15:10, 12; 1 John 2:3-4, 7-8; 3:22-24; 4:21; 5:2-3; 2 John 4-6) to the point of laying down one's life as Jesus did (John 10:14-18). The keeping of God's command is no mere exercise in conformity, for, as Jesus says, "I know that his command is eternal life" (12:50). No doubt this keeping of God's commands would also be informed by the numerous times the word "keep" appears in the seven prophetic messages the resurrected Jesus speaks to the seven churches. Specifically, such language is used with reference to keeping Jesus' works (Rev 2:26) and words (3:8, 10), as well as keeping the things they have received (3:3). "The rest of her seed, who keep the commands of God" is thus understood to be those who are faithful in living out a sacrificial love for God and others, even to the point of death. Closely related to this designation is the rest of the phrase, "and have the witness of Jesus." It is perhaps significant that, for the first time in chapter 12, the male child is identified by name as Jesus (cf. John 1:17 and 1 John 2:3).[317] The words of the hymn in Rev 12:11, "And they overcame him through the blood of the Lamb and the word of their testimony and they did not love their lives unto death," explicitly state that the individuals against whom the dragon is preparing to make war are themselves prepared to give the ultimate faithful witness by following Jesus in death. Both qualifying statements — "those who keep the commands of God" and "who have the witness of Jesus" — thus convey the same reality, a point confirmed by both phrases in the Greek text having the same article governing them.

"And he stood upon the sand of the sea." Apparently, the preparation and means of this war will emerge from the sea, preparing the hearers for the ensuing war and those who wage it with and for the dragon.

The Two Beasts (13:1b-18)

"And I saw a beast coming up out of the sea, having ten horns and seven heads, and upon his horns ten diadems, and upon his heads a blasphemous name." The words "and I saw" reappear for the first time in more than two chapters (10:5). This expression marks the beginning of a series of things seen that begins with the sea (13:1) and climaxes with something like "a sea of glass" in heaven (15:2). Mention of this beast would remind hearers of the reference to the beast who comes up from the Abyss, who made war against, overcame, and killed the two

---

317. Hauret, "Ève transfigurée," 335.

prophetic witnesses earlier in 11:7. If this section (Rev 12–14) expands upon 11:3-13, mention of the beast in 13:1 would suggest that more is to be learned about this enigmatic figure. This beast bears a striking resemblance to the great red dragon, who at last mention was standing on the sand of the seashore, apparently awaiting the arrival of the beast. Like the dragon, the beast has ten horns and seven heads, indicating extraordinary strength and power (ten horns), as well as complete and absolute rule (seven heads).[318] Yet, the beast is not identical to the dragon, for the description of the beast's horns and heads appear in inverse order to the dragon's. While the dragon has seven diadems, the beast is described as having ten. The ten horns and the ten diadems suggest that this beast is even more powerful than the dragon, if such a thing could be possible! The beast is also described as bearing a blasphemous name upon his head. This name likely impinges in some way upon the identity and glory of God and his name.[319] The church in Smyrna earlier suffered "the blasphemy of those who say that they are Jews and are not but are a synagogue of Satan." As such, it is likely that the blasphemy they endured is now understood as a manifestation of the power of the dragon and his servant the beast. If in 2:9 such blasphemy was connected to the identity of God and his people, it is likely that the beast's blasphemous name would be understood as closely connected to God's identity and name,[320] perhaps even referring to a variety of divine names, which numerous contemporary rulers were so fond of appropriating for themselves.[321]

"And the beast that I saw was as a leopard and his feet as a bear and his mouth as the mouth of a lion." This beast is swift, powerful, and terrifying, for the speed of the leopard, the power of the bear, and the ferociousness of the lion were well known. This particular combination of animals would remind readers of the description of the four beasts found in Dan 7. There, the four beasts — the lion, the bear, the leopard, and the terrible fourth beast with ten horns — represent four consecutive kingdoms, which culminate in the fourth kingdom, which makes war against the saints (Dan 7:21) and excels all the other kingdoms, as it devours the whole earth (7:23).[322] The visions of Daniel and John are distinctive, for not only is Daniel's order of the beasts (lion, bear, and leopard) inverted in Revelation (leopard, bear, and lion), but unlike Daniel, John does not see four separate beasts (kingdoms) but one composite terrible

---

318. Resseguie, *The Revelation of John*, 180.
319. H. W. Beyer, "Βλασφημία," *TDNT* 1:621-24.
320. Resseguie, *The Revelation of John*, 182.
321. Mounce, *The Book of Revelation*, 250.
322. Andrew of Caesarea (*Commentary on the Apocalypse*, 13.2 [ACCS 12, 199]) identifies the leopard as the Greeks, the bear as the Persians, the lion as the Babylonians, and the antichrist as the king of the Romans.

beast that appears to combine dreadful characteristics of them all.[323] If Daniel's vision implies chronological progression, John's vision suggests the culmination of all the kingdoms in one hideous beast.[324] "And the dragon gave to him his power and his throne and great authority." To this point the word "power" has been used only in association with God (4:11; 7:12; 11:17; 12:10), Jesus (1:16; 5:12), and believers (3:8). That the dragon gives his power to the beast not only indicates that the power standing behind the beast is that of the dragon but, owing to its previous associations with God and/or Christ, also suggests that the dragon's giving of power to the beast may parody the activity of God and his Christ.[325] Likewise, reference to the dragon giving his throne to the beast is conditioned by the numerous previous references to the word "throne" in Revelation; with one exception, they are mentioned only in association with God, the Lamb, or his followers. Reference to the dragon giving his throne to the beast would likely be taken as a continuation of the parody of the relationship between God and the Lamb,[326] especially in that Jesus promises that the one who overcomes will sit on Jesus' throne, just as he has overcome and sits on the Father's throne (3:21). Similarly, the dragon's giving the beast great authority is again conditioned, in that the occurrence of authority elsewhere in Revelation is always an authority that appears to have come from God or Jesus, either directly or indirectly (2:26; 6:8; 9:3, 10, 19; 11:6; 12:10).

"And one of his heads was as slaughtered unto death, and the plague of his death was healed." The phrase "as slaughtered" used to describe one of the beast's heads is the identical phrase earlier encountered in the description of the Lamb, who looked as though he had been slaughtered. Owing to the salvific implications of the slaughter of the Lamb, it would seem that the beast's slaughtered head would represent salvific claims on the part of the beast. Perhaps the slaughter of the beast's head is alluded to in 11:7, with the prophetic ministry of the two witnesses resulting in the slaughter of one of the beast's heads,[327] a slaughter so severe that the death of the beast is imminent. There may even be an echo of the Gen 3:15 prediction that the seed of the woman would bruise the head of the serpent.[328] "And the plague of his death was healed." The occurrence of the word "plague" would confirm earlier suspicions with regard to

---

323. Osborne, *Revelation*, 492.
324. Gause, *Revelation*, 178.
325. Resseguie, *The Revelation of John*, 183.
326. Allo, *Saint Jean: L'Apocalypse*, 185.
327. Kiddle (*The Revelation of St. John*, 245) observes, "John believed that the death of the martyrs was of cosmic importance," and Sweet (*Revelation*, 210) notes, "The *obedience* and *testimony* of Jesus and his saints wound the beast's *head*."
328. Michaels, *Revelation*, 156.

the occasion of the wounding, for this very word is used to describe some of the prophetic activities attributed to the two witnesses in 11:6 just before the introduction of the beast into the story line.[329] The pronoun "his" in "the plague of his death" appears to refer to the beast, not just his wounded head (i.e., the wound to one of the beast's heads was a mortal wound to the beast himself). The verb that describes the healing of the beast's mortal wound appears in the passive voice. To this point, verbs appearing in the passive voice have almost uniformly been forms of the divine passive, referring to the activity of God, and such may be the case here as well. Because of the number of ways in which the description of the dragon and the beast is a parody of God and the Lamb, however, one wonders whether the words "was healed" are a continuation of this theme, with this so-called divine passive referring to the activity of the dragon. "And the whole earth was astonished after the beast." Perhaps the presence of the words "was astonished" is a continuation of the parody of the previous sentences, as this very term occurs in John's gospel to describe the response of the disciples (John 4:27) and the Jews (5:20, 28; 7:15, 21) to the activity of Jesus. The way in which the beast rivals Jesus is thus underscored once again.

"And they worshipped the dragon, because he gave the authority to the beast, and they worshipped the beast saying, 'Who is like the beast, and who is able to war with him?'" Aside from the rest of those who would not repent and who worshipped demons or idols (9:20), to this point only God and the Lamb are the objects of worship in Revelation (4:10; 5:14; 7:11; 11:1, 16).[330] For those steeped in the OT and the heritage of Israel, the worship of other beings in the place of God (and the Lamb) would be especially heinous and would reveal the extreme threat posed to believers by the dragon and the beast. The worship rendered to the dragon is owing to the authority he gave to the beast. It would appear that the term "authority" includes "his power and his throne and great authority." No doubt the beast's similarity in appearance to the dragon and the healing of the beast's wounded head are part of such authority. Along with the dragon, the beast is also worshipped. The worship of the beast includes a song of praise sung to him, "Who is like the beast, and who is able to war with him?" This hymn's mimicry of the hymns offered to God (4:8, 11; 7:10, 12; 11:15, 17-18; 12:10-12) and the Lamb (5:9-10, 12-13) earlier in the book is clear.[331] The absurdity of the claims to invincibility in war made on behalf of the beast is obvious, since the dragon, who gives the beast authority and power, is himself

---

329. Sweet, *Revelation*, 210.

330. Even the appearance of the term in Rev 3:9 seems to have ultimate reference to the worship of Jesus.

331. Gause, *Revelation*, 179.

not strong enough to win the war he makes in heaven but loses his place there. While the "whole earth" might be foolish enough to engage in such empty praise, discerning hearers are not! Clearly, this psalm is reminiscent of a variety of OT songs that acclaim God's incomparable nature (Exod 15:11-12; Deut 3:24; Pss 18:31; 86:8; 89:8; 113:5; Isa 40:25-26; 44:7; Mic 7:18), suggesting that the song sung to the beast is a parody of Judaic praise as well.[332] In these words of praise, then, the lines of demarcation are drawn all the more clearly. The dragon and the beast are diametrically opposed to God and the Lamb, and those who side with the dragon and the beast engage in false worship and give them a place that belongs only to God.[333]

"And there was given to him a mouth speaking great and blasphemous things, and there was given to him authority to act forty-two months." These words would bring to mind the fourth beast with ten horns, three of which are displaced by the emergence of yet another horn with a mouth speaking great things who makes war against the saints and prevails against them (Dan 7:20). The double appearance of "there was given" (Rev 13:5) underscores that the beast's authority and power is a derived authority and power. The most immediate referent to one who gave something to the beast is the dragon, who is worshipped because he gave authority to the beast (13:4). Yet to this point in Revelation every occurrence of "there was given" has had reference to God or the Lamb. Perhaps in these passives reference is made to both the dragon and to God. Such an understanding would fit nicely with the dragon, who continues to mimic the activity of God, with even the divine passive now referring to him. Conversely, a reference to God would make sense, as he is ultimately in control and without rival in the book, and clearly he is the one who would place the limits of forty-two months upon the beast.[334] The mouth given to the beast is one that utters great and blasphemous things. There is a connection between the blasphemous name upon the heads of the beast (Rev 13:1) and the blasphemous things spoken by his mouth. These great and blasphemous things are likely closely connected to God's identity and name. The beast was given authority to act for forty-two months. The words "there was given to him authority" would hearken back to vv. 2 and 4, where the dragon is twice described as giving authority to the beast. Here, however, there is a temporal limitation on the period during which the beast may act, forty-two months, a limitation that appears to have a divine origin. The first occurrence of this temporal indicator was with reference to the trampling of the holy city described in 11:2. The reappearance

---

332. Smalley, *Revelation*, 339.
333. Prigent, *L'Apocalypse de Saint Jean*, 314.
334. Beasley-Murray, *Revelation*, 213, and Smalley, *Revelation*, 340.

here of this temporal indicator suggests that the period of the beast's activity is coterminous with the trampling of the holy city.

"And he opened his mouth unto blasphemy to God to blaspheme his name and his dwelling, those who dwell in heaven." The description of the beast as opening his mouth would call to mind the actions of the horn in Dan 7:25, who speaks great words against God, underscoring the significance of the words that are to follow, perhaps indicating that the beast speaks in an official capacity.[335] The emphasis upon the blasphemous activity of the beast is conveyed by the use of both the noun and the verb forms of the word occurring in this verse. The nature of the beast's blasphemous name and blasphemous speech is made explicit in the words of v. 6, for this verse clearly identifies the objects of his blasphemous acts. Though neither the blasphemous name of the beast nor the content of his blasphemous words is revealed, it is likely that his blasphemous activity challenges the identity and nature of God. The beast's blasphemous activity toward God includes his name, his dwelling, and those who dwell in heaven. This activity is thus a comprehensive challenge to God's identity, person, dwelling, and people. Since in antiquity one's name was thought to be identical with one's person, blasphemy of God's name was considered to be blasphemy of God himself.[336] The beast's blasphemous activity of God's "dwelling" would be understood as a direct attack upon God's person, for in Rev 7:14 God promises the eschatological provision that "the one who sits on the throne . . . will dwell" upon those coming out of the great tribulation. We could add to this evidence the testimony in John's gospel that the Word "tabernacled among us" (John 1:14). Blasphemy of God's dwelling would thus include not only his person but also those who witness and are enveloped by his dwelling. This latter understanding is made explicit in the final words conveyed in Rev 13:6, where the phrase "those who dwell in heaven" appears to modify "his dwelling." Perhaps the instruction to "the heavens and those who dwell in them" to rejoice at the casting down of the dragon (12:12) would come to mind. There is clearly a great deal of continuity between these who dwell in heaven and the believing community in heaven and, by extension, the believing community upon the earth.[337] Consequently, the blasphemous activity of the beast includes the believing community both past and present (2:9-10). This dimension of the beast's blasphemous activity would hardly be surprising, since the object of the

---

335. Aune, *Revelation 6–16*, 744. Gause (*Revelation*, 180) goes so far as to propose that this expression might very well remind the hearers of prophetic, oracular speech enabled by Yahweh. If so, such associations would suggest that the mimicry of God and the Lamb by the dragon and the beast continues to develop.

336. L. Hartman, "Ὄνομα," *EDNT*, 2:519.

337. Pattemore, *The People of God in the Apocalypse*, 168.

dragon's wrath is the rest of the woman's seed. The beast blasphemes God and all that is associated with him.

"And there was given to him to make war against the saints and to overcome them, and there was given to him authority over every tribe and people and tongue and nation." For a second time in three verses there is a double occurrence of "there was given" with reference to the beast. Clearly, the giving of the ability to make war against the saints is something that forwards the agenda of the dragon, who is described as making war with the rest of the seed of the woman (12:17). So perhaps these divine passives yet again refer to the dragon, who continues to mimic God. But it is clear that nothing happens upon the earth and/or to God's people without God's express permission. Consequently, these passives may point to the activity of both the dragon and God. The ascription to the beast of the ability "to make war against the saints and to overcome them" would remind hearers of the actions of the beast against the two prophetic witnesses in 11:7, where, upon the completion of their witness, "the beast from the Abyss made war against them and overcame them and killed them." Such near-identical wording suggests that the experience of the two witnesses and the saints at the hands of the beast is coterminous and, once again, confirms that the description of the beast in chapter 13 is an expansion of his brief enigmatic mention in 11:7. The word "saints" would reinforce the connection between this text and Dan 7:25, while indicating that the woman's seed is indeed identical with the saints. It also serves as an ominous warning that the saints can expect similar treatment at the hands of the beast, as did the two prophetic witnesses. The beast also receives "authority over every tribe and people and tongue and nation." Such language underscores the ultimate source of the beast's authority as the dragon. It is difficult to imagine that these words would not be taken as yet another point at which the activity of the beast parodies that of God and the Lamb (5:9; 7:9). Conversely, these very groups are those to whom John and the two prophetic witnesses are to prophesy (10:11; 11:9). Their mention in 11:9 would be especially poignant, as these are the ones who see the (dead) body of the two witnesses in the street of that great city.

"And all the inhabitants upon the earth will worship him." It follows that, if the beast has "authority over every tribe and people and tongue and nation," such authority would manifest itself in universal worship (cf. 13:4). Earlier encounters with the phrase "the inhabitants of the earth" also prepare us for this statement. To find that all the inhabitants of the earth worshipped the beast instead of God and the Lamb would hardly come as a surprise, based on the previous occurrences of this phrase (3:10; 6:10; 8:13; 11:10; 13:3). The comprehensive nature of the beast's worship is underscored, as this is the only occurrence of the word "all" with this phrase in Revelation.[338] Significantly, the primary verb, "will worship," appears in the future tense rather than the past tense, as in the preceding verses, indicating that such comprehensive worship lies at some point in the future.[339] The identity of the worshippers is made all the clearer in the words "each one whose name was not written in the book of life of the Lamb, who was slaughtered from the foundation of the world." The shift from the plural "all" to the singular "each one" refocuses attention upon the fact that, ultimately, the worship of the beast is rendered by individuals who have rejected the Lamb's salvific provisions. Mention of the Lamb's book of life would remind readers of its previous occurrence in 3:5, where the one who overcomes is promised by Jesus that his or her name will not be erased from it. Significantly, the book of life is explicitly identified with the Lamb, whose salvific work is underscored, emphasizing the close relationship that exists between the Lamb's death and the inscription of names in the book of life. The recurrence of the word "slaughtered" in this verse would be a powerful reminder of the central role Jesus' death and shedding of blood play in Revelation (1:5-6; 5:6, 9; 7:14; 12:11). This emphasis would reveal the significant differences between the beast's slaughtered head and the Lamb, who had been slaughtered "from the foundation of the world." Such a claim would rather clearly bring to mind Jesus' words to the Father, "You loved me before the foundation of the world" (John 17:24), a reference to their pretemporal relationship, when Jesus shared glory with the Father before the world began (17:5).[340] Though modern interpreters sometimes stumble at this idea,[341] such a disclosure would be very much in keeping with the understanding of Jesus' preexistence and relationship with the Father and the world. In contrast, worshippers of the beast are tied to a transitory and passing figure.[342] And though it is possible for the Lamb to erase names from the book of life (Rev 3:5), yet their names having been written in the slaughtered Lamb's book of life indicates that they will be able to withstand the temptation to worship the beast. This assurance arises from the basis of their salvation, which predates the world itself.

"If anyone has an ear, let that one hear." Such words remind hearers of the words of Jesus with which each of the seven prophetic messages conclude,

---

338. Aune, *Revelation 6-16*, 746.
339. Smalley, *Revelation*, 342.
340. O. Hofius, "Καταβολή," *EDNT*, 2:255.
341. Cf. discussion in Aune, *Revelation 6-16*, 746-47.
342. Gause (*Revelation*, 182) astutely observes, "Here is the irony of God's economy. This is the book of life, but it is based on the death of the Lamb, and it is a death that was and is established from eternity. Eternal life is given for an eternally established death. The saints conquer the beast that conquers them. His conquest is temporal and physical. Theirs is eternal and spiritual."

where Jesus' words were also words the Spirit speaks to the churches. It is likely that these words here in chapter 13 would once again be taken as coming from the resurrected Jesus and/or the Spirit. As such, they would carry with them something of their meaning in chapters 2–3, where they call for response on the part of the churches. Thus, "the Spirit-inspired voice of prophecy" gives divine guidance as to how believers are to respond.[343] Significantly, this pneumatic guidance stands at the very center of John's words about the two beasts found in chapter 13. This familiar call to pneumatic discernment is actually the first line of a poetic section devoted to this topic, the first three lines of which all begin with the words "if any":

If anyone has ears, let that one hear.

If anyone into captivity,
into captivity that one goes.

If anyone by the sword is to die,
he by the sword is to die.

While these prophetic words, which incorporate the prophetic words of Jer 15:11 and 43:11 (50:11 LXX), speak of punishment upon those who disobey God, the words of Rev 13:10 are not spoken to the beast and his followers but are addressed to believers,[344] as encouragement and as warning. These daunting words suggest that captivity and death by the sword are calamities potentially awaiting faithful witnesses. Yet, while such frightful fates could be a cause for drawing back and even capitulating to the power of the beast, they would remind readers of the similar fate of Jesus, Antipas, and the two prophetic witnesses. Such pneumatic discernment reveals that believers are not to resist the fates marked out for them;[345] rather, they must accept them as somehow integral to their prophetic witness and as part of God's will and plan for the believing community, perhaps echoing words spoken to the souls under the altar (6:11). These Spirit-inspired words of Jesus conclude with yet another call for pneumatic discernment, "Here is the patient endurance and the faith of the saints." This call emphasizes the saints' patient endurance and faith, with both terms being accompanied by the definite article in the Greek text.[346] Such

---

343. Pattemore, *The People of God in the Apocalypse*, 171.
344. Caird, *The Revelation of Saint John*, 169.
345. Ladd, *Revelation*, 182.
346. Aune, *Revelation 6–16*, 751.

patient endurance is understood to be "in Jesus" (1:9), belonging to him (3:10), and would carry with it the idea of following Jesus in rendering one's witness even to the point of death. "The faith of the saints" is also closely associated with Jesus, as he speaks both of "my faith" and "my faithful witness Antipas" in 2:13. Such language would remind believers of their solidarity with Jesus' witness, being a call to the kind of faithfulness characteristic of an overcomer. In this call to pneumatic discernment, despite the impending universal reign and worship of the beast, believers are thus called to faithful, patient endurance. The time of the beast is limited to forty-two months, and they stand with Jesus, identifying and standing with him and his own faithful witness.[347]

"And I saw another beast coming up out of the earth, and he had two horns as a lamb, and he spoke as a dragon." These words introduce readers to the third member of this triumvirate of evil, who comes alongside the dragon and the beast with seven heads to oppose God. The beast's existence suggests that the parody of God and the Lamb continues, only here the parody extends beyond God and the Lamb to include the Spirit. The beast's place of origin, earth, makes clear the comprehensive nature of this triumvirate's opposition, as they come from heaven (the dragon), the sea (the beast with seven heads), and the earth (the beast introduced here),[348] the latter perhaps being a fulfillment of the woe of warning spoken to the earth and sea from the great voice in heaven in 12:12. The description of the beast as having two horns like a lamb would be especially intriguing, as lambs do not have horns![349] While the ram with two horns in Dan 8:3 might be an analogy,[350] it is much more likely that the two horns (like those of a lamb) would be taken as a reference to the Lamb's two prophetic witnesses, in whom all prophetic abilities appear to converge (Rev 11:3-13).[351] In the triumvirate of evil, this beast would therefore be a parody of the Spirit.[352] Despite this beast's appearance, his speech indicates a more sinister relationship, for "he speaks as a dragon." While the beast with seven heads bears a physical resemblance to the dragon, this beast speaks as a dragon.

"And he exercises (lit. 'does') all the authority of the first beast before him, and he makes the earth and those who are inhabitants in it worship the first beast, whose plague of death was healed." The first words of the (Greek) text, "and the authority of the first beast," reveal the sentence's emphasis. The authority exercised by this beast is the same authority originally derived by the

---

347. Prigent, *L'Apocalypse de Saint Jean*, 318.
348. Kiddle, *The Revelation of St. John*, 253.
349. Aune, *Revelation 6–16*, 757.
350. Aune, *Revelation 6–16*, 757.
351. Sweet, *Revelation*, 215.
352. Gause, *Revelation*, 183.

first beast from the dragon himself (13:2, 4-5, 7), which may include the waging of war (13:7). Significantly, here the verb tense shifts from past to present, perhaps suggesting that this beast's activity is an ongoing reality for John and his church. Reference to the first beast follows mention of this beast's activity, as the exercising of this authority is done "before him" or "in his presence." In the Greek sentence references to the first beast thus form an inclusio around the mention of this beast, making clear the dependency of the latter upon the former. For the action of this beast to be described as "before him" would be yet another way in which a parody of God and his work would be detected, as to this point in Revelation, with few exceptions (2:14; 3:8-9; 12:4) the term "before" rather consistently occurs with reference to God (1:4; 3:2, 5; 4:5-6, 10[2x]; 7:9, 11, 15; 8:2-4; 9:13; 11:4, 16; 12:10) or Jesus (5:8; 7:9), reminding readers of OT texts that use this language to denote "serving before the Lord" (1 Kgs 17:1; 18:15).[353] The parallel between this word to describe the relationship between this beast and the first beast and the relationship of the two lampstands (which are the two prophetic witnesses) and the Lord of the earth (Rev 11:4) would be additional reason to see in this beast a parody of the Spirit. Significantly, this authority is exercised in order that the earth and those who are inhabitants in it might worship the first beast, explaining how it is that the whole earth comes to worship the dragon and the beast (13:4). Such worship is the result of the activity of this beast. Here the implicit connection made earlier between the healing of the first beast's plague of death and his worship by the world (13:3-4) is made explicit (13:12).[354]

"And he does great signs, namely, he even makes fire to come down unto the earth before men." Owing to the christologically conditioned nature of "signs" within the Johannine community, the doing of great signs by this beast underscores the way in which he continues to parody the activity of the Spirit. He is even able to make "fire fall from heaven unto the earth before men." The mention of fire from heaven would bring to mind Elijah, whose sacrifice was consumed by fire that fell from the Lord (1 Kgs 18:38). This beast is thus able to do what the prophets of Baal could not.[355] Mention of fire would also remind hearers of the two prophetic witnesses, from whose mouth fire came to devour their enemies.[356] In this way the actions of this beast reveal his continued parody of the work of the Spirit. The attribution of many great signs to this beast also likely calls to mind the words of Deut 13:1-5, which warn of an alleged

---

353. Kiddle, *The Revelation of St. John*, 254.
354. Allo, *Saint Jean: L'Apocalypse*, 190.
355. Beasley-Murray, *Revelation*, 217.
356. Osborne, *Revelation*, 513.

prophet who performs signs or wonders and leads the people to worship other gods. These signs, especially the calling down of fire from heaven unto the earth, were specifically done "before men."

"And (the second beast) deceived those who dwell upon the earth by means of the signs that had been given to him to do before the beast, saying to those who dwell upon the earth to make an icon/image to the beast, who has the plague of the sword and lived." As before, "deceive" language reminds readers of those who would deceive themselves (John 7:47; 1 John 1:8; 2 John 7) or others (John 7:12; 1 John 2:26; 3:7), the false prophetess (called "Jezebel" by Jesus), who "deceives my servants" (Rev 2:20), and most recently the agent of deception par excellence, the great dragon, who stands behind all the human agents of deception (Rev 12:9). This beast is one who deceives others, which also makes clear his relationship to the false prophetess Jezebel, and may even indicate that he himself should be considered the archetypal false prophet. The intended audience of these signs are "those who dwell upon the earth," earlier described as worshipping the first beast (13:8). These signs were done "before the beast." Significantly, this beast encourages the worship of the first beast by instructing the inhabitants upon the earth to make an image of the beast. Discerning hearers would find in this instruction a violation of the divine prohibition against the making of such images (Deut 4:16). It is indeed telling that this beast does not make the image himself but encourages the inhabitants of the earth to do so, for such an act constitutes a tangible step on their part in the direction of worshipping the first beast. As observed earlier (13:3-4), there is a concrete connection between the worship of the first beast and his having survived a mortal wound, as the beast is identified with the words "who has the plague of the sword and lived." For the first time it is revealed that the plague, or wound, suffered by the beast was inflicted by a sword. While this detail could be a subtle reference to the death of Nero, who took his own life with a dagger (Suetonius, *Nero* 49), the reference to the sword could perhaps be taken as indicating the severity of the wound and the dangerous nature of the instrument that inflicted it. If this wound suffered by the beast is to be identified with the activity of the two prophetic witnesses, there is irony in the fact that those destined to be put to death by the sword (13:10) may themselves inflict a mortal wound upon the beast, perhaps with the very sword that he wields. Even though the beast suffered a mortal wound, "he lived," just as Jesus lived after his death!

"And it was given to him to give life to the image of the beast, in order that the image of the beast might even speak, and he acted in order that whoever did not worship the image of the beast might be killed." The derived nature of this beast's authority is conveyed by the passive "it was given," which precedes the description of his activities. This beast was given the authority to give "life" or "spirit" to the image. While numerous examples from antiquity can be assembled with regard to the way in which statues and/or images could be made to appear alive,[357] there is no indication in the text that this or other activities of this beast are achieved by trickery.[358] By some means this beast gives the spirit of life, in a way that mimics God's gift of the Spirit of life to the two witnesses earlier (11:11), perhaps even being a parody of Ezekiel's prophetic activity where dead bones live (Ezek 37).[359] The activity of this living image even includes speaking, which would be understood as oracular in nature. The speech that comes from the image of the beast would be the words of the first beast himself.[360] It appears that the oracular words coming from the beast's image insist both on the universal worship of the image of the beast and the putting to death of anyone who does not participate in such worship.[361] Perhaps such oracular speech further defines the great and blasphemous things the first beast earlier uttered (13:5-6). It thus becomes clear that, in the war waged by the dragon, the first beast, and now this second beast, those who withstand the onslaughts of this triumvirate face certain death. But who are these who would oppose such universal worship of the beast and his image? These are the ones who keep the commands of God and have the testimony of Jesus (12:17), whose names are written in the book of life of the Lamb slaughtered from the foundation of the world (13:8), and who face captivity and sword (13:10). Could they be other than the souls under the altar, who had been slaughtered on account of the word of God and the witness that they had (6:9), or those coming out of the great tribulation, who have washed their garments in the blood of the Lamb (7:14)? If it has not been understood before, it certainly is now. The battle requires a patient endurance that is faithful unto death (13:10). The lines of demarcation are clearly drawn; one must align oneself fully either with God or with the dragon. There is no middle ground, no room for compromise.

"And he makes all, the small and great, and the rich and the poor, and the free and the slaves, in order that there be given to them a mark upon their right hand or upon their forehead." These words reveal the means by which those who worship the image of the beast are to be identified. Conversely, the absence of the beast's mark would also be the way in which those not worshipping the image could be identified. The comprehensive list of categories makes

357. Cf. Caird, *The Revelation of Saint John*, 173.
358. Murphy, *Fallen Is Babylon*, 310.
359. Sweet, *Revelation*, 214.
360. Aune, *Revelation 6–16*, 762-64. Lucian's account in *Alexander the False Prophet* (24) is perhaps the best-known example of this phenomenon and its oracular significance.
361. Aune, *Revelation 6–16*, 765.

clear the universal intent of this oracle.[362] All are expected to receive a mark in one of two prominent places on their bodies: either upon their right hand, the hand of honor, oaths, and business transactions, or upon their forehead, the place where religious articles were sometimes worn bearing the name of a particular deity indicating to which god or goddess one belonged. Clearly, the purpose of such a mark is identity, so that those who worship the image of the beast could be easily identified. How would the hearers likely understand this particular "mark" or "brand"? Perhaps they would see in it a practice similar to that of the branding or tattooing of fugitive slaves, or the sign of a conquering people that was sometimes placed upon the vanquished (Plutarch, *Nicias*, 29), or a religious symbol branded upon a subject people (3 Macc 2:28-30). But it would not be lost on them that the 144,000 have earlier been sealed by God upon their foreheads as a sign of his protection and ownership (7:3; 9:4). Consequently, this mark of the beast would be seen as yet another parody of God and his people.[363] As the seal of God signifies ownership by him, so this beast's mark would signify ownership by the beast.[364] As God's seal signifies protection for his people against the events that accompany the sounding of the trumpets, so the beast's seal signifies protection from death inflicted by him for those who worship him. To bear the seal of God or the mark of the beast reveals the identity of the worshipper, as well as the identity of the one worshipped. There is absolutely no middle ground. Temptations to accommodate to the beast and his system are therefore not to be viewed as minor points of nonconformity to God and his Lamb, but they carry in themselves the seeds of identification with the beast. They lead one to the worship of the beast and the receiving of his mark!

"In order that no one might be able to buy or sell except the one who has the mark, the name of the beast, or the number of his name." These words reveal a close connection between the worship of the image of the beast, the bearing of his mark, and participation in commercial and economic life. The scope of the beast's authority is now understood to encompass all economic categories. Failure to worship the beast and bear his mark bars one from entry into the commercial and economic systems upon which life depends. Thus, even if it were possible for one to refuse to receive the beast's mark and somehow escape death at the moment of refusal, one cannot escape death altogether. In the light of the relationship between worship of the beast's image and access to commercial and economic life, the words of the resurrected Jesus with regard to eating

---

362. Kiddle, *The Revelation of St. John*, 258.
363. Resseguie, *The Revelation of John*, 188.
364. Beale, *The Book of Revelation*, 716.

food sacrificed to idols (2:14, 20) might be seen in a more comprehensive light. Perhaps such a retrospective understanding would cause the hearers to examine more carefully their own current involvement with commercial and economic entities, especially those connected to eating meat sacrificed to idols. Is it possible that they could already be facing the temptation to worship the beast and bear his mark by the participation in various commercial and economic systems? Too much attachment to and/or dependence upon a world order or its systems that may be connected to the beast is futile. Eventually, all who do not enter fully into participation and cooperation with the beast will be excluded from them and ultimately put to death. Any temptation to compromise with this world and its systems is seen for the false choice that it is. Specifically, the beast and his system are to be viewed as diametrically opposed to those who keep the commands of God and the witness of Jesus. The beast's mark is described as "the mark, the name of the beast, or the number of his name." Here, the nature of the mark is revealed to signify that such ones belong to him. But the beast's name is not explicitly given, though it may be assumed that it is the same blasphemous name that appears upon his heads. Rather, they seem to be given a kind of numerical punning.[365]

"Here is wisdom. Let the one who has understanding calculate the number of the beast, for it is the number of man, and his number is 666." The last encounter with the "here is . . ." formula followed words that appear to have come from the resurrected Jesus and/or the Spirit (13:10) with regard to "the patient endurance and faith of the saints." Owing to the close proximity of these words to those in 13:18, it is likely that the reappearance of the formula "here is . . ." would carry with it a similar sense of prophetic, pneumatic instruction as had those in 13:10. "Here is wisdom" would be an especially potent instruction, for to this point in the book wisdom has been ascribed only to the Lamb (5:12) and to God (7:12). The wisdom here invoked thus has divine associations and, consequently, is entirely appropriate in an appeal for pneumatic discernment.[366] "Let the one who has understanding calculate the number of the beast." What would "understanding" likely mean? Given its context, it could hardly refer to mere human intellect. Rather, it would appear to be closely associated with "wisdom." Owing to this close association, the hearers might be wondering whether the term νοῦς (*nous,* "understanding") would not carry with it a similar sense of divine endowment. Interestingly enough, a similar idea is found near the close of 1 John, where readers are assured that they "have been given the ability to

---

365. Sweet, *Revelation,* 217.
366. Contra Aune (*Revelation 6–16,* 769), who sees no explicit mention of a need for divine help in order to understand.

understand" (1 John 5:20). On that occasion, the Greek word διάνοια (*dianoia*, "the ability to understand") occurs with reference to the process by which understanding comes, rather than to "knowledge" or "understanding" proper. As such, it bears a striking resemblance to the idea of "the anointing" that teaches the readers all things, making the need for human teachers superfluous (2:20, 27).[367] Such an interpretation fits nicely with the occurrence of "understanding" found in the call to pneumatic discernment in Rev 13:18. Specifically, those who have such understanding are encouraged to "calculate the number of the beast." On one level, there would be various ways by which the number of a person or thing could be calculated. And yet, the calculation to which the hearers are called is no mere parlor game, or a calculation that may be completed owing to one's own ingenuity. Rather, this calculation must take place in the Spirit! That is to say, this calculation must be undertaken in the Spirit of pneumatic discernment.

"And this is the number of man." Such a statement must be a bit startling, for to this point there is little in the description of the beast that would have encouraged him to be viewed in human terms. Yet, these words might bring a growing realization that the beast is more like a human than first thought. For example, the beast wears diadems (13:1), receives and gives authority (13:2, 12), is wounded and healed (13:3), is worshipped owing to his abilities to make war (13:4), and even speaks (13:6). There is therefore an explicit identification of the number and name of the beast with that of a "man," though the anarthrous construction "of a man" underscores that the number is that of a human being, not necessarily that of a specific individual. Additionally, the specific number of the beast is given: "and his number is 666." Owing to the way in which other numbers in Revelation function, this number too would likely be taken as having a symbolic or figurative quality.[368] The number of the beast would likely generate a whole matrix of meaning, not a simple identification of a specific figure, and yet it may do that as well.

Perhaps the first thing to note is that this very number, 666, appears on one occasion in the OT, where it is used to designate the weight of gold talents that came annually to King Solomon (1 Kgs 10:14).[369] This evidence might suggest that such kingly associations reveal something of the kingly aspirations of the beast. The implications of such monetary associations would not be insignificant for those who have recently learned that, without the beast's mark or number, one is denied access to commercial and economic life.

---

367. Thomas, *1 John, 2 John, 3 John*, 278.
368. Smalley, *Revelation*, 352.
369. An observation made by John Sweet to the author in private conversation.

The first clear hint given — that the beast's number is the number of man — would indicate that, despite the beast's mythological-like qualities, he is to be calculated in human terms. In other words, the beast himself will be manifested in some way in human form, a realization that might cause the hearers to suspect that there are ways in which they already are encountering the beast in a variety of human forms around them, even as they await the kind of manifestation described in 11:7 and 13:1b-18. That the number of the beast is the number of man speaks to genre. At the same time, it is very difficult to imagine that the call for pneumatic discernment to calculate the number of the beast would not bring the idea of gematria to mind. For at the time in which Revelation was written, letters in the Greek and Hebrew alphabets served a dual function as both letters and numbers. Specifically, Greek letters were assigned the following numerical values:

α'	=	1	ιβ'	=	12 etc.	σ'	=	200
β'	=	2	κ'	=	20	τ'	=	300
γ'	=	3	κα'	=	21 etc.	υ'	=	400
δ'	=	4	λ'	=	30	φ'	=	500
ε'	=	5	μ'	=	40	χ'	=	600
ς'	=	6	ν'	=	50	ψ'	=	700
ζ'	=	7	ξ'	=	60	ω'	=	800
η'	=	8	ο'	=	70	ϡ'	=	900
θ'	=	9	π'	=	80	,α	=	1000
ι'	=	10	ϙ'	=	90	,β	=	2000
ια'	=	11	ρ'	=	100	,γ	=	3000[370]

Using these values, it was possible to count up the numerical value of the Greek letters in any word. The practice was popular and widespread, even being found in graffiti written on the walls of various structures. Perhaps the most famous, and certainly most oft-cited, is the piece of graffiti found in Pompeii from sometime before 79 CE, which reads, "I love her whose number is 545."[371] The meaning of such a statement would be understandable to the person who wrote it and perhaps to the one "whose number is 545," but probably not to too wide a circle. Gematria made it possible to create a pun out of the numerical value of the letters contained in certain words and names, a method known as

---

370. For a concise discussion of this use of the Greek alphabet, cf. B. M. Metzger, *The Text of the New Testament: Its Transmission, Corruption, and Restoration* (3rd ed.; Oxford: Oxford University Press, 1992), 190 n. 1.

371. As cited in A. Deissmann, *Light from the Ancient East* (Grand Rapids: Baker, 1979), 277.

isopsephism.[372] According to Suetonius (*Nero* 39), even the emperor Nero was subjected to such sport. One pun reads:

> Nero, Orestes, Alcmeon their mothers slew.
> A calculation new.
> Nero his mother slew.[373]

This isopsephism is based on Nero's being known to have killed his own mother and on the numerical value of "Nero" in Greek being 1005, which is equivalent to the numerical value of the Greek words meaning "the slayer of one's own mother."

It would seem safe to assume that the hearers would likely make use of gematria as they proceed in their discernment.[374] If so, and if as seems likely from 9:11, some of the hearers were familiar with Hebrew, then perhaps they would notice that the numerical value of the Greek word θηρίον (*thērion*, "beast") is 666 when transliterated into Hebrew characters.[375] Hebrew letters were assigned the following numerical value:

א	=	1	ל	=	30
ב	=	2	מ	=	40
ג	=	3	נ	=	50
ד	=	4	ס	=	60
ה	=	5	ע	=	70
ו	=	6	פ	=	80
ז	=	7	צ	=	90
ח	=	8	ק	=	100
ט	=	9	ר	=	200
י	=	10	ש	=	300
כ	=	20	ת	=	400

---

372. Bauckham, *The Climax of Prophecy*, 386.

373. Cited according to the translation of J. C. Rolfe, *Suetonius*, vol. 2 (London: Heinemann, 1965), 156-59.

374. It should be apparent that it would be much easier to discern the practice of gematria if one starts with the name and arrives at the number, rather than beginning with the number and arriving at the name, for in the latter case, one would think the possibilities limitless, as they seem to be with 666!

375. Cf. W. Hadorn ("Die Zahl 666, ein Hinweis auf Trajan," *ZNW* 19 [1919-20]), who identifies the numerical value of the transliterated word תריון as 666 — that is, ת/400 + ר/200 + י/10 + ו/6 + ן(נ)/50.

The Struggle of God's People in Cosmic Perspective (12:1–14:20)

Such a calculation would serve to confirm that the number of the beast is indeed 666, and that they are calculating in the right way. But the call for pneumatic discernment in 13:18 seems to entail much more. Following these calculations, perhaps the hearers would figure out that, when the Greek name "Nero Caesar" is transliterated into Hebrew, it too calculates to 666.[376] What would be the implications of such a pneumatic discerning? Perhaps that in the person of Nero, whose excesses were widely known and who seems to have embodied many of the characteristics of the beast, the hearers would be able to see how the larger-than-life beast could be manifested in human form. Thus, if for the hearers the beast now has a face, Nero appears to have sat for the portrait.[377] And if the beast has the face of Nero, what are the implications for other details of the beast's description? Perhaps the hearers would begin to discern ways in which the beast and the empire were related (and this "head" to the others?). Yet, it does not seem likely that the hearers would have equated the beast with Nero full stop and ceased their calculations, for there are several ways in which the image of the beast is at odds with what is known of Nero.[378] The two differ in their death. One of the beast's heads is said to have suffered the plague of death by the sword, while Nero's own self-inflicted death was not a wound to the head with a sword but inflicted to his body with a dagger. Also, by the time of Revelation, Nero is surely dead, and despite arguments to the contrary, there is no evidence that the tradition of Nero's return included the idea of his death and resurrection, an idea that is clearly present in the description of the beast in Rev 13.[379] Perhaps on this understanding, the hearers would be reminded of their initial calculations of the beast, "It is Nero all over again."[380]

Some of the Johannine hearers would likely be familiar with another form of calculation that involves "triangular numbers." These are numbers that can be represented by dots arranged in a triangular shape, with the top row having one dot, the second row having two dots, and so forth. As illustrated in figure 1 on page 248, the first four triangular numbers are 1, 3, 6, and 10.

---

376. Cf. Bauckham (*The Climax of Prophecy*, 387), who identifies the numerical value of the transliterated word נרון קסר as 200 = ר + 60 = ס + 100 = ק + 50 = ן + 6 = ו + 200 = ר + 50 = נ, for a total of 666. It is significant that, when the final "n" is left off the Hebrew transliteration, following the Latin name rather than the Greek, the name calculates to 616, which might go some way toward explaining an early variant reading found in a few manuscripts of the NT that read 616 instead of 666 at this point.

377. Koester, *Revelation and the End of All Things*, 130.

378. In fact, it appears that, by the time of Irenaeus, Nero was not even considered to be one of the possible solutions to the calculation, as he is not one of the three proposals suggested by Irenaeus (*Adversus Haereses* 5.30.3).

379. Bauckham, *The Climax of Prophecy*, 407-23.

380. Koester, *Revelation and the End of All Things*, 133.

Figure 1. The first four triangular numbers

As early as the time of Augustine (*Homilies on the Gospel of John* 122.9), Bible students observed that 153, the number of fish caught by the disciples in John 21:11, is a triangular number. That is, 153 is the sum of each whole number from 1 to 17, which (at least for some students) makes this number significant. How much more significant could it be, then, that 666, the number of the beast, is also a triangular number, being the sum of each number between 1 and 36? (See fig. 2.)

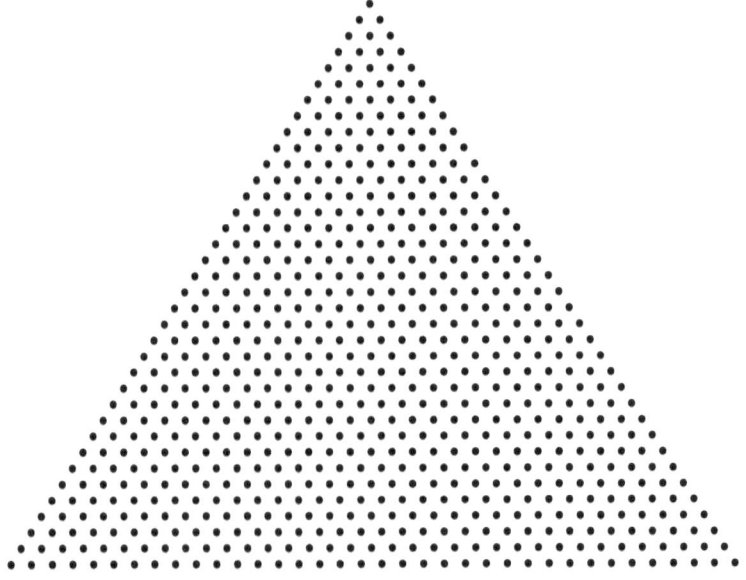

Figure 2. The triangular number 666

Furthermore, 666 has the added distinction of being a *doubly* triangular number. That is, the number of dots in its bottom row is 36, which itself is a triangular number, being the sum of the numbers from 1 to 8. Doubly triangular numbers (triangular numbers that are built on another triangular number) are uncommon, with 666 being only the eighth of the first thirty-six triangular numbers (1, 6, 21, 55, 120, 231, 406, 666). In addition, 36 is the only triangular number that is also a perfect square. We may portray both of these oddities as in figure 3.

Figure 3. The number 36: doubly triangular and a perfect square

What is the significance of all this mathematics for the meaning of the number of the beast? Because the number 36 was especially honored among the ancients,[381] and because 666 is the triangular number of that triangular number, it might not be going too far to see this number of the beast as one that had cosmic proportions — perhaps a king among numbers![382] That is to say, this "triangular" calculation of the number 666, along with the calculations by means of gematria, could reveal something of the identity of the beast, who not only exercises unrestrained authority on earth but appears and acts as a king by the wearing of the ten diadems (13:1). Perhaps in the number 666 the readers discern a cosmic number, a "king" of a number for a beast who would himself be a divine king and control the cosmos! As a result of their calculations in the Spirit, the hearers would thus have discerned two primary points. First, by means of gematria, they have discovered something about his identity. Specifically, they have come to know that the number of the beast is indeed 666 and have gone so far as even to peer into his face. And though his resemblance to Nero is remarkable, they know that the beast is not simply to be equated with Nero full stop, for Nero is dead, but the beast is not. Second, by means of calculations involving triangular numbers, the hearers

---

381. Plutarch (*De Iside et Osiride* 75) notes that the number 36 was held to be particularly sacred by the Pythagoreans: "The so-called *tetraktys*, namely thirty-six, was the greatest oath, as is well known, and was called the Cosmos [or "and Cosmos was its name"]; it was made up by the sum of the first four even (on the one hand) and (first four) uneven numbers (on the other hand)." Cited according to the translation, with the addition of some Greek words, of J. G. Griffiths, *Plutarch's De Iside et Osiride* (Cambridge: University of Wales Press, 1970), 239. Cf. F. H. Colson, "Triangular Numbers in the New Testament," *JTS* 16 (1915): 70.

382. Colson ("Triangular Numbers in the New Testament," 70-71) observes, "When we take into account the identity of what we call digits in 666, it seems likely that in Pythagorean or Nicomachean circles 666 would be a very king amongst numbers."

now have a better sense as to the kind of beast he is. Through their reflection on the number 666, they have discovered things about his aspirations, character, and power. He sees himself as enveloping, in himself, the cosmos (36) and even fancies himself as the divine king of all, traits consistent with the description of his actions encountered earlier in chapter 13. Consequently, the hearers' pneumatic calculations do not serve to satisfy a sense of curiosity to understand history written in advance so much as to arm themselves with discerning wisdom to prepare them for their next encounter(s) with him, both now and in the future.

The Lamb and the 144,000, the Harvest and the Winepress (14:1-20)

"And I saw, and behold the Lamb standing upon Mount Zion and with him 144,000 having his name and the name of the Father written upon their foreheads." If the triumvirate of evil stands ready to make war against the saints by every means necessary, the Lamb and those with him stand at the ready to enter into battle. The words "I saw, and behold" indicate a change of topic as a new aspect of the overall vision is now recounted. John sees another vision of the Lamb. Two aspects from the most recent mention of the Lamb (13:8) are carried forward to the description of the Lamb and his followers in 14:1. The first is the close relationship that exists between the Lamb and those whose names are written in his book. The second aspect is the emphasis once again placed upon the nature of the Lamb's death, for he is described as the one who had been slaughtered, bringing to mind the nature of the war the Lamb and his followers are prepared to wage against the triumvirate of evil. The phrase "and I saw . . . upon Mount Zion" would continue the upward trajectory of the things John sees, beginning in 13:1 from the sea (13:1), to the earth (13:11), and now to Mount Zion (14:1). The description of the Lamb standing on Mount Zion would reaffirm the understanding of the Lamb as "the Root of David" (5:5), owing to its close association with David, being known as the city of David (2 Sam. 5:7). Given its numerous OT associations (Pss 2:6; 9:11; 76:2; 132:13; Isa 24:23; 25:7-10), the Lamb's location here suggests that the eschatological promises are now seeing their fulfillment. Thus, the question whether Mount Zion is located on earth or in heaven is a bit misplaced, for at this point in the book heaven and earth appear to be very close together.[383] It would not come as a surprise that the Lamb has companions with him on Mount Zion, though the specific group of companions may indeed be unexpected, for there were with him 144,000. Despite no definite article standing before this number in

---

383. Smalley, *Revelation*, 354.

the Greek text, it is almost impossible to believe that the hearers would not think of the 144,000 sons of the tribes of Israel described earlier in Rev 7:1-8 when encountering this number.[384] Thus, when the 144,000 reappear in 14:1, this image of the transformed Israel has itself been transformed in the light of the innumerable crowd, suggesting that the 144,000 are now forever identified with the innumerable crowd (see 7:9), not unlike the way in which the Root of David is now forever identified with the slaughtered Lamb. The 144,000 are here described as standing with the Lamb on Mount Zion, while the innumerable crowd was "seen" as "standing before the throne and the Lamb"! In 14:1 the 144,000 stand with the Lamb in opposition to the triumvirate of evil, ready to do battle. Earlier the 144,000 received the seal of God upon their foreheads (7:3). Now, the content of that seal is revealed, for the 144,000 bear the name of the Lamb and the name of his Father. Clearly, the names that appear upon the 144,000 indicate possession, ownership, and protection,[385] specifically calling to mind the promise of the resurrected Jesus to the one who overcomes, "And I will write upon him the name of my God" (3:12).[386] They are like the one with whom they stand. The mention of the Father would likely trigger a recollection of the previous associations this language has had to this point in the book.[387] As they stand with the Lamb, they are a kingdom and priests to God (1:6), who have authority over the nations (2:26-27). As they stand with the Lamb, they are those whose names are not only written in, but have not been erased from (3:5), the book of life of the Lamb, who was slaughtered from the foundation of the world. As they stand with the Lamb, they are those entitled to sit on the throne with Jesus, who sits on the throne of his Father (3:21). The 144,000 thus represent those who overcome, who stand with the Lamb, who stand ready to fight as he has fought. The explicit contrast between those who bear the mark of the beast, with his blasphemous name on their foreheads, and those who bear the name of the Lamb and the name of his Father on their foreheads could hardly be missed!

"And I heard out of heaven as a voice of many waters and as a voice of great thunder, and the voice that I heard was as harpists harping on their harps." The focus of attention now shifts to heaven, the location of the voice or sound.

---

384. On this point, Beale (*The Book of Revelation*, 733-34) notes, "The lack of the article before '144,000' does not distinguish this group from the one in 7:4-9, where the article does occur. Throughout the Apocalypse images are repeated, sometimes without the article in later occurrences.... An article of previous reference is not needed here, since other features in the scene point clearly enough back to 7:4-9."

385. Beale, *The Book of Revelation*, 734.

386. Collins, *The Apocalypse*, 99.

387. Smalley, *Revelation*, 355.

There is a mysterious relationship between things seen and things heard in the book (1:10, 12-13; 5:5-6; 7:4, 9), sometimes with what is heard preceding what is seen (8:1-2). When the focus of attention shifts from what John saw to what he heard in 14:2, there is a buildup in anticipation. The voice(s) that come from heaven concern the 144,000 — their identity, their activities, and their character. The description of this voice as a voice of many waters would remind readers of the voice of Jesus (1:15). The description of the voice as a voice of great thunder would bring to mind the voice of one of the four living creatures crying "Go" as the first seal is being opened by the Lamb (6:1), with thunder having come to be closely associated with the activity of God (4:5; 8:5; 10:3-4; 11:19). This voice is also described as "harpists harping on their harps." In this peculiar description the subject ("harpists"), verbal form ("harping"), and object of the preposition ("harps") are all part of the same word family, a construction that places a great deal of emphasis upon this particular aspect of the voice's identity. The last time harps were mentioned, they were in the hands of the twenty-four elders in heaven (5:8). As harps accompany singing on that occasion, perhaps it might be expected that this sound from heaven in 14:1-2 would be accompanied by singing as well. This dramatic means of expression would thus likely be deemed as an appropriate sound to come from heaven and one closely associated as coming from those very near the throne and the one who sits on it, namely, the twenty-four elders.[388] This emphatic description goes some way toward preparing for the possibility that this remarkable sound comes from a number of individuals rather than one, as the mental image is of numerous harpists harping on their harps.

"And they sing a new song before the throne and before the four living creatures and the twenty-four elders, and no one was able to learn the song except the 144,000, those who had been purchased from the earth." In 5:8 the mention of harps is accompanied by singing, only here it appears the voice as harpists harping on their harps is actually the sound of numerous voices singing. Significantly, this song stands in stark contrast to the one sung by those enslaved to the beast (13:4).[389] Although there is some uncertainty with regard to the subject of the verb "they sing," which could be another of the third person impersonal forms here translated as "there was singing," it is likely that this third person plural verb would be taken as referring to the 144,000.[390] Despite the way in which the whole of v. 2 separates the subject (v. 1) from the

---

388. As Sweet (*Revelation*, 222) says, "Here the harping comes, by allusion, from the throne itself, and confirms the redemptive sense of John's vision."
389. Allo, *Saint Jean: L'Apocalypse*, 196.
390. Despite the protest of Aune, *Revelation 6–16*, 784.

verb (v. 3),[391] the rest of v. 3 makes clear that the 144,000 are uniquely qualified to sing this song. Notably, the voice of the 144,000 resembles the voice of the Lamb, depicted "like the sound of many waters."[392] "New song" language is holy war terminology, where a hymn of praise is offered for a new victory that a divine warrior wins over his foes (Pss 98:1-3; 144:9-10; Isa 42:10-13),[393] further underscoring the military nature of this scene. This new song is sung "before the throne and before the four living creatures and the elders," undoubtedly reminding hearers of the last time a new song was sung (5:8-10). There the new song is sung before the Lamb, and it appears to be sung by the twenty-four elders. The location of the song in 14:3 is the most appropriate place for it to be sung — the redemptive center of the universe — sung in the very presence of God! This song seems restricted to the 144,000, "and no one was able to learn the song except the 144,000, those who had been purchased from the earth." Interestingly, in Rev. 14:3 it is the ones who have the name of the Lamb and the name of his Father on their foreheads who are able to learn this new song. The 144,000 are further identified as "those who have been purchased from the earth," making explicit the connection between this group and all the redeemed. Those purchased by the blood of the Lamb come out of every tribe and tongue and people and nation (5:9b), and the blood of Jesus is clearly the means by which this purchase is accomplished (5:9a). The passive voice of the participle "the ones who have been purchased" further underscores the divine activity involved in this purchase.[394]

> These are the ones who have not been defiled by women, for they are virgins.
> These are the ones who follow the Lamb wherever he goes.
> These have been purchased from men as firstfruits to God and the Lamb, and in their mouth is found no lie, for they are blameless.

In these chiastically structured statements the hearers' skills in pneumatic discernment are put to the test. Though the first line might suggest that the 144,000 are to be understood as an all-male, celibate community,[395] this interpretation ultimately fails to convince. There is nothing in the Johannine literature to suggest that women were thought of as a group to be avoided in

---

391. Pattemore, *The People of God in the Apocalypse*, 184.
392. Pattemore, *The People of God in the Apocalypse*, 184.
393. Bauckham, *The Climax of Prophecy*, 230.
394. Gause, *Revelation*, 189.
395. So Collins, *The Apocalypse*, 100. For early Christian writers who defend this position, cf. ACCS 12, 217-21.

social interaction, or to be avoided sexually within the bounds of marriage. In fact, every specific woman mentioned in John's gospel turns out to be a model of belief in Jesus. To this point in Revelation the only negative female example is "the woman called Jezebel," who is not condemned for her gender but because she is a false prophetess. Neither would these words likely indicate an attitude suspicious of sexual relations as defiling; the wedding at Cana appears to indicate otherwise (John 2:1-11). Though male imagery has been used to describe the 144,000, as both the sons of the tribes of Israel (7:4) and those who have not been defiled by women (14:4), this group is one that ultimately encompasses all of the redeemed.[396] One of the things that would likely inform the interpretation of these words would be the "holy war" context in which they occur. OT holy war regulations include stipulations with regard to sexual abstinence before battle (Deut 23:9-10; 1 Sam. 21:5; 2 Sam. 11:11). Given that the 144,000 appear ready to join the Lamb in battle against the triumvirate of evil and that their sealing is reminiscent of a military roll call (7:4-8), the words they "have not defiled themselves with women" would likely be taken as a sign of their dedication to and preparation for battle. Owing to the emphasis placed upon the language of "fornication," "eating food sacrificed to idols" (Rev 2:14, 20), and "committing adultery" (Rev 2:22), all of which are used in a religiously qualified sense, and the refusal of "the rest of men" to repent for such activity (9:20-21),[397] it is likely that the idea of not being defiled would convey a sense of fidelity in witness and faith on the part of the 144,000 when faced with the temptation of such contamination.[398] Such an understanding is even more likely, given that the previous occurrence of the word that appears here as "they had been defiled" (3:4) describes those who had not defiled their clothing and whose names will not be erased from the book of life (3:5). The final statement, "for they are virgins," would then take on a rather thick meaning, which combines the ideas of preparation, dedication, and purity unto the Lamb.[399]

The second statement about the 144,000 stands at the center of the chiastic section marked out by the word "these," suggesting that primary focus would be given here. "These are the ones who follow the Lamb wherever he goes." This sentence would have a very special meaning, for the language of "following" is Johannine discipleship language par excellence (John 1:37-38, 40, 43; 8:12; 10:4-5, 27; 21:19-22). This aspect of following appears to be particularly in view in Rev 14:4b, for it is the Lamb who has been slaughtered that the 144,000 follow. The

---

396. Murphy, *Fallen Is Babylon*, 317.
397. Pattemore, *The People of God in the Apocalypse*, 186-87.
398. Sweet, *Revelation*, 221.
399. Pattemore, *The People of God in the Apocalypse*, 187.

144,000 thus follow Jesus even in death, with the phrase "wherever he goes" driving this point home, for Johannine hearers understand that this idea of going, with reference to Jesus, is unquestionably associated with his going to the Father (John 7:33; 8:14, 21-22; 13:3, 33; 16:5, 10, 17). Perhaps the most telling aspect of this verb for hearers of Rev 14:4 is found in the story of the dialogue between Jesus and his disciples before he goes to his friend Lazarus, who had just died. The disciples prophetically say, "Rabbi, now the Jews are seeking to stone you, and again you go there?" In John's gospel, as in Rev 14:4, where the Lamb goes inevitably involves suffering and death. Therefore, the meaning of this description of the 144,000 could hardly be missed: they follow the Lamb wherever he goes, even to death,[400] which, as it turns out, is the means by which this war is waged against the dragon and his beasts. Such a walk goes hand in glove with the first "these" statement, making clear the level of dedication and preparation on the part of the 144,000 for this battle.

The third statement with regard to the 144,000 forms a parallel to the first statement: "These have been purchased from men as firstfruits to God and the Lamb, and in their mouth is found no lie, for they are blameless." The 144,000 are those who have been purchased from the earth by means of the blood of the Lamb (14:3). This reality is one of the components of the new song (5:8-10), and it is to this characteristic of the 144,000 that the third statement returns. The imagery of firstfruits conveys that these have been dedicated to God and the Lamb in a special way, for they are pure, not contaminating themselves with the religious adultery, sexual immorality, and idolatry, with which they are confronted. Such imagery would also create an expectancy that these are the first of many to join the Lamb in the great harvest that is to follow. In this way, the relationship of the 144,000 to the conversion of the nations stands in parallel to the relationship of the 144,000 to the innumerable crowd (7:1-17). Similarly, the 144,000 also stand in parallel to the two prophetic witnesses, whose witness, including their death and resurrection, leads to the conversion of the vast majority of the universal city's inhabitants (11:3-13). Such language would encourage an expectation of a great harvest of belief to follow on from these firstfruits.[401] These who are firstfruits are further identified by the words "and in their mouth no lie was found, for they are blameless." Unlike the mouth of the beast, which boasts great and blasphemous things, and in contrast to those who lie (John 8:44; 1 John 1:6; 2:21, 27; Rev 2:2; 3:9), in the mouth of the

---

400. Eusebius (*The Ecclesiastical History* 5.1.10) cites this text in describing an early Christian martyr named Vettius Epagathus.
401. R. Bauckham, "Revelation," in *The Oxford Bible Commentary* (ed. J. Barton and J. Muddiman; Oxford: Oxford University Press, 2001), 1298.

144,000 there is found no lie.[402] Rather, these bear a likeness to the Lamb, who speaks words of truth, words of the Spirit, words that are true and are not lies (1 John 2:21, 27). In this respect, they bear a likeness to the remnant of Israel who speak no lies (Zeph. 3:13b). That they are truthful and do not lie would be of special significance, owing to the temptations to compromise their witness to the Lamb in the face of persecution and even death.[403] The words "for they are blameless" both reinforce the imagery of sacrifice, known from various OT texts, and underscore the issue of moral purity. The 144,000 are not only "blameless" as in a sacrifice without spot or defect, but they are also blameless with regard to moral purity.[404] In this as well, they resemble the Lamb, with whom they stand.

"And I saw another angel flying in mid-heaven, having an eternal gospel to preach unto those who are sitting upon the earth and unto every nation and tribe and tongue and people." This occurrence of "I saw" continues the upward trajectory of the things John sees, beginning with from the sea (13:1), to the earth (13:11), to Mount Zion (14:1), and now to the mid-heaven (14:6). The location of this other angel, in mid-heaven, is identical to that of the eagle described earlier, who pronounced with a great voice three coming woes (8:13). Such a location ensures that the angel could be seen and heard by everyone.[405] While the eagle proclaimed the negative message of woes, this other angel proclaims a positive message, having an "eternal gospel to preach."[406] The word play found in the Greek text would be easy to detect, as would the emphasis of this phrase upon the gospel, as both the direct object and the infinitive verb come from the same Greek root. Interestingly, this is the only occurrence of the term "gospel" in the Johannine literature, with only the verb form having appeared earlier. In the only other reference to this Greek word in Revelation, God himself is said to have preached "the mystery of God" to his own servants the prophets (10:7). Perhaps there is some connection between the eternal gospel this angel preaches and the mystery of God that he himself has preached. In any event, the eternal character of this gospel might very well be seen as quite fitting, coming as it does from the God who is earlier identified as "the one who is and the one who was and the one who is coming" (1:4). The hearers might also discern a contrast between (1) this eternal gospel and its offer of eternal life and (2) the transient message of the triumvirate of evil and its offer of "life" for only a brief

---

402. Michaels, *Revelation*, 172.
403. Smalley, *Revelation*, 360.
404. Bauckham, *The Climax of Prophecy*, 232, and Smalley, *Revelation*, 360.
405. Aune, *Revelation 6–16*, 824.
406. Bauckham, "Revelation," 1298.

time.[407] The scope of this gospel's intended audience appears to be as wide as it is eternal, for it is intended for all the inhabitants of the earth, described in the familiar fourfold fashion, "every nation and tribe and tongue and people," the sixth and final time this group of four demographic entities appears in Revelation. From its previous occurrences (5:9; 7:9; 10:11; 11:9; 13:7), three things are clear. First, these demographic groups are present in heaven, and their presence there offers hope and encouragement with regard to the ultimate redemption of these groups. Second, these groups are under the influence of, and side with, the first beast over against God and his people in the present battle on earth. Third, these groups are those to whom God, the Lamb, and his church are to bear witness for the purpose of their conversion. That the previous appearances of these groups convey such diverse ideas suggests that the hearers would find themselves facing those same tensions: between the hope of the conversion of the nations, the current reality of their obstinate opposition to God and his people, and the unrelenting call to bear prophetic witness to these very groups at the cost of the witnesses' lives.

"Saying with a great voice, 'Fear God and give him glory, because the hour of his judgment has come, and worship the one who made the heaven and the earth and the sea and the springs of water.'" The message to fear God and give him glory would be an unmistakably clear call for repentance, as fear leads to the giving of glory (11:11, 13), and God has given rewards to those who fear his name (11:18).[408] The giving or ascribing of glory to God in Revelation is consistently on the lips of believers (1:6; 4:9, 11; 5:12-13; 7:12; 11:13). The other angel's message is thus one that calls for a conversion on the part of humankind — from fearing the beast and worshipping him, to fearing God and giving glory unto him.[409] The urgency of this eternal gospel is revealed in the phrase "because the hour of his judgment has come,"[410] where the certainty of the arrival of the hour of judgment is spoken of as though it has already happened.[411] The words "the hour of his judgment" would likely be understood as referring to *the* final judgment,[412] the Day of the Lord, when all those who bear the name of God and the Lamb on their foreheads will be saved, and when all those who worship the image of the beast and bear his name will be destroyed. Thus, despite the obstinate refusal to repent and the continued worship of the image of the beast, the angel's proclamation of the eternal gospel reveals that it is still not

---

407. Smalley, *Revelation*, 361.
408. Osborne, *Revelation*, 535.
409. Collins, *The Apocalypse*, 102.
410. Prigent, *L'Apocalypse de Saint Jean*, 339.
411. Smalley, *Revelation*, 363.
412. Aune, *Revelation 6-16*, 828.

too late to repent![413] Specifically, this angel calls on those who hear his voice to "worship the one who made the heaven and the earth and the sea and the springs of water." The contrast between the worship rendered to the dragon and the beast by the inhabitants of the earth and the true worship rendered to the creator of it all could hardly be missed. Perhaps in "the heaven and the earth and the sea" there is reference to the places of origin of the dragon and the two beasts, indicating that, though they are powerful foes, God is the creator of everything.[414] Perhaps the hearers would also detect that the eternal gospel preached by this angel is none other than that spoken of in Ps 96:2, a psalm in which the entire content of the angel's message could be found.[415]

"And another angel, a second (one), followed, saying, 'Fallen, fallen is Babylon the Great, who out of the wine of the passion (wrath) of her sexual immorality gave all the nations to drink.'" This angel is described as following the first, which suggests that he too was flying in mid-heaven and preparing to proclaim a most important message. The emphasis of the angel's message would be easy to detect, for it stands at the beginning of the sentence, a position of emphasis in Greek grammar, and appears in duplicate form.[416] The occurrence of the word "fallen" in the aorist tense treats the fall of Babylon the Great, which is future, as though it has already taken place,[417] being yet another example of the prophetic perfect in Revelation (6:17; 11:18).[418] It is significant that the first mention of "Babylon the Great" in Revelation comes in a declaration of its utter and total demise! The name Babylon the Great would generate a variety of associations on the hearers' part, as Babylon would be remembered as a place of luxury and moral corruption,[419] as well as the destroyer of Jerusalem in 586 BCE. Neither would the parallels between the ancient Babylon and contemporary Rome, both as cities and empires, be missed. The description "great" might also remind hearers of "the great city" described in Rev 11, with the majority of its inhabitants, though opposed to God and his servants, eventually giving glory to God. Here, however, Babylon the Great is defined simply as the one "who out of the wine of the passion (wrath) of her sexual immorality gave all the nations to drink."

---

413. Ladd, *Revelation*, 193.

414. Koester, *Revelation and the End of All Things*, 137-39.

415. Cf. Bauckham, *The Climax of Prophecy*, 286-89, who suggests that Psalms 96–100 are all in view in the words of Rev 14:7.

416. Wall, *Revelation*, 184.

417. Tyconius (*Commentary on the Apocalypse*, 14:8 [ACCS 12, 225]) observes, "This is a common way of speaking in the Scripture, which often refers to events as past when they are yet in the future, esp. when he knows that what it predicts will inevitably be fulfilled."

418. Beale, *The Book of Revelation*, 754.

419. Smalley, *Revelation*, 264.

The Struggle of God's People in Cosmic Perspective (12:1–14:20)

The four genitive constructions that make up the Greek phrase translated "of the wine of the wrath of her sexual immorality" reflect the close connection of all the constituent elements (wine, wrath, sexual immorality, and "her"). Despite the idea that her wine is wine of passion borne of sexual immorality, it is simultaneously a wine of wrath, akin to the wrath of the dragon (12:12). The objects of her "affections" are "all the nations," those to whom the first angel has just preached the eternal gospel. That her wine is the wine of sexual immorality might well remind readers of the language of sexual immorality used to describe the activities of the woman called Jezebel by Jesus (2:20-21). Its appearance here might well serve to suggest that, in their encounter with the teaching of the Nicolaitans (2:15) and Jezebel, the hearers are actually already encountering Babylon the Great, which, it should be remembered, is as good as fallen.

"Another angel, a third (one) followed them, saying in a great voice, 'If anyone worships the beast and his image and receives a mark upon his forehead or upon his hand, he himself will drink of the wine of the wrath of God, which has been mixed, though unmixed in the cup of his anger, and he will be tormented in fire and sulfur before the holy angels and before the Lamb.'" This angel too would be understood as flying in mid-heaven and continuing the proclamation that the others have begun. It would not surprise hearers that the preaching of the eternal gospel includes the warnings of coming judgments for those who fail to heed this message and convert. This third angel picks up on the very phenomenon of the universal worship of the beast and the requisite receiving his mark, themes that are all too familiar from the extended discussion in chapter 13. This reference makes clear the connection between drinking the wine of the passion of sexual immorality given by Babylon the Great and the worship of the beast and the receiving of his mark. It would appear that the beast (and those who stand with him), like Babylon the Great, already stands under the judgment of "Fallen, Fallen" as well.

Such ones will also drink of the wine of the wrath of God. The same word that appears with reference to the wine of Babylon the Great to describe its passionate character appears here with the meaning "wrath." Through this word play we learn that drinking the wine of the passion of sexual immorality is actually drinking from the wine of God's wrath! While four genitive constructions occurred in the description of Babylon's wine, five occur in the description of God's wine. Perhaps most interesting is the occurrence together of the words "mixed, unmixed." The former expression refers to the practice of mixing wine with other substances to increase its strength. The latter refers to wine that has not been diluted by mixing it with water.[420] The meaning of this

---

420. Smalley, *Revelation*, 365.

"In the Spirit in Heaven" (4:1–16:21)

unusual combination would be that this wine of God's wrath will be drunk at full potency. It has not been diluted; it is at full strength! If this is not enough, God's wine is now described as "the cup of his anger." Reference to "cup" carries with it a variety of OT associations with regard to God's judgment (Pss 11:6; 75:8; Isa 51:17, 22; Jer 25:17, 28; 49:12; 51:7; Lam 4:21; Ezek 23:31-33; Hab 2:15-16; Obad 16; Zech 12:2);[421] for Johannine hearers, "cup" would forever be associated with Jesus himself having drunk the cup of the Father (John 18:11), which led to death.[422] The occurrence of the word "anger" or "rage" to describe the cup of his anger would remind readers of its previous occurrences with reference to the anger or wrath of the Lamb (6:16-17) and of God (6:17; 11:18). Apparently, drinking from the cup of God's anger will involve being "tormented in fire and sulfur before the holy angels and the Lamb." Torment has appeared as part of the means that God uses in Revelation when seeking to bring humankind to repentance (9:5; 11:10) and is even something the woman clothed with the sun experiences (12:2). In 14:10 the nature of the torment involves the incinerating effects of fire and sulfur, elements that appear in OT scenes of judgment (Job 18:15; Ps 11:6; Isa 30:33; 34:9), the best known of which is in the account of the destruction of Sodom and Gomorrah (Gen 19:1-29), which became a notorious example (cf. Deut 29:23).[423] Surprisingly, this tormenting punishment takes place in the presence of "the holy angels and the Lamb."[424] If the reference to the holy angels is thought to include the three other angels described in this passage devoted to the eternal gospel, it follows that they would stand ready to serve as witnesses to the message they have proclaimed.[425] Similarly, since reference was earlier made to "the wrath of the Lamb" (6:16-17), it would not be all that exceptional to find that the Lamb himself is witness to the judgment of God that falls upon those who obstinately refuse to repent from their worship of the beast.

"And the smoke of their torment goes up forever and ever, and they have no rest day and night, the ones who worship the beast; and if any receive the mark of his name, they have no rest day and night." The image of smoke going up would be familiar from the OT (Gen 19:28; Josh 8:20; Judg 20:40), where it serves as a sign of complete and utter destruction. In Rev 14:11, then, we conclude that this divine torment is eternal, complete, and inescapable.[426] Such a description creates a "ghastly counterpart" to the description of the prayers of

---

421. Aune, *Revelation 6–16*, 833.
422. Smalley, *Revelation*, 365.
423. Smalley, *Revelation*, 366.
424. Aune (*Revelation 6–16*, 835) notes that such is without parallel in antiquity.
425. Mounce, *The Book of Revelation*, 276.
426. Beasley-Murray, *Revelation*, 226.

the saints, which ascend to heaven like clouds of incense before the throne of God (5:8; 8:4; 14:11).[427] The phrase "they have no rest day and night" is identical to one in 4:8, where these words describe the never-ending praise of God offered by the four living creatures, creating an unforgettable contrast between unceasing worship and unending torment.[428] The recipients of such torment are those who worship the beast and his image and who receive the mark of his name. Significantly, these words are the same as those with which the angel's words began in v. 9, thus forming an inclusio around the words about the nature of punishment that awaits those who refuse to repent.

"Here is the patient endurance of the saints, those who keep the commands of God and the faith of Jesus." The call in 14:12, the third of four such calls encountered in Revelation (13:10, 18; 14:12; 17:9), emphasizes the saints' patient endurance. The mention of patient endurance would carry with it the previous nuances of the phrase (1:9; 2:2-3, 19; 3:10), where it is understood to be "in Jesus" (1:9) and belonging to him (3:10), with the idea of following Jesus in rendering one's witness, even to the point of death. The definition of patient endurance here offered, "those who keep the commands of God . . . ," would no doubt bring to mind the last occurrence of this phrase, where it appears synonymously with the rest of the woman's seed, against whom the dragon makes war (12:17). The words "and the faith of Jesus" remind readers that faith is used by the resurrected Jesus as a characteristic or work of the churches in Pergamum (2:13) and Thyatira (2:19). As with patient endurance, faith is closely associated with Jesus, as he speaks both of "my faith" and "my faithful witness Antipas" (2:13). In 14:12 the phrase "the faith of Jesus" would perhaps be taken as an objective genitive, placing emphasis on faith *in* Jesus,[429] though in typically Johannine fashion, it might at the same time convey something about *Jesus'* faith, as an equivalent to Jesus' testimony.[430] Such language focuses attention on solidarity with Jesus' faith and witness, being a call to the kind of faithfulness characteristic of an overcomer. This call to pneumatic discernment is thus a call to participate in the proclamation of the eternal gospel to a world drunk on the wine of the passion of Babylon the Great, which worships the beast and his image. Despite any hostile opposition, the hearers are called to faithful, patient endurance in "keeping the commands of God and the faith of Jesus."

"And I heard a voice out of heaven saying, 'Write: Blessed are the dead, those who die in the Lord from now on.' 'Yes,' says the Spirit, 'in order that

---

427. Koester, *Revelation and the End of All Things*, 138.

428. Aune, *Revelation 6–16*, 836.

429. Ladd, *Revelation*, 197.

430. On this phrase as both an objective and a subjective genitive, cf. Beale, *The Book of Revelation*, 766-67.

they might rest from their labors, for their works follow after them.'" Again an unidentified voice comes from heaven directing John to write. There would be no mistaking that such an instruction is a divine one, conveying a sense of importance,[431] even urgency, to the words that are to be written down. If the directive to write comes from the resurrected Jesus, the content of what is to be written would come from Jesus as well. In the book's second beatitude (14:13), the hearers learn that, while the death of those who worship the beast will be cursed with unending torment, those who die in the Lord die a blessed death.[432] The construction "in the Lord" refers to the sphere of the Lord as the place where death occurs.[433] Though it might be tempting to take the words "from now" as suggesting that only from this moment are those who die in the Lord blessed, its occurrences in John's gospel (John 13:19; 14:7) suggest that the idea is a bit more flexible (cf. also Rev 12:10), focusing more on the eschatological and spiritual than the temporal and spatial.[434] These comforting words are affirmed and witnessed by the Spirit himself with "Yes"! It would certainly not surprise the hearers to hear directly from the Spirit at this point. To this blessing the Spirit adds, "in order that they might rest from their labor, for their works follow them." This message about those who die in the Lord being said to rest from their labors would be heard in sharp contrast to those who worship the beast having no rest day and night from their torment (14:11); these words reveal one aspect of the blessing of dying in the Lord, rather than dying in obstinate opposition to him. It would not be lost on the hearers that they are to rest from their "labors," owing to Jesus' previous words that those in Ephesus have not "labored out" in their labor (2:2-3)! That this terminology appears in Jesus' words about the harvest among the Samaritans (John 4:38) might be additional reason to see a connection between their labor and the missiological nature of their labors.[435] Just as the 144,000 follow the Lamb wherever he goes, so their works follow them. Their works are known by the resurrected Jesus, indicate the condition of one's relationship with him, and are the basis of judgment by him (Rev 2:23). That they follow after them, even after their death, reveals the intimate connection that exists between one's person and one's works. Just as the Spirit's anointing upon the two prophetic witnesses did not cease with their death but extended beyond it, so too their works continue the witness given while they are alive, making clear yet another dimension of the blessing for the dead who die in the Lord.

431. Smalley, *Revelation*, 369.
432. Gause, *Revelation*, 195.
433. Smalley, *Revelation*, 370.
434. Smalley, *Revelation*, 370.
435. Sweet, *Revelation*, 231.

The Struggle of God's People in Cosmic Perspective (12:1–14:20)

"And I saw, and behold a white cloud, and upon the cloud (one) sitting as a Son of Man, having upon his head a golden crown and in his hand a sharp sickle." This occurrence of "I saw" continues the upward trajectory of the things John sees: from the sea (13:1), to the earth (13:11), to Mount Zion (14:1), to the mid-heaven (14:6), and now a white cloud (14:14). The appearance of a "white" cloud would prepare readers for a positive character or action on the part of the one described,[436] as white is uniformly associated with God and/or the Lamb (1:14; 2:17; 3:4-5, 18; 4:4; 6:2, 11; 7:9, 13). Unlike the "mighty angel," who is clothed with a cloud (10:1), and the two prophetic witnesses, who go up to heaven in a cloud (11:12), this figure is described as "sitting upon the cloud," reminding readers of the prophetic word about Jesus. This identical phrase is used with reference to him in the inaugural vision (1:7).[437] Clearly, this title would remind hearers of Dan 7:13, where reference to the Son of Man also appears. Johannine hearers would be familiar with its rich theological heritage from John's gospel as well (3:14; 5:27; 6:27, 53; 9:35; 12:23, 34; 13:31). Such an understanding of Jesus as Son of Man in the Johannine tradition combines the elements of heavenly location, authority to judge, and the giving of eternal life to those who believe. All this heritage suggests that these words refer to the return of Jesus with the clouds.[438] The golden crown upon his head indicates that he himself is an overcomer (Rev 2:10; 3:11; 4:4).[439] Reference to "a sharp sickle" in his hand would likely remind readers of the sharp sword that comes from the mouth of the resurrected Jesus (1:16), which can be an instrument of war (2:12) wielded against those who do not repent (2:16). At the same time, mention of the sickle would no doubt carry with it the idea of harvest, perhaps even the final harvest of judgment, of which Joel 3:13 speaks.

"And another angel came out of the temple crying out with a great voice to the one sitting upon the cloud, 'Send your sickle and harvest, because the hour to harvest has come, because the harvest of the earth has been ripened (dried up).'" Unlike the previous three other angels of 14:6-11, this other angel (14:15) comes out of the temple, suggesting that he came from the very presence of God,[440] being as good as the voice of God himself.[441] This divine command, issued to the one who sits on the cloud, focuses exclusively upon the activity of harvesting, with a form of the word "harvest" appearing three times in the

---

436. Smalley, *Revelation*, 371.
437. Fee, *Revelation*, 203.
438. Collins, *The Apocalypse*, 105.
439. Allo, *Saint Jean: L'Apocalypse*, 222.
440. Gause, *Revelation*, 197.
441. Allo (*Saint Jean: L'Apocalypse*, 223) suggests that it is Divinity himself who speaks with Jesus.

span of ten words in the Greek text. The command makes clear the purpose of the sharp sickle in the Son of Man's hand. For Johannine hearers the activity of harvesting would be conceived of in wholly positive terms, as the appearance of both the noun and verb forms in the missiological discussion of Jesus with his disciples in John 4:35-38 reveals. Such a missiological backdrop would make it altogether likely that this command includes a reference to the salvific harvest by the Son of Man of those who respond to the proclamation of the eternal gospel (14:7).[442] Like the first "other angel," this angel uses the imagery of "the hour," here as "the hour to harvest." It is spoken of in the past tense, indicating the certainty of its occurrence, even though this activity still lies in the future. This angel speaks of the harvest of the earth as "having been ripened" or "dried up." This word carries with it the idea of something drying up, as branches that are cut off from the vine and cast into the fire (John 15:6), but when used in the context of harvest, it indicates that the harvest has ripened to the point that it will spoil if not harvested.[443] The ripening of the harvest reveals that the hour of the harvest has arrived; it is the optimal moment for the harvest.

"And the one who sits upon the cloud cast his sickle out upon the earth, and the earth was harvested." These words make absolutely clear that it is the Son of Man, Jesus himself, who harvests the earth, reinforcing the depiction of the Son of Man in 14:14-15. The occurrence of the passive tense "was harvested," the fourth appearance of a form from the same word family in two verses, continues to emphasize the centrality of the harvest as the primary activity of the Son of Man in these verses and its significance.

"And another angel came out of the temple of the one in heaven, also himself having a sharp sickle." Like the other angel described in 14:15, this angel too is referred to simply as another angel, without enumeration. This other angel also comes out of the temple, with the temple explicitly identified as "the temple of the one in heaven," making clear the connection between the activity of this angel and God himself. Like the Son of Man, this angel also has a sharp sickle, indicating that he too is prepared to harvest, even though the earth has just been harvested!

"And another angel came out of the altar having authority over the fire, and he called with a great voice to the one having the sharp sickle saying, 'Send your sharp sickle and gather the clusters of the vineyard of the earth, because its grapes are ripe.'" The emergence of this other angel from the altar would indicate that he is very closely associated with the prayers of the souls under the altar (6:9) and the saints (8:3) for justice, the activity of divine judgment

---

442. Bauckham, *The Climax of Prophecy*, 294.
443. Aune, *Revelation 6–16*, 789-90.

The Struggle of God's People in Cosmic Perspective (12:1–14:20)

(9:13), and the worshippers of God (11:1). This angel has authority over fire, which, along with 8:5, 7-8 and 9:17-18, suggests a change in focus from the idea of harvesting to that of judgment. This other angel, the sixth to be mentioned since 14:6, calls out the divine command to the angel holding the sharp sickle to send his sickle and "gather the clusters of the vineyard of the earth, because his grapes are ripe." This divine command is reminiscent of the divine command given to the Son of Man, though this one focuses upon the gathering of clusters of grapes that are ripe for harvest. Grape and vineyard imagery would bring to mind the wine imagery that has appeared earlier, specifically, the wine of the passion of sexual immorality of Babylon the Great and the wine of the wrath of God, unmixed in the cup of his anger. The hearers may thus very well understand the divine command of 14:18 as being directly connected to the warning with regard to God's wine of wrath (14:10).

"The angel cast his sickle into the earth and gathered the vineyard of the earth and cast it into the great winepress of the wrath of God." Like the Son of Man before him, this other angel casts or swings his sickle into the earth, but unlike the Son of Man he does not harvest; rather, he gathers the vineyard of the earth. The imagery of Joel 3:13 is almost palpable, as the activity of judgment can hardly be missed. For as wine comes out of the winepress when the grapes are crushed underfoot, so the wine of God's wrath is produced when the clusters of grapes gathered by this other angel are crushed underfoot in the great winepress of God's wrath. The clear implication of the words in Rev 14:19 would be that those who worship the image of the beast and receive his mark, who refuse to repent and give glory to God, will find themselves in the great winepress of God's wrath, experiencing this excruciating punishment under the divine foot itself!

"And the winepress was trodden outside the city, and blood came out of the winepress up to the bridles of the horses for 1,600 stadia." The passive voice verb "was trodden" suggests it is God himself who does the treading. The description of the activity of treading in the great winepress of God's wrath would stand in contrast to and in critique of the activity of the nations, earlier described as treading underfoot the outer court of the temple (11:2). The great winepress of God's wrath is described as being outside of the city. Such language may remind hearers that the nations would tread under foot the court located outside of the temple (11:2) and that the place where Jesus was crucified was outside the city (John 19:20; cf. also Heb 13:12 and Matt 21:39).[444] On either understanding, it would appear that the punishment fits the crime.[445] Instead

---

444. Smalley, *Revelation*, 377.
445. Murphy, *Fallen Is Babylon*, 328. As Aune (*Revelation 6–16*, 847) observes, "This judgment constitutes a kind of poetic justice."

of the juice of the grapes coming out of the winepress, blood comes out of the great winepress of God's wrath! The mention of blood not only underscores the gruesome nature of the divine judgment (cf. also Rev 8:7-8) but also stands in contrast to the way in which the blood of the Lamb and those who are faithful to him carries with it redemptive connotations. The blood that emerged from the winepress is first measured by depth or height, for it is as high as the bridle of horses, a height that is the rough equivalent to the stature of most of the individual hearers! If one were to experience such a horrendous sight, the blood would be of such a magnitude that it would cover practically all living beings! The blood is also measured in terms of length, as it covers 1,600 stadia. This distance, the rough equivalent of the length of Palestine, would convey the idea that this judgment is universal and complete. By this point the hearers would likely expect the number 1,600 to convey a significance on its own, and not simply as a means of measuring geographic distance. If so, it is likely they would note that this number is explicable by several means of calculation (4×400, $4 \times 4 \times 100$, $4^2 \times 100$), carrying within itself the sacred number 40×40[446] and reflecting the universal geography of Revelation itself.[447] On any reckoning, the measurement of 1,600 stadia would convey the idea of universal and absolute judgment.[448]

Seven Angels with Seven Bowls of Plagues (15:1–16:21)

Once again the hearers of Revelation may be forgiven if they mistakenly think that they have come to the end of John's words, for the description of the dual activities of harvesting the faithful of the earth (14:14-16) and the gathering of grapes for the great winepress of the wrath of God (14:17-20) suggests just that. And yet, the vision continues.

Another Great Sign in Heaven: The Seven Angels (15:1-8)

"And I saw another great and marvelous sign in the heaven, seven angels having the seven last plagues, because in them the wrath of God has been completed." "I saw" continues the upward trajectory of the things John sees beginning in 13:1: from the sea (13:1), to the earth (13:11), to Mount Zion (14:1), to the mid-

---

446. Allo, *Saint Jean: L'Apocalypse*, 225.
447. Prigent, *L'Apocalypse de Saint Jean*, 350.
448. Resseguie, *The Revelation of John*, 202.

Seven Angels with Seven Bowls of Plagues (15:1–16:21)

heaven (14:6), to a white cloud (14:14), and now in heaven (15:1). The mention of "another great and marvelous sign in heaven" would remind hearers of the great sign in heaven encountered in 12:1.[449] It thus becomes clear that chapters 12–14, which appear to reveal the contents of the unsealed scroll, are enveloped by reference to these two great signs, forming an inclusio around this section, indicating that Rev 12–14 is coming to an end. If reference to this other "great and marvelous sign" would cause the hearers to look back to the mention of the first great sign in 12:1, mention of "seven angels with the seven last plagues" (15:1) would cause them to look further back to the seven angels with seven trumpets described in 8:6–9:21 and 11:15-19. The similarities between these two sets of seven angels and the fact that the seven angels mentioned in 15:1 are said to have the seven last plagues underscore the connection between these sets of seven angels. Mention of the seven angels with the seven last plagues would continue the story line of the seven angels with the seven trumpets, not unlike the way in which the description of these latter angels had earlier continued the story line of the opening of the seven seals. This identification thus suggests some connection between what has preceded in 12–14 and that which follows. The seven last plagues clearly convey the idea of finality, bringing to mind the connection between the activities described and the plagues of Egypt. Perhaps also these seven angels with their plagues would be understood as fulfilling the words of Lev 26:21-24, which speak of the sevenfold punishment of plagues that awaits those who do not obey the law of the Lord.[450] The reason they are last is "because in them the wrath of God has been completed." God's wrath (Rev 14:10, 19) is here spoken of as already having been completed,[451] which the aorist passive indicates. Again, God's future actions are understood as so certain that they are spoken of as already accomplished,[452] with the divine passive suggesting that it is God himself who completes his wrath through these last seven plagues.

"And I saw as a glass sea mixed with fire and those who overcome (out of) the beast and (out of) his image and (out of) his number standing upon the glass sea having harps of God." Almost nothing in these words is not informed by words and/or images previously encountered. Mention of the glass sea immediately recalls the inaugural vision of heaven (ch. 4), where a sea of glass stretches out before the throne. Here the description of the glass sea

---

449. Contra Beasley-Murray (*Revelation*, 234), who explains the similarities as an accident of language.
450. An interpretation prominent in the early church, for which cf. the discussions in ACCS 12, 239-41.
451. Gause, *Revelation*, 201.
452. Prigent, *L'Apocalypse de Saint Jean*, 354.

as mixed with fire would likely remind readers that the theophanic elements that come from the throne (4:5) appear to be reflected in the glass sea before it (4:6),[453] an indication that even the objects that have negative connotations, as "sea" did in antiquity, somehow reflect the glory of God. Since both the seals and the trumpets, which conclude with a display of theophanic elements in growing intensity, are designed to lead humankind to repentance, the hearers would likely understand the reflection of the theophanic elements in the glass sea as pointing to God's redemptive judgments, an understanding confirmed by 15:2, where the glass sea is described as "mixed with fire."[454] Owing to the previous occurrences of fire in the book (1:14; 2:18; 3:18; 4:5; 8:5, 7-8; 9:17-18; 10:1; 11:5; 14:10, 18), mention of this glass sea mixed with fire would be pregnant with meaning, suggesting that, even though the last seven plagues indicate the end of God's wrath, God's desire for the repentance of humankind has not yet come to an end. Furthermore, standing "upon" or "around" it are "those who overcome the beast and his image and his number." These individuals appear identical to those described in 12:11, who have overcome the great dragon, the ancient serpent, the one called Devil and Satan, the deceiver of the entire inhabited world, and who are themselves heirs to the promises given by the resurrected Jesus, in the seven prophetic messages to the seven churches, to those who overcome (2:7, 11, 17, 26-28; 3:5, 12, 21). Such associations would create a heightened sense of expectancy that the eschatological promises are not far from fulfillment! Here, reference is made to this opponent's identity in triplicate form. He is *the beast*, the one who made war against the offspring of the woman clothed with the sun; *the image of the beast*, which generates oracular speech and before whom all must worship; and *the number of the beast*, the mark that designates ownership by the beast, without which one cannot enter into commercial life and the refusal of which ultimately leads to death. That "the ones who overcome" is a present participle may suggest that those upon/around the glass sea are even now in the act of overcoming. That each reference to an aspect of the beast's identity is preceded by "out of" may convey something of the intensity of the faithful witnesses' conflict with the beast. The description of the overcomers as "standing" upon or around the glass sea would likely remind readers of the question raised by the inhabitants of the earth, "Who is able to stand?" before the face of the one who sits on the throne and the wrath of the Lamb when the day of their wrath has come (6:16-17). This question receives an answer in 7:9, where the innumerable crowd is "standing before the throne and before the Lamb." The description of the overcomers

---

453. S. Légasse, "Μείγνυμι, μειγνύω," *EDNT*, 2:402.
454. Smalley, *Revelation*, 384.

as standing in 15:2 would clearly provide a point of continuity between these two groups. The language of "standing" in 15:2 might be an allusion to the first resurrection, which reflects not only the posture of those in 7:9 but also that of the Lamb, who looked as though it had been slain but who stands (5:6).[455] The phrase "having harps of God" would also suggest a certain continuity between these overcomers and the twenty-four elders with harps around the throne (5:8) and the "harpists harping on their harps," who appear to be the 144,000 (14:2).[456] The mention of harps in 15:2 makes clear their divine origin, as they are identified as God's harps and thus would be understood as a divine gift or reward. Their presence here would also create an expectancy that singing could not be far away.

"And they sang the Song of Moses the servant of God and the song of the Lamb, saying. . . ." To this point, explicit mention of the singing of songs has occurred only in the immediate presence of God (5:9; 14:3). These earlier associations between singing and the redeemed would further underscore the emerging continuity between these who overcome, the twenty-four elders, and the 144,000 before them. Unlike the songs of chapters 5 and 14, this song is not identified as a "new" song but rather as "the Song of Moses the servant of God and the song of the Lamb." "The Song of Moses the servant of God" would call attention to the place of Moses in Israel's redemptive history, for not only is the descriptive title "the servant of God" one used for Moses on numerous occasions in the OT (Exod 14:31; Num 12:7; Deut 34:5; Josh 1:1, 15; 8:31; 9:24; 1 Kgs 8:53, 56; 2 Kgs 18:12; 21:8; 2 Chr 24:9; Neh 1:8; Ps 105[104]:26; Mal 4:4), but it also makes clear that Moses himself is a prophet of God (cf. Rev 10:7).[457] Mention of the Song of Moses would bring to mind one specific moment in redemptive history, when the Song of Moses was sung in celebration of Israel's deliverance from Egypt, culminating in the crossing of the Red Sea (Exod 15). Such associations would suggest a connection between those who overcome the beast, his image, and the number of his name and those who experienced the deliverance at the Red Sea. There may be a visual connection between the crossing of the Red Sea and those who stand beside (have passed through) the glass sea.[458] If mention of the Song of Moses calls to mind the song recorded in Exod 15, mention of the song of the Lamb would recall the new song of Rev 5:9-14, in which the worthiness of the Lamb is extolled by every creature in the universe owing to the Lamb's slaughter, his

---

455. Smalley, *Revelation*, 385.
456. Caird, *The Revelation of Saint John*, 197-98.
457. Bauckham, *The Climax of Prophecy*, 300.
458. Resseguie, *The Revelation of John*, 205.

purchase out of all peoples, and his making kings and priests unto God. As the new song of Rev 5 concludes, the praise of the Lamb is placed alongside that of the one who sits on the throne.

> Great and marvelous are your works,
>   Lord, God, the All Powerful One;
> Righteous and true are your ways,
>   the King of the nations.
> Who will not have feared you, Lord,
>   and will glorify your name?
> For you alone are holy,
>   for all the nations will come
>   and will worship before you,
> for your righteous acts have been manifested.

Semitic parallelism is revealed in the first four lines of this song. At the center of the song is an emphatic rhetorical question, reminiscent of those found in OT hymns (Exod 15:11; Pss 6:3; 15:1; Isa 40:25; Mic 7:18).[459] Scarcely a word in the song is not richly informed by its place in the OT. As the words of the song emerge, it becomes evident that John describes not two songs but one. For in the words of this song is an incredible convergence of words and images from the OT, as well as from Revelation and John's gospel, which goes some way toward revealing the intriguing relationship between the Song of Moses and the song of the Lamb. The relationship between the two songs appears on the same order as the relationship between the Lion of the Tribe of Judah and the Lamb that looked as though it had been slain in Rev 5. The songs are thus to be understood in the light of one another and yet are, at the same time, one song![460]

The extraordinary nature of this song is revealed, in part, by its opening lines:

> Great and marvelous are your works,
>   Lord, God, the All Powerful One;
> Righteous and true are your ways,
>   the King of the nations.

---

459. Smalley, *Revelation*, 388.
460. Cf. R. Meynet, "Le cantique de Moïse et le cantique de l'Agneau (Ap 15 et Ex 15)," *Gregorianum* 73 (1992): 46, and J. N. Musvosvi, "The Song of Moses and the Song of the Lamb," *Journal of the Adventist Theological Society* 9.1-2 (1998): 44-47.

Seven Angels with Seven Bowls of Plagues (15:1–16:21)

The opening line brings to mind the ways in which the mighty salvific works of God have been described in the OT (Exod 15:11; Pss 92:5; 98:1-2; 111:1-2; 118:1; 139:14; 1 Chr 16:9), as well as the way the activity of God and/or his agents is often spoken of as "great" in Revelation.[461] Such an emphasis also fits nicely with the way in which the works of God are portrayed in John's gospel (John 4:34; 5:20, 36[2x]; 6:29; 7:3, 21; 9:3-4; 10:25, 32[2x], 33, 37-38; 14:10-12; 15:24; 17:4), where his work is designed to result in belief (6:29). Conversely, there is a significant contrast between the great and marvelous works of God and the works of those who refuse to repent but continue in their worship of demons and idolatry (Rev 9:20). There is also an explicit connection between "the great and marvelous works" celebrated in this song and the "other great and marvelous sign" with which this section begins, indicating the tight connection between the assessment of God's judgments as "great and marvelous" and the seven angels with the seven last bowls of plagues (15:1).

This opening line is followed by the invocation "Lord, God, the All Powerful One," familiar from its numerous appearances in the OT, where it occurs in prophetic oracles in which Yahweh warns of impending judgment (Amos 3:13; 4:13; 5:16, 27; 9:5; Nah 3:5; Zech 10:3), in texts that refer to his work as creator (Amos 5:8; 9:6), and in texts referring to the promise of restoration (Hos 12:5; Amos 5:14-15; 9:15). The invocation is also familiar from its refrain-like occurrences in Revelation (1:8; 4:8; 11:17). Its occurrence in the song of 15:3 would thus draw together the idea of God as creator — as unrivaled power in the universe — and as judge.

The second part of the Hebraic parallelism stands in tandem with the song's opening. In hearing the ways of God described as "righteous and true," a number of emphases would converge. While the hearers would know that God and his ways are spoken of in similar terms in the Torah (Deut 32:4) and the Psalter (145:17), Johannine hearers would be especially aware of the close connection between Jesus (1 John 1:9; 2:1, 29; 3:7), his activity of righteous judgment (John 5:30; 7:24), and the righteous Father (17:25). Also in Johannine thought God is "true God" (John 3:33; 7:28; 8:26; 17:3; 1 John 5:20), and his Son is "the truth" (John 1:14, 17; 14:6; cf. also Rev 3:7, 14). In this line of the hymn (Rev 15:3), the hearers might discern a partial response to the prayer of the saints for judgment and vindication in 6:10, where God is invoked with the words "O Master, the Holy and True One." Perhaps in the words of those who sing this hymn in 15:3, the testimony of those who have been slain is present, namely, that they are satisfied that the God whom they implored to act has indeed acted in

---

461. The term μέγας (*megas*, "great") appears some forty-five times in the Apocalypse, many of which with reference to God, his activities, and/or his agents.

his own ways and in his own time. This line of thought is further borne out by the name attributed to God in this portion of the parallelism, "the King of the nations." This idea has a rich OT heritage, where it carries with it the idea of the absolute superiority of God over the nations and their gods (Jer 10:7; Pss 22:28; 47:8; 96:10; 99:2; 1 Chr 16:31). In this title a whole range of meanings converges from Revelation itself as well. In the prologue Jesus has been called "the ruler of the kings of the earth" (1:5). The title indicates that, despite the rebellious actions of the kings of the earth (6:15), God is still their sovereign, and in contrast to theirs, his reign is an eternal one (11:15) that even now has begun (11:17-18). Despite the rebellious actions of the kings of the earth, they continue to be the objects of God's prophetic call to repentance (10:11). This kingdom was made for God by Jesus through his blood; kingdom members who have overcome will join in the reign of God (1:6, 9; 5:10; 11:15-18; 12:10-12).

The structural center and theological heart of this song next appears in the rhetorical question:

> Who will not have feared you, Lord,
>   and will glorify your name?

Recognizable from the OT (Exod 15:11; Pss 6:3; 15:1; Isa 40:18, 25; Mic 7:18), this question follows well upon the previous titles used for God in this hymn — "Lord, God, All powerful One" and "King of the nations." His role as cosmic deliverer serves to highlight further his unique role and person. This question seems to be a direct response to and critique of the rhetorical question raised about the "incomparability" of the beast, "Who is like the beast, and who is able to make war against him?" and the description of the universal worship of the dragon and the beast in 13:4 and 13:8, respectively.[462] It also seems likely that the rhetorical question of 15:4 would be taken by the hearers as in some way a response to the angelic proclamation of the eternal gospel in 14:6-7 to "fear God and give him glory,"[463] especially since both fear (11:11, 13, 18) and giving glory (1:6; 4:9, 11; 5:12-13; 7:12; 11:13) are closely connected with repentance and the worship of God, respectively. The glorification of God's name would convey the glorification of God himself, as his name is coterminous with his presence, which is coterminous with his person. Perhaps in these words the prophetic words of Mal 1:11 are fulfilled, "'From the rising of the sun until its setting my name will have been glorified, and in every place where incense and a pure offering are offered; for my name is great among

---

462. Resseguie, *The Revelation of John*, 206.
463. Caird, *The Revelation of Saint John*, 198-99.

the nations,' says the Lord God All Powerful."⁴⁶⁴ Once again future realities are spoken of with such prophetic certainty that they are regarded as already having taken place, again underscoring the certainty of the conversion of the nations.

The hymn's conclusion takes a threefold structure, each line beginning with "because" or "for":

> For you alone are holy,
> for all the nations will come and will worship before you,
> for your righteous acts have been manifested.

The lines of this stanza appear to build on the hymn's rhetorical center, offering a series of justifications for its claims. Though God is previously called ἅγιος (*hagios*, "holy") in Revelation (4:8; 6:10), this is the first of only two times he is referred to as ὅσιος (*hosios*, "holy") in the book (cf. 16:5). This occurrence of the term, joined by the only occurrence of μόνος (*monos*, "only") in Revelation, underscores the earlier praise of God's incomparability. Such an attribution brings to mind Deut 32:4, where the Lord is described as "holy," and Ps 144:17 (LXX), where his works are described as such. This line thus offers an initial reason why all fear the Lord and will glorify his name — "for he alone is holy"!

The second line also begins with the word "because" or "for"; it too builds upon the hymn's rhetorical center, and it too hearkens back to ideas found in the parallelism of the first stanza. Specifically, this line indicates that even the nations will be drawn to the King of the Nations. These words, which echo those of certain eschatological promises found in the prophets (Isa 2:2-4; Mal 1:11), would continue to cultivate in the hearers the call to and hope for the conversion of the nations. It is likely that the language "will worship before you" would convey the idea of vindication and righteous acknowledgment, reminding hearers of the virtually identical language used by the resurrected Jesus in his words to the church in Philadelphia about that which awaits those of the synagogue of Satan: "They will come and will worship before your feet." Such would be an indication that the nations are joining with all other worshippers of the true God, described at various points throughout the book.⁴⁶⁵ These words also underscore the contrast between these worshippers and those engaged in the illegitimate worship of the dragon and the beast (13:4, 8, 12, 15; 14:9, 11). Since

---

464. Gause, *Revelation*, 204-5.
465. Contra Kiddle (*The Revelation of St. John*, 309), who caricatures such worship as having "a turncoat flavor" to it.

there is surely some overlap between some who have been described as involved in illegitimate worship and those who will worship God, it would stoke the fire of the hearers' passion to work for the conversion of the nations.

The third line of the third stanza is like the first two lines in that it too begins with the word "because" or "for," builds upon the hymn's rhetorical center, and hearkens back to ideas found in the parallelism of the first stanza. Here, the manifestation of God's righteous acts offers additional rationale for the rhetorical question standing at the hymn's center, which expresses truth about God. The Johannine hearers' encounter with "have been manifested" would likely be informed by its prominence in John's gospel, where it often occurs in describing the manifestation of the work and glory of Jesus (John 1:31; 2:11; 3:21; 7:4; 21:1, 14) and that of his Father (3:21; 9:3; 17:6). The occurrence of "your righteous actions" at this point in the hymn would not only direct the hearers' attention back to the second part of the parallelism with which the hymn begins, where God's ways are described as "righteous" — giving the hymn a chiastic sense of structure — but it would also be additional explanation for the extraordinary response of humankind described in the hymn's rhetorical center. God's acts of judgment are not random acts but are indeed righteous acts designed to encourage true worship, even among those who rebelliously worship the dragon, the beast, and the image of the beast.[466]

"And after these things I saw, and the temple of the tabernacle of witness in heaven opened, and the seven angels having the seven plagues came out of the temple wearing clean, shining stone and being girded with golden sashes around their chests." "I saw" continues the upward trajectory of the things John sees beginning in 13:1 from the sea (13:1), to the earth (13:11), to Mount Zion (14:1), to the mid-heaven (14:6), to a white cloud (14:14), to heaven itself (15:1), and now to the temple of the tabernacle of witness in heaven (15:5). The words of 15:5 seem to invite the hearers closer, to an even more intimate knowledge of God's presence, as "the temple of the tabernacle of witness" is itself opened. Perhaps these words are an indication that the ark of the covenant, which was itself opened in 11:19, only now reveals its sacred contents: the two tablets of God's witness that signify his covenant faithfulness (Deut 31:26; 1 Kgs 8:9). Or perhaps the explicit mention of the temple of the tabernacle of witness would shift the focus of their attention from the tablets of witness to the faithful Witness himself, who sits on the throne with God,[467] and/or the witness to which those who overcome are called.[468] In any case, there would

---

466. Prigent, *L'Apocalypse de Saint Jean*, 356.
467. Gause, *Revelation*, 206.
468. Smalley, *Revelation*, 390.

be in these words an extraordinary convergence of ideas that focus on the very presence of God, his tabernacle (and his tablets?) of witness, and his Faithful Witness, making it clear that the things that follow come from the very presence of God himself.

"And the seven angels having the seven plagues came out of the temple wearing clean, shining stone and being girded with golden sashes around their chests." These words hearken back to the words of 15:1 and 11:19, suggesting that the seven bowls pick up precisely where the seven trumpets leave off.[469] Thus, despite the cosmic interlude of chapters 12–14, here the events associated with the seven bowls are intimately connected to those associated with the seven trumpets and the opening of the seven seals before them. The expression "wearing clean, shining stone," often thought by modern interpreters to make no sense whatsoever,[470] would in fact highlight the resemblance between the appearance of these angels and the appearance of the one who sits on the throne, whose own appearance resembles that of the stones jasper and sardius, stones that appear on the sacred breastpiece worn by the high priest. Hence, this expression would convey the way in which these seven angels resemble the God from whose temple they come. They are also described as "being girded with golden sashes around their chests," a description nearly identical to that of the appearance of the risen Jesus in 1:13. Thus, their very appearance indicates that their mission is a divinely sanctioned one and that they are the very agents of God and Jesus.

"And one of the four living creatures gave to the seven angels seven golden bowls being full of the wrath of God, the one who lives forever and ever." That one of the four living creatures would reappear in the story line would not be surprising, for they have been located in extraordinary proximity to the throne of God (4:6-9; 5:6, 8, 11, 14; 7:11-12; 14:3) and have been instrumental in carrying out a variety of activities on God's behalf (6:1, 3, 5-7). The appearance of one of the living creatures here highlights the divine commission of the seven angels, as the living creature gives them the seven golden bowls. The mention of the seven golden bowls would bring to mind that the prayers of the saints had earlier been closely associated with golden bowls

---

469. Michaels, *Revelation*, 184.

470. Such is reflected in the almost universal preference for the reading λίνον (*linon*, "linen") rather than λίθον (*lithon*, "stone") as the original reading at this point in the Greek text. The manuscript tradition, which is somewhat evenly divided among the several variants, is not conclusive. Though *lithon* is clearly the more difficult of the readings, many interpreters consider it to be too difficult. This reading, however, as indicated in the interpretation offered here, while being difficult is neither too difficult nor without meaning in the context of Revelation. It does have the support of such manuscripts as A and C, among others.

(5:8),[471] further underscoring the deep connection that exists in Revelation between the prayers of the saints and the redemptive judgments that come from the hand of God (cf. 6:9-11; 8:3-5).[472] Here, however, these golden bowls are full of the wrath of God,[473] words that remind readers that, with these seven last plagues, the wrath of God has been completed (15:1). Reference to God as "the one who lives forever and ever" heightens the hearers' sense of access to the divine presence (4:9-10). Such a title here underscores that it is the God who is not limited by time or space, the creator of all things, whose wrath is full and will soon be poured out completely.

"And the temple was filled with smoke out of the glory of God and out of his power, and no one was able to enter into the temple until the seven plagues of the seven angels had been completed." The seven bowls are filled with God's wrath, while the temple is filled with the smoke of his glory and power, which makes clear the connection between the impending actions of the angels and his own person. The temple being full of his glory and power would also be informed by those places in the OT where the glory of God comes down and fills the tabernacle (Exod 40:34-35) and temple (2 Chr 7:1-3) to such an extent that entry was impossible. Such language also brings to mind the experience of the prophets (Isa 6:1-4; Ezek 44:4) who encounter the living God. Such associations indicate that God is fully present in majesty and glory to accomplish his purpose.[474] That the smoke comes from his glory and power continues the integrated, holistic understanding of God as glorious and powerful. It might also be remembered that, when the seventh seal was opened, there had been silence in heaven for half an hour (8:1) before the seven trumpets were given to the seven angels, suggesting a connection between the silence and the trumpeting that follows. Now, no one is able to enter the temple until the seven plagues of the seven angels have been completed, owing to the smoke of God's glory and power, indicating the tight connection that exists between the smoke and the activity of the seven angels.[475] This section, which begins with a reference to "the wrath of God being completed," concludes with a reference to "the seven plagues of the seven angels having been completed," forming an inclusio around this entire section, further indicating that, in these words, the hearers encounter the completion of God's wrath.[476]

---

471. Ladd, *Revelation*, 207.
472. Smalley, *Revelation*, 391.
473. Koester, *Revelation and the End of All Things*, 147.
474. Beasley-Murray, *Revelation*, 238.
475. Caird, *The Revelation of Saint John*, 200.
476. Aune, *Revelation 6-16*, 880.

The Pouring Out of the Seven Bowls (16:1-21)

"And I heard a great voice out of the temple saying to the seven angels, 'Go (forth) and pour out the seven bowls of the wrath of God into the earth.'" This voice would likely be taken as the voice of God, for it comes from the temple, and at this point no one was able to enter the temple because it was full of the smoke and power of God (15:8). Only here in Revelation does the adjective "great" precede the noun "voice."[477] Perhaps the intertext of Isa 66:6, where the sound of God's voice from heaven is placed within the context of the repayment to his enemies all they deserve to receive, would come to mind. The instruction for the angels to "go [forth]" carries divine authority, as earlier (10:8; 13:10; cf. also 14:4). The command "pour out" indicates that this may be a liturgical action, as this term appears in the OT in cultic contexts (1 Sam 7:6; Isa 57:6), sometimes in the context of judgment (Jer 7:20; 10:25; 14:16; Ezek 9:8; 14:19; Ps 79:3-6; Lam 2:4).[478] "The voice of God" makes reference to "the seven bowls of the wrath of God" even more ominous, as the anticipation of his wrath has been building significantly over the course of the last two chapters (cf. 14:8, 10, 19; 15:1, 7).

"And the first angel departed and poured out his bowl into the earth, and there came a bad and evil sore upon the men who have the mark of the beast and those who worship his image." The speed of the angel's response and the literal fulfillment of the command — he is told to "go forth and pour out his bowl into the earth," so he "departs and pours out his bowl into the earth" — serves to reinforce the expectation that God's commands will indeed be fulfilled. The enumeration "the first angel" suggests this series of seven is in some degree of continuity with the previously enumerated sevens. Surprisingly, the effect of the bowl's contents does not seem to afflict the earth as such, but rather, particular individuals upon it. Mention of the "bad and evil sore" would be especially thick with meaning, with the severity of the sores conveyed in part by the grammatical construction, which includes a combination of the adjectives "bad" and "evil" to describe the sores. This imagery would also be informed by the plague of festering sores sent by God upon the Egyptians, sores so severe that the Egyptian magicians could not stand before Moses owing to their affliction, and Job's affliction with sores by Satan, with God's consent (Job 2:1-10), but with a very different ending. These texts converge to convey the information that the seven last bowls of plagues of God's wrath are in continuity with God's previous activity in the exodus events and that such liturgical

---

477. Aune, *Revelation 6-16*, 882.
478. Smalley, *Revelation*, 400.

activity holds out the possibility of repentance on the part of those so afflicted.[479] It would be especially poignant that the affliction resulting from the pouring out of this bowl affects those who "have the mark of the beast and those who worship his image," as the objects of these sores are those who have trusted in the beast by receiving his mark of protection, avoiding death at his hands, and worshipping his image, choosing to obey its oracular commands instead of the voice of God. In this first bowl, God directly confronts the idolatrous behavior advocated by the beast,[480] revealing the futility of such identification with the beast and the limits of his powers to protect those who so identify with him. The contrast between the mark received from the beast and the sore (singular) sent by God could hardly be missed. The beast's mark is replaced by God's sore on those who worship the beast.[481]

"And the second (angel) poured out his bowl into the sea, and it became blood as of (someone) dead, and every living soul died, the things in the sea." This second angel pours his bowl into the sea, suggesting that "earth" in 16:1 is to be understood in a comprehensive fashion. The effects of the second trumpeting (8:8-9) and the first plague sent upon the Egyptians (Exod 7:14-24) inform these words.[482] The events accompanying the pouring out of the second bowl reveal a comprehensiveness and intensity that make clear the unparalleled nature of this bowl. Specifically, the description of the sea becoming blood "as one dead" is especially gruesome and repulsive, conveying something of the cause and effect of the scene.[483] When the water of the Nile River was turned to blood, all the fish died, and the people could not drink the water, having to dig wells along the Nile for drinking water, and when the second angel trumpeted his trumpet, a third of the sea was turned to blood, resulting in the death of a third of the creatures in the sea and the destruction of a third of the ships on the sea. When the second bowl is poured out in Rev 16:3, however, "every living soul died, the things in the sea." Based upon Rev 8:8-9, the appositional construction "every living soul . . . the things in the sea" would appear to include both human beings and aquatic life. Such comprehensive destruction would be indisputable evidence that the wrath of God is indeed being brought to completion in these seven last plagues. The intensity of God's redemptive judgments thus continues to build, from the opening of the fourth seal, when a fourth of the inhabitants of the earth were slain (6:8), to the trumpeting of the seven trumpets, when a

---

479. Cf. the suggestive canonical comments of Wall, *Revelation*, 196-97.
480. Smalley, *Revelation*, 400.
481. Koester, *Revelation and the End of All Things*, 148.
482. Beale, *The Book of Revelation*, 814-15.
483. Mounce (*The Book of Revelation*, 294) notes, "The sea becomes like the blood of a dead person — that is, coagulated and rotting."

third of the people or things afflicted were affected, to the death of every living soul, the things in the sea, when the first bowl is poured out.

"And the third (angel) poured out his bowl into the rivers and the fountains of water, and it became blood." The actions of the third angel would convey the sense that there is absolutely no reprieve from the completion of God's wrath. In a sense, the effects of this bowl build upon that of the second bowl, in that now it appears the water supply is completely contaminated. Since blood replaces the entire water supply, the amount of blood is absolutely unfathomable. The effects of the third trumpeting (Rev 8:10-11) and the first plague sent upon the Egyptians (Exod 7:14-24) inform these words.[484] But while the Egyptians were apparently able to dig along the Nile River for drinking water (Exod 7:24), and the third trumpeting affected a third of the rivers and fountains of water causing the death of a third of the people, the effects of the third bowl being poured out seem to be more intense and absolute.

And I heard (the voice) of the angel of the waters saying,

Righteous are you, the one who is and was, the Holy One,
for you have judged these things,
for blood of saints and prophets they have poured out,
and blood you have given to them to drink,
(as) they are worthy.

The angel who speaks may be the third angel responsible for pouring out the third bowl, from which the rivers and fountains of water turn into blood.[485] The words of the angel are hymnic, informed by numerous OT texts (Neh 9:33; Pss 7:11; 9:4; Jer 46:28; Dan 9:14), as well as the hymn found previously in Rev 15:3-4.[486] The song not only celebrates God's person and work by means of various descriptive titles, each drawing attention to some specific element of his being, but also offers an insight into the true significance of the bowls.[487] The angelic words "you are worthy" remind hearers of the Song of Moses and the song of the Lamb, where the ways of God are described as "righteous." If these wrathful activities of God are thought too severe, the hearers are immediately reassured that they come from the hand of a righteous God, whose ways are "true and righteous" (15:3). The title that follows, "the one who is and the one who was," carries with it all the weight of the threefold form that appears on

---

484. Beale, *The Book of Revelation*, 816.
485. Mounce, *The Book of Revelation*, 294-95. Contra Smalley, *Revelation*, 402.
486. Smalley, *Revelation*, 402.
487. Prigent, *L'Apocalypse de Saint Jean*, 361.

three previous occasions in Revelation, providing a sense of continuity. The same God whom John describes as sitting upon the throne (1:4), who identifies himself with this title (1:8), whom they know from the heavenly throne-room vision (4:8), is now described as righteous. The one who transcends time, encompassing the beginning and the end, is the righteous God, who sends these bowls of wrath. The twofold form of this title, first introduced in 11:17, underscores the reign of God as a present reality — he is no longer the one who is to come, for he has already come! This God is now called "the Holy One," a title that hearkens back to the hymn in 15:2-4, where the words "you alone are holy" are ascribed to God in a text that holds out hope for the conversion of the nations. In 16:5 the title "the Holy One" stands in continuity with its earlier reference (15:4). Significantly, this title appears in the context of the pouring out of the bowls of God's wrath. In 16:5 the title "the one who was and the one who is" is surrounded by the ascription that God is righteous and by the title "the Holy One," offering insight into the divine significance of the bowls of God's wrath. The second line of the hymn offers the justification for the lofty language of the opening line: "for you have judged them." This statement would be seen in some continuity with the cry of the souls under the altar, "How long ... will you not judge?" (6:10), and the words of the twenty-four elders in still another hymn, "The time has come to judge the dead" (11:17). The intricate connection between the lofty titles and ascription given to God and the justification for them indicates that the pouring out of the bowls of God's wrath are not capricious, one-off acts of a ruthless and unethical tyrant, but they are demanded by the very nature of this righteous and holy God, whose ways are righteous and true!

> For blood of saints and prophets they have poured out,
> and blood to them you have given to drink.

These parallel lines each focus on the word "blood," which stands in an emphatic position at the beginning of the lines, describing the pouring out or giving of blood and revealing who it is that acts in such ways. The phrase about the blood of the saints and prophets being poured out comes to represent the cost of giving faithful witness to Jesus, an idea present in numerous places in Revelation (1:5; 2:13; 6:10; 11:7-12; 13:10, 15; 14:4; 15:2-4). Reference to saints and prophets would perhaps be taken as a reference to the people of God as a whole and the prophetic witness to which they are called. Specifically, the saints are those whose prayers are always before the throne (5:8; 8:3-4), are worthy to receive their reward (11:18), are warred against by the beast (13:7), and are the recipients of divine assistance for the task of pneumatic discernment (13:10;

14:12); on their part, prophets preach the mystery of God (10:7), their death brings delight to the inhabitants of the earth (11:10), and they themselves are worthy of their reward (11:18). The verb "they poured out" suggests their actions were "liturgical" activity offered in the worship of the beast. It also provides a philological link between their activities of pouring out the blood of saints and prophets and the pouring out of the bowls of God's wrath. They pour out the blood of his saints and prophets; he in turn pours out bowls of wrath. Even more, "and blood to them you have given to drink." Line 4 thus goes further to explain why the second and third bowls of God's wrath have turned water into blood. The God who has given them blood to drink had earlier given them the blood of the Lamb for them to be loosed from their sins, but by rejecting the faithful witness of his saints and prophets, they have refused him, his Son, and his Spirit. The final line of this angelic hymn thus makes clear that these judgments are not capricious but righteous. The giving of blood to drink is something of which "they are worthy," a final testimony about the righteousness of God's judgments and the direct contrast to those faithful in Sardis who have not stained their clothes and who, as a result, will walk with Jesus in white, "for they are worthy" (3:4). The occurrence of "they are worthy" to describe both groups would be impossible to miss, driving home the sad but stark truth: those who pour out the blood of the saints and the prophets are as deserving of the bowls of God's wrath as the saints in Sardis are to walk with Jesus in white!

"And I heard one from the altar saying, 'Yes Lord, God, the All Powerful One, true and righteous are your judgments.'" Standing alongside the testimony of the angel of the waters is another testimonial hymn that comes from "one from the altar," likely a reference back to the souls under the altar (6:9), who had been slaughtered and who cry out to God, "How long, O Master, the Holy and True One, will you not judge and vindicate our blood on those who dwell upon the earth?"[488] The divine response to their cry for justice was to wait a little longer (6:11) until the number of their brothers who were about to be killed was full. In the intervening chapters there has been no direct mention of the souls under the altar, though reference to their prayers may appear in 8:3-4 and a partial response to their cry may be implied in the hymn in 15:3. Thus, in 16:7, where one of those under the altar speaks,[489] or the corporate voice of the martyrs is heard,[490] the hearers would be keen to discover the content of their words, for they have been waiting a very long time indeed! The first word, "Yes," has occurred on two occasions in Revelation to this point (1:7; 14:13). In

---

488. Skaggs and Benham, *Revelation*, 162.
489. Aune, *Revelation 6–16*, 888.
490. Pattemore, *The People of God in the Apocalypse*, 100.

keeping with those occurrences, in 16:7 it functions as an affirmation, an "amen" to the words of the hymn spoken by the angel of the waters. Specifically, this Yes affirms both the affirmation and the titles of which the angel has spoken and affirms the truth of these statements with regard to the pouring out of the blood of saints and prophets and the verdict that they are worthy to drink blood as a result. Following this affirmation, the voice from the altar acknowledges God by the threefold formula "Lord, God, the All Powerful One." This combination of titles, which begins as a self-designation for God in a prophetic utterance (1:8), appears in contexts of worship (each time in a hymn) on the lips of the four living creatures (4:8), the twenty-four elders (11:17), and most recently those who have overcome the beast and his image and the number of his name (15:3). It underscores God's incomparability, his absolute power, and the fact that nothing is beyond his reach. The words "true and righteous are your judgments" are intricately connected to both the cry from those under the altar and the words of the angel of the waters. The judgments of "the Master, the Holy and True One" (6:10) are "true and righteous judgments" (16:7). The judgment resulting from the pouring out of the bowl that turns the waters into blood, which is brought upon those who pour out the blood of saints and prophets (16:4-6), is in direct correlation with the cry of the souls under the altar for God to "judge and vindicate our blood" (6:10). The righteous God (16:5) is one whose judgments are themselves righteous (16:7). Thus, at this crucial moment in the unfolding of Revelation, the final word with regard to the righteousness of God and his judgments in these bowls is not left to an angelic being but to the martyrs,[491] whose own testimony indicates that they themselves, who have suffered so much and waited so long, are satisfied that the ways of God are indeed true and righteous!

"And the fourth (angel) poured out his bowl upon the sun, and there was given to it to scorch men with fire." The similarities with the Egyptian plague sequence include the fact that, like the effects of this bowl, both the fourth trumpeting and the ninth Egyptian plague affect the sun (and/or other sources of light), and in the case of the ninth plague, the effects could be felt. Whereas the former intensifies the sun's heat, the latter affected the sun's ability to illuminate the earth. Specifically, a third of the sun and moon were darkened after the fourth trumpeting, while the ninth plague brought darkness upon the Egyptians so severe it could be felt. The results of this bowl stand in stark contrast to the eschatological promises given to those coming out of the great tribulation, namely, that "the sun will not beat upon them nor any scorching heat" (7:16),[492]

---

491. Prigent, *L'Apocalypse de Saint Jean*, 362.
492. Osborne, *Revelation*, 586. Cf. the comments of Sweet (*Revelation*, 245), who compares

the same root word appearing in both 7:16 and 16:8. The statement that men will be scorched "with fire" reinforces the idea that this is indeed a judgment of God (Rev 8:5, 7-8; 9:17-18; 11:5; 14:10, 18).

"And the men were scorched with great scorching heat, and they blasphemed the name of God, the one having the authority over these plagues, and they did not repent to give him glory." The phrase "scorched . . . with great scorching," a grammatical construction known as a cognate accusative (the same root word appearing in both the verb and the direct object), conveys the extent of the suffering. Although these individuals rightly discern that these phenomena come from the hand of God,[493] they choose to blaspheme his name instead.[494] These individuals thus reveal their deep and intimate identification with the beast, who is the only character to this point to blaspheme the name of God (13:1, 5-6); they have wholly taken on the character of the one they worship.[495] The nature of their blasphemy impinges in some way upon his identity and glory and name (cf. 2:9). The plural "plagues" may suggest that their response to God is based on the effects of all the plagues to this point.[496] Yet, despite recognizing the ultimate source of the plagues, they cannot recognize the immediate cause, their unrepentant lives;[497] they refuse to repent and thus give him glory![498] This refusal to repent is reminiscent of the consistent actions of Pharaoh when confronted with the plagues God sent on Egypt (Exod 7:13, 22; 8:15, 19, 32; 9:7, 12, 34-35; 10:1, 20; 11:9-10; 14:4),[499] as well as the trumpet sequence in Rev 9:20-21.[500] These humans explicitly reject the message of the angel in 14:7, where nearly every word is significant for that described in 16:9. Specifically, the hour of God's final judgment has come upon the earth (16:2), the sea (16:3), the fountains of water (16:4), and the heaven (16:8-9), yet these human beings refuse to repent, to give God glory, though such appears possible even at this late hour (11:13; 14:7). For those who reject such a proclamation, the judgment of God has come already.

---

the promise of Rev 7:16 with Dan 3:22, 27, noting that "the three who refused to worship Nebuchadnezzar's image were not even singed by the scorching furnace."

    493. Ladd, *Revelation*, 211.
    494. Resseguie, *The Revelation of John*, 212.
    495. Caird, *The Revelation of Saint John*, 202.
    496. Smalley, *Revelation*, 405.
    497. Sweet, *Revelation*, 245.
    498. Primasius (*Commentary on the Apocalypse*, 16:9, cited in ACCS 12, 253) comments, "It is the habit of blasphemers that they prefer to blame God for wickedness and iniquity rather than themselves, and therefore [they] do not seek penance after plagues but, even though tormented, continue to throw insults."
    499. Aune, *Revelation 6–16*, 889.
    500. Beale, *The Book of Revelation*, 822.

"And the fifth (angel) poured out his bowl upon the throne of the beast, and his kingdom became dark, and they were gnawing their tongues out of agony." With the pouring out of the fifth bowl, God's wrath is directed to the very center of the beast's power, his throne, given to him by the dragon, along with the dragon's power and authority (13:2). From this position of power he blasphemes God (13:5-6), makes war with the saints (13:7), and is worshipped by all the world's inhabitants except "those whose names were written in the book of life of the Lamb, who was slaughtered before the foundation of the world" (13:8).[501] Apparently one manifestation of this throne is in Sardis. This bowl results in the beast's throne becoming dark, reminiscent of the fourth trumpet and the ninth Egyptian plague. This darkness appears to be felt as well, for the agony of those associated with the throne of the beast is so great that they were gnawing on their tongues, the imperfect tense of the especially harsh term "were gnawing" indicating that this gnawing was ongoing.[502]

"And they blasphemed the God of heaven out of their agony and out of their sores, and they did not repent of their works." Incredibly, the same tongues that were being gnawed are used to blaspheme the God of heaven![503] These, too, willfully reject the opportunity for repentance from their works, choosing to blaspheme God owing to their suffering. The pouring out of the previous bowls is likely felt in a cumulative fashion, as the sores inflicted in 16:2 appear to be felt still.[504] The reference to "sores" further underscores the relationship between the beast's mark and the sores inflicted by God.[505] In 16:2 the beast could offer no protection for his followers from the wrath of God; in 16:10-11 he can offer no protection for his own throne!

"And the sixth (angel) poured out his bowl upon the great river the Euphrates, and its water was dried up, in order that the way of the kings from the raising of the sun (the east) might be prepared." Unlike the preceding bowls directed to bodies or sources of water, the purpose of this pouring out is to dry the water up altogether! Owing to its great length and abundance, the Euphrates was never known to have dried up.[506] Clearly, the drying up of this river stands in contrast to the drying up of the Red Sea (Exod 14:21-22) and the Jordan

---

501. Koester, *Revelation and the End of All Things*, 151.
502. C. Schneider, "Μασάομαι," *TDNT* 4:514.
503. Gause, *Revelation*, 213.
504. Michaels, *Revelation*, 187.
505. Aune observes (*Revelation 6–16*, 890), "There is an inconsistency in the text in that there is no evident connection between darkness and the experience of pain and sores." Perhaps this point of commonality between these bowls addresses one aspect of this perceived "inconsistency."
506. Smalley, *Revelation*, 407.

River (Josh 3:14-17), where the people of God pass through during the period of the exodus and entry into the promised land, respectively. The language of preparing the way for the kings of the East closely parallels Isa 11:15, which also speaks of the drying up of the Euphrates so that the remnant of God's people might return from exile, further developing the contrast between judgment and salvation.[507] The reference to "the kings from the rising of the sun" (or "kings from the East") stands in some continuity with the "kings of the earth," who have appeared earlier in Revelation (6:15) and are a natural correlative to the drying up of the Euphrates.

"And I saw out of the mouth of the dragon and out of the mouth of the beast and out of the mouth of the false prophet three unclean spirits as frogs." The phrase "out of the mouth of" stands in a position of emphasis and also occurs three times in this verse. Such emphasis upon what comes from the mouths of this triumvirate of evil, mentioned here together for the first time in the book,[508] would remind hearers of the things that have been said to come from their mouths previously (12:15; 13:5-6) — all in contrast to the double-edged sword that comes from the mouth of Jesus (1:16; 2:16), of God (9:17-19), and of the two witnesses (11:5).[509] Most poignantly, they would be reminded that, in the mouths of the 144,000, no lies were found (14:5). Here for the first time the beast from the earth is called "the false prophet." What comes from the mouths of these figures are "unclean spirits, as frogs." This is the first mention of "unclean spirits," not to mention frogs, in the entire Johannine tradition. The first hint as to their meaning is the adjective "unclean." Whatever else they might be, these spirits are unclean. The second hint comes in the form of the somewhat enigmatic words that they came out of their mouths "as frogs." On one level, this designation continues the juxtaposition of the previous verse in that, while God sent a plague of frogs upon the Egyptians (Exod 8:5), here the enemies of God send the frogs. The phrase "as frogs" also conveys that these spirits are unclean, for frogs were deemed unclean in the Torah (Lev 11:9-12, 41-47), contact with which necessitated ritual cleansing.[510] It is even possible that mention of the frogs would conjure up images of magicians and sorcerers.[511]

"For they are spirits of demons (demonic spirits) who do signs, which are sent out to the kings of the whole inhabited world to gather them together into the war of the great day of God, the All Powerful One." The identification

---

507. Prompting Beasley-Murray (*Revelation*, 244) to conclude that this "miracle of redemption has become an eschatological miracle of judgment."
508. Osborne, *Revelation*, 591.
509. Sweet, *Revelation*, 249.
510. Smalley, *Revelation*, 409.
511. So Prigent, *L'Apocalypse de Saint Jean*, 366.

of these unclean spirits as demonic spirits now makes clear that the worship of demons in 9:20-21 was closely associated with the dragon, the beast, and the false prophet. In Rev 16:14 these demonic spirits do signs, as the beast from the earth did earlier to deceive the inhabitants of the earth (13:13-14). A similar agenda is at work here, as the signs performed by these demonic spirits appear to be linked to their ability to gather the kings together.[512] Ironically, the activity of the evil triumvirate takes place in tandem with the activity of God, for at the very time the sixth bowl is being poured out, demonic spirits go forth from the triumvirate to gather together all the kings of the inhabited world for the war of the great day of God, the All Powerful One! It appears that "the kings from the East" have morphed into "all the kings of the inhabited world," as the focus moves from a single compass point to the whole world.[513] The articular form "the war" suggests that the identity of this war is well known.[514] Could it be other than the final cataclysmic war to end all wars, the Day of the Lord, the day on which John writes?

"Behold, I come as a thief. Blessed is the one who watches and keeps his garments, in order that he not walk naked and they see his shame." Like a lightning bolt, these words of the resurrected Jesus break into the account of the bowls. While his words may be seen as an intrusion into this account, none of the hearers would be surprised to hear the voice of the resurrected Jesus in the midst of a discussion of the Day of the Lord![515] The same voice heard in the seven prophetic messages breaks in here to underscore the direct relevance of the events described in 16:12-14 to those given earlier.[516] Specifically, Jesus' words reveal that the war to end all wars is intimately connected with his return. Earlier (3:3) the resurrected Jesus has issued a very similar warning, "I come as a thief." There, the suddenness is underscored to an even greater degree with the words "you will not know the hour when I come." In 16:15 the promise is not conditional, predicated on their repenting or not repenting. Rather, the emphasis is upon the suddenness and certainty of his coming in salvation and judgment, and the warning not to be unprepared for it, and consequently unaware of its timing. This promise is followed by the book's third beatitude (cf. 1:3; 14:13), quite reminiscent of the promise/warning given to the church in Sardis. Specifically, the word "awake" or "watchful" appears, combining the idea of vigilance with eschatological expectation. In the prophetic message to Sardis (3:4) the imagery of clothing also appears, there with regard to those who

---

512. Murphy, *Fallen Is Babylon*, 343.
513. Smalley, *Revelation*, 410.
514. Aune, *Revelation 6–16*, 896.
515. Michaels, *Revelation*, 188.
516. Sweet, *Revelation*, 249.

have not soiled their clothes but walk with Jesus in white, for they are worthy. In the prophetic message to Laodicea, they are warned about their nakedness and instructed to buy white garments to wear so that they can cover their nakedness and avoid exposure to shame (3:17-18). Clearly, the convergence of these terms and themes underscores the gravity of this divine warning. Their vigilance with regard to their prophetic pneumatic witness necessitates lives whose works are praised and honored by Jesus himself. The language of "walking about naked" and "they will see their shame" confirms that one's relationship to Jesus is visible, not only to Jesus, but to those around as well.[517]

"And they gathered them into the place called in Hebrew, Har-Megiddon." The demonic spirits apparently have been successful in drawing together all the kings of the earth through the performance of signs. Though the throne of the beast has been attacked, he, through his envoys, is still able to dominate, if not all the inhabitants of the earth, at least all the kings. The kings have come for the great day of the war of God, the All Powerful One, though they are apparently still unaware that it was God who initiated this gathering in the first place by the drying up of the great Euphrates River.

Perhaps the most difficult aspect of these words to discern is the identity of "the place called in Hebrew, Har-Megiddon." Part of the complication is that a fair amount of uncertainty exists even with regard to the actual spelling of the name.[518] The name Har-Megiddon is a Hebrew name, which in Revelation can often mean more than its face value (2:14, 20; 9:11; 11:8; 14:8; 16:19).[519] The hearers would likely suspect that the Hebrew name Har-Megiddon comes from two Hebrew words, הר (*har*, "mountain") and מגדון (*magedon*, "Megiddon"), a combination that literally means "Mountain of Megiddon." Since there is no literal Mount Megiddon, they would likely understand that this is an image that emerges from the convergence of a variety of intertexts. Perhaps the first hint to its meaning would be that, in the OT, the city of Megiddo was associated with a number of significant battles (Judg 5:19; 2 Kgs 9:27; 23:29), even eschatological weeping (Zech 12:11). Battle imagery would be further enhanced in that the Jezreel Valley stretches out before Megiddo, where numerous battles have been fought, the vista of this site being particularly stunning from the vantage point of Mount Carmel, some ten kilometers to the northwest. The Hebrew name Har-Megiddon would thus carry with it associations of war, as perhaps no other location would. But there is more, for in the OT, mountains are tied to

---

517. As Sweet (*Revelation*, 249) observes, "Clothing signifies the righteousness and holiness which God will accept (cf. 19:8); nakedness signifies its lack."

518. Metzger, *Breaking the Code*, 84.

519. Koester, *Revelation and the End of All Things*, 152-53.

significant battles, even eschatological ones. Perhaps this would be enough for the hearers to recall the mountains of Israel (Ezek 38–39), important in one such eschatological context, and perhaps the possibility in the hearers' minds that, if there is a valley of Megiddo where the nations shall mourn (Zech 12:11), there must be a mountain of Megiddo as well.[520] Perhaps the mountains mentioned in association with the destruction of Babylon in Isa 13 are in the back of their minds also informing this name.[521] There is thus every likelihood that the Hebrew place-name Har-Megiddon would be deemed a most appropriate place for the war to end all wars, with a variety of images converging at this point.[522] As the words of 16:16 conclude, the kings of the earth stand at the ready, gathered together for the war of the great day of God, the All Powerful One!

"And the seventh (angel) poured out his bowl upon the air, and a great voice came out of the temple from the throne saying, 'It is Done!'" With the words "It is Done" the hearers are closer than ever to the end of all things. With this seventh bowl the pouring out the bowls upon the earth has moved from the earth itself to the air, which surrounds it. Neither would there be any confusion with regard to the identity of the one who speaks. It is the voice of God! The voice of God thus envelops the entire bowl sequence. His words indicate that their work has been accomplished and the end has arrived, with the perfect tense "it is done" indicating a past event, the results of which are felt into the present. The fact that this bowl is said to come not just from the temple but also specifically from the throne would also remind readers of the way in which this, the longest portion of the vision, began, with a vision of the one who sits on the throne (4:1–5:14). Thus, not only is the bowl sequence enveloped by God's voice, but this, the longest section of Revelation (4:1–16:21), is also enveloped by reference to the throne of God.

"And there were flashes of lightning and sounds and thunder, and there was a great earthquake, which had not been since before man had been upon the earth, so great was this earthquake." The display of the theophanic elements points back to 4:5 as well, where these elements are first recounted in Revelation, reminding readers of the way the sequence of seven bowls is connected to the

---

520. On this whole question, cf. esp. J. Day, "The Origin of Armageddon," in *Crossing the Boundaries: Essays in Biblical Interpretation in Honour of Michael D. Goulder* (ed. S. E. Porter, P. Joyce, and D. E. Orton; Leiden: Brill, 1994), 315-26.

521. Cf. M. Jauhiainen, "The OT Background to Armageddon (Rev 16:16) Revisited," *NovT* 47:4 (2005): 381-93.

522. Schüssler Fiorenza (*Revelation: Vision of a Just World*, 94) warns, "The multivalence of the author's mythological-symbolic language cannot be reduced to a single one-dimensional definition! Such multivalence expresses the author's interest in giving prophetic interpretation rather than geographical-eschatological information."

opening of the seven seals and the trumpeting of the seven trumpets, for the display of theophanic elements accompanies the conclusion of each sequence, with each sequence being more intense than the preceding one. Here the intensification comes initially by means of the reference to the earthquake of unparalleled magnitude. This intensification among the theophanic elements serves to bring to mind the direct connection between the one who sits on the throne and the pouring out of the seven bowls. It also provides a certain linear shape and movement to this section of Revelation and the book as a whole. The hearers would likely understand this earthquake in the light of the numerous OT texts where a great earthquake is part of the eschatological expectation (Isa 13:13; Hag 2:6-7; Zech 14:4-5).[523]

"And the great city came into three parts, and the cities of the nations fell. And Babylon the Great was remembered before God to give to her the cup of the wine of the wrath of his anger." The great city was earlier pneumatically called Sodom and Egypt (11:8-10), the place where their Lord was crucified and which has inhabitants from all over the world, a tenth of whom die from an earthquake, while 90 percent feared and gave glory to the God of heaven. In 16:19 the great city is literally broken apart, while the cities of the nations fall. Though the kings of the inhabited world had gathered together for war with God, rather than conquering him, their cities fell.[524] The expression "Babylon the Great was remembered by God" reveals that God is righteous and true in his judgments, and that he also has a memory! Nothing will go unrewarded; nothing will go without judgment. Here this reality is conveyed by the emphatic phrase "the cup of the wine of the wrath of his anger," which, according to the third angel of 14:9-10, awaits those "who worship the beast and his image and receive his number." The relationship between the beast and Babylon could not be clearer. "And every island fled, and mountains could not be found." The world comes undone![525]

"And great hail as a talent (ca. 100 pounds each) comes down out of heaven upon the men, and the men blasphemed God owing to the plague of the hail, because her (Babylon the Great's) plague was extremely great." After the breaking apart of the great city, the falling of the cities, the fleeing of every island, and mountains that could no longer be found, the words of this verse might be a bit surprising, especially that any human beings are still around! These final words in the bowl sequence return to the theme of the theophanic elements that appear in 16:18, indicating that the intervening events are envel-

---

523. Beasley-Murray, *Revelation*, 246.
524. Michaels, *Revelation*, 191.
525. Murphy, *Fallen Is Babylon*, 347.

oped within the display of these elements. This mention would complete expectations for hail to occur, given the place of great hail in the theophanic display at the conclusion of the trumpet sequence (11:19). Significantly, God not only sent great hail upon the Amorites in their battle with Israel (Josh. 10:11) but will also send hail upon Gog and Magog in the eschatological battle that is to come (Ezek 38:22). The weight of such great hail might remind hearers of the rocks used by the Roman army, specifically of its conquest of Jerusalem (Josephus, *Jewish Wars* 5.270).[526] With the appearance of this great hail this portion of Revelation draws to a close. Sadly, as before, this expression of God's righteous judgment results not in repentance but in blasphemy.[527]

---

526. Cf. Prigent, *L'Apocalypse de Saint Jean*, 368.
527. Andrew of Caesarea (*Commentary on the Apocalypse*, 16:21 cited in ACCS 12, 264) writes, "And so they will be like Pharaoh, or rather they will be even more intransigent than he was. For he at least to some extent was softened by the plagues sent from God and confessed his own ungodliness, but these persons will blaspheme even in the midst of being tormented."

"In the Spirit" — Carried to a Wilderness (17:1–21:8)

As the second and largest section of Revelation comes to a close, the next major section begins with the occurrence of the third "in the Spirit" phrase (17:3). This extended passage takes the hearers from the destruction of Babylon the great city to the New Jerusalem descending from heaven. In this section the hearers thus encounter an accounting of the final things. Beginning with a detailed description of Babylon the great city (17:1-18), the section moves to an extensive description of her destruction (18:1-24). Following this is an account of the great shouting in heaven that accompanies the marriage supper of the Lamb (19:1-10), the victory of the King of Kings and Lord of Lords over his enemies (19:11-21), the thousand-year reign of Jesus and those who overcome (20:1-6), Satan's final rebellion and defeat (20:7-10), the final judgment (20:11-15), and the initial description of the New Jerusalem descending from heaven (21:1-8).

The Woman on the Beast: Babylon the Whore (17:1-18)

"And one of the seven angels having the seven bowls came and spoke with me saying, 'Come, I will show you the judgment of the great whore who sits upon many waters, with whom the kings of the earth have committed sexual immorality and the inhabitants of the earth have become drunk with the wine of her sexual immorality.'" This angelic figure would likely be identified as the seventh angel who poured out the seventh bowl,[1] leading to the destruction of the great city, now described as the great whore, suggesting that the description of judgment to follow is closely connected to the pouring out of the bowls that precedes.[2] For the first time an angel addresses John directly. While the very first word from the angel, "Come," could be taken as a simple command, Johannine hearers would recall that its only other occurrence in the Johannine tradition is Jesus' command to Lazarus to "come forth" from his tomb (John 11:43). In this angelic command John thus encounters a divine invitation. "I will show" was previously encountered in Rev 1:1 and 4:1, where it is closely associated with the things that must take place soon, suggesting that the judgment of the great whore must itself take place soon. "Showing" also has a rich history in John's gospel, often describing divine revelation that comes from Jesus and or God (John 5:20; 10:32; 14:9; 20:20).[3] Specifically, the angel promises to show

---

1. Smalley, *Revelation*, 426.
2. Prigent, *L'Apocalypse de Saint Jean*, 375, and Murphy, *Fallen Is Babylon*, 348.
3. G. Schneider, "Δείκνυμι, δεικνύω," *EDNT*, 1:280-81.

John "the judgment of the great whore who sits upon many waters," perhaps an answer to the prayer of the souls under the altar for God to judge those who shed their blood (6:10; cf. also 11:18; 14:7; 16:5, 7), suggesting that a description of the final judgment immediately awaits. The word πόρνης (*pornēs*, "whore") would remind readers of its earlier occurrences and introduce a word group that will have near-unrivaled prominence as the section unfolds. The verbal form of this term appeared in close association with eating food sacrificed to idols (2:14), with reference to the activities of the woman who calls herself a prophet but whom the resurrected Jesus calls Jezebel (2:20). There the resurrected Jesus warned that judgment awaits her and her children if she does not repent of her sexual immorality (2:21-23). Perhaps the hearers would see in the judgment of the great whore in 17:1 an ultimate fulfillment of the warning the resurrected Jesus gives in his prophetic message to the church in Thyatira. Significantly, this term is often applied in the OT to Israel (Hos 5:3) and a variety of cities, including Jerusalem (Isa 1:21; Ezek 16:15; 23:3-4), Tyre (Isa 23:16), and Nineveh (Nah. 3:4). The description of the great whore in Rev 17:1 as "who sits upon many waters" would bring to mind the description of Babylon in Jer 51:13,[4] as well as the physical qualities of historic Babylon, through which the Euphrates ran and which was crisscrossed with canals.[5] It would also reveal something about the great whore's idolatrous ambitions, as it is Yahweh who is enthroned upon the flood (Ps 29:10).[6] Furthermore, she is identified as the one with whom the kings of the earth ἐπόρνευσαν (*eporneusan*, "have committed sexual immorality") and from whose wine of πορνεία (*porneia*, "sexual immorality") the inhabitants of the earth have become drunk.[7] Such repetitive vocabulary underscores her role in the seduction of others in her idolatrous activity. The fact that both "the kings of the earth" and "the inhabitants of the earth," a phrase that normally has negative associations in the book (3:10; 6:10; 8:13; 11:10; 13:8, 12, 14), are described as her active partners in sexually immoral activities indicates that her seduction to idolatrous activity has been universally successful, including both the world's leaders and its constituency. Mention of the wine of her sexual immorality serves to heighten the context of judgment in which these words occur, given the hearers' earlier encounter with this phrase in 14:8, suggesting a connection between the great whore and Babylon the Great.

4. Prigent, *L'Apocalypse de Saint Jean*, 375.
5. Aune, *Revelation 17-22*, 929.
6. Smalley, *Revelation*, 427.
7. Unlike a courtesan, who would devote herself to one man of means and social standing, the language πόρνη (*pornē*, "whore") indicates that the "one who sits on many waters" is indeed a street prostitute who has many lovers. Cf. J. A. Glancy and S. D. Moore, "How Typical a Roman Prostitute Is Revelation's 'Great Whore'?" *JBL* 130.3 (2011): 551-69.

"And he took me away into the wilderness in the Spirit." For the third time the hearers encounter the phrase "in the Spirit." As before, since there is no hint that John is no longer "in the Spirit" as chapter 17 begins, the phrase's appearance here would convey a sense of continuity between John's previous experience (Rev 1–3 and 4–16) and his experience in chapter 17 and following. Additional prophetic words from or about Jesus are thus expected. As Revelation has unfolded, it has become clear that this phrase is central to the book's structure, meaning that the revelation is given "in the Spirit." There continues to be a connection between specific geographic locations and being "in the Spirit." It was Patmos in 1:9-10 and in heaven in 4:2, and here (17:3) John is transported to the wilderness while "in the Spirit," bringing to mind Ezekiel's experience (3:12, 14; 8:3; 11:1, 24; 37:1; 43:5). Surprising to some contemporary hearers, in the Johannine tradition the wilderness is a place where God is active in prophetic and redemptive ways. The wilderness is the location of the prophetic work of John the Baptist, who is likened to "a voice crying in the wilderness" (John 1:23); also, the redemptive sign of the serpent being lifted up also takes place in the wilderness (3:14).[8] In the Bread of Life discourse Jesus twice refers to the gracious provision of manna for Israel in the wilderness (6:31, 49). The wilderness also functions as a place where Jesus and his disciples take refuge after the raising of Lazarus from the dead (11:54). From Rev 12:6, 14 the wilderness is known as a place prepared by God for the protection and sustenance of God's people. Thus, when John is transported to the wilderness "in the Spirit," the hearers would discern that what awaits John will be no less filled with prophetic and salvific significance than other "wilderness" events have been.[9]

"And I saw a woman seated upon a scarlet beast, full of blasphemous names, having seven heads and ten horns." In the Spirit John sees the great whore who sits upon many waters morph into a woman who sits upon a scarlet beast. Her presumptuous, idolatrous enthronement upon the waters is revealed to be an enthronement upon an idolatrous beast. This beast's color is somewhat reminiscent of that of the great red dragon,[10] while its physical appearance bears a striking resemblance to the beast that emerges from the sea (13:1), which also has ten horns, seven heads, and blasphemous names.[11] Her enthronement on the scarlet beast makes clear her character and intentions. Her power comes from the great red dragon, who is cast down out of heaven. The description of this beast (17:3)

---

8. On the soteriological dimension of this text, cf. Thomas, *Spirit of the New Testament*, 175-89.

9. Contra Aune, *Revelation 17–22*, 933, who suggests that "wilderness" here carries a negative connotation.

10. Ladd, *Revelation*, 223.

11. Murphy, *Fallen Is Babylon*, 335.

as full of blasphemous names reveals his presumptuous and idolatrous actions and nature. If the woman is enthroned upon such a one, there can be absolutely no doubt as to her own presumptuous and idolatrous actions and nature.

"And the woman was clothed in purple and scarlet and covered with gold in gold and precious stones and pearls, having a gold cup in her hand full of abominations and the uncleanness of her sexual immorality." The occurrence of the term "clothed" would draw attention to the contrast between how this woman is described and the last time this verb is used, where it describes the woman clothed with the sun (12:1). Every occurrence of the verb "clothe" to this point carries with it a positive connotation (3:5, 18; 4:4; 7:9, 13; 10:1; 11:3), suggesting that the contrast is not simply between these two women, but also between this woman and all those clothed in white. Specifically, this woman is clothed in purple, a color that conveys at the very least pretensions to royalty,[12] but which to Johannine hearers would forever be associated with the mockery of Jesus by the soldiers during his passion, who clothe and display him in a purple garment (John 19:2, 5), mocking him as "the king of the Jews" (19:3). Being clothed in scarlet would make it clear that she is dependent upon the beast for her authority, also that she is sharing in his nature.[13] She is literally "covered with gold in gold," wording that underscores the extraordinary amount of gold she wears, the same root word appearing in both verbal and noun forms, revealing a contrast between all individuals and things associated with gold to this point in Revelation (1:12-13, 20; 2:1; 3:18; 4:4; 5:8; 8:3; 9:13, 20; 14:14; 15:6-7) and this opulent portrayal.[14] Significantly, to this point only God and one of the angels have been described as wearing stones (4:3; 15:6), and only to God and to the Lamb has the related term "honor" or "value" been ascribed (4:9, 11; 5:12-13; 7:12). Mention of her pearls also conveys a similar message, though this detail will not become clear until later (21:21). Thus, in ways not always apparent to modern interpreters, the attire of this woman reveals a great deal about her presumptuous and idolatrous nature and character. In contrast to the golden bowl filled with the prayers of the saints (8:3), her golden cup is filled with abominations and the uncleanness of her sexual immorality.[15] Both "abominations" and "uncleanness" appear in the plural, underscoring the extent of her abominable and unclean activities. While "abominations" might convey the general idea of that which is loathsome before God,[16] in the Prophets it often appears with reference to idols (Jer 13:27; 32:35 [39:35 LXX]; 44:22 [51:22 LXX]; Ezek 5:9, 11;

---

12. Aune, *Revelation 17–22*, 935.
13. Gause, *Revelation*, 221.
14. The only possible exception to this positive usage is found in 9:7.
15. Wall, *Revelation*, 206.
16. J. Zmijewski, "Βδέλυγμα," *EDNT*, 1:209-10.

6:9).¹⁷ Perhaps in the words "uncleanness of her sexual immorality" there is reference to the unclean spirits of idolatry that come from the mouths of the dragon, the beast, and the false prophet (16:13), who through demonic seduction gather the kings of the whole inhabited world together to make war with God (16:14).¹⁸ It is clear that the appetites of this woman match her appearance. She constantly drinks in idolatrous abominations and the uncleanness of her own sexual immorality, which characterizes her own idolatrous identity.

"And upon her forehead a name had been written, mystery, 'Babylon the Great, the mother of whores and the abominations of the earth.'" The forehead is the place where the seal of God (7:3; 9:4) and/or his name (14:1) has been placed upon those who identify with him; in addition, it is the place where the mark of the beast has been placed upon those who identify with him (13:16; 14:9). A name has been written upon her forehead in the past that continues to be valid, as the perfect tense "had been written" indicates. The earlier occurrences of mystery (1:20; 10:7) would suggest that the name of the woman must be discerned, as must many of the other names that have occurred (Balaam, Jezebel, Sodom, Egypt, the city where their Lord was crucified, the number of the beast, etc.).¹⁹ Perhaps the most obvious thing would be that this Babylon the Great is the same as the Babylon the Great of 14:8. The Babylon the Great named in 17:5 is the same one who, in the context of judgment (16:17-21), was remembered before God to give her the cup of the wine of the wrath of his anger (16:19). The hearers might also think of Babylon the Great, which destroyed Jerusalem, exiled her inhabitants, was seated on the waters, and whose king eventually acknowledged the God of heaven (Dan 4:34-37). If so, perhaps they would discern that, just as the beast continues to exist despite the death of Nero, so Babylon the Great continues to exist despite the destruction of Babylon of old.²⁰ Her name also includes the words "the mother of whores and the abominations of the earth."²¹ Such words make it clear that the great whore

---

17. Prigent, *L'Apocalypse de Saint Jean*, 377.
18. Smalley, *Revelation*, 431.
19. Aune, *Revelation 17–22*, 936.
20. Cf. P. W. Cheung, "The Mystery of Revelation 17:5 and 7: A Typological Entrance," *Jian Dao* 18 (2003): 18.
21. This graphic depiction of the Great Whore has led J. E. Bruns ("The Contrasted Women of Apoc 12 and 17," *CBQ* 26 [1964]: 459-63) to conclude that Valeria Messalina, the wife of Emperor Claudius (41-54 C.E.), sat for this portrait. Her exploits, as depicted by Juvenal (*Satire* 6.116-32), Tacitus (*Annals* 11.1, 2, 12, 26-38), and Pliny (*Natural History* 11.171), suggest that "Messalina was remembered . . . as (1) a Roman Empress who (2) literally played the Harlot and (3) crowned her adulteries amid the luxurious surroundings of a drunken orgy." According to Juvenal's description, she actually bore an assumed name (on her forehead?) — "Lycisca," or "The Wolf Girl." Bruns suggests that her ignominious death parallels that of the Great Whore in Rev 17:16.

"In the Spirit" — Carried to a Wilderness (17:1–21:8)

and Babylon the Great are indeed the same; this one is the source or origin, the "mother," of all whores, those who practice and advocate idolatrous activity. This "mother of whores" stands in direct contrast to the woman clothed with the sun, who gives birth to the male child who is taken up into heaven (12:1-6) and the rest of her seed, who are characterized by "keeping the commands of God and having the witness of Jesus" (12:17).[22] In contrast, the mother of whores brings forth those like the false prophetess Jezebel, who commits and advocates sexual immorality (2:20-21). The description of Babylon the Great as the mother of "the abominations of the earth" makes doubly clear her relationship to the abominations of idolatry, for she holds in her hand a gold cup filled with such abominations (17:4), and she produces children who both practice and actively propagate idolatrous activity.

"And I saw the woman drunk out of the blood of the saints and out of the blood of the witnesses of Jesus." The second occurrence of "I saw" in this passage confirms that the woman John saw sitting upon a scarlet beast (17:3) is the same woman whom he now sees drunk on the blood of the saints. It appears that the blood of the saints and the blood of the witnesses of Jesus here emphasized are tightly connected to the blood of the souls under the altar (6:10) and the blood of the saints and the prophets (16:6). Mention of the blood of the saints and the blood of the witnesses *of Jesus* once again draws attention to Jesus' own faithful witness, involving the shedding of his blood, from which salvific consequences result. Those who would follow the Lamb wherever he goes (14:4) must be prepared to follow him into death. Perhaps there is a connection between the blood from which this woman has become drunk and the gold cup in her hand, which is full of abominations and sexual immorality. In Revelation an increase in idolatrous activity upon the earth brings the death of the saints in its wake (12:17; 13:15). Those who remain faithful in their witness to Jesus and refuse to worship the beast, his image, his name, or his number inevitably face death. The contents of the gold cup and the blood from which the great whore becomes drunk thus share a deep connection;[23] the increase of the one entails the increase of the other. There might also be a connection between the wine of her sexual immorality, "out of" which the inhabitants of the earth have become drunk, the gold cup full of abominations and the uncleanness of her sexual immorality, and the blood of the saints and the blood of the witnesses of Jesus, "out of" which the great whore has become drunk. The great whore is not alone in her culpability; it is shared by the kings of the earth who have committed sexual immorality with her (17:2) and the inhabitants of the earth who have

---

22. Smalley, *Revelation*, 432.
23. Smalley, *Revelation*, 432.

become drunk from her wine, having worshipped the beast (13:8, 12, 14). One might also wonder as to the relationship between the blood of the saints and the witnesses of Jesus from which she has become drunk and the blood that God has given his enemies to drink because they have poured out the blood of his saints and prophets (16:6). The hearers would no doubt appreciate the deep connection that exists between the faithful witness of the saints, their blood that is shed, the prayers they offer, and God's ultimate judgment of the earth. Her drunken state, resulting from the orgy of idolatrous activity that leads to the death of the saints and witnesses of Jesus, reveals that the great whore has become intoxicated and unable to function in a clear-headed fashion, having consumed the very witness that could have led to her salvation!

"And I marveled, seeing her a great marvel." Grammatically, the words "seeing her" stand in the middle of the Greek sentence, surrounded by a cognate accusative, with both the verb and the direct object from the same Greek root: "I marveled . . . a great marvel." The sight of this woman is surrounded by John's marveling, thus underscoring that her appearance has generated such an effect. Significantly, this verb has appeared once before in Revelation to describe the response of the whole world to the healing of the beast's wounded head (13:3), which results in the universal worship of the dragon and the beast (13:4).[24] Is it possible that John could here be susceptible to the same idolatrous seduction that has resulted in the worship of the dragon and the beast by the whole world?[25] If John, who is "in the Spirit" at the time, could be so tempted, could anyone be immune from such seduction? At the same time, this term occurs in describing a response that often accompanies aspects of Jesus' teaching or actions that prove difficult to understand for various individuals in John's gospel (John 3:7; 4:27; 5:20, 28; 7:15, 21). In addition to heightening the significance of vigilance with regard to temptations to idolatrous worship, these words may be an indication of John's puzzlement in interpreting this detail of the vision.[26]

"On account of what are you marveling?" the angel asked John. "I will show you the mystery of the woman and the beast who bears her who has seven heads and ten horns." The angel's question can hardly be taken as anything other than a rebuke to John.[27] This question would provide some space, however brief, for reflection upon John's response to the great whore. Perhaps it would also provoke the hearers to answer the same question themselves. Is there some seduction in this vision that could result in idolatrous activity on their part? The

---

24. Caird, *The Revelation of Saint John*, 213.
25. Schüssler Fiorenza, *Revelation: Vision of a Just World*, 96.
26. Aune, *Revelation 17–22*, 938.
27. Gause, *Revelation*, 223.

hearers, like John, are to receive additional divine assistance in their pneumatic discernment when told that the angel will explain the mystery of the woman and the beast who bears her. They learn of the close relationship that exists between the woman and the beast, as their mystery is to be explained together.[28] In discovering that the woman is being borne by the beast "who bears," the hearers would think of the contrast between this beast and what it bears and the church in Ephesus, which was "not able to bear evil ones or things" (2:2) but who "have patient endurance and bear on account of my name" (2:3).

"The beast that you saw was and is not and is about to come up out of the Abyss and go into destruction, and the inhabitants of the earth will have been made to marvel, those whose names have not been written upon the book of life from the foundation of the world, seeing the beast that was and is not and will be present." "The beast" stands first in the Greek sentence, as a point of emphasis, followed by the words "that you saw," a literary marker directing attention to various details of the angel's interpretation of the vision.[29] The beast is described with an appellation, "was and is not and is about to come up out of the Abyss," a parody of both the one who sits on the throne and the Lamb, bringing to mind the threefold description of God as "the one who is and the one who was and the one who is coming" (1:4, 8; 4:8). This appellation reveals the beast's idolatrous presumption. The description of the beast as "and was not" refers to the slaughter suffered by one of the beast's heads (13:3), indicating that it is a parody of the Lamb, who himself was slaughtered (5:6). The description "about to come up from the Abyss and go into destruction" reveals something of his character,[30] confirming that this beast is identical to the one who makes war against and overcomes the two witnesses (11:7), as he too comes from the Abyss. "The inhabitants of the earth are made to marvel" reminds hearers of the world's earlier astonishment at the healing of the beast's slaughtered head, which led to the universal worship of the dragon and the beast (13:3-4) and which has caused John himself to be astonished at the sight of the great whore (17:6). For a second time the description "whose names have not been written upon the book of life from the foundation of the world" appears. Earlier, the book of life has been closely associated with the resurrected Jesus (3:5) and the Lamb slaughtered from before the foundation of the world (13:8). Those who choose to identify with the beast have disregarded the salvific provisions made

---

28. Ladd, *Revelation*, 226.

29. The phrase ὅ/ἅ/ἣν εἶδες (*ho/ha/hēn eides*, "that/whom you saw") occurs five times in 17:8-18 (vv. 8, 12, 15, 16, 18).

30. Caird (*The Revelation of Saint John*, 216) describes these features as permanent qualities of the beast, not a description of one-off events; the beast is always arising from the Abyss and always heading for destruction.

by the slaughtered Lamb, provisions that predate the foundation of this world and are grounded in the pretemporal relationship of the Father and the Son. The amazement of the inhabitants of the earth comes from "seeing the beast that was and is not and will be present," coming up out of the Abyss. The description of the inhabitants of the earth, who are astonished at the beast and whose names have not been written in the book of life, is bounded on either side by descriptions of the beast that consist of a threefold appellation underscoring his presumptuous and idolatrous character. The sentence ends with the word "comes," used exclusively for the activity of Jesus in John's gospel (John 7:6; 11:28) and is the verb from which the noun "coming" is derived,[31] used in 1 John 2:28 for the return of Jesus. The parody by the beast of the one who sits on the throne and the Lamb thus continues in the last word of Rev 17:8.

"Here is the understanding, the one who has wisdom. The seven heads are seven mountains, where the woman sits upon them. And they are seven kings." It hardly matters whether this call is one to reflect back on the words of 17:8[32] or one that calls forward to the explanation offered by the angel, for the words of 17:8 and those that follow are intricately connected. This call to pneumatic discernment is reminiscent of a similar call in 13:18, where, following the words "Here is wisdom," a call is given for "the one who has understanding" to calculate the number of the beast.[33] Significantly, the call in 17:9 combines the words "understanding" with "wisdom" and is one concerned with spiritually discerning the aspects of the beast's identity, suggesting that the discernment called for in 13:18 and 17:9 are not unrelated activities. In 17:9 the angel reveals that the seven heads are seven mountains, perhaps prompting the hearers to think of the seven hills of Rome, owing to such a description in numerous ancient authors (Virgil, *Geor.* 11.535 and *Aen.* 6.783; Horace, *Carm.* 7; Ovid, *Trist.* 1.5.69; Martial, *Epigrams* 4.64; Cicero, *ad Att.* 6.5.).[34] Just as there had been a resemblance between Nero and the beast in 13:18, so there may be a resemblance between Rome and the beast in 17:9. But just as the beast was not confined to the identification with Nero, so it is not likely that the imagery of the seven mountains would be exhausted by the identification of Rome with the beast.[35] Owing to the significance of the number 7 throughout Revelation, it is difficult to believe that it would suddenly be reduced to conveying a literal and concrete meaning at this point. Rather, it is likely the imagery of the seven hills

---

31. G. Schneider, "Πάρειμι," *EDNT*, 3:36.
32. So Aune, *Revelation 17–22*, 941, and Smalley, *Revelation*, 435.
33. Murphy, *Fallen Is Babylon*, 359.
34. Caird, *The Revelation of Saint John*, 216.
35. Smalley, *Revelation*, 435.

would be taken to convey the idea of universal power,[36] not unlike the way in which mountains and hills were closely associated with political power in the OT (Jer 51:25).[37] But amazingly, the image of the seven heads that has morphed into the seven hills, morphs into the image of seven kings. Though sometimes challenging to modern interpreters,[38] such a transformation confirms that the hills do indeed refer to political powers, even universal political powers. The imagery of the seven kings might also remind readers of Rome, for in Roman and Etruscan histories (Tacitus, *Histories* 3.72; Pliny, *Natural History* 34.139) there were seven kings (Romulus, Numa Pompilius, Tullus Hostilius, Ancus Marcus, Tarquinus Priscus, Servius Tullius, and Tarquinius Superbus), with later historians going so far as identifying minor figures with major ones to preserve the number 7.[39] The imagery of seven kings would reinforce the idea of universal or complete rule, which the seven hills first generate and the beast earlier exhibits in chapter 13.

"And five have fallen, one is, another has not yet come, and when he comes, it is necessary for him to remain a little (while)." The seven kings' corporate description now takes on a threefold shape, quite reminiscent of the threefold way in which the beast is described: "was and is not and is coming up from the Abyss" (17:8),[40] suggesting that the identity of the seven kings is intimately connected to the identity of the beast. The words "five have fallen, one is, another has not yet come" indicate that the hearers have already encountered the beast in the form of the "five who have fallen," are currently facing the beast in the form of the one that is, and are sure to face him in the form of another "who has not yet come" but will reign for a little while. The hearers indeed stand near the end of all things, for they await the emergence of the one who brings the "seven" to their completion.[41] Saying that it is necessary for him to remain "a little (while)" might well bring to mind similar words spoken of the devil, who knows that he has but "little " time (12:12), underscoring the connection between the devil, the beast, and the seven kings. Reference to "remaining a little (while)" might even call to mind the relatively short length of the beast's forty-two-month reign (13:5), again pointing to the connection between the identity of the seven kings and the beast. Attempts to calculate the identity of these seven kings would be virtually impossible, owing to the

---

36. Resseguie, *The Revelation of John*, 220-21.
37. Wall, *Revelation*, 207.
38. For example, Ladd (*Revelation*, 227) sees no connection between the seven hills and the seven kings, preferring to take the seven kings as representing seven kingdoms.
39. Aune, *Revelation 17-22*, 948.
40. Resseguie, *The Revelation of John*, 223.
41. Beasley-Murray, *Revelation*, 257.

high number of variables involved, such as the starting point for the calculations (does one begin with Julius Caesar, Augustus, or even Tiberius?), the parameters that determine which kings are included and which are excluded (does one include all those who ruled, even the relatively minor figures Galba, Otho, Vitellius?), and the identity of the "one who is" (Galba? Otho? Vitellius? Vespasian? Titus? Domitian?).[42] Though little consensus would likely emerge even among the hearers as to the identity of the seven kings,[43] it is altogether likely that the close connection between the devil, the beast, and the seven kings would be clear.[44]

"And the beast which was and is not, and he is eighth and is of the seven, and he goes into destruction." Together with the words in the last part of 17:8, these words serve as an inclusio around the mystery that the hearers are called to discern in vv. 9-10. The threefold formula by which the beast has come to be known in a parody of both God and the Lamb[45] is expanded in this verse. Here, the beast is identified as "the eighth," a somewhat startling detail, since reference has been made only to seven kings. Have the seven kings morphed into an eighth king? Such an interpretative option would not appear likely, owing in part to the prominence of the number 7 throughout the book generally and its prominence with regard to the beast in particular. Rather, it would seem that this enigmatic detail would likely generate more reflection by the hearers upon the identity of the beast. Perhaps reference to the beast as "eighth" would remind them of their earlier calculations of the name of the beast and his number, 666. There they discerned that the number 666 is a triangular number, the sum of every number from 1 to 36, and that the number 666 is only the *eighth* such triangular number to occur (1, 6, 21, 55, 120, 231, 406, and 666).[46] Such reflection would further reveal the connection between the seven kings and the beast. Thus, the beast is not the eighth king after the seven, but is "eighth," whose number is 666. The beast is ἐκ (*ek*, "out of") "the seven," not one of the seven.[47] His identity is coterminous with the seven as a whole, not as one of the seven individually. Significantly, the words with which this verse concludes, "and he goes into destruction," are a reminder that, despite the beast's relationship to the seven kings, he is ultimately doomed for destruction. It is characteristic of his identity, a detail he cannot escape!

42. For the various possibilities, cf. the helpful overview by Aune, *Revelation 17–22*, 945-50.
43. For a similar point, cf. Kiddle, *The Revelation of St. John*, 350.
44. For a similar conclusion, cf. Murphy, *Fallen Is Babylon*, 358.
45. Skaggs and Benham, *Revelation*, 175.
46. Bauckham, *The Climax of Prophecy*, 395-96.
47. Mounce, *The Book of Revelation*, 316.

"And the ten horns that you saw are ten kings, who have not yet received their kingship, but they will receive authority as king for one hour with the beast." Again, the words "that you saw" indicate the revelation of a new detail: specifically, that the beast's ten horns are divinely revealed to be ten kings. Here, a number of previous ideas with regard to the number 10 would likely converge (2:10; 12:3; 13:1; 17:3, 7, 12), suggesting they are all intimately connected to the great dragon, the ancient serpent, the one called Devil and Satan, the one who deceives the entire inhabited world (12:9). Once again the work of the beast is concretized in human terms. Perhaps the hearers would see some continuity between the ten kings and the ten eschatological horns/kings of Dan 7:24 and the kings from the East (Rev 16:12), who appear to morph into all the kings of the whole inhabited world (16:14). This connection[48] would fit nicely with the way in which 10 is itself a number of completion in Revelation. The description of the ten kings as "not having received their kingship" and "receiving authority as king for one hour" (17:12) stands in remarkable parallel to the previous description of the last of the seven kings, described as "the other has not yet come, and when he comes, it is necessary for him to remain a little (while)" (17:10), underscoring the tight connection between these ten horns of the beast and one or more of the beast's seven heads. The short duration of the reign of these ten kings, one hour, stands in stark contrast to the forty-two-month reign of the beast (13:5), indicating that their reign is for only the shortest portion of his activity.[49] The derived nature of their authority is clear in that they have authority as kings "with the beast." The relationship of the ten kings to the beast is made even clearer in the statement that "these have one purpose, and their power and authority they will give to the beast." The grammatical construction of this sentence suggests that their "one" purpose is the giving of their power and authority to the beast. When the hearers encounter one (the ten kings), they encounter the other (the beast)!

"These will make war with the Lamb, and the Lamb will overcome them, because he is Lord of Lords and King of Kings, and those with him are called and chosen/elect and faithful." In ways reminiscent of the demonic seduction of all the kings of the whole inhabited world (16:14), these ten kings will make war on the Lamb. Despite previous statements about war upon God's people (11:7; 12:7, 17; 13:4), 17:14 is the first text to state that war was made upon the Lamb! Unsurprisingly, these efforts at war upon the Lamb by the ten kings (the

---

48. Beale, *The Book of Revelation*, 878.
49. On the proportionality of the periods of time in Revelation, cf. Resseguie, *The Revelation of John*, 225.

The Woman on the Beast: Babylon the Whore (17:1-18)

ten horns of the beast) end in utter defeat, for this Lamb is uniquely connected with overcoming in Revelation (3:21; 5:5; 12:11). It is this Lamb, who earlier had promised to make war with the sword of his mouth upon those who refuse to repent at Pergamum (2:16), who proves victorious against (overcomes) the ten kings (of the beast). The Lamb overcomes, "for he is Lord of Lords and King of Kings!" The term "Lord" has been frequently applied to "the one who sits on the throne," "the Lord, God, the All Powerful One" (1:8; 4:8, 11; 11:4, 15, 17; 15:3-4; 16:7), with the word used in reference to Jesus once (11:8). In 17:14 this title would express the close relationship between God and the Lamb and the superiority of Jesus over all the kings of the earth (the ten kings in particular). In the Johannine tradition, Jesus' identification as king is a rich one (John 1:49; 6:15; 12:13, 15; 18:33, 37, 39; 19:3, 12, 14-15, 19, 21). In Revelation, Jesus is the ruler of the kings of the earth (Rev 1:5), kings who are sometimes at enmity with God and the Lamb (6:15; 16:12, 14) and/or to whom prophetic witness is to be given (10:11). On occasion, God himself is spoken of as King (15:3). For the Lamb to be called the King of Kings thus underscores Jesus' inherent identity as king — he is the ruler of all the kings of the earth, especially these ten warring kings! In this role he is also king over the beast (and his horns). Furthermore, the Lamb does not stand alone, but just as in 14:1-5 he has certain ones with him. They are referred to as "called and chosen and faithful." While the term "called" does not appear elsewhere in the Johannine literature, the verb form from which it is derived would likely inform its usage here, as it is closely associated with discipleship, being used to describe the renaming of Simon as Cephas by Jesus (John 1:42), as well as being a term of invitation for the disciples to the wedding at Cana (2:2), where they are described as believing in Jesus (2:11). In Revelation this term is one that reveals the identity and even spiritual significance of places and/or individuals (Rev 1:9; 11:8; 12:9; 16:16). The occurrence of "called" would thus indicate that those who stand with the Lamb are his disciples, who have been named or called by Jesus himself. The second term, "chosen" or "elect," would also be of significance, for this term of honor is used for either an individual or a community in right standing with the Elder (2 John 1, 13). In John's gospel the verb form is always found on the lips of Jesus in contexts underscoring his divine selection or choosing of his disciples (John 6:70; 13:18; and esp. 15:16). For those who stand with the Lamb to be called "chosen" or "elect" thus underscores that their relationship with the Lamb rests upon divine initiative. The third term, "faithful," has become the term par excellence for the faithful obedience unto death exemplifying Jesus (Rev 1:5; 3:14), those called upon to withstand the suffering inflicted by the devil even unto death (2:10), and Antipas, who was killed owing to his faithful witness (2:13). Such "faithful" ones as these, like the 144,000 who follow the Lamb wherever he goes, are overcomers because of their faithfulness even unto death![50]

"And he says to me, 'The waters that you saw, upon which the whore sits, are peoples and crowds and nations and tongues.'" The third occurrence of the words "that you saw" in this angelic explanation is a return to the whore with whom this vision began. Here the waters are identified as people by means of the familiar fourfold listing: peoples, crowds, nations, and tongues. For a seventh time this fourfold formula appears (with slight variations), conveying a sense of universality.[51] It has designated all those who worship God and the Lamb (5:9; 7:9), those who are opposed to God and are under the authority of the beast (11:9; 13:7), those to whom John must prophesy a second time (10:11), and those to whom the everlasting gospel must be preached (14:6). Again, the blasphemy of the whore, who presumes to sit in the place of God (17:1), is underscored. The hearers would also understand that those to whom their pneumatic witness is to be directed are under the oppressive authority of the whore, under the authority of the beast (13:7).

"And the ten horns that you saw and the beast will hate the whore and will make her ruined/desolate and naked and will eat her flesh and will burn her in fire." The fourth occurrence of the words "that you saw" reveals that yet another dimension of the vision is to be explained. Mention of the ten horns and the beast serves to underscore the solidarity of the actions of the ten kings and those of the beast. Amazingly enough, the beast (and his ten horns), who has to this point supported the whore and her domination of the peoples of the world, turns upon her with a viciousness normally associated with the actions of wild animals.[52] Their treatment of the whore would generate a visceral response as the hearers encounter the language of hatred, desolation, nakedness, eating flesh, and burning with fire. Specifically, such graphic language would remind hearers of the words of Ezekiel (23:1-49) in describing the divine judgments brought on by the actions of two whoring sisters, Oholah (Samaria) and Oholibah (Jerusalem). Owing to their opulence and unrestrained adulteries and sexual immoralities, they are turned over to those who hate them, they are stripped naked, their flesh is mutilated, and their remains are burned with fire![53] That the beast and the ten horns will hate the whore might suggest that their actions are tied to God's judgment in some way, as the resurrected Jesus

---

50. It may be that these terms would be understood as building upon one another, as Prigent (*L'Apocalypse*, 383) observes, "Cette fidélité c'est la réponse de l'homme qui reconnaît et accepte la vocation et l'élection."

51. Smalley, *Revelation*, 440.

52. Ladd, *Revelation*, 233.

53. Murphy, *Fallen Is Babylon*, 364.

himself has earlier claimed to "hate" the works of the Nicolaitans (Rev 2:6). The whore being made naked makes clear the nature of her spiritual state, as it had with the church in Laodicea (3:17), exposing her shame (16:15). There is a stark juxtaposition of her naked state with her earlier opulent attire. These gruesome words also remind readers of Jezebel's ultimate fate (2 Kgs 9:30-37).[54] Owing to the close association between burning (8:7) and the display of fire as a near-universal activity of God in Revelation (the lone exception being 13:13), mention of her fiery fate could hardly be taken as anything other than divine judgment.

"For God gave into their hearts to do his purpose and to do one purpose and to give their kingship to the beast until the words of God might be fulfilled." Just as the pouring out of the sixth bowl caused the Euphrates to dry up so that the kings of the East might invade (16:12), now the hearers learn that God himself has a hand in the cooperative venture of the ten kings and the beast. Their "one purpose" is in reality his "one purpose." Such activities are part of the divine plan bringing to completion "the words of God."[55] The occurrence of the term τελεσθήσονται (*telesthēsontai*, "will have been completed") would be of special significance, for not only is it the same verb that Jesus utters at the end of his life on the cross ("It is completed" — John 19:30), but it also functions in Revelation to describe the completion of extraordinarily important things: the mystery of God (Rev 10:7), the witness of the two prophetic witnesses (11:7), and the wrath of God (15:1, 8). These "words of God" are likely coterminous with "the words of this prophecy" (1:3; 22:7, 9-10, 18-19). The actions of these ten kings, which are in accord with the divine will, are also being revealed in the book that John has written!

"And the woman whom you saw is the great city that has the kingship over the kings of the earth." The mystery of the woman, which the angel earlier promised to reveal (17:7), is now taken up directly, as she is identified with the great city. The first mention of the great city in Revelation described the city in which the body of the two prophetic witnesses would lie, a city called pneumatically Sodom, Egypt, the place where their Lord was crucified. This universal city was a location, the identity of which could be discerned only by means of the Spirit (11:8). In conjunction with this city the first mention of the beast in Revelation occurs (11:7), underscoring the close relationship between the two. In 17:18 this woman is identified with this "great city," which is none other than Babylon the Great. Such words would remind readers that, despite her unrivaled power, this woman's fate is as certain as that of Babylon the Great, who had earlier fallen!

---

54. Aune, *Revelation 17-22*, 957.
55. As Gause (*Revelation*, 227) notes, "Even in their sinful purposes, they are in actual fact fulfilling the will of God."

The Destruction of Babylon (18:1-24)

"After these things I saw another angel coming down out of heaven having great authority, and the earth was enlightened out of his glory." This verse indicates that a new section[56] of this third major part of the vision (Rev 17:1–21:8) is now about to unfold. The phrase "after these things" often denotes a transition in thought in the Johannine literature, "and I saw" frequently indicates a new direction in the book's development, while the appearance of another angel suggests a change from or development of the previous scene. This angel's introduction would bring to mind the activity of the angel whom John encounters in chapter 17, who is clearly identified as one of the seven angels who has the seven bowls of plagues. Though not the same angel,[57] some similarities between their roles and functions are evident. The description of this angel as "coming down out of heaven" makes clear that he comes from the very presence of God and that his words will carry with them divine authority.[58] The angel's great authority would remind hearers that the beast has earlier been described as receiving "great authority" from the dragon (13:2), with the contrast between the origins of their respective great authority hard to miss. The extraordinary characteristics of this angel would remind hearers of the angels previously encountered in Rev 5 and 10. Specifically, if the angel in Rev 5 introduces the slaughtered Lamb, who is worthy to take the book and open its seals, and the colossal angel in Rev 10 reaches from earth to heaven and is instrumental in John's commission to prophesy again "to the people and nations and tongues and kings" (10:11), might this authoritative angelic figure have a message of no less significance? Remarkably, "the earth was enlightened out of his glory." This is the only angel to whom glory is attributed in Revelation, an attribution made to this point only to God (4:9, 11; 5:13; 7:12; 11:13; 14:7; 15:8; 16:9) and to the Lamb (1:6; 5:12-13).[59] This glory would likely be understood as the result of the angel's origin from heaven, having been in close spatial proximity to God. The angel's glory enlightens the world, which suggests a tight connection between the residual glory of the angel and his ability to enlighten the world, indicating that the enlightening of the earth comes from God via the angelic mission.[60] That the earth is enlightened

---

56. Resseguie, *The Revelation of John*, 228.
57. Contra Beale (892) and Aune (*Revelation 17–22*, 985), who identify this angel with the previously mentioned one.
58. Osborne, *Revelation*, 634.
59. Smalley, *Revelation*, 443.
60. As H. B. Swete (*The Apocalypse of St. John* [London: Macmillan, 1909], 226) observes, "So recently has he come from the Presence that in passing he flings a broad belt of light across the dark earth."

underscores the global significance of this authoritative angel's mission.[61] The soteriological implications of this statement would be understood in the light of the fact that the term "enlightened" appears in the prologue of John's gospel to describe the person and work of the Logos (John 1:9).

> And he cried with a strong voice, saying,
> "Fallen, fallen is Babylon the Great,
> and she has become a habitation of demons
> and a prison of every unclean spirit
> and a prison of every unclean and hateful bird."

This is the first angel in Revelation to cry with a "strong" voice, ensuring that it is heard by the whole earth, just as the angel's glory had enlightened it. It is certainly in keeping with his divine origin and the significance of his message.[62] His words "Fallen, fallen is Babylon the Great" remind readers of Rev 14:8, where this exact phrase occurs, being spoken about the Babylon the Great of old (Isa 21:9), perhaps underscoring that this Babylon the Great will fall under the judgment of God as surely as did its predecessor. Significantly, this future event is described with a past tense verb, the prophetic perfect, underscoring the certainty of the future judgment.[63] The fallen state of Babylon the Great results in its transformation from a city of opulent splendor into a place of unclean creatures of every description, with each of the three lines that describe Babylon the Great in her fallen state underscoring the unclean nature of the place. The first line — "she has become a habitation of demons" — includes the first and only appearance of the noun "habitation," reminding hearers of the numerous occurrences of the verb "inhabit" or "dwell" in the book in association with those who oppose God and or his people (3:10; 6:10; 8:13; 11:10; 13:8, 12, 14; 17:2, 8), especially those who enter into the idolatrous worship of the beast (13:8, 12, 14; 17:2, 8). Babylon the Great has become, as she was, a place of idolatrous worship. In Revelation, demons have been intimately associated with the deception of false prophecy that leads to idolatrous worship (9:20; 16:13-14). Babylon the Great in her fallenness is what she was before, a place of demonic deception that leads to idolatrous worship. The second line, "a prison of every unclean spirit," reinforces the first. While it is possible to take the term φυλακή (*phylakē*, "prison") as "haunt" or a general word for "habitation" or "domain," its use elsewhere in the Johannine literature (John 3:24) and Revelation in particular (Rev 2:10) sug-

---

61. Gause, *Revelation*, 228.
62. Smalley, *Revelation*, 443.
63. Aune, *Revelation 17–22*, 985.

gests that it would likely mean "prison" here.[64] Perhaps the idea is that Babylon the Great, who has imprisoned many by her domination, "sitting upon many waters," has now become a prison where every unclean spirit is captive. In the Johannine world unclean spirits are themselves closely associated with deception (1 John 4:1-6) and idolatrous worship (Rev 16:13-14). The third line, "and a prison of every unclean and hateful bird," continues the emphasis upon the unclean nature of Babylon the Great, while reminding readers of Isaiah's words with regard to the fall of Edom and the unclean birds that take it over (Isa 34:11-15). These birds are described as "hateful," which may even suggest that these unclean birds may somehow be the instruments of God's activity (cf. 2:6; 17:16-17).

> Because out of the wine of the wrath of her sexual immorality all nations have drunk,
> and the kings of the earth have committed sexual immorality with her,
> and the merchants of the earth out of the power of her extravagant luxury have become rich.

The first line of this angel's words replicates exactly the words of the second other angel associated with the eternal gospel (14:8). Whereas the angel in 17:1 provides continuity with the seven bowls of plagues described in chapter 17, this other angel provides continuity with the message of the second other angel described in Rev 14. The four separate genitive constructions that make up the Greek phrase translated "of the wine of the wrath of her sexual immorality" indicate that all of the constituent elements (wine, wrath, sexual immorality, and "her") are closely connected. The words τοῦ θυμοῦ (*tou thymou*, "of the passion" or "of the wrath")[65] have already been encountered in the description of the dragon, who, after being cast down from heaven, had great θυμός (*thymos*, "wrath") (12:12). Thus, despite the clear contextual idea that her wine is wine of passion, born of sexual immorality, it is also a wine of wrath, akin to the wrath of the dragon. Ominously, this wine of her passion has resulted in her being made to drink from the cup of the wrath of God's anger (16:19). As in 14:8, the objects of her "affections" are "all the nations," those to whom the first other angel in 14:6-7 had preached the eternal gospel. The nations form the first of three groups described in the verse. The second line continues the emphasis upon sexual immorality, where the kings of the earth are said to commit sexual immorality with the great whore, reinforcing the way she has been successful in the seduction of the leaders of the world into idolatrous activity. This is the

---

64. As, for example, Mounce (*The Book of Revelation*, 323) and others argue.
65. Sweet, *Revelation*, 268.

very language used to describe the activities of the woman called Jezebel by Jesus (2:20-21). Its appearance in the first two lines in 18:3 might suggest that, in the encounter with the teaching of the Nicolaitans (2:14) and Jezebel, the hearers are actually already encountering Babylon the Great, who is as good as fallen.[66] The third line introduces yet another group, "the merchants of the earth," who "out of the power of her extravagant luxury have become rich." The word "merchants" would likely be colored by the negative connotations its associated term "market" or "emporium" has in John's gospel, where Jesus charges that the house of his father has been made into an emporium (John 2:16), implying that trade has replaced true worship in an idolatrous fashion. This relationship is described in economic terms, for they have become rich by means of "the power of her extravagant luxury," making more explicit the connection between idolatrous sexual immorality and the economics controlled by Babylon the Great. Such words bring to mind the prophetic words of the resurrected Jesus to the church in Laodicea (3:17), whose riches he reveals to be poverty, in contrast to his own riches. Perhaps such reflection would result in the realization that the riches acquired by the church in Laodicea were worthless, since their origin was found in the extravagant luxury of Babylon the Great, a realization that would reveal the extent of their complicity with an idolatrous system. The grammatical construction "the power of her extravagant luxury," known as a genitive of source, makes clear that the power of Babylon the Great derives from its extravagant wealth.[67]

And I heard another voice out of heaven saying,

"Come out of her, my people,
   in order that you might not share in her sins
      and out of her plagues
   in order that you might not receive."

The voice's heavenly origin makes clear that it too comes from the very presence of God, and thus its words are coterminous with the words of God.[68] The first occurrence of "my people" would convey an extraordinary sense of intimacy with God, in contrast to his relationship with Babylon the Great, who is as good as fallen. These words are reminiscent of various expressions found throughout the OT, where God's people are warned to flee from a given location

---

66. Koester, *Revelation and the End of All Things*, 164.
67. Smalley, *Revelation*, 445.
68. Cf. Prigent, *L'Apocalypse de Saint Jean*, 389.

(Gen 12:1; Num. 16:23; Isa 48:20; 52:11; Jer 50:8; 51:6, 45; Zech 2:6-7).[69] But how would the hearers understand this call for God's people to come out of Babylon the Great? Would they hear in it a call to physically depart from the city?[70] This possibility seems to stand at odds with the way in which faithful witness has been characterized throughout the book, most clearly in the two prophetic witnesses in Rev 11:3-13, who do not withdraw from the great city; rather, they confront it.[71] This call is to a different kind of separation, from complicity with this city to resolute opposition to its injustice, murder, and idolatry.[72] The purpose of this instruction is expressed by means of a double ἵνα (*hina*, "because") clause that takes a chiastic form, with the word "because" standing at the beginning and end of the phrase. The first "because" makes clear its purpose, "in order that you might not share in her sins," sins in which all the nations, kings of the earth, and merchants of the earth have participated, for which she and they will be judged. The second "because" clause — "in order that you might not receive" — follows the words "out of her plagues" in the Greek text, making clear that those who do not separate themselves from Babylon the Great will find themselves victim of the plagues reserved for her.[73]

"Because her sins have piled up unto heaven, and God remembered her unrighteous deeds." This biblical image of evil piled up (Jer 51:9; Jonah 1:2; Ezra 9:6) indicates that her sins are so high that they can no longer be ignored;[74] they encroach upon heaven itself. Whether such an image would suggest that Babylon's sins threaten the sovereignty of God,[75] it at least indicates that they at long last must be addressed. Ominously, when God remembers, it is an indication that God has decided to act.[76] These details indicate that God's judgment upon her is imminent. The specific mention of her "unrighteous deeds" would no doubt remind hearers that the God whose ways are "righteous" and true (15:3), who is "righteous" (16:5), whose judgments are true and "righteous" (16:7), and whose "righteous deeds" have been manifested (15:4), is himself the one who remembers her "unrighteous acts" and will judge them with righteous judgment (16:7). This emphatic language would make the warning to those called "my people" all the more stark.

---

69. Wall, *Revelation*, 214-15.
70. A possibility raised by Wall, *Revelation*, 214.
71. Sweet, *Revelation*, 226.
72. Schüssler Fiorenza, *Revelation: Vision of a Just World*, 100, and Resseguie, *The Revelation of John*, 229.
73. Smalley, *Revelation*, 446.
74. Beasley-Murray, *Revelation*, 265
75. Aune, *Revelation 17–22*, 992.
76. Murphy, *Fallen Is Babylon*, 370.

In 18:5 God is spoken of in the third person, suggesting these "divine" words are spoken by an angel or that there was an unidentified change of speaker between vv. 4 and 5. In the next "heavenly" words, commands are given to unidentified agents,

Give to her even as she has given,
and repay her double according to her works;
in the cup that she mixed, you mix for her double.

On first encounter, these words would appear to be addressed directly to the hearers,[77] but the things commanded rather clearly require divine action and power. These commands would likely be taken as addressed to others, understood in the light of the preceding narrative describing the destruction of the great whore, where it is learned that the ten kings and the beast will hate her and, ultimately, destroy her.[78] Perhaps these commands would thus be taken as directed to the ten kings and the beast, into whose hearts God puts the destruction of the great whore. The first line, "Give to her even as she has given," calls to mind the *lex talionis*, indicating that the punishment she is to receive is just and that it fits her crime. The double use of the term "give," which stands at the beginning and the end of this first line in the Greek text, serves to underscore the connection between the acts of Babylon and the punishment that is to be dispensed. The second line, "repay her double according to her works," heightens the emphasis upon the justice of Babylon's judgment by use of a phrase "repay double," a Greek construction that underscores the extent of the punishment by placing side by side the verb and the object, both from the same Greek root. This idea conveys the idea of full and complete requital,[79] with similar language used in Jer 16:18[80] to describe the double recompense destined for those who profane the land by evil works, sins, and abominations. The third line, "in the cup that she mixed, you mix for her double," not only underscores the emphasis of the first two, but goes beyond them in certain ways. It too contains a play on words, with "she mixed" and "you mix" standing side by side in the Greek text, underscoring the connection between the action of Babylon the Great and the act of punishment that is commanded. The reappearance of the words "cup" and "double" connects this line, not only with that which immediately precedes ("double"), but also with a very potent image

---

77. So Aune, *Revelation 17–22*, 994.
78. Wall, *Revelation*, 215.
79. Mounce, *The Book of Revelation*, 235.
80. So Sweet, *Revelation*, 267, and Aune, *Revelation 17–22*, 992.

of judgment ("cup") that awaits Babylon the Great and is even now imminent (14:10; 16:19; 17:4).

"As much as she glorified herself and she lived opulently, so much give to her torment and mourning because in her heart she says, 'I sit enthroned and I am not a widow, and I will never see mourning.'" Her idolatrous activity is made clear in that she has "glorified herself," an activity for which only one is worthy (15:4),[81] as glory is attributed in Revelation only to God (4:9, 11; 5:13; 7:12; 11:13; 14:7; 15:8; 16:9), the Lamb (1:6; 5:12-13), and the residual glory of the angel (18:1). This illegitimate glorification is closely related to her opulent lifestyle, an opulence from which the merchants of the earth have been made rich (18:3). The judgments that God has visited on a variety of individuals who oppose him will now be visited upon Babylon the Great: torment (9:5; 11:10; 14:10-11), with the added judgment of mourning. Babylon the Great's only words recorded in the book,[82] words that come from her heart, testify against her, "I sit enthroned and I am not a widow, and I will never see mourning." Her claim to enthronement would remind hearers of her being seated "upon many waters" (17:1), who are "the peoples and crowds and nations and tongues of the earth" (17:15), a position that belongs to God alone (Ps 29:10). Her claim "I am not a widow" reveals something of her thoughts of invincibility, as widowhood was associated with vulnerability and being a victim of war.[83] This claim would prove ironic coming from one said to have had so many sexual partners, perhaps a reminder of her adulterous activity. Her claim "I will never see mourning" may suggest that she harbors delusions of her own eternality.[84] Yet, mourning is on its way to her while these words are on the lips of her heart. If she thinks there is no God or that she is divine, she is wrong!

"On account of this, in one day her plagues will come, death and mourning and famine, and in fire she will be burned up, because strong is the Lord God, the one who judges her." Her preceding boasts (Rev 18:7) and her activities described previously in this chapter become the basis for her judgment, as "on account of this" makes clear. Despite delusions about her own eternality, her judgment comes quickly, in one day. The judgment comes in the form of "her plagues." There can be little question as to the origin of such plagues, as throughout plagues have come from God and/or his agents (9:18, 20; 11:6; 15:1, 6, 8; 16:9, 21; 18:4). Here the plagues are identified as death, mourning, and famine. The naming of such plagues would remind readers of the activities associated

---

81. Murray, *Fallen Is Babylon*, 372.
82. Michaels, *Revelation*, 205.
83. Mounce, *The Book of Revelation*, 326.
84. Collins, *The Apocalypse*, 127.

with the rider on the pale horse (6:7-8)[85] and the way such mourning stands in contrast to the boasts of Babylon the Great in 18:7. Just as the ten kings and beast will burn the great whore with fire (17:16), so Babylon the Great too will be burned up,[86] the same fate as both Sodom (Gen 19:28) and Edom (Isa 34:10).[87] Despite her claims to the contrary, "strong is the Lord God, the one who judges her." Such strength, attributed to God (7:12), the Lamb (5:12), and his messengers (5:2; 10:1; 18:2), stands in contrast to the lack of strength on the part of the great red dragon and his angels (12:8). The Lord God is strong to judge (cf. 6:10; 11:18; 14:7; 16:5, 7), he has no rival — not even Babylon the Great!

Not all rejoice in the judgments of God upon her. "And they will cry and will lament over her, the kings of the earth, those who with her were sexually immoral and opulently wealthy, when they see the smoke of her fire." Emphasis is placed upon the crying and lamenting that comes from these kings, as these terms stand first in this sentence in the Greek text. Earlier, John is described as crying (5:4), an activity prohibited by one of the elders (5:5), who directs his attention to the Lion of the Tribe of Judah. Johannine hearers might also recall that this very verb occurs in the description of Mary crying at the death of her brother (John 11:31, 33), the disciples' predicted crying at the departure of Jesus (16:20), and Mary's crying at the tomb of Jesus (20:11, 13, 15). Perhaps the term's occurrence in Rev 18:9 would convey something of the deep sense of loss experienced by the kings of the earth at the destruction of Babylon the Great. In Revelation the term has appeared earlier to describe the mourning all the tribes of the earth will experience at the appearing of Jesus with the clouds (1:7). Learning the identity of those who cry and mourn the destruction of the great city would explain the reason for such emotional responses, for the kings of the earth have committed sexual immorality with the great city (cf. 17:2) and with her enjoyed opulent wealth. This intimate relationship is based upon idolatrous activity that results in economic advantage.[88] Specifically, the crying and mourning results when the kings of the earth see the smoke of her fire — a sure sign of her destruction, a sign that all is lost as far as the great city is concerned!

These kings were "standing from afar, on account of the fear of her torment, saying, 'Woe, woe, the great city, Babylon the strong, because in one hour your judgment came.'" Their location, "standing from afar," may suggest a reverential distance for those suspected of being under divine judgment (cf. Ps 38:11 [37:12]). "The fear of her torment" would indicate that even the kings of

---

85. Smalley, *Revelation*, 450.
86. Murphy, *Fallen Is Babylon*, 371.
87. Sweet, *Revelation*, 271.
88. Bauckham, *The Climax of Prophecy*, 372.

the earth understood the great city to be under the judgment of God (cf. Rev 9:5; 11:10; 12:2; 14:10-11; 18:7), which would be understood as the direct result of the command given in 18:7 above. Their dirge reveals their continued infatuation with her, for even now she is still referred to by the kings as "great," revealing something of their own adulterous nature.[89] Their misplaced fascination is further revealed when they refer to her as "Babylon the mighty city," since "mighty" is the very term used earlier to describe "the Lord God, who is mighty to judge her" (18:8)! The dirge's final line, "because in one hour your judgment came," reveals its reason. The second person pronoun "your" reveals something of the kings' affections for her. The suddenness of her judgment would bring to mind the "one hour" for which the ten kings will reign (17:12)[90] and the destruction of the great whore, which is part of their one purpose placed into their hearts by God (17:13, 16-17)!

"And the merchants of the earth are crying and mourning about her, because their cargo no one buys any longer." Earlier (18:3), the merchants were said to have become rich by the power of the great city's opulent wealth. The description of the merchants of the earth differs from that of the kings in that the merchants, not their activities, stand first in the Greek sentence. Like the kings, however, they are at first described as crying, suggesting a deep sense of loss on their part. They too are described as mourning, but the word used to describe this activity earlier appears to describe the judgment that awaits the great city (18:7-8), even while she denies that such grieving is a possibility for her (18:7). Their grief might be taken as the direct result of the grief and mourning that God sends upon the great city as judgment. The merchants' crying and mourning turns out to be based on the loss of their means of sharing in the power of her wealth, "because their cargo no one buys any longer." Clearly, their interest in her was primarily economical. Ironically, while the beast upon whom the great whore sits appears to have the power to determine who can buy and who can sell (13:17), ultimately such decisions reside with God, for whom peoples are purchased through the blood of the Lamb (5:9; 14:3-4) and from whom gold fired by fire may be purchased (3:18).

The kinds of cargo no longer sold include "cargo of gold and of silver and of precious stone and of pearls and of linen garments and of purple clothing and of silk and of scarlet, and every kind of citron wood and every kind of object of ivory and every kind of product of precious wood and of brass and of iron and of marble, and cinnamon and amomum and incense and myrrh and frankincense and wine and oil and fine flour and grain and cattle and sheep,

---

89. Smalley, *Revelation*, 452.
90. Caird, *The Revelation of Saint John*, 225-26.

and horses and carriages and bodies, even souls/lives of men." Each of the items is connected by the word "and," revealing their individual significance.[91] There are numerous similarities between this list of cargoes and the extensive list (of forty cargoes) found in Ezek 27:12-24, describing Tyre's trading partners. In contrast to the Ezekiel list, this one is structured around categories of cargo,[92] moving from most valuable to least valuable. Yet, this intertextual connection might well remind hearers of the far-reaching origins of the cargo here identified, including Spain, Morocco, North Africa, Asia Minor, Syria, India, and China. The similarity between the beginning of this list of cargo (18:12) and the description of the attire of the great whore (17:4) reinforces the idea that the great whore and the great city are the same and that it is she to whom the merchants come to sell their goods.[93] The majority of items in this list are luxury items[94] characteristic of opulent lifestyles sometimes lived out in almost hyperbolic fashion.[95] There are twenty-eight items listed, perhaps a significant number in itself. There may be a sevenfold division of items into groups of (1) metals (gold and silver), (2) precious stones (including pearls), (3) cloth (fine linen, purple, silk, scarlet), (4) costly articles (citron wood, ivory, precious wood, brass, iron, marble), (5) spices, fragrances, and food products (cinnamon, amomum, incense, myrrh, frankincense, wine, oil, fine flour, grain), (6) chattels (cattle, sheep, horses, carriages), and (7) humanity (slaves and souls).[96] Standing at the conclusion of the list are "and bodies," which was "the common term for slaves in the slave markets,"[97] indicating that slaves are regarded as no more than chattel to the merchants who mourn the loss of their market. If this list is arranged in descending order of value,[98] the occurrence of slaves at the very end reveals a great deal about the values of the great city and the merchants, perhaps not wholly unexpected in an empire where as many as

---

91. Resseguie, *The Revelation of John*, 230.
92. Bauckham, *The Climax of Prophecy*, 350-51.
93. Bauckham, *The Climax of Prophecy*, 369, and Smalley, *Revelation*, 453.
94. Koester, *Revelation and the End of All Things*, 165.
95. Contra the argument of Iain Provan, "Foul Spirits, Fornication, and Finance: Revelation 18 from an Old Testament Perspective," *JSNT* 64 (1996): 81-100, who argues that an economic critique is not the point of this passage. For examples of the way in which several of these items became the objects of excessive opulent indulgence, cf. Mounce, *The Book of Revelation*, 329, and Aune, *Revelation 17-22*, 998-1003.
96. So Smalley, *Revelation*, 454. Cf. Ladd, *Revelation*, 240, for a slightly different sevenfold division.
97. Bauckham, *The Climax of Prophecy*, 371.
98. Clarice J. Martin, "Polishing the Cloudy Mirror: A Womanist Reading of Revelation 18:13," in *From Every People and Nation: The Book of Revelation in Intercultural Perspective* (ed. David Rhoads; Minneapolis: Fortress Press, 2005), 99.

60,000,000 people were enslaved.[99] But the words "even souls/lives of men" reveal that, despite their relatively low economic value, slaves are not simply commodity items but are themselves human beings. Standing in apposition to "bodies," these words reveal that, for the great city and those with whom she does business, even human life is a commodity.[100] Such a critique suggests that the prosperity and luxury that characterize her way of life are condemned as being in diametric opposition to that to which John and his hearers are called, perhaps underscoring the vigilance required in discerning the extent to which they could be involved in the economic life in their locales.

> And the fruit of your soul/life's desire has departed from you,
> and all the luxuries and the splendors have been destroyed/lost from you;
> they will no longer find them.

In the first line of this tripartite form, reference to "the fruit of your soul/life's desire" would be taken as intimately connected to the list of cargo that immediately precedes. Elsewhere in the Johannine tradition references to "desire" or "lust" carry negative connotations, including references to the "desires" or "lusts" of "your father" the devil (John 8:44) and references to the "desires" or "lusts" of the world (1 John 2:16-17). The fruit of the desires of this great city would thus clearly be understood as being diametrically opposed to the desires of God. Often in Revelation the appearance of the term "depart" is closely associated with divine activity (Rev 9:12; 11:14; 16:2), further underscoring the idea that the loss of the things that she desires is owing to God's own activity of judgment. The second line builds upon the first, with the opulence of the great city being reenforced by reference to her luxuries, which have now been lost. The occurrence of "the splendors" would remind readers of her idolatrous desires/lusts, for in its previous occurrence (15:6) it describes the shining stone that the seven angels wore. The second line concludes with allusions to the activity of God, for her luxuries and splendors are described as being "lost" to her, as in Johannine thought ἀπόλλυμι (*apollymi*, "lose" or "destroy") often carries the idea of loss of eternal proportions (John 3:16; 6:12, 27, 39; 10:10, 28; 11:50; 12:25; 17:12; 2 John 8).[101] The third line of these "heavenly" words offers an emphatic conclusion, for the Greek construction contains an unusual and

---

99. Mounce, *The Book of Revelation*, 331.

100. Martin ("Polishing the Cloudy Mirror," 89-90) suggests that the language "even souls/lives of men" is an intentional critique of Aristotle's view of slaves as "soulless bodies" or as possessing souls but not being "ensouled."

101. Cf. A Kretzer, "Ἀπόλλυμι," *EDNT*, 1:136.

somewhat grammatically awkward triple negative construction,[102] which emphatically states that "these things" — the fruit of her soul's desires, the luxuries and splendors — have absolutely and decisively disappeared, not to be found any longer.[103]

"These merchants, those who became rich from her, from afar stood on account of the fear of her torment, crying and mourning." Attention is once again focused on these merchants' relationship with the great city (cf. 18:3). From her they stand afar; the Greek construction underscores the contrast by having the preposition "from" stand on either side of the pronoun "her." The location of the merchants ("standing from afar") may suggest a reverential distance for those suspected of being under divine judgment, as the appearance of "afar" here and in Ps 38:11 (37:12 LXX) implies. The explicit attribution of their reverential distance to "the fear of her torment" would indicate that even these merchants understood the great city to be under the judgment of God, as this word family is reserved for the activity of God and/or his agents in Revelation (9:5; 11:10; 12:2; 14:10-11; 18:7) and would certainly be understood as the direct result of the command given in 18:7. As in 18:11, so here the merchants are referred to as crying and mourning, suggesting a deep sense of loss on the merchants' part, as well as a recognition that their mourning is connected to the judgment that awaits the great city (18:7-8).

> Woe, Woe, the great city
> The one who wears fine linen
> and purple and scarlet
> and covered with gold in gold
> and precious stones and pearls,
> because in one hour such great wealth was laid waste.

This dirge also begins with the double "woe," perhaps suggesting again that her destruction is divine in origin (8:13; 9:12; 11:14). As with the dirge of the kings, this dirge reveals a continued infatuation with Babylon, for despite her destruction, she is still referred to by the merchants as great. But unlike the previous dirge, here the city is described in minute detail, in near-identical fashion to 17:4, leaving no question that Babylon the Great and the great whore are identical. Though the final line of this dirge begins identically to the final line of the first dirge, "because in one hour . . . ," on this occasion, instead of the words "your judgment has come," we have the words "such great wealth was

---

102. Aune, *Revelation 17-22*, 1003.
103. Gause, *Revelation*, 234.

laid waste," underscoring the commercial nature of the merchants' relationship with the city Babylon the Great. The language "was laid waste" serves again to connect the great city with the great whore (cf. 17:16). Such vocabulary would bring to mind the "one hour" for which the ten kings will reign (17:12) and the destruction of the great whore, which is part of their one purpose, placed into their hearts by God (17:13, 16-17).

"And every shipmaster and everyone who sails for port and sailors and whoever works the sea, from afar they stand and are crying out seeing the smoke of the fire from her, saying, 'Who is like the great city?'" Whether or not the fourfold division of this group of mourners refers to four distinct groups of mariners in descending order of grade,[104] these four groups would convey the idea of completeness to include all those who work the sea. Such a comprehensive understanding would go some way toward underscoring the image of Babylon the Great as the center of the commercial universe. Again their infatuation with the city endures beyond her destruction, for even as they witness the smoke of the fire of her destruction, they cry out, "Who is like the great city?" Such words are in keeping with those who worship the beast (13:4), "Who is like the beast, and who is able to make war with him?"[105] Such similarity not only makes explicit the mariners' reverence, perhaps even worship, for the great city, but it also underscores the implicit connection between Babylon the Great (the great whore) and the beast.

"And they were casting dust upon their heads and were crying out, weeping and mourning saying,

> 'Woe, woe, the great city
> in whom all those having ships in the sea were made rich
> out of her wealth
> because in one hour she was laid waste.'"

The mariners' intense pain at the destruction of Babylon the Great is conveyed by their action of casting dust upon their heads, a sign of mourning throughout the Near East,[106] occurring only here in Revelation. They, too, are described as "weeping and mourning." Their grief would perhaps also be seen as the direct result of the grief and mourning that God sends upon the great city as judgment. As with the dirge offered by the kings and the merchants before

---

104. As the text of Ezek 27:27, to which Rev 18:17 appears to have reference, may suggest; so Prigent, *L'Apocalypse de Saint Jean*, 394-95.
105. Sweet, *Revelation*, 273.
106. A. Sand, "Χοῦς, χοός," *EDNT*, 3:471.

them, so this dirge proper begins with the double "woe." This dirge reveals their continued infatuation with Babylon, for even though her destruction is before their eyes, she is still referred to by the merchants as great. Such heartfelt grief is closely tied to the fact that her destruction affects all those who have boats upon the sea, who have been made rich out of the magnificence of the fullness of her wealth. Once again, the grief expressed for Babylon the Great underscores the economic nature of their relationship to the city. For a third time in this chapter the reason for mourning is revealed in a "because" or "for" clause. The words of this third dirge would remind hearers of that offered by the merchants, as the first three words found in these two clauses are identical. But whereas the words "was laid waste" in 18:17 refers to "such great wealth," in 18:19 the verb clearly refers to the city itself: "in one hour she was laid waste." At this point it may be evident that the stated reasons for these three individual dirges stand in a chiastic structure with the middle phrase "because in one hour such wealth was laid waste" (v. 17) standing between "because in one hour your judgment came" (v. 10) and "because in one hour she has been laid waste" (v. 19).

"Rejoice over her, heaven and the saints and the apostles and the prophets, because God has judged your judgment upon her!" Babylon the Great's demise is not met with grief on the part of everyone.[107] The imperative of 18:20 likely comes from heaven, or at least has its implicit authority. The language "rejoice over her" was used earlier to describe the activity of the inhabitants of the earth when they saw the fate of the two prophetic witnesses whom the beast overcame and killed and left unburied in the streets so that all could witness their complete humiliation (11:10). At the same time, in 12:12 a great voice from heaven commands, "On account of this rejoice, heavens and those who dwell in them." Such a close connection would suggest that, in the destruction of Babylon the Great, the hearers are witnessing the coming of the salvation, power, kingdom of our God, and authority of his Christ, as well as the casting down of the accuser of the brothers (12:10). The command to rejoice suggests that these words are directed to all those within the heavens.[108] Such a command would not surprise the hearers, for to this point the heavens have been teeming with those who praise God and the Lamb for a variety of things. While the grammatical form of the list — the saints and the apostles and the prophets, with the article accompanying each of the nouns — might normally suggest that three distinct groups are here in view,[109] additional considerations suggest otherwise. "Saints and prophets" have appeared together earlier in Revelation (16:6) with

---

107. Murphy, *Fallen Is Babylon*, 237.
108. Michaels, *Revelation*, 207.
109. Aune, *Revelation 17–22*, 1007.

apparent reference to the people of God as a whole and the prophetic witness to which they are called. Both the contours of the theological characterization of the saints (5:8; 8:3-4; 11:18; 13:7, 10; 14:12; 16:6; 17:6) and prophets (10:7; 11:10, 18; 16:6) generally, and, more specifically, the convergence of a variety of prophetic emphases in the description of the two prophetic witnesses in chapter 11 suggest that the community may well have understood itself as a "prophethood of all believers."[110] From its earlier appearance (2:2), the term "apostle" apparently conveys the idea of a divine sending, being informed by the extensive sending language in John's gospel and 1 John, suggesting that there are individuals whom God commissions for specific tasks, especially being sent to participate in the harvest of the world (John 4:38; 17:18; 20:21). The occurrence of "sent" language elsewhere in Revelation (1:1; 5:6) tends to deepen this understanding further. Such sent ones are likely special envoys[111] that God has sent into the global harvest to bear witness to the Lamb. The placement of "the apostles" between "the saints" and "the prophets" would underscore the fact that the people of God, who have a prophetic vocation, are indeed "the sent ones" of God himself. Thus, standing in the midst of saints and prophets in 18:20, the appearance of apostles would underscore all the more the idea that those who have shed their blood on behalf of the Lamb are now called upon to rejoice at the destruction of Babylon the Great, who had become drunk on their blood, for she has now been judged. The reason for such rejoicing is made explicit in the "because" clause with which the verse concludes: "because God has judged your judgment upon her." Initially, the hearers might be struck by the fact that in the Greek text the word "God" is bounded on either side by words that speak of judgment, the verb "has judged" and the object "your judgment" making explicit the emphasis upon the divine nature of the judgment of Babylon the Great. Neither should it be overlooked that the verb "has judged" and the noun "judgment" are from the same Greek word family, further underscoring the idea of judgment. By means of this unusual phrase, "God has judged your judgment upon her," the hearers learn that the judgment Babylon the Great has rendered upon these faithful witnesses has been brought upon her. Such a construction would remind readers of the Torah (Deut 19:16-19).[112] She who was drunk on the blood of the saints has been given blood to drink. God has judged and vindicated the blood of the souls under the altar (6:10). As in the case of the two prophetic witnesses, over whom the inhabitants of the earth rejoiced, there has been a divinely enacted inversion so that such ones as these, who gave their

---

110. Cf. esp. Waddell, *The Spirit of the Book of Revelation*, 176-77.
111. So Prigent, *L'Apocalypse de Saint Jean*, 395.
112. Sweet, *Revelation*, 275.

faithful witness and followed the Lamb wherever he goes, are now called upon to rejoice over their fallen enemy, for the time has come.

"And one strong angel took up a stone as a great millstone and cast it into the sea, saying, 'In the same way with wrath will be overthrown Babylon the great city and will be found no longer.'" This is the third angel in Revelation to be described as "mighty" or "strong." Owing to the significant roles played by each of the first two mighty angels (5:2; 10:1), the hearers may well deduce that this mighty angel also fulfills a most significant role, if not a culminating one.[113] This angel takes up a stone as great as a millstone[114] and casts it into the sea. This mighty angel's words follow, "In the same way with wrath will be overthrown Babylon the great city and will be found no longer." The play on words describing the action of the angel (who "cast" or "threw" the great stone) and the action to be enacted upon Babylon the Great (it "will be overthrown") underscores the tight connection between this angel's prophetic action and the prophetic judgment that accompanies this prophetic sign, suggesting a deep intertextual connection between this prophetic activity and that of Jeremiah, who instructs Seraiah to take a book in which the prophet had written all the evil that would come upon Babylon, read all of its contents, bind it with a stone, cast it into the midst of the Euphrates, and say, "Thus shall Babylon sink, to rise no more, because of the evil that I am bringing upon her" (Jer 51:59-64). Such intertextual connections would go some way toward reemphasizing the deep connection between this Babylon the Great and Babylon the Great of old. Significantly, Babylon the great whore, who is oft described as wearing precious stones (17:4; 18:12, 16), would in the end be destroyed by a stone of judgment. Finally, the pronouncement of judgment upon the city is stated by means of the phrase "and will be found no longer," a phrase that will figure prominently in the words that follow.

> And a voice/sound of harpists and musicians and flutists and trumpeters
> will be heard in you no longer
>
> And every craftsman/artisan of every craft/art
> will be found in you no longer
>
> And a voice/sound of a mill
> will be heard in you no longer

---

113. Smalley, *Revelation*, 462.

114. Aune (*Revelation 17-22*, 1008) notes the millstone would be the stone often pulled by a donkey.

> And a light of a lamp
> will shine in you no longer
>
> And a voice/sound of a bridegroom and bride
> will be heard in you no longer.

The first vignette focuses upon the voice or sound made by a cross section of musicians, as well as perhaps those who sing. Clearly, this vignette emphasizes that the normal musical sounds that mark the major events, transitions, and moments of life from celebration to mourning will be absent from Babylon the great city. While the sound of harpists will be missing in the great city, harpists are present in abundance in heaven (5:8; 14:2: 15:2), a reality that contrasts with the silence in the great city in deafening tones. The absence of the sound of the trumpeters would bring to mind the numerous trumpet-like sounds that accompany the activities of God (1:10; 4:1; 8:2, 6-8, 10, 12-13; 9:1, 13-14; 10:7; 11:15). Significantly, in this verse we have the last mention of trumpet-like sounds in Revelation, underscoring this ominous silence all the more. The portentous refrain "will be heard in you no longer" adds to the foreboding sense of the vignette. The second vignette focuses upon the craftsmen and artisans normally plying their trades in any large city. In Rev 18:22 the complete absence of such normality is conveyed in the words "every craftsman of every craft," which includes the double "every . . . every," suggesting that all craftsmen of every craft are here in view, as well as the play on words "craftsman . . . craft," which further underscores this all-inclusive understanding. These details, along with the refrain "will be found in you no longer," not only make clear the absolute absence of such craftsmen and crafts, but also remind hearers that, just as Babylon the great city "will be found no longer," the same is true of normal craftsmen and their crafts. Similarly, the third vignette focuses upon the absence of a normal sound[115] — that of the millstone at work grinding in the city to provide food for its inhabitants. Ironically, the stone like a great millstone, which the mighty angel cast into the sea, has made the use of the ordinary millstone unnecessary. The ominous refrain "will be heard in you no longer" makes clear the absolute absence of this normal (and essential) sound. The fourth vignette focuses upon an image familiar throughout antiquity, the light of the lamp, without which there is no illumination after sunset, when darkness approaches. The absence of such a common sight would thus be an additional indication that life has been extinguished in the great city. Discerning Johannine hearers might find even a

---

115. In addition to its appearance here, φωνή (*phōnē*, "sound" or "voice") occurs in the first and fifth vignettes as well, forming a somewhat concentric structure.

deeper meaning in hearing these words. For in the Johannine literature "light" is christologically conditioned, having numerous explicit intimate connections to Jesus (John 1:4-5, 7-9; 8:12; 9:5; 12:46). In John's gospel John the Baptist, while not the Light, is explicitly called a lamp by Jesus himself (John 5:35), whose witness shines forth. Johannine hearers might discern that the Light of the lamp's witness will no longer shine to bring her inhabitants to faith or, in the case of Revelation, to repentance. The fifth vignette concludes this set of word pictures by focusing on yet another normal activity in the life of a community and its members: the joyous occasion of a wedding. For a third time in the five vignettes the word "voice" or "sound" appears, giving a certain symmetry to the whole, as the term occurs in the first, third, and fifth vignettes. In Rev 18:23 intertexts from Jeremiah again would be discerned, as the imagery of silencing the voice or sound of the bridegroom and bride occurs on three occasions in connection with proclamations of judgment (Jer 7:34; 16:9; 25:10). This vignette occurs last in the series, suggesting that it would be understood as the most important element in the group.[116] If there are no wedding sounds found in the great city, the city itself has no future; without parents, there are no children.

> Because your merchants were the great men of the earth,
> because with your enchantment all nations have been deceived
> and in you was found the blood of the prophets and saints
>   and all those slaughtered upon the earth.

The first reason offered for such silent devastation of Babylon the great city goes back to the merchants. Their mention would remind hearers of the extent and scope of their trade, powerfully conveyed by the extensive, if not comprehensive, list of cargo found earlier (18:12-13), as well as the merchants' intimate economic relationship, which was wholly dependent on the great city. These merchants, who became rich from her opulent wealth (18:15), were the great men of the earth. Such men have already appeared in the sevenfold list of humanity that opposes God, for they beg the mountains and the stones to fall upon them and to hide them from the face of the one who sits upon the throne and the wrath of the Lamb (6:15-16). A number of its occurrences in the OT would reveal that the term "the great men" often appears in contexts that reveal such individuals to be trusted companions, officials, and courtiers of the king and his family (2 Chr 36:18; Isa 34:12; Dan 2:24; 4:33; 5:1-3, 9, 23; 6:17; Jonah 3:7), who normally have their position owing to God (Prov 8:15-16). Such nuances

---

116. So Ruben Zimmerman, "Nuptial Imagery in the Revelation of John," *Biblica* 84.2 (2003): 161.

underscore the idea that the close economic relationship between the great city and her merchants is what has elevated them to the status of "the great men" of the earth, not their relationship with God. The initial "because," however, indicates that the destruction of the great city is not unrelated to the economic relationship that makes of her merchants the great men of the earth. The second reason for the silent devastation of Babylon the Great also comes in the form of a "because" clause: "because with your enchantment all the nations have been deceived." While at first glance it might appear that these two reasons have little to do with one another, further reflection reveals their deeper connection. While the mention of "sorcery" or "magic" might call to mind any number of ideas from magic to magic potions, incantations, or magic spells, its meaning here is likely "enchantment," as it is by this means that all the nations have been deceived. Such enchanting deception would be informed by numerous specific examples in Revelation (2:20; 12:9; 13:14). In this context the enchantment that deceives would be closely tied to the deceptive power of the great city's wealth and power, which leads to an enchanted state for those caught up in such deception. Such enchanting deception involves the false worship of idolatry,[117] an activity with which the great whore is intimately connected.

The third reason for the great city's silent devastation, joined to the first two simply by the word "and," is clearly the culminating charge.[118] In an ironic twist, the close connection that exists between the things that will be found no longer, described in the five vignettes earlier, and the one thing that is (still?) found within her is blood![119] In explicit language, the blood of prophets and saints and all those slaughtered upon the earth is the culminating charge. While the judgment inflicted upon the great city owing to the blood of the saints and the prophets is by now familiar (18:20), in 18:24 the great city's culpability expands to include the blood of "all those slaughtered upon the earth," a charge that is both astonishing and enigmatic at the same time. Perhaps such culpability is because the great city is depicted as the ruling sovereign of the entire world and as such has a certain responsibility for all its inhabitants,[120] or that her guilt is so immense that it subsumes culpability for all shedding of blood.[121] The word that appears here to describe all those slaughtered upon the earth is the same word used to describe the slaughtered Lamb (5:6, 9, 12; 13:8) and the souls under the altar (6:9),[122] making clear that, while the blood of God's people

---

117. Gause, *Revelation*, 236.
118. Kiddle, *The Revelation of St. John*, 374.
119. Smalley, *Revelation*, 465.
120. Mounce, *The Book of Revelation*, 335.
121. Murphy, *Fallen Is Babylon*, 378.
122. Prigent, *L'Apocalypse de Saint Jean*, 397.

From Babylon the Great to the New Jerusalem — from the Last Judgment to the New Creation (19:1–21:8)

At the midpoint of the third major section of Revelation, marked by another ἐν πνεύματι (*en pneumati*, "in the Spirit") phrase, following the detailed description of Babylon the great city (17:1-18) and the extensive description of her destruction (18:1-24), the hearers encounter a stretch of text that in many ways brings the story to its climax by narrating a number of final things, taking them from the judgment of Babylon the Great to the New Jerusalem. Specifically, they encounter the great rejoicing in heaven and on earth that accompanies the judgment of Babylon the Great and the invitation to the marriage supper of the Lamb (19:1-10), the appearance of the King of Kings and Lord of Lords (19:11-16), his victory over his enemies (19:17-21), the thousand-year reign of Jesus and those who overcome (20:1-6), Satan's final rebellion and defeat (20:7-10), the final judgment (20:11-15), and the initial description of the New Jerusalem descending from heaven (21:1-8).

Rejoicing in Heaven and on Earth and the Marriage Supper of the Lamb (19:1-10)

"After these things I heard as a great voice of a great crowd in heaven saying, 'Hallelujah, the salvation and the glory and the power of our God. . . .'" For the only time in Revelation the words "after these things" is joined with "I heard."[123] This unique combination marks a new transition in the story line, while contrasting nicely with the many things that "will be heard no longer" (18:22-23) in the great city. This contrast continues, for that which John hears is also "a voice" or "a sound," the term occurring three times in 18:22-23. Here, John hears a great voice or sound as of a large crowd in heaven. Such language would remind readers of other great crowds, in 7:9-10 and 12:10. These similarities suggest that this great crowd includes the redeemed in heaven.[124] The first word, "Hallelujah," a Greek transliteration of the Hebrew word הללויה (*hallelujah*, "praise Yahweh"), has not appeared elsewhere in Revelation, nor in the whole of the NT. It's some-

---

123. Aune, *Revelation 17–22*, 1024.
124. Caird, *The Revelation of Saint John*, 232, and Prigent, *L'Apocalypse de Saint Jean*, 402.

what unrivaled place in Israel's worship of Yahweh, where it introduces Pss 106, 111–13, 117, 135, 146–50, would indicate a sharp contrast in tone and mood from the previous passage, which includes destruction and mourning.[125] This distinctive term would likely indicate that the command to the heavens to rejoice over the destruction of the great city (18:20) is beginning to be fulfilled.[126] The words "the salvation and the glory and the power of our God" follow fast on the heels of the Hallelujah and are reminiscent of other worship scenes earlier encountered. Like its previous two occurrences (7:10; 12:10), the attribution of salvation to God in praise conveys a sense of finality, focusing upon salvation in its most comprehensive, eschatological sense. It stands first in this series owing to its foundational and fundamental role in the accomplishment of God's will in the world.[127] The attribution of glory to "our God," often offered in heaven (4:9, 11; 5:12; 7:12) and earth (11:13; 14:7), here stands in sharp contrast to those who refuse to give God such praise and/or who, in the case of Babylon the Great (18:7), give glory to themselves. Neither is the attribution of power surprising, for God is constantly praised in such a manner in Revelation (4:11; 7:12; 11:17; 12:10; 15:8), here also standing in sharp contrast to the idolatrous use of power occasionally encountered in the book (13:2; 17:13; 18:3).

> Because true and righteous are his judgments,
> because he judged the great whore who corrupted the earth with her sexual immorality,
> and he avenged (gave justice to/vindicated) the blood of his servants out of her hand.

The explanation takes the familiar triple form, with the first two reasons introduced by "because" clauses. The first reveals the primary reason for such exalted praise by the phrase "true and righteous are his judgments." Such words hearken back to several previous passages in Revelation (6:10; 15:3; 16:7), suggesting that some of the voices heard earlier are to be found among this heavenly crowd and underscoring the idea that, even though God's judgments may seem to be delayed or absent altogether, they are nevertheless true and righteous. The second reason for such praise occurs in the second "because" clause. God's true and righteous judgments have been seen most recently in his judgment of "the great whore who corrupted the earth with her sexual immorality." Not only is his judgment of the great whore the example par excellence

---

125. Smalley, *Revelation*, 476.
126. Beasley-Murray, *Revelation*, 270.
127. Smalley, *Revelation*, 477.

of his true and faithful judgments, but it also reminds readers of the reason for her judgment:[128] she is said to have "corrupted the earth with her sexual immorality." The imperfect verb form "corrupted" or "ruined" would convey something of the continuously corrupting influence of the great whore upon the world.[129] The meaning of the term φθείρω (*phtheirō*, "corrupt" or "ruin") logically includes the idea of destruction,[130] a meaning that the related compound word διαφθείρω (*diaphtheirō*, also meaning "corrupt" or "ruin") conveys in its three previous occurrences in Revelation (8:9; 11:18[2x]). The words of 19:2 thus indicate that the destruction of the great whore is the result of her own destructive corruption of the earth.[131] God's salvation and glory and power are also celebrated with the Hallelujah because "he avenged (gave justice to/vindicated) the blood of his servants out of her hand." The occurrence of the verb "avenged" or "vindicated," which at its root is the word to judge, would bring to mind the words of the souls under the altar, who cry out to God with a great voice for him to judge and avenge/give justice to/vindicate their blood. As 19:2 and 6:10 are the only two places in the whole of Revelation where the verb ἐκδικέω (*ekdikeō*, "avenge" or "vindicate") occurs, it is virtually impossible not to believe that this description of God's action is an indication that the prayers of the souls under the altar have been answered![132] His salvation and glory and power are praised, for his judgments are indeed true and righteous, for he has vindicated the blood of the saints who died at the hands of the great whore, the blood with which she had become drunk (17:6). Clearly, reference to "the blood of his servants" would be a reminder that God's people are indeed his prophetic servants who bear faithful witness to him. The close parallel between these words and those of 2 Kgs 9:7 would further underscore the prophetic identification of the servants in Rev 19:2, as well as suggest another connection between the Jezebel of old and the Jezebel with whom the church in Thyatira contends (2:20-23).[133]

"And a second time they said, 'Hallelujah! And her smoke goes up forever and forever.'" These words come from the same great voice of the great crowd in heaven that utters the first Hallelujah.[134] The second occurrence of the word Hallelujah in the span of three verses would raise the intensity of the praise

---

128. Prigent, *L'Apocalypse de Saint Jean*, 403.

129. Smalley, *Revelation*, 477.

130. F. Merkel, "Destroy," *NIDNTT*, 1:469.

131. Beasley-Murray (*Revelation*, 272) suggests that, in corrupting the earth, the Great Whore is undoing the work of creation.

132. Ladd, *Revelation*, 245.

133. Aune, *Revelation 17-22*, 1025.

134. Aune, *Revelation 17-22*, 1026.

and heighten the dramatic quality of the scene considerably.[135] This Hallelujah stands in parallel to the first, as a word of praise, for it too is accompanied by words of explanation. The specific reason is again closely connected to the destruction of the great whore, in this case, a celebration of the manner and permanence of her destruction. The mention of her smoke that rises forever and forever would remind hearers of very similar words already spoken about her destruction (14:11; 17:16; 18:8, 18). This is no accident but the judgment of God.[136] These words would perhaps also remind readers of the similar fate experienced by Sodom of old (Gen 19:28), revealing that this Babylon the Great has shown herself to be another Sodom, a name given pneumatically to the great city in Rev 11:8.[137] The rising of her smoke forever and forever would stand in ghastly contrast to the smoke of the incense that rises to God in heavenly worship, mentioned at various points throughout Revelation (5:8; 8:4; 14:11).[138] The phrase "forever and forever" leaves little doubt that her destruction is permanent, absolute, and irreversible,[139] taking on even greater significance, since the only other places this phrase occurs in Revelation are in reference to the unending praise due to the one who sits on the throne and to the Lamb (1:6; 5:13; 11:15).

"And the twenty-four elders and the four living creatures fell down, and they worshipped the God who sits on the throne, saying, 'Amen! Hallelujah!'" The praise of God for his righteous judgments is now complete, as the twenty-four elders appear to represent all the redeemed who overcome, and the four living creatures appear to represent the entire created order.[140] These heavenly characters, introduced during the inaugural vision of God (4:4, 7), have punctuated the narrative with their praise and adoration at periodic intervals throughout. Their first appearance in the throne-room scene and their last appearance here in 19:4 surround the entire portion of the narrative given to the judgments of God,[141] continuing to underscore the fact that indeed God is sovereign! Here as previously, the twenty-four elders and four living creatures are described as falling down before the one who sits on the throne (4:10; 5:8, 14; 7:11; 11:16), with the word "fell down" standing first in the Greek sentence. Such prostration appears to be the way in which God is to be worshipped in Revelation, perhaps suggesting that it is an involuntary response to the divine presence. Significantly, this is one of the few places where the one who sits on

---

135. Mounce, *The Book of Revelation*, 338.
136. Prigent, *L'Apocalypse de Saint Jean*, 403.
137. Beasley-Murray, *Revelation*, 272.
138. Smalley, *Revelation*, 278.
139. Gause, *Revelation*, 239.
140. Prigent, *L'Apocalypse de Saint Jean*, 403.
141. Murphy, *Fallen Is Babylon*, 381.

the throne is explicitly identified as God in the title itself (cf. also 7:10; 11:16). The twenty-four elders and the four living creatures join their voices with the great voice of a great crowd that comes from heaven and says, "Amen, Hallelujah!" Thus for a third time in the span of four verses the word Hallelujah occurs! Their word of Hallelujah continues the fulfillment of the command for the heavens to rejoice (18:20). A certain sense of finality might be conveyed in the combination of these terms as these very words, "Amen, Hallelujah," appear at the end of the fourth division of the Psalms in the Hebrew Bible (106:48) as an invitation to the hearers to respond to the book as a whole.[142]

"And a voice from the throne came out, saying, 'Praise our God all his servants, those who fear him, the small and the great.'" The reference to "our God" suggests that this voice is that of one of the heavenly beings closest to the throne, perhaps one of the four living creatures.[143] But as the verb of origin "came out" makes clear, if this is not the voice of God, the words that follow are the words of God.[144] These divine(ly authorized) words are reminiscent of OT passages (LXX) where the people of God are instructed to praise God (e.g., Pss. 112; 135; 148; 150).[145] The command is directed to all those who are in right relationship with God, including his servants (1:1; 7:3), whose prophetic vocation is central to their identity (10:7; 11:18), and to whose blood justice has been given (19:2). These servants are identified as those who fear him, confirming a previous identification of God's people (11:18), indicating their obedience to the angelic command to "fear God" (14:7). "The small and the great" who are called upon to praise God stand in diametric opposition to those both small and great who worship the beast and receive his mark (13:15-16).[146] These words underscore the comprehensive nature of this command to praise; all, regardless of social standing, are commanded to praise God. All these terms have earlier appeared together in 11:18 in a passage that (1) promises a reward to his servants the prophets and the saints and to those who fear his name, both small and great, and (2) speaks of a judgment of destruction upon those who have destroyed the earth. The relationship between the praise here prescribed and God's activity of rewarding and judging could hardly be more evident.

"And I heard as a voice of a large crowd and as a voice of many waters and as a voice of strong thunder saying, 'Hallelujah! Because our Lord God, the All Powerful One, reigns.'" For the first time the hearers encounter an extraordinary voice that brings to mind three of the loudest sounds possible within

---

142. J. Goldingay, *Psalms*, vol. 3: *Psalms 90-150* (BCOT; Grand Rapids: Baker, 2008), 241-42.
143. Kiddle, *The Revelation of St. John*, 378.
144. Aune, *Revelation 17-22*, 1027.
145. BAGD, 22.
146. Sweet, *Revelation*, 279.

their context. This unique combination of sounds distinguishes this voice from that heard in 19:1, as does the anarthrous construction of the voice; it is "a" voice rather than "the" voice, suggesting that this voice, while standing in some continuity with the first, is both more extensive and may well even include the previous one. If so, what is envisioned would bring to mind the scene in chapter 5, where every creature in the universe offers praise to the one who sits on the throne and to the Lamb![147] This voice would at the least include all those addressed in 19:5, the redeemed of all time, the universal church.[148] This deafening voice utters the fourth Hallelujah within this six-verse span, continuing the explosive intensification of praise offered, praise so great the hearers might wonder if it is possible for them to participate in anything more grand or engaging. This fourth Hallelujah is accompanied by a rationale for such praise, which takes the form of still another "because" clause. The reason offered is that "the Lord our God, the All Powerful One, reigns." The verb with which this sentence begins in the Greek text actually stands in the aorist tense, a form known grammatically as an ingressive aorist, here conveying the idea that at some point in the past God's reign has begun and is now a recognizably present reality.[149] As such, the meaning of the verb in 19:6 would likely remind hearers of earlier occurrences (11:15, 17), where it stands in both the future and the aorist forms, testifying to something of the trans-temporal nature of this divine reign. The hearers might well understand the beginning of this reign as in some way connected with the judgment and destruction of the great whore. The combination of titles for God in this verse — "Lord, God, All Powerful One" — has occurred five times before in Revelation in contexts of praise (1:8; 4:8; 11:17; 15:3; 16:7), with the term All Powerful One underscoring the idea of God's unrivaled power (1:8; 16:14) and immense greatness.[150] This, the great God, whose current reign has already begun, is victorious over the great whore and is worthy of the praise of all.

"Let us rejoice and let us be glad and let us give glory to him because the marriage of the Lamb has come, and his bride has prepared herself!" A careful reading of the verse reveals that its forward thrust is quite conscious of, if not rooted in, the past judgment of Babylon. Each of the commands takes the grammatical form of a hortatory subjunctive, a construction that here would serve to intensify the sense of eschatological joy as they combine both a recognition of the provisions of God's reign and the role those who hear are to play. The

---

147. Smalley, *Revelation*, 481.
148. Allo, *Saint Jean: L'Apocalypse*, 275.
149. Murphy, *Fallen Is Babylon*, 382.
150. G. Braumann, "Strength," *NIDNTT*, 3:718.

verb in the first hortatory subjunctive, "rejoice," often appears in what might be called Johannine eschatological contexts (John 3:29; 4:36; 8:56; 11:15; 14:28; 16:22; 20:20). This hortatory subjunctive to rejoice would thus be informed by a host of christological and eschatological dimensions, which would contribute to making their eschatological rejoicing all the richer. It would also be informed by the rejoicing of the opponents of Jesus and his followers (John 16:20; Rev 11:10), tying their rejoicing specifically to the vindication of their blood by God! The second hortatory subjunctive, "let us be glad," would also convey special meaning, as it too is informed by its place in the tradition of John's gospel (John 5:35; 8:56). The third hortatory subjunctive would be no less significant, as the giving of glory to God is quite important in Revelation (4:9; 11:13; 14:7; 16:9). Clearly, the hearers would understand that, by obeying the command of this third hortatory subjunctive, they stand on the side of God and are invited to be active participants in this momentous activity. The rationale for this threefold exhortation is made clear in the following words: "because the marriage of the Lamb has come, and his bride has prepared herself." These words convey a transition from the rejoicing that accompanies God's judgment of destruction upon those who destroyed the earth to rejoicing over the rewards that he now gives to his faithful servants. Although this wedding imagery might at first seem to come out of nowhere,[151] Johannine hearers would no doubt be aware of marriage/wedding imagery being used in the OT on various occasions to describe the relationship between God and his bride, Israel (Hos 2:7; Isa 1:21; Jer 2:2).[152] This imagery often appears in negative contexts depicting Israel's unfaithfulness, which seems to have led to an expectation that this ideal relationship would be fulfilled only in the future.[153] They would be familiar already with the idea of Jesus as bridegroom from the words of John the Baptist in John's gospel (John 3:29). Since the voices of the bridegroom and bride will no longer be heard in the great city as a result of its judgment (Rev 18:23), the appearance of wedding imagery at this point in Revelation would perhaps not take the hearers completely by surprise. The occurrence of such multifaceted imagery at this point in Revelation would indicate that the narrative is being pushed along to its dramatic conclusion.[154] It is also noted that his bride (literally "woman") has prepared herself. The hearers are likely to understand these words within the context of ancient Jewish two-stage weddings, where after the betrothal, at which point the couple is legally married, the bride continues

---

151. Prigent (*L'Apocalypse de Saint Jean*, 405) says that it appears brutally in this context.
152. Caird, *A Commentary on the Revelation of St. John the Divine*, 234.
153. Wall, *Revelation*, 222.
154. Metzger, *Breaking the Code*, 90.

to live in the house of her father, where she prepares herself as she awaits her husband's arrival, at a date in the future, to take her to his house.[155] Clearly, the bride of the Lamb is preparing herself for this extraordinary event, owing in part to the occurrence of "herself" as the object of her preparations. The specific vocabulary used to describe this preparation would suggest a cooperative, if not reciprocal, activity between the bride of the Lamb and God, as this verb's six other occurrences in Revelation (8:6; 9:7, 15; 12:6; 16:12; 21:2) always describe the direct activity and intervention of God. As God's other preparations have not been altered or retarded, so the hearers would understand that the bride's preparations will result in the plan of God being accomplished in her as well.[156]

"And there was given to her in order that she might be clothed with fine linen, bright and pure." Both aspects of their reciprocal relationship appear in these words. The occurrence of the divine passive "there was given" implies that God (or the Lamb) is the one who gives this garment of fine linen to the bride of the Lamb.[157] The purpose of this gift is made clear by the verb "to be clothed," a middle voice indicating that she is to clothe herself in this gift. The verbs thus underscore the reciprocal nature of the relationship shared by God and the bride of the Lamb. The bright and pure characteristics of the bride's attire would remind readers of the bright and pure stones with which the seven angels that come from the temple of the tabernacle of witness in heaven are clothed (15:6), suggesting that the bride too is in a very close relationship with God. The bride's "fine linen, bright and pure," would also stand in striking contrast to the fine linen of the great whore. While the latter's attire is the result of idolatrous opulence, the attire of the former is the result of an intimate relationship with the Lamb, perhaps underscoring his bride's sexual innocence in contrast to the sexual exploits of the great whore.[158] Unexpectedly come the words "for the fine linen is the righteous deeds of the saints." Obviously, the fine linen here described is the same fine linen that was divinely given to the bride, with which she clothed herself. But though this linen is a divine gift, it is here identified as "the righteous deeds" of the saints. This word would be conditioned by the hearers' earlier encounter with it once before in Revelation, where it refers to the righteous deeds of God (15:3-4). There his righteous deeds of judgment are also described as great and marvelous works, as well as righteous and true ways. This occurrence, along with the fact that the root

---

155. D. A. McIlraith, "'For the Fine Linen Is the Righteous Deeds of the Saints': Works and Wife in Revelation 19:8," *CBQ* 61.3 (July 1999): 524.

156. Prigent, *L'Apocalypse de Saint Jean*, 406.

157. Gause, *Revelation*, 242.

158. Allo (*Saint Jean: L'Apocalypse*, 276) refers to the bride's attire as "vestments of innocence."

From Babylon the Great to the New Jerusalem (19:1–21:8)

from which the "righteous" family of words come refers only to God in Revelation,[159] indicates a close association between God and the saints. Conversely, the activities of Babylon are described as "unrighteous deeds," indicating that the contrast between the attire of the bride of the Lamb and the attire of the great whore has its basis in their diametrically opposed activities.[160] It is difficult to imagine that the righteous deeds of the saints would be understood by Johannine hearers apart from the idea of works that has proven so important throughout Revelation. In this light, the identity of the righteous deeds and the works of the saints could hardly be thought to be anything but coterminous. Specifically, such language brings to mind the activities of love, labor, patient endurance, keeping faith/keeping my (Jesus') word, faithful witness, service, moral purity, and discernment.[161] The fact that the fine linen given to the bride is at the same time the righteous deeds of the saints well captures something of the divine-human cooperation essential to a proper understanding of salvation in Revelation.[162] The twofold occurrence of the term "the righteous deeds" describes the righteous deeds of God carried out on behalf of the saints (15:4), while also describing the righteous deeds of the saints carried out on behalf of God.[163] Their righteous deeds are consistent with his righteous deeds; their actions reflect the God who has given them salvation. The identification of the fine linen with the righteous deeds of the saints confirms that the bride of the Lamb is indeed identical to the saints.[164]

"And he says to me, 'Write: Blessed are those called to the marriage supper of the Lamb.' And he says to me, 'These are the true words of God.'" The words of 19:9 appear to have divine authorization, though the identity of the speaker is uncertain.[165] For the first time since 14:13, John is instructed to write,

---

159. Aune, *Revelation 17–22*, 1031.

160. McIlraith, "For the Fine Linen Is the Righteous Deeds of the Saints," 526-27.

161. On this whole question, cf. the helpful discussion in McIlraith, "For the Fine Linen Is the Righteous Deeds of the Saints," 512-29.

162. Prigent (*L'Apocalypse de Saint Jean*, 399) calls the righteous deeds "les manifestations humaines du salut, les signes terrestres du royaume . . . les preuves evidentes de la puissance de Dieu," while Sweet (*Revelation*, 277) notes that her clothing is the sanctified lives of her members, who have washed their robes in the blood of the Lamb (7:14).

163. Smalley, *Revelation*, 484.

164. Michaels, *Revelation*, 212.

165. On the basis of a parallel to this passage occurring later in the book (22:8-9), where a fellow servant is explicitly identified as an angel, it is tempting to identify the one who speaks in 19:10 as an angel. But nowhere in 19:10 are the hearers told that this speaker is an angel. If the hearers discern that this speaker is indeed an angel, it is not altogether clear with which angelic figure they would identify him. On the one hand, the hearers might think him to be the last angel mentioned in the narrative, who both cast a boulder into the sea and spoke words of doom over

with the command accompanied by a beatitude, the fourth such beatitude the hearers have encountered in the book (1:3; 14:13; 16:15). This beatitude, like its predecessors, conveys a blessing (and warning!) of eschatological proportions, "Blessed are those called to the marriage supper of the Lamb." Earlier (17:14), those who stand with the Lamb are referred to as the "called," a term informed by the verb form from which it is derived and informing its usage here, in 19:9. In John's gospel the verb "call" is closely associated with discipleship (John 1:42; 2:2, 11), while in Revelation it reveals the identity and even spiritual significance of places and/or individuals (Rev 1:9; 11:8; 12:9; 16:16). Those invited to the marriage supper of the Lamb are those who follow the Lamb wherever he goes (14:4), who stand with him in battle (17:14). Oddly enough, they are none other than the saints, the bride herself! Thus, once again, one image has morphed into another before the very eyes and ears of the hearers. That "those invited" is a perfect participle in 19:9 suggests that their call has been issued in the past and that this invitation is still valid. The idea of the marriage supper would likely bring to mind the eating imagery found already within the seven prophetic messages to the seven churches (2:7, 17; 3:20)[166] and the theologically significant locations of the term "supper" in John's gospel (John 12:2; 13:2, 4; 21:20). The words "These are the true words of God" convey a certain sense of finality and authority. Yet, there is a certain ambiguity in them as well, for they would function equally well as an emphatic call to discerning obedience to the beatitude that immediately precedes (19:9), to all the words devoted to the mystery of the great whore (17:1–19:9),[167] and/or to all the words that precede it in Revelation to this point (1:1–19:9).[168] Owing to such ambiguity, perhaps these words would be understood in a multivalent way. In that light, these are the true words of God spoken with regard to (1) the marriage supper of the Lamb and those called to attend,[169] (2) Babylon the Great, and (3) the revelation of Jesus Christ given to John, which must be heard and kept!

"And I fell before his feet to worship him." There can be no misunderstanding these words, for not only does John fall before the feet of this figure, an action that functions in Revelation as one of the defining acts of worship (1:17; 4:10; 5:8, 14; 7:11; 11:16; 19:4), but he also uses the term "worship" to convey his intention, a term that has earlier been used for the worship of God (4:10;

---

the city (18:21-24; so Smalley, *Revelation*, 484). On the other hand, they might well take this angel to be the one whom John encounters in 17:1, who shows John the mystery of the Great Whore (so Kiddle, *The Revelation of St. John*, 380, among others).

166. Sweet, *Revelation*, 277.
167. Beasley-Murray, *Revelation*, 275.
168. Murphy, *Fallen Is Babylon*, 384.
169. Sweet, *Revelation*, 280.

5:14; 7:11; 11:1, 16; 14:7; 15:4; 19:4) and the Lamb (5:14), demons (9:20), the dragon (13:4), the beast (13:4, 8, 12; 14:9, 11), and the image of the beast (13:15; 14:9, 11; 16:2). This is the first time in the book that the word is ever directly associated with John. Perhaps John's actions are in part the result of the ambiguity surrounding the identity of this speaker, thinking that if he speaks such divinely authorized words, perhaps he shares in the divine power and is himself divine.[170] But whereas John's earlier falling "at the feet of Jesus as though dead" (1:17) appears to have been an involuntary reflex, his action here appears to be less involuntary and more intentional, somewhat reminiscent of the way in which he had marveled a great marvel at the appearance of the great whore (17:6; cf. also 13:3-4). If John's earlier temptation to worship the great whore was met by an angelic rebuke (17:7), here he is met with a more urgent and direct rebuke[171] in the form of a prohibition meaning something like, "See that you do not do it!" The implication of John's intended worship is that it amounts to idolatrous worship, because the one before whose feet he has bowed is not divine but a fellow servant. Here the hearers discover that their stance against idolatrous worship, one of the dominant themes of this book, must be a comprehensively discerning one. For the temptation to idolatrous worship can infiltrate the church to the extent that the servants of God, rather than God, are worshipped![172]

The next words, "I am your fellow servant of you and of your brothers who have the testimony of Jesus," would no doubt remind hearers of the only other place in the book where nearly all of this vocabulary occurs together. When the fifth seal is opened, the souls under the altar, who have been slaughtered owing to the word of God and the testimony that they had, are told to wait until the number of their fellow servants and brothers who are about to be killed is full (6:9-11). Such remarkable similarities might suggest that the speaker of these words is a fellow servant, perhaps one of the souls under the altar who has been killed to make the number of martyrs full.[173] As a representative of all the redeemed, he steps out of the chorus of 19:6-8 and speaks individually to John — words of prophecy, true words of God, spoken on behalf of the holy and true Sovereign (6:10). On this view, John's intention to worship this speaker might better be understood. If he is one of the souls slaughtered for his faithful witness and is an heir to a number of promises made to the one who overcomes (2:17, 26-28; 3:21), then perhaps in John's mind he is worthy of worship, for he would be thought to share extensively in Jesus' identity. But the speaker forbids

---

170. K. E. Miller, "The Nuptial Eschatology of Revelation 19–22," *CBQ* 60.2 (1998): 307.
171. Michaels, *Revelation*, 213.
172. Caird, *A Commentary on the Revelation of St. John the Divine*, 237.
173. Contra Beale, *The Book of Revelation*, 946.

such veneration, for he is a fellow servant of John, as he is of John's brothers, those who have the testimony of Jesus. He is their brother in tribulation and kingdom and patient endurance (1:9). This fellow servant continues with the command, "Worship God!" This message conforms to that of the entire book and redirects John's worship to its appropriate object. Only God is to be praised — not the dragon or the beast or the image of the beast or the great whore, not even those who have been slaughtered because of the word of God and the testimony of Jesus — only God is to be praised! The fellow servant's message to worship God is connected to the following statement — "for the witness of Jesus is the Spirit of prophecy" — by the postpositive "for," indicating a certain linkage between the two, suggesting that the worship of God is grounded in and supported by the witness of Jesus, the Spirit of prophecy. Such linkage underscores the truth that, from its first chapter, Revelation has been concerned with the witness of Jesus, a witness intricately connected to the Spirit, and that this witness affirms and points again and again to the worship of God and the avoidance of idolatrous worship.[174] While modern interpreters debate whether the phrase "the witness of Jesus" is grammatically a subjective genitive or an objective genitive (i.e., whether Jesus' own witness or the witness about Jesus is in view), it is unlikely that the hearers would make such a distinction at this point,[175] for they have witnessed firsthand how integrated these two dimensions of Jesus' witness are in Revelation, for the witness about Jesus is indeed a message from Jesus.[176] Jesus is the faithful witness par excellence, who is the firstborn of the dead, whose blood washed us from our sin and made us a kingdom, priests unto God (1:5-6; 3:4). His own faithful witness is shared and/or emulated by his followers like John (1:2, 9), Antipas — my faithful witness (2:13), the souls under the altar (6:9-11), the two prophetic witnesses (11:3, 7), believers in general (12:11, 17; 17:6), as well as the 144,000 (14:4). In this witness, they are faithful unto death (3:10). By this time the extraordinarily close relationship that exists between Jesus and the Spirit is abundantly clear. As Revelation opens, they are described together with the one who sits on the throne in the prologue (1:4-6). In the inaugural vision of Jesus, he stands in the midst of the seven lampstands. In the seven prophetic messages to the seven churches, the words spoken by Jesus and the words spoken by the Spirit are coterminous (2:7, 11, 17, 29; 3:6, 13, 22), indicating that what Jesus says, the Spirit says.[177] In the throne-room scene, the intimate relationship between Jesus and the Spirit

---

174. Koester, *Revelation and the End of All Things*, 170.
175. Murphy, *Fallen Is Babylon*, 385.
176. Michaels, *Revelation*, 213.
177. Mazzaferri, *The Genre of the Book of Revelation from a Source-Critical Perspective*, 310.

is conveyed by the Lamb's having seven eyes, which are identified as the seven Spirits of God that are sent out into all the earth (5:6).[178] The hearers also know that this same Spirit is closely associated with the life and ministry of Jesus' own faithful witness. Not only is this association borne out in the example of the two prophetic witnesses, who receive Jesus' witness to prophesy, who are the two olive trees and lampstands that stand before the throne (11:3-4), and the apostles who are sent out in the power of the seven Spirits before the throne (5:6), but also by the way in which the hearers are called to pneumatic discernment throughout (2:7, 11, 17, 29; 3:6, 13, 22; 11:8; 13:9-10, 18; 17:9-10). The witness of Jesus and the Spirit of prophecy are thus intricately connected to one another and in Revelation cannot be understood apart from each other. The witness of Jesus is quintessentially pneumatic, prophetic, dynamic, and active. The Spirit who goes out into all the world is the same Spirit who empowers the church's prophetic witness.[179] The Spirit who speaks prophetically to the church is the same Spirit who speaks prophetically to the world, and in 19:10 these ideas are united. For the community, participation in the faithful witness of Jesus is fueled by the Spirit of prophecy.[180] It too is active and dynamic. It is the kind of pneumatic witness that is very much at home in a prophetic community where the prophethood of all believers seems to be a basic understanding.[181] If the fellow servant who speaks in 19:9-10 is thought to be one of the souls under the altar, these words about the Spirit of prophecy themselves come from this Spirit and are prophetic words spoken to a prophetic community! This is the Spirit who guarantees and underlies the truthfulness of their witness.[182]

The King of Kings and Lord of Lords (19:11-16)

"And I saw heaven opening, and behold a white horse, and the one who sat upon him was called Faithful and True, and in righteousness he judges and makes war." For the first time since 18:1 the words "I saw" appear, indicating a new direction or the beginning of a new section in the book. With John, the hearers have witnessed a number of heavenly revelations made possible by the opening of heaven to various degrees: a door standing open in heaven (4:1); the

---

178. Bauckham, *The Climax of Prophecy*, 162-66.
179. Smalley, *Revelation*, 478.
180. Caird (*The Revelation of Saint John*, 238) notes, "It is the word spoken by God and attested by Jesus that the Spirit takes and puts into the mouth of the Christian prophet."
181. On this idea, cf. Bauckham, *The Climax of Prophecy*, 161-62, and Waddell, *The Spirit of the Book of Revelation*, 189-91, 193-94.
182. Miller, "The Nuptial Eschatology of Revelation 19–22," 308.

temple of God in heaven being opened, revealing the ark of his covenant in his temple (11:19); and the opened temple of the tabernacle of witness in heaven (15:5). But the opening of heaven in 19:11 suggests even greater access to the heavenly presence, for coming from heaven will be the long-awaited return of Jesus himself![183] The appearance of a white horse with the accompanying "Behold!" would remind readers of the emergence of a white horse (from heaven) that accompanied the breaking of the scroll's first seal by the Lamb (6:1-2). The appearance of the white horse in 19:11 could invite reflection about whether these two white horses are the same. Would the hearers suspect that the white horse in 19:11 and its rider are also connected to such overcoming? Such a question would seem to receive an immediate answer when the one who sits upon the white horse of 19:11 is identified as the one called "Faithful and True." Since Jesus is initially identified as the faithful witness in 1:5 and as the faithful and true witness in 3:14, there could be little confusion as to the identity of this figure. Not only would the term "faithful" bring to mind Jesus' own faithfulness unto death and that of his followers, for five of the eight occurrences of the term in Revelation refer to dying (1:5b; 2:10, 13; 3:14; 17:14), but the term "true" would also tie this rider to Jesus (3:7, 14) and to God, who is true (6:10), as are his ways and judgments (15:3; 16:7; 19:2, 9). As such, the very name of this rider reassures readers of the faithfulness and truthfulness of God and of Jesus.[184] Just as the rider of the first white horse went out to overcome, standing at the beginning of the judgments of God intended to bring humankind to repentance, so this rider goes out "and in righteousness judges and makes war," executing the final judgment(s). Thus, the recounting of the judgments of God in Revelation is enveloped by white horses whose riders are intimately connected to executing the eschatological judgments of God. The resemblance between these two horses and riders hardly seems fortuitous.[185] This rider's actions of judging and making war are grounded in righteousness, underscoring the tight connection between this rider and God, who is righteous both in his person (16:5) and in his ways (15:3; 16:7; 19:2). It also emphasizes the relationship between the rider and the bride of the Lamb, who has been given a garment that consists of the righteous deeds of the saints.[186] Significantly, the verbs used to describe the actions of the rider, judging and making war, are both found in the present tense, perhaps suggesting that these are ongoing

---

183. McIlraith ("For the Fine Linen Is the Righteous Deeds of the Saints," 313) notes that heaven itself is now opened.

184. T. B. Slater, *Christ and Community: A Socio-Historical Study of the Christology of Revelation* (JSNTS 178; Sheffield: Sheffield Academic Press, 1999), 213-14.

185. Prigent, *L'Apocalypse de Saint Jean*, 415-16.

186. McIlraith, "For the Fine Linen Is the Righteous Deeds of the Saints," 314.

activities of this rider.[187] The making of war has earlier been attributed to the Lamb with regard to his church (2:16), as well as his enemies (17:14).[188] These actions would rather clearly include salvific acts on behalf of his people.[189]

"His eyes as a flame of fire, and upon his head many diadems, having a name written that no one knew except him." The words "his eyes as a flame of fire" would remind hearers of the stunning vision of Jesus with which the revelation begins (1:14) and of his prophetic message to the church in Thyatira (2:18). This imagery would remind readers of his penetrating prophetic vision, from which nothing is hidden.[190] His eyes as a flame of fire are intimately connected to the seven Spirits before the throne of God (1:4), which in fact are the seven eyes of the Lamb sent out into all the earth (5:6). Clearly, this rider is the resurrected Jesus described in Rev 1–3.[191] In contrast to a "crown," normally given to one who overcomes, the "diadem" signified kingship over a particular kingdom or kingdoms; unlike the laurel wreath of the crown, the diadem was a band worn around a tiara.[192] The great red dragon was described as wearing seven diadems (12:3), representing absolute power, and the beast as wearing ten diadems, one for each king and their respective kingdoms (13:1). This rider, however, is described as wearing many diadems, suggesting a number far greater than 7 or 10,[193] indicating that his authority is unlimited and corresponds perfectly to the one called the Lord of Lords and King of Kings (17:14).[194] It is not clear whether the next phrase, "having a name written that no one knew except him," would mean that this name was written upon the diadems that the rider wears or upon the rider's head, as seems to be the case with the blasphemous names of the beast in 13:1. Although the name is both written (seen) and unknown to all but the rider himself, it is likely that the hearers would be able to make their way through such an enigmatic paradox.[195] The name itself would have a special significance as "written," as a variety of things written (and unwritten!) in Revelation are of eschatological significance (1:3, 11, 19; 2:1, 8, 12, 17-18; 3:1, 7, 12, 14; 5:1; 10:4; 13:8; 14:1, 13; 17:5, 8; 19:9). Such written things often indicate one's spiritual identity in the book. Its written

---

187. Allo, *Saint Jean: L'Apocalypse*, 279.
188. Sweet, *Revelation*, 282.
189. M. Rissi, *Die Zukunft der Welt: Eine exegetische Studie über Johannesoffenbarung 19,11 bis 22,15* (Basel: Verlag Friedrich Reinhardt, 1966), 19.
190. Kiddle, *The Revelation of St. John*, 384, and Mounce, *The Book of Revelation*, 344.
191. Slater, *Christ and Community*, 222.
192. C. J. Hemer, "Crown, Scepter, Rod," *NIDNTT*, 1:405.
193. Beasley-Murray, *Revelation*, 279.
194. Prigent, *L'Apocalypse de Saint Jean*, 417, and Aune, *Revelation 17-22*, 1054.
195. McIlraith, "For the Fine Linen Is the Righteous Deeds of the Saints," 313.

nature implies that it is observable, at least to John, and has some sort of testamentary function that both reveals and conceals. Its unknown nature, except for the rider, underscores the power of its bearer.[196] If to know one's name implies that one can gain some knowledge and mastery over the one known, to have a secret name indicates something of the depth of power that resides in its bearer.[197] This imagery would bring to mind Jesus' words in 2:17, "I will give to him a white stone and upon the stone a new name written that no one knows except the one who receives it," a promise taking on greater significance as the new name they will receive is the unknown name written upon the rider on the white horse. The fact that both he and they know this name would be yet another example of the way in which the followers of Jesus share in his identity and eschatological rewards, revealing that they too will have access to its power and depth.

"And he was wearing a garment dipped in blood, and his name is called the Word of God." The rider's garment dipped in blood might well remind hearers of the judgments of God (8:7-8; 11:6; 16:3-4) and the Lamb's ability to make war (17:14).[198] But this mention of blood would also be informed by previous references to the death of Jesus and his saints (1:5; 5:9; 6:10; 7:14; 8:8; 12:11; 14:20; 16:6; 17:6; 18:24; 19:2). This rider is the one whose shed blood has loosed us from our sins and has purchased for God those out of every tribe and tongue and people and nation. The garment dipped in blood points to the nature of his victory or overcoming that enables him to confront all the nations of the earth, for he has been slaughtered for them, shedding his blood for them,[199] a past act to which this perfect passive participle points. The judging and making war he carries out are thus salvific acts based on his atoning life and death.[200] The imagery of the robe dipped in blood might even remind readers that this very verb is used by Jesus in John's gospel in his words that identify his betrayer, "'That is the one to whom I dip the morsel and will give to him.' Therefore, dipping the morsel, he received and gave it to Judas Simon Iscariot" (John 13:26). Even in this picture of the returning Jesus, the mention of his shed blood thus carries with it a reminder of his betrayal. The hearers next discover that he also has a name with which they are familiar but have not encountered as a name before, "And his name is called the Word of God." This name would call to mind the prologue of John's gospel, where the Logos is described as existing before the

---

196. Kiddle, *The Revelation of St. John*, 385.
197. Gause, *Revelation*, 244.
198. Ladd, *Revelation*, 254.
199. Koester, *Revelation and the End of All Things*, 176.
200. Origen (*Commentary on John* 6.173) understands this detail as a symbol of Christ's incarnation and sacrifice. Cf. Kovacs and Rowland, *Revelation*, 196.

creation of the world (1:1-18). The Logos through whom everything was created is the same Logos through whom the purpose of creation is fulfilled by means of his judging and making war in righteousness.[201] The one who was not received by his own (John 1:11) will "come with the clouds, and every eye will see him, even those who pierced him, and all the tribes of the earth will mourn because of him" (Rev 1:7). The perfect passive verb "was called" suggests that this name is one of long standing. In this case, the past goes back all the way to eternity.

"And the armies in heaven follow him upon white horses, wearing white, pure fine linen." The only other mention of armies to this point in Revelation is the army of 200,000,000 riders and horses that was dressed for battle and inflicted punishment and death in order that the rest of humankind might repent (9:16-19). Since the armies of 19:14 are said to be in heaven, perhaps they comprise myriads of angels, though nothing in the text itself suggests such a conclusion other than their location. These armies follow the rider on the white horse, reminding readers of the 144,000 who follow the Lamb wherever he goes (14:4) and of the called and elect and faithful who are with the Lamb, who makes war (17:14), which suggests that these armies comprise those who are faithful witnesses to the Lamb.[202] These armies are on white horses as well, indicating that they stand as one with the one who is faithful and true and that they too are overcomers and will overcome even as he.[203] Their clothing in white, pure fine linen reveals that, instead of being dressed for battle, as the armies in 9:16-19, these armies are dressed for a joyous festival of celebration.[204] Their attire is identical to that of the bride of the Lamb,[205] prepared for the marriage supper of the Lamb. Just as the image of the saints has morphed from bride to wedding guest, so it now morphs into the heavenly armies who accompany the rider on the white horse.

"And out of his mouth comes a sharp sword in order that he might strike the nations, and he will shepherd them with a rod of iron; and he tramples the winepress of the wine of the anger of the wrath of God, the All Powerful One." Remarkably, despite the presence of the armies that accompany this rider, he alone is described as being armed for battle. The only weapon mentioned is the sharp sword that comes from his mouth.[206] In the stunning vision of the resurrected Jesus with which the book begins, a sharp two-edged sword comes from his mouth (1:16). This detail appears later as a mark of identification on

---

201. Beasley-Murray, *Revelation*, 280.
202. Sweet, *Revelation*, 283.
203. Caird, *A Commentary on the Revelation of St. John the Divine*, 244.
204. Koester, *Revelation and the End of All Things*, 177.
205. McIlraith, "For the Fine Linen Is the Righteous Deeds of the Saints," 525.
206. Metzger, *Breaking the Code*, 91.

"In the Spirit" — Carried to a Wilderness (17:1–21:8)

the lips of Jesus as he speaks to the church in Pergamum (2:12), also in his words of warning to this same church that, if they do not repent, "I will come to you quickly, and I will make war with them with the sword of my mouth" (2:16). In 19:15 the purpose of the sharp sword that comes from his mouth is made clear by the purpose clause that follows: "in order that he might strike the nations." The imagery of striking would be familiar from the authority of the two prophetic witnesses to strike the earth with every kind of plague (11:6); it suggests that the nations will finally receive their due punishment. But this making of war by the sword of his mouth is not an end in itself, for "he will shepherd them with a rod of iron." In Revelation the messianic imagery of shepherding with an iron rod (Isa 49:2) refers to the Lamb, who has the authority to perform this task (Rev 7:17; 12:5), as well as to give this authority to the one who overcomes (2:27). The idea appears to be wide enough to include kind and gentle tending of the flock, as well as the strong and dominating action that is sometimes required. Such shepherding is mentioned after the action of striking, which may be taken as a hopeful sign, suggesting that, even in the context of the return of Jesus, who judges and makes war in righteousness, hope for the conversion of the nations has not been completely lost or forgotten.[207] "And he tramples the winepress of the wine of the anger of the wrath of God, the All Powerful One." Reference to the rider's action of trampling would remind hearers that the holy city has previously been described as being trampled for forty-two months by the nations/Gentiles (11:1-2). Such associations may suggest that the nations, who had earlier trampled the holy city, are now themselves to be trampled by the rider on the white horse. The winepress of the wrath of the great God has earlier been encountered, with the effects of the trampling being the production of blood up to the bridles of the horses (14:19-20), with mention of "the cup of the wine of the anger of his wrath" that Babylon the Great was given because God remembered her (16:19).[208] A variety of ideas would here converge in a phrase that is the longest string of words in the genitive case in the whole of Revelation:[209] the winepress "of the wine of the anger of the wrath of God, the All Powerful One," where ten consecutive words in the Greek text appear in the genitive case. In this construction the winepress of God's judgment and the displeasure of God with unrepentant humanity combine with the twofold name of God. The eschatological judgment of God culminates in the activity of the rider on the white horse, who judges and makes war in righteousness.

"And he has upon his garment/robe and upon his thigh a name written:

207. Sweet, *Revelation*, 283.
208. Smalley, *Revelation*, 494.
209. Aune, *Revelation 17–22*, 1062.

King of Kings and Lord of Lords." Apparently the rider bears these familiar names upon his garment and in his person, indicating the extent to which this name is connected to and representative of his person. The thigh, normally the place where one's sword was worn, may underscore the significance of the rider's sword all the more.[210] The name King of Kings and Lord of Lords, in the reverse order, appeared earlier (17:14). For Jesus to be identified as King of Kings draws upon the rich Johannine tradition about his kingship (John 1:49; 6:15; 12:13, 15; 18:33, 37, 39; 19:3, 12, 14-15, 19, 21; Rev 1:5; 6:15; 10:11; 15:3; 16:12, 14). For the Lamb here to be called the King of Kings underscores Jesus' inherent identity as king, indicating that his power is unrivaled. The second part of this extraordinary attribution would remind hearers that, to this point in Revelation, the term Lord has been frequently applied to "the one who sits on the throne," "the Lord God, the All Powerful One" (1:8; 4:8, 11; 11:4, 15, 17; 15:3-4; 16:7), with the word used only once with reference to Jesus (11:8). The use of this title for the Lamb in 17:14 would impress readers further regarding the close relationship between God and the Lamb and the superiority of Jesus over all the kings of the earth. Together, these titles make his absolute sovereignty clear.[211] Perhaps such language, "King of Kings and Lord of Lords," unrivaled in Jewish messianic expectation,[212] would reinforce the conclusion that only the rider on the white horse is armed for battle and that he alone, the King of Kings and Lord of Lords, will fight it.[213]

Victory over the King's Enemies (19:17-21)

"And I saw one angel standing in the sun, and he cried with a great voice to all the birds that were flying in the mid-heavens, 'Come, gather into the great supper of God in order that you might eat flesh of kings and flesh of captains and flesh of the mighty and flesh of horses and those sitting upon them and flesh of all free and slave and small and great.'" For the first time since 19:11 the hearers encounter another "I saw," with attention focused upon an angel whose prominent position on or in the sun ensures a universal hearing,[214] bringing

---

210. Smalley, *Revelation*, 495.

211. P. W. Skehan ("King of Kings, Lord of Lords," *CBQ* 10.4 [1948]: 398) argues that "the combination 'King of Kings, Lord of Lords,' in Aramaic מלך מלכין מרא מרון, adds up to 777," though the fact that the word "and" must be omitted in order to arrive at this numerical value makes its significance less certain.

212. Slater, *Christ and Community*, 219.

213. Beasley-Murray, *Revelation*, 281.

214. Smalley, *Revelation*, 479.

to mind the eagle in 8:13 and the other angel in 14:6-7.[215] The angel of 19:17, like his predecessors, speaks with a great voice, so great it appears that all the birds flying in the mid-heaven can hear it. The angel's message for them to "come" is filled with urgency, like the invitation of the Samaritan woman to the villagers to "come see a man . . ." (John 4:29), as is the command to "gather together," which in the Johannine tradition can appear with both positive (John 4:36; 6:12-13; 11:52; 18:2) and negative connotations (11:47; 15:6), but never without theological significance. In Revelation this term is used to describe the gathering together of the kings of the whole earth for the war of the great day of God the All Powerful One (Rev 16:14), at a place named Har-Megiddon (16:16).[216] The invitation to the birds of the air to gather together is not unrelated to these previously described gatherings for war. Specifically, these birds are invited to "the great supper of God." While this supper might be thought to be the same supper mentioned earlier, namely, the marriage supper of the Lamb, it stands as a ghastly counterpart to the marriage supper of the Lamb![217] The birds of the air are invited in order that they might eat the flesh of all humans (and of horses too!). The list that follows is a remarkable one, reminding hearers of a similar list in 6:15, where humankind that opposes God is divided into seven divisions comprising the kings of the earth and the great men and the captains and the rich and the strong and each slave and free. While five of the same groups reappear in the list of 19:18, this latter list is distinctive in several ways. Here the word "flesh" occurs five times. The only previous occurrence of "flesh" in Revelation refers to the flesh of the great whore, which is to be eaten by the ten kings and the beast they serve (17:16). The fivefold mention of flesh might be understood as providing a basic structure revealing the five groups into which all humanity might be divided. Nine different groups are actually named in this verse, which reveals a sense of growing intensity, perhaps suggesting that this list is an even more comprehensive list than its counterpart in 6:15. The inclusion of the flesh of horses perhaps suggests its availability owing to war. Significantly, this invitation is issued even before these enemies are described as assembled, underscoring God's absolute sense of sovereignty.[218] The extraordinarily graphic nature of this verse would offer a stark warning (and promise) to hearers who might be tempted to settle for the complacency of accommodation to the beast and Babylon the Great rather than to maintain faithful witness.[219] The message is very clear: absolutely no one will be exempt from the judgment

---

215. Schüssler Fiorenza, *Revelation: Vision of a Just World*, 106.
216. Sweet, *Revelation*, 285.
217. Beasley-Murray, *Revelation*, 282.
218. Beale, *The Book of Revelation*, 965.
219. Koester, *Revelation and the End of All Things*, 178-79.

inherent for those who stand in opposition to the rider on the white horse. No one will escape; no favoritism will be shown.[220]

"And I saw the beast and the kings of the earth with their armies gathered together to make war with the one who sits upon the horse and with his army." The words "I saw" focus attention upon those who have now gathered together for battle. This gathering of powers is quite reminiscent of those who have been gathered together by the demonic spirits to the war of the great day of God (16:14), the battle of Har-Megiddon (16:16).[221] The similarities suggest that the battle of Har-Megiddon has finally arrived![222] The last mention of the beast was in the context of the destruction of the great whore (17:17),[223] where ironically the beast's actions are part of the completion of the words of God. The destruction of the great whore has been documented (17:1–18:24); could the destruction of the beast be far behind? The appearance of the rider on the white horse, the one called Faithful and True, results in united opposition to him by those who remain unrepentant, despite all the opportunities given to repent and worship God.[224]

"And the beast was seized and with him the false prophet, the one who did signs before him, with which he deceived those who received the mark of the beast and those who worshipped his image." The hearers might well be surprised that this battle is not described in any great detail. In fact, it is not really described at all, only its results. The army dressed in white, pure fine linen that accompanies the rider is not involved in the combat at all — the rider on the white horse does all the fighting![225] Beginning with the first word (after "and") in the Greek text, this understanding is conveyed, as the term "was seized" takes the form of a divine passive, the implication being that such action is the activity of God — in this case, the rider on the white horse. Though this is the only occurrence of the term "seize" in Revelation, it would be familiar to Johannine hearers, for it describes the intentions of Jesus' opponents to seize or arrest him (John 7:30, 32, 44; 8:20; 10:39; 11:57), and it even occurs to describe the catching of fish (21:3, 10).[226] The appearance of this word would set the tone for what follows in this verse. That which is seized is none other than the beast himself and, with him, the false

---

220. Slater, *Christ and Community*, 228.
221. Smalley, *Revelation*, 497.
222. Ladd, *Revelation*, 257.
223. Prigent, *L'Apocalypse de Saint Jean*, 423.
224. J. W. Mealy, *After the Thousand Years: Resurrection and Judgment in Revelation 20* (JSNTS 70; Sheffield: JSOT Press, 1992), 91.
225. Aune, *Revelation 17–22*, 1065.
226. Allo, *Saint Jean: L'Apocalypse*, 282.

prophet. No struggle ensues, no battle rages. The beast and the false prophet are completely outmatched. They are not equal to the King of Kings and Lord of Lords! Significantly, the false prophet is described in considerable detail. Called "the false prophet" for only the second time in the book (16:13), the description of his activities reveals that he is none other than the other beast who comes from the earth; though he looks like a lamb, he speaks as a dragon (13:11). Specifically, his description reminds hearers of the signs that the false prophet performed "before the beast," a phrase that conveys the idea of worship, and the role these signs played in deceiving those who ultimately received the mark of the beast and who worship his image.[227] If the testimony of Jesus is the Spirit of prophecy (19:10), in the false prophet they encounter the diametric opposite, one who deceives rather than leads to the truth, one who leads to and promotes idolatrous worship instead of one who leads to the true worship of God. Not only did the work of the false prophet result in the deception of the inhabitants of the world to receive the mark of the beast[228] and worship his image, but it also results in the death of all those who would not join in his deception and engage in the idolatrous worship he promotes (13:15-17). The words of 19:20 reveal that, not only are the origins of the beast and the false prophet intimately connected (13:1b-18), but their end is intimately connected as well.[229] The next words make this conclusion all the clearer: "The two were cast living into the lake of fire kept burning with sulfur." The order of the Greek text — "living were cast the two into the lake . . . " — emphasizes the nature of their punishment, perhaps recalling the fate of the rebels in Num 16:30,[230] with the first word "living" underscoring the fierceness of the punishment. Such language may suggest something more than annihilation,[231] especially since this term is often used of Jesus (Rev 1:18; 2:8) and God (7:2), underscoring the eternality of the latter (4:9-10; 10:6; 15:7)! The place where the beast and false prophet are cast would also be of significance for the hearers. They might well recall the words of the angel who warned that those who worship the beast and receive his mark would suffer this very punishment (14:9-10). The beast and the false prophet are thus now seen to suffer the very punishment that their deceptive idolatry led others toward. The contents of this lake — ongoing fire and noxious sulfur — would

---

227. Murphy, *Fallen Is Babylon*, 349.
228. Resseguie, *The Revelation of John*, 241, and Christopher C. Rowland, "The Book of Revelation: Introduction, Commentary, and Reflections," in *The New Interpreter's Bible*, vol. 12 (ed. L. E. Keck; Nashville: Abingdon, 1998), 700.
229. Michaels, *Revelation*, 219.
230. Sweet, *Revelation*, 286.
231. Smalley, *Revelation*, 499.

indicate that this lake is an abode of death, not life, the imagery even suggesting an ongoing death.²³² Thus, despite the claims of the beast and the false prophet to determine who lives and who dies (13:7, 15), they themselves inherit a place of ongoing death! It might well be recalled that one of the signs that the false prophet performed in order to deceive the inhabitants of the earth was to call down fire from heaven. Ironically, the false prophet now meets his demise in the lake of the burning fire of God's judgment. While the mention of sulfur might well bring to mind the punishment of Sodom and Gomorrah (Gen 19:24),²³³ the hearers might now regard the earlier encounters with the sulfur that came from the mouths of the instruments of God's redemptive judgments in 9:17-18 as gracious invitations to those who witnessed such to avoid as their destiny a lake of sulfur, of which they stood as anticipations! In one verse the hearers thus learn of the dispatch of the beast and the false prophet at the hands of the rider on the white horse.

"And the rest were killed with the sword of the one who sits upon the horse, (the sword) that comes out of his mouth, and all the birds gorged themselves out of their flesh." The rest of those involved in the battle would obviously be thought to include the kings of the earth and their armies (19:19),²³⁴ which would no doubt include all those who have assembled to make war with the rider on the white horse. As with the seizure of the beast and the false prophet and their subsequent casting into the lake of fire, so the battle between the rest and the rider on the white horse is short and to the point. Again, only the rider on the white horse is involved in the fighting,²³⁵ as the rest are all put to death by the sword that comes out of his mouth. All the birds gorge themselves on their flesh, which underscores that the victory by the one who rides the white horse is one-sided, again demonstrating that this King of Kings and Lord of Lords has no rivals. He is indeed the ruler of all the kings of the earth (1:5)! The victims of this war are eaten by the birds of the air, indicating that they have been denied a proper burial, a humiliation that might be thought an avenging judgment for the similar treatment of the two prophetic witnesses earlier in the book (11:8-10).²³⁶ The birds now gorge themselves on the flesh of the fallen, which fulfills the purpose of their angelic call to gather together for the great supper of God (19:17) with which this section begins, forming an inclusio around the action of 19:17-21. All together, these verses appear to have the following structure:

---

232. Sweet, *Revelation*, 285, and Prigent, *L'Apocalypse de Saint Jean*, 424.
233. Mounce, *The Book of Revelation*, 349.
234. Aune, *Revelation 17–22*, 1067.
235. Gause, *Revelation*, 250.
236. Kiddle, *The Revelation of St. John*, 389.

> The birds are invited to the great supper of God (19:17).
>> The armies are described (19:18).
>>> The beast gathers his armies (19:19).
>>>> The beast and the false prophet are captured and thrown into the lake of fire (19:20).
>>> The armies are killed by the sword of the rider's mouth (19:21).
>> The birds feast on the flesh of the slain (19:21).[237]

In gruesome contrast to the marriage supper of the Lamb and the fullness that resulted from Jesus' feeding the 5,000 in John's gospel (6:12), the sight of the birds gorging themselves graphically drives home the point that compromise with the beast and the great whore leads to absolute desolation, death, and humiliation! With this act, the vindication of the saints appears to be complete, for those who have opposed God and his people have now met their ultimate fate.[238]

The Thousand-Year Reign (20:1-6)

"And I saw an angel coming down out of heaven having the key of the Abyss and a great chain in his hand." The words "and I saw" stand in continuity with the previous frequent occurrences of the phrase beginning in 19:11 and continuing in strategic locations throughout this section of Revelation (19:17, 19), suggesting a continuity with what precedes and in some sense of chronological development. The sudden shift to an angel would create a great sense of expectancy, for this angel reminds them of other significant angelic figures in the book doing the work of God, while the physical description of what this angel bears is quite intriguing on its own. The origin of this angel, "coming down out of heaven," indicates that he comes with divine authority and a sense of divine commission, which the instruments in his hands reveal. The key to the Abyss would remind hearers of the star that was given the key to the shaft of the Abyss at the time the fifth angel trumpeted (9:1), whose actions released an army of locusts that torment the inhabitants of the earth. The angel introduced in 20:1 might be thought to be the same angel as the one described in 9:11, where he is given the names Destruction and Destroyer, in Hebrew and Greek respectively, names reminiscent of the Destroyer of Exod 12:23. If so, the instruments in his hands indicate his authority over the Abyss and his ability to subdue any opponent with the great chain he possesses. While in Revelation the Abyss is the place of

---

237. Michaels, *Revelation*, 218.
238. Slater, *Christ and Community*, 229.

From Babylon the Great to the New Jerusalem (19:1–21:8)

origin of the tormenting locusts (9:1-2, 11) and of the beast (11:7; 17:8), it is clear that God himself controls the Abyss and that God has authority over it. Since the rider on the white horse has apparently destroyed all his opponents but one, perhaps the hearers anticipate that the appearance of this angel is connected to the judgment of the final cosmic opponent, the dragon.

"And he seized the dragon, the ancient serpent, who is Devil and Satan, and he bound him for a thousand years." For a second time the dragon's full identity occurs, with the names Dragon, Ancient Serpent, Devil, and Satan standing together, as in 12:9, underscoring his identity in all its intensity. The name Dragon would remind readers of his role as the persecutor of the woman clothed with the sun (12:3), his attempt to kill her child (12:4), the loss of his place in heaven (12:7-9), his persecution of the rest of the woman's seed (12:13), his giving power to the beast (13:2), his receiving idolatrous worship (13:4), and his being the source of unclean, frog-like spirits (16:13). Mention of the ancient serpent would bring to mind the Genesis story (Gen 3:1-7), where the serpent tempts Adam and Eve to eat from the fruit of the tree in the midst of the garden. Nor would the correlation between the dragon's intention to devour the woman's child at birth and the enmity between the serpent and Eve's seed (Gen 3:15) be lost on the hearers (Rev 12:14). He is the ancient serpent, the liar and murderer from of old (John 8:44), the one who sins from the beginning and whose works are destroyed by the Son of God (1 John 3:8). Earlier (Rev 2:10) the hearers learned that "the devil is about to cast some of you into prison in order that he might test you. Be faithful unto death, and I will give you the crown of life."

Joined to the name Devil in 20:2 is Satan, who in John's gospel entered Judas just before this disciple goes out into the night (John 13:27). In Revelation this sinister figure is especially associated with Jewish opposition to the church, the synagogue of Satan (Rev 2:9; 3:9), the powerful presence of Satan (2:13), and the ominous nature of his "deep things" (2:24). For the great dragon to be identified as identical to Satan concretizes the nature of the dragon's activity and power. As in 12:9, the remarkable convergence of this impressive cacophony of titles and names does not overwhelm, for the hearers remember that this very opponent has earlier been "cast down." This creature, with pretensions to deity, is seized and bound not by God directly, but by an unnamed angelic creature,[239] whose authority becomes clear by his actions, as well as by the creature's full identity being surrounded by verbs that describe his impotence. This angel "seized" and "bound" the dragon, apparently using the great chain in his hand. The dragon is bound for a thousand years, an extraordinarily long period of

---

239. Gause, *Revelation*, 251.

"In the Spirit" — Carried to a Wilderness (17:1–21:8)

time. Nothing to this point in Revelation compares with the thousand years of binding, which dwarfs all other periods of binding and persecution of the saints in the book. While Satan may indeed throw some of the saints in Smyrna into prison for ten days (2:10), Satan himself is to be bound for a thousand years — a ratio of one hundred years of being bound for each day he has imprisoned the saints. While the temple will be trampled underfoot and the beast will speak blasphemy for forty-two months (11:2; 13:5, respectively), the dragon will be bound for a thousand years — a ratio of some 280 years of binding for each year of persecution. While the bodies of the two prophetic witnesses will lie in the streets of the great city for all the world to see for three and a half days (11:9), Satan will be bound a thousand years — a ratio of some 280 years of binding per day of humiliation. While the ten kings who serve the beast will rule for one hour (17:12), Satan will be bound for a thousand years — a ratio of a thousand years of being bound to but a single hour of reign. In the light of this binding of Satan, the saints' periods of persecution, imprisonment, and humiliation lose some of their potency and are seen from a different perspective. For the saints may indeed suffer unto death, but Satan will be bound a thousand years!

"And he cast him into the Abyss, and he shut/locked it and sealed over it in order that he might not deceive the nations until the thousand years have been completed; after these things it is necessary for him to be loosed for a short time." The angel's next action is reminiscent of Michael's action (12:9), for here too the dragon is cast down. Perhaps this development marks a progression in this cosmic story, with the dragon being cast down out of heaven unto the earth by Michael, and then being cast down (from the earth?) into the Abyss by this angel.[240] There is poetic justice in that the devil, who would cast some in Smyrna into jail for ten days (2:10), is now being cast into the Abyss, a place in Revelation over which God and his agents have authority. Authoritatively, the unnamed angel both shuts/locks and places a seal upon the Abyss, where the dragon has been cast, reminiscent of the divine activity encountered in Jesus' words, "I have the key of David, the one who opens and no one can close, and closes and no one can open" (3:7), and the prophetic powers of the two witnesses, who have the authority to shut the heavens (11:6). When the angel seals over the Abyss, he not only ensures that the prisoner cannot escape unobserved[241] but also matches vocabulary for sealing used previously in Revelation (7:3-5; 10:4 and 5:1-2, 5, 9; 6:1, 3, 5, 7, 9, 12; 7:2; 8:1; 9:4; cf. also John 3:33; 6:27), which takes place through divine initiative; this sealing would be no different. The purpose of this angelic activity is "in order that he might not

---

240. Resseguie, *The Revelation of John*, 244.
241. Beasley-Murray, *Revelation*, 285.

deceive the nations until the thousand years have been completed." The relationship between deception and the dragon would hardly surprise the readers, for he is "the one who deceives the whole inhabited world" (Rev 12:9). In fact, the dragon is the one who stands behind all human agents of deception (John 7:12, 47; 1 John 1:8; 2:26; 3:7; Rev 2:20), as well as the false prophet (13:14; 19:20) and Babylon (18:23).[242] However, when the dragon is locked in the Abyss, there will be a thousand-year period in which the nations will not be subjected to his deception. Surprisingly, those to be protected from the dragon's deceptive activity are the nations, who apparently were slain by the sword of Jesus' mouth in the preceding passage (19:21). Who, then, are these nations mentioned in 20:3? Are they the remnants of the nations as a whole that opposed God but for some reason were not completely destroyed?[243] Are they representative of the nations?[244] Are they nations that did not join in the war of opposition against the rider on the white horse? Are they the ghosts of the nations that had earlier been described as slain by the rider?[245] Perhaps the hearers' previous pneumatic discernment would lead them to understand that, just as numerous things in Revelation have disappeared only to reappear later, so the (re)appearance of the nations serves a similar function, suggesting that there is even more to the linear development of the nations. The major theme of the conversion of the nations thus continues in a somewhat unexpected way. For although the nations have apparently been completely destroyed by the rider on the white horse, they (re)appear here in a context suggesting that, at long last, they may be able to respond to the witness of the church without the deceptive influence of the dragon. Their (re)appearance here, as in 19:15, confirms that they have not yet been completely forgotten! A second mention of the thousand years in the span of two verses would reinforce the conclusion that this extraordinary period of time serves a specific function, namely, as a period in which the nations are not to be deceived by the dragon[246] and a period of time that must run its course for the divine will to be accomplished, as the theologically significant Johannine "has been completed" indicates (John 19:28, 30; Rev 10:7; 11:7; 15:1, 8; 17:17). The words "it is necessary" not only would convey that the conclusion of the period serves a divine necessity,[247] but also would indicate that Satan's release is no escape but is itself part of the divine plan.[248] As incredulous as this detail

---

242. Prigent, *L'Apocalypse de Saint Jean*, 436.
243. Mounce, *The Book of Revelation*, 353, and Caird, *The Revelation of Saint John*, 251.
244. Ladd, *Revelation*, 263.
245. Rissi, *Die Zukunft der Welt*, 34-36, and Mealy, *After the Thousand Years*, 181-86.
246. Gause, *Revelation*, 252.
247. Sweet, *Revelation*, 288.
248. Gause, *Revelation*, 252.

might at first appear, perhaps the hearers would suspect that, if the nations are being given an opportunity to respond to the witness of the church without the deceptive influence of Satan during this thousand-year period, then perhaps they would not be surprised that any such positive response on the nations' part must of necessity be tested by the deception of the dragon.

"And I saw thrones, and they were seated upon them, and judgment was given to them, and (I saw) the souls of those beheaded on account of the witness of Jesus and on account of the word of God, and (I saw) those who did not worship the beast or his image and did not receive his mark upon their forehead and upon their hand. And they came to life, and they reigned with Christ a thousand years." On this occasion John sees thrones, a familiar detail because of the frequent reference to the throne of God (and the one who sits upon it) throughout the book (1:4; 3:21; 4:2-6, 9-10; 5:1, 6-7, 11, 13; 6:16; 7:9-11, 15, 17; 8:3; 12:5; 14:3; 16:17; 19:4-5). It also reminds readers of the throne of Jesus, which he will share with believers (3:21), and the thrones of the twenty-four elders (4:4; 11:16). In addition, there are references to the throne of Satan (2:13) and the throne of the beast (13:2; 16:10). While the throne of God and those of the twenty-four elders are located in heaven, the throne of Satan and the beast appear to be on earth. Owing to the earthly orientation beginning in 19:11 and extending through 20:10, the hearers might suspect that the throne of Satan and the beast have given way to other thrones, perhaps in keeping with the promise of Jesus to those who overcome (3:21), an idea supported by the fact that the verb "sit" occurs only in 3:21, where the promise is made, and here in 20:4. As the vision progresses, it becomes clear that the things seen take on a kaleidoscopic form, with a variety of images described one after the other, images that appear to converge as they pile one on top of the other. In addition to the thrones, there were those seated upon them, yet another somewhat ambiguous individual detail — perhaps they are the twenty-four elders or the overcomers themselves? But they immediately encounter yet another somewhat ambiguous individual detail, "and judgment was given to them." While these words might imply that those on the thrones are involved in the dispensing of judgment,[249] it is likely that those who sit on the thrones have received judgment in the sense of vindication (cf. 17:1; 18:20; cf. also John 9:39).[250]

But yet another somewhat ambiguous individual detail is encountered: "And (I saw) the souls of those beheaded on account of the witness of Jesus and on account of the word of God." Mention of "the souls" would remind hearers of the souls under the altar who had been slaughtered owing to the word of

---

249. Mealy, *After the Thousand Years*, 109.
250. Pattemore, *The People of God in the Apocalypse*, 108, and Smalley, *Revelation*, 506.

God and the testimony that they have, who cry out to God for him to judge and vindicate their blood (6:9). It appears that it is they who have now been given judgment. Surprisingly, these are identified as the souls of those who have been beheaded — the only time in the whole of Scripture that the verb "behead" appears. If reference to the souls in 20:4 is taken in continuity with reference to the souls under the altar, then the manner of death by beheading stands in direct continuity with the previous description of their death as slaughtered. Clearly, the death of these respective souls is owing to their relationship with the witness of Jesus and the word of God (14:4; 19:10). The death of these souls being directly tied to the word of God would remind readers of John's own suffering because of the prophetic activity of God (1:9) and would reinforce the tie to Jesus, who has recently been called the Word of God. Reference to this graphic manner of execution would intensify the visceral nature of the description of their death from the more generic "slaughtered" (a fairly visceral term itself!) to the more specific "beheaded." Perhaps there is a contrast between the fate of these beheaded ones and that of the beast who had suffered a mortal wound to one of his heads. While both the beast and these souls suffered mortal head wounds, the latter being much more severe, it is they and not he who in fact have received the judgment of life! And then yet another somewhat ambiguous detail is encountered: "and those who did not worship the beast or his image and did not receive his mark upon their forehead and upon their hand." This phrase appears to be inclusive enough to include all those who offer faithful witness to Jesus by worshipping God, not the beast in any form, whether their faithful witness results in a martyr's death or not. The paradoxical ambiguity of these phrases, standing side by side, reinforces yet again the importance of being faithful unto death.[251]

With the next words the seemingly disparate individual, somewhat ambiguous pieces of this verse converge: "And they came to life, and they reigned with Christ a thousand years." With these words the hearers discover that the souls of the beheaded ones, those who did not worship the beast in any form, to whom the verdict of judgment was given, who are seated upon the thrones, themselves experience resurrection, just as had their Lord (1:18; 2:8) and the two prophetic witnesses (11:11),[252] and they reign with Christ in accord with his promises to those who overcome (2:26; 3:21; 5:10) for a thousand years.[253] While ambiguities abound, it would appear certain that the hearers would understand this coming to life as similar to, and standing in continuity with,

---

251. Mealy, *After the Thousand Years*, 109-19.
252. Sweet, *Revelation*, 289.
253. Ladd, *Revelation*, 264.

the coming to life of Jesus, as the same word found here appeared earlier in Revelation to describe the resurrection of Jesus (2:8). Such an understanding would be consistent with the idea found in 1 John 3:2 that "we shall be like him, because we will see him as he is," and with the descriptions of the resurrected Jesus in John 20 and 21. Thus, while modern interpreters may be fascinated with the idea that this coming to life is a spiritual, not a physical, resurrection,[254] such an idea would likely be quite foreign to Johannine hearers. Rather, this is the moment at which the souls of those who had been beheaded are resurrected in bodily form, as had been their Lord. The judgment rendered to them is thus integrally connected to their being brought to life. In this respect they experience more fully the eternal life with which Johannine hearers are quite familiar, and they share more immediately in their identification with God, who is often described in Revelation as the one who lives forever and ever (4:9-10; 7:2; 10:6; 15:7). They also reign with Christ for a thousand years, the sheer temporal magnitude of which would dwarf all other reigns mentioned in Revelation to this point, whether it be the forty-two-month reign of the beast (13:5) or the one-hour reign of the ten kings (17:12). The hearers thus learn that, during the entire time the dragon is bound in the Abyss, those who have been faithful witnesses experience a different reality altogether — they reign with Christ! Despite the numerous OT intertexts encountered throughout the book, at this point there is a stark and striking absence of OT references. The description of this thousand-year reign is extraordinarily restrained and sparse in its description. The focus of attention is placed upon the relational nature of the thousand-year period.[255] Specifically, those brought to life will be with Christ for the thousand years. Thus, not only will the deceptive influence of Satan be absent during this period, the overcomers will also be with Christ for this entire period; they will be with the same resurrected Lord whom they experience even now via the Spirit's prophetic witness. The resurrected Lord, whom they know in their worship and faithful witness, whom they follow wherever he goes, whose return is imminent, is the same Lord with whom they will reign. All that Christ is as Redeemer, they will now be as redeemed.[256] These resurrected overcomers will be with their resurrected Lord for longer than any of the hearers could imagine or fathom — for a thousand years! Owing to the relational nature of this reign, issues about over whom or over what they reign with Christ

---

254. P. Gaechter, "The Original Sequence of Apocalypse 20–22," *Theological Studies* 10 (1949): 491.

255. Koester, *Revelation and the End of All Things*, 184-85.

256. Gause, *Revelation*, 254.

would not appear to be of primary concern. Since Satan is unable to deceive the nations during this period, perhaps their reign would be connected to the nations in some way. If one of the purposes of this extraordinarily long period is to give the nations yet another chance to respond in faith, perhaps the reign of these resurrected ones involves a continuation of bearing their prophetic, faithful witness, not unlike that borne by the two witnesses whom the Spirit of life from God raised up (11:11-14)! The idyllic conditions of this thousand-year reign might also bring to mind the conditions at the beginning in the Garden of Eden, where the human being was given charge over the creation and creatures within it (Gen 1:26-28).[257] On this view, the thousand-year reign with Christ would be designed in part to be a visible sign of the redemption of creation itself, with resurrected human agents reigning with Christ in a way that fulfills that initial command and commission.

"The rest of the dead did not come to life until the thousand years were complete. This is the first resurrection." The rest of the dead would likely be thought to consist of the opponents of the rider on the white horse (19:21),[258] as well as all those who do not believe in him.[259] Again, a physical resurrection of the dead appears to be in view.[260] The idea of two separate resurrections appears to be consistent with the teaching of Jesus, who says, "Do not be astonished at this, because an hour comes in which all those who are in their graves will hear his voice and will come out, the ones who have done good into resurrection of life, but the ones who practice evil into resurrection of judgment" (John 5:28-29). But unlike the overcomers, the rest of the dead do not come to life until after the thousand years; they are in their graves for this entire period. Mention of the thousand-year period, the fourth such mention in a span of five verses, again underscores the magnitude of the loss for the rest of the dead who lie in their graves while the overcomers reign with Christ. "This is the first resurrection" directs attention back to the description of those who came to life and reign with Christ for the thousand years. In this context, the first resurrection is so named owing to its chronological and theological precedence over the resurrection of the rest of the dead. Though a "second resurrection" is nowhere named as such in the Johannine literature,[261] since the first resurrection identifies the resurrection of the overcomers who reign with Christ a thousand years and precedes the resurrection of the rest of the dead, hearers would in all

---

257. Mealy, *After the Thousand Years*, 116.
258. Mealy, *After the Thousand Years*, 115.
259. Ladd, *Revelation*, 265.
260. Aune, *Revelation 17-22*, 1090.
261. Wall, *Revelation*, 239, and Prigent, *L'Apocalypse de Saint Jean*, 429.

likelihood understand that two resurrections, separated by a thousand years, are indeed here described.[262]

"Blessed and holy is the one who has a part in the first resurrection; over these the second death has no authority, but they will be priests of God and of Christ, and they will reign with him a thousand years." For a fifth time a beatitude is encountered, and for the first time it contains a compound predicate: to the characteristic "blessed" is added "and holy."[263] This unique addition of "holy" reinforces the idea of those faithful witnesses who have stayed awake and kept their garments with them (16:15); they have been deemed worthy of invitation to the marriage supper of the Lamb, having prepared themselves through righteous acts (19:8-9). The word here translated "holy" is the same Greek word as is elsewhere translated "saint," reinforcing the conclusion that all the saints will have part in the first resurrection. The theologically significant word "share" or "part" — in John 13:8 closely identified with eternal life, solidarity with Jesus' destiny, mission, martyrdom, and resurrection[264] — here emphasizes the depth of identification and solidarity between Jesus and the faithful witnesses who participate in the first resurrection. "Over these the second death has no authority" reminds hearers of the promise of the resurrected Jesus to the church in Smyrna (Rev 2:11), making even clearer that the one who participates in the first resurrection has no fear of the second death. Those who participate in the first resurrection will be in the very presence of God and Christ, serving as priests[265] and reigning with Christ for the thousand years. The word "priests" reminds us that it is through Jesus, the one with whom they will reign for a thousand years, that they have been made into a kingdom — priests to God (1:6; 5:10). By his death they gain admission to the divine presence[266] and minister to God and Christ. Such language may well suggest that the overcomers still have an active role to play in the conversion of the nations and that their reigning with Christ may well involve such a priestly dimension as they continue to act as faithful witnesses to the witness of Jesus and the Word of God — for a thousand years![267] The fifth mention of the thousand years underscores that the hearers shall serve as priests to God and Christ and reign with Christ for a thousand years.[268] In this reign they will enjoy their time with Christ, seek the conversion of the nations, and fulfill the command given to Adam and Eve in the Garden.

262. Aune, *Revelation 17-22*, 1091.
263. Murphy, *Fallen Is Babylon*, 399.
264. Thomas, *Footwashing in John 13 and the Johannine Community*, 92-95.
265. Smalley, *Revelation*, 510.
266. Gause, *Revelation*, 254.
267. Caird, *The Revelation of Saint John*, 255-56.
268. Metzger, *Breaking the Code*, 93.

From Babylon the Great to the New Jerusalem (19:1–21:8)

Satan's Final Rebellion and Defeat (20:7-10)

"And when the thousand years were completed, Satan will be loosed out of his prison." The theologically significant "were completed" not only would indicate that the thousand years (and its purposes) have now come to completion,[269] but, by using the passive form, would also remind hearers that this period was brought to its completion by God himself. Satan's confinement in the Abyss is now revealed to have been an imprisonment, for after the thousand years he will be loosed from "his prison." The passive "will be loosed" indicates that, just as God is active in bringing the thousand years to completion, so the loosing of Satan is no escape but is in accord with the divine purpose and is indeed God's own activity.

"And he will go out to deceive the nations, those in the four corners of the earth, Gog and Magog, to gather them together into war, the number of them being as the sand of the sea." Satan, who in 20:3 was bound for a thousand years so he could no longer deceive the nations, is the same Satan who emerges from his prison to deceive the nations in 20:8. The first word the hearers encounter in this verse after "and," translated "he will go out," would be known to discerning Johannine hearers as a term closely associated with deception and betrayal, as it describes Judas's departure to betray Jesus in John 13:30 and describes the missionary activity of the many deceivers who have gone out into the world in 2 John 7.[270] Despite his long imprisonment in the Abyss, Satan emerges as ready as ever to deceive the nations and is prepared to do so in as comprehensive a fashion as possible.[271] The extent of his intended deception is conveyed by the wording "the nations, those in the four corners of the earth," the proverbial furthest points of the earth, and these nations called by the names Gog and Magog. Gog was the chief prince of Meshech and Tubal (Ezek 38:2), and Magog was known as the son of Japheth (Gen 10:2) and became identified as the territory located in the uttermost parts of the north (Ezek 38:6).[272] As with other names in the book, these two names likely have a deeper meaning, perhaps thought of as the eschatological enemies of the north[273] that attack the people of God after a period of peace.[274] The purpose of Satan's going out to deceive is "to gather them together into war" (Rev 16:14).[275] Such similarity would remind hearers,

---

269. Gause, *Revelation*, 255.
270. Thomas, *1 John, 2 John, 3 John*, 45, and Smalley, *Revelation*, 511.
271. Koester, *Revelation and the End of All Things*, 187.
272. Mounce, *The Book of Revelation*, 362.
273. Allo, *Saint Jean: L'Apocalypse*, 288.
274. Caird, *The Revelation of Saint John*, 257.
275. Aune, *Revelation 17–22*, 1095.

not only of similar hostile intentions of the nations, but also of their ultimate demise on that occasion as well. The success of Satan's deception is revealed by the fact that the nations gathered together for war are numbered as the sand of the sea, a phrase that indicates the overwhelming success of his deceptive work and also draws upon the ominous associations this phrase has from its earlier appearance, where the dragon stands upon the sand of the sea looking for the emergence of the beast (12:18).[276] Such language stands in stark contrast to the promise given to Abraham with regard to the number of his descendants,[277] indicating something of the diametric opposition of the purposes of God and those of Satan. The words of this verse suggest that, despite the thousand-year period, in which Satan is kept from deceiving the nations and in which Christ himself reigns with those faithful to him, the nations are as susceptible as ever to the deception of Satan. Despite the millennium-long ideal circumstances, the nations refuse to repent and worship God and the Lamb.[278]

"And they went up upon the breadth of the earth and circled the camp of the saints and the beloved city." The actions of these deceived nations is no less significant than their numbers — they traverse the face of the earth and encircle their intended targets, an ancient strategy, where cities are circled to cut their inhabitants off from the outside world. Mention of the camp of the saints reveals the intended target of the nations' planned attack — the saints, those holy ones who have a part in the first resurrection and reign with Christ for a thousand years — and it reminds us yet again of the tight connection that exists between the Johannine believers and the heritage of Israel (cf. esp. 7:1-8). Specifically, the phrase "the camp of the saints" brings to mind Israel's dependence upon God as he led them through the wilderness via a cloud by day and a pillar of fire by night (Exod 13:21-22),[279] imagery that would likely remind Johannine hearers of the pneumatic activity that is an essential part of their life together. Mention of "the beloved city" would have special significance, calling up memories of Yahweh's special love for Zion, the city of Jerusalem (Pss 87:2; 132:13; cf. also Jer 11:15; 12:7), the place where Yahweh chose to dwell,[280] and as such could well be taken as an anticipation of the New Jerusalem, which the hearers know is to come down out of heaven (3:12). To learn that, even at the end of the thousand years, the people of God face attacks inspired by Satan would also remind the hearers that, from start to finish, they are totally dependent upon God for their protection, security, and defense. Despite expectations of the description of

---

276. Sweet, *Revelation*, 292.
277. Aune, *Revelation 17-22*, 1096.
278. Cf. the esp. perceptive comments of Mealy, *After the Thousand Years*, 186 and 189.
279. Sweet, *Revelation*, 292.
280. Sweet, *Revelation*, 292.

a great final battle, as was the case with previous war scenes, no battle takes place.[281] Rather, the fire of judgment comes from heaven and consumes the nations gathered together for war, reminiscent of the way fire comes from the mouths of the two witnesses and consumes their enemies (11:5). The fact that the fire comes from heaven makes the origin of this victory unmistakable,[282] and reminds hearers of the fire of judgment that falls upon Gog (Ezek 38:22) and Magog (Ezek 39:6).[283] Yet again, the people of God stand vindicated!

"And Satan, the one who deceives them, was cast into the lake of fire and sulfur, where both the beast and the false prophet (were cast), and they will be tormented day and night for ever and ever." At long last, the archenemy of God and his people receives his final judgment. Satan is identified as "the one who deceives them," reminding the hearers of 12:9, where he is called "the one who deceives the whole inhabited world." This description would tie his fate directly to his activity of deceiving the nations. On a third occasion Satan is described as having been "cast down" (12:9 and 20:3). Whereas Satan had earlier been cast down to earth (12:9) and into the Abyss (20:3), he is now described as having been cast into the lake of fire and sulfur, revealing that Satan goes to the same place to which his accomplices, the beast and the false prophet, have preceded him (19:20).[284] Their appearance together here makes very clear that all opponents and opposition to God, his Lamb, his Spirit, and his people have no future but judgment and eternal punishment, regardless of the strength they may currently exhibit in their persecution of the faithful witnesses of the prophetic community. They are doomed to judgment! Just as they had acted together to deceive the nations and the inhabitants of the whole earth, so they are judged together and are to be tormented together. The appearance of the passive verb "they will be tormented" indicates that the torment that awaits comes from the hand of God. The third person plural form of the verb makes clear that the torment that awaits includes all three opponents: Satan, the beast, and the false prophet. This verb also confirms that the time that awaits the triumvirate in the lake of fire and sulfur is not only a time of confinement, but a time of punishment in the form of torment as well. The time of their torment is unfathomably constant and long, being conveyed by the phrase "day and night,"[285] indicating something of the unrelenting nature of the torment that awaits. Perhaps such constancy of torment is an appropriate judgment for "the one who accuses the

---

281. Ladd, *Revelation*, 270.
282. Gause, *Revelation*, 257.
283. Mounce, *The Book of Revelation*, 363.
284. Beasley-Murray, *Revelation*, 298.
285. Smalley (*Revelation*, 515) labels these words a hendiadys, generating the meaning "without interruption."

brothers day and night before our God" (12:10). Conversely, there is a contrast between the torment of this triumvirate of evil and the four living creatures, who do not cease praising God day and night (4:8), and those who are coming out of the great tribulation, who are before the throne of God serving him day and night (7:15). The phrase "day and night" may reveal some continuity between the smoke of destruction of God's enemies that goes up forever and ever (14:11; 19:3) and the torment of this triumvirate. At the same time, the hearers can take comfort, knowing that the reign of God lasts forever and ever (11:15) and that God and/or the Lamb receive worship forever and ever from every creature in the universe (5:13), from the angels, the four living creatures, and the twenty-four elders (7:11-12). It would be quite clear that both the constancy of the torment and its duration point to an eternal death for Satan, the beast, and the false prophet rather than merely to their annihilation.[286]

The Final Judgment (20:11-15)

"And I saw a great white throne and the one sitting upon it, from whose face the earth and heaven fled, and a place was not found for them." The description of this throne as great would serve to emphasize its magnitude and judicial function. It is the throne of judgment. Its description as white would bring to mind that in Revelation white is the color of Jesus (1:14; 14:14; 19:11), the angels (4:4), the stone (2:17), as well as the dress of faithful believers (3:4-5, 18; 6:11; 7:9, 13-14; 19:14), conveying in 20:11 the qualities of holiness and vindication.[287] While the Lamb might be the one who sits upon the throne of judgment,[288] the vast preponderance throughout the book of references to God as the one who sits upon the throne makes it likely that the reference in 20:11 alludes to God. At the appearance of the face of the one who sits upon the throne, both the earth and heaven fled. Here the verb "fled" might convey a somewhat more active meaning than merely an involuntary response.[289] If so, it would appear that the fleeing of the earth and heaven has to do with the character of the one who sits upon the throne and the character of the earth and heaven. Perhaps they flee owing to the moral grandeur of God or the glory of his presence.[290] Or because of the judicial significance of this throne, perhaps judgment itself

---

286. Murphy, *Fallen Is Babylon*, 403.
287. Smalley, *Revelation*, 516.
288. Gause, *Revelation*, 258, and Aune, *Revelation 17–22*, 1101.
289. Caird, *The Revelation of Saint John*, 258.
290. Ladd, *Revelation*, 271, and Metzger, *Breaking the Code*, 95.

begins with the known elements of the world — the earth and heaven.[291] Or perhaps this is the physical dissolution of the universe in the direct presence of God and his throne.[292] What would be clear is that the earth and heaven have no more use and as such find no place for existence. Their time has expired; their usefulness has run its course.[293] The boundaries of the old order no longer exist.[294] All that remains is the great white throne and the one who sits upon it, suspended in space by God's own power. Nothing any longer separates God from humanity.[295]

"And I saw the dead, the great and the small, standing before the throne, and books were opened; and another book was opened, which is the book of life; and the dead were judged out of the things written in the books according to their works." The qualifications of this group as both "the great and the small" suggest that all the dead are present; the phrase "small and great" has appeared earlier in the book as a designation of universality (11:18; 13:16; 19:5, 18). In 20:12 the order is reversed from its normal appearance, which may suggest that absolutely no one, beginning with the great people of the earth and going to the least, is absent or exempted.[296] No one is too important or unimportant;[297] all claims to privilege are given up.[298] All the dead are seen, joining the great white throne and the one who sits upon it as the only things visible, since earth and heaven have fled. The scene would perhaps remind readers of those earlier described as standing before the throne (5:6; 7:15)[299] and those who had cried out, asking for the mountains and rocks to fall upon them (6:16), the latter text suggesting that standing before the throne is inevitable. Neither would it surprise readers to learn that "books were opened" on this occasion, as books of judgment normally accompany judgment scenes (cf. esp. Dan 7:10). These as yet unidentified books are joined by another book that has been opened, which *is* identified. It is the book of life, a book encountered already on several occasions. The hearers know a number of things about this book (3:5; 13:8; 17:8). Thus, when they learn that one of the books opened at the great white throne event is the book of life, they would understand that redemption is not absent and that, for those who overcome, whose names have been written in the book

---

291. Michaels, *Revelation*, 229.
292. Mounce, *The Book of Revelation*, 365-66.
293. Murphy, *Fallen Is Babylon*, 404.
294. Sweet, *Revelation*, 294.
295. Resseguie, *The Revelation of John*, 248.
296. Metzger, *Breaking the Code*, 95.
297. Mounce, *The Book of Revelation*, 365.
298. Kiddle, *The Revelation of St. John*, 404.
299. Smalley, *Revelation*, 517.

of life owing to their faithful witness, Jesus himself stands ready to confess their names before the Father and his angels. At this point the identity of the other opened books is confirmed, for "the dead were judged out of the things written in the books according to their works." These books would provide the evidence for judgment written by the lives of every human being,[300] ensuring that the judgment that comes from the great white throne is not capricious but accurate[301] and indisputable![302] Nor would the hearers be unaware of the importance of works and their eternal destiny, for they here find that such works form the basis of their judgment, which is consistent with the continuous emphasis upon works found throughout Revelation (2:2, 5-6, 19, 22-23; 3:1-2, 8, 15; 9:20; 14:13; 15:3; 16:11; 18:6).

The words of v. 12 anticipate those that follow in v. 13:[303] "and the sea gave up the dead in it, and Death and Hades gave up the dead in them, and each one was judged according to their works." Death at sea held a special horror in the ancient world, in part because a proper burial was impossible for its victims.[304] But here it is revealed that even those who seem to have disappeared into nothingness are remembered by God[305] and that the manner and place of death make no difference.[306] Perhaps even more astounding is Death and Hades giving up the dead in them. The resurrected Jesus has the keys of Death and Hades (1:18), indicating his absolute power and authority over them. Death and Hades are companions when the fourth seal is opened, as they are given authority over a fourth of the earth to kill with the sword and with famine and with death and authority over the beasts of the earth (6:8). For a second time in the span of two verses the hearers are told that each one was judged according to their works, and here the specificity of each one's works is emphasized even more than before.

"And Death and Hades were cast into the lake of fire. This is the second death, the lake of fire." Death and Hades suffer a similar fate to the dragon, the beast, and the false prophet, for they are cast into the lake of fire. Hades is never mentioned except as a companion of Death, and Death is always mentioned first, perhaps suggesting that in some way Death rules over or has authority over Hades.[307] To discover that these final foes now meet their eternal fate re-

---

300. Mounce, *The Book of Revelation*, 365.
301. Smalley, *Revelation*, 517.
302. Mealy, *After the Thousand Years*, 171.
303. Allo, *Saint Jean: L'Apocalypse*, 304.
304. Caird, *The Revelation of Saint John*, 260.
305. Prigent, *L'Apocalypse de Saint Jean*, 447, and Smalley, *Revelation*, 519.
306. Metzger, *Breaking the Code*, 96.
307. Aune, *Revelation 17-22*, 1103.

veals that the horrors of both are now banished forever.[308] The death of Death would be extremely encouraging to those who face death daily owing to their faithful witness to Jesus.[309] The hearers have long known that the one who overcomes cannot be harmed by the second death at all (2:11); the second death has no authority over them (20:6). Now they learn that their earlier suspicions are confirmed, that the lake of fire is the second death. They learn that, while those who experience physical death will be brought to life again, those who experience the second death experience eternal death, from which no escape is possible! It is unmitigated death, complete separation from God.[310]

"And if anyone was not found written in the book of life, that one was cast into the lake of fire." Stern words appear yet again about the judgment. On this occasion the emphasis is upon whether or not one is found written in the book of life. Specifically, if anyone is not found written in this book, he or she also is cast into the lake of fire. The implications could not be clearer. If one identifies with Satan and the beast and the false prophet in this life, that one will suffer eternal death with them. At the same time, despite the ominous scene of the great white throne and the judgment that accompanies it, the hearers would be assured that they have no need to fear, not even a list of evil works in one or more of the opened books, for they are written in the book of life and have overcome, having offered faithful witness to Jesus.[311]

The Descent of the New Jerusalem (21:1-8)

The narrative continues in an amazing fashion. "And I saw a new heaven and a new earth, for the first heaven and the first earth had departed, and there is no more sea." This discovery would be breathtaking. The word that describes the newness of this heaven and earth, καινός (*kainos*, "new"), designates something new in kind, not just a new thing of the same kind;[312] it is a newness hitherto unknown.[313] To this point heaven has been the dwelling place of God, the one who sits on the throne, the place from which his righteous and holy judgments come, the place where those who have been martyred reside, the place of praise and thanksgiving, and the place of divine self-revelation. If this extraordinary place stretches the bounds of the imagination, what could possibly await in the

---

308. Kiddle, *The Revelation of St. John*, 408.
309. Smalley, *Revelation*, 519.
310. Metzger, *Breaking the Code*, 97.
311. Gause, *Revelation*, 262.
312. Sweet, *Revelation*, 297.
313. Smalley, *Revelation*, 524.

new heaven? At the same time, thoughts of a new earth would in many ways be just as perplexing and engaging. For while the thousand-year reign with Christ, which awaits those who overcome (20:1-10), might provide a sampling of what ideal life in the future might look like, a new earth would indicate that this existence is even more radically different than anything that could be imagined! Significantly, the hearers are reminded of its necessity by means of reference to the departure of the first heaven and first earth (20:11). This explicit reference would perhaps call to mind that their fleeing was a part of the last judgment, that the first heaven and first earth had served their purpose. While the language of "first heaven" and "first earth" may suggest some continuity between them and the new heaven and new earth, the disappearance of the former and the radical newness of the latter would lead the hearers to give pride of place to the latter. This new creation — the new heaven and new earth — stands in remarkable discontinuity in at least one specific respect, for now "there is no more sea."[314] In the first heaven (4:6) and the first earth (12:12; 13:1), there is reference to the sea. Just as the first heaven and first earth had served their purpose, so the sea had served its purpose, and now as part of the last judgment, its place too has been exhausted. The numerous associations of the sea with evil in Revelation would likely suggest that evil itself has no place in the new creation.[315] Just as the hearers had learned in the first reference to the sea (4:6) that the glory of God is reflected even in those objects that have negative associations, so now in the last reference to the sea in Revelation they learn that the purpose of this mixed image has passed.[316] There is no more sea, for there is no more evil.[317] These words may even suggest that there is no longer any need for the glory of God to be reflected or mediated, perhaps leading them to suspect that, in this new heaven and new earth, the glory of God is experienced more immediately and directly.[318]

"And the holy city New Jerusalem I saw coming down out of heaven from God, prepared as a bride adorned for her husband." For the only time in Revelation, here the conjunction and verb ("and I saw") are separated by the direct object,[319] adding further emphasis to and focus upon the object, "the holy city New Jerusalem." Earlier in the book the people of God have metaphorically been called the holy city (11:2), suggesting some degree of continuity between

---

314. Beasley-Murray, *Revelation*, 307.
315. Schüssler Fiorenza, *Revelation: Vision of a Just World*, 110.
316. Fee, *Revelation*, 291.
317. P. Lee, *The New Jerusalem in the Book of Revelation: A Study of Revelation 21–22 in the Light of Its Background in Jewish Tradition* (WUNT 129; Berlin: Mohr Siebeck, 2001), 269.
318. Kiddle, *The Revelation of St. John*, 411.
319. Aune, *Revelation 17–22*, 1120.

this holy city and the people of God here in 21:2. The name New Jerusalem has appeared earlier in the form of a promise from the resurrected Jesus to the one who overcomes — "I will write upon him the name of my God and the name of the city of my God, the New Jerusalem" (3:12).[320] In both texts New Jerusalem is identified as "coming down out of heaven from God," a twofold attribution making clear the city's divine origin. The last phrase in 21:2 makes explicit the connection between the city and the people of God, for she is "prepared as a bride adorned for her husband." This description would bring to mind the radical difference between this city, described as a bride, and fallen Babylon, in which the voice (or sound) of the bride will be heard no longer (18:23), contrasting yet again the impotence of the great whore with the promise of the bride. The language of 21:2 would call to mind the marriage supper of the Lamb and his bride — in this instance, γυνή (*gynē*, "woman") — who has prepared herself for her marriage by means of her righteous acts (19:7-8). It would thus be difficult not to take the holy city New Jerusalem as the bride of the Lamb,[321] perhaps indicating that the marriage supper of the Lamb has indeed come at last.[322] Her preparations are coterminous with her having adorned herself for her husband, an activity that is now past, the effects of which are still felt, as the perfect "adorned" indicates, standing in stark contrast to the adornment of the great whore in chapters 17–18. The kind of discontinuity that exists between the first heaven/first earth and the new heaven/new earth would thus likely also exist between the Jerusalem of old and the holy city New Jerusalem. For this is not another Jerusalem of the same kind as the first; rather, it is the New Jerusalem. Since some of the eschatological promises found earlier in Revelation appear to be fulfilled in the new heaven and new earth, the hearers might well wonder, Is it not possible that the eschatological promises with regard to eschatological Jerusalem, scattered throughout the biblical tradition, would be fulfilled in New Jerusalem?[323]

"And I heard a great voice out of the throne saying, 'Behold the dwelling of God is with men, and he will dwell with them, and they will be his peoples, and God himself will be with them.'" This is the first time we encounter a "great voice" from the throne. The combination of the adjective "great" and the voice's origin would heighten the dramatic quality of the narration, suggesting the significance and great eschatological consequence of the following words.[324] These divine words from the throne once again take on third person form, be-

---

320. Mounce, *The Book of Revelation*, 370.
321. Zimmermann, "Nuptial Imagery in the Revelation of John," 169.
322. Ladd, *Revelation*, 277.
323. Smalley, *Revelation*, 535.
324. Smalley, *Revelation*, 537.

ing words spoken about God. The first words, "Behold the dwelling of God is with men," indicate that the nature of God's relationship with his people in the new creation will be direct and unhindered.[325] A number of OT texts appear to converge at this point. The language of dwelling would point to the presence of God in the tabernacle among Israel during its wilderness wanderings (Lev 26:11-12), echoing the continuity between God's past salvific activity and what lies ahead.[326] Discerning Johannine hearers would be aware that, in the life and ministry of Jesus, the presence of God among them was made even more immediate (John 1:14). The dwelling of God, previously encountered in heaven (Rev 15:5), is now among human beings, confirming that divine access is now more immediate and direct. The dwelling of God is said to be "with men," which would remind readers yet again of the wideness in God's mercy, for although significant numbers of men have perished earlier in Revelation (8:11; 9:15, 18), the dwelling of God "with men" would give additional hope for the conversion of the nations.[327] The next line, "and he will dwell with them," also echoes numerous OT texts and reinforces the words of the previous line, with the verb "will dwell" corresponding to the noun "dwelling." Such language points to the fulfillment of the eschatological promises for those who come out of the great tribulation, where the one who sits upon the throne "will dwell upon them" (7:15). The next line, "and they will be his peoples," drives the point home even further, again underscoring the fulfillment of the eschatological promises of many OT texts, while affirming the large scope of the soteriological reality.[328] Here the term "peoples" is plural, rather than singular, as in Lev 26:12 and Jer 24:7, perhaps suggesting that the eschatological people of God, Israel, has expanded to include *all* peoples,[329] in accord with Rev 5:9; 7:9.[330] The emphasis upon the intimate relationship between God and his peoples continues in the final line of v. 3, where it is emphatically stated that "God himself will be with them," the emphatic construction "God himself" occurring here alone in the whole of Revelation.[331] It is he of "the dwelling of God" who will dwell with them, he whose peoples they are; it is this very God himself who will be with them!

---

325. Beasley-Murray, *Revelation*, 311.

326. Gause, *Revelation*, 265.

327. D. Mathewson, "The Destiny of the Nations in Revelation 21:1–22:5: A Reconsideration," *TynB* 53.1 (2002): 128.

328. Bauckham, *The Climax of Prophecy*, 311-13.

329. Pattemore, *The People of God in the Apocalypse*, 201.

330. R. H. Gundry, "The New Jerusalem: People as Place, not Place for People," *NovT* 29 (1987): 257.

331. Smalley, *Revelation*, 538.

"And he will wipe away every tear from their eyes, and death is no more, neither is there any longer mourning or crying or pain, because the first things have departed." As the new creation was described in part by what is missing ("there is no more sea"), so these words describe the intimate relationship with God in the new creation by what is missing. In fact, the things that are missing in the new creation stand in chiastic parallel to one another, further defining the lack of a sea as an indication that the sea stands in continuity with the trouble, evil, and suffering of the first heaven and first earth.[332] The specific elements encountered in 21:4 are very similar to those earlier found in 7:16-17. The shedding of tears will be wiped away by the one who will not wipe away (erase) the name of the one who overcomes from the book of life (3:5). Death is no more, which not only reminds hearers that death itself experiences eternal death in the lake of fire and sulfur, but also again underscores the contrast between New Jerusalem, where death is found no longer, and fallen Babylon, where all signs of joy and life are found no longer (18:21-23).[333] Closely connected with the absence of death is the absence of its close associates: mourning, crying, and pain. For as surely as death continually experiences eternal death, so mourning, crying, and pain are found no more — for they are characteristics of the first things, the first heaven and first earth,[334] which have now departed. These experiences find no place in the new creation, where the presence of God is experienced so intimately.

"And the one who sits upon the throne said, 'Behold I make all things new.' And he says, 'Write, because these words are faithful and true.'" Not since 1:8 and 16:17 have the hearers encountered words explicitly identified as coming from God.[335] This startling announcement indicates the importance of these divinely spoken words, which stand in close continuity with those in 21:1 (regarding a new heaven and new earth), as the one who sits on the throne says, "Behold I make all things new." The emphasis of this sentence in the Greek text is on the newness of all things, as "new" stands first in the sentence immediately after "behold." This same word, occurring earlier to describe the radical newness of the new heaven and the new earth, makes it clear that the "all things" made new are not new things of a previous kind but new things that are hitherto unknown. They also imply that it is the one who sits on the throne who is creating the new heaven and new earth, New Jerusalem, and all

---

332. D. Mathewson, "New Exodus as a Background for 'The Sea Was No More' in Revelation 21:1c," *Trinity Journal* 24 (2003): 245.
333. Sweet, *Revelation*, 299.
334. Aune, *Revelation 17-22*, 1124.
335. Caird, *The Revelation of Saint John*, 265.

things associated with it.³³⁶ The present tense verb "make" suggests that God is even now making all things new. His words continue with the command for John to write. Although John has received such instructions from the resurrected Jesus (1:11, 19; 2:1, 8, 12, 18; 3:1, 7) and a voice from heaven (14:13) earlier in Revelation, this is the first and only time that this instruction comes from the one who sits on the throne. Here, the words "these words are faithful and true" are a divine authorization of the trustworthiness of the words spoken by the one who sits on the throne and, by extension, all the words found in this book. They are guaranteed by the authority of the one who speaks them!³³⁷ As before, the combination of the words "faithful and true" would remind hearers of the same words used earlier to describe the resurrected Jesus (3:14) and the rider on the white horse (19:11);³³⁸ they would draw attention to the close and intimate relationship between God and the Lamb.

"And he said to me, 'They are completed. I Am the Alpha and the Omega, the Beginning and the End. I will give to the one who is thirsty a gift out of the fountain of living water.'" These words remind readers of those spoken in 16:17, where a great voice coming out of the temple from the throne says, "It is done."³³⁹ Previously, this Greek term had reference to the completion of the seven bowls of the judgments of God, which led to the destruction of Babylon the Great (16:18-21). This utterance stands just before the conclusion of the second major section of Revelation (4:1–16:21), which gives way to the third section of the book, which examines more closely the destruction of Babylon the Great and the emergence of the New Jerusalem (17:1–21:8). The appearance of "they are done" in 21:6 stands in parallel with its counterpart in 16:17, only here the term is a third person plural form and may refer to the completion of God's words that are faithful and true, God's words that stand behind the new creation. This term likely signals the end of the book's third major section and anticipates a fourth, where the New Jerusalem will be examined in more detail.³⁴⁰ For a second time a prophetic utterance comes from God himself, the words of which are identical and quite familiar to Johannine hearers. The words "I Am" are often on the lips of Jesus in John's gospel. In Rev 21:6, as in Rev 1:8, the predicate to the "I Am" statement is "Alpha and Omega," which refers to God himself. All of creation, the first heaven and first earth, as well as the new heaven and new earth, stand within his purview and are enveloped by his presence and power.³⁴¹

336. Smalley, *Revelation*, 540.
337. Beasley-Murray, *Revelation*, 312.
338. Prigent, *L'Apocalypse de Saint Jean*, 462.
339. Murphy, *Fallen Is Babylon*, 412.
340. Bauckham, *The Climax of Prophecy*, 7.
341. Beale, *The Book of Revelation*, 1055.

Standing alongside it is the additional title "the First and the Last," well known from Isa 44:6, where God's claim to exclusivity as the only God is made clear. These two identifications, standing side by side, convey the idea that God is indeed the Beginning and the Ending, the First and the Last; he is the all in all. Perhaps this combination of titles would even suggest that the end is not an event but a person.[342] It is this unrivaled God who promises to the thirsty a gift out of the well of living water, in which a number of eschatological promises converge (Isa 55:1; John 4:7-15; Rev 7:16-17).[343] The sources of this well are deep and never ending![344]

"The one who overcomes will inherit these things, and I will be to him God, and he will be to me son." The language of overcoming reminds readers of the eschatological promises to those who overcome found in the seven prophetic messages (2:7, 11, 17, 26-28; 3:5, 12, 21).[345] The one who overcomes will inherit all these things and the eschatological promises of 21:3-4,[346] which culminate in the words "I will be to him God, and he will be to me son." It would be difficult to overestimate the impact of these words upon the hearers. These words echo the divine promise given to David with regard to his seed (2 Sam 7:14), suggesting that this Davidic promise is inherited by those who overcome, offering further support for the understanding that Johannine believers are indeed part of the transformed Israel represented in the 144,000 who are sealed by God (7:1-8). Unlike in the promise of 2 Sam 7:14, the one who sits on the throne is referred to as God rather than Father, perhaps reminding the hearers that only once in the Johannine literature is God referred to as the Father of believers (John 20:17).[347] The rest of the promise contains a most astounding and exhilarating detail. The Johannine tradition is very careful to make a clear distinction between Jesus as *Son* of God and believers as *children* of God. That is, the term υἱός (*huios*, "son") is never used in John's gospel or 1–3 John to describe believers as sons of God. This term is reserved to describe the unique Son of God, Jesus. And yet in Rev 21:7, the eschatological promise of God to the one who overcomes is that such a one will be *huios* of God! It is difficult to know what kind of impact such an unexpected and startling use of words would have. It would be clear that the fierce monotheism found within Revelation would rule out the idea that any created being is to be considered divine or worshipped, an idolatrous idea that the words of this prophecy condemn all the way through.

---

342. Caird, *The Revelation of Saint John*, 266.
343. Sweet, *Revelation*, 299.
344. Smalley, *Revelation*, 541.
345. Mounce, *The Book of Revelation*, 375.
346. Beasley-Murray, *Revelation*, 313.
347. Prigent, *L'Apocalypse de Saint Jean*, 465.

But part of the implications would no doubt cause the hearers to reexamine the various eschatological promises encountered earlier in order to discern more deeply other nuances of these promises. Specifically, all of them (2:7, 11, 17, 26-28; 3:5, 12, 21) sound a bit richer in the light of the fact that the one who overcomes will be to God "son." This statement may also have implications for the close and intimate relationship between Jesus and the believer. Would this wording encourage the hearers to think in terms of an embryonic theosis, or some other form of sharing in the divine nature? Whatever the full implications, it is clear that it would at the least indicate that the close relationship that exists between God and the overcomer is even more intimate than anticipated to this point, a further illustration of the immediacy between God and his people that characterizes the New Jerusalem.

"And for the cowardly and unfaithful and those who commit abominations and murderers and sexually immoral and magicians and idolaters and all liars, their part will be in the lake of burning fire and sulfur, which is the second death." This is no ordinary list of sinners. Each of the categories found here appears to represent groups of believers who have succumbed to temptations that kept them from being faithful until the end as overcomers,[348] for almost all of these categories have a special meaning that derives from Revelation itself.[349] This list has the effect of a warning to Johannine believers not to lose their way and stop short of offering faithful witness to the end.[350]

The term "cowardly," which would be taken as the antonym of "overcomer" in this context,[351] would have less to do with one's general disposition and more to do with the lack of courage to offer faithful witness in following the Lamb wherever he might go, specifically to death. By saving one's life before the threats of the beast and his false prophet, these cowardly in point of fact lose their lives. Giving in to the fear of suffering and death, they are unable to join those in Smyrna (2:10) and Pergamum (2:13-15) in offering faithful witness.[352] The term "unfaithful" (or "unbelieving") stands with the first in identifying those Christians who, owing to their fear of the beast and/or the seduction of the great whore, are unable to offer the faithful witness that reflects their Lord and his followers.[353] They are similar to Jesus' words to his disciple Thomas, who was in danger of losing his way, that Thomas no longer be unbelieving but

---

348. Gundry, "The New Jerusalem," 258.
349. Murphy, *Fallen Is Babylon*, 415.
350. G. D. Cloete, "'And I Saw a New Heaven and a New Earth, for the First . . . Were Passed Away' (Revelation 21:1-8)," *Journal of Theology for South Africa* 81 (December, 1992): 58-59.
351. Aune, *Revelation 17-22*, 1131.
352. Sweet, *Revelation*, 300.
353. Michaels, *Revelation*, 239.

believing (John 20:27). The term translated "those who commit abominations" would be defined in Revelation by its being wholly associated with the activity of the great whore (17:4), who is identified as the mother of the abominations of the earth (17:5).[354] By succumbing to the seduction of the great whore and participating in her abominations, these individuals now share in the punishment that awaits her rather than sharing in the eschatological promises to the one who overcomes. In Revelation those who commit murder are numbered among the rest of people who refuse to repent of murders (9:21).[355] And though a different word is used to describe their murderous activities, in John's gospel Jesus describes Satan as a murderer from the beginning (John 8:44). In Revelation refusal to worship the beast results in death for such offenders (13:15). This category would thus suggest that those who identify with the beast are complicit in his activity of murdering those whose names are written in the Lamb's book of life.[356] Joining these other categories are the sexually immoral. This word and its word family in Revelation are also closely identified with the activity of the great whore (17:1-2, 4-5), whose idolatrous charms result in the sexual immorality of the kings of the earth (18:3, 9), a temptation with which even the church must contend (Rev 2:14, 20).[357] For this activity the great whore is judged (17:16; 19:2), as are all those who are sexually immoral owing to their economic and idolatrous relationship with her. Next are mentioned the magicians. This activity too is described as a work of their hands, for which the rest of "men" did not offer repentance (9:21), as well as being the means by which the great whore had deceived all the nations (18:23). Such an understanding might well lead the hearers to conclude that those who have been enchanted by her magic themselves share in this activity and will suffer a similar fate to the great whore. In Revelation idolatrous activity is closely associated with sexual immorality and eating meat sacrificed to idols (2:14, 20). Ultimately, those who worship the beast and/or join in the idolatrous activity of the great whore, even those who worship the servants of God, commit idolatry. Only God is to be glorified; all who engage in idolatrous activity betray him and forsake true worship. The designation "all liars" would be rich in meaning. By this time readers well know that, when the devil lies, he speaks his native tongue (John 8:44), that the one who lies is diametrically opposed to the truth (1 John 2:21, 27), and that there are those who claim to be apostles or Jews but are not, for they lie (Rev 2:2; 3:9). Perhaps this category would include those who have be-

---

354. Prigent, *L'Apocalypse de Saint Jean*, 466.
355. Ladd, *Revelation*, 279.
356. Mounce, *The Book of Revelation*, 375.
357. Pattemore, *The People of God in the Apocalypse*, 211.

lieved the lie of the beast and the great whore and, by their participation with them, have perpetuated that lie.[358] At the least, there is a stark contrast between those who lie and the followers of the Lamb, in whose mouths no lie is found (14:5). Owing to the close association with the beast and the great whore, all such ones as these — cowardly, unfaithful, those who commit abominations, murderers, sexually immoral, magicians, idolaters, and all liars — have a share or portion in the same eternal punishment that awaits the dragon, the beast, and the false prophet (19:20; 20:10). Those who identify with and/or are seduced by the beast and the great whore choose to share in their destiny rather than in that which awaits the overcomers.[359] Instead of being called "son" by God and experiencing the fellowship this title portends, these individuals who have not offered faithful witness unto death now experience eternal death — the second death — a death that holds no power over the overcomers. Such warnings at this point are clearly intended for the church.[360]

---

358. Beasley-Murray, *Revelation*, 314.
359. Caird, *The Revelation of Saint John*, 268.
360. Sweet, *Revelation*, 300.

"In the Spirit" — Carried to a Great High Mountain: The Description of the New Jerusalem (21:9–22:5)

The final major section of Revelation is introduced by the fourth and final "in the Spirit" phrase (21:10). A detailed description is given of the New Jerusalem, noting its appearance (21:9-21), the role of God and the Lamb as temple and light (21:22-27), and the tree of life and the direct immediacy of the presence of God and the Lamb (22:1-5).

"And one of the seven angels having the seven bowls full of the seven last plagues came and was speaking with me saying, 'Come, I will show you the bride, the wife of the Lamb.'" The first twelve words in the Greek text of 21:9 are exactly like those with which 17:1 begins. This verbatim repetition would indicate that a contrast is intended between the judgment of the great whore and the marriage of the bride of the Lamb.[1] The reappearance of one of the angels having the seven bowls would be a reminder that the God who rewards is also the God who punishes, continuing the implicit warning to the community to avoid contamination from the seductions of the great whore and to offer a faithful witness to God and the Lamb to the end. The angel who speaks with John uses identical words to those in 17:1 in issuing the invitation, "Come, I will show you." The word "come" is a divine invitation, not unlike the one Jesus issues to Lazarus in John's gospel (John 11:43). As in 17:1 the next word from the angel, "I will show" is the term closely associated in Revelation (Rev 1:1; 4:1) with those things that must take place soon, and a word with a rich history in John's gospel (John 5:20; 10:32; 14:9; 20:20).[2] Thus, in Rev 21:9, as in 17:1, the term would strike the hearers as pregnant with divine revelatory meaning. What is to be shown to John on this occasion, in contrast to the judgment of the great whore, is "the bride, the wife of the Lamb." This mention of the bride of the Lamb would bring to mind the radical difference between this city, described as a bride, and fallen Babylon, in which the voice (or sound) of the bride will be heard no longer (18:23). It would likely resurface the expectation of the marriage supper of the Lamb, which was announced earlier in 19:7-8. The words τὴν νύμφην (*tēn nymphēn*, "the bride") and τὴν γυναῖκα (*tēn gynaika*, "the wife"), which stand side by side in the Greek text, could be taken as superfluous duplication, but they might actually convey significant information to the hearers, in two respects. First, this construction makes clear that the bride of the Lamb is identical to the wife of the Lamb, whose bright shining linen garment is defined as the righteous acts of the saints (19:7-8), indicating that the bride

---

1. Mounce, *The Book of Revelation*, 377.
2. G. Schneider, "Δείκνυμι, δεικνύω," *EDNT*, 1:280-81.

and the church are coterminous. Second, the occurrence of these two nouns side by side might also convey something more about her theological identity, with the term "bride" pointing to virginal purity,[3] newness, and intimacy, and the word "wife," to covenant fidelity, intimacy, and fruitfulness.[4]

"And he carried me in the Spirit unto a great and high mountain and showed me the holy city Jerusalem coming down out of heaven from God, having the glory of God." For the fourth time, the "in the Spirit" phrase appears. As before, the appearance of this phrase would convey a sense of continuity between John's experience in chapters 1–3, his experience in chapters 4–16, and his experience in 17:1–21:8. It has become evident that this phrase is central to the book's structure, indicating that the means by which the revelation is given is "in the Spirit." As in 17:3, John is again transported "in the Spirit," only here in 21:10 he is not taken to the theologically rich wilderness but to a great and high mountain. In the OT, mountains function as a place of the divine presence (Gen 22:2; Exod 17:9-10; 1 Kgs 18:42), communication, and revelation (Exod 19), as well as prophetic activity (Judg 9:7; 1 Kgs 18:20-46) and eschatological expectation (Isa 2:2-4; Mic 4:1-3).[5] The mountain functioned as a place of solitude and refuge for Jesus in John's gospel (John 6:3, 15). John's experience in 21:10 is similar to that of Ezekiel, who was also set upon a high mountain to see the cleansed and rebuilt Jerusalem (Ezek 40:1-2).[6] The description as great and high might well be taken as an indication of its supernatural size.[7] Rather than simply being brought to a high vantage point, John is taken to this enormous mountain, as it is the location of the city that he sees. Though the angel promises to show John the bride of the Lamb, John is shown "the holy city Jerusalem coming down out of heaven from God." This shift from bride to the holy city Jerusalem would be reminiscent of the interplay between the description of the destruction of the great whore that morphs into the destruction of Babylon the Great. What John is shown in 21:10 is identical to what he saw in 21:2. Just as the destruction of Babylon the Great was introduced in 16:19 before its more detailed description in 17:1–19:2, so the New Jerusalem, which was introduced in 21:1-2, here in 21:10 begins to be described in greater detail. As noted in 21:2, there is a close connection between this holy city and the people of God, who themselves are the holy ones. The divine origin of the city is underscored in a twofold fashion, as this city continues to be described as "coming down out

---

3. Allo, *Saint Jean: L'Apocalypse*, 316.
4. Celia Deutsch, "Transformation of Symbols: the New Jerusalem in Rv 21:1–22:5," *ZNW* 78 (1987): 112-13, and Smalley, *Revelation*, 545.
5. C. Brown, "Ὄρος," *NIDNTT*, 3:1009-10.
6. Sweet, *Revelation*, 303.
7. Smalley, *Revelation*, 456.

of heaven" and as "from God." This city not only originates with God, it also bears the glory of God, a phenomenon that fits with the direct and immediate nature of God's relationship to his people in New Jerusalem. For if his dwelling is indeed with them, his shekinah would be certain to shine forth, not unlike the way in which Moses' face shone with the glory of God after being in his presence on Mount Sinai (Exod 34:29-35).[8] If the unmediated eschatological presence of God shines forth with nothing to obstruct it in all its intensity,[9] it is met among his people, his sons (and daughters), who continue to give him glory in the praise and adoration they offer.

"Her radiance is as a precious stone, as a stone of translucent jasper." The comparison of the unbelievable brilliance of the city to that of a precious stone would remind hearers of the precious stones with which the great whore sought to give the impression that such adornment was an accurate indication of her person and worth (17:4; 18:12, 16). In stark contrast, the value and beauty of a precious stone can be used only in comparison to the radiance of God's glory, with which the city is characterized. Specifically, this brilliance is compared to translucent jasper, a stone closely connected to the appearance of the one who sits on the throne (4:3) and also is the final stone found upon the breastplate of the high priest (Exod 28:17-21). The description of this stone as "clear," "translucent," "clear as crystal" may convey something of its purity and value,[10] indicating that it, as the holy city, is especially formed and suited to reflect the glory of God, a characteristic also attributed to the crystal sea before the throne of God (4:6). Significantly, the two occurrences of this root word in Revelation both are closely associated with reflecting the glory of God.

"Having a wall great and high, having twelve gates, and upon these gates twelve angels, and names have been written that are of the twelve tribes of the sons of Israel; from the east three gates and from the north three gates and from the south three gates and from the west three gates." The city and mountain John sees are described exactly, as great and high, suggesting that the wall is in keeping with the mountain upon which the city apparently sits. As the description includes various combinations of the number 12, each occurrence would remind readers of the theologically significant ways in which the multiples of the number 12 have previously occurred (4:4, 10; 5:8; 7:4-8; 11:16; 12:1; 14:1, 3; 19:4). This theologically significant number is in some ways indistinguishable from the city itself, for it is deeply embedded in its very essence and being. Such emphasis would likely suggest perfection in all details. As such, the wall

---

8. Murphy, *Fallen Is Babylon*, 418.
9. Prigent, *L'Apocalypse de Saint Jean*, 451.
10. Aune, *Revelation 17–22*, 1154.

of the city has the perfect number of (twelve) gates, attended by the perfect number of (twelve) angels, with the names of the perfect number of the (twelve) tribes of the sons of Israel! The twelve gates suggest perfect access,[11] while the twelve angels convey the idea of divinely appointed perfect oversight of access. The names that have been written on the gates include all the names of those encountered earlier when the 144,000 of the tribes of the sons of Israel were divinely sealed (Rev 7:4-8). Twelve gates, each of which bears the name of one of the tribes of the sons of Israel, would thus testify to the way in which God's people and the holy city are identical.[12]

The gates are symmetrically distributed around the city, with three gates on each side, but in the peculiar geographic order east, north, south, and west.[13] The enumeration of these twelve gates that open in all directions would suggest universal access,[14] as no corner of existence stands without three entrances to the holy city.[15] Normally such a description would follow a north, east, south, west direction (e.g., Ezek 48:30-35). Here, the place of prominence is given to the east, the direction that the door of the Jerusalem temple faced,[16] perhaps suggesting that this city, which the wall encloses, is itself a temple, owing to the brilliant radiance of the glory of God present in it and its eastern orientation. Would the three gates on the east wall of the holy city bring to mind the way prepared for the kings of the East to make their way to the war of the great day of God the All Powerful One (16:12-16), suggesting that there is hope even for these kings from the East, kings who violently opposed God, to enter the holy city? When thinking of the gates on the north, would the hearers think of the ways in which Gog and Magog, the traditional enemies from the north (Ezek 38:6), gathered together to make war with the camp of the saints, God's beloved city (Rev 20:8)? If so, would they be inclined to think that these gates are opened to them and all others from the four points of the earth (20:8) that have opposed God? When contemplating the gates on the south side of the wall, would they be reminded of the city pneumatically called Sodom and Egypt that humiliates the two Spirit-inspired prophets (11:8)? Is it possible that there exists access to the holy city even for these? And would thoughts of the three gates on the west remind them of the great sea, which is no more? Is there hope even for those who are in its grip?

"And the wall of the city having twelve foundations, and upon them twelve

11. Lee, *The New Jerusalem in the Book of Revelation*, 281.
12. Gause, *Revelation*, 271.
13. Sweet, *Revelation*, 304.
14. Smalley, *Revelation*, 548.
15. Resseguie, *The Revelation of John*, 254.
16. Yet another observation for which I am indebted to my colleague L. R. Martin.

"In the Spirit" — Carried to a Great High Mountain (21:9-22:5)

names of the twelve apostles of the Lamb." Attention is next directed to what stands under the wall: its supports, and remarkably there are twelve foundations, signifying a perfect foundation. Apparently these foundations are visible,[17] so that the names of the twelve apostles of the Lamb are revealed. This is the first occurrence of "apostle" (referring to the Twelve) in Johannine literature. Although "the Twelve" appears on three occasions in John's gospel (John 6:67, 70, 71), the Twelve are never named there as such; only nine seem to be specifically mentioned (Andrew, Simon Peter, Philip, Nathaniel, Judas Iscariot, Thomas, Judas not Iscariot, the sons of Zebedee), or ten, if one includes the Beloved Disciple, who does not seem to make an apostolic claim for himself. The phrase "the twelve apostles of the Lamb" is interesting because the term "apostle" never appears in John's gospel or in 1-3 John outside of one proverbial use (John 13:16). Nor has the term appeared in the technical sense of the twelve apostles earlier in Revelation (cf. Rev 2:2; 18:20). From its previous occurrences the term "apostle" conveys the idea of a divine sending, being informed by the extensive sending language in John's gospel and 1 John, suggesting that there are individuals whom God commissions for specific tasks, especially being sent to participate in the harvest of the world (John 4:38; 17:18; 20:21). The term ἀποστέλλω (*apostellō*, "send") appears on one occasion with reference to the seven Spirits of God, who are sent out into all the earth (Rev 5:6), and on two other occasions to describe the activity of God, who sends his angel to make known to his servants all that is to happen quickly (1:1; 22:6). Such sent ones are likely thought of as special envoys[18] whom God has sent into the global harvest to bear witness to the Lamb. The placement of "the apostles" between "the saints" and "the prophets" in 18:20 underscores the idea that the people of God, who have a prophetic vocation, are indeed "the sent ones" of God himself. The first and only reference to the twelve apostles of the Lamb in 21:14 thus seems to combine the idea of the Twelve from John's gospel with that of the special envoys sent by God into the world harvest and their close association with the Lamb. Their relationship to the Lamb, whose mention would remind the hearers of his death,[19] may suggest, along with the appearance of the term "apostles" in 18:20, that they too have followed the Lamb even unto death. Such a foundational role for the twelve apostles of the Lamb fits well with the general meaning of the term, but here the term appears to be used in a more technical way. The fact that the names of the twelve apostles appear along with the names of the twelve tribes of the sons of Israel would indicate the way in

---

17. Allo, *Saint Jean: L'Apocalypse*, 318.
18. So Prigent, *L'Apocalypse de Saint Jean*, 395.
19. Aune, *Revelation 17-22*, 1157.

which both the twelve tribes and the twelve apostles are foundational for the redemptive community, a reality to which the twenty-four elders may point as they themselves appear to stand for all the redeemed.[20] The corporate image of these two groups of twelve would convey to the hearers a sense of the perfection of God's people in the holy city.[21]

"And the one speaking with me had a measuring rod of gold in order that he might measure the city and her gates and her wall." The appearance of the angel leads us to expect that John will be shown even more about the holy city. The mention of a measuring rod of gold would well remind readers that John himself had earlier measured the temple of God and the altar and those who worshipped in it, a measurement that conveyed protection to the things measured (11:1). But in 21:15 it is not John who measures but the angel. If John's measuring signified protection for the temple, altar, and worshippers for forty-two months, perhaps this angelic measurement of the holy city would signify eternal protection and/or security for the people of God. The fact that the measuring rod is made of gold would convey something about the importance and value of that which is being measured;[22] it is altogether suitable for measuring a holy city that descends from heaven from God.[23] To this point, gold seems to be valued as the purest of metals and has regularly been associated with heaven and heavenly objects (4:4; 5:8; 8:3; 9:13; 14:14; 15:6-7).

"And the city lies as a square, and her length is as the breadth. And he measured the city with the rod upon twelve thousand stadia; the length and the breadth and the height of her is equal." What the hearers now learn continues to push their imaginative abilities beyond their boundaries![24] Like the temple that Ezekiel (45:2) sees, this city lies square, its length being equal to its breadth. The square itself seems to be a shape associated with perfection.[25] But the size of the holy city that the angel measures dwarfs Ezekiel's city (48:8-9, 30-35) by a ratio of almost 1,000:1,[26] for it measures 144,000,000 square stadia. This number equals one thousand times the number of those sealed from the twelve tribes of the sons of Israel introduced in Rev 7:5-8, the 144,000 who appear with the Lamb who have his name and the name of his Father written upon their foreheads (14:1-4). It is of enormous, almost supernatural size.[27] One stadion

20. Beasley-Murray, *Revelation*, 321.
21. Gause, *Revelation*, 271.
22. Smalley, *Revelation*, 550.
23. Aune, *Revelation 17–22*, 1159.
24. Caird, *The Revelation of Saint John*, 272.
25. Kiddle, *The Revelation of St. John*, 429.
26. Koester, *Revelation and the End of All Things*, 196.
27. Smalley, *Revelation*, 551.

is about 400 cubits, or about 214 yards, which means that the size of this city is about 1,450 miles on each side![28] Such a city has never been seen, for even ancient Babylon, which was itself an enormous size, measured only 120 stadia per side (Herodotus 1.178).[29] The holy city would stretch across the known world and into the heavens itself, perhaps indicating that the new heaven and new earth unite in the New Jerusalem![30] It is the perfect home for the people of God, who number 144,000, plus the innumerable crowd as well.[31] The holy city actually takes the form of a cube, implying perfection, reminding readers of the shape of the holy of holies in the temple, which was twenty cubits long, wide, and high (1 Kgs 6:20),[32] making clear that the holy city is itself a temple — indeed, the entire city is a holy of holies! Such a reality would fit well with the immediacy and direct access believers have to God in New Jerusalem (Rev 21:1-8), for the city is itself a temple.

"And he measured her wall, being 144 cubits, a measure of man, which is of an angel." Once again, a multiple of 12 appears in the description of the holy city and its wall, with the measurement of the wall being 144 cubits. Such a measurement continues the idea of perfection, in this case suggesting that the wall itself is a perfect fit for the city, fulfilling its function perfectly.[33] But while 144 cubits (= 230 feet) is not an insignificant measurement for a wall, in comparison to the size of the city itself, this measurement is almost ludicrously small.[34] If the total length of the various walls is 144,000 stadia (ca. 17,500 miles), the wall itself is measured at 144 cubits (ca. 230 feet). While it is possible that the wall's breadth is here in view, serving as a graphic boundary of demarcation,[35] given that the wall has earlier been described as great and high (21:12), like the mountain to which John was transported, perhaps the hearers would take the wall to be 144 cubits high, a good height for a wall, to which only a few on earth would compare. Or perhaps the measurement would refer to both the height and breadth of the wall, in keeping with the symmetrical dimensions of the city itself. While comparatively small, perhaps the wall's dimensions would accentuate the unbelievable enormity of the holy city that lies behind these walls. Perhaps this wall designates protection and security as city walls in the

---

28. O. R. Sellers, "Weights and Measures," *The Interpreter's Dictionary of the Bible* (ed. G. A. Buttrick; Nashville: Abingdon, 1962), 4:838.
29. Sweet, *Revelation*, 305.
30. Beasley-Murray, *Revelation*, 322.
31. Michaels, *Revelation*, 242.
32. Mounce, *The Book of Revelation*, 380.
33. Gause, *Revelation*, 271.
34. Sweet, *Revelation*, 305.
35. Sweet, *Revelation*, 305.

ancient world normally would. Perhaps the comparatively small size of the wall would draw attention to the fact that God's ability to protect and secure the holy city is not dependent upon walls or other fortifications.[36] Curiously, the measurement is described as "a measure of a man, which is of an angel." On one level the hearers would understand these words as indicating that the measurement of the wall is given in terms of the human measurement of cubits but is actually measured by an angel,[37] suggesting that such a task would seem to be well beyond the abilities of any human. But perhaps this somewhat odd notation would spur the hearers to discern on the order of earlier discernment with regard to the number of the beast, which is "the number of man," or 666. Interestingly enough, when the Greek word "angel" is written in Hebrew characters, its numerical value is 144.[38] Such a realization could perhaps provide a contrast for the hearers: between humanity debased to the level of the beast (666) and humanity exalted to the level of the angels (144), surrounded by the square of 12.[39]

"And the material of her wall is jasper, and the city is pure gold as pure glass." The material of the wall, jasper, is the very stone that earlier describes the appearance of the one who sits on the throne (4:3),[40] as well as the radiance of the holy city Jerusalem, through which the glory of God shines. Thus, like God and his city, the wall is characterized by the glory of God, so that the walls of this holy of holies shine forth the glory of God rather than hide it.[41] Not surprisingly, the material out of which the holy city is made is transparent gold, clear as glass or crystal, which itself reflects all the more the glory of God that is within the city. The gold out of which the city is constructed underscores the value of the city,[42] demonstrating the way in which this holy city far transcends any of its earthly rivals, even the earthly temple, in which jasper and gold were used in its construction (1 Kgs 6–7). The spectacular splendor of the holy city shines forth the glory of God in ways that stagger the imagination.[43]

"The foundations of the wall of the city were adorned with every precious

---

36. Beasley-Murray, *Revelation*, 323.

37. Ladd, *Revelation*, 282.

38. 144 = א/1 + י/50 + ג/3 + ל/30 + ס/60. On this point, cf. Bauckham, *The Climax of Prophecy*, 298.

39. Bauckham (*The Climax of Prophecy*, 300) concludes, "Thus whereas humanity debased to the level of the beast bears the triangular number 666, humanity raised to the level of the angels in the new Jerusalem is surrounded by the square of 12."

40. Sweet, *Revelation*, 305.

41. Mealy, *After the Thousand Years*, 198 n. 1.

42. Prigent, *L'Apocalypse de Saint Jean*, 474.

43. Gause, *Revelation*, 272.

stone; the first foundation jasper, the second sapphire, the third chalcedony, the fourth emerald, the fifth sardonyx, the sixth carnelian, the seventh chrysolite, the eighth beryl, the ninth topaz, the tenth chrysoprase, the eleventh jacinth, and the twelfth amethyst." There is a connection between the bride "adorned" for her husband (21:2) and the foundations that are "adorned" with these precious stones (21:19), further underscoring the relationship between the bride and the city. The value of the holy city would be emphasized owing to such elaborate foundations, reminding readers that great and costly stones were used as a foundation for the house of God that Solomon built (1 Kgs 5:17).[44] Such a vision would also likely remind hearers of the promise that Yahweh will lay foundations of sapphire in the ideal days to come (Isa 54:11).[45] Several of the stones that appear here would bring to mind Ezekiel's lamentation to the king of Tyre, the list of precious stones in the Eden of God (Ezek 28:13).[46] It is likely that the hearers would recall the description of the breastplate of the high priest, on which were twelve precious stones in four rows of three,[47] where several of the stones in Rev 21:19-20 appear. This convergence of intertexts would convey the sense that, in the very foundations of the holy city Jerusalem, a number of OT prophecies and ideas are fulfilled. The hearers would also recall that, in the inaugural vision of heaven, the one who sits on the throne has the appearance of jasper and carnelian, with a rainbow around the throne that resembles emerald (4:3), reinforcing all the more the relationship of the foundations with the special presence of God. Here the enumeration of the respective foundations makes it even clearer that each foundation is made of a specific precious stone, perhaps conveying the idea of the foundations lying on top of one another.[48] As the hearers reflect on this combination of colors,[49] perhaps they would be struck by the wide range of hues represented: various shades of the primary colors — green (jasper, chalcedony, emerald, beryl, chrysoprase), blue (sapphire, jacinth), and red (sardonyx, carnelian) — as well as yellow (chrysolite, topaz) and purple (amethyst). Thus, even the foundations of the holy city are found to be perfectly suited to it![50]

44. Sweet, *Revelation*, 306.
45. Beasley-Murray, *Revelation*, 324.
46. Kiddle, *The Revelation of St. John*, 433.
47. Aune, *Revelation 17-22*, 1165.
48. Smalley, *Revelation*, 545.
49. For the relationship between these precious stones and their respective colors, cf. Mounce, *The Book of Revelation*, 382.
50. An intriguing Christological interpretation of the specific order of the precious stones that adorn the foundations comes from M. Wojciechowski ("Apocalypse 21:19-20: Titres christologiques cachés dans la liste des pierres précieuses," *NTS* 33 [1987]: 154), who points out that the

"And the twelve gates are twelve pearls; each one of the gates was out of one pearl. And the street of the city was pure gold, as clear as glass or crystal." The gates of the city are not inlaid with pearl; rather, each of the gates *is* one pearl, a detail that could not help but push the hearers' imaginative abilities to their limits.[51] But perhaps this amazing detail would call for more pneumatic discernment. For example, this mention of these gates of pearls might remind readers of the only other times the word "pearl" appears in Revelation, where it has been exclusively associated with the great whore (17:4), Babylon the Great (18:16), and her merchants (18:12). In each case, the mention of pearls underscores the opulent wealth of the great whore, as she is bedecked in pearls, appearing to have no rivals. But here it is revealed that the woman with whom she is compared, the bride of the Lamb, is adorned to such an unbelievable extent that the great whore's claims to wealth are revealed to be almost laughable. For if she makes claims by wearing pearls around her neck and upon her clothing, the bride of the Lamb has (wears?) whole gates that are composed of single pearls — a most staggering comparison indeed. Not only do gates of pearls stand as entrances to this rich city, but once inside, those who enter also walk on a street of gold. It is not altogether clear whether "the street of the city" refers to the central street or the plaza of the city or is a collective referring to all the streets of the city.[52] However, mention of the street of gold could hardly help but remind readers that, just as the priests of the OT ministered on a floor inlaid with gold (1 Kgs 6:30), so those who enter the holy city walk on streets of gold that are not just covered with gold but are made of solid gold that is clear as glass.[53] The words might also hearken back to the similar phrase "the street of the great city," where the body of the two prophetic witnesses lay for three days in utter humiliation (11:8). The contrast between the shame the saints experienced in the street of the great city and the eternal glory that awaits in the holy city is striking.[54]

"And a temple I did not see in it, for the Lord God the All Powerful One and the Lamb is the temple." The grammatical construction of the Greek text

---

first letter of each stone produces the following combination of sacred names and titles IC XC CC X B T X Y A, which he says stands for "Jesus, Christ, Savior, Christ, King and Telos, Christ, Son of Man." This configuration underscores the title of Christ, presenting his eschatological mission as the realization of the prophets about the king, Messiah, and about the Son of Man. While it is not altogether clear that the hearers would arrive at such a result via their pneumatic discernment, one of the things in favor of such a possibility is the fact that all of these names and titles would be familiar to Johannine hearers.

51. Metzger, *Breaking the Code*, 101.
52. Aune, *Revelation 17-22*, 1166.
53. Mounce, *The Book of Revelation*, 383.
54. Wall, *Revelation*, 254-55.

suggests that John expected to see a temple in the holy city.[55] Sufficient temple language in the book suggests that a temple does indeed exist in heaven (7:15; 11:19; 14:15, 17; 15:5-6, 8; 16:1, 17),[56] an understanding that might lead to the expectation of a temple in the holy city as well. Ezekiel's seven-chapter description (Ezek 40–46) of the eschatological temple and its activities[57] might also lend credence to the idea of a temple here. Yet, the Lord God the All Powerful One and the Lamb is the temple. The holy city's shape as a cube like the holy of holies (21:16), the eastern orientation of its twelve gates (21:13), the fact that the overcomer is promised to be made a pillar "in the temple of my God" (3:12), the unmediated presence of God in the New Jerusalem (21:1-8),[58] the priestly language scattered throughout the book (1:6; 5:10; 7:15; 20:6), and Jesus' body being spoken of as a temple in the Johannine literature (John 2:19-20)[59] — all these ideas converge in a new and comprehensible fashion. The relationship between God and his people in the holy city Jerusalem represents complete integration of God with his people, with the mention of the Lamb underscoring the means by which salvation itself is accomplished.[60]

"And the city has no need of the sun or the moon in order that they might enlighten it, for the glory of God lightens it, and his lamp is the Lamb." Taken together, these words would certainly bring to mind Isaiah's near-identical wording with regard to the future that awaits God's people (Isa 60:19-20).[61] The city has no need of the sun or the moon, which is closely connected to there being no temple in the city, owing to the radiance of God's direct presence. If the sun previously is a point of reference for comparison (Rev 1:16; 10:1; 12:1; 19:17), now even it is outdistanced in its ability to illuminate. The holy city radiates with the glory of God (21:11), but now the holy city is enlightened by the glory of God, a glory so powerful that it makes redundant the need for the sun or the moon! The word "enlighten" carries with it soteriological associations, as it is the term used to describe the Logos shining in the darkness and the inability of the darkness to comprehend or extinguish it (John 1:5). The way in which the glory of God enlightens the holy city thus carries with it salvific overtones; its light enables not simply physical sight, but soteriological sight as well! Not only does the glory of God act in such a way, but so too does the Lamb, who reflects the glory of God in an especially impressive way, for the Lamb is the

---

55. Smalley, *Revelation*, 556.
56. Murphy, *Fallen Is Babylon*, 423.
57. Mounce, *The Book of Revelation*, 383.
58. Resseguie, *The Revelation of John*, 256.
59. Aune, *Revelation 17–22*, 1168.
60. Gause, *Revelation*, 273.
61. Prigent, *L'Apocalypse de Saint Jean*, 478.

lamp for the holy city, through whom the glory of God shines forth in its comprehensive salvific fashion. Unlike the judged city Babylon the Great, where the light of a lamp no longer enlightens it (18:23), this holy city is enlightened by the Lamb himself!

"And the nations will walk by means of its light, and the kings of the earth bring their glory into it." These words remind hearers of yet another Isaianic promise, in near-identical wording (Isa 60:3) with regard to the ideal age to come. There could be little doubt that the hearers would understand this language to mean that the nations who walk in its light are those who have experienced his salvation, as in Johannine thought the word "walk" functions metaphorically as a description of one's relationship or fellowship with God, Jesus, and/or the Light (John 6:66; 8:12; 11:9-10; 12:35; 1 John 1:6-7; 2:6, 11; 2 John 4, 6; 3 John 3-4), and this very word has been encountered earlier in Revelation to describe fellowship with the resurrected Jesus (Rev 2:1), eschatological reward (3:4), and ethical conduct (16:15). The words of 21:24 follow on quite naturally from the optimistic impression left by the perfect and universal access to the holy city (21:13). It thus appears that the rebellious nations will find a place in God's salvific light that fills the holy city, fulfilling the hearers' previous expectations based upon descriptions of the nations in precisely these terms (5:9; 7:9; 11:9-13; 15:3-4), nations that are the specific objects of faithful witness and prophecy (10:11; 11:9-13; 14:6). Yet, the nations have previously been spoken of almost entirely in negative terms (11:9-13, 18; 13:7; 14:8; 16:19; 17:15; 18:3, 23; 19:15; 20:3, 8). That the nations, perhaps these very nations, are spoken of as walking in the light of the holy city, the very glory of God, would force the hearers to hold these dialectical possibilities together — the possible implication being that God is even more gracious and longsuffering than they could ever have imagined! These first words of 21:24 clearly suggest that the nations who walk in the light of the holy city are indeed converted. They go further, however, being pregnant with meaning and calling for reflection on the incongruities of these two ends of the dialectic — perhaps those who have expressed such open hostility and opposition to God and his people somehow experience his salvific light! Not only are the nations said to walk in the light of the holy city, but it is also said that "the kings of the earth bring their glory into it." As with the previous words in this verse, these remind readers of the same Isaianic promise with regard to the ideal age to come, where almost identical wording occurs (Isa 60:3). The kings of the earth in this verse are seen, not only as entering the holy city, but also as bringing their glory into it. In Revelation, "glory" is closely associated with worship (1:6; 4:9, 11; 5:12-13; 7:12; 11:13; 14:7; 16:9; 19:1, 7),[62]

---

62. Mathewson, "The Destiny of the Nations in Revelation 21:1–22:5," 130.

indicating that the kings of the earth too are engaged in the worship of the God, whose own glory enlightens the entire city. These words would appear even more challenging than those with regard to the nations, for aside from the first reference to the kings of the earth (1:5), there is no other place in the whole of Revelation where the kings of the earth do not function as the enemies of God (6:15; 17:2, 18; 18:3, 9; 19:19), except in 21:24[63] — in point of fact, they appear to have been destroyed by the rider on the white horse! And yet, here they are spoken of as bringing their own objects of worship into the holy city.[64] Would not such an inversion suggest that a remarkable conversion takes place among the kings of the earth, whose idolatrous greed, self-serving pursuit of power, and opposition to God and his people have been transformed so that they now worship God with the very things they had formerly sought for themselves?[65] As with the nations, it would be clear that these kings of the earth have indeed been converted as a result of the faithful witness of God's people, but would the absolute polarities and incongruities encountered in the text not push the hearers to contemplate a greater wideness in God's mercy than they have hitherto been prepared to explore or for which even to hope?[66] If so, would not such a marvelous optimism serve to encourage their faithful pneumatic witness all the more[67] — knowing that the conversion of the nations and their kings might possibly include even greater numbers than they are able to see or have heard in the words of this prophecy, and therefore that they cannot begin to calculate its importance? If so, the significance of encountering here the two positive references to the kings of the earth in Revelation, which might override the earlier negative references, would not be lost on the hearers.[68]

"And its gates are never closed by day, for night is not there, and they will bring the glory and honor of the nations into it." The twelve gates provide perfect and immediate access, for unlike the city gates of the ancient world, these gates never close during the night; the angelic sentries and God himself ensure its security. These gates provide around-the-clock access to the holy city

---

63. Aune, *Revelation 17–22*, 1171.
64. Caird, *The Revelation of Saint John*, 279.
65. Beasley-Murray, *Revelation*, 328; Sweet, *Revelation*, 308; and Bauckham, *The Climax of Prophecy*, 315.
66. Pattemore, *The People of God in the Apocalypse*, 202.
67. As R. Herms [*An Apocalypse for the Church and the World: The Narrative Function of Universal Language in the Book of Revelation* (BZNW 143; Berlin: Walter de Gruyter, 2006), 260] notes, "... universal language does not necessarily presuppose universal salvation; rather, it serves to vindicate the faithful community, and validate their present circumstances in light of a future reversal."
68. Herms, *An Apocalypse for the Church and the World*, 211.

(Isa 60:11),[69] for there is no night there! The radiance of the glory of God means that darkness is never manifested in the holy city. Whenever the words "day" and "night" occur in close proximity in Revelation (4:8; 7:15; 12:10; 14:11; 20:10), with one exception (8:12), the meaning conveys the idea of around-the-clock activity or access. In Johannine thought both night (John 3:2; 9:4; 11:10; 13:30; 19:39) and darkness (1:5; 6:17; 8:12; 12:35, 46; 1 John 1:5; 2:8-9, 11) often have ominous spiritual connotations. There is no place in the holy city for the unbelief and doubt of night and/or darkness — for all is light in it.[70] The kings of the earth thus will have ample opportunity to bring into it the glory and honor of the nations. The combination of the words "glory" and "honor" bring to mind that particular combination in 4:9, 11 and 5:12-13, where they describe the worship given to the one who sits on the throne and to the Lamb,[71] indicating that the kings and nations offer genuine worship to God as they enter into the holy city. Perhaps we have here a contrast between the earthly kings who brought their glory into the Babylon of old[72] and the kings of the earth who bring in their glory in accord with the eschatological hopes found in various places in the OT (Isa 45:20, 22, 24; Zech 2:11; 8:23; Dan 7:14). Such a contrast would further reinforce the dialectical relationship confronting the hearers between the conversion of the nations and the judgment of those who fail to repent,[73] who appear to be punished in the lake of burning sulfur (20:15).

"And every impure thing and the one who engages in abominations and falsehood will never enter into it, except those who have been written in the Lamb's book of life." While the previous verses have made clear that the nations and the kings of the earth will be present in the holy city, they do not make explicit at what point these entities convert, nor do they explain how these opponents of God, who apparently are punished by God in the lake of burning sulfur, are transformed into those worthy to gain admission to the holy city. Without resolving such tensions, the words of 21:27 reveal that, however such a transformation comes about, those who enter the holy city, including the nations and the kings of the earth, will not enter it as impure entities or as those who are characterized by abominations, like the great whore (17:4-5; 21:8), or falsehood, like the beast (21:8). Rather, they must of necessity have their names written in the Lamb's book of life (3:5; 13:8; 17:8; 20:12, 15),[74] an indication that they too have experienced the salvation offered by the Lamb who had been

---

69. Beasley-Murray, *Revelation*, 329.
70. Smalley, *Revelation*, 560.
71. Smalley, *Revelation*, 558.
72. Sweet, *Revelation*, 310.
73. Aune, *Revelation 17–22*, 1173.
74. Michaels, *Revelation*, 246.

slaughtered (5:6) and whose blood has loosed them from their sin (1:5; 5:9), and they too have rejected the beast and joined in offering faithful witness to the Lamb.

"And he showed me a river of living water clear as crystal, coming out of the throne of God and of the Lamb in the middle of the street." A number of ideas likely converge in this image: the original river that came out of the Garden of Eden feeding four fountainheads (Gen 2:10), the river Ezekiel describes that brings life to all things it encounters (Ezek 47:1-12), the rivers of living water of which Jesus speaks in John's gospel (John 7:38), and the most recent reference in Rev 21:6. In 22:1 the image of this river of living water, which is clear as crystal (cf. Rev 4:6; 21:11), is central, underscoring its immediate and ready access to all those who inhabit New Jerusalem. The pneumatological promises known from John's gospel find their ultimate fulfillment and consummation in the holy city. The divine origin of this river of living water is made clear in that it flows from the very throne of God and the Lamb, an unrivaled image of the presence of God in New Jerusalem. This river is God's river; it is the Lamb's river. It is their salvific gift to all those who believe in and offer faithful witness to them; it is a complete gift that provides abundantly for all soteriological needs. Significantly, there is but one throne, not two, shared by God and the Lamb[75] in accordance with the words of the resurrected Jesus to the church in Laodicea (3:21),[76] underscoring yet again the extraordinarily intimate nature of the relationship of God and the Lamb and the theme of the unbelievably immediate and direct access that God's "son" (or "daughter") has to his presence and that of the Lamb in the holy city. Mention of the Lamb would remind the hearers once more of his own faithful witness offered unto God, which is the basis of the redemption of all those who believe in him. The river flows prominently down the city's street,[77] which suggests that all who inhabit the holy city surround and have access to this soteriological provision.

"And on either side of the river a tree of life bearing twelve fruits, each month giving its fruit, and the leaves of the tree for healing of the nations." The potency of the river of living water is underscored in that it is surrounded on both sides by plantings of the tree of life.[78] Mention of the tree of life would remind hearers of the tree found in the Garden of Eden, the fruit of which was prohibited for human consumption after Adam and Eve ate the fruit of the tree of the knowledge of good and evil, lest they take the fruit of the tree of life and

---

75. Murphy, *Fallen Is Babylon*, 428.
76. Ladd, *Revelation*, 286.
77. Smalley, *Revelation*, 562.
78. Gause, *Revelation*, 276. The Greek expression translated "tree of life" is a collective, standing for this whole genus of trees.

live forever; cherubim and a flaming sword were placed at the entrance of the Garden to protect this tree of life (Gen 3:22-24). But in the very first prophetic message the resurrected Jesus promises to the one who overcomes to eat of the tree of life in the paradise of God (2:7)![79] The anticipation created by this initial eschatological promise of life, given by the resurrected living one (!), is finally fulfilled. The presence of this tree signals the reversal of the curse brought on by the disobedience of Adam and Eve, again making clear the immediate and direct access the overcomers have to God, for this tree is a sign that the previous separation and enmity between God and humankind is now completely removed.[80] This holy city thus bears the characteristics of a garden. The inexhaustible supply of eternal life in this New Jerusalem is exhibited in that the tree of life brings forth a staggering amount of fruit, far exceeding even that described in Ezekiel's vision (Ezek 47:12),[81] producing the perfect amount of eternal sustenance — generating twelve crops, with these twelve crops of fruit given every month — that is, twelve times a year! This supply of eternal life is more than enough and never ending; "the leaves of the tree are for the healing of the nations." It would be clear that the leaves of this tree of life, a tree that stands on both sides of the river of life, are closely associated with eternal life and, consequently, are signs of its bestowal. These words stand with the other statements in the description of New Jerusalem that underscore a view of a wideness in God's mercy that includes the conversion of the nations (21:3, 12-13, 24-26).[82] In John's gospel there is a deep connection between signs of healing and salvation, that is, belief in Jesus. Each physical healing there described is directly connected to the experience of eternal life based in the atoning life and death of Jesus (John 4:46-54; 5:1-18; 9:1-41; 11:1-57).[83] The healing of the nations thus includes healing in its most holistic and comprehensive fashion, encompassing both physical and spiritual healing, for both are part of the salvific work of Jesus.[84] This comprehensive understanding of the healing of the nations indicates that provision for the conversion of the nations is part of the very fabric of the New Jerusalem. Perhaps this healing would even include the healing of the wounds of the nations incurred in their rebellion against God and the Lamb.[85]

"And there is no curse any longer. And the throne of God and the Lamb is there, and his servants serve (worship) him, and they will see his face, and

79. Kiddle, *The Revelation of St. John*, 441-42.
80. Mayo, "*Those Who Call Themselves Jews,*" 196.
81. Aune, *Revelation 17-22*, 1178.
82. Mathewson, "The Destiny of the Nations in Revelation 21:1–22:5," 139
83. Cf. Thomas, *Spirit of the New Testament*, 175-89.
84. Resseguie, *The Revelation of John*, 258.
85. Sweet, *Revelation*, 311.

his name will be upon their foreheads." The first words in 22:3, "and there is no curse any longer," would likely have at least a double meaning. It is very difficult to imagine that the lifting of the restriction on the fruit of the tree of life and its immediate availability in the New Jerusalem could be seen as anything other than the removal of the curse incurred by humanity via the disobedience of Adam and Eve.[86] The recent emphasis upon the healing of the nations would likely suggest that reference to the absence of a curse in 22:3 would convey the sense that the nations are also in mind, specifically, that the ban of destruction placed upon the enemies of God has now been lifted (Zech 14:11).[87]

The throne is again identified, as in 22:1, as that of God and the Lamb. Remarkably, in what follows singular pronouns are used to describe God and the Lamb.[88] "His" servants worship "him"; they shall see "his" face; "his" name is written upon their foreheads! This theological reality breaks apart the Greek grammar! Each of these statements reveals that the relationship of God and the Lamb with his people is unprecedented, reaching an unrivaled climax. As his servants who "minister" to him, his people fulfill their priestly function in the very presence of God, a function anticipated at various points throughout the book (1:6; 3:12; 5:10; 7:15; 20:6). In contrast to those who seek to hide or flee from his face (6:16; 20:11), such ones as these "will see his face." While indicating the idea of admission into the immediate presence of God,[89] the hearers would well know that no human can see God's face and live (Exod 33:20; John 1:18; 6:46; 1 John 4:12)! And yet the longing to see his face continued to be expressed among his people (Pss 11:7; 17:15; 42:2),[90] showing up in modified form in the Johannine tradition (1 John 3:2). To see the face of God is to be in perfect and complete harmony with God. It is the beatific vision. It is transformative in that the one who sees his face is made unto his likeness (1 John 3:2). Those who see his face experience in an even greater way the extraordinarily holy and transformative power of his presence. Absolutely nothing stands in the way of such incredible intimacy that awaits in New Jerusalem.[91] Such communion is the end for which humanity is created, for which it is intended, for which it longs! Such ones as these are those who bear the name of God and the Lamb upon their forehead — who belong wholly to him (3:12). They are those who have been sealed by him (7:3; 9:4; 14:1). They bear his name, for they bear his nature.[92]

---

86. Murphy, *Fallen Is Babylon*, 429.
87. Mathewson, "The Destiny of the Nations in Revelation 21:1–22:5," 139-41.
88. Sweet, *Revelation*, 312.
89. Metzger, *Breaking the Code*, 103.
90. Michaels, *Revelation*, 248.
91. Resseguie, *The Revelation of John*, 258.
92. Caird, *The Revelation of Saint John*, 280-81.

Just like the high priest, they bear the name of God upon their foreheads; these servants who serve before his throne actually see his face!⁹³ Perhaps the hearers may be forgiven if they have nearly forgotten the mark, name, and number that the beast seeks to place upon them, for what he has to offer can in no way compare to that which awaits in New Jerusalem.

"And night is not there, and they have no need for a light of a lamp and a light of the sun, because the Lord God shines upon them and they will reign for ever and ever." These words sum up all that has preceded from 21:9 to this point, bringing to mind the fundamental characteristics of the holy city. The words "night is not there" bring to mind 21:25, where there is no spiritual night or darkness of unbelief (in the Johannine sense), nor is access to the holy city ever closed off. All evil is absent; access to the holy city is always available. Such words reveal that the incomparable glory of God makes the need for other forms of illumination unnecessary, reminding hearers that such divine illumination is salvific, making it possible for the nations to walk in it, as well as for the kings of the earth to bring their glories into the holy city. Finally, New Jerusalem is characterized by the fact that, along with God and the Lamb, its inhabitants will reign forever and ever! Such a statement would remind readers of the eternal reign described earlier in Revelation (5:10; 11:15, 17), underscoring the relationship between God's people and the God who lives forever and ever (4:9-10; 7:12; 10:6; 15:7). Just as the thousand-year reign dwarfed the forty-two-month reign of the beast (13:5) and the one-hour reign of the ten kings (17:12), so now the prospect of a reign that lasts forever more than dwarfs even the unbelievably long thousand-year reign! This reign is eternal and perfect, in complete continuity with the other characteristics of the unmediated presence of God and the Lamb and the believers' identification with them in New Jerusalem. Not only are they in his presence, they share his reign; dare one say, they sit on his throne, which he shares with the Lamb.

---

93. Koester, *Revelation and the End of All Things*, 200.

Epilogue (22:6-21)

The words of 22:6-9 function both as the conclusion of the fourth major section and as the introduction of the book's epilogue. "And he said, 'These words are faithful and true, and the Lord, the God of the S/spirits of the prophets, sent his angel to show his servants that which is necessary to take place quickly.'" The phrase "these words are faithful and true" earlier occurred near the end of the third major section of Revelation (21:5), devoted to the fall of Babylon the great whore and the emergence of New Jerusalem coming down from heaven. In 22:6 this phrase stands near the conclusion of the fourth major section of the book, affirming the trustworthy nature of the vision about New Jerusalem (21:9–22:5), as well as the contents of the book itself. Encountering this phrase at two such strategic locations serves to compare and contrast the two women/cities to which these two major sections have been devoted. In 21:5 these words were spoken by the one who sits on the throne, yet here, the Lord God is spoken of in the third person, suggesting that the speaker on this occasion is the Lamb. The identification of the Lord as the God of the S/spirits of the prophets might be taken as referring to individual human spirits of the individual prophets in the community, that is, the psychic power of the prophets.[1] Discerning Johannine hearers, however, would well know the ways in which the community is called upon to test the spirits that inspire the prophetic activity within the community (1 John 4:1-2) to determine whether the prophetic activity is inspired by the Spirit of Truth or is inspired by the spirit of deception (1 John 4:6).[2] By this point the hearers of Revelation have come to understand the tight connection between the seven Spirits of God (Rev 1:4; 4:5; 5:6) and the prophetic activity of the Spirit-anointed community in the world. It would thus seem likely that this phrase underscores both the origin of the inspiration of the community of prophets and the close connection of such inspiration to the one who sits on the throne, before whom the seven Spirits appear (1:4; 4:5), and the Lamb, who has seven eyes, which are the seven Spirits of God sent out into all the earth (5:6). The mention of the mission of God's angel in 22:6 would recall his initial mention (1:1) and the ways he has "shown" his servant John (and God's other servants) that which is necessary to take place soon. By this point, the hearers realize the many ways in which they have been called upon to engage in pneumatic discernment, an activity dependent upon the prophetic activity of the Spirit in their midst. As they draw near the end of the book, the hearers

---

1. Aune, *Revelation 17–22*, 1182.
2. On the whole matter of the source of prophetic activity, cf. Thomas, *1 John, 2 John, 3 John*, 197-214.

Epilogue (22:6-21)

are reminded yet again of the nearness to them of the things described — "it is necessary for them to take place quickly!" Perhaps they would now realize that they are already experiencing some of the things that must take place quickly in the course of their daily activity, for they are connected to eschatological events and activity.

"And behold I am coming quickly. Blessed is the one who keeps the words of the prophecy of this book." There is no mistaking the speaker's identity in 22:7, as the words "Behold I am coming quickly" could hardly come from anyone but Jesus! The connection between the things that must take place "quickly" and Jesus' description of his return as taking place "quickly" indicates that, among the things that must soon take place, is his own coming. These words occur twice before in Revelation, to describe Jesus' coming to the church in Pergamum to make war with the sword of his mouth (2:16) and as a warning to the church in Philadelphia not to allow anyone to take their crown (3:11). In this third occurrence, their previous meanings would likely converge, tying present and future together, indicating that this Jesus who comes quickly can come in judgment at any moment and will surely come quickly at the consummation as well. Just as the hearers already experience in their daily activities eschatological realities in the things that must take place quickly, so they experience the coming of Jesus here and now in their community worship and activities, a coming that is tied to the eschatological reality of his return in the consummation. A sixth beatitude next occurs, which, with the very first one (1:3), frames the contents of the book.[3] The command to keep is supported here by reference to "the words of the prophecy of this book," underscoring all the more the authority and significance of the book's contents. Primarily, such obedience would be understood as maintaining one's faithful witness to God and the Lamb through a Spirit-empowered prophetic life that offers one's witness to a hostile world, with a view toward the conversion of the nations. Such obedience entails pneumatic discernment in one's daily activities so that such a witness might not be compromised owing to the seductions of the beast, the false prophet, and/or the great whore. Keeping the words of this prophecy is a call to pneumatic discernment, whether such seductions are encountered in the church or in the world; a call to offer the same faithful witness as did the slaughtered Lamb; a call to follow the Lamb wherever he goes; a call to engage in the eschatological harvest of the conversion of the nations. This is a call to active participation in the pneumatically empowered witness of the church.

"Even I, John, am the one who hears and sees these things. And when I heard and I saw, I fell to worship before the feet of the angel who is showing

---

3. Murphy, *Fallen Is Babylon*, 436.

these things to me." For the first time since 1:9, John's name appears,[4] perhaps an indication that the end of the book is near, with John's name framing the entire work. John's words about that which he hears and sees reveal the content of his witness to those things shown to him by the angel, a witness to which he refers at the book's opening as well (1:2). The cumulative effect of this revelation upon John, as he confesses, was to cause him to fall before the feet of the angel who shows all these things to him. On two previous occasions John has been tempted or attempts to worship someone other than God; when John marvels a great marvel upon seeing the great whore (17:6-7), a marveling akin to that which leads to the beast's worship by the whole world (13:3-4), and when John falls to the feet and attempts to worship his fellow servant and brother who speaks divinely authorized words (19:10). Regarding the latter, it appears that John's temptation to worship him is based upon his identity as one of the souls slaughtered for his faithful witness, who is heir to the numerous promises made to the one who overcomes, including reception of a new name that no one knows (2:17), authority to rule over the nations with an iron scepter and the morning star (2:26-28), and authority to sit on Jesus' throne with him (3:21). But John finds that even this redeemed one is not to be worshipped; God alone is deserving of such. Significantly, this event takes place just after a divine affirmation that the words of this prophecy are the true words of God (19:9), just as John's falling before the angel in 22:8 follows similar words of Jesus in 22:6. John's action of falling at the feet of the angel extends the theme of legitimate worship further, for surely the one who is showing him all these things is worthy of veneration, sent by God for this specific revelatory purpose and indeed even speaking for God![5]

"And he says to me, 'See that you do not do it! I am the fellow servant of you and your brothers the prophets and of those who keep the words of this book. Worship God!'" The angel in 22:9 forbids John's attempt at worship, using the same words as his counterpart in 19:10: "See that you do not do it," underscoring that he, like John and his brothers, is on the creaturely divide between Creator and creation. Here the angel underscores his solidarity with John and his brothers the prophets, as well as those who keep the words of this book. The description of John's brothers the prophets emphasizes the relationship this angel shares with John and his brothers the prophets in the revelatory experience of Revelation. At the least, these words suggest an active role for them in the pneumatic discernment to which they are called, continuing to drive home the point that this is a prophetic community, perhaps even one that includes

4. Michaels, *Revelation*, 250.
5. Beasley-Murray, *Revelation*, 336.

an understanding of the prophethood of all believers. The message of the fellow servant continues, identical to that of his counterpart in 19:10, "Worship God!" These words reinforce the overriding message of the book as a whole. Only God (and the Lamb) is worthy of worship. Any other form of worship is idolatrous, whether that worship be offered to the beast, the great whore, one who overcomes via faithful witness, or a revelatory angel of Revelation itself![6] Perhaps it becomes apparent that the words of 22:6-9 function as a conclusion to the previous section, devoted to the bride of Christ, just as those of 19:9-10 function as a conclusion to the section devoted to the great whore.[7] These verses also form a transition to the epilogue of the book proper.[8]

"And he says to me, 'Do not seal up the words of the prophecy of this book, for the time is near.'" Next we hear either the voice of the resurrected Jesus or his words through the revelatory angel. Unlike the command that Daniel and John seal up portions of their revelations (Dan 12:4;[9] Rev. 10:4),[10] here in 22:10 John is clearly directed *not* to seal up the words of the prophecy of this book. This instruction stands in continuity with the commands he earlier receives to write what he sees and hears (1:11, 19). The reason for such urgency is revealed in the words "for the time is near," a phrase that takes the hearers back to the book's opening, when near-identical wording occurs with regard to those who read, hear, and keep the words written in this book (1:3).[11] The words of the prophecy of this book are thus enfolded by words underscoring their urgency in the light of their eschatological context.

"The one who does evil, let that one do evil still; and the filthy, let that one be filthy still; and the righteous, let that one do righteousness still; and the holy one, let that one be holy still." The proverbial form of this verse has the authority of the resurrected Jesus. Nearly all its words have been encountered elsewhere in the book. Four kinds of individuals and activities are identified, two negative examples followed by two positive. The first term, "do evil" or "harm," is normally used of divine commands and activity or that of God's agents in Revelation (6:6; 7:2-3; 9:4, 10, 19) or his protection against such (2:11). Here, the meaning of this phrase would likely be shaped by 11:5, where the term occurs twice to describe those who seek to harm or do evil to the two prophetic

---

6. Bauckham, *The Climax of Prophecy*, 136.

7. Bauckham, *The Climax of Prophecy*, 133.

8. Cf. B. W. Longenecker, "'Linked like a Chain': Rev 22:6-9 in Light of Ancient Translation Technique," *NTS* 47.1 (2001): 105-17, who argues that this passage is a carefully linked transition similar to those found in 3:21-22; 8:1-5; 15:1-4.

9. Schüssler Fiorenza, *Revelation: Vision of a Just World*, 115.

10. Smalley, *Revelation*, 570.

11. Michaels, *Revelation*, 251.

witnesses. The first part of this verse thus focuses on those who seek to oppose God and his people by seeking to do them harm. The term to describe the second category of individuals in 22:11, "filthy," would perhaps bring to mind the contrast between the one whose filthy garments are taken away, being replaced by clean ones in Zech 3:3-7, and those described here. Such language would also no doubt bring to mind the admonitions in Revelation to keep one's garments clean and dress appropriately, avoiding nakedness (Rev 3:4; 16:15). Those who are filthy clearly stand alongside those who seek to persecute the people of God as displeasing to him. There is a clear contrast between these first two groups and those that are next described, for in Revelation the language of righteous and righteousness is closely associated with God and the Lamb (15:3; 16:5, 7; 19:2, 11), indicating that the righteous here described bear a characteristic resemblance to God and the Lamb and as such belong to him. If such connections are true of the righteous, they are even more so with regard to the language of "holy" or "saint" that describes the last group, language intimately connected to God, the Lamb, and his people throughout the book. Thus, the proverb's content is clear — but what of its meaning? Given the eschatological context and the repeated invitation in the book to repent, even for those who do evil (11:3-13), these words would perhaps be understood as conveying the ominous message that the end of all things is indeed near. While it is possible that the words of this prophecy will not be kept by those who hear them, they will be ignored at one's own peril. The stark reality is that one's response to the words of this prophecy is revealed by the life of the one who hears them,[12] a response that will be clear to all.

"Behold, I come quickly, and my reward is with me to give to each according to his/her work." This is the second time in the book's conclusion (cf. 22:7) that the phrase "Behold, I come quickly" occurs, language that clearly underscores the importance of keeping the words of this prophecy. This has been the clarion message heard from the beginning of the book. The second occurrence of this phrase within a span of six verses would reiterate the nearness to the end: if Jesus comes quickly, the time is indeed near! As before, these words would tie present and future together, reminding the hearers that this Jesus, who comes quickly, can come in judgment at any moment. On this occasion, Jesus' words are accompanied by words of judgment: "And my reward is with me to give to each according to his/her work." Works have been part of the theological landscape throughout. Not only does Jesus know the works of the churches he addresses in the seven prophetic messages (2:2, 19; 3:1, 8, 15), but works also form the basis of divine judgment both now (2:23) and at the final judgment

---

12. Prigent, *L'Apocalypse de Saint Jean*, 492.

(20:12-13). The ominous nature of these words is heightened in that emphasis is placed upon the specificity of the reward that is given to each one according to one's individual works, thus reinforcing the dualistic warning of 22:11.[13]

"I Am the Alpha and the Omega, the First and the Last, the Beginning and the End." Jesus' identity is conveyed by means of three titles that appear together only here in the whole of Revelation.[14] Each of these titles is formed by a combination of two antithetical terms, revealing that the person who bears them encompasses both extremes.[15] Two of these titles have been used exclusively for God to this point. God's self-designation as "the Alpha and the Omega" and "the Beginning and the End" (1:8; 21:6) conveys the claim that all of creation, the first heaven and first earth, as well as the new heaven and new earth, stands within God's purview and is enveloped by his presence and power! These two identifications convey the idea that God is the beginning and the ending of everything, the all in all. Nothing exists outside of him. Astonishingly, however, these titles are now claimed by Jesus, underscoring the intimate relationship between God and Jesus. Significantly, the other title, "the First and the Last," which has been used exclusively for Jesus in Revelation (1:17; 2:8), stands between the titles earlier used by God as a self-identification. "The First and the Last" might also remind hearers of Isa 44:6, where God's claim to exclusivity as the only God is made clear, a claim that is now shared by Jesus. Not only does Jesus share these titles with God, but he also shares God's throne as well! Perhaps this extraordinary combination of titles would also make it clear that the end is not so much an event as a person,[16] and that this person has authority to come with his reward with him.

"Blessed are those who wash their robes, in order that they might have their authority to the tree of life, and through the gates they might enter into the city." This is the seventh (and final) beatitude encountered in the book. As with the beatitudes found in 14:13 and 19:9, the plural form "blessed" appears here.[17] This pronouncement of blessing by the resurrected Jesus continues the theme of warning that characterizes the epilogue. This blessing is pronounced upon those who wash their robes, which would call attention to the way in which clothing has functioned in the book (7:14; 16:15). In 7:14 we have the aorist past tense verb "have washed," indicating that they have washed their robes in the blood of the Lamb at a particular point in the past, while in 22:14 we have a present participle, "those who wash," indicating that these are the ones who

---

13. Michaels, *Revelation*, 253.
14. Smalley, *Revelation*, 573.
15. Aune, *Revelation 17–22*, 1219.
16. Sweet, *Revelation*, 316.
17. Aune, *Revelation 17–22*, 1219.

continually wash their robes.[18] Only those who are vigilant about their lives of purity and continue to wash their robes in the blood of the Lamb will be heirs to the promises of this beatitude. The idea of such ongoing cleansing is consistent with Johannine thought (cf. esp. 1 John 1:5–2:2; 3:4-10, 19-24; 5:14-17), perhaps reminding hearers of one of the community practices that embodies this very phenomenon: the rendering and receiving of footwashing.[19] Such active participation would be seen as the saving and purifying effect of the blood of the Lamb.[20] Those upon whom this beatitude is pronounced are promised access to the tree of life and to the (holy) city itself. The hearers would be well aware of these eschatological rewards, having encountered both items in the previous description of New Jerusalem (21:9–22:5). Perhaps they would also remember that the promise to eat of the tree of life was the first given to the one who overcomes in the very first prophetic message to the church in Ephesus (2:7). Both images convey the promise of eternal life in the holy city, in the former, recalling the abundance of the fruit of the tree of life, and, in the latter, the richness and beauty of the bride of Christ, in contrast to that feigned by the great whore. It almost goes without saying that admission into and enjoyment of the holy city is contingent upon the continual washing of one's robes, the purifying of one's life, in the blood of the Lamb.

"Outside are the dogs and the magicians and the sexually immoral and the murderers and the idolaters and everyone who loves and makes a lie." This warning would remind readers of a similar one in 21:8, where many of the same terms occur. The list encountered in 22:15 is a specific warning regarding the consequences of not keeping the words of the prophecy of this book. Most, if not all, of the terms in this list have special meaning derived from Revelation. Those who are "outside" are those excluded from access to the city, not those in close proximity to it.[21] The meaning of οἱ κύνες (*hoi kynes*, "the dogs") is not altogether clear, as it appears only here in Revelation. The reputation of dogs as the scavengers of the ancient world, who come to represent the extremes of base behavior[22] and consequently would be unclean and deemed unfit to gain admission to the holy city,[23] is easy enough to surmise. In addition, dogs func-

---

18. Smalley, *Revelation*, 573, and Resseguie, *The Revelation of John*, 259.
19. For this suggestion, cf. Mounce, *The Book of Revelation*, 393. For the sacramental significance of footwashing in the Johannine community, cf. Thomas, *Footwashing in John 13 and the Johannine Community*.
20. Metzger, *Breaking the Code*, 105.
21. Metzger, *Breaking the Code*, 105.
22. S. Pederson, "Κύων, κυνός," *EDNT*, 2:332.
23. M. Philonenko, "'Dehors les Chiens' (Apocalypse 22:16 et 4QMMT B 58-62)," *NTS* 43.3 (1997): 445-50. Citing a text from Qumran, where dogs are prohibited from the camp owing

tion in the Psalter (22:16, 20) as malicious people who oppose and persecute God's anointed.[24] In the Torah the word "dog" is a metaphor for a male prostitute, whose person and money are deemed unclean and therefore cannot be brought into "the house of the LORD your God" (Deut 23:18).[25] The occurrence of "abominations" in this same passage in the Torah suggests that the word "dog" might be a synonym for one who commits abominations, paralleled in the list of Rev 21:8 and the reference in 21:27.[26] Listed next are the magicians, in noun form unlike the participial form in 21:8. Earlier references to such activity (9:21; 18:23; 21:8) suggest that those who have been enchanted by the great whore's magic share in this activity and will suffer a similar fate to hers. Joining these first two categories are the sexually immoral, a familiar word family in Revelation, very closely identified with the activity of the great whore (17:1-2, 4-5) whose idolatrous charms result in the sexual immorality of the kings of the earth (18:3, 9), a temptation with which even the church must contend (Rev 2:14, 20).[27] For this activity the great whore is judged (17:16; 19:2), as are all those who are sexually immoral owing to their economic and idolatrous relationship with her. In Revelation, murders appear on a list of activities of "the works of their hands," for which the rest of men refuse to repent (9:21).[28] Though a different word is used to describe their murderous activities, they are reminiscent of Jesus' words that Satan is a murderer from the beginning (John 8:44) and would remind hearers that in Revelation refusal to worship the beast results in death for such offenders (13:15). This category might thus suggest that those who identify with the beast are complicit in his murderous activity of those whose names are written in the Lamb's book of life.[29] Closely associated with the previous categories are the idolaters. In Revelation such activity is closely associated with sexual immorality and eating meat sacrificed to idols (2:14, 20), activities that imply corruption by participation in the economic system, which is in collusion with the beast and the great whore. Ultimately, those who worship the beast and/or join in the idolatrous activity of the great whore, even those who worship the servants of God, commit idolatry. Only God is to be glorified — all who engage in idolatrous activity betray him and forsake true

---

to the danger they pose to eating the bones from the sanctuary, Philonenko argues that dogs in Rev 22:15 is given a spiritual interpretation on the order of the spiritual interpretation given to the New Jerusalem.

24. Ladd, *Revelation*, 293.
25. Aune, *Revelation 17-22*, 1222.
26. Smalley, *Revelation*, 575.
27. Pattemore, *The People of God in the Apocalypse*, 211.
28. Ladd, *Revelation*, 279.
29. Mounce, *The Book of Revelation*, 375.

worship. The end of the list — "everyone who loves and does a lie" — would remind hearers that, when the devil lies, he speaks his native tongue (John 8:44), that the one who lies is diametrically opposed to the truth (1 John 2:21, 27), that there are those who claim to be apostles or Jews but are not for they lie (Rev 2:2; 3:9), and that all liars will have their part in the lake of burning sulfur (21:8). Perhaps this category includes those who have believed the lie of the beast and the great whore and by their participation with them have perpetuated that lie.[30] The contrast is stark between those who lie and the followers of the Lamb, in whose mouths no lie is found (14:5). All such ones as these (the dogs, the magicians, the sexually immoral, the murderers, the idolaters, and each one who loves and does a lie) are "outside," excluded from access to the holy city.

"I, Jesus, sent my angel to witness to you these things to the churches. I Am the Root and Offspring of David, the Bright Morning Star." For the first and only time in Revelation, Jesus refers to himself by name.[31] Jesus makes clear that he, along with God (1:1-2), has a role in the sending of the angel, now referred to as "my angel." Just as John and those in the community have done, so now the angel of Jesus is said to have witnessed the things found in this book to "you." Such shared witness underscores that this angel is truly a fellow servant with John and his brothers the prophets in offering witness to Jesus. "You" here is plural, referring either to John and his brothers the prophets in the community[32] or to the angels of the churches to which the seven prophetic messages are directed.[33] In either case attention is drawn to the chain of revelation by which this revelation of Jesus Christ comes: from Jesus to his angel to his servants (either prophetic or angelic or both) to the churches, a chain of revelation reminiscent of that found at the book's beginning (1:1-2). Such an inclusio would again indicate that the book's conclusion is approaching. Jesus' self-references are preceded by the theologically significant "I Am," underscoring further Jesus' shared identity with God, as well as his own divine authority. The title "the Root and Offspring of David" would remind readers that the resurrected Jesus holds the key of David (3:7) and is identified by John as the Lion of the Tribe of Judah, the Root of David (5:5). Here, the combination of "the root" and "the offspring" or "the shoot" of David would underscore that Jesus is indeed the Alpha and Omega, the First and the Last, the Beginning and the End, for he is both the origin of Davidic kingship and its culmination. The second title, "the Bright Morning Star," would also be familiar, for the morning star is promised

---

30. Beasley-Murray, *Revelation*, 314.
31. Michaels, *Revelation*, 255.
32. G. Biguzzi, "The Chaos of Rev 22,6-21 and Prophecy in Asia," *Biblica* 83.2 (2002): 197.
33. Smalley, *Revelation*, 575-76.

to the one who overcomes in 2:28. In this title might be reference to yet another messianic title via Num 24:17, which speaks of a star that will come forth from Jacob.[34] In the context of Rev 22:16, the messianic character of this title, underscoring all the more the importance of the Jewish heritage for both Jesus and the church, would be hard to miss. He is the origin and culmination of Davidic kingship and the star that comes from the patriarch Jacob, the fulfillment of all the messianic promises and longings; as the Johannine hearers know, he is even greater than "our father Jacob" (John 4:12).

"And the Spirit and the Bride say, 'Come.' And the one who hears, let that one say, 'Come.' And the one who is thirsty, let that one come, the one who desires to receive living water without cost." There is no compelling reason to suggest that the identity of the speaker changes in 22:12-20; that is, we can well take these as the words of the resurrected Jesus.[35] The first invitation comes from the Spirit and the Bride, whose identities would hardly be mistaken. The strategic and indispensable role the Spirit plays in the pneumatic witness offered to the kings and nations of the earth is clear (1:4, 19-20; 2:7, 11, 17, 29; 3:6, 13, 22; 4:5; 5:6; 11:3-13; 17:3; 19:10; 21:10; 22:6).[36] This same Spirit now says "Come" to those who have ears to hear — and also to those who do not, for this Spirit speaks both to the churches and to those beyond them. Neither would the identity of the Bride be a mystery, for the Bride and the saints are identical (19:7-8).[37] Their prophetic, pneumatically empowered message is identical to the message that comes from the Spirit. For it is the Spirit that empowers their own faithful witness, which is offered to a hostile and unbelieving world. The Bride offers this invitation, for she knows that somehow her faithful witness is intimately connected to the conversion of the nations, a result that will exceed her wildest dreams. The words encountered in the second phrase, "The one who hears, let that one say, 'Come,'" contain a twofold invitation. In this verse the resurrected Jesus calls for pneumatic discernment and obedience to the words of this prophecy on the part of the one who has ears to hear. A positive response would manifest itself by the one who hears, joining in the proclamation of the Spirit and the Bride, which in turn would result in the issue of the invitation to the kings and nations of the earth to "come." The hearers might furthermore also discern in these first two invitations the longing of the Spirit, the Bride, and the one who hears for the soon coming of Jesus. Owing to the broader context, this secondary meaning of the invitation to "come" would likely be present in

---

34. Bauckham, *The Climax of Prophecy*, 323-25.
35. Michaels, *Revelation*, 256.
36. Smalley, *Revelation*, 578.
37. Smalley, *Revelation*, 578.

their thinking. In the verse's third phrase, the invitations of the Spirit and the Bride and the one who hears are joined by an invitation from the resurrected Jesus to the one who is thirsty to come, the one who desires to receive the water of life without cost, a call Johannine hearers would well recall from the call of Jesus in John's gospel (John 7:37-39). Not only are the previous invitations clarified by this one — the invitation to come and drink of the water of life — but it also would make clearer to the hearers the connection between the availability of this water of life in the present and in the holy city.[38] One's response to these invitations has eternal consequences.

"I witness to each who hears the words of the prophecy of this book; if anyone adds unto them, God will add unto him/her the plagues written in this book; and if anyone takes away from the words of the book of this prophecy, God will take away his/her part from the tree of life and out of the holy city, written in this book." The hearers are addressed directly by the resurrected Jesus.[39] In order to keep (i.e., obey) the words of the prophecy of this book, they must embrace it in its entirety, not giving in to the temptation of compromising it by adding to it or by diluting its message by deletion. Such a witness of warning reminds hearers of the stern admonition given to Moses and Israel with regard to obedience to God's Torah (Deut 12:32).[40] These words warn the prophets and others within the community who, owing to the words' uncompromising and unrelenting nature, might be tempted to soften or make them more palatable to the churches to which they are read.[41] Specifically, for those tempted to add to these words, God will add to the plagues contained herein. The warning of Deut 29,[42] the manifestations that accompany the opening of the seven seals or the trumpeting by the seven angels, and the seven plagues poured out upon the earth described in Rev 15–16, the last plagues of God, would here converge. In the failure to keep the words of the prophecy of this book, they will have sided with those who reject God, refusing to repent for the works of their hands, entering into the sexual immorality of idolatrous activity.[43] For those tempted to take away from these words, God will take away from them their share. To lose one's "part" or "share" means to loss one's relationship with Jesus by disobedience, as Peter learned in the account of the footwashing (John 13:8).[44] In Rev 22:19 this

---

38. Bauckham, *The Climax of Prophecy*, 168.
39. Michaels, *Revelation*, 257.
40. Michaels, *Revelation*, 258.
41. Beasley-Murray, *Revelation*, 346.
42. R. M. Royalty, Jr., "Don't Touch This Book! Revelation 22:18-19 and the Rhetoric of Reading (in) the Apocalypse of John," *Biblical Interpretation* 12.3 (2004): 282-99.
43. Sweet, *Revelation*, 319.
44. Thomas, *Footwashing in John 13 and the Johannine Community*, 92-95.

share is spoken of in terms very similar to those found in the seventh and final beatitude of 22:14, which mentions access to the tree of life and entrance into the holy city. Clearly, failure to keep the prophecy in its entirety disqualifies one from the eternal life that awaits in New Jerusalem. Four times, within the span of two verses, reference is made to what is written in this book. There can be no mistaking: one's response to the words of the prophecy of this book is of eternal consequence.

"The one who witnesses says these things, 'Yes, I am coming quickly.' 'Amen, come, Lord Jesus.'" On this occasion Jesus is identified as "the one who witnesses (or testifies to) these things." The one who bears witness here in 22:20 is the same one who bears witness of warning in 22:18. And for a third time in the epilogue, Jesus promises, "I am coming quickly."[45] On this occasion these words of promise are preceded by an emphatic "Yes" in the place of "Behold," which accompanies its first two occurrences (22:7, 12). This third occurrence of "I am coming quickly" in the span of fourteen verses could not fail to underscore and reinforce the conviction that the revelation of Jesus Christ that John and his hearers receive is informed by this extraordinary promise. This emphatic promise clearly picks up on the words of warning by the resurrected Jesus that he will come in judgment to those churches who do not hear (and keep) what the Spirit is saying to them in the seven prophetic messages and the words of the prophecy as a whole. These words also emphasize the way in which the consummation of this promise is the consummation of all the eschatological promises, of all prophetic words — for in a very real way, the return of Jesus is indeed the climax of prophecy, even of history itself! The convergence in this promise of the extraordinary images, texts, visions, sights, sounds, smells, touches, and tastes experienced in Revelation would perhaps be overwhelming for John and his hearers. Such an extraordinarily rich convergence of eschatological ideas generates John's own response, "Amen, come, Lord Jesus." The word "amen" initially occurs in the book as an affirmation of Jesus' redemptive work (1:6) and as a conclusion to the word of prophecy with which the book commences (1:7). Not only is the amen christologically conditioned in these verses, but "the Amen" is also a self-designation used by the resurrected Jesus in addressing the church in Laodicea (3:14). The term also occurs in contexts of worship as a final affirmation, especially on the lips of the twenty-four elders (5:14; 7:12; 19:4). The current context of worship in which the amen is offered is made clear by John's next voicing his own eschatological prayer for the Lord Jesus to come (quickly). This prayer indicates that John has heard and is keeping the words of this prophecy. John's prayer for Jesus to come quickly would be

---

45. Caird, *The Revelation of Saint John*, 288.

an invitation for the resurrected Jesus, who stands at the door and knocks, to come into the church (3:20) to fulfill his promises and warnings, and for Jesus to come quickly in all his eschatological power and glory — to make possible the unmediated spectacular intimacy that awaits in New Jerusalem. John's prayer, as his earlier falling at the feet of Jesus as though dead (1:17), would be an invitation for his hearers to join him in this final act of worship described within the words of the prophecy of this book! "Amen, come, Lord Jesus."

"May the grace of the Lord Jesus be upon all." Modern interpreters often see this conclusion as somewhat ill-fitting, for it is unusual for an epistle to end with a benediction.[46] However, the meaning of such unusual concluding words of blessing would extend the context of worship in which the hearers experience the book. Neither would the significance of the word "grace" be missed. The only other occurrence of the term in the entire book stands at its beginning and is also part of John's words (1:4), indicating that, despite the ominous contents of this book of prophecy, the entire book is enfolded by grace. Johannine hearers would no doubt remember that it is the Word made flesh who is full of grace and truth, and that it is "out of his fullness we have all received one grace after another" (John 1:14-16). The hearers might thus now appreciate the way in which this book's unfolding is indeed the revelation of one grace after another as Jesus Christ is more fully revealed than ever before, further underscoring the fact that this book is actually a means of grace! This extraordinary grace is pronounced upon all those in the community who heed its call to pneumatic discernment, which manifests itself in prophetic faithful witness to a hostile world, with the goal of the conversion of the nations — for indeed Jesus is coming quickly!

---

46. Mounce, *The Book of Revelation*, 396.

Theological Horizons of Revelation

God

Revelation and Biblical Theology

I. Howard Marshall notes, surprisingly, that "God is the character who is most often neglected in studies of New Testament theology."[1] This admission seems strange, given that God is by far the chief topic of theology, as the term itself implies.[2] The God-centered nature of theology is rooted in the biblical story. Biblical theology is mainly about God's identity, purposes, and works. God is the chief player in the drama of the biblical narrative, for "from him and through him and to him are all things," as Paul notes in Rom 11:36. Rev 1:8 puts it this way: God is the Lord "who was, who is, and who is to come." God is the chief subject matter of the entire biblical drama, of the drama of creation itself, from beginning to end. In fact, an argument can convincingly be made that, in the second third of the twentieth century, Karl Barth helped to inspire the rise of the biblical theology movement by turning the attention of a generation of theological students to the "strange new world within the Bible," which was chiefly about God's address to humanity, rather than the human religious or moral quest for God, as claimed earlier by liberal scholars.[3] The Bible is God centered and not human centered. What an irony that studies in the field of NT theology would now tend to neglect the topic of God!

---

1. I. Howard Marshall, *New Testament Theology: Many Witnesses, One Gospel* (Downers Grove, IL: InterVarsity Press, 2004), 121-22.
2. The term "theology" comes from the Greek terms θεός (*theos*, "God") and λόγος (*logos*, a reasoned discourse about or study of something). The term thus literally means "study of God."
3. See Brevard Childs, *Biblical Theology in Crisis* (Philadelphia: Westminster Press, 1970).

Revelation

The book of Revelation, however, clearly gives its attention to God as the chief player in the narrative of salvation history. The worship of God as the only Creator and Redeemer dominates the book. It begins with greetings from the triune God surrounding the throne of grace: "Grace and peace to you from him who is, and who was, and who is to come, and from the seven spirits before his throne, and from Jesus Christ, who is the faithful witness, the firstborn from the dead, and the ruler of the kings of the earth" (1:4-5). The triumph of the triune God in the battle for the loyalty of the nations is already prefigured in this greeting. The triune God is faithful to redeem, despite all the opposition that can be raised against divine love for creation.

In a way reminiscent of Isa 6, the heavenly host cries out, "Holy, holy, holy is the Lord God Almighty, who was and is and is to come." The elders also worship God, throwing their crowns before the throne and saying, "You are worthy, our Lord and God, to receive glory and honor and power, for you created all things, and by your will they were created and have their being" (Rev 4:11). Praise, honor, glory and power are lifted up to God and to the Lamb (5:13). Indeed, "salvation belongs to our God," according to the host of the redeemed (7:10), which is followed by a string of accolades: praise, glory, wisdom, thanks, honor, power, and strength (7:12). Praise and thanks are also offered to the Lord God Almighty for beginning to reign (11:17). God is especially praised for being just in judgment (16:5, 7; 19:2). God is indeed praised for "great and marvelous deeds" and for being just and true in them all. For God alone is holy, and all nations will come to praise before the throne (15:3-4). One could almost hear the heavenly host echo, "The whole earth is full of his glory" (Isa 6:3), or John say, "Here am I. Send me" (Isa 6:8). "Then I was told," he wrote, "You must prophesy again about many peoples, nations, languages, and kings" (Rev 10:11).

The throne of God also dominates the heavenly city, into which John was able to peer through spiritual discernment (4:9-10; 5:1, 7, 13; 6:16; 7:10, 15; 11:16; 19:4; 21:5). "God reigns" is more than an empty slogan in Revelation. God functions throughout Revelation as the principal actor who determines the outcome of the drama, for God is the First and the Last (Exod 3:14; Isa 44:6), the Alpha and the Omega, who remains consistently faithful over all of the changing and threatening moments of history. This is the God who was, who is, and who is to come (Rev 1:8), the same yesterday, today, and forever (cf. Heb 13:8), the eternal God. God was before all time, is faithful to the divine purposes throughout all times, and is coming to establish a kingdom that will remain forever (Rev 11:15). There are no times outside of God's purposes, since these purposes precede all times and will represent their *telos* long after time as we know it has ceased.

Reminiscent of the throne scene of Isa 6, Revelation proclaims the sovereignty of God over all of the affairs of history. Nothing occurs "behind God's back," so to speak, or outside the realm of God's redemptive purposes. The divine passives of Revelation, in which God is the implied agent, indicate that the divine hand is providentially the source of grace or judgment throughout all of the affairs of history, even those that seek to thwart God's redemptive purposes (Rev 6:4, 8; 7:2; 8:2; 9:1, 5; 13:7; 16:8). These redemptive purposes are fulfilled through God as the heavenly Father (1:6), the crucified and risen Lamb, Jesus Christ (1:5), and the Holy Spirit (1:4), who inspires the discernment and prophetic witness of the people of God. All three function to fulfill redemption, sharing in the authority and glory that belong to God alone, for there is no savior but God: "Salvation belongs to our God, who sits on the throne, and to the Lamb" (7:10). Such a text harkens back to Hos 13:4: "You shall acknowledge no God but me, no savior except me." Here we find the raw materials for the later Trinitarian confession of the church. The one God of Israel who rules over all, who redeems, and to whom all loyalty belongs is "one" in a way that involves a plurality of three agents. God's oneness is relationally complex.

At the base of God's sovereignty in Revelation is the OT affirmation of God alone as the creator and sustainer of life (4:11; 10:6). Only the Creator has a rightful claim over the creation. Only the Creator can redeem and create anew, sharing a taste of glory with the creation and receiving glory from it. The rainbow surrounding the divine throne (4:3) reminds us of God's covenant with all living things and with the earth after the flood. Echoes of God's commitment never again to allow a flood to destroy the earth are found in God's repeated restraint with regard to the extent to which the effect of the plagues is allowed to go. In the light of this sovereign God's exclusive claim to creation, the dragon's attempt to mimic divine authority, divine ability to grant life, and divine right to receive glory in chapter 13 is nothing short of an effort to usurp the place of the Creator. But God will vindicate God's own right as Creator by raising Jesus from the dead (ch. 1), defeating the dragon (ch. 12), and making all things new (ch. 21). The drama of creation found in the OT, in which God conquers the chaos to bring life (Gen 1:1-3), finds its fulfillment in Revelation in God's victory over the dark forces in order to make all things new. As Brevard Childs notes, the creation narrative of the OT is pictured as God's initial transformation of the opposing forces of chaos, establishing righteousness or justice as the foundation of God's continuing rule. This narrative thus assumes a unity of creation and redemption in God's ongoing reign over history. In Isaiah, for example, God is the First and the Last (Isa 46:10) as the Creator, whose purposes for the salvation of the creation result in the advent of new things previously unknown (42:9; 43:18-19; 46:13). The Priestly account of creation culminates in the covenant (Exod 31:16), with a linkage to the building of the tabernacle (24:15-18), which shows that the goal of creation is not only exodus and the victory over the opposition but God's dwelling with the faithful.[4] Such is the God of Revelation, who, as the First and the Last and the creator of all things, fulfills covenant promises by ruling, redeeming, making all things new, and dwelling with humanity (Rev 21:1-6). The God of Revelation is thus defined as the Creator, as the one who will deliver the covenant people from the world in a new exodus that involves plagues that are analogous to (and even greater than) those originally witnessed in Egypt. This God raised Israel from Egypt and now raises Jesus in victory over the opposition in order to renew all things and to dwell with humanity. The Father, the Lamb, and the Spirit are the one God who creates, saves, and renews.

The justice of God's judgments in Revelation assumes the divine claim on all of creation (4:11; 10:6). It also assumes the vindication of those who bear witness to God as alone the Lord of creation. Revelation does not take up the question as to why the righteous suffer except to locate the source in a cosmic rebellion against God, but it does assure the audience that God is involved in their suffering, hears their cries, and is acting to fulfill justice by remaining true to covenant promises. No explanation is given as to the time that it will take for the final victory to occur; rewards are promised only to those who patiently endure. The sovereign God is mysterious, but the divine will to redeem is clear. When those who deny God's grace persecute and kill prophetic witnesses, God vindicates their witness and even avenges them through acts of judgment (16:4-5). Such is also reminiscent of the OT, where God defeats the enemies of redemptive purposes in righteous judgments (Exod 15:6). As Childs notes, "The identity of Israel's God emerges in all of its mystery, holiness, and burning righteousness."[5] The entire book of Revelation is filled with doxologies of praise for the justice of God's judgments (1:6; 4:9-11; 5:12-13; 7:12; 11:13). The book urges the audience to see the falsehood of alien claims to lordship and to worship only God. The arch of justice bends from the beginning to the end of the book, and the sovereign Creator is praised for being its source, sustainer, and *telos*.

God's righteous judgments emerge from a holy God who cannot be seduced by evil but, rather, conquers it. The holiness of God is a major theme in the praises offered to God in Revelation. As noted above, one finds in Revelation echoes of the throne scene in Isa 6, in which the angelic host cries, "Holy, holy, holy is the Lord Almighty; the whole earth is full of his glory" (Isa 6:3). The

---

4. Brevard Childs, *Biblical Theology of the Old and New Testaments: Theological Reflection on the Christian Bible* (Minneapolis: Fortress Press, 1992), 387.
5. Childs, *Biblical Theology of the Old and New Testaments*, 353.

angelic host in Revelation also cries, "Holy, holy, holy is the Lord God Almighty, who was and is and is to come" (Rev 4:8). The martyrs cry out for justice to the God who is "holy and true" (6:10). At a decisive point in the narrative, the heavenly hosts worship God by asking and stating, "Who will not fear you, O Lord, and bring glory to your name? For you alone are holy. All nations will come and worship before you, for your righteous acts have been revealed" (15:4; note also 16:5). There is no question but that the exalted God who reigns in Revelation is holy.

The sovereign God of justice in Revelation, however, is also fundamentally a loving God. The divine sovereignty and holiness of God accented in the drama of Revelation are not meant to lead the audience to the conclusion that this God is distant or untouched by suffering. Remember that the acts of divine judgment are a response to the cry for justice by the martyrs (6:10; 16:4-5). God is neither untouched by their pain nor forgetful of their sacrifice. God does not forget the prayers of the saints either, even those that have gone unanswered for so long (8:3-5); the divine purposes are fulfilled only as God dwells with the redeemed and can wipe away their tears, as a loving parent cares for a weeping child (7:17; 21:3-4). As in Isa 57:15, the God of Revelation is lofty but dwells with those of a contrite heart. The God upon the throne acts through the crucified Lamb and creates a path for victory among those who conquer by the Lamb's spilled blood (5:6; 12:11). The sovereign God of the universe is driven by self-giving love and is able to be wounded in reaching out to humanity.

The mercy of God in Revelation, however, is not limited to the contrite. In Revelation, justice is ultimately fulfilled in mercy, including the mercy extended to the sinner. The book is accented by efforts to reach the lost with the good news of God's mercy and celebrates the multitudes who receive God's grace and goodness (7:9-17; 10:9-11; 11:3; 14:6-7). Even the nations that are judged in chapter 19 reappear in chapter 20 to enjoy a magnanimous opportunity to repent during the thousand-year reign of peace, a reign that towers over the years of trial in length of time ("where sin increased, grace increased all the more," Rom 5:20). The leaves of the tree of life in the New Jerusalem are in fact earmarked for the healing of the nations (22:2). Not even the final judgment of chapter 20 nullifies this hope. Consistent with this hope, the gates of the new city remain open and facing in the directions from which the opposition to God's purposes had come (21:13, 25). Even the wrath poured out comes forth from God's wounded love and flows most directly forth from the violence of evildoers who oppose that love (ch. 6). True, those who ultimately seek to spurn this love fall beneath the shadow of judgment cast by the cross, but God's sovereign purposes symbolized by the Lamb's blood are dominated by the will to redeem. Only the evil forces seek to destroy out of violent and destructive purposes (11:18).

There is a creative tension between divine sovereignty and love in Revelation that has deep OT roots in its overarching preference for mercy and redemption. As Walter Brueggemann has noted, there is an inner tension in the OT between divine sovereignty and pathos. There are texts that seem to suggest that the sovereign God acts out of self-regard in order to uphold divine holiness (Ezek 20:41) or to sanctify the divine name (36:23). God delivers Israel to gain glory over Pharaoh (Exod 14:4-7). In other texts, however, God is willing to suffer rejection and humiliation for the sake of Israel (Hos 1–2) and desires to extend grace even to the oppressors of Israel like the Assyrians (cf. Jonah) or the Philistines (Amos 9:7). Yahweh moves back and forth between self-regard and regard for others, "between sovereignty and pathos."[6] In Hosea, for example, God appears as both a roaring lion and a spurned lover (1:2; 2; 4; 5:3, 14-15). Revelation similarly pictures Christ as the Lion and the Lamb. The two are compatible in that the divinity of God is also absolute and undying love.[7] This accent on divine love as that which represents God's overall purpose becomes for T. C. Vriezen "the most characteristic element of the structure of Israelite religion."[8] As Walther Eichrodt has argued, divine love actually ascends over (without eclipsing) divine sovereignty in the OT, qualifying fear of the Lord so as to eliminate the sense of terror and to add the element of knowing God as the loving Creator and covenant partner. Even divine judgment comes to serve redemptive purposes.[9] Brueggemann maintains that the central thrust of the OT is thus to resolve the tension between sovereignty and love through a convergence of sovereignty and fidelity in God's saving deeds. God's righteous self-regard as sovereign Lord is fulfilled in God's merciful and saving deeds (Isa 45:8, 23-24; 51:6-8; Pss 71:19; 89:17; 96:13; 98:9; 111:3; Dan 9:16-18). God is glorified in showing mercy. In fact, "such convergence of sovereignty and compassion is the staple of Israel's faith,"[10] functioning as "normative for theological interpretation."[11] Referring to the NT, Eichrodt even speaks of a "cruciform discernment of the nature of God . . . who completely risks sovereignty in solidarity."[12] Such is the God of Revelation — except sovereignty is not so much "risked" in this

---

6. Walter Brueggemann, *Theology of the Old Testament: Testimony, Dispute, Advocacy* (Minneapolis: Augsburg/Fortress, 2005), 309.

7. See not only Brueggemann here but also T. C. Vriezen, *An Outline of Old Testament Theology* (Oxford: Basil Blackwell, 1958), 135, 144.

8. Vriezen, *An Outline of Old Testament Theology*, 137.

9. Walther Eichrodt, *Theology of the Old Testament*, vol. 2 (Philadelphia: Westminster, 1972), 291.

10. Eichrodt, *Theology of the Old Testament*, 306.

11. Eichrodt, *Theology of the Old Testament*, 309.

12. Eichrodt, *Theology of the Old Testament*, 311.

end-time drama as fundamentally qualified in its very definition by the overarching goal of mercy and redemption. Yet, even this love is also qualified in some sense by sovereignty. Divine love in Revelation is not weak sentiment but an all-powerful redemptive force that casts a dark shadow of judgment over those who continue to oppose its liberating work in the world.

Revelation thus takes evil seriously as genuine opposition to God. God is not secretly behind it but opposes it. In being sovereign, the God who sits upon the throne takes sides on the side of salvation and justice. God never sides in Revelation with the forces of the dragon or the beast. This God does not write the script for evil oppression, but neither is there anything that cannot be used in the service of God's redemptive outcome. God's self-disclosure in the figure of the crucified Lamb is a powerful witness to the fact that God stands on the side of redemption. God's granting the opposition space in which to resist is not meant to be understood as a divine sanction. There is no contradiction between the God who sits on the throne and the God revealed in the crucified Lamb. The cosmic warfare described from chapter 13 onward urges the readers to take sides in the battle for redemption and justice. The thought that "God reigns" was a battle cry for the saints, as well as a source of comfort. The readers were encouraged and comforted by the fact that the resistance of evil agents to God will be turned against them. The cry of the martyrs for justice is answered by God's acts of judgment upon the world (6:10; 16:5-6) toward those who carelessly seek to destroy the earth (11:18). Violence and wickedness build to the point of overflowing. It becomes clear that things cannot remain as they are. God answers the cry that arises from injustice by putting a decisive end to the injustice.

The dark forces behind human resistance to God thus imply a stark dualism, but one that is qualified by God's sovereignty. There is no absolute dualism here in which God and the dragon struggle in perpetual combat over the outcome of history. The contrasts between God and the dragon, the Lamb and the beast, and the false prophet and the faithful witnesses of God are sharp and striking. Yet, though the dragon and the beast seek to intimidate with their vast shows of strength, God alone is all powerful in Revelation (4:8; 11:17; 15:3; 16:7, 14; 19:6; 21:22), having already conquered sin and death in Christ (1:18). This decisive event of Christ's resurrection sets the stage for the final victory in the making of all things new (21:5). God works to draw the affairs of history, even human rejection, into the fulfillment of redemptive purposes. Only those who discern in the Spirit can understand something of the mystery of God's ways, of how God is accomplishing divine purposes in history. The God of Revelation has the first and the last word of history, as well as the decisive words in between. In this light, the defeat of the dragon and the beast in chapter 12 makes

Theological Horizons of Revelation

their pretension to rule in the next chapter laughable. The audience is drawn to the conclusion that their awesome shows of strength cannot ultimately thwart the divine purposes. The ways in which the dragon and the beast seek to mimic God's roles as divine ruler (13:1-2), author of life (13:15), and object of praise (13:4) are ridiculous. Given that the dragon has already been decisively defeated (1:18; 12:1-12), such pretensions appear at best empty. Their resistance creates the conditions of a real battle in which the saints suffer temporary losses, but the victory is assured to those who struggle and patiently endure.

Gospel of John and 1–3 John

God in John's gospel is a mystery as well, not having been seen at any time but appearing in the Word made flesh (John 1:14, 18; 1 John 1:2). Not even with Moses does one have the light of truth that came through Christ (John 1:4, 17-18). God created all things through the Word of truth, in whom burned the very radiant light and glory of God (1:1-5). Unique to John's gospel is a strong accent on Jesus' revealing this mystery to be a heavenly Father who loves him with an eternal love that existed before the worlds began (John 3:35; 5:20; 10:17; 15:9; 16:27; 17:23-24). This emphasis on the timeless love between the heavenly Father and the Son involves them in a rich communion in which the Son is in the Father and the Father is in the Son (17:21). The Spirit is implied in the eternal love and glory shared between them (17:24). The beloved community participates in this eternal love and glory shared between the heavenly Father and his Son in the Spirit (17:21; 20:21-22; 1 John 4:7-8). God is love; whoever does not love does not know God (1 John 4:8). God is love; whoever lives in love lives in God, and God in him or her (4:11). No one has ever seen God, but God lives in those who love completely (4:12). This love casts out fear of judgment because there is no fear in love (4:17-18). Indeed, God so loved the world that "he gave his one and only Son," not to condemn the world, but to save it (John 3:15-17; cf. 1 John 4:9). The fundamental revelation of divine love does not come from us but from God, whose love is demonstrated in Christ's death for sinners (4:10). The judgment enacted against the world is precisely the darkness chosen by the unrepentant in willful rejection of God and of the divine light of truth revealed in the Word of the Father (John 3:18). Judgment is less direct here than it is in Revelation, but it is no less dark and devastating.

As in Revelation, John's gospel does assume widespread resistance to the truth of the divine self-disclosure. Also consistent is God's provision of signs in chapters 2–12 that bear witness to the divine triumph over darkness in Jesus, a witness that will be vindicated as true. The Spirit will also bear witness to the judgment of God against darkness and to Jesus as the light of the world (16:8-11). The revelation of the light of God is the overarching goal for history, but the shadow side of this light means condemnation for those who choose to oppose it by following the devil, who is the cosmic deceiver (8:44). By contrast, God is truthful (3:33). As with Revelation, God's judgment is faithful and true, for "God is light; in him is no darkness at all" (1 John 1:5). Christ and the divine Spirit thus bear witness to the truth. God is Spirit, and those who worship God do so in Spirit and truth (John 4:24). Those who reject the light of truth live under the wrath of darkness (3:36). The glory and truth of the Word are revealed in both the crucifixion and the resurrection (12:23-28), which serve to vindicate God's righteousness in the world.

Matthew and Mark

The Synoptic Gospels also reveal that the God of Israel is principally the heavenly Father of Jesus Christ. They stress in addition the connection between the Father and the reign or kingdom of God.[13] This kingdom involves the reign of the sovereign God. It has been brought near in Jesus and in the realm of the Spirit, coming as a liberating force upon those who repent. Matthew is clear on this point: "If I drive out demons by the Spirit of God, then the kingdom of God has come upon you" (Matt 12:28). God's reign is not only far (yet to come) but near (13:31-32). Repentance is absolutely essential to enter God's reign (3:1-2), as is a righteousness that is of the heart and that values God and the kingdom above all else (5:20; 6:33).

As Mark notes, the kingdom is given to those who receive it as a child (Mark 10:15) or as a servant in following the servant Son of Man (10:45). Those who come to God by following in the path of servanthood do not lord it over others, for God's reign is not oppressive but liberating. God's ways in Jesus' path to the cross are mysterious and difficult to fathom. Even Peter with his striking confession can see them only vaguely, much like a blind man who at first sees men only as trees walking (8:22-30). But the God over these events is the living God of Abraham, Isaac, and Jacob (12:26-27; cf. Matt 22:32). Peter will eventually see God's purposes clearly enough.

In Matthew, God seeks after the lost in order to bring them under the liberating reign of the kingdom and the loving care of God as Father: "Then

---

13. George Eldon Ladd, *A Theology of the New Testament* (rev. ed.; Grand Rapids: Eerdmans, 1993), 83.

the righteous will shine like the sun in the kingdom of their Father" (Matt 13:43; cf. 25:34; 26:29). Jesus' table fellowship invites sinners and those who regard themselves as righteous for the purpose of bringing both together in devotion to the heavenly Father. Jesus prays to God as "*our* Father," inviting others into his fellowship with the Father (6:9), even in Mark addressing God as "Abba," the intimate address to a father (Mark 14:36; cf. Rom 8:15; Gal 4:6).

God providentially cares for creation right down to the minutest detail (Matt 5:45; 6:26-27; 10:29). Yet, in both Matthew and Mark, the love of the Father is not shallow sentiment. Just before the text in which God remembers the insignificant sparrow (Matt 10:29), Jesus warns that we are to fear the one who can destroy both body and soul in hell (10:28). God's kingdom also involves judgment (3:12; 25:34, 41). Jesus pronounced judgment on cities where he proclaimed the kingdom (11:20-24). Judgment will also overtake Jerusalem (Matt 24; Mark 13; cf. Luke 21). God's love is a holy love that involves judgment for those who oppose it. Yet, the redemptive will is God's overall purpose, for the Son was sent to seek the lost. The Son who cries out to God from the alienation and darkness of the cross (Mark 15:33-34) will be raised to life by the Father. This is the hope of all who turn to God for mercy (10:45).

Luke and Acts

For Luke, the kingdom of God is especially good news to the poor and oppressed of this world, granting them the power and well-being to enjoy the goodness of the Father (Luke 4:18-19). Luke especially sees history as fulfilling a divine plan initiated in Jesus and fulfilled in the power of the Spirit.[14] God's mercy through mighty deeds extends to all generations "to those who fear him" (1:50-51), lifting up the humble. But God scatters the proud and brings down rulers from their thrones (1:51-52); God fills the hungry but sends the rich away empty-handed (1:53). These grand reversals reveal that God's ways do not necessarily fulfill social expectations; rather, they follow the values implicit in the divine plan for history. God, however, is rich in mercy (1:54).

God's goal in Acts is to pour out the Holy Spirit upon all flesh, upon all peoples who call upon the name of the Lord and cling to the promise of the Spirit's blessing (Acts 2:17-21, 38-39). The God of this historical plan does not show favoritism but wills to give all peoples a share in the Spirit (10:34). This plan is "the whole will of God" (20:27). To seek to hinder the forward move of this plan is to stand in God's way (11:17). Yet, nothing can ultimately thwart

---

14. Marshall, *New Testament Theology*, 141.

God's plan. The world condemned God's chosen Messiah unjustly, but God vindicated him as Lord and Judge (2:22-36). Indeed, the one who was condemned is the one whom the "God of Abraham, Isaac and Jacob, the God of our fathers, has glorified" (3:13). This is the God "of the people of Israel" (13:17) but also the Creator, who made the world and cannot be confined to temples made with human hands (17:24). This God needs nothing "but gives everyone life and breath and everything else" (17:25). All peoples are in fact God's offspring, for "in him we live and move and have our being" (17:28). The God to whom the church prays in times of threat is the "sovereign Lord," who made the heavens and the earth and all that is in them (4:24). People and not idols of wood or stone are thus meant to image God (17:29).

Paul

Paul also assumes with the OT that God is the creator of all things (1 Cor 8:6; 11:12; 2 Cor 4:6; Rom 11:36; Eph 3:9). The whole world is thus held accountable to God (Rom 3:19). The creation bears witness to God's deity and great power, so that no one is without excuse in his or her rejection of grace (Rom 1:19-20). The Creator is known most specifically by the resurrection of Jesus from the dead, which stands for Paul as God's distinguishing mark (1 Thess 1:10; 4:14; 1 Cor 15:12-19, 20-28). Indeed, even Abraham believed in the "God who gives life to the dead and calls things that are not as though they were" (Rom 4:17). The great power of the Creator, who called all things into existence by the mere spoken word, also called forth Jesus the Son of God from the dead "according to the Spirit of holiness" (Rom 1:4). Paul never tires of referring to God as Father, Son, and Spirit, even where the context does not require it (e.g., Eph 4:4-6; 1 Cor 12:4-6). The God who raised Jesus from the dead involves precisely these three players (Rom 1:4), compelling Paul to name God in this way.

God for Paul transcends time and is the source, means, and fulfillment of creation. Concerning God, Paul notes that, similar to the "I Am" of the OT and the "Alpha and Omega" of Revelation, "from him and through him and to him are all things" (Rom 11:36). God for Paul is sovereign, directing the affairs of history toward salvific purposes, even using human rejection and opposition to accomplish redemptive goals. In Rom 9–11 Paul weaves an intricate argument in which God favors Israel over the nations ("Jacob I loved, Esau I hated," 9:13) but then turns the tables, whereupon the *nations* achieve favored status because of Israel's rejection. Paul wants his readers to know, however, that God has not forgotten Israel. God will use the favored status of the nations to make Israel "envious" (11:11) so that they will want to reclaim their covenant promises. The ultimate goal of history is to relegate all peoples to the status of sinner (non-favored status because of disobedience) so that God may have mercy upon all through grace alone (11:32, an elaboration on 3:23-24). This is arguably the narrative substructure for Paul's letters. At the end, all will be willing to glorify God for a salvation that they did not deserve because of their rejection and will extol God's ability to work providentially beneath human rejection to bring all peoples to grace:

> Oh, the depth of the riches of the wisdom and knowledge of God!
>   How unsearchable his judgments,
>   and his paths beyond tracing out! (11:33)

Such praise could easily be placed within the pages of Revelation.

Also consistent is Paul's insight that God not only calls but also rejects (1 Thess 5:9). Election and calling are major themes for Paul (Rom 9–11; Eph 1; 1 Thess 2:12; 5:24; Gal 1:6; 5:8). Yet, so is the peril of rejecting God. God's grace is life to those who accept but death to those who oppose (2 Cor 2:16). God sticks by covenant promises, for God's gifts are irrevocable (Rom 11:29), but it is still possible to stumble in one's disobedience (11:11). The sovereign God is not mocked, for whatever a person sows, so shall that person reap (Gal 6:7). Consistent with John's gospel, Paul sees wrath as involving the darkness chosen by the disobedient heart. Three times in Rom 1 Paul notes that God "delivered over" sinners to their shameful lusts and deviant ways (vv. 24-28). This wrath is also revealed from heaven against the ungodliness of those who suppress the truth through their wickedness, especially against the idolatry of turning the creation that bore witness to God into an object of worship (1:18-23). Interestingly, however, Paul uses the same verb (παραδίδωμι [*paradidōmi*, "deliver over"]) with regard to Christ in Rom 4:25 and 8:32. The Father "delivered over" the Son to the same darkness chosen by the sinners in order to win them back. Of course, the Son also offered himself in obedience to the Father (Phil 2). As in Revelation, the divine rejection is not meant as the final word: "God has bound all men over to disobedience so that he may have mercy on them all" (Rom 11:32). God for Paul is the "Father of compassion" (2 Cor 1:3; cf. 2 Cor 4:1). Paul goes even further than Revelation in offering up doxologies that envision a universal adoration of Christ to the glory of the Father by every tongue (Phil 2:9-11). This is not to say that we necessarily have an unqualified universalism here, but the scope of praise to God assumed in Paul's eschatological vision of the future is even more staggering and bold than that found in Revelation.

Other New Testament Voices

For Hebrews also, God is principally the Father of the Lord Jesus Christ (Heb 1:5-6). The Father is the living God who shows mercy and judgment (3:12). It is a dreadful thing in the midst of rebellion to fall into the hands of the living God (10:31). God's Word is "living and active," judging the thoughts and attitudes of the heart (4:12). Nothing at all is hidden from God's sight; "Everything is uncovered and laid bare before the eyes of him to whom we must give account" (4:13). God is the "Father of our spirits" who sees the hidden things deep within (12:9). God is a consuming fire (12:29), disciplining those whom God loves, as a father disciplines a child (12:4-12).

God for Hebrews dwells in the most holy place (9:12) but is approachable through Christ for those of a pure heart with the assurance of faith (4:16; 10:22). God is the "God of peace" who makes atonement through Christ (13:20). It is not possible to please God without faith (11:6). Those who approach God "must believe that he exists and that he rewards those who earnestly seek him" (11:6). God is faithful and trustworthy, making an oath "to himself" (since there was no one greater to swear by) to bless all nations through Abraham, a promise that will be fulfilled, for "it is impossible for God to lie" (6:13, 18). Indeed, "the Lord has sworn and will not change his mind" (7:21).

In the Petrine letters, God is identified as the one who raised Jesus from the dead (1 Pet 1:21). This is the living God, whose eyes are on the righteous, with ears attentive to their prayers but whose face is turned against those who do evil (3:12). The God of awesome judgment knows how to rescue those who suffer unjustly (2 Pet 2:4-9). God is our shepherd (1 Pet 2:25) as the "God of all grace" (5:10) who cares for us, encouraging us to "cast all our anxieties upon him" (5:7).

God in James is the "Father of heavenly lights" who is good and unchangingly faithful to give every good gift (1:17). There is not a trace here of the triune structure in naming God as used by Paul. God is simply the Father, who is not tempted by evil and does not tempt with evil (1:13). The heavenly Father cares for the marginalized, for pure religion acceptable to God is to care for orphans and widows in distress (1:27). This God has chosen the poor in the eyes of this world to be rich in faith and to inherit the kingdom of God (2:5). God is the judge who stands at the door but who is also "full of compassion and mercy" (5:9, 11).

Conclusion

Though there are nuances of difference and shifting accents in the NT's understanding of God against the background of the OT, there is also a remarkable continuity of witness. They all accent God as alone the eternal Creator and Lord of the creation who rules, who fulfills covenant promises in mercy and righteous judgment, and who will fulfill all things by dwelling with creation. The God of Revelation, however, is at war with the opposition in the midst of the final conflict, which will bring God's purposes as creator and redeemer to fulfillment. Naturally, this overall purpose causes the author to highlight the sharp contrasts between God and the enemies of redemption, as well as the awesomeness of divine judgments, including vengeance for those unjustly crushed by violent forces who oppose God. Mercy for the nations is the overarching goal of Revelation, but this attention to judgment stands in creative tension with the equally strong love theme of the gospel and epistles of John or Jesus' open table fellowship with sinners that characterizes the Synoptics. Such is a tension in accent, of course, since, as we have noted, themes of both mercy and judgment qualify each other in some way in all of these voices. There is as well a creative tension between the understanding of judgment found in John's gospel (and Paul) as the self-willed path of alienation and darkness involved among those who oppose God (John 3:19; Rom 1:24-28) and that found in Revelation. Revelation also assumes that judgments involve the darkness that arises from evil hearts (note the horsemen of ch. 6), but Revelation goes beyond that to depict direct acts of judgment that come forth from the throne of God. Paul notes that vengeance is the Lord's (Rom 12:19), but Revelation lifts this point from being a minor note in the background of the NT canon and makes it the trombone section. Yet, even here, we dare not forget that Revelation trumps the negative side of judgment with grace. If vengeance temporarily blasts forth as trombones in the concert of Revelation, grace counterbalances these tones throughout and presents us with clashing cymbals at the end.

Revelation and Systematic Theology

God is the great theme of theology, the chief concern and point of reference. God is the one who was, is, and is to come. All of human history has its point of reference ultimately in God. To reflect on God is to reflect on the mystery at the core of all of life. In the context of systematic theological reflection on this divine mystery, perhaps the greatest challenge has arisen from the theme of Revelation on divine sovereignty: the fact that God reigns over all and will fulfill divine purposes through acts of judgment and mercy. This accent on sovereignty dominated what may be called the Augustinian/Calvinist wing of Christianity in the West but also, to some extent, classical theism, or the dominant view of God prior to the modern period.[15] Significant changes have occurred in the theology of God over the past century that have called into question this view of God. We first consider classical theism and then look at the resources that are available from Revelation for reconstruction. The goal will be to reconsider divine sovereignty without removing it altogether as an important feature of a contemporary theology of God. A useful category for doing so will be that of the kingdom of God.

The Sovereign God of Classical Theism

In the classical theism prior to the modern period, God's "relation" to the world was typically viewed as one-sided and unilateral rather than mutual. God tended to function as absolute and sovereign, acting unilaterally on the world but immune to being acted upon by the world or affected significantly as a result. This idea was influenced by Greek metaphysics, which represented an effort to describe the very essence or substance of reality in relation to the reality of God. Plotinus, for example, contrasted temporal and mutable worldly substance with the supreme spiritual substance of the divine life, which is immutable (not subject to change), unaffected and impassible (incapable of suffering). Centuries earlier, Aristotle had thought of God in a similar way. Following such influences, the classical understanding of God seemed to represent the very *opposite* of creaturely life. The divine-world relation was defined by a series of metaphysical oppositions. If creaturely life is temporal, God is timeless. If creaturely life is diverse, God is perfectly simple, having no parts or divisions. If creaturely life is changing, God is immutable. If creaturely life is moved, affected, and vulnerable to suffering, God is immovable and impassible, invulnerable to suffering. If creaturely life is limited, God is unlimited and can do anything. As Jürgen Moltmann noted, the picture of God influenced by Greek metaphysics is "defined by certain characteristics of the finite cosmos, and these are marked by negation."[16] The assumption seemed to be that God could be free and transcendent only if this freedom is *from us,* as *far* from us as the mind could possibly imagine, even further.

The God of classical theism was not entirely incorrect. The case can be made from the Bible (especially Revelation) that God does indeed reign and is

---

15. For a helpful description of the differences between the historic Augustinian/Calvinist view of God and that held in the East, see John Hick, *Evil and the God of Love* (New York: Pelgrave Macmillan, 2010).

16. Jürgen Moltmann, *The Trinity and the Kingdom* (San Francisco: Harper & Row, 1981), 11.

not limited by anything external to the divine life, nor is God subject to human manipulation. But the God of classical theism seemed so radically removed from the world that it became conceptually difficult to understand how God could be loving or involved in intimate and mutual *relationship* with the world at the same time. For example, if God genuinely loves another, especially one who is unfaithful as is the human race, how can God be unaffected, impassible, unmovable, and incapable of suffering? How can one who genuinely *loves* sinful humans even to the point of experiencing crucifixion on their behalf not be affected or suffer, or, on the other hand, take pleasure in their love?[17]

One might think that the premodern history of Trinitarian theology would have helped to offset this lack of relationality in the classical view of God, but such has not always been the case. One can think of stellar theologies of the Trinity such as that of Athanasius (fourth century), which were robustly relational. The challenges at that time against Christ's full deity (subordinationism) or against the eternal intrarelationality of Father, Son, and Spirit (modalism), however, caused the church to eventually focus the doctrine of the Trinity on God's inner life. Trinitarian theology in the Middle Ages became increasingly abstract and removed from the biblical narrative, which originally provided the context of interpretation. Trinitarian theology became embroiled in technical and complex debates over how the God who is one in essence is also three in person.[18] The issues raised have their value, but they are inadequate for a Trinitarian theology today. Rather than reading the triune life from the story of redemption, Trinitarian theology tended to be hammered out instead in the laboratory of abstract speculation. As Anne Hunt wrote of Aquinas's theology in the late Middle Ages, "Apparently, the interconnection of the Trinity with Jesus' death and resurrection is simply not a question in this stage in the tradition."[19]

By the time we reach the Enlightenment, we find Friedrich Schleiermacher concluding that the classical doctrine of the Trinity was an outmoded antique that required significant revision to be meaningful. For Schleiermacher, "our faith in Christ and our living fellowship with him" would be the same without the classical doctrine of the Trinity. Even the "main pivots" of church doctrine exist independently of this doctrine in Schleiermacher's judgment.[20] He capped his system with a Trinitarian understanding of God but one that

---

17. Ted Peters, *God as Trinity: Relationality and Temporality in Divine Life* (Minneapolis: Westminster John Knox Press, 1993), 32.

18. See, for example, Catherine M. LaCugna, *God for Us: The Trinity and Christian Life* (San Francisco: HarperOne, 1993), and Anne Hunt, *The Trinity and the Paschal Mystery* (Collegeville, MN: Liturgical Press, 1997).

19. Hunt, *The Trinity*, 5.

20. Friedrich Schleiermacher, *The Christian Faith* (Philadelphia: Fortress), 741.

was modalistic, without an adequately conceived understanding of the interrelationality of the divine persons. It was Karl Barth in the twentieth century who sought to restore the Trinity to its rightful place as the cornerstone of one's reflection on Christian doctrine. Barth saw that theology is not birthed primarily from speculation about human experience of God but rather within the church's proclamation and hearing of the Word of God. For Barth, the Word of God proclaimed from Scripture is most essentially the living Christ. This Word thus has a Trinitarian structure because the story of Jesus has a Trinitarian structure, describing God as Father, Son, and Spirit: Christ was sent by the Father, was anointed by the Spirit, and is known in the Spirit. As such, the Word of God at the base of theology calls forth a Trinitarian framework for all of theology, namely, the Father as Revealer, the Son as the Revealed, and the Holy Spirit as Revealedness, or the power of revelation.[21] Barth was influenced by the shift evident in Hegel from metaphysics to more personal or subjective categories for understanding God. God is absolute Subject in threefold revelation as Father, Son, and Spirit. What God's divine essence ends up being in relation to creation as revealed in the incarnate Christ depends ultimately on God's self-determination or elect will. By stressing the one divine Subject in threefold revelation, does Barth display a modalistic tendency that lacks full appreciation for the interrelationality of the divine persons? Not quite. Barth does criticize modalism early on for wrongly viewing the economic relationality of Father, Son, and Spirit as alien to the being of God and eventually came to describe the triune God in robustly relational terms.[22]

Rather than Trinitarian theology remaining nonessential to theology, Barth showed that it is vital to theology's very point of departure. In so doing, Barth attached theological speculation to the issue of the divine self-disclosure in the redemptive story of Jesus. More recently and in a similar vein, Kevin J. Vanhoozer has suggested a theological reflection on God that arises from God's triune self-communication, a self-communication that provides the occasion for communion with God. He writes of a "theodramatic metaphysics" that asks "what God must *be* to have *said* and *done that*" (Vanhoozer's emphasis).[23] Revelation can provide us with resources for discussing the triune God as the God who gives of Godself in communicative acts that redeem and renew creation while bringing it into the divine embrace. This trend holds promise for many in its potential to offset the lack of relationality typical of classical theism. The

---

21. Karl Barth, *Church Dogmatics*, vol. 1/1 (ed. Geoffrey William Bromiley and Thomas Torrance; Edinburgh: T&T Clark, 1956), 88-89.

22. Barth, *Church Dogmatics*, 4/2:70; 1/1:382; 3/1:185.

23. Kevin J. Vanhoozer, *Remythologizing Theology: Divine Action, Passion, and Authorship* (Cambridge: Cambridge University Press, 2010), 79.

triune God speaks and acts in creation without being wholly defined by the historical process. Following Karl Rahner's rule, the triune God's involvement in history is indicative (a living icon) of the immanent life of God as Father, Son, and Spirit.[24]

All of this is a response to classical theism's thorny conceptual problem, one that seemed unavoidable. Behind the concept of classical theism seemed to lie the idea that God had to be contrasted with finite reality to be transcendent and free. After all, the relational web of creaturely existence makes evil and suffering an interconnected and inescapable reality. The entire web of creaturely existence is also in flux and change, caught in the grip of sin, death, and dying. The sharp oppositions and negations traditionally assumed in classical theism between God and creation thus served to explain how the God who came to us in the figure of the suffering and crucified Christ was not swallowed up by the manipulative forces of sin or the seemingly unconquerable grip of death. God was not swallowed up, it was thought, because God is the *opposite* of finite creation. God was thought to enter into finite creation without having at essence the vulnerabilities of finite existence. It was thought that, if God were indeed vulnerable to suffering and change like the rest of us, God would seem to be finite, caught up as we are in the vicissitudes and evil forces of historical existence. There would be no "rock of ages" here on which to place one's trust and hope during the shifting and sinking sands of historical existence!

We thus seem caught within a difficult choice: either God is robustly relational and trapped within the vicissitudes and evils of historical existence, or God transcends the trap of creaturely existence by avoiding anything that might truly be regarded as relational. In more traditional theological terms, absolute sovereignty seems to preclude all-embracing love. As Ted Peters notes, "To speak of God as absolute seems to include the assumption that absoluteness is the opposite of relationality."[25] As noted above, more recent theologies of God are attempting to overcome this duality between absoluteness and relationality by speaking of the self-communicative triune God such as we have featured in Revelation. The God who reigns from the throne in Revelation is decisively revealed in the crucified and risen Lamb! The Lion is the Lamb. This God is certainly both absolute and relational, transcendent and revealed in self-sacrificial love.

Our readiness to hear the gospel of this book is due in part to certain conceptual changes that have occurred in the twentieth century. Most important, our times are characterized by an awareness of relationality as essential

---

24. See Vanhoozer, *Remythologizing Theology*, 70-72.
25. Peters, *God as Trinity*, 14.

to life, all of life, biological as well as social. Personhood and community are now typically viewed as overlapping concepts. It becomes difficult within this intellectual climate to understand how God can be *personal* without also being essentially and entirely *relational*. This problem is urgent, since it may also be argued that the absolute deity of classical theism even threatens God's *infinity and freedom*. An absolute existence set radically in *opposition* to the finite realm is hardly "infinite," as Hegel has noted.[26] An *infinite* God bordered off and defined over against finite creation makes no sense. Both realms, bordering on each other, would end up determinate in relation to the other. Both would be essentially and necessarily limited and therefore *finite*. Arguably, a God who *cannot* be affected or *cannot* suffer would be just as limited as those are who are caught up in the flux and flow of suffering. To be infinite or absolute, genuinely sovereign over *all* of the affairs of life, this God would need to be both transcendent and all-encompassing and all-embracing of finite existence, able to feel and experience all of its joys and sorrows and to move with it experientially but with an absolute freedom unknown to those who are finite. In short, it seems that we are stuck with relationality or love. There is simply no way to define either a personal or an infinite God without it. This insight leads us in the contemporary situation to the need for a reconstruction of divine sovereignty and absoluteness that embraces divine empathy, self-giving, and relationality, a project for which Revelation can function as a resource.

Doxology: The Point of Departure

If theology is done in the context of God's theodramatic self-communication to us as the triune God, then Scripture is the guide, and worship is the context, for theological reflection. We face the challenges of our social contexts by reasoning scripturally in a way that is continuous with the drama of worship. The book of Revelation can be a resource here. The message of Revelation is not given from an ivory tower. The primary context for envisioning God is not a theoretical problem, such as the one that eventually dominated classical theism. The issue is not how we can protect an infinite God from the vicissitudes of finite existence. In Revelation, the matter of God is raised first in the *worship* among the redeemed and their solidarity with a much more expansive praise that is going on among the heavenly host (4:8) and will go on eschatologically

---

26. F. LeRon Schultz, *Reforming the Doctrine of God* (Grand Rapids: Eerdmans, 2005), 29. Schultz quotes Hegel (*Hegel's Science of Logic* [trans. A. V. Miller; Amherst, NY: Humanity Books, 1999], 139-40) in pointing to this problem.

among all peoples (15:4). This worship itself recalls the dramatic framework of the Hebrew Scriptures and is described as an extended drama that is meant to be visualized and imagined as well as heard. This is the fundamental context for theological reflection for John. It is not that the author and his audience are out of touch with their concrete social contexts. The fact that they are so in touch is abundantly clear, especially in chapters 2 and 3. Yet, their understanding of God, influenced as it is by the Hebrew Scriptures (e.g., Isa 6), is brought to expression first in worship. All other activity, whether it be disciplined thinking about the faith, witness of the gospel in life, or moral virtue, is implicitly viewed as an extension of glorifying God. As Geoffrey Wainwright has argued, the Christian identity and vision come to expression first in the context of worship and lead to the praise of God in "worship, doctrine, and life."[27] Such, as Vladimir Lossky has shown, is the Eastern understanding of theology as well.[28]

God's great attributes and deeds in Revelation come to most eloquent expression in praise and worship. When John sees the risen Christ in chapter 1, John falls prostrate before him. What other language is as adequate to such a confrontation with eschatological glory, victorious love incarnate? This kind of response will become standard practice for all of the great redemptive deeds of God that are done throughout the book. The first, proper response to them all is praise. The theologian will take note of the language of praise (both bodily and in words) and will seek to see his or her disciplined reflection as an extension of this affection and this glory. After all, the Christian identity, the faith, is expressed most deeply here. Orthodoxy literally means "proper glory." As Steven J. Land has observed, orthodoxy must thus overlap with orthopathy (right affection) and orthopraxy (right action).[29]

What drives the narrative theology of Revelation is also the disparity between the vision of the nations as praising God (15:4) and the reality of the nations as angry against God (11:18). The disparity is felt among Christians who praise God for his final victory and for the glory that will one day cover the earth in vindication of God's mercy and justice in opposition to the reality of dark forces that currently dominate the nations and that threaten those who worship. Their suffering and potential fear must be tempered by the reality that is opened to them in worship. They live from that vision, are comforted by it, read their Scriptures from this context, and act boldly and patiently in ways

---

27. Geoffrey Wainwright, *Doxology: The Praise of God in Worship, Doctrine, and Life* (New York: Oxford University Press, 1980), 1-12.

28. Vladimir Lossky, *The Mystical Theology of the Eastern Church* (Yonkers, NY: St. Vladimirs Press, 1997).

29. Steven J. Land, *Pentecostal Spirituality: A Passion for the Kingdom* (JPTS 1; Sheffield: Sheffield Academic Press, 1993).

consistent with it. The vision of God that emerges in worship is indeed sovereign or high and lifted up. Yet, this God is also near and intricately involved in the renewal of all things to the divine glory. That the praise of the book begins at the feet of the risen Lamb, slain for the sins of the world, is telling indeed. The revision of classical theism will thus begin here, with John, prostrate before the risen Lamb.

The Sovereign God of Resurrection

The revision of the doctrine of divine sovereignty should begin with the fact that this sovereignty in Revelation is not only far but near, not only absolute but a force within the world for liberation and redemption. This is precisely how the kingdom of God can be defined, namely, as the sovereign reign of God brought near in Jesus Christ and the sevenfold Spirit to liberate the world from darkness and death.[30] The God who reigns is thus not known through abstract speculation projected out from human social or political realities but, rather, in the midst of redemptive deeds or within a drama that tells what this God is doing to bring the divine reign to the world. We do not project outward to form a God-figure; God projects Godself into human history through self-communicative action.[31] The principal act toward this end in Revelation is that of raising Jesus from the dead. Revelation's theology of God is not the result of an intellectually satisfying worldview in which freedom from finite existence is secured through a series of oppositions. Revelation's theology of God arises, rather, from God's opposition to sin and death, especially in God's act of conquering sin and death by raising Jesus from the dead and making all things new in his image. The theology of the God who reigns thus begins in Revelation, not in a metaphysical speculation on the divine/creature relation, but with John's falling as though dead in the presence of the risen Lord and having his tears and despair in the face of the slaughtered Lamb turn to praise when the Lamb rises to take the scroll from the hand of the sovereign God who sits upon the throne (5:1-10). The God who was, is, and is to come, who transcends time and space and is sure to renew all things, is decisively revealed in this risen Christ. This drama fulfills the one given in Israel's Scriptures, for God is also the one who freed Israel in the exodus. The drama of God's liberating reign revealed in the resurrection of Jesus in Revelation refers meaningfully back to Israel's

---

30. See, for example, Ladd, *Gospel of the Kingdom: Scripture Studies in the Kingdom of God* (Grand Rapids: Eerdmans, 1959).

31. Vanhoozer, *Remythologizing Theology*, 21.

Scriptures, since "Israel's hope in her God cannot be sustained if it is not verified by victory also over death."[32] Indeed, "God is whoever raised Jesus from the dead, having before raised Israel from Egypt."[33] This is the Creator, who fulfills what was begun at creation by calling all things out of the darkness and the emptiness into the glorious light of God (Rom 4:17).

The God of Revelation is thus not identified by human speculation but rather by *dramatic coherence* experienced in Scripture and worship between the God who raised Jesus from the dead and the God of both creation and the exodus.[34] The crisis of the drama is the crucifixion (5:1-9), just as death was the ultimate crisis of Israel's faith. Indeed, the OT sees death as something that not only borders but also threatens to destroy the validity of God's covenant faithfulness. Death in the OT cancels any distinction between the wise and the foolish, since the deeds of both are forgotten (Eccl 2:16), and it removes the creature's capacity to glorify God for divine faithfulness (Isa 38:18). God in the OT is thus the hope for redemption from death (Ps 49:15) or even ransom from its captivity (Hos 13:14). Jonah cries from the "grave" for deliverance and vindication (Jonah 2:2). God is vindicated as the Lord of life in the victory of life over death, for God will be known as the *Lord* when the dead dry bones are raised (Ezek 37:13-14). All those thrown into the ash heap of history find hope only in resurrection.

The resolution of the crisis in Revelation is thus found in the resurrection of Jesus, the subsequent new exodus of God's people in the midst of plagues, and the new creation, in which God dwells. The God who raised Jesus from the dead is identified as the eternal Creator, who will not yield the throne to death but who claims the rightful place as Lord by defeating death and making all things new. The connection between the resurrection of Jesus and God's eternal nature as the great Alpha and Omega is in the fact that God remains in this act the God who was, is, and always will be as the eternally faithful covenant partner to creation. This is the God who is changelessly faithful, who "is eternally himself in that he unrestrictedly anticipates an end in which he will be all that he ever could be."[35] God anticipates an end already revealed in the resurrection of Jesus, an end that will verify and fulfill that decisive salvific and revelatory act. Sin and death cannot lower a curtain that decisively and forever puts an end to the faithfulness of God. The resurrection of Jesus lowers a curtain rather on sin and death and distinguishes this God as the eternal Alpha and Omega, who reigns forever as the faithful covenant partner to creation.

---

32. Robert W. Jenson, *Systematic Theology*, vol. 1: *The Triune God* (New York: Oxford University Press, 1997), 44.

33. Jenson, *Systematic Theology*, 1:63.

34. Jenson, *Systematic Theology*, 1:64.

35. Jenson, *Systematic Theology*, 1:66.

The Sovereign God of Love and Grace

God's sovereignty is thus fundamentally tilted in the direction of redemption and life. It is not meant as an alienating concept, except to those who oppose them and opt instead for condemnation and death. The book of Revelation thus provides us resources for engaging the recent trends in contemporary theologies of God that have granted divine love ascendance over sovereignty. Revelation can offer us resources for thinking creatively about these trends without sacrificing either one. The God of Revelation is not a capricious tyrant who predestines the atrocities of history and then crushes those who perpetrate them. Rather, God's election is tied theologically to the Lamb slain before the creation of the world for the sake of humanity (13:8). The presence of the crucified and risen Christ at the beginning of the book, the unceasing proclamation of the gospel to the nations throughout the book, and the persistent efforts to reach the wayward nations even in the midst of the new creation at the end of the book show us a very different understanding of divine sovereignty. This is a sovereignty that is concretely to be understood as reigning love or grace. It has love and grace at its very heart, the wounded heart of the God who elected the slain Lamb from before time as we know it (13:8).

Is such a transformation of sovereignty meaningful in the current theological climate? Have we gone far enough in redefining it? Especially in feminist theology, sovereignty has come to be regarded as an alien concept. In an effort to rid theology of oppressive images, the God who rules from the throne has been replaced with the immanent God as the womb of life that gives rise to, nourishes, empowers, and heals. As Elizabeth Johnson has noted, "By drawing imagery and concepts for God almost exclusively from the world of ruling men, inherited speech functions effectively to legitimate structures and theories that grant a theomorphic character to men who rule but that relegate women, children, and other men to the deficient margins."[36] The result is the divine legitimizing of domination and violence throughout human communities in both politics and religion. The reaction to this modern problem of God has been to favor immanent views of God as a presence that invites participation, mutuality, and communion.

This pneumatologically oriented understanding of God must be taken seriously in the light of Revelation, since God is also pictured there as the universal (sevenfold) Spirit. The very fact that this God is decisively revealed in the crucified and risen Lamb is proof that God stands on the side of the

---

36. Elizabeth Johnson, *She Who Is: The Mystery of God in Feminist Theological Discourse* (Chestnut Ridge, NY: Crossroad, 2002), 18.

redemption wrought through suffering love and not on the side of those who perpetrate injustice and self-destructive violence. God's reign or kingdom is a liberating and not an oppressive force. In Revelation, however, the Spirit who proceeds from the throne comes forth from the reign of the heavenly Father and in witness to Christ. There is thus for Revelation no possibility of merely reducing God to a cosmic process or to the energy behind community and healing (though God certainly encompasses both). It is one thing to redefine sovereignty in the service of God's immanent presence and redemptive love; it is another to eliminate sovereignty altogether as an alienating concept. Revelation supports the former but not the latter. This is the significant role that Revelation can serve in this important discussion.

If we turn our backs on this part of the canon, what will be the cost? For one thing, one must do the same with so much else in the biblical canon that resonates with the images of divine sovereignty in Revelation. If images of sovereignty are entirely eliminated, what guarantees that self-giving love will prove to be the victor at the end of all things or even now in the midst of the darkness that surrounds us? How do we know that history will not end in a nightmare or in some sort of meaningless, frozen wasteland? Or do we stand as in Samuel Beckett's *Endgame* in a posture of not knowing what will happen, of simply saying "perhaps"? How do we know that the Lamb will prove to be the Lion who defeats injustice and evil? How do we know that the book he holds in his hand comes from the one who is truly almighty and who reigns eternally over all? How do we know that his sacrifice will prove to be something other than the mere symbol of all those who are crushed without any possibility of hope? Is not his resurrection from the dead authentic as the key to God's future relationship to the world? Is it not his Spirit who will give life and drink to those who thirst in the new heavens and new earth? How do we know that the cries for justice among those who have been thrown into the trash heap of history will be answered? The biblical slogan "God reigns" is surely the answer. We may indeed discuss the limits of the culturally embedded images used in Revelation to give life to this slogan. Here is where feminist theology can be of significant help to us. But the essential message at the core of these images cannot be dismissed. It bears witness to a truth that is without a doubt the only hope there is.

As noted earlier, we cannot overestimate the fact that in Revelation love and mercy are at the core of the sovereign God's intentions for the world. In Revelation the Father who sits upon the throne seems mysterious but is not unaffected by the sin and violence of the world. Divine election is tied to the Lamb slain before the creation of the world (13:8). This God is revealed in the Lamb, who maintains his wounds, bearing before the throne the marks that were the means of the world's redemption. God hands over the eternal right to reign to this perpetual symbol of wounded love. This God hears the cries of the martyrs for justice and responds in injured love by striking at the strongholds of the oppressors, using in part their own violence against them. Redemption is fulfilled when God draws near to wipe away the tears of those who have suffered, as a loving parent comforts a crying child (21:4).

In the battle for redemption, God has been wounded. To love another who is free to reject this love is to risk suffering. In fact, "If God cannot feel anguish, he cannot love."[37] Historically, the church has traditionally held that, as immutable, God is incapable of suffering. The doctrine of God's impassibility did not imply that God has no passion, only that God is immune from suffering. But the biblical witness tells another story. Brevard Childs could thus write of both Testaments, "Does God suffer? Most certainly he does (Isa 63:9)."[38] In response to the biblical witness concerning the suffering of God, the Council of Ephesus in 431 affirmed that God attained the capacity to suffer *in Christ*, by becoming flesh and going to the cross (Twelve Anathemas, article 12). We could add that the God of the OT suffers also by loving creation and granting it the freedom to resist. As Gen 6:6 notes, "The Lord regretted that he had made human beings on the earth, and his heart was deeply troubled." Yet, it was also thought among those who assumed that God suffered in Christ that God retained divine freedom, a reservoir of infinite power, the power of love, from which suffering could be overcome in Christ. God has an infinite capacity to suffer, so suffering could never overwhelm the divine life.

The question remained, however, Is there continuity between the infinite God who reigns and the Lamb who suffers? Of course there is. The Lamb in Revelation shares fully in God's eternal reign, and the one who sits on the throne is revealed in the figure of this Lamb. The God on the throne responds in injured love to a violent world, and the Lamb exercises divine sovereignty as the Lion of Judah. Is the sovereign God vulnerable to suffering? If so, where is the divine Achilles' heel? The answer is love, which is the strength of God hidden in weakness! The Japanese theologian Kazoh Kitamori noted that the capacity to suffer was implied in the very nature of the triune God because of the eternal divine willingness to love those who should not be loved or those deserving of wrath.[39] Naturally, God did not suffer before creating, but the will and capacity to suffer was already implied in the divine willingness to love the creation even in the midst of its rebellion. The Lamb in Revelation is indeed slain before the creation of the world (13:8), a reality buried deep

---

37. Paul Schilling, *God and Human Anguish* (Nashville: Abingdon, 1977), 253.
38. Childs, *Biblical Theology of the Old and New Testaments*, 357.
39. Kazoh Kitamori, *Theology of the Pain of God* (Richmond, VA: John Knox Press, 1965), 21.

within the eternal heart of the Creator. Because of humanity's wayward path, Kitamori wrote, "God himself was broken, was wounded, and suffered, because he embraced those who should not be embraced."[40] Kitamori criticized liberal Protestant theology for highlighting a shallow version of divine love that lacked the cross and thus missed the depth of divine suffering involved in the infinite richness of divine love.[41] Karl Barth had earlier criticized liberal theology in much the same way, complaining that Schleiermacher's notion of sin as a mere lack of God consciousness does not adequately explain the power of human opposition against divine love revealed in the way in which God was genuinely "assailed" and suffered in the cross.[42] In fact, Dietrich Bonhoeffer even saw this assailed and wounded God hidden beneath the weakness of the cross as the key to the renewal of theology in an increasingly secular age.[43] Kitamori added that the wounded love revealed in the God of the OT makes the cross the supreme revelation of divine love. God in fact used the human pain of Jesus in the cross to reveal the divine pain. Only in this joining of human suffering to God's suffering love for others is redemption possible.[44] The suffering love of God certainly judges or resists, but also extends an embrace to, all that threatens to break the union of love between God and the creature.[45]

A similar vision of the suffering love of God is advocated by Jürgen Moltmann. Moltmann came to develop an understanding of the cross as an intra-Trinitarian event, thus securing the link between the Trinity and the paschal mystery. The Trinity was not simply an intellectual puzzle; rather, it structured and explained the relational richness of the story of Jesus. Not only was the pain of God revealed in the pain of Jesus on the cross, but for Moltmann the pain of Jesus was taken up into the intra-Trinitarian life of God to have a significant effect on God.[46] So also in Revelation, the crisis of crucifixion depicted in chapter 5 is resolved as the Son rises to the throne to take from the heavenly Father the scroll that proclaims the gospel of redemption.

This vision of the suffering God of love does not necessarily eclipse the God who is holy and sovereign, as Revelation shows us. The image of God's reigning from the throne in Revelation prevents us from simply dissolving God into the process of human liberation and healing. The God who is revealed in

40. Kitamori, *Theology of the Pain of God*, 22.
41. Kitamori, *Theology of the Pain of God*, 24.
42. Barth, *Church Dogmatics*, 3/3:329.
43. Dietrich Bonhoeffer, *Letters and Papers from Prison* (London: SCM Press, 1967), 348-49, 360-61, 370.
44. Kitamori, *Theology of the Pain of God*, 80.
45. Kitamori, *Theology of the Pain of God*, 78.
46. This is Moltmann's major thesis in *The Trinity and the Kingdom*.

the crucified and risen Christ still reigns over all of the affairs of history. But providence is not identical in Revelation with "whatever happens"; instead, it is the redemptive purposes being worked out in the events of the end, purposes that must be spiritually discerned in their consistency with the crucified and risen Christ. Sovereignty is thus understood in a way that is integral to, even fundamentally defined by, divine love and pathos. So it is also with the God of Revelation.

The Sovereign God in Holiness

The above integration of sovereignty and grace in Revelation, however, is mediated by divine holiness. The holiness of God is difficult to define, since it is not depicted so much in Revelation as expressed in adoration. Obviously, God's transcendence, majesty, purity, goodness, and covenant faithfulness are all connected to the multifaceted meaning of this term. God's holiness in Revelation undergirds the righteousness of divine judgments in response to cries for justice. The God who reigns is not seduced by evil or manipulated by it; rather, God overcomes evil through redemptive self-giving and righteous acts of judgment. The blood of the Lamb and the all-pervasive presence of the Holy Spirit thus complement our understanding of the holy God. The blood of the Lamb cleanses from sin (7:14) and allows the saints to overcome evil in the world (12:11). This blood is the means by which the saints can participate in God's purity and victory over evil. The Holy Spirit allows the people of God to discern the words of Jesus and to obey them, thus furthering their clothing in righteous deeds. Yet, God's holiness is still infinitely transcendent and unique, an all-consuming fire, ultimately inaccessible to mere finite creatures. The Germans thus rightly distinguish between our holiness *(Heiligung)* and divine holiness *(Heiligkeit)*. The latter confronts and changes us but remains transcendent and infinite.

There is no question but that the holy God in Revelation both judges evil and reaches out to sinners in grace. Theologically, it is important to note that divine holiness helps us to understand the connection between these two realities of judgment and grace. God's love is a holy love, not one that is morally neutral. It does not seek to avoid conflict so as to let evil have its way. It does not cower in fear of evil, nor is it subject to being seduced by evil. Divine love is an almighty and a holy love that does not compromise with evil but rather overcomes evil in merciful and righteous judgments.

Though divine holiness points to God's transcendence and majesty, it is also a relational quality in the Bible that invites the creature within the faithfulness of the divine embrace. Divine holiness thus helps us to understand why the creature is in need of grace and redemption. It helps us to understand why atonement is necessary or why we burst forth with praise at the depth of mercy involved in this gift (5:9). In Isa 6 Isaiah cries out in unworthiness at the sight of the holy God and must be consecrated through atonement before he can proceed to fulfill God's purposes. So also in Revelation, the holy God is known only by the blood of the Lamb and the living prophetic witness of the Holy Spirit. In the light of such texts, Barth rightly notes that, if God "were not first the Creator and Father who is the Lord of our being, against whom we have sinned, whose wrath is thus upon us, but whose wrath is but the reverse side of His love as Creator and Father, how then could He be the Reconciler, the Peacemaker?"[47] Divine holiness further helps us to understand the moral fittingness of God's stance against evil and injustice, and the need for God to graciously turn to the sinner for reconciliation to occur. If the God of the covenant were not holy, grace would be an empty concept, and divine judgment against injustice a hypocritical sham. There would be no way of understanding the need for atonement or of the blood of the Lamb, no need to understand why knowing God should so overwhelm us with gratitude and praise.

Divine holiness is thus a vital component of God's relationship to the creature. In fact, if God were not holy, humanity would be forever lost, since evil would end up the decisive victor in history and over all of creation, even over God. In fact, the evil one would be God! Humanity must see in the holiness of God a vital part of ultimate hope for the victory of God over evil. In both grace and judgment, the holy God is thus for humanity, for creation, as the only real hope that evil cannot win and that grace will. God's love and judgments are holy because they are genuinely for the creature and against the evil that seeks to ultimately destroy creation.

Not only does holiness help us understand divine love or grace and how it relates to judgment, divine love also helps us to understand the depth of divine holiness. God is holy *love;* divine holiness is pure love. In this sense, it is important to note that God hates evil or responds in wrath against it because God loves creation so much and knows what evil does to it. Evil separates creation from God and destroys the creation. God thus strikes out against those destroying the creation in order to bring an end to it (Rev 11:18). God's holy love is an all-consuming fire ultimately for the sake of creation and not against it. God's wrath is ultimately meant to purge and aid in redemption. Barth thus quotes J. Wichelhaus: "Man cannot and will not understand that it is just be-

---

47. Barth, *Church Dogmatics*, 1/1:413.

cause God is good that He is holy."⁴⁸ Barth could thus comment in response, "To accept God's grace necessarily means, therefore, to respect God's holiness, and therefore to accept, heed and keep His laws, to fear His threats, to experience His wrath and to suffer His punishment."⁴⁹ One needs only to read Rev 2–3 to recognize this fact. In the light of divine holiness, grace judges, and judgment has a gracious purpose. In fact, divine holiness helps us to see that judgment and grace are not really so separate, since judgment points to grace, and grace implies a rejection of evil. Barth thus wrote that the "holiness of God consists in the unity of His judgment with His grace."⁵⁰

The Sovereign God at War

The relationship of God and violence in Revelation is a complex issue. Many are offended when reading of the sharp judgments that come from the divine throne, even though chapter 6 implies a human cause to the violence unleashed in judgment as well. Even the plagues given in response to the cries of the martyrs are described as halting such violence, including that which destroys the earth ("destroying those who destroy the earth," 11:18). Moreover, the church has always recognized Christ as the Lord of Scripture (its chief subject matter) and the drama of mercy and redemption offered through him as governing for interpreting the Scripture's larger prophetic witness.⁵¹ It has been suggested above that the convergence in Revelation of divine sovereignty and love and mercy under the category of the kingdom of God and of the slain Lamb would be an important step in the direction of dealing with the issue of God and violence. The role of the Lamb and the Spirit in judgment in revelation has at its core exposing and defeating the deception of the dragon, beast, and false prophet by Christ's discerning eyes or by the sword that proceeds from Christ's mouth (Rev. 1:16; 2:12, 16; 5:6; 19:15, 21). In this light, evil in Revelation has within itself the seeds of its own violent undoing, precisely in its opposition to the light of God's self-communicative action. As Miroslav Volf has shown, the overarching divine

---

48. Barth, *Church Dogmatics*, 1/2:365.
49. Barth, *Church Dogmatics*, 1/2:367.
50. Barth, *Church Dogmatics*, 1/2:363.
51. Luther even wrote, "The scriptures must be understood for Christ and not against him. . . . If, therefore, our adversaries should use scripture against Christ, we shall use Christ against the scripture." *The Works of Martin Luther* (ed. Paul Zeller Strodach; Philadelphia: Muhlenberg Press, 1915), 1:xxxix, 47. Of course, Christ is delivered to us through the scriptural witness, so ultimately one is discerning in the light of the Christ-event the larger witness of Scripture in order to understand the various parts within its light.

will to embrace must also involve divine exclusion or justice, or redemptive love cannot overcome their opposites.[52] Revelation belongs to "resistance literature," and its power lies "in the unmasking of the present order."[53]

Moreover, judgment is turned against the human perpetrators of deception, but with a redemptive purpose. In other words, the theology of Revelation occurs in conflict with the world for the sake of the world. Divine sovereignty, or the kingdom of God, is thus not a static concept in Revelation but is redemptive in its thrust. The sovereignty of the God of love, therefore, does not mean that the battle is over and that all the church has to do is to tread water until the end of the age comes. One striking point about the God of classical theism is that this God rests comfortably within a static reality disconnected from the battle to be fought and won. The overwhelming emphasis is on God's infinity and transcendence. God is essentially removed from the challenges of evil, cannot be wounded or assailed, has nothing really at stake. There is no unfolding drama that takes our breath away or causes us to weep or to rejoice as the audience to Revelation is provoked into doing. The problem of theodicy (justifying faith in God in the midst of evil and suffering) is solved by removing any real conflict.

In response to the accusation that he supported just such an understanding of God, Karl Barth entitled one entire section of his *Church Dogmatics*, "Jesus Is Victor." Though for Barth the Bible does not present an absolute dualism in which darkness and light are locked in eternal combat, neither do we have a monism in which the opposition of darkness to the light is brushed aside, with "its challenging and restricting of light of no account."[54] What we have instead is a "dynamic teleology" in which real opposition, injury, and loss occur and in which the light, though clearly on the way toward ultimate victory, must wrestle toward it. Barth concludes, "A history is here taking place; a drama is being enacted; a war waged to a successful conclusion."[55] This is not the abstract and speculative God of classical theism in which contrasts are made in the service of an intellectually satisfying worldview. This is theology that begins with the battle in history for redemption and justice. The kind of theology that is done in this context is not armchair theology but rather theology born of prayer, petition, conflict, and praise. Theology true to Revelation is wartime theology.

This wartime theology of God does not mean that theology is not also to be humble and dialogical. Those who are working on this aspect of theological method on the cutting edge of addressing the pluralist challenges facing Chris-

---

52. Miroslav Volf, *Exclusion and Embrace: A Theological Reflection on Identity, Otherness, and Reconciliation* (Nashville: Abingdon, 1996).

53. Johns, *The Lamb Christology of the Apocalypse of John*, 9-10.

54. Barth, *Church Dogmatics*, 4/3, first half, 168.

55. Barth, *Church Dogmatics*, 4/3, first half, 168.

tian theological claims might find the sharp dualisms of Revelation off-putting. One might then understandably turn to Luke, for example, for more helpful guidance. Luke notes that the cultural journeys of all peoples have been guided by God providentially so that they might reach out for God and perhaps find him, for God is near to all of humanity, in the breath that they breathe and in the vitality of their lives (Acts 17:24-28). In the midst of this understandable move to other canonical voices, however, James Cone has argued that a respectful engagement with theological pluralism should not eclipse the fact that, at decisive moments in history, the church and theology are called to take sides on behalf of those who cry out for justice.[56] Dialogue in the midst of pluralist options can sometimes be done without an equally strong recognition that theologians must also engage in conflict and take sides. Theology may at times need to utilize the battlefield context more than the table of dialogue, though both are always needed in some sense. God's commitment to hear and to respond to the cries for justice among the martyrs in chapter 6 means that unjust suffering for Revelation is at the very point of departure for the author's "theological method." God's solidarity with the oppressed in the figure of the slaughtered Lamb is determinative for how we view who God is and how we judge the divine involvement in the world. God's determination to make all things new in the figure of the risen Christ fulfills our understanding of God and grants us hope in the struggle for the justice of the kingdom of God in the world.

Yet, there is certainly more to say. Though Revelation focuses on justice for the persecuted Christian community, there is certainly room to invoke other canonical texts in an effort to bring in voices that cry for justice from outside the boundaries of the church. The divine guidance of the peoples of the world in Acts 17 was surely at work in Acts 8, leading the marginalized Ethiopian eunuch to the Isa 53 passage concerning the suffering servant, who lacked the privilege of any descendants. Drawn from a history of oppression, this spiritual connection between the eunuch and Isa 53 occurred before any Christian evangelist could explain what it meant. Such sensitivity to oppressed voices outside of the church is especially relevant in those times and places where the church (or at least sectors of the church removed from oppression) may even contribute more to the forces of injustice than to the forces for justice and healing. The sharp warnings of Revelation for the churches to repent are applicable here as well. I also cannot help but see in the glory and honor of the nations that are brought into the heavenly city and presented to the risen Lamb (21:26) the suffering and victories of these peoples over the long span of their histories in their search for God in the midst of evil and injustice.

56. James Cone, *God of the Oppressed* (Maryknoll, NY: Orbis, 1997), 78-83.

There is also the urgent need for seeing the slain Lamb as not only a means for the oppressed to be free but also as a means for saving the oppressor. After all, the boundary between oppressor and oppressed is sometimes difficult to draw, since we all have elements of both in us. As Volf notes, only in extending the possibility of grace to the oppressor can the oppressed face the danger of their own potential for violence and break the cycle of violence imposed by those who stand to benefit most from it. By extending grace while seeking freedom, the oppressed ultimately refuse to allow the oppressor to determine their course, the course of the future.[57] At the heart of extending grace in Revelation is God's opening up the hospitality of faith in Christ to the nations. Revelation offers far-reaching resources for thinking theologically about the hospitality of faith set before the nations so as to save them from the feast of destruction and preserve them for the marriage supper of God's Lamb. But not even the destruction of chapters 17 and 18 is the final word for the nations in Revelation. The sudden presence of the nations judged in chapter 19 in the millennial kingdom of chapter 20 and the vast expanse of time involving that kingdom (1,000 years) in comparison with the brief time of trial are powerful reminders of the breadth of grace in Revelation. The presence of leaves in the New Jerusalem for the healing of the nations (22:2) is proof that even the judgments of the book are not at all the final word when it comes to God's relationship to the nations. It is God's grace that sets the terms of the future, not the forces of violence.

Conclusion

The God of Revelation is sovereign; yet, this sovereign reign is not an oppressive reality but a liberating and redemptive one. So it is with the kingdom of God on earth. God's reign is mysterious, but it is also defined concretely in the resurrection of the crucified Christ, in the discernment of the Spirit, and in the coming new creation. This reign is transcendent, but it has also been brought near through the crucified and risen Lamb and the Spirit of discernment and witness. It is thus fundamentally defined by divine love and holiness, though it is also expressed in acts of judgment against the forces of injustice. It is not static but dynamic and is in the process of gaining ground until the final victory is accomplished. This victory is already inaugurated in the resurrection of the crucified Lamb, but it will come to fullness in the new heavens and new earth, in which God and all righteousness will dwell. Such a complex and redemptive

---

57. Miroslav Volf, *Exclusion and Embrace*.

view of divine sovereignty holds promise as a meaningful alternative to the static and oppressive understandings possible whenever sovereignty is detached from the work of the triune God to bring about redemption. Once the triune God is viewed as the one who structures the redemptive story of Jesus rather than simply an occasion for abstract speculation about the inner life of God, it becomes possible to reconstruct the reign of God in our time as a real source of hope for a liberating future.

Christ

Revelation and Biblical Theology

As Brevard Childs notes, Christian theologians widely assume that "the centre of Biblical Theology, in some sense, must be Christology, the biblical witness to the person and work of Jesus Christ."[58] Christ is indeed the key to understanding both the divine turn to humanity in grace and the human self-giving by way of response. Christ is thus the visible point of union between God and humanity. The focal point in the NT for where this union of God and humanity becomes most clearly visible is the story of Jesus: his birth, baptism, mission, death, resurrection, and ascension. Seen from the angle of God's work of redemption for humanity, the story of Jesus Christ can be seen as the "whole context of the Christian message."[59] It is not our consciousness of God, sense of moral "ought," or diverse cultural understandings of transcendence that provide the clearest indication of the divine/human relationship; rather, it is the story of Jesus Christ as the one who gave his life and rose again for the salvation of humankind and the renewal of creation. The ongoing and diverse contextualization of that liberating story throughout various communities of faith is vital to our richly expansive understandings of God's involvement in the world and our participation in God. But Christ and the biblical witness to him remain the living measure of all of our experiences of grace.

Revelation

The significance of Christ as the measure of God's involvement in the world and of our participation in the unfolding drama of redemption is clearly

---

58. Childs, *Biblical Theology of the Old and New Testaments*, 452.
59. Childs, *Biblical Theology of the Old and New Testaments*, 462.

supported in Revelation. The first two verses of Revelation identify the book as "the revelation of Jesus Christ," as well as the ongoing "word of God and the testimony of Jesus Christ." Both the revelation and the testimony point to Christ being the focal point of God's word, for he is the mediator of revelation in the book. The interpretive key for understanding Christ is not fundamentally the messianic expectations drawn from the OT but rather the image of the risen Christ who was crucified for the salvation of the world. The messianic ruler is thus portrayed mainly with the help of a conflation of images drawn from the heavenly or eschatological Son of Man (Dan 7:13-14) and the Suffering Servant/Lamb (Isa 53). Determinative is the slaughtered Lamb, who rises up as the Lion of Judah to open the scroll and to reign over God's kingdom (Rev 5).

The centrality of the Lamb in Revelation is connected to the Lamb as the object of worship. Revelation is unique among Jewish and Christian apocalyptic literature in the attention it pays to worship, even to the point of containing passages of a liturgical nature. It is telling in this light that John embarks on his visions "in the Spirit on the Lord's Day," prostrate before the risen Christ (1:10, 17). The drama that follows highlights Christ as the mediator between God and humanity within the overall restoration of the creature to its proper role in giving praise to the Creator. Revelation assumes that the intermediary role served by the Lamb warrants making him the object of worship. This striking assumption has much to do with the Lamb as revealer.

The worship of the Lamb in Revelation thus begins with the conviction that he participates in the impartation of revelation from God, or, more generally, in the divine self-giving as light in the midst of darkness. The book of Revelation qualifies the revelation imparted by Christ as that which *God gave him* to show his servants "what must soon take place" (1:1). However, Christ does not just serve to mediate revelation as mere servants of God do, for the Father does not give Christ the revelation in the same way it is given to them. In receiving the revelation from the Father, Christ becomes integral to the revelation itself, actively mediating it in a way that allows the revelation to flow forth *from him* as it does from God. Christ thus speaks revelatory words directly to the churches in the first person singular as the very source of the divinely given words discerned in the Spirit (2:7, 11, 17, 29; 3:1, 6, 13, 22). Radiating from the Father, he is indeed the light by which the nations walk in the New Jerusalem (21:23-25).

Revelation confirms in subtle ways that Christ's unique mediation of revelation is divine. Interestingly, when John falls prostrate before the messenger/guide in 19:10 and 22:8-9, it is precisely because of the messenger's role *in showing him what must come to pass*. But John is immediately informed that he has made a grave error here. The messenger does not mediate revelation as Christ does; the messenger is not the one to whom the Spirit of prophecy bears testimony. The messenger is, like John, a mere servant who exclaims, "Worship God! For it is the Spirit of prophecy who bears testimony to Jesus" (19:10). The indication in this verse is that there is a divide between Christ's mediation of revelation, which makes him the object of the Spirit's testimony, and the role of the servant messengers, which does not qualify them to be the object of the Spirit's testimony. Such a distinction helps us to understand why John is not rebuked when he falls prostrate before the risen Christ in chapter 1. Christ does not say, as the messenger says later, "Don't do that!" Christ is then described in ways typical of how the OT describes God. His hair is white as wool like the Ancient of Days in Dan 7:9, and he is "the First and the Last," a reference to Isa 44:6, one of the strongest monotheistic statements from the OT: "I am the first and I am the last; apart from me there is no God." Christ in Revelation is thus "King of Kings and Lord of Lords" (19:16).

The distinction between Christ's mediation of revelation and that of the servants provides the background for the pivotal throne-room scene in chapter 5, which features Christ as alone worthy to reveal the contents of the scroll. John is taken up in the Spirit to the throne so as to discover "what must take place" (4:1). The scroll that then becomes noticeable is key to the impartation of this revelation from God. Immediately upon noticing this scroll, however, John is confronted with a problematic question: Who is worthy to take the scroll from the hand of God, break its seals, and reveal its contents? The question is made all the more urgent in light of the fact that no creature from all of creation is able to do it: "No one in heaven or on earth or under the earth could open the scroll or even look inside it" (5:3). The utter sacredness and transcendence of the revelation place it outside the grasp of creaturely abilities. The creatures, who have their being from the divine will according to 4:11, do not have that will within their grasp.

John weeps at the absence of a worthy mediator between the transcendent scroll and the creaturely realm (5:4). The possibility that such a failure could occur at the throne of God seemed unimaginable to John. At this point, the assurance is given that the Lion of Judah, the Root of David, is able and worthy to open the scroll to reveal its contents (5:5). Surprisingly, standing before John at the very "center of the throne" is not a lion or the blazing image of the risen Christ that was encountered in chapter 1 but rather a Lamb "looking as if it had been slain" and encircled by the living creatures who had been worshipping God (5:6). The location of the slain Lamb at the center of the throne encircled by worshippers implies that he is to be the recipient of praise. His exalted state at the throne contrasts with his appearance as a little, vulnerable lamb, as the term ἀρνίον (*arnion*, "lamb") indicates.⁶⁰ The fact that this lamb has horns does not distract from the obvious contrast in image between the conquering Lion of Judah and the vulnerable little Lamb that had been slaughtered. The one who conquered and is worthy to stand with God in revealing the scroll is a vulnerable and slain Lamb.

Indeed, this embodiment of revelation by the Lamb is exactly the point, for it assumes that the Lamb's self-giving is a *divine* activity, God's self-communicative action. It is precisely because the Lamb has given of himself victoriously to redeem humanity that he is now worthy to unveil the revelation of the scroll that recounts this event and its projection into the future. The Lamb, who is the central player in the drama, is the only one who can unveil it. As the Lamb takes the scroll from the right hand of God to reveal its contents, the response is immediate and powerful. *The Lamb is worshipped.* The first round of praise to the Lamb comes from the living creatures and twenty-four elders, who fall down before the Lamb with harps and bowls of incense containing the prayers of God's people. This imagery implies that John considers the worship of the Lamb in heaven to be consistent with the worship practices of the churches with which he was connected, for he assumes continuity between the heavenly praise and the earthly praises of God's people.⁶¹ They praise the Lamb for being worthy to open the scroll because he has redeemed us by his blood (5:9-10). Two more rounds of praise then resound through heaven: first, involving the angelic hosts, and, then, every remaining living creature. The final round rings forth among all the creatures:

> To him who sits on the throne and to the Lamb
> be praise and honor and glory and power,
>   for ever and ever! (5:13)

The Lamb thus receives the same praise offered to the Father. He is identified with God.

Interestingly, this worship of the mediator Lamb did not to John's mind ease the demands of Jewish monotheism. I use the term "monotheism" cautiously here, aware of the problem involved in reading a modern understanding of that term into a first-century Jewish context. But as Richard Bauckham and Larry Hurtado have shown, the essential features of the Jewish monotheism that dominated first-century Judaism — namely, that there is only one God,

---

60. Johns, *The Lamb Christology of the Apocalypse of John*, 25-40.
61. Otto Piper, "The Apocalypse of John and the Liturgy of the Ancient Church," *Church History* 20.1 (March, 1951): 10-22.

who reigns over all and who is alone the object of cultic worship — provided the background for the worship of the Lamb in Revelation.[62] Within the threatening context of imperial Rome, John is well aware of the difference between worship of God and the worship of a mere creature. The difference between true and false worship is at the core of the book's entire message. It represents idolatry to worship anyone other than God, especially the dragon and the beast, who seek such adoration (2:14, 20; 9:20; 13; 21:8; 22:15), and worship is condemned even for beings appointed from heaven to do God's will (19:10; 22:8-9). The fact that the worship of the Lamb plays such a dominant role in a book so committed to its Jewish monotheistic roots is significant. The worship of Jesus in Revelation is thus not a result of a departure from Jewish monotheism but is rather a mutation within it, dependent on it for its exclusivity but qualified by the experience of Jesus as the risen Lord, who in imparting himself imparts revelation from God.

The worship of the Lamb in Revelation is not only based on the Lamb's mediation of revelation from God, it is also based on the Lamb's mediation of the creature's response of praise to God. The two are integral to each other. Consistent with his role in making creation a fitting offering to God, the risen Christ in chapter 1 is imaged with priestly garb as he walks among the churches that are symbolized by lampstands in the temple of God (1:12-13). The role of the churches as lights in the temple is mediated by the priestly ministry of Christ, who is the supreme light that shines forth from the Father (21:23). In Revelation the Lamb does not mediate the self-offering of the saints to the glory of God as creatures do. He mediates actively as God does by making the creatures worthy of divine glory. The saints are purified (7:14) and conquer during the time of trial (12:11) "by the blood of the Lamb." The two witnesses are murdered and rise again as Christ did (11:7-12), and the 144,000 faithful are said to be offered as firstfruits "to God and the Lamb," but only as they "follow the Lamb wherever he goes" (14:4). The assumption is that the Lamb is the supreme offering to God through which these witnesses are accepted as a holy offering, the firstfruits of the redeemed creation. This offering of creation through the offering of the Lamb is set within cultic imagery that connects heaven to earth, such as the altar before the throne (6:9; 8:3; 9:13; 11:1; 14:18; 16:7) and bowls of incense (5:8; 8:3-4), which contextualize the priestly ministry of the Lamb.[63] Christ makes them a kingdom and priests by mediating and perfecting their self-giving to God.

---

62. Bauckham, *Jesus and the God of Israel*, and Larry W. Hurtado, *Lord Jesus Christ: Devotion to Jesus in Earliest Christianity* (Grand Rapids: Eerdmans, 2003).

63. Johns, *The Lamb Christology of the Apocalypse of John*, 128-29.

The contrast between the vulnerable image of the slain, little Lamb and the powerful image of the Lion of Judah throughout the Lamb's redemptive activity is most striking.[64] This contrast turns on its head the notion of power assumed by the dragon, the beast, and the successes of Babylon. It is not through aggression and injustice that the decisive victories of the kingdom of God will be accomplished but, rather, through the self-sacrifice of the vulnerable Lamb of God. The heavenly Father has committed the victories of the divine kingdom to this slain Lamb, which speaks volumes about the nature of the kingdom of God. The victory of the Lion is enacted through the path of the vulnerable and slain Lamb. The one who will reign with an iron scepter came as a vulnerable child who was destined to be slain (12:4-5; 13:8). By electing the Son (12:5) to be the slaughtered Lamb from the very creation of the world (13:8), the heavenly Father also engaged in a profound form of self-determination as the God of the Lamb, or as the God who would forever be the self-giving, self-sacrificial covenant partner to humanity. This is the God who is vulnerable to suffering and who bears up under our sin and death in order to bring us into God's eternal reign. The vulnerable Lamb does not simply qualify our understanding of the ferocious Lion but is rather the lens through which the Lion's acts are to be understood. The God who is victorious over the dragon and the beast has won through the exercise of wounded love. The saints win by following this same self-sacrificial path as well (12:11; 14:4). One must keep in mind when reading further on in the book how divine wrath destroys "those who destroy the earth" (11:18b), that such wrath is the act of wounded love and, for the book, is necessary resistance to the destructive power of the beast and those who seek to be his instruments. The overarching goal of the wounded Lamb, however, is the healing of the nations (22:2). Divine love is wounded so that we may be healed.

The Lion, however, also helps us to understand the Lamb. The beast does draw from human rebellion to wound the Lamb, much as believers have been wounded. The slain Lamb stands in the midst of the throne! The wounding of human rejection pierces the very heart of God's reign over history. But Revelation assures believers that the wounded Lamb is also the Lion of Judah. There is no way that divine love can be conquered. It is wounded but will conquer through these wounds. Rather than allow this wounding to thwart the divine plan, God weaves it into salvation history as the vital core of the victory. God tastes our sin and death in order that we might taste righteousness and life. There is a joyful exchange taking place between Christ and sinners here. The Lion of God's kingdom partakes of the wounds and consequences of sin in order that we might partake of his kingdom. This is the praise of the saints:

---

64. See Johns, *The Lamb Christology of the Apocalypse of John*.

By his blood the Lion/Lamb has "made them to be a kingdom and priests to serve our God, and they will reign on the earth" (5:10). By becoming the Lamb, the Lion could bring those captive to and wounded by sin into the kingdom of those who intercede for a dying world. Through eyes of faith the saints can see the Lion through the image of the crucified Lamb, as well as the hidden presence of victory through the darkness that surrounds them and the wounds that pierce them.

Though the grace of God offered to sinful humanity is certainly at the heart of the image of the slaughtered Lamb, the reality of judgment in the face of the crucified is present in Revelation as well, for the cross casts a shadow upon those who continue to choose the path of rejecting grace. Grace offers healing from the wounds of sin, but it does not whitewash the sin as though it were no sin at all. This point is especially significant in relation to the forces of violence in Revelation that lead in the rejection of God's offer of grace. As S. Mark Heim has noted (under the influence of René Girard), the Bible does not allow the oppressors who persecute and murder the righteous to cover up the crime through scapegoating (blaming the victim or glorifying the victim in order to hide the evil of the crime perpetrated).[65] The Psalms, for example, leave unaltered the cries of innocence and injustice made against those who persecute and kill. Likewise, the murder of the Lamb in Revelation cannot be covered up as in the case of scapegoating, for he returns with his wounds and the brutality of humanity's crime against him fully exposed (1:7). The murderers of Jesus among the Jews and the Romans are not in control of how the crucifixion of Jesus is interpreted, for all that they can do is mourn. The risen Lamb, or the Lion of Judah, determines what the crucifixion will mean for them all. Though grace is always offered by the slaughtered Lamb, the reality of how humanity unjustly killed him must also be faced. Those who continue to live in that sin will face the Lamb as their judge and will have to face the reality of their self-chosen path of alienation and darkness, "for the great day of their wrath has come, and who can withstand it?" (6:17). As we will see when we discuss eschatology, grace never ceases to be offered to the unredeemed in the book of Revelation, but this point cannot be used to downplay the seriousness of sin.

In chapter 1 the risen Christ is pictured as both coming and present. Christ is referred to as coming in both judgment and salvation, an awesome event accompanied by mourning among those who murdered him (1:7). The hope for Christ's future coming then leads in Rev 1 to a blazing portrayal of the

---

65. S. Mark Heim, *Saved from Sacrifice: A Theology of the Cross* (Grand Rapids: Eerdmans, 2006). See also René Girard, *The Scapegoat* (Baltimore, MD: Johns Hopkins University Press, 1989).

risen Christ walking in the midst of the seven lamps, which are the churches, addressing each one directly (1:12-16). The future coming of Christ is juxtaposed with the Christ who is present in the midst of the churches, grasped by the discernment of the Spirit. The coming Christ is, in a sense, already present. Christ is present as the one who is the focal point of the churches, for they gather around him to hear his word. He speaks words of judgment and salvation that belong to God alone: "I am he who searches hearts and minds, and I will repay each of you according to your deeds" (2:23).[66] The word of Christ is presented to them and then through them to the world. This combination of Christ's absence (yet to come) and spiritual presence (as discerned in the Spirit) will help to explain the "not-yet/already" nature of Christian experience, or the longing for Christ fueled and comforted by an experience of Christ in the Spirit.

The presence of the risen Christ is especially significant, given the context of suffering, for John identifies himself as "your brother and companion in the suffering and kingdom and patient endurance that are ours in Jesus" (1:9). Suffering makes the patience for the arrival of Christ all the more difficult to achieve. The presence of the risen Christ, however, offers readers who suffer in the midst of a dark world a glimpse of the coming victory, as well as a foretaste of its future glory. What a boost to their patient endurance this must have been! Moreover, the presence of the risen Christ who had been crucified offers them the hermeneutical key to understanding the destiny of suffering believers, as well as an earth severely battered in the coming time of trial. Christ is the living one who holds the keys of Death and Hades (1:18) and whose resurrection has inaugurated the resurrection of the dead and the new heavens and new earth. The coming victory is already foreshadowed in the presence of the risen Christ as discerned in the Spirit. If believers know that they will one day rise victoriously from the dead in order to occupy a new heaven and a new earth, they are indeed able to patiently endure in the midst of suffering. They can have the "confidence in what we hope for and assurance about what we do not see" (Heb 11:1).

This assurance is indeed put to the test, which means that believers must overcome and patiently endure. It is put to the test by the violence of persecution. Such a challenge to faith sets the stage for the ultimate test that is found in the dramatic image of the slain Lamb in Rev 5 who reveals the contents of the scroll. In worshipping the Lamb as a result, believers can affirm their own victory over death in continuity with the Lamb. They know that their own victory is tied to the Lamb's and their own faith and hope thrive in worship-

---

66. See Richard B. Hays, "Faithful Witness, Alpha and Omega," in *Revelation and the Politics of Interpretation* (ed. Richard B. Hays; Waco, TX: Baylor University Press, 2012), 71.

ping the Lamb. Their worship is a form of resistance to the lies of the forces of opposition.

As noted earlier, the Lamb is parodied by the beast who also seeks to be worshipped and to reign over all (13:6-8). The beast thus implicitly seeks to repeat the sin of Adam, who attempted to exalt himself to the place of God by heeding the words of the serpent (Gen 3:5). The Lamb, however, came to reverse the sin of Adam by giving of himself in obedience to the Father. In so doing, the Lamb in Revelation clashes with the beast. The beast seeks to reign and receive praise through violence and self-exaltation, while the Lamb will reign through self-giving or by the blood of his self-sacrifice for the sake of a redeemed humanity. While in Babylon, humans are sold and purchased as slaves in a violent world that dehumanizes. Christ purchases humanity through his blood in order to restore unto them the dignity of sharing in God's reign (Rev 5:9). If there is violence coming from the Lamb, it is essentially an antiviolence campaign aimed at stopping the violent forces that seek to destroy the earth (11:18) and dehumanize (18:13).

The conflict between the Lamb and the dragon in chapter 12 is thus the ultimate war over the question of lordship. Who will reign? Christ or the dragon and his beast, self-giving love or self-assertive violence, righteousness or sin, life or death? The result is clear, was clear from the start of the drama, but becomes strikingly clear as the drama unfolds. Despite his flashy displays of power in the world, the beast cannot win, for Christ, the slaughtered Lamb, is the one who is the First and the Last, the Risen One who holds the keys to hell and death, who stands in the midst of the heavenly throne, and who is coming again to reign. The saints only need to keep this in mind when the beast rises up against them with awesome displays of power.

Gospel of John and 1–3 John

What stands out in the Christology of the Gospel of John is the preexistence of Jesus as the Word of the heavenly Father (John 1:1; cf. Rev 19:13). The Word, or Logos, is not Philo's divine mind but, rather, the agent of creation (John 1:2-3), in whom was the life that was the light of all humankind (1:4). Just as the Father has life, so also the Father has granted the Son to have the same (5:26). This is the new life that raises the dead, a privilege granted by the Father to the Son (5:21). Jesus is the resurrection and the life, who will raise those who believe in him (11:25; 6:40). He breathes forth the Spirit of life (20:22) in a way that recalls God's giving Adam the breath of life in Gen 2:7. Obviously, the very Spirit or breath of God belongs as well, and in the same sense, to the Son. The Logos is the Son who gives forth not only life but also light (John 1:4-5) and grace, truth, and glory (1:14). The Word, or Son, of the Father preexisted with the Father from the beginning (1:1-2; 17:5, 24) and became flesh to reveal the Father (1:14, 18). This Word, or Son, is distinct from the Father but is still referred to as well with the title God or Lord (1:1; 20:28). This unity of nature with the Father is not surprising, given that the Son shares in the uniquely divine privileges of creating, imparting the Spirit, raising the dead, and giving forth life, grace, and truth. The Spirit is even identified as the very breath of Jesus (20:22), meaning that the Spirit belongs as uniquely to Jesus as the Spirit belongs to God.

Jesus thus has a uniquely intimate relationship to the Father in John. Jesus refers to God as his Father 106 times in John alone.[67] He is the "one and only Son, who is himself God and is in closest relationship with the Father," for only the Son knows directly and can reveal the Father (1:18; cf. 6:46). The Father is seen in seeing Jesus (14:9). The Son is thus the only path to the Father (14:6). The Son and the Father are one (10:30), having shared divine love and glory from eternity (17:5, 24). Indeed, the Word is God (1:1). Jesus' unique reference to God as his Father implies an "unheard of closeness" or intimacy of union between himself and God.[68] In reporting that Jewish leaders complained about Jesus' making himself equal to God by referring to God as his Father (5:18), John does not in any way imply that they had misread him, but follows with Jesus' statement that the Father has entrusted all judgment to the Son, precisely so that "all may honor the Son just as they honor the Father" (5:22-23). Jesus has always been in the Father and the Father in him in intimate communion (10:38; 17:21). Jesus' deity is also supported by the many "I Am" statements of John (4:26; 6:20; 8:24, 58; 18:5, 6, 8), a phrase that is "a divine self-declaration which encapsulates Yahweh's claim to unique and exclusive divinity."[69]

The Son shares deity with the Father but is also willingly dependent on the Father for all things. The Father loves the Son and has placed everything in his hands (3:35). The Father has placed all things under the Son's power (13:3). The Father has entrusted all judgment to the Son (5:22) and has placed the divine seal of approval on him (6:27). Whatever the Father does, the Son also does (5:19), including, as we have seen, creating, imparting the Spirit, giving new life, and raising the dead. His entire mission is described as a being sent by the Father in order to return to him after dying for the world and rising again (16:28).

67. Ladd, *Theology of the New Testament*, 283.
68. Jürgen Moltmann, *The Way of Jesus Christ* (Philadelphia: Fortress Press, 1992), 142.
69. Richard Bauckham, "Monotheism and Christology in the Gospel of John," in *Contours of Christology in the New Testament* (ed. Richard N. Longenecker; Grand Rapids: Eerdmans, 2005), 158.

Jesus' mission in John has a messianic element (11:47-48; 6:15). But John goes to great lengths to contrast Jesus' actual fulfillment of this mission from popular Jewish expectations, especially of a political king come to fulfill nationalistic hopes. People expect the Messiah in John (1:20, 41; 4:29; 7:31), and they try to make him the Davidic king by force (6:15). Jesus' reign, however, is not of this world but of the world to come, and the truthfulness of witness to its reality already invades the here and now (18:36-37). For John, Jesus' glorious reign as Messiah is connected to Jesus' death on the cross (10:11, 15, 17-18). When he as the heavenly Son of Man is lifted up, he will draw all people to himself (12:32; 8:28). Pointing toward the cross, his washing the disciples' feet was a powerful expression of his love for them and of his servanthood (13:1-11), as well as an implicit initiation of what was meant to be an ongoing part of the church's sacramental life.[70] His death will in fact be the means of imparting life, for "unless a kernel of wheat falls to the ground and dies, it remains only a single seed. But if it dies, it produces many seeds" (12:24). Jesus is thus the vine that the Father cultivates to give forth branches that will bear fruit for the Father (15:1). In order to impart new life, Jesus will lay down his life for his sheep as a deliberate act (10:18). He is in fact God's gift of life to the entire world (3:16-17). As the Lamb of God, he will take away the sin of the world in order to give life (1:29).

For John, it is precisely the crucified Christ who rises to fulfill his role as the one who imparts life. He still bears his wounds, even in his risen state (20:26-27). The risen Christ is no mere ghost; the battered body of Jesus is not left behind. Jesus rises with his entire history of suffering, except this history has been transformed by the renewing power of God. So also can we be healed by believing in Christ. John places great weight on the challenge of believing in the one who was glorified in both death and resurrection for the salvation of the world (20:29-31; 3:16-17). Implicit is a defense that Jesus came in the flesh (1 John 4:2). This faith must also be "incarnated" in deeds of love: "Whoever claims to live in him must live as Jesus did" (2:6; cf. 4:7-8).

Matthew and Mark

Matthew highlights Jesus' role as the Messiah, the Son of David (Matt 1:18-25; 21:9; 22:41-46), born in Bethlehem (2:5). Jesus is "the Christ" (16:16). As the Son of David or the Christ, Jesus is King of the Jews (2:2; 27:11), who rides into Jerusalem on an ass to signify an understanding of his reign that was unexpected by the crowd (21:5). In Matthew the messianic title Son of David or Christ is not

---

70. See Thomas, *Footwashing in John 13 and the Johannine Community*.

a projection of the nationalistic or political hopes of the people but, rather, is defined by God's coming rule on the earth. The Son of David is also to be called Lord (22:44-45), for in him the reign of God will come. His casting out demons by the Spirit of God is already bringing God's reign to the earth and signifying its future direction (12:28). His death also contains signs of his coming victory and of its witness to the nations (27:51-54). After his resurrection, all authority is given to Jesus, who will reign, and it is to him that people of all nations will be discipled (28:18-20).

Jesus was reticent to apply the Davidic title to himself because of the nationalistic hopes attached to it. Jesus actually preferred the title of the heavenly or eschatological Son of Man. He applied the title to himself sixty-five times in the Gospels.[71] Referring back to the exaltation and vindication of the heavenly Son of Man in Dan 7:13-14, the title is not used of him by others, implying that it may have been Jesus' most cherished self-designation.[72] At the time of Jesus the term was a messianic title and not merely a designation of his humanity, in contrast to his deity.[73] There is a creative tension between the Son of David, who fulfills Jewish messianic hopes, and the eschatological Son of Man, who is more directly relevant to the blessing of the nations.[74] The Gospels do not abandon the idea that Jesus fulfills messianic hopes but expands these in the direction of the eschatological Son of Man.

In Mark especially, Jesus did not use the Son of Man title primarily in support of his exaltation and vindication (following the lead of Dan 7) but rather, uniquely, of his suffering servanthood and death. Jesus thus conflated the motifs of the Son of Man and the Suffering Servant (of Dan 7 and Isa 53). Jesus as the Son of Man came not to be served but to serve and to give his life as a ransom for many (Mark 10:45). The Son of Man thus came to seek and to save the lost from their captivity. At the very core of Mark's gospel is the conviction that Peter and the others will not understand the Messiah or what it means to follow him unless they understand his mission to give his life in service to others (8:27-38). But Jesus did not ignore the eschatological future of the Son of Man. Standing before the Jewish tribunal, Jesus noted that the roles will one day be reversed as they all stand before him when he returns on clouds of glory as the vindicated and glorified Son of Man (13:26; cf. Matt 26:64).

Jesus is also referred to in Matthew and Mark, as in all of the Gospels, as the Son of God. Not used commonly in Judaism as a messianic title but known

---

71. Ladd, *Theology of the New Testament*, 144.
72. Ladd, *Theology of the New Testament*, 144.
73. Cf. the *Similitudes of Enoch* (1 Enoch 37–71).
74. See Moltmann, *The Way of Jesus Christ*, 17-18.

in the Gentile world as that of a miracle worker or demigod, Jesus did not use the title of himself.[75] He did view himself as the Son, however. Indeed, the "relationship between the Father and the Son is interwoven throughout the entire fabric of the Gospels."[76] From the beginning, Mark's gospel is about Jesus, the Son of God (Mark 1:1). Interestingly, Luke also notes that he is the holy Son of God at his conception (Luke 1:35), and all three Synoptics highlight his being designated as the beloved Son of the Father at his baptism (Matt 3:17; Mark 1:11; Luke 3:22) and transfiguration (Matt 17:5; Mark 9:7; Luke 9:35). Peter in Matthew rightly confessed him as Messiah, Son of God (Matt 16:16), only to be rebuked afterward for attempting to disassociate the mission of the Son from the path to the cross (16:22-23; cf. Mark 8:31-33). Jesus' temptation in the wilderness challenged his sonship also, as the tempter sought to lure Jesus into proving it in ways that would have caused him to be disobedient to the Father (Matt 4:1-11; cf. Luke 4:1-13). Jesus was determined, however, to be the faithful Son of the Father. Sonship no doubt involved several ideas here, including Jesus as elect and favored of the Father, holy and set apart for accomplishing the Father's will, and faithfully obedient to that will all the way to the cross. But in Mark especially it also referred to his power over the spirit world (Mark 3:11; 5:7). We already saw that in John, "His designation of himself as the Son included elements that go beyond the Messianic and point to a unique oneness with God."[77]

As the beloved Son of the Father, Jesus inaugurated God's liberating reign in the world by the Spirit, according to Matthew: "If it is by the Spirit of God that I drive out demons, then the kingdom of God has come upon you" (Matt 12:28). In fact, Matthew and Mark share with all of the Gospels the conviction that Jesus bears the Spirit in order to impart the Spirit to others. He will baptize in the Spirit for judgment and restoration (Matt 3:11-12; Mark 1:8; Luke 3:16-17; John 1:33). His ministry, however, is especially directed to restoring the outcasts. His table fellowship was open to the poor and the outcast (Mark 2:13-17), while judgment will fall on the house of Israel for their disobedience (Matt 24; cf. Mark 13; Luke 21). The temple is already earmarked for judgment, and he will become the focal point of God's presence and favor. The temple will be permanently destroyed, but when his body (temple) is destroyed, it will be raised up in three days (Matt 27:40; Mark 14:58; cf. John 2:19). He relied on the Father for everything and urged others to do the same, shunning the lure of riches or of worry about the attainment of material things (Matt 6:19-34). He put the kingdom of God first in all things. He supported the heart of the law,

75. Ladd, *Theology of the New Testament*, 162.
76. Ladd, *Theology of the New Testament*, 283.
77. Ladd, *Theology of the New Testament*, 171.

which is love for God and mercy and justice for others (Matt 23:23). The Spirit of God rested on Jesus at his baptism as Jesus took his first public step toward identifying with the lost. The Spirit led Jesus into the wilderness to be tested and was present later at the garden as the willing Spirit leading Jesus on toward the cross during his time of weakness (Mark 14:38).[78] As the man of the Spirit and the one who imparts the Spirit, Jesus will bear our alienation from God in order to grant us a share in his Spirit. Since only God can give forth the Spirit, Jesus' role in doing this affirms his deity.

Jesus' awareness of the cross as his messianic destiny is apparent in the Synoptic Gospels (as it is in John). Jesus predicted his passion after Caesarea Philippi (Mark 9:12, 31; 10:33; Matt 17:12; 20:18-19; Luke 17:25). This point is highlighted in Mark, leading some to remark that this gospel is a passion narrative with an extended introduction.[79] The cross as key to the fulfillment of his messianic mission is especially clear in the texts of the Last Supper (Matt 26:28; Mark 14:24-25). This understanding of Jesus' messianic mission must be original to Jesus; otherwise it becomes difficult to fathom how the theology of his atoning death could have arisen so early in the history of the church (cf. 1 Cor 15:3-4).[80] Jesus' death is sacrificial, substitutionary, and will ransom or deliver the lost (Mark 10:45; 14:24; Matt 26:28).

Jesus' resurrection narratives are crucial to the Gospels as well (except for Mark). Having just betrayed Jesus and now hiding out in fear, the disciples were met by the risen Christ with greetings of peace, an offer of grace, and a willingness to commission them for the fulfillment of his work in the world (Matt 28:8-10, 16-20; cf. John 20:19-23). The cross was meant to lead to grace, not judgment. The climax of the messianic mission in the resurrection of the crucified Christ meant that the meaning of this mission was not taken primarily from messianic texts of the OT but rather from the actual life, death, and resurrection of Jesus. The OT texts that provided the raw materials for understanding these events in the story of Jesus were then fitted around these events as fragments of a story that would become clear only within the context of their fulfillment in the story of Jesus. After meeting the risen Christ, the disciples will proclaim him to the world under the power of the Spirit, knowing that his grace has already rewritten the narratives of their own lives. Jesus has conquered death and canceled sin. The world will never be the same!

78. D. Lyle Dabney interprets the Spirit in this text as the Holy Spirit leading Jesus to the cross. See Dabney, "Naming the Spirit: Towards a Pneumatology of the Cross," in *Starting with the Spirit,* Task of Theology Today, vol. 2 (ed. Stephen Pickard and Gordon Preece; Hindmarsh, Australia: Australian Theological Forum, 2001), 50-52.

79. Childs, *Biblical Theology of the Old and New Testaments,* 469.

80. Childs, *Biblical Theology of the Old and New Testaments,* 183-84.

Luke and Acts

In Luke, Jesus is the bearer of the Spirit to proclaim the year of the Lord's favor and to set at liberty those who are oppressed (Luke 4:18). The Spirit as the power of the Most High hovers over Mary's womb in order to bring the holy Son of God into the world (1:35). This same Spirit rests on Jesus at his baptism as the power of the prophetic mission for which he was set apart from his conception (3:21-22). He will impart the Spirit with judgment and restoration (3:16-17). Jesus brings God's favor with signs and wonders that signal the coming kingdom or reign of God: "The blind receive sight, the lame walk, those who have leprosy are cleansed, the deaf hear, the dead are raised, and the good news is proclaimed to the poor" (7:22). In a way reminiscent of Moses' intention to share his prophetic anointing with seventy elders in Num 11, Jesus shares his prophetic ministry with seventy as well. They return rejoicing, "Lord, even the demons submit to us in your name," at which point Jesus sees Satan fall from heaven and grants these disciples authority "to overcome all the power of the enemy" (Luke 10:17-19). As the one who bears the Spirit, Jesus not only proclaims the Lord's favor but is the very presence of this favor on earth. As with the rest of the Gospels, he can bestow the Spirit and the prophetic authority that goes with it. Jesus thus shows God's lordship to be a dynamic and liberating presence that is concentrated on Jesus and on the Spirit's witness to him. In Luke especially, "The God of Israel is thus so concentrated in the figure of Jesus that they can share an identity."[81]

In Acts, Christ is the one ascended on a cloud to the right hand of the throne of God (Acts 1:9; cf. Dan 7:13-14) in order to impart the Spirit to us on behalf of the heavenly Father (Acts 2:33). As the one anointed of the Spirit to fulfill the Father's will, Jesus now passes this Spirit on to us in order that we can participate in his mission to Israel and to all nations (1:1-8; 10:38-39). He is the one unjustly condemned and killed (7:52), but God did not abandon him; God raised him from the dead and vindicated him as Savior and Lord (2:30-32). Christ now turns to his murderers in grace through the preaching of his followers. The one condemned on the cross is now the Judge and Savior of all (17:31). The destiny of all peoples is now in his hands, for there is no other name on earth by which to be saved (4:12). The unique journeys of all peoples point ultimately to him, and he will be the focal point of unity for the coming together of Jew and Gentile in the one mission of God (17:22-34). The prophetic voices of the church now urge all to repent and to call upon

---

81. Christopher Kavin Rowe, *Early Narrative Christology: The Lord in the Gospel of Luke* (BZNW 139; Berlin: Walter de Gruyter, 2006), 201.

the name of the Lord for salvation, something that was done especially in baptism (22:16).

Paul

Unlike in the Gospels, Paul did not write much about the story of Jesus. The relative silence concerning the details of Jesus' earthly life and teachings implies that "Paul found little of theological importance in these historical details."[82] He focused instead on a number of christological leitmotifs used in Christian preaching and meaningful to Paul's own life and mission. Christ was without question "the central content of Paul's symbolic universe."[83] This new orientation to Paul's own identity and mission began at his encounter with Christ on the Damascus road, when Paul gained a new orientation to the crucified Christ (1 Cor 9:1; 15:8; 2 Cor 4:6; Gal 1:12-16; Phil 3:4-11). Jesus had in fact not died under God's curse; rather, God was on Christ's side. Christ instead bore the curse of Israel so that the blessing of Abraham, the Spirit of God, might come to the cursed Gentiles, thus fulfilling Israel's call to be a channel of Abraham's blessing to all nations (Gal 3:13-14). Christ thus becomes the focal point of a narrative of salvation history in which all people, Jew and Gentile, are shown to be under the curse of disobedience so that the blessings of salvation may be seen to be by grace and not the law (Rom 3:24; 9–11).

For Paul, Christ's death and resurrection were of vast cosmic significance. The whole creation groans under the burden of sin and death in anticipation of the liberty won by Christ in his death and resurrection (Rom 8:18-25). Christ is the focal point of deliverance from slavery to sin (7:14) and from "this body that is subject to death" (7:24). The law cannot of itself set free, since we are unable in our weak flesh to grasp its promise of life; only Christ's atoning death can reconcile us to God (8:3). Besides, the law as a witness to life cannot give life. Only the crucified and risen Christ can do this (Gal 3:21-22). Paul thus gave up all efforts at extolling his credentials as a Pharisee devoted to the law so that he might win Christ by faith and thus attain the resurrection of the dead (Phil 3:7-11). The law, which prepared the way for faith in Christ (Gal 3:24), is now fulfilled by the love of Christ (Rom 13:10).

Paul draws from different metaphors to describe the redemptive power

---

82. Douglas J. Moo, "The Christology of the Early Pauline Letters," in *Contours of Christology in the New Testament* (ed. Richard N. Longenecker; Grand Rapids: Eerdmans, 2005), 180.

83. Udo Schnelle, *Theology of the New Testament* (trans. M. Eugene Boring; Grand Rapids: Baker Academic, 2009), 226.

of Christ's death and resurrection. In addition to the metaphor of redemption from slavery, Paul also parallels Christ as the one who inaugurates the new creation, with Adam as a symbol of the original creation. Christ is the last Adam, who came from heaven (rather than from dust, as with the first Adam) in order to bring humanity to immortality. Adam became a living being, but Christ a life-giving spirit (1 Cor 15:45). The last Adam reversed the sin of Adam by emptying himself in obedience to the Father all the way to the cross in order to be exalted as Lord on our behalf (Phil 2:4-11). Christ brought righteousness and life in order to rescue those under the curse of sin and death (Rom 5:12-20). In addition to the notion of redemption, Paul assumed some idea of substitution. Christ died "for our sins" (1 Cor 15:3-4). He was offered up for our transgressions and was raised for our justification (Rom 4:25). Christ is, moreover, the point of reconciliation between God and humanity (5:10-11; 11:15; 2 Cor 5:18-19). He is also the fountain of new life, for it is by faith in him that we receive the Spirit of God (Gal 3:1-2). "For we were all baptized by one Spirit so as to form one body — whether Jews or Gentiles, slave or free — and we were all given the one Spirit to drink" (1 Cor 12:13).

For Paul, Christ is not only the central player in the drama of salvation history but the one in whom Paul participated by faith in intimate union. Paul knows Christ in the power of his resurrection and in participation in his suffering (Phil 3:10). He is crucified with Christ and lives by the faith of the Son of God (Gal 2:20). We are raised and ascended with Christ in heavenly places (Eph 2:6), for we have died to self-centered interests so that our lives are now hidden with Christ in God (Col 3:3). Baptism signifies our participation in Christ's death and resurrection (Rom 6:4-5), as does the Lord's Supper (1 Cor 10:17). Christ is the one who breaks down the barrier between Jew and Gentile so as to form a new people united as his body (Eph 2:11-18).

Christ is elect of the Father to be the doorway to all spiritual blessings (Eph 1:3-4). Salvation is typically from God "through" or "in" Christ (e.g., Rom 5:21; 6:11, 23). Yet, Christ is also the Savior for Paul (Phil 3:20). Since only God can save from sin and death and impart life in biblical theology, Paul ends up identifying Jesus with God by granting Jesus these same functions. Paul also uses the terms God and Christ interchangeably. The kingdom of God is the kingdom of God's Son (Col 1:13). Faith in God is faith in Christ (Col 1:4). God as Lord translates into Christ as Lord (1 Cor 12:3). Church of God becomes the church of Christ (Rom 16:16). The gospel of God is also the gospel of Christ (Rom 15:19). Grace and peace come from both God and Christ (2 Cor 1:2). The grace of God (1 Cor 15:10) is thus also the grace of Christ (2 Cor 8:9). Most striking is the fact that the Spirit of God is also the Spirit of Christ, implying that the Spirit belongs as uniquely to Christ as to God (Rom 8:9).[84] In Paul, "God and Christ were resolutely thought of together."[85]

Faithful to the story of Jesus, Paul couches the name of Christ within triadic references to God as Father, Lord, and Spirit (or God, Lord, and Spirit; Eph 4:4-6; 1 Cor 12:4-6), even though there is nothing in the larger context of these passages that necessitates it. Behind these references is Paul's devotion to the gospel of the God who raised Jesus from the dead "according to the Spirit of holiness" (Rom 1:4). The God of the resurrection of Jesus (and of the entire story of Jesus) is Father, Son (Lord), and Spirit.

Paul, more so than the Gospel writers, developed his Christology around the crucifixion and resurrection of Jesus and not directly from OT messianic texts. Paul uses Christ as a common name and the Son of David title to highlight Christ's earthly lineage. These points should not be overplayed so as to strip these titles of all messianic significance in Paul. Yet, the connection to messianic hopes in Paul is not as obvious as it is in the Synoptics. Crucial for Paul, rather, is Christ's resurrection by the agency of the Holy Spirit, by which Christ is declared the Son of God (Rom 1:3-4). Childs rightly states that, for Paul, "The past messianic traditions of Judaism were pushed to the distant background in the light of the overwhelming reality of the resurrected Christ."[86]

Other New Testament Voices

All prophetic voices have pointed to Christ. From the very start of Hebrews, the author stresses the uniqueness of Christ in relation to the prophetic voices of times past. They all bore witness in various ways, but none of them are to be compared to the Son. The Son has the advantage of a privileged relationship with God, for only he is appointed heir of all things and serves as the agent in their creation (Heb 1:2). Only he is the very "radiance of God's glory and the exact representation of his being" (1:3). Only he upholds all things by his mighty word, provided for their purification, and now occupies the place of divine glory at the right hand of the Majesty in heaven (1:3). As the agent of creation, he was the agent in the very first word that gave rise to all things. His word now sustains all things, and he will have the final word over all things, for in these latter days he is the one through whom God is decisively revealed (1:2). He

---

84. See Walter Elwell, "The Deity of Christ in the Writings of Paul," in *Current Issues in Biblical and Patristic Interpretation: Studies in Honor of Merrill C. Tenney Presented by His Former Students* (ed. Gerald F. Hawthorne; Grand Rapids: Eerdmans, 1975), 297-308.

85. Schnelle, *Theology of the New Testament*, 222.

86. Childs, *Biblical Theology of the Old and New Testaments*, 459.

not only speaks the word, but as the exact representation of God's very being and the radiance of God's glory, he *is* that word. His word is all-encompassing: past, present, and future. There is no prophet whose word is not taken up as a reference to him, and there is no word that can precede or supersede him. The cloud of witnesses that point to him is drawn from all times and places (12:1).

Christ is thus superior to prophetic voices, including Moses himself, as well as priestly figures and heavenly angelic beings. Yet, not only his privileged relationship with God as the radiance of God's glory grants Christ his role as the mediator of salvation, but also his obedient life on earth as a human being who offered his life up as a perfect sacrifice. The law and the sacrifices were only a shadow that points to his perfect sacrifice as the redemptive event of all history, for OT sacrifices could not remove sin (10:1-4). Obedience will provide the ultimate sacrifice, the obedience of the favored Son. It is thus his coming to do the will of the heavenly Father that is foretold in the Hebrew Scriptures and that provides atonement for sins (10:5-10). "Son though he was, he learned obedience from what he suffered, and once made perfect, he became the source of eternal salvation for all who obey him" (5:8-9). It is his life of dedication that God uses to redeem humanity. His priestly office is therefore not based on human ancestry but, rather, on "the power of an indestructible life" (7:16). It is also by the power of the eternal Spirit that Christ poured out his life as an offering for sin (9:14). His indestructible life stood in our place in order to mend those who live under the destruction of sin and death. He partook of our flesh ultimately in order to taste death on our behalf so as to provide freedom from it and from the fear felt among those living under its shadow (2:14-15). His death is thus also a ransom that delivers us from slavery to sin and death (9:15).

He is now the ascended high priest who still helps us in times of weakness (4:14-16). He occupies the very right hand of the Majesty on high, as well as a heavenly tabernacle not made with human hands. His high priestly ministry is thus connected directly to God (8:1-2; 9:24). As the fulfillment of the law, his sacrifice is once and for all and is not repeated, unlike the OT sacrifices. He is the head of the new and final covenant, in which the law is written on the hearts of his followers, and God remembers their sins no more (8:10-13). Christ is coming again not to remove sin (he had done that once and for all) but to bring salvation (or to perfect salvation) for those waiting for him (9:28). Our eyes are thus to be fixed on him as the author and perfecter of our own faith (or faithfulness; 12:2). Our faithful response to God is perfected by him, by way of his perfect mediation.

In 1 Peter, Christ is the perfect Lamb chosen before the creation of the world to redeem us (1 Pet 1:18-20). He bore our sins so that we could be free of their hold and live righteously before God. He was wounded so as to heal us in our sin-sick souls (2:24). He still functions as the Shepherd and Overseer of our souls (2:25). He is the living stone rejected by the original builders of Israel but used by God as the cornerstone of the new spiritual tabernacle dedicated to God (2:4-7). In 2 Peter, the Lord's future coming will be like a thief. "The heavens will disappear with a roar; the elements will be destroyed by fire, and the earth and everything done in it will be laid bare" (2 Pet 3:10). Christ will come suddenly to transform the world into the final dwelling place of God.

Conclusion

Several lines of interpretation tie together the diverse witness of the NT concerning Christ. First, though the Gospels are more attentive to the OT Scriptures, especially to messianic texts, than Paul is, they all have as their basic point of departure the death and resurrection of Jesus Christ. His conception (incarnation), life (including baptism), ascension, and future coming are vital as well. The OT texts were then organized around these events to provide depth to the narrative, as well as continuity with the past. The God who raised Israel up from Egypt and from the valley of dry bones also raised the crucified Christ from the dead. In other words, it was not as though the significance of Jesus was taken from an exegesis of OT texts and then applied to Jesus; the NT writers went from fulfillment to that which foreshadowed it.

Second, Christ without a doubt is the central focal point of the NT kerygma. Of course, the Gospel is ultimately Trinitarian, so that the vital roles of the Father and of the Holy Spirit are by no means to be neglected. But viewed from the vantage point of God's objective turn toward creation in grace, the story of Jesus is the focal point of concern, or the fundamental narrative that tells this story for us. It is a Trinitarian story, but one that focuses especially on Christ as the incarnate Son of the Father and the bearer of the Spirit.

Third, a variety of overlapping titles or designations are used to describe Christ's central role in the redemptive drama, including Son of David, Suffering Servant, Son of Man, Son of God, Word of God, the anointed Christ, Lamb of God, and Last Adam. They are used in ways determined mainly by the story of Jesus but also connected (more or less) with their OT and Jewish backgrounds. The most novel breakthroughs are in the conflation of Son of Man and Suffering Servant images and in the implications in titles such as Word of God or Son of God or a divine Messiah, someone who not only bears the Spirit but will impart the Spirit to us. A variety of themes are accented, such as ransom, redemption, reconciliation, substitution, sacrifice, vindication, and new creation. Throughout these overlapping titles and themes is the central drama of a God who acts

Christ

decisively in Christ to embrace a sinful and dying world in order to forgive, cleanse, deliver, and transform it by the divine Spirit.

Last, the two themes that dominate the picture of Christ's role as Savior and Lord are his intimate union with the heavenly Father (and identification with God) and his obedience to the Father toward the fulfillment of his messianic mission as the man of the Spirit. The worship of Christ as Savior and Lord is key to the assumption of the NT that Jesus is to be identified with God. But Jesus is also the perfect sacrifice, which implies the ideal pattern of faithful worship and service to God. Implied here is the idea that Christ is the living union between God and faithful humanity, the objective point of meeting, reconciliation, and intimate communion between God and the world. The NT pictures of Christ thus have us see in the eyes of Christ both the face of God and the face of God's faithful servant.

Revelation and Systematic Theology

Christological Method

In Revelation, the slain Lamb rises up as the Lion to open the scroll, which sets in motion the final victory over evil. God's sovereign will for creation is thus revealed in the story of this Lamb, and he functions as the key to its discernment. Any discernment of the *telos* of history apart from the story of this Lamb is bound to dissipate into vague abstractions or veer dangerously into erroneous directions. All that we know about God in relation to humanity is to be developed in a way that is consistent with the story of this Lamb.

There is no question but that Christology is to serve a criteriological function in one's theology and, as such, has played a seminal role in the renewal of theology in the twentieth (and into the twenty-first) century. Karl Barth's attempt to suggest just such a renewal received its decisive thrust when he turned to Christology in the 1930s as the means of furthering the earlier protest developed in his *Römerbrief* against the rising liberal Protestant attempt to speak of God from within the world of human faith and culture rather than more objectively from the context of divine revelation in history as given to us in the biblical narrative and in proclamation. Barth saw very insightfully that an abstract theology of God developed apart from the story of God's self-giving in Jesus bears little resemblance to the God of the Scriptures, who is the self-giving God in election, creation, and redemption. He also saw that an abstract anthropology developed apart from Jesus also fails to come to grips with the Last Adam, who, living from and dedicated to God, came to reveal true humanity.

Barth saw in Christology a way of arriving at the biblical picture of both God and humanity, of both the self-giving God as covenant partner to humanity and the faithfully responsive human servant who is called to covenant relation with God. The slain Lamb who is worshipped as the Redeemer but who offers himself in devotion to God on behalf of the world reveals both in dynamic union.

Barth developed the larger theological significance of his christological focus directly from his doctrine of election. Barth noted that Calvinism did not describe election with a clear enough devotion to the actual story of Jesus. As a result, the theology of the free God of election was developed in isolation from the actual story of God's election of humanity in the events of Jesus' life as a life for us. "It cannot be denied," Barth wrote, "that there has taken place such an absolutising of the concept of electing, or of its freedom, with the accompanying influence of a non-Christian conception of God in the history of the doctrine."[87] The God of election has been described in a way closer to that of a capricious monarch than of the self-giving God depicted in the story of Jesus. Barth was equally wary of an abstract anthropology taken fundamentally from philosophical considerations rather than from the actual story of Jesus as the faithful servant.

Against this trend, Barth proposed a point of departure for election in the "decision of the divine will that was fulfilled in Jesus Christ, and which had as its goal the sending of the Son of God."[88] Since the Son of God is the eternal Word, who was always with the Father as the Father's self-giving (John 1:1-14), there can be no elect will for creation that is somehow prior theologically to Christ.[89] Barth thus criticized the historic Protestant tendency to posit an eternal "absolute decree" *(decretum absolutum)* that is theologically prior to Christ, "which is independent of Jesus Christ and is only executed by Him."[90] Under this decree, Christ becomes a subordinate and secondary decision, reduced to an instrumentalist function of bringing about that which was theologically prior to him. Barth responds to this absolute decree by remarking, "What an abyss of uncertainty is opened up!"[91] One then cannot know for sure who this God is who elects or what lies at the basis of this will to act. An election that is meant to be a source of security, gratitude, and joy now becomes a source of uncertainty and anxiety. Rather than looking to the depth of Jesus Christ as the Lamb slain before the creation of the world (13:8) in fathoming God's elect will

---

87. Karl Barth, *Church Dogmatics*, vol. 2: *The Doctrine of God*, pt. 2 (ed. G. W. Bromiley and T. F. Torrance; Edinburgh: T&T Clark, 1957), 25.
88. Barth, *Church Dogmatics*, 2/2:25.
89. Barth, *Church Dogmatics*, 2/2:101.
90. Barth, *Church Dogmatics*, 2/2:65.
91. Barth, *Church Dogmatics*, 2/2:65.

for creation, we end up looking for something prior to and other than Christ, which for Barth can only be "nothingness, or rather the depth of Satan."[92] Likewise, one can find in Christ the image of the elect person called of God to fulfill a liberating purpose in history. For Barth, Jesus was the electing God and the elect person in dynamic union.

More recently, Wolfhart Pannenberg has developed christological method in line with Barth's concrete christological focus but with an even stronger emphasis on the actual emergence of christological themes "from below," that is, from the actual history of Jesus Christ. Pannenberg notes that, in the early development of christological dogma, the tendency was the opposite ("from above"), with a point of departure in the incarnation of the preexistent Son, from which was read his relation to both God the Father and creation. The danger in this approach from above was that of arriving at abstract notions of deity and humanity within the context of an incarnation doctrine and then proceeding from there to a lengthy and technical discussion of their hypostatic union without first noting carefully what actually emerges about God and about the Christ from within the story of Jesus.

We noted earlier that Paul and, to a degree, other NT authors are not preoccupied with the actual precrucifixion story of Jesus but develop Christology largely from the pivotal event of Jesus' crucifixion and resurrection. Interestingly, Pannenberg makes the bold move of including in the history of Jesus' life and mission not only Jesus' crucifixion but his resurrection as well. He is convinced that the resurrection of Jesus is anticipated in the story of Jesus and culminates this story as its necessary vindication. Pannenberg arrives at the dogmatic Christology from above via the approach from below because the resurrection vindicates Jesus' intimate union with the Father that develops throughout his life, thus indicating his preexistence as the eternal, divine Son of the Father.[93] This move by Pannenberg is decisive and enormously important. In terms that are used in Revelation, the story of the slain and risen Lamb helps us to understand the entire story of Jesus, as well as the election of the eternally preexistent Word of the Father as "the Lamb slain before the creation of the world" (Rev 13:8). What Jesus tells us about God and about humanity in relation to God is taken centrally from the story of this Lamb crucified and risen.

There are various angles from which one can develop this Christology from below. Besides Jesus' intimate union with the Father, one could stress the socially liberating thrust of Jesus' resistance to the oppressive expectations

---

92. Barth, *Church Dogmatics*, 2/2:25.
93. Wolfhart Pannenberg, *Systematic Theology*, vol. 2 (trans. Geoffrey W. Bromiley; Grand Rapids: Eerdmans, 1994), 277-97.

of those who wished to use violence to accomplish their own ends, a reading that would be consistent with Revelation. His acts of healing and deliverance among the outcasts took them out of the dehumanizing system in which they lived and placed them primarily within the liberating story of God's kingdom in the world. This insight would be quite in line with the way in which the slain Lamb redeemed those who were purchased as slaves in Babylon in order that they could reign as priests in the kingdom of God (5:9-10; 18:13). Jesus is both the liberating God revealed in the exodus and the liberated servant devoted to the work of the kingdom of God in the world.

Other accents are possible too. Jesus as the man of the Spirit (and not only the incarnate Word) is also an accent worthy of note. The inauguration of the Spirit's liberating work in the world is initiated in the story of Jesus as the faithful servant, especially his path to the cross, and continues on at Pentecost, when Jesus culminates his redemptive work by bestowing the Spirit upon us. He is the faithful Son who not only receives but also pours forth the Spirit. The Spirit gave the Son a Spirit-indwelt body so that, through the Son, all bodies could become the holy dwelling place of God. In line with Revelation, we could accent as well Jesus' entire life as one of a sacrifice of praise to the heavenly Father. He reveals both the self-sacrificing God and the self-sacrificing servant by way of response to God's liberating grace. In traditional categories, Jesus is the charismatic prophet who bears faithful witness, the king who will rule on the earth (1:5), and the high priest who makes intercession (1:13). All of these angles (and others) from below overlap and intersect in interesting ways.

The point is that, in Jesus, one finds the intersection and revelation of God and humanity in concrete relation. Jesus offers us the pattern both of the God who gives of Godself for humanity and of the human who receives from and faithfully obeys God in analogous self-giving. The Jesus of Revelation, as the one who receives the worship that belongs to God *and* leads the self-sacrificial life of humans offered up to God in obedience and praise, grants us a picturesque foundation for this Barthian revolution enhanced by Pannenberg. Actually, the image of the Lamb as both receiving worship and being the archtypical sacrifice of self-giving praise to God points to the significance of doxology or worship as an important context for Christology.

Worship and the Mediation of the Lamb

The christological method of Barth and Pannenberg naturally assumes that Jesus is both divine and human. By viewing Jesus' resurrection as the culmination of his liberating story, Pannenberg implicitly points us to doxology as a vital context for understanding the meaning of the divine Christ for our time. After all, one does not respond to Christ as the risen Lord primarily from an intellectual ivory tower but rather prostrate before him as John was in Rev 1:17 and as the elders and living creatures were in 5:8-14. In Revelation John prostrates himself in front of the risen Christ at the beginning of the book, a classic act of Jewish worship (1:17; an act refused at the end of the book by John's fellow servants to the visions, 19:10; 22:8-9), and the elders and living creatures worship the Lamb at the decisive moment of his accepting the scroll from the hand of the heavenly Father at the throne (5:8-14). What emerges from that context in our discernment of the story of Jesus is a view of God's lordship as given to us in self-sacrificial love and of Jesus' self-sacrificial mission as the ideal pattern of human praise, not only the praise done collectively in church or individually in one's private prayer life but also in all of life. The dynamic union between God and humanity played out in the story of Jesus is one that has doxology at its heart.

Helpful for this direction of reflection on Christology is the chapter on Christology in Geoffrey Wainwright's book *Doxology: The Praise of God in Worship, Doctrine, and Life*. He starts this chapter with the striking fact that Christ was worshipped in the NT and also in the liturgical life of the centuries of church history that immediately followed.[94] Since the publication of Wainwright's work, his insight has received considerable support.[95] There is no assumption in Revelation that the one who shares in our suffering and death to mediate *from and to* the Father must somehow be less than divine. *The Lamb is thus worshipped precisely because of this mediation.* In contrast, the mediating role of Christ involved a certain "reserve" in the early centuries of the church leading up to Nicaea when it comes to the worship of Christ. Aside from gnostic sources, the worship of Christ in the second and third centuries is largely confined to the hymns and prayers offered individually or outside of the formal structure of the liturgy. The evidence from the larger worship of the church for worshipping Christ is indeed striking and has been well documented.[96] As Martin Hengel notes, the early Christian hymns celebrated the redemptive work and heavenly exaltation of Christ to the divine throne so that he may receive the praise of all of creation, much as one finds occurring in Rev 5.[97] Maurice Wiles has made a convincing case that these early centuries are characterized as well by a popular devotion to Christ that

---

94. Wainwright, *Doxology*, 47-48.
95. See Hurtado, *Lord Jesus Christ*.
96. See Bauckham, *Jesus and the God of Israel*, 132-39; Wainwright, *Doxology*, 50-53.
97. Martin Hengel, "Hymns and Christology," in *Between Jesus and Paul* (trans. John Bowden; London: SCM, 1983).

exercised considerable influence on the doctrinal development of the church.[98] For example, Eusebius notes that early-third-century resistance to the heretic Artemon, who denied Christ's deity, occurred because of his contradicting "all the psalms and songs written from the beginning by faithful brethren, which celebrate the Word of God, even Christ, and speak of him as God."[99] Still, liturgical worship in these centuries largely follows the pattern of worship *to* the Father *through* Christ and in the Spirit.

This liturgical pattern is not in itself problematic, since Christ is obviously the object of praise precisely as the mediator of praise. However, the reserve with regard to the worship of the Lamb comes to radical and problematic expression in Origen, when he assumed that the Lamb's mediating role in worship excluded him from receiving the praise that is properly given to the Father. As is well known, Origen reserved prayer (προσευχή [*proseuchē*, "prayer"]) "in its full meaning" to God the Father: "But if we accept prayer in its full meaning, we may not ever pray to any begotten being, not even to Christ himself, but only to the God and Father of All, to whom our Savior both prayed himself, as we have already instanced, and teaches us to pray."[100] Origen, however, also defended the worship of Christ against those who criticized this practice as polytheistic, and he even inserted praises to Christ in his homilies.[101] His belief in the eternal generation of the Son from the Father gave Origen a conceptual means for maintaining some kind of continuity between them and between the two types of prayer, "full" and "secondary." Origen was still able to maintain within this distinction (at least occasionally) that Jesus is the legitimate object of praise.

Arius, however, rejected the remaining link in Origen between the Father and the Son. Arius considered Origen's eternal generation of the Son doctrine as pagan, as frightfully close to the emanating deities of Hellenistic religion. Deity is "unoriginate" and cannot emanate forth from a higher source. Arius thus wrote to Alexander of Alexandria that the Son as the Father's offspring "is not, as Valentinus taught, an emission of the Father."[102] Arius consequently felt compelled to replace Origen's filial "generation" doctrine with what was to his mind a more biblical category, namely, "creation." The Word of the Father was created by the Father as the most exalted of all creatures. Arius thus raises

---

98. Maurice Wiles, *The Making of Christian Doctrine: A Study in the Principles of Early Doctrinal Development* (Cambridge: Cambridge University Press, 1975), 66-67.

99. Eusebius, *Church History* 5.28.5; quoted in Wainwright, *Doxology,* 52.

100. Origen, *On Prayer* ch. 10, www.tertullian.org/fathers/origen_on_prayer_02_text.htm.

101. See Josef A. Jungmann, *The Place of Christ in Liturgical Prayer* (Collegeville, MN: Liturgical Press, 1989), 160.

102. As given by Athanasius, *De synodis* 16.

the question implied by Origen with glaring clarity, namely, Does the Lamb's role as mediator and object of worship necessitate an ontological identification between the Lamb and the heavenly Father? Put differently in terms reminiscent of Revelation, would Arius's Christology confine the Lamb to the creatures who cannot reveal the scroll or even look inside it? Could he redeem creation by his blood?

The evidence indicates that the Arians still worshipped Christ. They attempted to justify this practice with reference to the worship of angels.[103] But such justification is strictly forbidden in Revelation. Angels cannot mediate as the Lamb does. Arius's Christology ended up, according to Athanasius, "degrading him to the creatures," thus removing his right to be the object of worship.[104] Following the strict requirements of Jewish monotheism, it was unimaginable to Athanasius that the Arians were actually worshipping Christ, since they regarded him as a mere creature. He wrote of the Arians, "If they do not worship the Son, let them admit it, and the case is settled."[105] Nicaea settled it by founding the Son's role in worship on the confession that he was "begotten, not made," for the Son did not originate from someone other than the Father, but rather from the Father, with whom he is *homoousios*, or of one nature. Rather than the generation of the Son implying an origination that contradicts monotheistic faith, it indicates instead a view of the one God as an eternally flowing stream of self-giving or self-communicating love. As Athanasius wrote, without the generation of the Son from the Father, "it will follow that there is no longer a Fountain, but a sort of pool," when it comes to the divine nature.[106] In Athanasius's judgment, the Father is thus as dependent on the eternally generated Son as the Son is on the Father as the eternal fount of deity for a fuller understanding of the divine self-giving. We can worship Christ because his role as mediator of worship is the very fulfillment of the divine self-giving for humanity. The Lamb's self-giving is a divine act.

This basing the role of Christ as object of worship on his role as mediator of worship was precisely the point that also undercut the modalist option. Interestingly, the fourth-century modalist Marcellus of Ancyra was able to affirm the Nicene Creed as the only true basis for adoring the Son.[107] It was possible to exalt Christ as the object of worship from within a modalist theology — but what about its basis in Christ as mediator of worship? Marcellus assumed that

---

103. Jaroslav Pelikan, *The Emergence of the Catholic Tradition (100-600)* (The Christian Tradition 1; Chicago: University of Chicago Press, 1971), 199.
104. Athanasius, *De synodis* 45.
105. Athanasius, *Orations against the Arians* 1.8.
106. Athanasius, *Defence of the Nicene Definition* 4.15.
107. Pelikan, *The Emergence of the Catholic Tradition*, 207-8.

Christ was only *temporarily* the mediation to the Father in his life, death, and resurrection.[108] Yet, how does the church then *continue* to justify adoring Christ as the *ongoing* link between worshippers and the Father? Christ's ongoing role as the point of mediation implies a distinction between him and the Father, a distinction that is inconsistent with modalism. Founding the worship of Christ on his role as mediator of worship provided a barrier to both modalism and Arianism. Since Christ's mediation of worship made him the *object* of worship, it excluded Arianism, and since Christ as object of worship was based on his role as *mediator* of worship, it undercut modalism.

As Josef Jungmann has shown, Christ is worshipped more frequently in the liturgical life of the churches after Nicaea in critical response to the Arian threat. Imagery from Revelation is evidenced in this trend. The shift of emphasis in the liturgy to Christ as object of worship brought with it a stress, not on what unites us to God (Christ as our representative), but on what separates us from God (Christ in the place of God's infinite majesty).[109] This imbalance reveals an inherent weakness in the tradition that the Apocalypse can strengthen, for the exaltation of Christ as object of worship in Revelation does not leave behind his role as our representative self-offering. In fact, the former is based in part on the latter. It is not merely the case that Arius "degraded Christ to the creatures," as Athanasius wrote. It is even more fundamentally the case that Arius had wrongly exalted the creatures, for the Lamb cannot exalt them if he is only one of them. The Lamb *could* exalt them only if his creaturely suffering, death, and victorious exaltation was a divine act. There is nothing wrong with degrading Christ to the creatures (he degraded himself), so long as one identifies this act as essentially God's own self-degradation for the exaltation of creation. The Lamb receives glory as God because he mediates glory as God precisely within and through the degradation of flesh.

Nicaea's conclusion that Jesus is *homoousios* (of one nature) with the Father did not necessarily use the best term that could have been used. It seemed to many to be a crudely material term for describing the ontological connection between the Father and the Son. The point of it was to highlight the ontic relation between Jesus as the divine Son and the Father, namely, that the two persons are essentially one, sharing "being." A constructive Christology will seek to be faithful to the revelatory power of the victorious Lamb of God in language that makes sense to us today. As noted above, the worship of Christ as Savior and Lord helped to guide the church toward its creedal affirmation of Christ's equality with the heavenly Father. Later, more than a century after the

---

108. Pelikan, *The Emergence of the Catholic Tradition*, 207-8.
109. Jungmann, *The Place of Christ in Liturgical Prayer*, 172-220.

Council of Nicaea, the Council of Chalcedon (451) affirmed a unity of natures in Christ that did not dissolve the distinction between them. Christ was affirmed as one person who had two distinct but inseparable natures, divine and human. The purpose of Chalcedon had mainly to do with salvation, namely, to view salvation as a union with God in which God participates in all dimensions of life in the flesh without ceasing to be God, and we participate in the divine nature but in a way that fulfills (and does not dissolve) our God-intended personhood. Christ was viewed as the meeting place between God and humanity, so it was important not to eclipse either nature in Christ (divine or human). Jesus was fully God and fully human, and the two natures were viewed as distinct (i.e., not to be confused). Yet, an inseparable union was needed between them as well so as to allow Christ to be one person (the real incarnation of the divine Son in flesh). The unity of natures in Christ also preserved the facts that the divine Son was fully involved in all aspects of life in the flesh (including suffering and death) and that we in Christ participate in God entirely by grace in the midst of all aspects of life. In a sense, the mediation of Christ as divine and human in its entirety took place in God or in the context of the divine self-giving, as does our participation in redemption. Only a Christ who was both divine and human in inseparable unity but also in a way that the natures are fully preserved in all of their God-intended distinctiveness would do.

In all of these considerations, there is no denying that the ancient substantialist language of "natures" and "substances" made sense in that time and place. These were the conceptual tools available to the ancient Greek world in which Christianity had flourished. Nowadays, we tend to speak more often of identities than of natures or substances, and we are prone to view identity in more functional terms. For this reason, Richard Bauckham has focused on the NT assumption that Jesus was *identified* with God in his person and work precisely as the Son of the heavenly Father. This focus on identity provides a more understandable way of talking about Christ's deity, without resorting necessarily to substantialist language.[110] Similarly, Pannenberg referred to the divine and human in Jesus as "two complementary total aspects of his existence" as the Son of the Father.[111] Others today will stress Jesus' revelation of the self-giving God and the faithfully responsive servant as functional in significance. Jesus *functioned* as God in relation to us, and as the ideal servant (our representative) in relation to God. As Oscar Cullmann noted, "When it is asked in the New Testament, 'Who is Christ?', the question never means

---

110. Richard Bauckham, *Jesus and the God of Israel: "God Crucified" and Other Studies on the New Testament's Christology of Divine Identity* (Grand Rapids: Eerdmans, 2008).

111. Wolfhart Pannenberg, *Jesus: God and Man* (Philadelphia: Westminster Press, 1968), 337.

exclusively or even primarily, 'What is his nature?', but first of all, 'What is his function?'"[112]

Functional Christology, however, as vital as it is as a point of departure for a Christology meaningful for our time, cannot avoid some kind of ontological implication. After all, Christ not only *functioned* as God in creation and redemption, he was *worshipped* as God as well. This worship implies that he *is* God, and this "is" implies a divine identity, even, if you will, a divine "nature." But Jesus is God as the *Son,* who became flesh for our salvation. Jesus' identification with God specifically as the divine *Son* explains Jesus' mediatorial role as God in relation to us and us in relation to God, since the Son was from all eternity the Word or Son of the Father. There is thus ultimately no way of separating function, identity, and nature in contemporary Christology. Christ is the only mediator and link between God and humanity. He is God's turning to us, and our turning to God. He conveys God's turning to us as an incarnate reality, and he takes up our redeemed response and perfects it through his heavenly mediation. He is the necessary link between us and God, the Lamb slain to reveal God's self-giving to us and to reveal the ideal servanthood, through which we offer ourselves self-sacrificially by way of response to God.

Christ and the Challenge of Pluralism

The above understanding of Christ as the only divine-human mediator has not only been revised in contemporary discussion so as to become more understandable, it has been replaced in a way that removes Christ's deity and, by implication, his right to be the object of the church's worship. As we will note, this "adjustment" was done especially in an effort to relate Christian faith to the growing challenge of religious pluralism. In the nineteenth century Friedrich Schleiermacher came to view this "two-nature" Christ (as both divine and human) as merely symbolic of Christ as a man wholly directed in life by "God consciousness." Jesus' uniqueness was thus not in his possession of a divine nature but rather in "the constant potency of his God consciousness, which was a veritable existence of God in him."[113] Schleiermacher found the literal two-nature doctrine of Christ problematic because of the difficulty involved in attributing a "nature" to God that can exist somehow united with a finite

---

112. Oscar Cullmann, *Christology of the New Testament* (trans. Shirlie C. Guthrie and Charles A. M. Hall; Philadelphia: Westminster, 1963), 3.

113. Schleiermacher, *The Christian Faith*, 385.

human nature.[114] Schleiermacher held that a revision is needed of what he saw as a mythological union of natures, so that Christ's deity may be viewed as the existence of "the God consciousness in him," which "was absolutely clear and determined each moment, to the exclusion of all else, so that it must be regarded as a continual living presence, and withal a real existence of God in him." Every element of Christ's sinless humanity is related to the power of this divine presence through Jesus' dominant God consciousness, making it possible that, through his human life, we can grasp this power for ourselves as a source of redemption.[115]

Schleiermacher undoubtedly wants to support the contention that Jesus is the embodiment of revelation, of a life entirely revelatory of divine grace. In the end, however, Schleiermacher's view of Jesus' mediating role as divine and human collapses into an ideal human archetype: Jesus as the man wholly given over to God. This replacement of Chalcedon's two-nature Christology is similar in some ways to Paul Tillich's later understanding of Christ as merely the "new being" (archetype of existential wholeness, or "the undistorted manifestation of essential being under the conditions of existence"),[116] or to Hendrikus Berkhof's reduction of the church's belief in the incarnation to Jesus' being permeated entirely by God's Spirit.[117] We may indeed imitate such an ideally human Christ, even with God's help "grasp" something of his consciousness of God, new being, or openness to the Spirit. But he would differ from us or any other prophet of old only by the degree to which he yields to God. His entire person would still rank with us in creaturely dependence on God. Such a Christ could never be worshipped as Savior and Lord. He could not stand, as did the Lamb at the throne of God, to receive the same praise as God the Father. He could not call himself "the First and the Last" or rank with the eternal Word or Son of the Father who became flesh in order to defeat sin and death and to raise us to immortality. He could not mediate by representing God entering flesh and taking it up into the divine embrace; he could only call us as one human being to another, much as Moses or John the Baptist did. In this case, we would still be waiting for the mediator to come so that we can say with John, "We are not that light; we came only to bear witness to it" (John 1:8). Schleiermacher's Christ pales by comparison to the Christ of Revelation.

More recently, something similar to Schleiermacher's Christology has

---

114. Schleiermacher, *The Christian Faith*, 392-95.

115. Schleiermacher, *The Christian Faith*, 397.

116. Paul Tillich, *Systematic Theology*, vol. 2 (Chicago: University of Chicago Press, 1957), 119.

117. Hendrikus Berkhof, *Christian Faith: An Introduction to the Study of Faith* (Grand Rapids: Eerdmans, 1991), 287.

been revived by some who struggle to meet the pluralist challenge. The challenge is this: Is it not terribly narrow to assume that *only* Christ is the way to God, when there is such a vast plurality of religious faiths in the world today that are sincerely and even admirably relating to God? Some believe that we have to qualify what the NT says about Christ's being the only way to the Father as the Way, the Truth, and the Life (John 14:6), or about there being no other name under heaven given to us whereby we are saved except Jesus (Acts 4:12). The elevation of the Lamb in Revelation as "the First and the Last" who shares the throne with the Father, as well as the praise appropriate only to God, is not meant to be taken too literally, is it?

These statements are taken with utmost seriousness by John Hick. Hick maintains that the worship of Christ in the NT or his elevation to the level of God is not meant to be taken literally. This language of worship to Jesus is poetic language, the language of love and devotion. It is much like the man who says that his wife is the most beautiful woman in the world or that she is the only possible woman for him. We do not take this language literally and are willing to forgive its exaggerations.[118] Hick, by making Christ only one way to God among others, ends up dismissing the theological implications of the worship of the Lamb in Revelation or the insistence that only he is the risen Lord and Savior. Hick is forced by way of implication to deny Christ's deity, as well as his bodily resurrection. He attributes Jesus' postresurrection appearances to altered mental states of the disciples.[119] Jesus' real uniqueness is in his "extremely intense God-consciousness . . . sustained firm prophetic assurance and charismatic power."[120] Of course, the same could be said of John the Baptist or of John the author of Revelation. Surely, the one before whom John lay prostrate in Rev 1 deserves a loftier theological definition than Hick's.

Specifically to the point of worship, Hick and other pluralists are prone to speak of a fundamental confusion in orthodox Christianity between the image of God revealed in Christ and the reality of God, or between the medium of worship in the figure of Christ and the object of worship. Such a blurring of lines may be understandable, given the gushing devotion to Jesus in Christianity, but more precise theological reflection will seek to correct it. By way of response, we can note that, although the NT and theological tradition indeed tend to prefer worship (and salvation) as *in* or *through* Christ, they both also note that Christ can himself be viewed as the Savior and as the object of worship. Wainwright

---

118. John Hick, *The Center of Christianity* (New York: Harper & Row, 1978), 31-32.

119. John Hick, *The Metaphor of God Incarnate: Christ in a Pluralist Age* (Louisville, KY: Westminster John Knox Press, 1983), 23.

120. Hick, *The Metaphor of God Incarnate*, 18.

notes that this combination of factors may best be understood when we see that Jesus is *divine*, but divine precisely as the *Son*, who from all eternity was earmarked as God to mediate God to creation, while the Father should be seen as the eternally inexhaustible self-giving. All worship of Jesus as Savior and Lord (in praise and in all of life), though legitimate and indeed indicative of his deity, is ultimately to be viewed as directed to the heavenly Father. Worship is always in and through Christ, even if it be directed *to* him.[121] Christ as the exclusive divine-human mediator does not preclude the reality of truth and light in other religions. Light in other religions points implicitly to Christ, going to him and through him to the glory of the heavenly Father. One thinks, for example, of how the glory and honor of the nations will be brought into the heavenly city and presented in glory to the Lamb (Rev 21:26). Certainly this glory and honor will be culled from their history and culture, including their search for God and its positive fruit. Yet, "there is one God and one mediator between God and mankind, the man Christ Jesus" (1 Tim 2:5). He alone is the Lamb, who has conquered sin and death for us all as the Lion.

Given the dependence of Revelation on the OT, a word should be added about Jesus as the hope of Israel. The Lamb of God connects the church to Israel in that he will be the light of the New Jerusalem and is already the one who came to fulfill the promises first given to Israel. Yet, the confession of him as Lord also currently separates the church from much of Israel. The current rejection of the church's confession of Jesus as Lord and Savior has been succinctly expressed by Martin Buber. His basic problem is that, in Jewish expectation, the coming of the Messiah will usher in the kingdom of God and the redemption of creation. But it seems clear to Buber that these events have not occurred with the coming of Christ. He wrote, "We know more deeply, more truly, that world history has not been turned upside down to its very foundations — that the world is not yet redeemed." Buber is not convinced by the Christian claim that the kingdom in Christ is currently grasped in the Spirit: "An anticipation of any single part of the completed redemption of the world — for example the redemption beforehand of the world — is something we cannot grasp." He is willing to concede that Judaism also contains a concept of "redeeming and redemption" in our mortal hours, but the length of time from Christ until now makes such a possibility as a christological reality too incredible to believe, for God "does not linger in this way."[122]

By way of response, Moltmann notes that a similar challenge exists in rela-

---

121. Wainwright, *Doxology*, 57-60.
122. Martin Buber, *Der Jude und Sein Judentum* (Hessen: Melzer Verlag, 1963), 562; quoted in Moltmann, *The Way of Jesus Christ*, 29.

tion to Israel's election. Can Israel's faith be maintained in the light of the divine promises to be fulfilled through the nation being also seemingly unfulfilled in the world? And he asks, "Can one already be a Jew in this Godless world? After all the cruel persecutions of human beings, and in forsakenness by God, can one still be a Jew?"[123] To pursue this line of inquiry further, we can ask, As one appreciates Israel's prophetic calling among the nations, is it so inconceivable that one could also embrace the witness of the Spirit of prophecy to the crucified and risen Lamb in the midst of a godless world? Precisely in the face of this godlessness, this unredeemed world, Christ cried out to the Father from the cross. The resurrection is the Father's answer, one that can currently be felt in the Spirit of Christ as the hope of the world, for Israel and the nations. This answer confronts the reader from the first chapter of Revelation.

Toward a Nonviolent Christology

Do the judgments of Revelation undermine genuine hope through the Lamb? The elevation of the Lamb to the throne of God as the victor over sin and death and as the recipient of praise means judgment as well as salvation. Those who reject this grace face "the wrath of the Lamb" (Rev 6:16). Does this mean that the Lamb of revelation is oppressive and violent? Is his elevation and praise as the one who will open the scroll and return in victory a message of doom to Israel and the nations?

The relationship between Christology and violence in Revelation is a difficult issue. The issue is complicated by Revelation speaking of Christ using "holy war" rhetoric. At his return, people mourn (1:7), and those who oppose the Lamb seek to hide themselves from his wrath (6:16). He comes on a conquering steed to exact war and judgment (19:11). He will strike down the nations and rule over them with an iron scepter (19:15). There is no question but that Jesus is Victor in Revelation in a way that casts a dark shadow upon those who resist the truth and grace of God given through the Lamb. Can this be good news for Israel and the nations?

A closer examination of this rhetoric is needed. Looking closely at Rev 19:15, one notices that the sword that strikes down the nations is the sword "coming out of his mouth," implying that it is the sharp sword of truth (cf. Isa 41:2). He is indeed the one who is called "faithful and true" (Rev 19:11), and on his thigh will be written the word of God, the very word of truth (19:13). Those who live by the web of deception weaved by the forces of darkness that oppress

---

123. Moltmann, *The Way of Jesus Christ*, 30.

and dehumanize will be struck down in judgment by the faithful *witness* of the Lamb to the truth and justice of God. The truth of his righteousness will be seen even by those who crucified him, and they will be made to mourn (1:7). The resurrection and future coming of Christ in Revelation vindicate God's redemptive act through the Lamb as faithful and true. So are the judgments against those who continue in rejecting the grace released in Christ's redemptive act. The truth of his vindication by the Father as the faithful Lamb worthy to take the scroll and to reveal its contents will shake all denials to the contrary at their very foundations.

It is also to be remembered that it is the *Lamb* who is the Lion. The Lamb is not a deceptive cover for something more hideous beneath, a ruthless and violent lion in sheep's clothing, so to speak. The Lamb fundamentally grants us the lens through which to view the Lion, so that the ferocious power of the Lion is seen as the power of self-sacrificial love. The Lamb conquers and rules as the presence of self-sacrificial love. It is not hate, deception, and violence that rule at the end of history; rather, it is the self-sacrificial Lamb of God, who gives himself without qualification and condition for the salvation of the world. He has won and will win, he rules and will rule, which is the only hope there is for the world. Without his victory, the darkness and deception will destroy us all.

The Lamb is thus primarily aimed at stopping the violence and healing the wounds left in its wake. He stands for self-sacrificial love, truth, and justice, for at his triumphant return those who have pierced him will see the results of what they had done (1:7); his robe will be dipped in the blood spilled for the redemption of the world, and on his thigh will be written the word of God (19:13). As Mark Bredin notes, the rhetoric of holy war is transformed in Revelation into a war of self-sacrificial love and truth against violent hate and deception. The result is a picture of Jesus "as a non-violent, faithful witness whose message is for all nations."[124]

In Revelation, Jesus' victory over sin and death through atonement involves violence to be sure, but the root of this violence is in those who have crucified him. This is not meant to imply, as some do who advocate "nonviolent" atonement theories, that the violence of crucifixion was a coincidental price to be paid for the radical love revealed in Jesus' mission to a dark and violent world. The Lamb is slain before the creation (13:8); God's decision before all time is to lay down his life or to offer it up for the salvation of the world. But in electing crucifixion as the means of atonement, God is not revealing the

---

124. Mark Bredin, *Jesus, Revolutionary of Peace: A Non-violent Christology in the Book of Revelation* (Paternoster Biblical Monographs; Waynesboro, GA: Paternoster, 2003), 215.

bloodthirsty side of a parental abuser. God was choosing, rather, our ultimate rejection of grace and truth as the means of embracing us. God elected to use our ultimate and worst rejection as the means of healing us through the Lamb. When one thinks of it, there could be no greater or more fitting means of redemption than this.

Word of the Father and Man of the Spirit

The crucified and risen Lamb in the book of Revelation is the Word of the Father and the man of the Spirit. This is the Lamb who "holds," or bears, the seven Spirits of God (Rev 3:1), the Spirit who goes out into the entire world from the Lamb and the throne of God (5:6). The words of the Lamb are discerned in the Spirit (e.g., 3:13), and the Spirit invites Jesus to return in concert with (and presumably through) the church, which is the bride (22:17).

Jesus as the man of the Spirit is an important complement to the confession of Jesus as the Word of the Father. The early stress on Jesus as the incarnate Word of the Father made sense in the light of the currency of the term *logos* in Hellenistic culture and of the early threat of adoptionism, which held Jesus to be only an anointed Son who was not divine. The disadvantage of the dominant stress on Logos Christology, however, was the tendency to neglect the concrete history of Jesus' Spirit-led sojourn to the cross and the resurrection. Also neglected was the fact that Jesus bore the Spirit in order to impart the Spirit to us. The neglect of this insight led to understandings of atonement that excluded the Holy Spirit. The impartation of the Spirit in the West then tended to be viewed as an additional bonus added on to an understanding of Christ's redemptive work that was developed quite apart from it.

Though the theme is undeveloped, Jesus as the Word of the Father and as the man of the Spirit are inseparably connected in Revelation, in that the Spirit is the means by which the church discerns the presence and words of Jesus (e.g., 3:13) and shares in the victory of Christ's death and resurrection (11:11-12). It is from the crucified and risen Lamb that the Spirit goes out into the entire world (5:6). As the Word of the Father *and* man of the Spirit, the Lamb reveals not only the self-sacrificial God but also the ideal human who is driven by the love of God to offer up his or her entire life as a praise offering to God. In this role, Jesus is the ideal pattern of a life devoted to the glory of God. He rescues us from sin and death through his atonement and impartation of the Spirit; then he provides the pattern and the grace for the Spirit-indwelt life that has been redeemed. In the history of Jesus' sojourn on earth as the divine Word of the Father and as the bearer of the Spirit, the suffering Son of Man grants us a complex and colorful drama of a life given over as an offering to God, the supreme measure of the committed life. The cross stands as the supreme image of the kenotic God and the kenotic man; the former gives to set the latter free, and the latter gives back in gratitude and praise that which has been given, a life set free and consecrated for the glory of God. In the end, the Spirit will enter us to raise us up from the dead, much as Christ as the man of the Spirit was raised. Our testimony will be vindicated just as his was. This is the assurance that followers of Jesus have as they face their darkest moments and their most severe persecution.

The Spirit goes throughout the entire world from the crucified and risen Lamb, which means that Christology is "on the way" as diverse communities of faith discern the words and path of Jesus for their time and place. The foundational narrative of Jesus' life, death, and resurrection continues to serve a most critical function in determining the validity of that discernment, but the discernment is ongoing. In other words, the Christology of Revelation is profoundly contextual as Christ speaks to the churches and the churches discern his words in the Spirit in ways specific to their time and place. What it means to follow Christ in various times and places will vary in the details, but they all have as their general direction the liberating call of the risen Lamb sacrificed for the redemption of the world.

The risen Christ experienced in his word and in his supper (3:20) is present. He is also coming. To borrow from a Pauline metaphor, we now see as in a mirror dimly, but then face to face. We currently walk by faith and not by sight. We have only a foretaste of the coming victory and must cling by faith to him and to the promise of the vindication of our testimony. Currently, we must bear up under the challenges thrown at us from the powers of darkness and seek through patient endurance to lay claim to the promises. The glimpse of the risen Lord granted in Rev 1 grants us the encouragement that we need. We have the assurance that the Word of the Father will not only raise us from the dead but also renew the entire suffering and battered creation. As Jürgen Moltmann has noted, Jesus' sufferings were fundamental to the birth pangs of the coming new creation, representative of the entire suffering creation. His resurrection is the inauguration of the new creation.[125] The key to understanding the suffering of creation in the time of trial and the conclusion of Revelation in the new creation is already given in the vision of Christ as the risen Lamb in chapters 1 and 5. He is the key to the hope of the church and to the yearning of the entire suffering creation. When he returns, this hope will be vindicated and verified by sight in a way that is obvious to all, for the king-

---

125. Moltmann, *The Way of Jesus Christ*, 249.

doms of this world will become the kingdoms of our God and of his Christ, and he shall reign forever and ever (11:15). God stood by the crucified Lamb, vindicated his sacrifice, and used it to redeem the world. God's judgments are faithful and true.

Conclusion

The worship of the sacrificed Lamb in Revelation can offer us resources for uncovering important features of a constructive Christology that is founded on Scripture and sensitive to both ancient tradition/worship and contemporary contexts. The ancient struggles to clarify the relationship of the Son to the Father and the union of the divine and human natures in Christ can fruitfully be understood in the context of worship, or more generally, from within a view of the entire Christian life as one of praise directed to the glory of God. The Lamb of Revelation is obviously both the divine redeemer who is worshipped and the faithful human offering to God's glory. The modern efforts of Schleiermacher and others to revise this two-nature Christology end up reducing Jesus to an ideal servant, thus leaving unexplained how he could conquer death or impart new life and why he should be worshipped as Savior and Lord. Efforts to meet the pluralist challenge by denying his deity so as to reduce him to only one way to God among others runs contrary to the worship of the Lamb in Revelation.

The Christology of Revelation thus helps to safeguard Christ's deity, as well as the vital role of his true humanity as the ideal offering of praise to God. In the Lamb who is worshipped, we find a beautiful image of the suffering, self-sacrificing God and the faithful self-sacrificial offering to God. Seen from one angle, one sees the self-giving God, but then seen from the other angle, one sees the ideal human servant giving that life back to the glory of the Father. The Christ of Revelation reveals the dynamic union of the two, the very wellspring of liberating grace. If there is a "holy war" in Revelation, it is the fight for the opening of this covenant to all of humanity, and the Lamb leads the way in the struggle. It is ultimately the struggle for truth and righteousness against darkness and deception. Faithful and true are the judgments of grace against sin and for the redemption revealed in the crucified and risen Lamb and applied to creation through trial and new creation. By way of the Spirit who goes out from the Lamb, we can participate in this struggle in a way that glorifies Jesus (and the Father through him) and mimics Jesus as the one who glorifies the Father. The goal is the ultimate transformation of all things in the image of the Lamb. May the whole earth be full of his glory!

Holy Spirit

Revelation and Biblical Theology

The term "Spirit" is a subtle word in the English language that impacts many hearers as both intriguing and ambiguous. The clarity of the term, however, is granted within the narrative framework of the biblical text. The drama of the book of Revelation uses the term in key places as significant to the unfolding and fulfillment of God's will for humanity. The term is mysterious and meant to strike awe and wonder in the audience of Revelation, but it is also specifically defined in the context of the Spirit's role in revealing God (and the Lamb) and the human participation in the truth of that revelation, as well as in God as the source of life.

Revelation

Right from the beginning of the book of Revelation, we encounter a cryptic reference to the "seven spirits" before God's throne (Rev 1:4-5). As noted earlier, a strong case can be made that this is a reference to the Spirit of God. What strikes one as immediately apparent is that the seven spirits are mentioned in this text within a triadic framework where one would expect the Spirit, also involving the one who sits upon the throne and the Lamb, as though they are all three in unison, joining in the greeting from the divine throne:

> John,
>   To the seven churches in the province of Asia:
>   Grace and peace to you from him who is, and who was, and who is to come, and from the seven spirits before his throne, and from Jesus Christ, who is the faithful witness, the firstborn from the dead, and the ruler of the kings of the earth.

The inclusion of the seven spirits in this triadic greeting involving God and the Lamb leads to a further triadic reference to these spirits as the seven spirits *of God* held by *Christ* (3:1). As part of this triad, the seven spirits are before the throne (4:5) and function as the very eyes of the Lamb (cf. eyes of the Lord, Zech 4:10), which proceed out from the Lamb to go throughout the earth so as to fulfill his and (implicitly) the Father's mission in the world. The dramatic inclusion of the seven spirits within these implicitly triadic texts involves these seven spirits in bringing to eschatological fulfillment in the world the divine actions that come forth from the throne. The audience would have identified the presence and work of these "seven spirits" as divine in nature. Since the number 7 can refer in this context to the "fullness and wholeness of God's work" in the world,[126] the implication is that the seven spirits is a symbolic reference to the work of the Holy Spirit as perfecting or bringing to eschatological fulfillment the will of the one who sits upon the throne and the work of the Lamb. Thus we have implicit support for viewing the Father as creator (4:11), the Son as redeemer (5:9), and the Spirit as the giver of life (11:11), or as the one who perfects redemption eschatologically as the seven spirits (or Spirits).

The function of the Spirit of God in Revelation seems multilayered and significant to the entire revelation and its fulfillment given in the book. First, the Spirit is closely connected to the heavenly Father, who sits upon the throne. The Spirit is designated as the Spirit *of God* (3:1; 4:5; 5:6), more specifically, of the Creator, who imparts the "breath of life" (11:11, echoes here perhaps of Gen 2:7 and Job 33:4). These passages imply that the Spirit located so closely to the throne works on behalf of God the heavenly Father, the Creator, who gives the breath of life and who sends forth the Son to redeem humanity.

Second, the Spirit in Revelation is intimately connected to Jesus. The Spirit speaks the words of Jesus and provides the wisdom for discerning these words in life. Not only does the Spirit speak the words of Jesus, but these words are also discerned (understood, contextualized) in the Spirit (2:7, 11, 17, 29; 3:6, 13, 22). The discernment not only is conceptual but involves wisdom for life. It involves repentance, patient endurance, and faithful living. The discernment of the words of Christ in the Spirit among the faithful is part of their consecration unto God as the lampstands of the temple. The Spirit functions most intimately with the risen Christ to consecrate the people of God for life and witness. It is not warranted to say that the Spirit is indistinguishable from Christ in Revelation in some absolute sense. The Spirit is also related to both God the Father and the discernment of the people of God. In fact, the phrase "in the Spirit" occurs at key places in Revelation, serving to introduce each new act in the unfolding revelatory drama (1:10; 4:2; 17:3; 21:10). The discernment in the Spirit is the means by which the revelation given through Christ is received by John. This discernment then extends to a wider circle to involve the churches so that they would have the wherewithal to understand the words of Christ and the revelations that follow.

Third, the Spirit not only helps the people of God to discern the mind of Christ and commit themselves to it; the Spirit also empowers the faithful to bear prophetic witness to Jesus in the world. The Christ who has the Spirit of

---

126. Schnelle, *Theology of the New Testament*, 760.

discernment imparts the same Spirit throughout the world as a testimony to Jesus. The Spirit is the Spirit of prophecy (19:10). The Spirit accompanies Christ as the seven eyes of the Lamb that then go out from Christ to penetrate the darkness in the world so as to reveal the truth that the Lamb represents and came to offer. The Spirit does so through the witness of John and of the faithful to Jesus in the world. Richard Bauckham has shown that the witness to the nations by the Spirit of prophecy through the church is at the core of the message of Revelation.[127] The two witnesses of chapter 11, who play such a pivotal role in bearing witness to Jesus during the time of trial, are connected to Zech 4 in their description as the two olive trees and lampstands (Rev 11:4). Zech 4 (see vv. 6, 14) promises that the two anointed trees are servants who will serve the Lord of all the earth in the Spirit. The two witnesses are thus implicitly symbolic for John of the prophetic people who will go forth in the Spirit of the Lamb into all the earth to testify to Jesus and to the truth of God that Christ represents. They do so in truth and with signs and wonders of God's power. When slain at the conclusion of their witness, they are vindicated by being raised up and by ascending to the throne. The Spirit is thus the Spirit of prophecy who testifies of Jesus and who vindicates the witness of the faithful to Jesus. As Christ was parodied by the dragon and the beast, so also the prophetic witness of the Spirit through the faithful is set in stark contrast to the forces of darkness who seek to parody it. Evil spirits pour forth from the mouths of the dragon, the beast, and the false prophet to perform signs and to go out to the kings of the whole earth in order to gather them for battle against God (Rev 16:13-14). There is in the world a spirit of anti-Lamb or, if you will, an anti-Spirit. As the Spirit speaks in testimony to Christ through the witness of the faithful throughout the earth, so the evil spirits go out from the dragon, the beast, and the false prophet to the whole earth in service to them in order to foment rebellion against God. The evil spirits seek to inspire a world movement in fulfillment of the mission of the forces of darkness, but there is no discernment in their work. They are not the eyes of the Lamb; they do not discern the truth of God, nor do they bear witness as the true Spirit of prophecy. They spread only darkness and deception, words without insight or truth. They proceed only from the mouth and not from the eyes, for they are blind to the truth of genuine wisdom. They are bound to be exposed by the light of the Spirit of Truth. Their mission will never find fulfillment. When they are crushed, they will not rise again; their witness will not be vindicated, nor will they have the final word.

Fourth, the Spirit of prophecy in Revelation has implications for the

---

127. Bauckham, *The Climax of Prophecy*, 150-73. See also Waddell, *The Spirit of the Book of Revelation*.

church's worship. John was in the Spirit on the Lord's Day, implying that the Spirit was the path to worship. Notice that the text concerning the role of the Spirit of prophecy in testifying of Jesus (19:10) is given in the words of the fellow servant who had just refused John's worship and had directed John to worship God instead: "At this I fell at his feet to worship him. But he said to me, 'Don't do that! I am a fellow servant with you and with your brothers and sisters who hold to the testimony of Jesus. Worship God! For the Spirit of prophecy is testimony of Jesus'" (19:10). Recall that John had also fallen prostrate before the risen Christ in chapter 1 but without any such correction. Evidently, worshipping a servant of God contradicts the Spirit's prophetic testimony to Jesus but not worshipping Christ. One worships God and Christ in "Spirit and Truth" for Revelation. The Spirit of prophecy directs the congregation to exalt Christ and to worship God. Moreover, the Spirit's invocation with the bride to "come" in 22:17 implies an invitation for Christ to reign on the earth as the Lord (11:15). The Spirit is enabling the people of God to exalt Jesus as Lord. The worship inspired among the people of God brought together by the Spirit of prophecy involves every nation, tribe, and language (7:9-10). The unity in the Spirit of Truth and worship never dissolves the colorful diversity of God's creation.

Fifth, believers drink from the Spirit of life and invite others to do so (22:17). But this drinking is not the ultimate in the riches of life in Christ, since they are still urged in the Spirit to yearn for the coming of Christ. Note the full text of 22:17: "The Spirit and the bride say, 'Come!' And let the one who hears say, 'Come!' Let the one who is thirsty come; and let the one who wishes take the free gift of the water of life." Notice that the Spirit is the principal speaker, who seems to invite Christ to come in the larger context of 22:16-20 (Christ seems to answer in v. 20: "Yes, I am coming soon"), an invitation given in response to Christ's statement in 22:16. Those who discern in the Spirit join their voices to the Spirit's in yearning for and inviting Christ to come, but they also extend an invitation to those who are thirsty to come in order to drink from the free gift of the water of life (implicitly from the Spirit of God, 22:17). Those who invite others to come and drink have presumably already drunk themselves of the water of life. The Spirit functions in Revelation not only to convey the words of Jesus or to empower the witness to Jesus in the world but also as part of the treasure hidden in the good news itself, namely, as the very water of life. One is reminded of John 7:38-39: "Whoever believes in me, as Scripture has said, rivers of living water will flow from within them. By this he meant the Spirit, whom those who believed in him were later to receive." The Spirit who spoke Christ's words to them now speaks with and through them, yearning for Christ's coming and inviting others to come and drink from the well of new life in Christ. The Spirit is the eschatological Spirit who provides new life but also urges a yearning for the fullness of life to come.

Gospel of John and 1–3 John

"A deep stratum of Johannine theology is constituted by its pneumatology."[128]

God is Spirit (John 4:24), implying that the Spirit is divine. The Holy Spirit is also distinguished from the Father as sent forth from him into the world (15:26). At the same time, the Holy Spirit in John's gospel is intimately connected to Jesus. Jesus is the resurrection and the life, granting everlasting life to those who will believe on him (3:16; 10:10; 11:25-26). Yet, the Spirit is also distinguished from Christ as "another Paraclete" (14:16). The Spirit's resting upon Jesus signified to John the Baptist that Jesus is the one who baptizes in the Spirit. After Christ is glorified, the disciples will experience this dimension of the Spirit's work. The Spirit will burst beyond all containment and flow through the depths of believers' souls as an overflowing river (7:38-39). Reminiscent of Rev 22:17, the call thus goes out: "Let anyone who is thirsty come to me and drink" (John 7:37). The Holy Spirit, who is divine, is distinct from, but also intimately connected to, the life of Jesus and his followers. The Spirit forges the deep union of love between them (15:9). This deep inner tie between Jesus and his followers is indicated by 1 John 4:13: "This is how we know that we live in him and he in us: he has given us of his Spirit." Jesus will breathe forth the Spirit upon his followers from the inner depths of his communion with the Father (John 20:21; 17:20-23), which may be an "acted parable" of the bestowal of the Spirit after Jesus ascends.[129] Jesus bears the Spirit in order to impart the same Spirit to others, thus incorporating them into his communion with his heavenly Father.

Jesus himself possesses the Spirit with unlimited richness. The Spirit was given excessively ("without measure") to this one who speaks the words of God, remaining on him in unqualified union (3:34). The entire life, words, and deeds of Jesus are the work of the Spirit. These words imparted from Christ are themselves "full" of the "Spirit and life" (6:63). The Spirit is dedicated to Christ's words as the very link between Christ as the man full of the Spirit and believers, who are allowed to drink of the Spirit in him. They worship God in Spirit and truth because of this intimate connection between the Spirit and the words of Jesus (4:23-24) and with Jesus himself as the embodiment of truth. The Spirit is the Spirit of Truth (14:17; 15:26; 16:13; 1 John 4:6; 5:6), who will remind the disciples of everything that Christ said to them (John 14:26). The Spirit will make known to them that which was received from Christ, much as Christ made known what he received from the heavenly Father (16:15). The Spirit will

---

128. Schnelle, *Theology of the New Testament*, 704.
129. Ladd, *Theology of the New Testament*, 325.

guide the disciples into all truth: "He will not speak on his own; he will speak only what he hears, and he will tell you what is yet to come" (16:13). The Spirit who proceeds out from the Father will testify of Jesus (15:26).

Following Jesus in the Spirit implies a commitment radical enough to be described as a new birth. Those who embrace Jesus Christ are "born of God" (1:13), or of the Spirit, who blows "wherever he pleases," describing a mystery that now defines the lives of those dedicated to the way of Christ in the world ("so it is with everyone born of the Spirit"; 3:6-8). The unfettered Spirit is not at our disposal, and neither is the new life that the Spirit opens to us. This spiritual rebirth grants Jesus' followers entry into the kingdom, or reign, of God (3:5), which is lived out in the love of Christ following the commandments (1 John 3:24). The Spirit will be their "Paraclete" (παράκλητος [*parakletos*]), another paraclete besides Jesus to help the disciples and to be with them forever (John 14:16). Jesus himself is present with his followers through the Spirit (14:18), "reaching them, reminding them of what he said, revealing to them what is to come, and protecting them from the world's hatred."[130]

Matthew and Mark

In Matthew the virgin Mary is said to have conceived Jesus through the Holy Spirit (Matt 1:18-20; cf. Luke 1:35). The Spirit then appears at Jesus' baptism, resting upon Jesus as the Father expressed love for Jesus as the faithful Son (Matt 3:16; Mark 1:10-11; cf. Luke 3:22). The Spirit is indeed the presence of God's liberating reign for Matthew: "If it is by the Spirit of God that I drive out demons, then the kingdom of God has come upon you" (Matt 12:28). By the Spirit, Jesus drives out the dark powers in order to bring people into the freedom of God's kingdom. By the Spirit, he will proclaim justice to the nations (12:18).

Jesus' role in imparting the Spirit is connected for Matthew with the proclamation and arrival of the kingdom of God (3:2). In the context of the coming reign of God, Jesus is identified as the one who bears the Spirit in order to impart the Spirit (3:11-12). The Spirit will bring both judgment and restoration in fulfillment of eschatological salvation. Those who repent in hope for the coming day of salvation will know the restoring power of the Spirit (3:11-12; cf. Luke 3:15-18). There is no hope for those who blaspheme by attributing the Spirit's liberating work to the forces of darkness (Matt 12:22-32). Such alienation from the life of the Spirit cuts one off from the coming kingdom, which has consequences for this life and the one to come.

130. Schnelle, *Theology of the New Testament*, 704.

Especially in Mark, the Spirit leads Jesus to encounter such darkness in the wilderness as he is tested by the devil, an important step in the direction of the supreme trial that Jesus will face at the cross (Mark 1:12; cf. Matt 4:1; Luke 4:1). The Spirit is experienced as the power of God in the depth of trial and testing. When Jesus says that the "spirit" is willing but the flesh is weak at the Garden Gethsemane, he may have had in mind the Holy Spirit. The Spirit is the one who is willing in the midst of Jesus' human weakness, leading Jesus to the cross, just as the Spirit led Jesus into the wilderness (Mark 14:38; cf. Matt 26:41).[131]

Luke and Acts

For Luke, the Spirit by which the Son of God is conceived as "holy" is called "the power of the Most High" and is depicted as "hovering" over Mary's womb. Luke adds that the Spirit rests upon Jesus at the baptismal waters to proclaim good news to the poor, to proclaim freedom for the prisoners and the recovery of sight for the blind, and to set the oppressed free (Luke 4:18). The Spirit is especially active in prophetic ministry. The Holy Spirit is promised as the one who will grant the wisdom to speak in witness to Christ (12:12). The Spirit is the Spirit of prophecy, inspiring Simeon with foresight into the coming Messiah (2:25), John the Baptist as well (1:15-17). Elizabeth and Zechariah prophesy as those filled with the Spirit (1:40-42, 67). The disciples were told by Jesus after his resurrection to wait in Jerusalem until the promise of the Father is given — namely, the Spirit as the power from on high — so that they could serve as witnesses to all nations (24:49). The Spirit is the one who bears witness to the salvation that comes from the Father and is inaugurated in the Son.

Luke's Acts promises the baptism in the Holy Spirit toward the fulfillment of the mission of the church to bear witness of Christ to the ends of the earth (Acts 1:8). At stake is the fulfillment of the kingdom of God (1:1-8). At the Day of Pentecost, the church is filled with the Spirit and joins in the cause of the kingdom. Jesus ascends to receive the Spirit from the Father once more, but this time so as to pour forth the Spirit upon the disciples (2:33). At the initial bestowal of the Holy Spirit, the church speaks in tongues that are understood in the languages of the nations as a sign of the global outreach of the church's mission (2:4-12). Miraculous signs of the age to come accompany the proclamation of the gospel. The people of God are brought together for fellowship, breaking bread, giving to the poor, and receiving apostolic teaching (2:42-47).

---

131. See D. Lyle Dabney's comments on Mark in "Naming the Spirit: Towards a Pneumatology of the Cross," 50-52.

Barriers between people groups are broken down in the presence of the Spirit so that all — male and female, young and old, rich and poor — may join what may be called the prophethood of believers.[132] At each bestowal of the Spirit, there is a breakthrough in the fulfillment of the church's mission to reach the nations: the Samaritans and most decisively the Gentiles, in Palestine and beyond (chs. 9, 10, 19). At nearly every bestowal of the Spirit there is an inspired utterance in tongues and/or prophecy (2:4-12; 4:31; 10:44-46; 19:6), as the Spirit inspires truthful speech in ways that transcend human wisdom or knowledge. The Spirit is reaching out beyond Israel to the nations toward the fulfillment of the kingdom of God.

Paul

Paul wrote of the Holy Spirit as the one by whom God raised Jesus from the dead, declaring him as the Son of God (Rom 1:4). The Spirit is thus mentioned along with God the Father and the Lord Jesus as one of the principal players in the drama of redemption (Eph 4:4-6; 1 Cor 12:4-6). The Spirit of wisdom is given by the Father so that we may know him (Eph 1:17), for by the Spirit we have access to the Father (2:18). The Spirit searches out the deep things of God to reveal them to us (1 Cor 2:10). The Spirit is also of the Son, who causes us to cry "Abba" Father (Rom 8:15; Gal 4:6), which may be a reference to an act of worship.[133] In receiving the Spirit by faith, believers are set within communion with Christ and are thus within salvation (1 Thess 4:8; 1 Cor 2:12; 2 Cor 1:22; 11:4; Gal 3:2, 14; Rom 5:5; 8:15). The Spirit is the power that leads to faith in Christ (1 Cor 2:4-5), enabling the confession of Jesus as Lord in the worship of the congregation (1 Cor 12:3). The Spirit regenerates those who believe on Christ (Titus 3:5) and brings the love of God into their hearts (Rom 5:5), the love that fulfills the law (Rom 13:10). To belong to the Spirit is thus to belong to Christ, for the Spirit of God is also the Spirit of Christ (Rom 8:9). When we are included in Christ, we are sealed with the promised Holy Spirit (Eph 1:13). We are washed, justified, and sanctified in the name of Christ and by the Spirit of God (1 Cor 6:11). We are saved by the sanctifying work of the Spirit (2 Thess 2:13). Indeed, we are being transformed into Christ's image by the Lord, who is the Spirit (2 Cor 3:18). One can see this text as a reference to the Spirit's exercising lordship in the church in witness to Christ.

---

132. See Roger Stronstad, *The Prophethood of All Believers: A Study in Luke's Charismatic Theology* (Cleveland, TN: CPT Press, 2010).

133. Wainwright, *Doxology,* 90.

The church is the temple of the Spirit (1 Cor 3:16). We are all baptized by one Spirit so as to form one body consisting of Jew and Gentile, bond and free, and we are all given the one Spirit to drink (12:13). There are many gifts of the Spirit that are meant to edify the body of Christ so that all may grow up into the fullness of Christ as each member does its part (ch. 12; Eph 4:14-16). These manifestations and ministries of the Spirit have as their supreme fulfillment the love of God, without which they lose their purpose (1 Cor 13). Paul himself preached with various miraculous signs of the Spirit, which allowed his ministry to resemble Christ's (1 Cor 2:1-5). Paul was no stranger to prophetic ecstasy (2 Cor 12:4), but he valued above all the power that emerges in the midst of weakness, in a life dedicated to the self-sacrificial life and ministry of Jesus (12:6-10). In the Corinthian assembly, Paul encouraged the use of prophetic utterance that was understandable, even though ecstatic tongues were not to be forbidden in public if interpreted, and they had a cherished place in private, self-edification (1 Cor 14: 5, 17-18).

The new being in Christ is in harmony with the Spirit, led by the Spirit (Gal 5:25; 1 Cor 5:7; Rom 6:2, 12; Phil 2:12-13). We walk in the Spirit when we crucify the flesh with its passions and desires and live instead according to the fruit of the Spirit (Gal 5:16-25). Implicit is the fact that, by the Spirit, we are crucified with Christ but live now by faith in the one who gave himself for us (2:20). Against this way of life there is no law (5:23). The law cannot save us because of the weakness of sinful flesh (Rom 8:3) and because there is no commandment that can give life (Gal 3:21). Not the letter but the Spirit gives life (2 Cor 3:6). The Spirit teaches the truths of Christ preached by the apostles (1 Cor 2:13).

The Spirit is the foretaste of the life to come. If the Spirit of the Father who raised Christ from the dead dwells in us, so shall our mortal bodies be raised (Rom 8:11). We yearn for the immortal body, for which we were made, and we have received the Spirit as the down payment of this fullness of life to come (2 Cor 1:22; 5:5; Eph 1:13-14). The Spirit is thus the firstfruits of the fullness of redemption yet to come in the resurrection (Rom 8:23). The Spirit as the Spirit of life is not an escape from the life of the body but rather its guarantee of renewal.

Other New Testament Voices

Hebrews notes that God testified of the gospel "by signs, wonders and various miracles, and by gifts of the Holy Spirit distributed according to his will" (Heb 2:4). In witness to Christ, the Spirit says, "Today, hear his voice" (3:7). Every aspect of the sacrificial system was used by the Spirit to point toward the fulfillment to come in Christ (9:7-9). The Spirit now testifies to the sufficiency of Christ's sacrifice on the cross, the effect of which is to have the law of God written on our hearts and minds (10:14-16). The Spirit is essential to the very meaning of the cross, for Christ offered himself up "by the eternal Spirit" (9:14) "on the basis of the power of an indestructible life" (7:16). It is possible to deafen one's ears to the Spirit's witness even after tasting of the heavenly gift of eternal life shared in the Spirit (6:4). Those who come to trample the Son of God underfoot in this way insult the Spirit of grace (10:28-30). We keep ourselves in God's love by building ourselves up in faith and praying in the Holy Spirit (see Jude 20-21).

First Peter mentions the Spirit within a Trinitarian context in which the Father elects, the Son redeems through his blood, and the Spirit sanctifies (1 Pet 1:2). As with Hebrews, the Spirit is said to have spoken through the prophets of old to foretell the coming crucifixion of Jesus "and the glories that would follow" (1:10-11). The prophets spoke not of their own genius but rather as "carried along by the Holy Spirit" (2 Pet 1:21). The Spirit was also active in the fulfillment of the OT witness to Christ. Christ was indeed put to death in the body but raised by the Spirit, by whom he preached to imprisoned spirits that were once disobedient during the time of Noah (1 Pet 3:18-20). Believers now preach the gospel "by the Spirit sent from heaven" (1:12). The pure milk of the Word is "spiritual milk" that we drink as we are built into a spiritual household in which we offer spiritual sacrifices acceptable to God through Jesus (2:2-5).

Conclusion

The Holy Spirit's work throughout Revelation and the entire NT is free and mysterious but by no means devoid of meaning. The Spirit's work is multilayered. Most fundamentally, the Spirit proceeds forth from the Father to reveal, provide access, inspire worship, and make all things new. The Spirit is also closely tied to Jesus, joining in the fulfillment of his work (including the cross and resurrection). Jesus imparts the Spirit to us in order to constitute us as the people of God and to bring us into the life and fulfillment of the kingdom of God. The Spirit breaks down barriers between people in the expanding fellowship and mission of the church. Speaking forth Christ's words in and through the congregation, the Spirit guides the contextual discernment of the people of God. The Spirit is indeed the Spirit of prophecy who bears witness to Christ through the people of God. The unfettered Spirit gushes forth in abundant fullness from a life dedicated to God as the people of God bear witness through word and deed. The Spirit who proceeds from the Father and through the Son also justifies, sanctifies, and glorifies in Christ's image. The Spirit is the eschatological Spirit who raises the dead and gives us a foretaste (down payment) of the glory to come. In inviting people to come to Christ, we also invite them to come and drink from the well of life.

Revelation and Systematic Theology

The Spirit is still arguably the neglected member of the Godhead in Western theology and worship, though the churches in Western contexts have come a long way toward including the Spirit in their liturgies and theological reflections. The *Geistvergessenheit* (forgetting the Spirit) is still noticeably with us. It is possible to draw from Revelation in giving the Spirit greater weight in the need for discernment and also for reflection on the drama of redemption, especially with regard to its eschatological substance and fulfillment.

The Need for Discernment

The Spirit in Revelation is the Spirit of prophecy (Rev 19:10). This statement is powerful in its brevity and is relevant to contemporary pneumatology. Michael Welker notes that the term "Spirit" is notoriously vague and susceptible to being hijacked in the contemporary context by self-serving and destructive forces. Every movement or institution can boast of having a noble or virtuous "spirit." Indeed, these sources of massive influence in our world do seem to exercise a spiritual influence of sorts, but how truly virtuous is it? The mass media tend to create the illusion that social processes are under the control of common sense and tried and true moralities. Beneath the veneer of this imagined morality are deeply entrenched and competing public interests that often discriminate and oppress. Discernment becomes difficult because of the tendency in the West to see the Spirit as a nonmaterial and detached phantom or ghostly figure, which is easily discredited in the modern world (people know there are no such things as ghosts!).[134] Meanwhile, spiritualities abound that are harnessed to vague goals revolving around self-discovery or personal health, wealth, and the "good life." It has become customary to deal with a plethora of problems within the context of personal "spirituality." While the term sounds meaningful on the surface (and can become genuinely meaningful), we struggle to know what it means.

The image of the Spirit as nebulous in meaning is strengthened by theologies that have stressed the Spirit's transcendence and otherworldliness, as

---

134. Michael Welker, *God the Spirit* (Minneapolis: Fortress Press, 1992), 5-7.

mysterious and numinous, beyond finding out. Welker notes that discernment has thus become urgent to pneumatology in the contemporary context. It is not that the Spirit is not free and mysterious, but Revelation informs us that the Spirit's freedom is defined in specific ways that resist human idolatry and that follow in the path of freedom opened up for us in the story of Jesus as the risen Lamb. The nature of the Spirit's transcendent mystery and supernatural quality must become clear through discernment into the Spirit's intervention in the present. "The Holy Spirit makes God's power and God's righteousness knowable."[135] The Spirit of prophecy, of truth, is involved in discernment and interpretation. There is a great need for a discernment of the truth that genuinely sets free and makes whole. There is at base a need to recognize the role of the Holy Spirit *of God* and *of Christ* as the Spirit of Truth or of prophecy, as stressed in Revelation (19:10). The Spirit in Revelation is the Spirit of prophecy because the discernment that the Spirit offers does not arise fundamentally from human goals or competing interests but from the reign of God and the story of the Lamb's self-sacrificial life for the redemption of humanity. The Spirit discerns the words of this crucified Lamb spoken to us in the churches today.

The Spirit's role in discernment runs throughout Revelation, even, as noted above, structuring the entire book. At decisive points in Revelation, each new series of visions involves John's being taken up in the Spirit (1:10; 4:2; 17:3; 21:10). This experience of being in the Spirit or carried by the Spirit must have involved an experience of rapture or even ecstasy. John is being gripped by another reality that fundamentally contradicted and subverted the world in which he lived, a world dominated by violent powers opposed to the justice and mercy of the kingdom of God. Yet, the world of the Spirit is not escapist. It does not involve ecstasy for ecstasy's sake. It does not involve an invitation to bathe in alternative forms of consciousness. The world of the Spirit is the world of truth and prophetic discernment. The mighty deeds of God recalled in the Hebrew Scriptures and in the early preaching concerning Christ as the risen Lamb provide the lens through which John sees his world in a different light. John's vision of the risen Lamb in chapter 1 is shrouded in OT allusions that recall the promise of the coming of the Son of Man to bring God's liberating reign to the earth (Dan 7:13-14). John is taken up into fiery visions that tell the dramatic story of the fulfillment of that promise. One is reminded of the earliest company of believers, who spoke in tongues concerning "the wonderful works of God" (Acts 2:11). This is ecstasy taken up with prophetic insight. One is also reminded of Paul's being taken up into the seventh heaven, in which he heard things no one could tell, and yet, the power of God was still felt for him

---

135. Welker, *God the Spirit*, 21, see also, 30-31.

most profoundly in the life lived out according to the wisdom of the crucified Christ (2 Cor 12:4-10). John knew that he too had to swallow the bitter pill of following the crucified Lamb in a violent world (Rev 10:10-11). His rapture in the Spirit gave him added insight into that task. John's was a "sober ecstasy" of prophetic discernment.

Before the Christian community can clearly discern the implications of Christ for their world, they must first understand the words of Christ for themselves. The Spirit of prophetic discernment begins at home. The story of the risen Lamb must fundamentally shape their corporate life and worship before they can properly discern with prophetic insight the conflict between prophetic truth and corporate deception in the world. The challenge is to note the difference between the Spirit who goes out into the world in witness to the Lamb of God and the deceptive spirits that go out from the mouths of the dragon, the beast, and the false prophet. Notice that the Spirit goes out from the eyes of the Lamb (with discernment), while the evil spirits go out only from the mouths of the dragon, the beast, and the false prophet (16:13). One cannot see this difference in the world unless one also sees the difference at home within the community gathered around Jesus and dedicated in the Spirit to his truth. One is struck in chapters 2 and 3 by the repetitiveness of the phrase "the one who has an ear, let that one hear what the Spirit says to the churches" (2:7, 11, 17, 29; 3:6, 13, 22). It is spoken over and over for emphasis. It is mentioned seven times. The sevenfold Spirit thoroughly penetrates the world of the seven churches with a sevenfold call for discernment. No stone is meant to be left unturned. Every church is addressed in particular, and every aspect of the life of the churches is to be placed under the glaring light of prophetic truth. The goal is to help the churches to see the world through the seven eyes of the Lamb. Before they can do that, they must first see themselves clearly. Their own eyes must first be cleared of any and all sources of blindness. This is not a rigid perfectionism that tolerates no weakness. They are still regarded as lamps surrounding Christ, even in their weakness, though the church of Ephesus is threatened with removal if it does not repent (2:5). Rather, this is a call for clarity and focus, for repentance and discipline, as an ongoing way of life for the community of faith in the world. Prophetic discernment involves not just intellectual insight but, more broadly, a wisdom that penetrates thought and life. Life is restructured in a way that is fitting to its role as witness to the life and truth of the Lamb of God.

The discernment of the Spirit in Revelation thus gains its content from what the Lamb reveals. The Spirit proceeds from the throne of God dedicated to God's reign, and from the eyes of the Lamb dedicated to his discerning truth. The Spirit is thus not raw power that can be harnessed in any direction; rather, it is the power of the Lamb's discernment or wisdom. The discerning eyes of the Lamb recall Jesus' self-sacrificial path to the cross. They recall Jesus' faithfulness to the heavenly Father, including Jesus' opposition to the tempter's lies. They recall Jesus' dedication to the truth of God in the world, the only hope for a world blinded by darkness and deception. They recall Jesus' commitment to the reign of God in the world, to the liberation of the oppressed and the healing of the sick. They recall freedom for the victims and for those who benefit from their plight but who lay their privilege down in repentance. They recall the penetrating insight of Jesus into the future reign of God in the world, into its judgment upon all that stands in resistance against it, and into the hope that exists for those who will lay their idols down in order to glorify God alone. The Spirit is the eyes of the Lamb, the power of discernment in the sojourn of the Lamb, and the power of discernment among the people of God, who will go throughout the earth in witness to the Lamb. We cannot view the Spirit as our eyes until we first see the Spirit as the eyes of the Lamb. The Spirit links our wisdom to the Lamb's.

We may thus refer to the need to advocate for an "objective pneumatology" that witnesses for God and for Christ and that is not trapped within the inner recesses of human subjectivity. Karl Barth, for example, credited Friedrich Schleiermacher with seeking a theology of the third article in his emphasis on enlightened human consciousness of God.[136] But interestingly, Barth faulted him for using anthropology rather than the outpouring of the Spirit at Pentecost as his fundamental point of departure. It is not that the Spirit is trapped within the ancient story of Jesus or the pages of the canon without ongoing historical and contextual significance. In his provocative essay on Spirit baptism, Barth resists such an implication, which he calls "Christomonistic," interpreting the Spirit's discernment as merely a way of hearing the ancient words of Christ. The Spirit also shows what these words mean for community life in the world, for history, and for our ultimate hopes. But neither are we to slip into an "anthropomonism" in which Christ becomes nothing more than a symbol of our corporate hopes and fears, our own constructed identity in the world. The Spirit of God is faithful to the Lamb's words and actions, but within the context of their historical significance and ongoing eschatological fulfillment.[137] The Lamb's wisdom must always be contextualized anew but always in ways fundamentally faithful to the Lamb.

We in the churches today may not share in John's direct vision of the risen

---

136. The third article of the Apostles' Creed deals with matters in the realm of the Holy Spirit. See Karl Barth, *Protestant Theology in the Nineteenth Century: Its Background and History* (new ed.; Grand Rapids: Eerdmans, 2002), 411-59.

137. Karl Barth, *Church Dogmatics*, vol. 4, pt. 4: *The Doctrine of Reconciliation* (Edinburgh: T&T Clark, 1969), 3-40.

Christ, but we do have this vision before us in Revelation and other passages of Scripture. The words of Christ in Revelation come to us less directly than among the churches of Asia Minor, but they apply to us just the same. We too are called to discernment of our own life together. Such a call has profound implications for theological method and pastoral leadership. In his *Drama of Doctrine*, Kevin Vanhoozer calls theologians and pastors to the task of guiding the community of faith in its "performance" of the truth and wisdom of Christ as they come to us in the pages of the biblical canon.[138] He accepts the recent tendency of postliberal theology to see interpretation not only as an exegetical science but also as wisdom for life that finds expression in core practices. We interpret the Word of God through core practices that involve doctrine, worship, and life witness. Doctrine is to regulate these practices as grammar regulates language. Vanhoozer fears, however, that the tendency of postliberal theology is to dissolve the meaning of the canon's presentation of the living Christ into the church's core practices. Christ ends up meaning what we construe him to mean, and doctrine merely regulates our theological constructions so that they remain consistent with prior community practices. Prophetic discernment requires more. It requires us to constantly lay our idols down under the impact of the Spirit of prophecy, who comes to us with the words of Christ (and of the canon) as the living measure of our lives and witness. Toward this end, Vanhoozer suggests a dramatic or theatrical model for theology. Theology serves the Spirit in discerning and following the Spirit's direction of the ongoing performance among believers who seek to perform and embody the scripted drama given for us in the pages of the canon. The canon that centers on the story of Jesus comes alive in the church through the Spirit of discernment and is interpreted through our faithful practices, practices in worship and witness performed in ways that are informed by this acquired wisdom. Yet, the meaning is not determined fundamentally by the practices but rather by the words of Christ made alive by the Spirit or by the living Christ speaking these words to us by the Spirit. The canon functions as the living measure of our performance. Our faithful performance is also done in ways that are sensitive and challenging to the larger world. Our task is to call the world to repentance and to joining the drama of faithfulness to Christ and in faithfulness to the voice of the Spirit of discernment. Opposing dramas of reality and truth must be placed under the glaring light of this truth. Vanhoozer's project is just one way that theological method and pastoral leadership can be informed by the Spirit of prophetic discernment featured in Revelation.

---

138. Kevin J. Vanhoozer, *The Drama of Doctrine: A Canonical-Linguistic Approach to Christian Doctrine* (Louisville, KY: Westminster John Knox Press, 2005).

The Deity and Person of the Spirit

The Spirit in Revelation can speak to the churches in the very words of Christ because the Spirit is the Spirit of God, the Spirit of the Lamb. The Spirit of prophetic discernment does not arise in Revelation from a human source. This Spirit does not proceed from human imagination or corporate life. The Spirit's words or discernment is not fundamentally dependent on our interpretive constructions or experiences for meaning. The Spirit speaks for God and for Christ. This is one reason the deity of the Spirit is so important.

Divine revelation does not exclude human experience but is based in divine self-disclosure. The revelation of the Spirit involves profound experiences and changes of direction in life that contextualize and concretely clarify what the Spirit says to us. Jürgen Moltmann has noted that there can ultimately be no mutually exclusive relationship between divine revelation and human experience of God, since both are necessary to any theological concept of revelation. Pneumatology must certainly span both. There is no revelation if God does not reveal *and* if humans can have no experience of God.[139] Yet, revelation does contradict human sinfulness. Experience as fallible cannot be that which fundamentally guides the substance of revealed wisdom. Experience does not occur within a vacuum but is mediated by social, cultural, and personal realities. How we construe our experiences profoundly influences what they mean to us and how they shape us. There is no such thing as an immediate experience of God in the absolute sense of the term.[140] Our experiences are thus in constant danger of falsification or of being construed in support of self-serving agendas. Prophetic discernment based in revelation will thus play a seminal role in human experience of God. This role means that revelation must be determined first by God's own self-disclosure in Christ and the biblical witness to Christ. The Spirit's discernment is faithful to the words and actions of God and of the Lamb.

Here is where we need to raise the issue of the Spirit's deity, for the Spirit cannot be the prophetic discernment of the Lamb if the Spirit is not one in nature with the Lamb and the heavenly Father as "light from light." Note again that the Spirit is part of the triad involving the Father and the Son in Rev 1:4-5. The beginning greeting of the book may be said to have a Trinitarian structure. This follows other similar structures in the NT (Eph 4:4-6; 1 Cor 12:4-6; 1 Pet 1:2), implying the deity of the Spirit in Revelation. What may be termed the deity of the Spirit is basic to the Spirit's freedom and sovereignty in Revelation. We can

---

139. Jürgen Moltmann, *The Spirit of Life: A Universal Affirmation* (Minneapolis: Fortress Press, 1992), 5-10.

140. We may be able to speak of a mediated immediacy.

question whether or not the Spirit is referred to as "God" in Scripture, such as we have with Christ (John 1:1; 20:28; Titus 2:13). The closest candidates would be Jesus' statement that "God is Spirit" (John 4:24) or the reference to the glory that "comes from the Lord, who is the Spirit" (2 Cor 3:18). Some have pointed to the fact that Peter in Acts seems to equate lying to the Spirit with lying to God (Acts 5:1-5). Even more questionable is the possibility that the Spirit is worshipped in the NT. First Cor 6:20 ends with the phrase "honor God with your body" and not, as Augustine suggested, "honor the God in your body" (i.e., the Spirit).[141]

The church of early Christian history was thus slow to bring the belief in the deity of the Spirit to creedal expression. The focus of the early centuries was much more on the identity of the Son in relation to the heavenly Father. Amphilochius of Iconium thus noted in the fourth century, "It was quite necessary for the fathers then to expound more amply about the glory of the Only-Begotten since they had to cut off the Arian heresy."[142] Consequently, the original Nicene Creed of 325 merely mentioned at the end of the creed, "We believe in the Holy Spirit." The First Council of Constantinople in 381 added to the creed the belief in the Spirit as the "Lord and Giver of life," who, with the Son, is to be "worshipped and glorified." Yet, at the same time that this significant addition to the creed was penned, the level of ambiguity and uncertainty concerning the identity of the Holy Spirit remained. Notice this remarkable statement by Gregory of Nazianzus written in 380: "Of the wise men among ourselves, some have conceived of him [the Holy Spirit] as an activity, some as a creature, some as God; and some have been uncertain which to call him."[143]

Two major sources of encouragement for regarding the Spirit as divine were emerging from the NT and early tradition, however. First was the Spirit's titles. The Spirit is the *Holy* Spirit, which implied that the Spirit was sanctifying but had no need to be sanctified. The Holy Spirit was thus to be identified with God rather than with the creation. The biblical designations of the Spirit as the Spirit *of God* and *of Christ* (e.g., Rom 8:9) also served to solidify the connection between the Spirit and God. The second source of encouragement that led to the belief in the deity of the Spirit was the Spirit's works. The Spirit reveals God, gives life, sanctifies, raises the dead, and perfects the redemption that the Son came to give (Rev 11:11-12). Such things can be done only by God.[144] The same logic that was used to speak of the Son's deity (only God can redeem; the Son redeems; therefore, the Son must be divine) was applied to the Holy Spirit (only

---

141. Wainwright, *Doxology*, 92.
142. Quoted in Jaroslav Pelikan, *The Emergence of the Catholic Tradition*, 211.
143. Quoted in Pelikan, *The Emergence of the Catholic Tradition*, 213.
144. Pelikan, *The Emergence of the Catholic Tradition*, 213-16.

God can give life and raise the dead; the Spirit does such things; therefore, the Spirit is divine). The believer is baptized in the name of the Father, the Son, and the Holy Spirit (Matt 28:19), which was further proof that the Spirit is divine and plays a vital role in salvation. As noted above, the close connection between the Spirit and Christ in the NT (the Spirit of God as the Spirit of Christ, Rom 8:9) also served to support extending the deity attributed to the Son to the Holy Spirit. Athanasius can thus write that the Nicene formulation regarding Christ as "light from light" (Heb 1:3) applies to the Spirit as well, since Christ enlightens the heart by the Spirit.[145] Anti-Arian motives did lead after Nicaea to a tendency to elevate the Spirit from the enabler of worship to the object of worship. Already before Nicaea in the third century, however, the *Didascalia Apostolorum* noted: "We [the apostles] have fixed and determined that you shall worship God [the Father] almighty and Jesus, [his Son] the Christ, and the Holy Spirit."[146]

The Spirit in Revelation does implicitly enable true worship. John was in the Spirit on the Lord's Day (Rev 1:10), implying that the Spirit is the context of worship. The Spirit of prophecy in 19:10 implies the ability to discern the difference between legitimate and illegitimate worship. One recalls the Johannine worship in Spirit and truth. Moreover, the Spirit's invocation for Christ to "come" in unison with the people of God (22:16-20) implies an invitation for Christ to reign on the earth as Lord and Christ (11:15). Implied here is an exaltation of Christ as Lord. It may be said that the Spirit is worshipped along with the Lamb in Revelation, in that the Spirit as the Lamb's eyes is inseparable from the Lamb. The Spirit in the Scripture is the presence of God from which or by which we worship, but this role for the Spirit is no less a divine role than that which serves as the object of worship. For worship is by, through, and to God. When the church later glorifies the Spirit as divine, such may not be found as a practice in Revelation, but there is nothing in Revelation to forbid it. In fact, such a practice can be seen as a logical outcome of the role that the Spirit plays as the very eyes of the Lamb.

Is the Holy Spirit in Revelation implicitly a distinct personal agent? For example, Eduard Schweizer maintains that the Spirit in Revelation is not what may be termed the Holy Spirit in Christian theology (as a distinct person) but is merely the presence of the exalted Christ.[147] The Spirit speaks, but does so as the exalted Christ. There is indeed a very intimate relationship between the Spirit and Christ in Revelation. The Spirit is the eyes of Christ and speaks in the

---

145. Pelikan, *The Emergence of the Catholic Tradition*, 213, 217.
146. Quoted in Wainwright, *Doxology*, 97; see also 95.
147. Eduard Schweizer, "Πνεῦμα," *TDNT*, 6:449-50.

words of Christ. Yet, the Spirit also invites Christ to come in the larger context of 22:16-20. Moreover, there may be a conversation in 14:13 between God and the Spirit that implies a distinction as well between the Spirit and the Lord Jesus: "Then I heard a voice from heaven say, 'Write this: Blessed are the dead who die in the Lord from now on.' 'Yes,' says the Spirit, 'they will rest from their labor, for their deeds will follow them.'" Here the Spirit answers God concerning the Lord. Notice also that the statement begins with the command for John to write. Nearly all other commands to write in Revelation came from Christ (1:11, 19; 2:1, 8, 12, 18; 3:1, 7, 14) or from the throne, namely, from God (21:5). In one instance a servant tells John to write (19:9), at which moment John falls down to worship him (19:10), implying that John understood the command to write as coming typically from a divine source. The fact that the command in 14:13 comes "from heaven" implies just such a divine source. Thus, it may well be that 14:13 implies a conversation between God and the Spirit about those in the Lord. The fact that God calls those who die in the Lord blessed, to which the Spirit answers Yes, may imply some kind of distinction between the three: God, the Lord, and the Spirit. Such a distinction is implied also in the greeting of 1:4-5 and is typical of other parts of the NT (e.g., Eph 4:4-6; 1 Cor 12:4-6).

In fulfillment of such distinctions between divine agents, later Trinitarian theology will thus distinguish between the three persons as three distinct (though inseparable) *personae* or *hypostases* of the one God. The term "persons" in such ancient formulations would not have carried with it the modern psychological notion of an autonomous ego, but they would have implied a distinct personal agent of the one divine essence or life. It became particularly important to regard the Spirit as personal and as a personal agent distinct from Christ and the heavenly Father, without sacrificing the Spirit's deity. Against the modalists the early church had to defend the Spirit's distinct personhood in relation to the Father and the Son, and against the Arians it was vital to preserve the Spirit's deity.

Relating the Spirit to Christ has been a fascinating topic in its own right. On the one hand, the early centuries stressed the fact that Christ, as the divine Word or Son of the Father, imparted the Spirit as a witness to himself. Not much stress was placed on Christ as the one who bore and was led by the Spirit. The potent image of the Spirit as the discerning eyes of the Lamb that go forth from the Lamb to all the earth to witness of him grants us a resource for including both aspects: Jesus' bearing of the Spirit for his prophetic function on earth, and his pouring forth the Spirit as a witness to himself throughout the world. The result of the Spirit's witness is implicitly the coming of a multitude from every nation united in Christ (7:9-10). The Spirit's going forth in witness to the nations makes the one and only Son into a large family of sons and daughters.

The Spirit is the principle of the many, of global expanse and eschatological reach. Does the going forth of the Spirit from the Lamb as the eyes of the Lamb imply that the *filioque* clause advocating a procession of the Spirit from both the Father *and the Son (filioque)* is the preferred formulation? Though this question naturally does not involve an issue addressed in Revelation, it might be interesting to probe the flexibility of the imagery in terms of what it might suggest. We can note that the imagery of Revelation does not necessitate viewing the Spirit as proceeding from both the Father "and the Son." The Spirit in Revelation may be seen as proceeding from the throne of the Father alone but through Christ missionally in identification with, and furtherance of, his prophetic discernment and mission.

The Witness to the Nations

A case can be made that the Spirit in Revelation is mainly directed to the conversion of the nations to the Lamb of God. Jesus is himself the faithful witness as the one who died and was raised to free us from our sins (Rev 1:5). The love of God for humanity is revealed most profoundly by the crucified and risen Lamb. The Lamb is committed to overthrowing the dark forces in order to bring all of creation into the liberating reign of God's suffering love for humanity. The eyes of the Lamb discern the truth of God's liberating love, the very difference between darkness and light. The Spirit sends the Lamb's discernment into the world and makes it available to others, for the eyes of the Lamb, the seven Spirits of God, are sent throughout the entire earth (5:6). To attain this wisdom, one must repent and follow the Lamb. The Spirit is thus the power of witness to the Lamb's wisdom, the wisdom of the cross, of self-sacrificial love.

Arguably, the two witnesses of chapter 11 are symbolic of the people of God in their witness to the Lamb against opposition by the beast. They give forth powerful witness and are protected until their testimony is complete. Only then does the beast rise up to overpower and to kill them. In apparent imitation of Christ, they rise from the dead and ascend to God within three days of their martyrdom. John himself eats the scroll most likely containing the Gospel, which is sweet in the mouth but bitter in the stomach, symbolizing that John must suffer in his witness to the Lamb. His task is clear: he must still testify to many peoples, nations, languages, and kings (10:11). Even an angel flies through the air to proclaim the eternal gospel to those who live on the earth, "to every nation, tribe, language, and people" (14:6). The results of this witness will be staggering. John sees a vast multitude in heaven that no one can count from every nation, tribe, people, and language. When John asked who they are, an angel answered, "These are they who have come out of the great tribulation; they have washed their robes and made them white in the blood of the Lamb" (7:14). The discerning wisdom of the sacrificial Lamb has been sent out into all the earth by the Spirit of God. Though the nations are judged, there is a place for them in the New Jerusalem, for the nations will walk by the light of the Lamb, and their glory and honor will be brought into the gates of this new city (21:24-25). The leaves on the tree of life will be for the healing of the nations (22:2).

The Spirit is the global Spirit, who takes the blessings of God's grace beyond the borders of Israel to the nations. The mandate for history originally forged in God's covenant with Abraham was to bless the nations (Gen 18:18). Though the nations are judged in Israel's coming into the land of promise, Israel was also admonished to bear witness to the nations, a mandate powerfully represented for us in the story of Jonah. Israel is called to proclaim to the nations the marvelous things that God has done (Pss 9:11; 67:2; Isa 12:4) or to praise God among the nations (Ps 18:49). The goal is that the nations bring God glory (45:17). "May the nations be glad and sing for joy, for you rule the peoples with equity and guide the nations of the earth" (67:4); "Be still, and know that I am God; I will be exalted among the nations, I will be exalted in the earth" (46:10). Indeed, "May all kings bow down to him and all nations serve him" (72:11), something that will happen in the future (Ps 86:9). May all nations be blessed through this (72:17). God will bring peace to the nations, turning their swords into plowshares, their spears into pruning hooks (Isa 2:4). God will put the Spirit upon his servant, and he will bring justice to the nations (42:1). The mandate to witness to the nations is thus handed down from the risen Christ to the church (Matt 28:19), for the end will come only after this task is done (24:14). The Spirit will come upon the people of God to empower their witness to the ends of the earth (Acts 1:8).

The Spirit as the Spirit of prophecy in Revelation fulfills this mandate to bless the nations. The Holy Spirit in Revelation is the Spirit of wisdom and truth, who is meant for all the world. This Spirit cannot remain confined to the walls of the people of God or to the inner recesses of one's private piety. The Spirit of wisdom and truth spills out and overflows such confines. The Spirit moves the people of God outward beyond themselves to discover a fuller identity of themselves as a missionary people, the people of the global Spirit, the church for others. Following the Spirit in the world, they follow the discerning wisdom of the Lamb and seek to share this wisdom with others. Confronted with hatred and violence, they overcome by the self-sacrificial life that bears witness to Christ. Faced with darkness, they stand for the light of truth. They seek to overcome evil with good, for they follow the discerning eyes of the sacrificial Lamb in following the witness of the Spirit. Their witness conforms to Christ's and seeks to make his witness into a global movement.

The postmodern sensibility may cause some to reject the thought of a global movement of the Spirit. Any effort to globalize the truth of the Lamb can seem oppressive to this sensibility, since it seems to imply violence toward those who follow a different wisdom. After all, is it not the case that Christianity is not the only way of making sense of the world? Is not its way, like any other, simply the product of a community's effort to make sense of the world? By way of response, we can note that one is certainly not to impose the wisdom of the Lamb on others by force, for such a strategy would imitate the beast and not the Lamb. Moreover, the Spirit's witness may be found implicitly wherever there is truth, justice, and mercy. Yet, it is also important for the church not to shrink back from its global witness both in proclamation and deed, in prayer and acts in support of justice and healing in the world. We need to note again that the wisdom of the Lamb does not have its source within a particular community's constructed self-identity. The Spirit's mission in the world is not to spread Christianity as a culture or ideology. The Spirit is the discerning wisdom of the Lamb crucified and risen for the liberation of humanity from sin and death. This Spirit bears witness to a freedom and wholeness that is truly of global significance. All nations, tongues, and peoples can interpret the liberating story of the Lamb in diverse ways so that each cultural lens can remain true to its God-given uniqueness. The Spirit's witness will empower such contextually sensitive discernment. But the story of the Lamb to which the Spirit bears loyal witness remains unchanged in its promise to all peoples of all times.

The Spirit of Life

The Spirit in Revelation is not only the Spirit of prophecy who grants discernment into the wisdom of Jesus. The Spirit does not serve merely an interpretive function. This is not to say that the function of the Spirit in discernment is unimportant. This interpretive function of the Spirit has been significant to Protestantism in its stress on the Spirit's role in illuminating Scripture, especially in critical response to the modern Enlightenment quest for discovering the foundations of epistemological certainty. Pneumatology in modern Protestantism has come to stress the noetic dimension of the Spirit's work. As we have implied above, the role of the Spirit in discernment has to do with life and worship and not just conceptual illumination and certainly not merely for epistemological certainty. Moreover, the Spirit in Revelation works for more than discernment. The Spirit in Revelation is the *Spirit of life*.

This introduction helps us to return to the passage about the two witnesses. This passage does not just highlight the Spirit of prophecy evident in their witness; it also shows the vindication of their witness in the breath of life that conquers death. In Rev 11:11, after the witnesses are martyred and lie dead in the street for nearly three days, the Spirit (πνεῦμα [*pneuma*]) of life enters them. They are raised from the dead and taken up to heaven. One finds echoes here of Job 33:4, "The breath of the Almighty gives me life" (e.g., Gen 2:7), and especially of the Johannine Jesus, whose breathing on the disciples indicates his role as the one who gives new life (John 20:22). In Revelation, the seven Spirits are the eyes of the crucified Lamb, which are also by implication the eyes of the Lion of Judah raised from the dead as the chief partaker of eschatological glory. This Lamb, whom the violent forces of this world had thought to be condemned and destroyed, is vindicated as the Son of Man in his resurrection. This vindication of the risen Lamb theologically frames the breath of the Spirit of prophecy in chapter 11, who enters the two witnesses in order to raise them after the world had thought them to be condemned and conquered. They too are vindicated by the Spirit of new life in the very image of the Lamb. They too partake with Christ in eschatological glory. The risen Christ in chapter 1 thus provides the hermeneutical key for understanding the victorious witness of the people of God through the Spirit of prophecy. Their witness is vindicated and thus fulfilled by the Spirit of life. The beast comes to life after a fatal wound in an effort to vindicate his lordship (13:3-4), but the claim is empty compared to the raising of Christ and of the witnesses in imitation of Jesus by the Spirit of life. The second beast does miracles like the two witnesses and even gives life to the image of the first beast as if mimicking both the witnesses and the Lamb, through whom the Spirit of life proceeds into the world to empower God's people and to vindicate their witness through resurrection (13:13-15). Again, only the Spirit of life that comes forth from the Lamb and that empowers the church's witness is the true source of life. Imitations from the forces of darkness are empty and ridiculous deceptions.

This entire issue of the Spirit of life has become important to contemporary pneumatology, not only to expand pneumatology beyond the confines of the noetic realm, but also to soften the stark dualism of immortal and natural life. The relationship between the Holy Spirit and human life, breath, and vitality is theologically important. John Levison has recently written an important treatise on the Spirit in which he maintains that a creative tension exists between the role of the Spirit as human vitality and wisdom in the OT and the Spirit as the supernatural source of new birth and immortality in witness to the crucified and risen Christ in the NT.[148] On the positive side, the attachment of the Spirit to immortality in the NT bursts through the wall

---

148. John R. Levison, *Filled with the Spirit* (Grand Rapids: Eerdmans, 2009).

of death that limits the flourishing of life in the OT ("for dust you are, and to dust you will return," Gen 3:19b). The life that stands in the shadow of death in the OT becomes the death that cowers in the light of life in the NT (such is foreshadowed in texts like Ezek 37). On the more negative side, however, Levison maintains that the NT does not give much evidence of the role of the Spirit as the flourishing of natural life and human wisdom (the flourishing of the soul) as one has in the OT. The two Testaments complement each other but stand in creative tension.

There is no ontological identification between the Holy Spirit and the soul in the OT. But there does seem to be a conditional functional unity between them: "The breath of the Almighty gives me life" (Job 33:4). The Spirit creates us body and soul and sustains us in the flourishing of natural life in all of its dimensions: "When you take away their breath, they die and return to the dust. When you send your Spirit, they are created" (Ps 104:29b-30a). In the NT this role of the Spirit of creation is not neglected entirely but, rather, is assumed in such passages as those that depict Jesus' early growth in wisdom and stature (Luke 2:52), humankind's living, moving, and having its being in God (Acts 17:28), or Paul's *desire* to live by the law but inability to do so adequately (Rom 7).[149] The new birth in the Spirit through Jesus takes the limited flourishing of natural life to another level, one that is open to the ultimate eschatological work of the Spirit in overcoming the bonds of sin and death, "so that what is mortal may be swallowed up by life" (2 Cor 5:4). Indeed, we were made for this very purpose and remain unfulfilled without it (5:5). There is no continuous bridge from creation to new creation; one cannot evolve from one to the other. One must be born anew through faith in Christ.

All of life lives from the Spirit and is renewed by the Spirit. Significantly, Revelation climaxes with an invitation by the Spirit and the bride (the Spirit with and through the bride) for many to come to drink from the gift of the water of life (Rev 22:17). The Spirit who gives the breath of life (11:11) is here implicitly the gift of the water of life. One recalls the close association between the Spirit and the water of life in John's gospel (4:10-24; 7:37-39). For this call to go out at the climax of the book implies that the role of the Spirit as the gift of life is important to John. The Spirit of life conquers death, empowers and vindicates the witness of the people of God, and gives them a share in the eschatological glory of immortal life with God. The Spirit is the principle of eschatological freedom in which God opens life abundant to the vast reaches of the future. The final call of history is the invitation to drink. Not only is the Spirit the powerful means by which the good news is proclaimed, the Spirit as the very water of life

---

149. I would regard Romans 7 as having broad anthropological implications.

is part of the good news itself, namely, that those who come to the Lamb are able to drink of the water of life.

The Spirit is substantive to the gospel. "All the works of God end in the presence of the Spirit," wrote Jürgen Moltmann.[150] This provocative statement suggests that all soteriological categories, such as justification (our favor with God and its vindication), sanctification (our consecration for a holy purpose), or glorification (our resurrection in Christ's image), are fulfilled in the Spirit of life.[151] We were made to become immortal vessels of God's presence, drinking eternally from the Spirit of God (2 Cor 5:5; Rev 21:6; 22:17). We can thus be fulfilled only by drinking from the streams of the Spirit of life. In a sense, salvation can be viewed from beginning to end through the lens of the call to become immortal vessels of the Spirit of life. From this lens we see that the law of God bears witness to such abundant life but cannot grant it: "For if a law had been given that could impart life, then righteousness would certainly have come by the law" (Gal 3:21). Sin is not just the breaking of a commandment (something quantifiable) but is alienation from life abundant in the Spirit. Justification is not just "right relation" in some empty sense but participation by faith in the abundant life of God or of Christ via the Spirit of life. Sanctification is not just separation from sin but participation in life, not just dead works but works "*for* life as well as *from* life," as John Wesley so wisely wrote (Wesley's emphasis).[152] The Spirit can serve a much more substantive function in Christian preaching and theology, offering people who are thirsty for God, who want a living relationship with God as near and present, an understanding of Christian faith that is vibrant, communal, and transformative. The life of faith is meant to yearn for the filling of the Spirit and to experience it ever afresh in worship, communion with one another, and service.

Conclusion

If one of the great challenges of pneumatology today is discernment, Revelation can certainly grant us resources for reflection. This discernment cannot be merely conceptual. It reflects a wisdom that involves thought, worship, and

---

150. Jürgen Moltmann, *God in Creation: A New Theology of Creation and the Spirit of God* (trans. Margaret Kohl; New York: Harper & Row, 1985), 96.

151. See Frank D. Macchia, *Justified in the Spirit: Creation, Redemption, and the Triune God* (Grand Rapids: Eerdmans, 2010).

152. John Wesley, "Minutes of Several Conversations between the Rev. Mr. Wesley and Others, from the Year 1744 to the year 1789," in *Wesley's Works*, vol. 8 (Grand Rapids: Zondervan, 1979), 337.

life. It encourages the personal and communal righteousness of Rev 2–3, as well as the bold witness to the Lamb in the remainder of the book. It involves the ability to discern the difference between truth and deception in the world, the difference between the voice of the Lamb and that of the beast. It detects where there is true life and where death is beckoning us under the guise of life. It forges ahead in resistance to the violent and oppressive forces of darkness but always with patience and humility. In suffering and despair, it can see beyond to the New Jerusalem, where all peoples will walk by the light of the Lamb with a God-given dignity and honor unique to each one, where the invitation is always there to drink from the well of life abundant. This new life is the power that sustains us and the horizon toward which we strive as we invite the Lamb to come and reign on behalf of the heavenly Father. This is what the Spirit of prophecy can mean to Christian theology and church life.

Church

Revelation and Biblical Theology

"God institutes the church by not letting Jesus' resurrection be itself the End, by appointing the 'delay of the Parousia.'"[153] This provocative statement by Robert Jenson is a fitting entrance into the topic of the church. Involved in the reality of the church is the delay of the end, or, put more positively, the inauguration of a missional history that will precede and lead up to the fulfillment of the end. This communal and missional history necessitates the church in numerous ways, not the least of which is the "unfinished business" of the kingdom of God given in the OT mandate that Israel bless the nations. The widespread rejection of the Messiah by Israel and the nations at the point of Jesus' crucifixion occasions (ironically) God's self-offering to the world at the base of the communal and missional journey of the church. The church is called of God the Father from Israel, redeemed by Christ, and sanctified and empowered by the Spirit so that it may participate in divine communion and fulfill a latter-day mission to all nations. The purpose is so that the church may occasion the consent of all to being gathered by the Spirit into Christ (Eph 1:10) and taken up into God's sovereign and liberating reign (Rev 11:15). The purpose is also to glorify God: "We give thanks to you, Lord God Almighty, the one who is and who was, because you have taken your great power and have begun to reign" (11:16). It

---

153. Robert W. Jenson, *Systematic Theology*, vol. 2: *The Works of God* (New York, NY: Oxford University Press, 1999), 170.

is this cluster of convictions concerning the church that fuels the heart of NT ecclesiology and provides the focus for this reflection on the understanding of the church in Revelation. If faith in Jesus is to result in the gathering of a new humanity by the Spirit in Christ for the fulfillment of his mission in the world, the role of the church in the inauguration and fulfillment of the kingdom of God is mandated as meaningful. This point will guide us into our discussion of the ecclesiology of Revelation.

Revelation

Revelation begins with a vision of the risen Christ (Rev 1:12-16). This vision does not close the book; it opens it. One was accustomed in first-century Judaism to locating the resurrection at the end, but contrary to this expectation, the rising of the Messiah, the Son of Man, does not end the story of Revelation; it starts it. Indeed, Revelation notes that the "time is near" (1:3), but it is still *not yet*, for God is the one who was, is, and is *still to come* (1:8). Though the resurrection has begun, the end is not yet. It is precisely in this period of "now but not-yet" that the church plays its role in the overall inauguration and fulfillment of the kingdom of God. Both the now and the not-yet are important for the nature and purpose of the church. The resurrection of the crucified Christ and the impartation of the Spirit shape the "now" within which the church lives and functions. Yet, had Christ's resurrection and the impartation of the Spirit ended the age, the mission given to Israel to bless the nations would have remained unfulfilled. The delay of the end, the presence but also lack of eschatological fulfillment, gives the church the space in which to fulfill its mission. As Jenson notes, "When the Spirit descends eschatologically, yet without raising all the dead and ending this age, the time for the church is opened."[154]

The now of the church is constituted by the elect will of the Father, which was first realized in the calling of Israel to bless the nations (e.g., Gen 18:18; 22:18; Pss 9:11; 18:49; 46:10; 47:9; 96:3; Isa 2:2; 11:10; 12:4; 42:1; 51:4; 60:3; 66:18). Revelation assumes that the roots of the church are in Israel. The witnesses that typify the church in Rev 11 (the two olive trees) and 14 (the 144,000) are described with imagery or references that are drawn from Israel, even though their lives are most decisively shaped by the crucified and risen Christ. Without discounting the role of Mary the mother of Jesus in the image of the woman of chapter 12, Israel is implied in this image too, giving birth to the Messiah. The church proceeds through the world surrounded by plagues toward the New Jerusalem as

---

154. Jenson, *Systematic Theology*, 2:178-79.

a kind of new exodus. Those victorious over the beast sing the Song of Moses and the Lamb, connecting intricately the victories of the two exoduses (15:3). This connection remains into the eschatological future. The New Jerusalem will have on its gates the twelve tribes of Israel (21:9-12) alongside the names of the twelve apostles of the Lamb on the twelve foundations (21:14). The connection between the two implies that the twelve apostles represent the faithful remnant that will lead the mission of the eschatological Israel transformed by the Messiah and the bestowal of the Spirit to bear witness in the image of the crucified Lamb to all nations, thus fulfilling Israel's calling to bless the nations, a calling that began with the promise given to Abraham. There is no church without Israel and without the Messiah that was born from it. The church is forever tied to Israel as its root. Conversely, as is indicated by Israel's election, there is no Israel ultimately without the church and the nations to whom the church as the eschatological Israel of the Lamb is called to bear witness. Even the term the "synagogue of Satan" is qualified by the assumption that the designation concerns "those who say they are Jews and are not," as though Israel now belongs exclusively to the missions of Christ and the Spirit (2:9). The people of God as transformed Israel is thus also constituted by Christ, by his redemptive death and resurrection. The integral connection between Israel as God's people and the church of Jesus Christ (shown also in John's gospel) receives unique emphasis in Revelation.

Called from Israel, the church is redeemed and made a kingdom and priests to serve God from the death and resurrection of Christ, as well as from the Spirit, who proceeds through him into all the earth (5:6-10). The churches are the lampstands of the temple surrounding Christ (1:20). They are purchased from God by Jesus' blood "from every tribe and language and people and nation" (5:9; see 14:4). In the wicked city of Babylon, people are denigrated as property as they are "bought and sold as slaves" (18:13). But in the kingdom of God, people are liberated or redeemed from slavery unto a royal priesthood precisely by the unjust murder and just vindication of Jesus the Messiah. They are made by Christ to be a kingdom and priests to serve God, for they will reign upon the earth (5:10). This mixture of images that moves between a temple (priests) and a kingdom (reigning with Christ) has its meaningful context at the end of Revelation in the New Jerusalem, which will be a city with the Lamb as its temple. With Christ as the temple at the heart of the New Jerusalem (God's ultimate πόλις [*polis,* "city"]), the people of God will serve both a priestly and a reigning function. In this world, the people of God embody God's kingdom, or liberating reign, in anticipation of the fulfillment of the kingdom of God on earth. On this earth, the church also serves the priestly function of witnessing before the world and yearning for the coming kingdom. Though the martyrs ask for justice in chapter 6 against the oppressors, which God grants in the plagues that follow, such witnesses give their lives for the repentance and healing of the nations in chapters 12–14, which the conclusion of the book indicates will be the determining reality for both the church's passion for the world and the world's destiny within the God who fueled this passion. The prayers of God's people are a prominent feature of the altar of God in the heavenly city (5:8; 8:3-4). These prayers are even hurled to earth with theophanic signs of the coming fulfillment for which these prayers yearn (8:5).

Freed by Christ's atoning death and resurrection and by embracing Christ's gospel, the churches of Revelation gather around the risen Christ to continue to hear from, and respond favorably to, his Word (1:12-13). The Spirit of discernment calls out to the churches to hear what the words of Christ are saying to them (e.g., 2:7). Each and every church receives this admonition. This injunction is repeated seven times, once for each church. None are excluded, for the time is short and prophetically urgent. By application, all churches are urged to listen. In the now and not-yet of eschatological existence as the latter day draws near, the churches are constantly confronted with the unfinished business of the Word of Christ. Indeed, the church is the creature of the gospel in admonishment and comfort, command and promise. The churches must hear and obey this Word before they can embody and proclaim it before the nations. These words must shape and structure their corporate life together before these churches can show forth the goodness of God to the world. The church is not only to proclaim the gospel with words but must also embody it in numerous ways in their common life together. The church's participation in divine communion and its witness to the world overlap.

But even with the redemptive act and gospel of Jesus, the churches are still not fully constituted according to Revelation, for the churches will represent a prophetic witness to the nations only in the context of the Lamb's authority (seven horns) and discernment (seven eyes), which are the seven Spirits of God who are sent out into all the world (5:6). It is the wisdom imparted by the Spirit that allows the churches to "hear" properly and to keep (in all that this hearing and keeping involve) the words of Christ to them. It is in the power and authority of the seven Spirits sent out into the entire world that the churches will be sent to bear witness to the nations. If Jesus is the "ruler of the kings of the earth" (1:5), then the Spirit will need to provide the conditions and the power by which the kings and their domains are to become the domains of the risen Christ through the prophetic witness of the church. Christ speaks to the churches as the Spirit speaks, and the churches speak to the world only as the Spirit speaks. The Spirit is the means by which the Word of Christ goes forth and is heard and kept, whether it be *to* or *through* the churches.

The urgency of the church's prophetic task is thus the setting for understanding the messages to the churches. Each message involves intimate knowledge of a church's situation, works, and needs. Each involves admonishment and/or encouragement. Each message begins with a reference to the risen Christ and ends with a reference to the New Jerusalem. The messages thus govern the life of the churches in between their constitution as a church and the fulfillment of their mission in the coming of the kingdom of God to earth. This is not to say that the church brings the kingdom. The church can only yearn for that which Christ alone can bring (their prayer being for Christ and his kingdom to come, Rev 22:17). But the church can prepare the way for the coming kingdom, penultimately embody it, and find in it the fulfillment of its witness. Living in between the rising of Christ and the coming of the kingdom in power at Christ's return, the church lives from the Spirit in memory and hope, conviction and patient endurance. These are found together in the living communion with Christ and the reception of his Word by faith and obedience through the power of the Spirit.

Patient endurance is a key in the admonitions to the churches (2:3; 3:10). The churches see a violent and dark world when they look out beyond the walls of their worship services. Yet, John tells them of a different world, a heavenly city, from which God and his Christ reign and from which the Spirit comes forth to reveal the truth of Christ. God's reign is soon coming from heaven to earth, at which point a transference of sovereignty will occur from the world to Christ (11:15). The churches are to follow the Spirit into the entire world in witness to the crucified and risen Christ before the end comes. Spiritual preparation is needed for this task, especially since it will place the most radical demands on the church, requiring unconditional self-sacrifice in the image of the crucified Christ, perhaps martyrdom itself (as the story of the witnesses in ch. 11 indicates). The messages of chapters 2 and 3 will aid in this process of preparation. Until the fulfillment comes, the church requires patience, not an inactive patience, but rather a patient endurance in the faithful life until the end.

Patient endurance provides the context in the churches of Revelation for the holy life. God is holy (6:10; 15:4; 16:5), and Christ is holy (3:7). The words of Christ are holy, as is the city of God's dwelling (22:19). Holiness is proper to God alone (15:4), but God grants participation in righteousness and purity by the church, for the saints are God's holy people in Revelation (13:7; 16:6; 17:6; 18:24; 19:8). This holiness is manifested in good works. There is thus a strong accent on the works of God's people in Revelation. The churches are to hear and "keep" the word of testimony shared through the reading aloud of the book (1:3). The churches are made a kingdom and priests "to serve our God" (5:10). God knows the works of the churches (2:2, 19; 3:8, 15). Each will give an account of the works done by it (2:23); their works will follow them (14:13). Yet, the churches do not generate these works from their own resources. The fine linen worn by the bride of Christ and representative of her deeds is tellingly described as "given her to wear" (19:8). These righteous deeds do not have their ultimate source in human will or effort but rather in the holy works of God (15:3) and of Christ (2:26), for Christ is the faithful witness from which the church draws its inspiration (1:5). It is by the work of Christ and the power of the Spirit that the church can be purified of sin and, as a faithful bride (2:4), do the works that belong to their first love of Christ. The church is to exert effort in repenting and acting in concert with Christ, to be sure, but the fire that produces these deeds is fueled by the Spirit of God and burns in love for Christ.

The holiness of the church is connected in Revelation with the church's role in glorifying God. The world may refuse to repent and glorify God (16:9), but not the church. They are called upon to repent and to give God due glory in all things. From the beginning of the Christian life, the immediate response of those who repent is to give God glory (11:13). The very gospel of salvation calls upon the nations to fear God and to give God glory, for the divine Creator's judgment has arrived (14:6-7). The saints become the "firstfruits" unto God in the image of the slain Lamb, willing to make the ultimate sacrifice in service to Christ in the world. They follow the Lamb wherever he goes; no lie is found in their mouths, for they are blameless (14:3-5). Such holiness has its ultimate basis in grace. The church recognizes that it has *been made* a kingdom and priests unto God by Christ's redemptive work, with the conclusion that God is to be praised for such grace (1:5-7). The eschatological goal is for the nations to come to worship God (15:4), for "salvation and power and glory belong to our God" (19:1). In chapter 13 the dragon, the beast, and the false prophet seek to be worshipped, but the saints know that their claim is baseless, even absurd, for the dragon has already been decisively defeated (ch. 12).

Revelation from the beginning depicts worship to God as the context for hearing the words of the prophecy. John himself falls prostrate before the risen Christ in an act of worship at the start of the book in 1:17. In that position, the Lord places his hand on John, and the messages to the churches are given with John remaining in that posture of worship. Indeed, John is in the Spirit on the Lord's Day (1:10) and is able in this pneumatic state to peer into the worship among the heavenly hosts to Christ and God (5:11-14; 7:11). There are hymnic praises throughout the book (4:8-11; 5:9-14; 11:15-18; 15:3-5; 16:5-6; 19:1-8). The worship of the church allows the church to come into solidarity with the forces of heaven against the dark forces on earth. The dark forces may persecute and denigrate the church, but the church finds its true identity and courage in its worship. In worship, the churches of Revelation gain the power to endure. Near the end of the book, in chapter 19, a voice comes from the throne urging the saints to worship God:

> Praise our God,
>   all you his servants,
> you who fear him,
>   both great and small!

The response is resounding, "like the roar of rushing waters and like loud peals of thunder, shouting":

> Hallelujah!
>   For our Lord God Almighty reigns.

The worship of the saints in Revelation also involves the sacramental life of the church. The imagery of Revelation might even imply the marking of the divine name on the baptismal initiate (3:12; 14:1; 22:4) and the placing of the white garment on the newly baptized, who at baptism are wedded to Christ as his bride (7:14; 22:14).[155] In Rev 3:20 Christ calls the church to dine with him, a meal that should be understood also in the light of the reference in 19:7-9 to the marriage supper of the Lamb or the messianic banquet. Christ calls his church to commune with him in the context of a sacred meal. The Lamb of God presides at the meal, imagery that recalls the Passover Lamb of the OT.[156]

The church of Revelation is indeed deeply rooted in the OT narrative of the exodus and life of Israel. In chapter 14 the church is the 144,000 from the tribes of Israel that find their way through the wilderness trials of the latter days to the New Jerusalem. Chapter 15 depicts a new exodus involving plagues of judgment as the church journeys toward the new creation. Yet, the church is on a journey not for its own freedom alone but for the freedom of the nations. The wilderness wandering of the church thus involves preparation for its devotion to the Word of God and the mission of Christ.

The church is thus also the community of the Word of God. Christ walks in the midst of the lampstands, which symbolize the seven churches, in order to address them one by one. The churches gather around him, for from him they hear the words of life. Jesus himself is the Word of God (19:13), God revealed in the very person of Christ and in his life, death, and resurrection. The Spirit

---

155. Charles A. Gieschen, "Sacramental Theology in the Book of Revelation," *Concordia Theological Quarterly* 67.2 (April 2003): 149-62.
156. Gieschen, "Sacramental Theology in the Book of Revelation," 163-74.

of prophecy thus bears witness to Jesus (19:10), and John bears witness to the Word of God and the testimony of Jesus Christ (1:2). The words of prophecy that make up the book are to be read aloud in the churches. These words are the "true words of God" (19:9), trustworthy and true (21:5; 22:6). The saints triumph over the powers of darkness through the blood of the Lamb and the word of their testimony (12:11). The saints also suffer for the Word of God. John is on the island of Patmos because of the Word of God and the testimony of Jesus (1:9). He eats the scroll that comes from Christ, which is sweet in his mouth but bitter in his stomach (10:10). The martyrs are slain because of the Word of God and the testimony that they had maintained (6:9; 20:4). There is little question but that the church is a "creature of the gospel" in Revelation. It lives from and according to the Word of God, dedicated to its mission in the world.

The church lives from the Spirit of prophecy in Revelation. Though the witness of the apostles is foundational to Revelation (21:14), John does not claim to be an apostle, only a brother in persecution and prophetic witness (1:9; 19:10; 22:9). Nor is there any mention of an institutional, juridical authority at work in the messages to the churches, for there is a noticeable silence about the official ecclesial structures that one might have presupposed for the churches of Asia Minor at the time. The church in Revelation is a fellowship of brothers and sisters, a company of prophets who bear the Word of Christ in their words and in their self-sacrificial lives. All bear the words of Christ, all bear the Spirit of prophecy, and all are bound by the same faith and mission. This is not necessarily to say that there is no place for the ministry of oversight; but the unique accent of Revelation is elsewhere, namely, on the nature of the church as a company of faithful and prophetic witnesses. Revelation reminds us that all are ministers of the Word of God. All are called to bear the blessing and burden of prophetic witness in the world.

The accent of Revelation ecclesiologically is arguably on the church's call to suffer in bearing witness of the crucified and risen Christ to the nations. The conviction of the book is that the God of Israel has been decisively revealed in the slaughter and rising again of the Lamb. The God who raised Israel from Egypt has raised the Lamb from the dead, will raise the church to the New Jerusalem, and will raise the old creation to the new creation. The fulfillment of Israel's mission to bless the nations is now fulfilled in the Lamb. He is the true and faithful witness who will rule the nations (1:5). According to Revelation, the church is to witness to the Lamb in a way that will bring the nations into his liberating reign. Richard Bauckham has shown that this missionary call is focused on the scroll taken by the risen Lamb from the hand of the heavenly Father in chapter 5. The Lamb's conquest for the redemption of the world qualifies him to open the scroll and constitutes the church as the embodiment of the kingdom of God in a world given over to the powers of darkness (5:9-10). The church constituted by the Lamb is drawn to Christ as a multitude that no one can count from all nations (7:9).[157]

Bauckham maintains that the content of the scroll of chapter 5 is disclosed in chapters 10 and 11, which dramatize for us the mission of the church in the latter days. Mission is essential to the church of Revelation. John typifies the calling of the church in chapter 10 by taking the scroll and eating it in accepting his call to prophesy to the nations. In further symbolizing the latter-day witness of the church, the two witnesses of chapter 11 recall Moses (in turning the water into blood) and Elijah (in calling down fire from heaven and stopping the rain) as representative of the OT prophetic witness, but go beyond by giving their very lives for their witness. It is here that they exceed the two great OT prophets by following the crucified Lamb. After three and a half days, the Spirit of God enters them, and they rise from the dead as a clear vindication of their witness, which is an equally clear participation in the vindication of the Lamb, noted as occurring at the moment that he took the scroll in chapter 5. An earthquake follows, which leads to widespread repentance and glorifying God among the survivors. It is most interesting that what the plagues could not accomplish in chapter 9 is now achieved in the suffering witness of the church in chapter 11. This may indeed be the essential content of the scroll: the nations will come to the Lamb only through the suffering witness and martyrdom of his followers, who bear up under the nations' rejection of the gospel in a way that follows the path of the cross and shows forth the vindication of resurrection life.[158] This suffering witness and not the cry for vengeance against the oppressors is at the heart of what the martyrs mean for the scroll in Revelation.

The martyrs thus idealize the life witness of the churches for Revelation. The martyred church follows Christ everywhere and is a holy offering to God as firstfruits in Christ's image (14:4). Their cry for justice occasions the judgment of the nations (6:9-11), but their witness leads to repentance and forgiveness among the nations as well (as noted previously, 11:13). The martyrs are the noteworthies when the kingdom of peace comes to earth (20:4). As with the Lamb whom they follow, those condemned and martyred by the kingdoms of this world now judge over them, but not for vengeance; rather, with grace, peace, and liberty as the ultimate goals. Their willingness to pay the ultimate price in witness to the Lamb shows forth a commitment shared by the entire church, having proclaimed Christ crucified in baptism (John 1:31). The suffering of the martyrs is not without effect but unleashes a creative force in witness to Christ.

---

157. Bauckham, "The Conversion of the Nations," in *The Climax of Prophecy*, 257-58.
158. Bauckham, "The Conversion of the Nations," in *The Climax of Prophecy*, 258.

This force is redemptive and is wielded in the power of the Spirit against the forces of darkness. The church in Revelation is not only the faithful bride but also an army in the cause of transferring sovereignty from the nations to Christ. The company of faithful witnesses joins with the Spirit in linking heaven and earth, or, better, in bringing heaven to earth. The goal of the church is not to escape the earth in a flight to heaven but to prepare for the coming of heaven to earth, or to provide a witness in the here and now to God's coming reign. The liberating reign of God is already foreshadowed in the church but will one day be brought to earth to a significant degree through the church's prophetic witness.

Gospel of John and 1–3 John

For the Gospel of John, the church is not determined by issues of natural birth or lineage but rather from spiritual rebirth from above. Though neither the world nor Israel recognized the Word of life by whom all things were made, those who did receive him were given the right to share in his sonship and to participate in the reign of God that he brought (John 1:9-13, 18). Yet, salvation for John "is of the Jews" (4:22), and Nathanael calls him "the King of the Jews" (1:49). Though "the Jews" (used seventy-one times in John) is a term usually employed in John to describe those who are in resistance to Jesus, the focus of the term is mainly on the Jewish authorities.[159]

For John, transformed Israel participates in the kingdom, or reign, of God by believing in Jesus and by being born again according to the Spirit, an event that is as mysterious in its source and effects as the blowing of the wind (3:5-8). The Spirit is the Paraclete, the other comforter, or helper, who will be sent from the Father through the Son in order to teach the faithful community concerning Christ and to be with them forever (14:16, 26; 15:26).

Jesus will gather the church together unto himself through his crucifixion and resurrection, for in his death he will draw all people to himself (12:32), and this gathering includes more than Israel (11:52). The church consists of all those who are cleansed by Jesus' blood through faith (1 John 1:7). Faith is receiving Jesus himself, as well as the testimony of him (John 1:12). The original disciples doubted the news of Jesus' resurrection but upon receiving him at his appearance are nonetheless commissioned as ambassadors of forgiveness.

---

159. D. Moody Smith, "Judaism and the Gospel of John," in *Jews and Christians: Exploring the Past, Present, and Future* (ed. James H. Charlesworth; New York: Crossroad, 1990), 76-99. This is not to deny that a larger plot was at work. See James D. G. Dunn, "The Question of Anti-Semitism in the New Testament Writings of the Period," in *Jews and Christians: The Parting of the Ways, A.D. 70-135* (Grand Rapids: Eerdmans, 1999), 199.

They have seen the risen Jesus and give forth the testimony by which the future community will hear and believe without seeing (20:29). Whoever believes in Jesus receives this testimony (1 John 5:10).

The church comes together through faith in Jesus (John 3:18; 1 John 5:1). Jesus will abide in his disciples, and they will abide in him as branches of a vine. They will be wholly dependent on him for new life and fruit bearing (John 15:1-5). Abiding in Jesus involves a baptism in water and Spirit (3:5) and has eucharistic overtones (6:53-58). It also involves receiving Jesus' footwashing at the entry into his final hour, implying an ongoing practice in the community (13:1-20). This abiding will allow the disciples to know intimate communion with Jesus as Jesus has with his heavenly Father. Just as Jesus is in the Father and the Father is in Jesus, so are the disciples in them. This interpersonal communion is their dynamic unity and the quality of their common life (17:20-22). This communion existed between the Father and the Son before the creation of the world (17:24) and is opened to creation through the Word made flesh (1:14).

The disciples are bound to Jesus by keeping his word. They receive the words of God from Jesus (17:7-8) and have kept his word (17:6). He is their shepherd, and the sheep know his voice (10:11-15). They follow Jesus' commands, the chief of which is to love one another as Jesus has loved them (15:12-14; 1 John 2:3-6). Jesus regards them as friends rather than as mere slaves, because he has disclosed the Father's will to them and called them to join him in the fulfillment of this will (John 15:15). Their obedience in living out the love of Jesus is at the core of their witness, for the world will know that Jesus was sent by the Father through the quality of their common life together (17:21). The church's outward mission is inseparable from its inner life and communion.

Jesus sanctified himself in truth so that his disciples can be sanctified (17:19). They are given to the Son from the Father so that they belong to the Son and not to the world (17:9). Jesus also has chosen them from the world for himself (13:18). They are in the world but are kept from the evil one, for the Father will protect them by the power of his name (17:11). They are not of the world, just as Jesus is not of the world, for they partake of his sanctification in truth (17:16-19). As Jesus was sent, they are sent in the power of the Spirit to be agents of forgiveness or of exclusion from forgiveness (20:21-23). Yet, the Son did not come to condemn or exclude but to save. Those who prefer the darkness rather than the light bring condemnation on themselves (3:17-21), implying that exclusion is fundamentally the act of the unrepentant. Though the disciples reach out to the world, which God loves (3:16), they are not to love the things of the world that exist in resistance to God (1 John 2:15-16). They have fellowship in Jesus through the light of his truth and continue to walk in this light in ongoing fellowship (John 1:5-7).

Walking in the light of truth involves loving others (1 John 4:7-12) and confessing that Jesus has come from the Father into flesh (4:1-3), for the original circle of disciples beheld that Jesus partook of our flesh and blood for our salvation (1:1-4; John 1:14). The goal of the church is to be like Jesus, a reality fulfilled at Jesus' appearing (1 John 3:2). There is no fear when facing the final judgment, for the love of Jesus casts out fear (4:18). He took on flesh so that the faith community can become like him.

Matthew and Mark

There is no question that, according to the Gospels, Jesus, as John the Baptist before him, proclaimed the coming of the kingdom of God. For Matthew especially, Jesus brings God's liberating reign that is felt in Jesus' act of setting the captives free (Matt 12:28; 3:2). Jesus came to the lost house of Israel (15:24) and sought to bring the Pharisees and the outcasts of Israel to the banquet table of the kingdom of God (9:10-13; cf. Mark 2:13-17; Luke 15:11-31). He was to teach them the deeper meaning of the law in loving God and neighbor and in expanding the concept of neighbor to include those on the margins of Israel's life. The nets were to reach peoples outside of Israel as well, however, as the confession of the pagan centurion at the crucifixion implies (Matt 27:54). However, the rejection of the Messiah by Israel as a nation will mean that the mission to the nations will need to be carried out by a remnant people taken from Israel but expanded to involve others. The rejection of Jesus by much of Israel (23:37-39) and the judgment that was to come upon the nation as a result thus imply the rise of a new people, connected to Israel but still distinct from the nation as a whole. Jesus thus foretold judgment upon the temple and implied that he would replace it as the center of Israel's faith (12:6; 26:61; cf. Mark 13; 14:58; Luke 21; John 2:19). The concept of the faithful remnant is implied in the gathering of the disciples as the core of a new community of faith that, through Israel's Messiah, will inherit the promises given in the OT to Israel. The twelve disciples were symbolic of the twelve tribes of Israel, sitting in judgment over them (Matt 19:28; Luke 12:32; 22:30). "The twelve are destined to be the rulers of eschatological Israel."[160]

Though references to the church in the Gospels are sparse, the later rise of the church is inexplicable without them.[161] Such references are especially

---

160. Ladd, *Theology of the New Testament*, 107.
161. Donald Guthrie, *New Testament Theology: A Thematic Study* (Downers Grove, IL: InterVarsity Press, 1981), 702.

important to Matthew, where Jesus notes that he will build his church and the gates of Hades will not prevail against it (Matt 16:18). The concept of building up the people of God is in the OT (Ruth 4:11; Jer 1:10; 24:6; 31:4; 33:7; Pss 28:5; 118:22; Amos 9:11). The church in Jesus' mission was to be formed from Israel, but also from Israel's mission to bless the nations, for the end will not come until the gospel is preached to all nations (Matt 24:14). Not only is the new ἐκκλησία (ekklēsia, "gathering") that arises from Israel to reach the nations, they are to do so in loyalty to the Messiah. What is unique about Matt 16:18 is Jesus' reference to "my" church. Though rooted in Israel, this *ekklēsia* also belongs to Jesus, has its center in the Christ.[162] Matthew's entire gospel arguably comes to a climax in Jesus' admonition to the disciples that they make disciples to Jesus of all nations (28:19).

The disciples' witness of the risen Christ would set them apart as foundational to the church for Matthew. Peter as representative of the other disciples confesses Jesus as the Christ, thus functioning as the rock upon which the church is founded as a confessing community of the Messiah (16:18-19).[163] Bound to the risen Christ, not even Hades can prevail against the church, which may be a cryptic reference to the end-time resurrection (16:18). In Jesus' name, the disciples will exercise the ministry of binding and loosing, which must refer among other things to the binding of the dark powers and the loosing of people from their hold (16:19).[164] This is the work of the church as the sign and instrument of the kingdom of God on earth. The church is not the kingdom; rather, it serves the kingdom and seeks to be its chief sign and instrument. Indeed, "the kingdom creates the church, works through the church, and is proclaimed in the world by the church."[165]

For Mark also the church is formed from those who repent in response to the coming kingdom (Mark 1:15). Jesus is misunderstood, however, even by his closest relatives (3:20-21). Jesus' new family will consist of those who hear and obey his message (3:33-35). Though the disciples are called to be a shining light upon the hill (4:21-25), they are not yet prepared to be that light. They also have considerable difficulty understanding Jesus' message or identity. Peter gets it right but is then rebuked (8:27-30). Like the blind man who sees only dimly

---

162. Ladd, *Theology of the New Testament*, 107.

163. Oscar Cullmann, for example, notes that Peter is singled out in Matthew 16 to bear a special responsibility in leading the earliest Christian community in its confession of Christ but denies that this leads in Matthew to a church office handed down from generation to generation. See Cullmann's *Peter: Disciple, Apostle, Martyr* (repr.; Waco, TX: Baylor University Press, 2011).

164. R. H. Hiers, "'Binding and Loosing': The Matthean Authorization," *JBL* 104 (1985): 233-50.

165. Ladd, *Theology of the New Testament*, 115.

but will gain clarity later, Peter and the others are yet to discover Jesus' identity as the Suffering Servant and their own call to serve in the image of the Suffering Servant (8:22-26). If even the Son of Man is to serve and to give his life, the disciples are surely not to evade the way of the cross (10:45), for the greatest must become servants of all (10:43-44). The original ending concludes with the women at the tomb being afraid at the news of Jesus' resurrection. In Mark, the resurrection does not play the triumphant role in the founding of the people of God that it plays in Matthew. Mark stresses the role of the people of God in walking in the way of the cross, even if this means experiences of abandonment and confusion. But the implication is surely that the Suffering Servant whom they follow will also prove to be the reigning Son of Man.

Luke and Acts

The people of God in Luke are those who know the liberating presence of the Spirit through faith in Christ (Luke 4:18). They too will share in the Spirit of prophecy, much like their forerunners in Zechariah, Elizabeth, Mary, Simeon, and Anna (1–2). Forerunners also include the seventy-two who go out in representation of Christ, much like the seventy elders were to share in the ministry of Moses in Num 11. As Jesus healed the sick, so also the seventy-two rejoice that the demons were subject to them (Luke 10:1-24). The Spirit will teach the disciples what they will say before the Jewish and Roman officials (12:11-12). The disciples are assigned the title "apostles" in Luke (9:10; 17:5; 22:14; 24:10), but the overall accent is on their participation with all of the people of God in bearing prophetic witness to Christ. Like the men on the road to Emmaus, their hearts will be stirred when the Scriptures are read in the light of Christ, and they will know the risen Lord in the breaking of the bread (24:13-35). Their common life together will bear witness to the risen Lord. But they must wait for the Spirit to be "clothed with power" (24:49). Luke ends with the company of believers worshiping Jesus and praising God joyously (24:52-53). This worship also foreshadows the life of the church for Luke.

The book of Acts begins with the missionary mandate of the church, namely, to further the goals of the kingdom of God in the world by bearing witness of Christ to the nations. Jesus taught the disciples concerning the kingdom of God directly after his resurrection. When the disciples ask Jesus if the time has come for Israel to inherit the kingdom of God, they are told that it is not for them to know the times or dates set by the Father. They are to concentrate instead on receiving the Holy Spirit so that they may be Christ's witnesses in Jerusalem, Judea, Samaria, and to the ends of the earth (1:1-8). With this admonition, the church receives its very reason for being. The end does not come at Pentecost; rather, a new era begins: the mission of the church. This delay of the end is justified in part by Luke according to a missionary mandate. The Spirit will fall upon the people of God as living witnesses of Christ to both Jew and Gentile, Israel and the nations.

The entire book of Acts tells the story of how the church as a missionary people fulfills its eschatological mandate, its essentially ecclesial mandate. The earliest community speaks in tongues as a sign of the church's future journey to the ends of the earth (1:8) to witness of Christ to all nations and tongues (2:4; 10:44; 19:6; 17:26-27). Pentecost turns them into a community of the Spirit that heeds apostolic doctrine, enjoys fellowship, breaks bread in memory of Christ, prays together, shares of their substance with one another, and worships God with glad and grateful hearts (2:44-47). All of these realities are granted to the church by the Spirit. They are "core practices" bequeathed to the church from Christ and by the Spirit for participation in God and for the fulfillment of a missionary mandate, for the church will witness of Christ in multiple ways that are rooted in their life together as a community of disciples. The Lord adds to their number daily those who are being saved (2:47), which is just a foretaste of things to come.

Throughout the book of Acts, the church seems to enjoy its greatest missionary breakthroughs on the heels of its most severe challenges. The first persecution leads to a fresh filling with the Spirit and to both an outbreak of missionary zeal and a deepening of unity (4:30-31; 5:41-42). When martyrdom and persecution hit the church, the apostles scatter and preach the word wherever they go (8:4; 12:24). Saul's zeal against the church is turned into a missionary zeal at his conversion (ch. 9). Persecution along the path of Paul's missionary journeys only strengthens his and his companions' resolve to go further (13:49-52). Furthermore, the opening of the doors to the Samaritans (ch. 8) and the Gentiles (ch. 10) deeply impacts the understanding of the church concerning the all-encompassing implications of the gospel for church practice. The Spirit comes upon hearts of faith even in the absence of circumcision, teaching the Jewish believers to call no uncircumcised person of faith unclean (10:28; 15:8-10). The Spirit breaks down barriers between Jew and Gentile, as well as across cultural barriers related to age, social standing, and sex (2:17-21). The outpouring of the Spirit on all flesh is granted sociological specificity, canceling social privilege and crossing barriers. The church in Acts is both a reconciled and a reconciling community of the Spirit dedicated to witnessing to the world that the Messiah whom Israel and the Gentile rulers unjustly condemned has been vindicated by the Father and made Lord and Judge over all (10:41-43). The filling of the Spirit is closely connected to repentance, faith, and baptism in

Acts (2:38). Though fluid, this relationship seems fairly consistent throughout (8:14-17; 10:44-48; 19:4-6).

Paul

The Pauline corpus is rich with imagery and instructions concerning the nature and purpose of the church. Nearly half (44 of 114) of the occurrences of the term *ekklēsia* in the NT appear in the letters attributed to Paul. The term is used of a local gathering or congregation (1 Thess 1:1; 1 Cor 1:2), a group of congregations in a local area (2 Cor 1:1; Gal 1:2), and the churches everywhere as a whole (1 Thess 2:14; 1 Cor 10:32; 11:16, 22; 12:28; 15:9; Gal 1:13; Phil 3:6).[166]

The church or churches are united in praise to the heavenly Father, who is the source of all blessing (Rom 8:15; 15:6; Eph 1:3; Phil 4:20; Col 1:12) and from whom all families in heaven and on earth derive their name (Eph 3:15). The church is the field of God planted for the Father's glory (1 Cor 1:9).

Paul consistently implies that the Father has chosen the church "in Christ" to share in all of the blessings of sonship (Rom 8:15-16; Eph 1:3-4). The election of Israel is not denied, only fulfilled in Christ the Messiah. The rejection of the Messiah causes the nation to forsake its rights and privileges, but the promises given to Israel are not forgotten. They are transferred to a faithful remnant, for "at the present time there is a remnant chosen by grace" (Rom 11:5). The natural branches that reject the Messiah are taken out, and the unnatural branches among the Gentiles who believe are grafted in (11:17-21). There remains one tree, however, with its roots in Israel, its trunk in Christ the Messiah, and its many branches representing those who are in Christ by faith. It is Christ who represents the focal point of the church: its continuity with Israel, its current unity, and its future destiny in terms of its mission and eschatological fulfillment. Indeed, God willed "to bring unity to all things in heaven and on earth under Christ" (Eph 1:10).

The church is thus the body of Christ. The image of the church as Christ's body is organic, implying an intimate union between Christ and the church. Yet, there is no doubt about the identity of Christ as the head and the need for all of the members to function at his direction, for "he is the head of the body, the church; he is the beginning and the firstborn from among the dead, so that in everything he might have the supremacy" (Col 1:18). Everyone is baptized into this body by the Spirit. In all of their diversity, the members drink of the same Spirit and bear the words of truth (1 Cor 12:13; Eph 4:15). Everyone is thus gifted

---

166. Schnelle, *Theology of the New Testament*, 329.

to contribute toward the good of the whole (Eph 4:15-16). It is possible through disobedience to lose connection with the head (and thus with the body, Col 2:19). The ideal, however, is for every part of the body to function in harmony with Christ so as to grow toward him as their ultimate *telos* (Eph 4:15). In the process, the members bear one another's sorrows and joys (1 Cor 12:26). The least honorable members receive more honor (12:23); everyone belongs and is needed (12:15-19). There is a variety of gifts; not everyone is to strive to serve the same function. Yet, all are united by the same divine working (12:4-6). Though there are elders who exercise the ministry of oversight in the congregations (2 Tim 1:13-14), all put on Christ in baptism, so that the barriers of race, sex, or social status are removed, allowing for the church to function as a united body in which every part is dignified with the call to minister the truth of Christ in the Spirit (Gal 3:28). We submit to one another out of reverence for Christ (Eph 5:21). In the Spirit, all of the gifted members exalt Christ as Lord (1 Cor 12:1-3), function in harmony with divine love (13), edify or build up the saints (14:26), and exercise ministry decently and in order, according to the directives of God's word as given through an apostle (14:36-40). Through the many gifts, God's turning to the world in Christ is further concretized through the church's discipleship.

In 1 Cor 12–14, Paul confronts an infant church that lifted up certain spectacular gifts such as speaking in tongues over others in the church. Paul does not respond by denigrating tongues in any way, for he refers to himself as a prolific glossolalic (14:18), states that through tongues one edifies the self (14:4), and gives thanks "well" through the use of this gift (14:17). Paul thus instructs the Corinthians not to forbid tongues in their midst (14:39). To say that speaking in tongues is implicitly inferior because Paul focuses it on self-edification profoundly misunderstands Paul's ecclesiology. The personal dimension of self-edification is not excluded from the life of the church. Paul does not allow persons in fellowship to be swallowed up by the corporate *Geist*. There is a dignified place to be given to self-edification in the communion of saints. The bestowal of gifts involves this dimension of building up in the body of Christ. Yet, those gifts expressed publically cannot simply be confined to self-edification. These gifts must be geared to the common good, which is why tongues, as valuable as they are in the believer's prayer life, are to be interpreted for the common good if expressed openly in the public assembly (14:27-28). The major point that Paul seems to be making in response to the elevation of tongues among the Corinthians is not to denigrate tongues but rather to place it on par with other gifts within a broader diversity of giftings. He encourages greater use of prophecy in the public assembly (cf. 14:1) because this gift seems to have been neglected in favor of uninterpreted tongues. In chapter 13 Paul subordinates all gifts to the gift of divine love that bears all things and will never pass away. In chapter 14 Paul allows love to be the guiding force in the edification of persons and of the common whole through the variety of gifts intended for the church.

The church is also the new temple for Paul (1 Cor 3:16-17). Christ is the only foundation upon which the worker must build with lasting materials fitting for the task (3:10-14). Christ is also referred to as the chief cornerstone, which holds together the structure that is based on the NT apostles and prophets (Eph 2:20-21). The people of God are being built together in order to rise up through the Spirit into a holy temple (2:21). The church thus grows in holiness as the dwelling place of God through the Spirit. The church for Paul functions moreover as a mighty army that stands in the Lord's victory and might, bearing the armor that is able to withstand the powers of darkness and to further the cause of the kingdom of God in the world. This armor involves righteousness, faith, salvation, the Word of God, and prayer in the Spirit (6:10-20). Though the church fights the good fight of faith, it in Christ is more than conqueror, since he has already won the decisive victory. Nothing can now separate the people of God from the love of Christ (Rom 8:31-39).

For Paul, the church lives from the Word of God (Eph 4:15) but also from the fellowship of the Spirit, into which all are baptized by faith in Christ (1 Cor 12:13). All continue to experience the filling of the Spirit in acts of praise and ministry to one another (Eph 5:18-21). All participate in the body and blood of Jesus by breaking bread and drinking of the cup together (1 Cor 10:16), for in this meal they show themselves to be one body in Christ (10:17). They are to partake of this meal discerning this reality, the very body of the Lord, which is the only way to partake worthily or in a way that is fitting. To eat and drink in a way that neglects or humiliates others is to bring condemnation on oneself (11:17-34, esp. v. 29). As with any table fellowship in the ancient world, there are rules of conduct considered fitting or shameful in the Lord's Supper. With every sacred meal, we remember the Lord's death and proclaim his death until he comes again (11:26). The meal takes its place alongside the proclamation of the Word as basic modes of witness undertaken by the church as it awaits the coming of Christ.

In Paul's ecclesiology, all are to accept one another as Christ has accepted them, to the praise and glory of God (Rom 15:7). Justification by faith obviously has this ecclesial dimension, since the cross has broken down the barrier between peoples (especially Jew and Gentile) in order to form a new humanity from the separate streams (Eph 2:14-18). Neither Jew nor Gentile, bond nor free, male nor female determines status or privilege, for all have put on Christ (Gal 3:26-28). The unity of the church as Christ's body is a given for Paul, for Christ cannot be divided (1 Cor 1:10). Yet, the people of God are also to make every effort to maintain the unity of the Spirit (Eph 4:3). This new humanity in Christ is to be fashioned one day after the risen Christ as the last Adam (1 Cor 15:44-49). All were created as humans to bear the Spirit and to participate in Christ's immortality (2 Cor 5:1-5), for those he justified he also glorified (Rom 8:30). The people of God are sealed by the Spirit until the final day of redemption (Eph 4:30). They currently live from the down payment of the Spirit given to us (Eph 1:13-14) so that we could pray to God as Abba, Father (Rom 8:15-16).

Other New Testament Voices

The church in Hebrews is a pilgrim people on a journey toward the heavenly city, the New Jerusalem. Faith remains the assurance of such currently invisible realities (Heb 11:1), for which saints down through the ages have been willing to sacrifice all to inherit (ch. 11). The church is but the continuation of this story of faithfulness and perseverance, part of a cloud of witnesses to Jesus that began with the prophets and saints of old and continues on among those who join the covenant sealed by Christ's sacrificial death (9:16-28). This cloud of witnesses points the saints forward, encouraging perseverance in the journey (12:1-3). The church is to resist the temptation to go back to Judaism, for the witnesses of the old covenant are themselves pointing to Christ as the fulfillment.

The church consists of "holy brothers and sisters who share in the heavenly calling" and who fix their thoughts on Jesus, "whom we acknowledge as our apostle and high priest" (3:1). The brothers and sisters are to submit to the authority of elders, who keep watch over the house of God, so that the work of these leaders is a joy and not a burden (13:17). Christ, however, is the ultimate head over the church. As the eternal high priest, he serves in a heavenly tabernacle not made with hands (8:3-6). We have access with confidence through faith in Christ (4:16; 10:19). As Moses was the faithful servant of God's house of Israel, so Christ is the faithful Son in God's house, the church. "And we are his house, if indeed we hold firmly to our confidence and the hope in which we glory" (3:6). As Moses led the children of Israel out of Egypt, so, by way of implication, the church is to faithfully follow Christ in journeying through this life on the way to the heavenly city (3:16-19). The Lord disciplines the church through hardship along the way for its learning and increased faithfulness. The admonition is given: "Therefore, strengthen your feeble arms and weak knees" (12:12).

The church in 1 and 2 Peter is called God's elect who are chosen by God the Father, sanctified by the Spirit for obedience to Christ, and made clean by the blood of Jesus (1 Pet 1:2). Christ is the chosen one (1:20), from whom the church enjoys its election. In obedience to Christ, the church is not only sanctified and cleansed but is to be holy in life, for God is holy (1:15-16). Godliness will confirm the church's calling and make its election certain (2 Pet 2:10). The holy life is encouraged by the hope of Christ's coming (3:11-13). The holy life has its impetus in a renewal of life caused by faith in the Word of God. The church is born anew by the imperishable seed of God's Word (1 Pet 1:23). The Word is a reliable witness to what Jesus did for our salvation (2 Pet 1:16-18). As a faithful witness to Christ, Scripture is a light shining in a dark place that rises like the sun in the hearts of believers (1:19). Faithful to the Word, the church is to avoid false teaching and persevere in the faith (ch. 2).

James also exhorts believers to be single-minded in their faith so as to avoid being tossed to and fro in life (1:6-8). Their faith is also born from the Word of God: "He chose to give us birth through the word of truth, that we might be a kind of firstfruits of all he created" (1:18). The congregation is not only to hear but to obey the word of truth (1:22-25), for faith without its works in life is dead (2:14-26). The community of believers shaped by the word restrains its speech (1:26; 3:3-12) so as not to slander one another (4:11), and it cares for widows and orphans (1:27). Those of humble circumstances should take pride in their exaltation, while those of honorable estate should take pride in their humiliation (1:9-10). There is to be no favoritism granted to the rich (2:1-4). The elders of the church are to gather around the sick to pray for them, for the prayers of righteous persons avail much (5:13-18). If someone wanders from the faith, the believers are to seek to bring back that one (5:19). The church behind James is a just and a healing community.

Conclusion

The church in the NT arises from Israel in order to participate in the mission of the triune God to all nations. Israel as a nation rejected the Messiah, however, and consequently the nations were still not blessed with the gospel. All that existed at Christ's resurrection was the risen Messiah and a relatively small faithful remnant. There was a mission that God had chosen Israel to fulfill to the nations that the faithful remnant of Israel needs to take up. The church shares in the life of Christ and proceeds to the ends of the earth with Christ's mission in mind. The church in the NT is thus elect of the Father, established by Christ in his death and resurrection, and sanctified/empowered of the Spirit to be the sign and instrument of the reign of God on earth. The overarching purpose is the participation of the church in the life and mission of God toward the divinely intended eschatological fulfillment. The ultimate end is to glorify God among the nations. The mission of the church in the world is thus a broad and multifaceted reality that is rooted deeply in the church's life. The communion of saints participates in God, is governed by the love of God, and is directed by the mission of God in the world toward turning the world into the theater of God's glory.

Revelation and Systematic Theology

As noted above, the church in Revelation, as elsewhere in the NT, occurs in the delay of the end willed by Christ. In this delay, the church discovers its life of worship, fellowship, and mission as part of the now and not yet of God's kingdom, drawing from the now and reaching (yearning) for the not yet. The church thus has its reason for being largely in the worship of the saints and missionary call of the church to bless the nations with the goodness of God. As we noted at the start of our essay, the church takes up its mission to the ends of the earth when the end did not arrive at Christ's resurrection and the bestowal of the Spirit. The church had its very being in the delay of the end, a delay that has as its purpose the repentance and blessing of the nations. The mission of the church is thus fundamentally directed to this end, the glory of God on the earth. It is with these thoughts that we begin our exploration into the significance of Revelation for constructive ecclesiology.

The Trinitarian Founding of the Church

The church is grounded in the divine decision to embrace humanity in love and communion. It is fitting that Revelation should begin with a triadic greeting (Rev 1:4-6) and then proceed to show how the divine life opened up to the world through the decision of the Father to send the Lamb of God and to give the Spirit for the redemption of the world. The risen Christ and the sending forth of the Spirit give rise to the church. This divine decision gathers the people of God and sends them forth. The ἐκκλησία (*ekklēsia*, "gathering") in the ancient world was a gathering or assembly come together to make a political decision. But the *ekklēsia* of Christ and of the Spirit gather because of a decision already made by God and is now to be carried out in and through the assembly. Theologians have become increasingly aware of the need to conceive of the founding of the church as an act of the triune God, as an open invitation to participate in the κοινωνία (*koinōnia*, "communion [of God]"). The church is not simply a utility for accomplishing a mission but is more deeply a communion of saints within the embrace of the triune God. Its worship and mission involve the living reality of this communion at its base and as its *telos*.

All three divine persons featured in Revelation are needed for a balanced ecclesiology, or doctrine of the church. First, an ecclesiology that is focused only on the Father's sovereign will can make the church seem to be a privileged sect predestined from among humanity to function as the glory of creation. The nature of the church in Revelation as an open invitation to others to dine with Christ in the Spirit makes such an elitism impossible as a theological option. Even the Lamb's book of life belongs to the *Lamb* and is thus open to all who wish to follow. Second, a one-sided emphasis on the incarnate Christ as the founding principle of the church can lead the church into thinking that it is the prolongation of Christ in the world to an extent that the critical dialectic between the church and Christ (the body and its head) is relaxed and the church that is meant to live in humble witness to Christ seeks to rule in his stead. The image of the church as Christ's bride in Revelation leaves no doubt that the church cannot simply identify itself with Christ; it lives faithfully in covenant relationship with Christ, living from and imitating, but certainly not confusing its own reality with, Christ. Third, a pneumatologically founded church can slip into religious enthusiasm and chaos without the christological guidance and structure needed to maintain a unified and purposeful witness. The close connection between the slain Lamb and the suffering witness of the church in Revelation makes such a spiritual enthusiasm detached from Christ and his witness impossible as well. In response to such one-sided dangers, the tendency has thus been to view the founding of the church in the elect will of the Father, the redemptive act of Christ, and the communion of the Spirit poured forth from the Father and through the Son to bring the kingdom of God to earth through the church as its chief instrument and sign. The church lives from the *koinōnia* of the triune God as Father, Son, and Holy Spirit, which causes it to extend this communion to others and to worship God for divine goodness. Such communion holds much promise for an ecumenical ecclesiology today, a concept that helps us to view the doxological and missionary life of the church, not as an exercise in propaganda, but as an opening up of the hospitality of faith and justice to all peoples. The church that worships and missionizes does so from the rich wellspring of its shared life with God.

Revelation begins in 1:4-8 by greeting the churches from the eternal Father, the crucified and risen Son as the faithful witness, and the sevenfold Spirit, who 5:6 tells us will go out from the Lamb into all the world. The church is greeted from these three in part because these divine persons will represent the major players in the redemptive drama that is about to enfold. The churches from the beginning are to view themselves as secondary actors bearing witness and taking comfort from within the acting of these three principal players. The judgments and acts of the Father, the redemptive and self-sacrificial work of the Lamb, and the global reach of the discerning Spirit's witness will provide the dramatic setting in which the churches will understand their nature and purpose in the drama. They can navigate their way throughout their threatening and confusing world with the knowledge that they are called of the Father, following the way of the crucified and risen Lamb, and set apart and empowered by the global witness of the Spirit. They are bound together by participation in the love of the triune God and driven to bring this love to a dark and violent world.

Election in Revelation does not privilege the church as a "kingdom" in domination over the world. This is the passion of the beast and not those who follow the Lamb. The church conquers the evil forces not by force but rather by the blood of the Lamb's self-sacrifice (12:11). In fact, the dependence of chapter 11 on Zech 4 in describing the victory of the witnesses to Christ implies that Revelation is devoted to the basic principle found there: "Not by might, nor by power, but by my Spirit says the Lord Almighty" (Zech 4:6). Election is thus rooted for Revelation in the chosen Lamb, who was slain before the creation of the world (Rev 13:8). The church, elect in the eternal Lamb, is to follow in his self-sacrificial life for the sake of the world. There is no election in Revelation that does not arise from this eternal decision to make the self-sacrificed Lamb the key to the redemption of the world. The redeemed are elect in him, in his self-sacrificial life. There is no possibility of elitism in this notion of election, only life, worship, and service.

Christ thus founds the church in the victory of his life poured out for the world. It is the word of Christ that commands authority in the churches in chapters 1–3. The author of Revelation claims no juridical authority, though he prophetically conveys Christ's word to the churches. He is the brother in suffering and the kingdom (1:9), a prophetic figure leading a community of prophets (10:9-11). The saints gather around the risen Christ and are addressed by him as the focal point of unity. Yet, the twelve apostles of the Lamb are listed in the heavenly city (21:14), and their witness implicitly stands as the criterion for truth by which to judge false apostles (2:2). An apostolic legacy is implied in Revelation that the saints must protect against false apostles. But there is no hierarchical structure apparent in Revelation. The fellowship of suffering and the kingdom and the Spirit of prophecy seem to dominate the ecclesiology of Revelation.

The purpose here is not to score points for a Protestant or free-church ecclesiology. Those who hold to a hierarchical ecclesiology can also appreciate the reality of the church as a gifted body of believers who minister the words of

Christ in the power of the Spirit. And those who hold to a free-church ecclesiology can appreciate the unique gifting of those who are called to the ministry of oversight in the churches, a ministry that has an ancient apostolic legacy. The witness of this part of the canon, however, prevents our ecclesiologies from neglecting the charismatic structure of the church or the calling of all in the churches to bear the Spirit and the words of Christ in prophetic leadership of the church in its witness to the world. We all serve one another and the world *in persona Christi*. We not only speak the truth in love, we live the truth in love. We convey and interpret Christ's word with our lives.

The Spirit thus places within the body of Christ diverse giftings that are unified by the mission of Christ in the world. So as to avoid an overly juridical notion of the church, those who occupy church offices need to view themselves first as spiritual gifts in the body of Christ devoted to a universally exercised prophetic mission in conformity to Christ and the way of discipleship. The church is empowered by the outpouring of the Spirit at Pentecost, gifted with the diverse ministry of prophetic witness to Christ, and due to participate in its life and ministry in the new creation that is dawning in our midst. The Spirit is the very "soul" of the church, without which the church could not function as a living organism. But the church is not to be simply identified with the Spirit. The Spirit exercises lordship in the churches in witness to Christ (2 Cor 3:18). The Spirit is the great "Dialectician," who brings the church to sharp awareness of its weakness and constant need for renewal (2 Cor 4:7-12). Rev 2–3 is a striking example of this point. Let those who have an ear constantly hear what the Spirit is saying to the churches in witness to the word of Christ. The church lives from the word of prophecy and seeks to live out that word before the world.

In witness to the work of Christ, the Spirit bequeaths to the church core practices such as baptism, footwashing, Eucharist, proclamation, discipleship, gifted ministry, doctrinal faithfulness, and mission that aid in the overall mission of the church as Christ's faithful body. We can thus speak of "suffering" or bearing divine things as the body of Christ.[167] Christ is present in his word in chapters 2–3 but also in the communion of the meal (3:20). The church also accompanies Christ in the world when, as a living offering for the redemption of others, they follow the Lamb wherever he goes (14:4).

The church knows that it is the sanctified and empowered company of saints in its role as the firstfruits unto God. Even if not physically martyred, all of the saints have offered themselves to God, having lifted up the crucified Christ in faith and baptism. They die daily in imitation of Christ's self-giving

---

167. See Reinhard Hütter, *Suffering Divine Things: Theology as Church Practice* (Grand Rapids: Eerdmans, 1999).

for the world. Their holiness and empowerment are essential to their victory over the world in conformity to the blood of the Lamb. As Christ's bride, they are to wear the good works imparted to her by Christ (19:8). They are set apart unto God by following the Lamb as the firstfruits of the harvest of the new creation in glory to God (14:14-16). The larger harvest is to involve people of all nations and tongues, who are allowed to bring into the kingdom of God the glory of their national and cultural heritages in glory to God (7:9; 21:26). The Spirit does not dissolve the element of diversity in the communion of saints, ever. The peoples of all nations and tongues are indeed sanctified, for they don white robes. But their being set apart for the Lamb does not cause them to relinquish their cultural heritages, for those are sanctified too. They come with them into the heavenly city and they offer them in glory to Christ (21:26). In all of its diversity, the holy church is also one. The masses of the saints from every nation and tongue who have come out of the great tribulation offer one chorus of praise to God (7:9-17). Though diverse, the people of God journey toward eschatological unity. They are one, and they journey toward experiencing that unity before the throne of God and the Lamb.

There is a tantalizing hint here that can guide the church when confronting the pluralist challenges of our time. The unity of the church is meant to include an ever-increasing diversity from all nations. Although judgment comes upon the nations for killing the martyrs in Revelation after chapter 6, the prophetic vision of the book as a whole clearly depicts a heart of love for the nations that drives the witness of the church and that influences the victory envisioned at the end. The vision of the kings of the earth bringing the glory of the nations into the heavenly city (21:26) is telling. The hospitality of faith opened to the nations in the book is responded to favorably as the peoples enter at the end bearing gifts from their national and cultural heritages. The exclusivity of Christ does not dispel the vast inclusivity of the Spirit's witness to Christ, nor does it diminish the dignity of the gifts granted the nations by the Spirit in the context of their long histories and rich heritages.[168] The missionary life of the church should not cause the church to overlook or disparage these gifts. We are blessed by them as we seek to bless the nations, and we invite the peoples of the nations to bring these gifts with them to the communion of the saints and ultimately to the heavenly city. This is the fulfillment of the kingdom of God on earth.

---

168. See Veli-Matti Kärkkäinen, *The Trinity and Religious Pluralism: The Doctrine of the Trinity in the Christian Theology of Religions* (Hants, UK: Ashgate, 2004), and Amos Yong, *Hospitality and the Other: Pentecost, Christian Practices, and the Neighbor* (Maryknoll, NY: Orbis Books, 2008).

The church fulfills its worship and mission in the now and not-yet of the kingdom of God, which means that the church is a pilgrim people, as the Vatican II document *Lumen gentium* noted (ch. 7). The church lives from Christ and the Spirit, glorifying God, and participating in the fulfillment of God's kingdom on earth. Yet, the church does so in weakness, knowing that, as servants of God, it bears its treasures in vessels of clay. It journeys through the trials of life, always recognizing the critical dialectic that exists between itself and the kingdom that it proclaims. Its members journey as servants humble in their identification with the crucified Christ and grateful to be servants of God's grace in the world. They resist the lure of worldly power and influence and seek to be agents of justice and peace as they look forward to the heavenly city, wherein righteousness will dwell for all peoples.

The Worship of the Saints

The church prays what it believes and believes what it prays. It also prays what it yearns for in the world and takes its worldly concerns up into its prayers. Such is Wainwright's insight into the centrality of worship for theological reflection.[169] As the locus of Christian formation and identity, the church is eschatologically the firstfruits of praise in glory to God. Worship is not just a task given for the church to do, it is essential to the very nature and purpose of the church. We are the firstfruits of a harvest set apart as a holy offering for the glory of God. In fact, worship and mission overlap, since the church participates in the mission of God in the world to bring God glory. The church participates in the self-sacrifice of the Lamb as the holy offering to God's glory as the firstfruits unto the Father (Rev 14:4). It is to be the initial part of the larger harvest reaped from all nations that at the end would represent a holy offering in praise to God (7:9-10; 14:14-16; 21:24). Like mission, the worship of the church is essential to its very nature as the firstfruits of the harvest unto God and is not just a task that it takes on. The worship of the church flows into its missionary life and back again, for the church realizes that it is to be the sign and instrument of a much larger offering to God that will involve all peoples.

It is important that the church bring God glory as firstfruits. The Lamb is the supreme offering of praise to the Father, for the Lamb is pure and without blemish. The church is firstfruits only as attached to the Lamb and only in following the Lamb as his spotless bride. There is a sense here in which the church's worship in life and word is perfected by Christ as mediated through

---

169. Wainwright, *Doxology*.

him. In the power of the Spirit, the church is a worshipping body only as mediated through the Lamb.

In worship the church discovers its true identity as the firstfruits of a holy offering to God in the image of the slain and risen Lamb. A persecuted church does not accept the verdict of the larger society concerning the church's identity; rather, it embraces the verdict that is heard in worship: in proclamation, confession, the sacred meal, prayers, and songs. The church connects with a more ancient tradition and a future communion in affirming a reality that cannot be seen with the naked eye but can be experienced in faith. Worship connects with the church's dogmatic and creedal tradition both nourishing it and being guided by it. The church also connects with its missionary life, both nourishing it and being inspired by it. All of these realities are practices that make the church what it is as a communion of saints.

Though worship is essential to the church's life and purpose, it is thus also something that the church practices. These practices lift the church beyond the earthly sphere but also inspire hope for the renewal of the earth. In worshipping, the saints on earth feel a connection with the saints and angels above but also with the new heavens and new earth. John is in the Spirit on the Lord's Day in touch with such realities of hope, even though he is exiled from the company of the saints (1:10). God is worshipped in Revelation simply for being worthy of praise as Lord (ch. 5), for being the Creator (4:11; 14:7), for being mighty and wise (7:12; 11:17), for righteous acts and judgments, and for beginning to reign (15:4). The beast in chapter 13 wants glory in a deceptive bid for lordship. But the church sees through the deception and grants lordship to God alone. By worshipping God alone (and not the beast), the church not only has victory over the beast but also foreshadows the reign of God on earth, when all of creation will give God glory. One recalls here the vision of Isa 6:3:

> Holy, holy, holy is the Lord Almighty;
> the whole earth is full of his glory.

Such is the goal of the prophetic vision of Revelation as well. Such is at the heart of the life and mission of the church as well. In the light of the church's worship, we can better appreciate the Trinitarian founding of the church.

Missionary Ecclesiology

One fact is clear about the church in Revelation: it is a missionary church. The world did not end with the rising of Christ; Revelation in fact begins with the risen Christ. The end is delayed in part so that the church may fulfill its missionary calling to reach the nations. The destiny of Israel and the church in Revelation "is bound up with that of the nations."[170] For this reason the book of Revelation tells this missionary story in between the rising of Christ and the rising of the saints in the new creation. In referring to the missionary story, we do not refer here primarily to a church that necessarily sends people into foreign lands or seeks to expand the boundaries of the church beyond a given local area. We refer basically here to the role of the church both near and far to *live* and *proclaim* the reality of Jesus Christ before the world. The focus is participation in life and communication of its significance, not expansion. This point is illustrated in numerous ways in Revelation. The Christ around whom the church gathers in worship and obedience has seven eyes, which are the seven Spirits that go out into the entire world (5:6). As we noted earlier, the scroll opened by this Lamb in chapter 5 reappears at John's own call to prophesy again to many peoples, nations, languages, and kings (10:11). Its contents are arguably given in the account of the witness of the two olive trees in chapter 11, a witness that symbolizes the fulfillment of the church's missionary task. The 144,000 also bear witness to the word of Christ in a way that follows the Lamb wherever he goes, even if this means martyrdom (14:4). The church itself discerns the words of Christ in the Spirit in order to follow by imitating Jesus' own faithful witness before the world. It moves with the discerning eyes of the Lamb into all the earth toward this end.

What all of this means is that, for Revelation, mission cannot be conceived of as a mere task given to the church. To the contrary, the church has mission built into its very nature and reason for being in the world. As David Bosch wrote, "Christianity is missionary by its very nature, or it denies its very *raison d'être*."[171] To quote Lesslie Newbigin by way of elaboration:

> The truth is that the Church is not the Church in any New Testament sense unless it *is* mission. The Church is the outflowing of God's love into the world. It is the body of Christ who came to seek and save the lost and, if it is not all the time actively seeking and saving, it is — to that extent — not the Church.[172]

---

170. Joseph L. Mangina, "God, Israel, and Ecclesia in the Apocalypse," in *Revelation and the Politics of Interpretation* (ed. Richard B. Hays; Waco, TX: Baylor University Press, 2012), 101.

171. David Bosch, *Transforming Mission: Paradigm Shifts in Theology of Mission* (Maryknoll, NY: Orbis Books, 1991), 9.

172. Lesslie Newbigin, "The Evangelization of Eastern Asia," *International Review of Mission* 39 (1950): 142.

Newbigin was instrumental in popularizing what has come to be called a "missionary ecclesiology." The term "mission" is used here in the broad sense as rooted in the missions of the Son and the Spirit, or in the self-giving of the triune God through Christ and the Holy Spirit for the sake of a new humanity, a new creation. Mission is thus a participation in the mission of God in witness to Christ and in harmony with the Spirit's liberating work in the world. Though the proclamation of the good news of salvation in Christ is essential to mission, so is the larger participation in the realization of the values of the kingdom and love of God in the world, including justice, mercy, and faithfulness (Matt 23:23). A missionary ecclesiology lifts up what Dietrich Bonhoeffer termed the "church for others."

As the reference to Bonhoeffer indicates, Newbigin's understanding of the church as a missionary fellowship is part of a larger trend in ecclesiology influenced by the world missionary conferences and the Second Vatican Council, which helped to create a new vision for the church as a missionary presence in the world. Feeding it also were the Pietist, Wesleyan, and Pentecostal churches, which viewed the mission of God in the world to be part of the central focus of the church. This focus affects a number of issues related to the church. For example, the unity of the church takes on an increased urgency when viewed in the light of the church's missionary calling, especially since Jesus prayed for the church's unity precisely in the context of the church's task to show the world that Jesus was sent from the Father into the world for its salvation (John 17:20-21). Yves Congar has thus called for an ecumenism "for the world" that is not limited to mere comparative ecclesiology or (beyond that) an effort to negotiate historic differences among world communions (as important as this is). Ecumenism must also take up issues of doctrine and life that concern the world or the ways in which the kingdom of God challenges the world for its salvation and healing. Ecumenism is to have a worldly direction. The call here is for the end of ecclesiocentrism and the beginning of a theocentrism that places God's passion and mission for the world at the very center of the life and unity of the church. If Jesus came to seek and to save the lost, then the Spirit sanctifies and empowers the church to continue in this mission. As Revelation shows us, the church is to move with the Spirit in the image of the crucified Lamb into all the world to lead the world to repentance and healing.

David Bosch has shown that a missionary ecclesiology is to take note of the massive changes that took place in the church when it moved from an ancient, persecuted minority to an imperial church in the post-Constantinian era. The question becomes how a church that is at peace with the world and has grown comfortable with privilege and power can simultaneously manifest the justice and peace of the kingdom of God and the mission of the crucified

Christ in the world. Such an imperial church has a tendency to close in upon itself, become preoccupied with its own success, and to forget its Christlike call to serve. A "Christendom ecclesiology" tends to be institutionally based, focused on its own expansion and success. This church loses its prophetic edge and speaks in the voice of the dominant social order. It is attached to the state rather than to the kingdom of God.[173] There are many middle-class churches in the West today that face a similar danger. Such was certainly not common to the church of Revelation. John wrote as a brother in suffering and the kingdom of God (1:9). The witness of the churches to which he wrote was to thrust them into conflict with the empire, with its rebellion against God, its violence, its claims to lordship, and its illusion of peace. Their path was that of suffering love in witness to the Lamb who was slain. This was a church led by martyrs and not politicians.

Many find the collapse of Christendom in the modern era or the end to the hegemonic hold of the church on Western culture to be an opportunity for the church to rediscover anew its prophetic witness. The voice of the martyrs especially speaks to us from across the centuries, and from many locations in the world today where Christianity is still an oppressed minority, concerning the self-sacrificial witness to the redemption and justice of the kingdom of God to which the church is called. Guided by the life of the crucified Christ and driven by the winds of the eschatological Spirit, the church is to realize what the martyrs knew so well, namely, that this world as it exists is not ultimately our home. Our home is with the presence of God in the new heavens and new earth. Fueled by this hope, the church is to bear witness in this world of the world to come and to seek as much as possible to be both the sign and the instrument of the kingdom in the here and now. From this cluster of insights concerning the challenge and promise of a missionary ecclesiology, we turn afresh to the theological significance of the witness of the martyrs.

The Witness of the Martyrs

The ancient church honored its martyrs, a practice implied in Revelation. There is no cult of the martyrs in Revelation, for adoration is channeled to the Lamb alone (19:10). But the honor due to their witness as exemplary for the church is

---

173. Bosch, *Transforming Mission*, 181-261. See also H. Richard Niebuhr, Wilhelm Pauck, and Francis Miller, *The Church against the World* (Chicago: Willet, Clark, 1935), and José Míguez Bonino, "Fundamental Questions in Ecclesiology," in *The Challenge of Basic Christian Communities* (ed. Sergio Torres and John Eagleson; Maryknoll, NY: Orbis Books, 1988), 145-49.

assumed throughout. The martyrs in Revelation are the quintessential Christians, who show forth a witness that is to be held in some sense by all of the saints. Those who typify the witness of the church in Revelation (the two witnesses in ch. 11 and the 144,000 witnesses in ch. 14) are described as having made the ultimate sacrifice for their faith. The 144,000 follow the Lamb wherever he goes, even to death itself.

In contrast to the ecclesiology of Revelation, we do not remember our martyrs anymore, even though more Christians have been martyred in the modern era than in any other in the history of the church. We no longer grieve for them, honor them, or contemplate what they mean for the nature and purpose of the church in the world. For example, there is no question but that all Christians die with Christ in faith and baptism and are risen anew to a life dedicated to following him. The NT word for witness implies a connection with the contemporary word "martyr." The martyrs are arguably not making the ultimate sacrifice at their moment of death. That decision was implicitly made at their conversion and baptism. The decision made at the end of their lives represented a courageous act of following through from that original decision, to remain true to it no matter what price had to be paid to do so. In a sense, the martyr at the end of life feels that there is no other choice available. A life lived as buried with Christ and risen in identification with him cannot at the end be reversed in order to avoid physical death. To do so would be to nullify all that had gone before. To believe on Christ and be baptized into his body is to enter into the life of a martyr. The church of Revelation is the church of martyrs in faithfulness to the crucified and risen Christ. The church of the martyrs cannot rest at ease within a "state" or "culture" Christianity and remain true to its own core in the crucified Lamb.

The church that honors the martyrs knows that it cannot be wedded to the state and will resist any claims by a dominant culture to ultimate loyalty. Being a Christian is being a disciple of the crucified Christ, discerning the way of the cross and following in its wisdom. The church resists the lure of power and follows instead the path of empowered service ("not by might nor by power, but by my Spirit says the Lord"). The church led by the martyrs is loyal above all else to the justice and mercy of the kingdom of God. It avoids any hint of racism or oppression and works against these social evils. Moreover, the martyrs bear witness to God's rightful lordship over all of creation. The life that the community of Christians sacrifices belongs to God. For Revelation, the willingness of the martyrs to give up life in this world is rooted in the deeper truth that this life has always belonged to God as the creator and redeemer. All of life is thus a gift from the hand of God: "You are worthy, our Lord and God, to receive glory and honor and power, for you created all things, and by your will they were created and have their being" (4:11). We do not possess life as our own natural right, so in relinquishing life into the hands of God, the martyr merely recognizes the divine claim to what has always belonged rightfully to God. The effort by humanity to cling to life and to claim it as one's own is an illusion, a cryptic form of idolatry, a denial of the right of the Creator to all of life. When faced with the choice of denying God's lordship or facing death, the martyr remains faithful, recognizing that he or she cannot hold on to or misuse that which belongs to God alone. "It is in submission to his own martyrdom that the martyr witnesses to the real and proper relationship between God and man, namely, that it is God alone who gives life and man who receives it."[174]

The martyr thus leads the missionary church in bearing witness to the value of the kingdom of God over all else. He or she shows that no amount of years in the flesh is worth one's eternal life with God within the loving communion of saints. This belief cannot be confessed with the mouth alone but must be lived in all of life's circumstances. If put to the ultimate test, this faith, if authentic, must remain the determining factor in one's actions. The church in Revelation journeys through this world with the vision of the heavenly city before it. To turn one's gaze from this hope in order to cling to earthly life is similar to the desire of the Israelites to return to Egypt during the time of trial. The church of the new exodus follows the martyrs in keeping one's hope alive. The living martyrs are willing to sacrifice anything in this life to aid in the work of the kingdom of God. The sacrifice of the martyrs is to inspire the church in making such decisions on a daily basis. After all, if life in its entirety belongs to God, what dare we hold back from God in the present moment? The church challenges and subverts a materialistic culture that seeks wealth and power by any means necessary, including those that do violence to others. The church engages in its social witness as an aspect of its discipleship, in a way consistent with the path of the cross. It knows that the more it penetrates into the depths of its center in the crucified Lamb, the more profoundly social it becomes, for the Lamb was slain for the whole world. The more social it becomes, the more it can penetrate into the depths of its own center.

Finally, the martyrs remind the church of the victory of the risen Christ over the forces of death and alienation. The vision of the risen Christ in chapter 1 and the slain Lamb that rises up to take the scroll from the Father at the throne of God in chapter 5 connect with the slain witnesses that rise up in chapter 11 vindicated of God and victorious over the beast that had slain them. The power of their witness converts many. The witness of the church has its power precisely

---

174. William C. Weinrich, "Death and Martyrdom: An Important Aspect of Early Christian Eschatology," *Concordia Theological Monthly* 66.4 (Oct. 2002): 335.

in its participation by the Spirit in the life of the crucified and risen Christ. The comfort that comes to the people of God is from the knowledge that nothing can separate us from the love of God. The purpose is to give God glory in all things and to dedicate oneself to see the nations share in giving thanks.

Israel and the Nations

In Revelation, the church's self-sacrificial witness in the image of the risen Lamb has deep roots in the calling of Israel as the people of God to bless the nations. As we noted earlier, Revelation is filled with imagery that ties the church to Israel as the people of God. The witnesses that typify the church in chapters 11 (the two olive trees) and 14 (the 144,000) are described with imagery or references that are drawn from Israel, even though their lives are most decisively shaped by the crucified and risen Christ. In chapter 12 Israel is implied in the image of the woman giving birth to the Messiah. The church proceeds through the world surrounded by plagues toward the New Jerusalem as a kind of new exodus. Those victorious over the beast sing the Song of Moses and the Lamb, connecting intricately the victories of the two exoduses (15:3). This connection remains into the eschatological future. The New Jerusalem will have on its gates the twelve tribes of Israel, while the names of the apostles are on its foundations. The connection between the two implies that the twelve apostles represent the faithful remnant that will lead the mission of the eschatological Israel transformed by the Messiah and the bestowal of the Spirit to bear witness in the image of the crucified Lamb to all nations, thus fulfilling Israel's calling to bless the nations, a calling that began with the promise given to Abraham. There is no church without Israel and without the Messiah that was born from her. The church is forever tied to Israel as its root.

Such provocative insights from Revelation are relevant to the challenges of an ecumenical ecclesiology today, for the church of Jesus Christ founded on the apostles is still so divided from the twelve tribes of Israel. What the heavenly city places side by side is anything but united in today's world. Improvements have been achieved in the relationship between Israel and the church of Jesus Christ. There is no question but that Christian theology in a post-Holocaust era is casting off its older prejudicial judgments about Judaism. It is now widely assumed that ancient Judaism was not simply legalistic.[175] Moreover, Christian biblical and theological scholarship has largely followed the advice of the World

---

175. See Frank Thielman, *Paul and the Law: A Contextual Approach* (Lombard, IL: IVP Academic, 1995).

Council of Churches that we should listen carefully and learn from how Jews define Judaism (ancient and modern) "in their own terms."[176] The churches as well are rediscovering anew their ties to Israel's spiritual legacy, which the church and historic Israel hold in common. As *Nostra aetate* of the Second Vatican Council affirmed, NT faith is deeply rooted in the Hebrew Scriptures:

> The Church of Christ acknowledges that, according to God's saving design, the beginnings of her faith and her election are found already among the Patriarchs, Moses and the prophets. She professes that all who believe in Christ — Abraham's sons according to faith (cf. Gal 3:7) — are included in the same Patriarch's call, and likewise that the salvation of the Church is mysteriously foreshadowed by the chosen people's exodus from the land of bondage. The Church, therefore, cannot forget that she received the revelation of the Old Testament through the people with whom God in His inexpressible mercy concluded the Ancient Covenant. Nor can she forget that she draws sustenance from the root of that well-cultivated olive tree onto which have been grafted the wild shoots, the Gentiles (cf. Rom 11:17-24).[177]

The God who raised Israel up from Egypt and from the grave of despair (Ezek 37) raised Christ from the dead for the rise of a transformed, eschatological Israel that will involve the Gentiles. Though the church is constituted directly by the missions of Christ and the Spirit, it also has its roots in the OT people of God, called by the same triune God as an *ekklēsia* in its own right. Vatican II's *Lumen gentium* thus adds that:

> Israel according to the flesh, which wandered as an exile in the desert, was already called the Church of God. So likewise the new Israel which while living in this present age goes in search of a future and abiding city is called the Church of Christ. For He has bought it for Himself with His blood, has filled it with His Spirit and provided it with those means which befit it as a visible and social union.[178]

Regarding Israel, *Nostra aetate* notes further that "God holds the Jews most dear for the sake of their Fathers; He does not repent of the gifts He makes

---

176. Considerations approved by the WCC Central Committee, 1.7, given in *The Ecumenical Movement: An Anthology of Key Texts and Voices* (ed. Michael Kinnamon and Brian E. Cope; Grand Rapids: Eerdmans, 1997), 421.

177. *Nostra aetate: Declaration of the Relationship of the Church to Non-Christian Religions*, §4.

178. *Lumen gentium: Dogmatic Constitution on the Church*, §9.

or of the calls He issues."[179] Such a statement implies hope for a gathering of the nation of Israel into the eschatological fulfillment of God's kingdom in Christ. Other ecumenical documents besides Vatican II have affirmed such a hope. In 1948 at the first assembly of the World Council of Churches, in Amsterdam, the council affirmed (partly in response to the Holocaust), "To the Jews our God has bound us in a special solidarity linking our destinies together in his design."[180] The fact that the New Jerusalem has the names of both the twelve tribes of Israel and the twelve apostles on its gates and foundations implies that the church of Lamb of God is tied to Israel in both heritage and eschatological destiny.

This link between Israel and the church is forged by the triune God with a particular focus on Christ. It is not the church that fulfills Israel but Christ, and both Israel and the church find their destiny in him.[181] The Father who elected Israel as the chosen people did so in preparation for the coming of his Son, the eternally chosen Messiah of Israel (the Lamb slain before the creation of the world, Rev. 13:8). According to Revelation, he is the Lamb, called out of Israel to fulfill its calling to bless the nations. As Marcus Barth wrote, "Therefore, Christians are bound to affirm that Jesus is not just a Jew, but the Jew of Jews, the affirmation and culmination of Israel's history among and for the nations."[182] Barth is clear that Christ as the fulfillment of Israel does not cause Israel to pass from God's elect will. To the contrary, Barth affirms that Israel maintains significance as having its eternal election and calling bound to Christ: "Should anyone want to honor Jesus at the expense of Israel by presenting him as an alternative or substitute for the salvation which was to come from the Jews, he would disprove himself as a follower of Christ, the Son of Mary."[183] Thus, we cannot simply ask in a generic way as the medieval theologian Anselm did, "Why the God-Man?" *(Cur Deus Homo?)*. In the light of the inseparable connection between Christ and Israel, we should ask, "Which God-Man?" The answer is not just the Word made "flesh" in a generic sense but as John understood it, namely, as this particular man, the Jewish Messiah come to fulfill Israel's calling to bless the nations. The salvation that comes from Christ is the salvation that God eternally elected should come from the Jews for the nations. The Father willed it and sent Christ and the Spirit to fulfill it. It

---

179. Nostra Aetate, §4.

180. Quoted in Paul M. Van Buren, "Israel and the Church," *Dictionary of the Ecumenical Movement* (ed. Nicholas Lossky et al.; Grand Rapids: Eerdmans, 1991), 536.

181. Mangina, "God, Israel, and Ecclesia in the Apocalypse," 87.

182. Marcus Barth, *Israel and the Church: Contribution to a Dialogue Vital for Peace* (Richmond, VA: John Knox, 1969), 29.

183. Barth, *Israel and the Church*, 29.

is God's salvation (Rev 7:10), but it is still the salvation that comes historically in God's election from the Jews for the nations, especially the Jew of Jews, the Lamb slain before the creation of the world.

The Lamb was slain before the creation, meaning that the very act of creation had him in view. Thus, there is also a sense in which Christ is made flesh in a way that encompasses all of humanity, for he is not only the Lamb born from Israel but the Son of Man, who will be worshipped by "all nations and peoples" (Dan 7:14; cf. Rev 7:9-10). Israel's calling as a people to bless the nations thus pushes the election of Israel back to Abraham, the one to whom the promise was given that through him *all nations* would be blessed. The blessing of Abraham is described within a Genesis narrative that starts with Adam and Eve. Without denying the special calling of Israel in the fulfillment of the promise to bless all peoples, this calling is not to be centered on Israel but on God's plan for humanity in Christ (a reminder that the church has needed with regard to its own history and mission). Palestinians (including Christians) and others sympathetic to their cause will note that Abraham does not belong only to the Jewish people. There is no justification for a reading of Revelation that elevates Israel above the nations and deafens our ears to the legitimate concerns of other peoples in that region as elsewhere (just as we are not to deafen our ears to the concerns of Israel). The call of Israel to give of itself as a blessing to the nations is tied to a calling that transcends Israel from the beginning. According to Revelation, this beginning even predates Abraham and the creation of humanity. The risen Lamb who was slain before the creation lies eternally at the base of God's elect will implied in Adam and Abraham for all peoples, for Israel and the Arabs, and for all nations, for there can be no elect decision theologically prior to the Lamb of God. We refer here to God's own eternal self-determination as Father, Son, and Spirit to create and to redeem humanity. The church, which traces its origins back to the redemption of the slain Lamb, and the Spirit, who proceeds through him to the ends of the earth (5:6), know that Israel is bound in its election to this same Lamb and to this same Spirit in hope as well as in truth. The goal is that, through the Lamb and the mission of the church, Israel will come to realize the fullness of its own calling and destiny.

This hope recognizes that, as the eternal source of Israel's and the church's election, the Lamb is the source of both promise and judgment when it comes to Israel. There is no avoiding the rift that occurred between the nation Israel and its Messiah (and the eschatological Israel that is bound to him) because of Israel's rejection of Christ. Though language we would for various reasons not use today, the reference to the "synagogue of Satan" in 2:9 is a potent reminder of this reality. Israel cannot be viewed today as the people of God in the same way that it was before the rejection of its Messiah, as though there are two peoples of God, Israel and the church, awaiting eschatological reconciliation. This is not to say, however, that God has forgotten Israel or its unique calling in the world to bless the nations. The listing of the twelve tribes on the gates of the heavenly city leaves open the hope that Jesus will yet gather the nation Israel into its true destiny within eschatological Israel as the people of the crucified and risen Lamb and of the Spirit that proceeded through him into the world to bless the nations. This is not a reference to the assimilation of Israel into Christianity to be defined by the largely Gentile church of Jesus. This is rather an assimilation into Christ the Messiah, which is sure to alter the church in every aspect of its life and thought as it alters historic Israel. If the Lamb is the light of the New Jerusalem in which all peoples walk, the eschatological fulfillment of Israel and the nations can only be in him and to his glory, shaped ultimately in his glorified image.

Conclusion

Revelation can speak powerfully to contemporary ecclesiological concerns. Though there are vast differences among the world communions (and even within them) over a myriad of specific issues related to the nature, boundaries, location, practices, and missionary purpose of the church, Revelation can help to bring to our attention several salient points that can inform our differences and common vision. Revelation speaks to a communion ecclesiology that lives from the embrace of the triune God, from the elect will of the Father, the crucified and risen path of the Son, and the powerful discernment and life of the Spirit. The worshipping and missionary lives of the church overlap as dimensions of a church deeply committed to the missions of the Lamb and the Spirit in the world. The church is led by the prophetic discernment of all the people of God and not just by those who possess the gift of oversight. Throughout its journey the church seeks to bring to full expression its holiness and its unity, and it lives in hope of reconciliation with both Israel and the nations. Revelation also speaks to a martyr church that forsakes the lure of power and seeks instead the self-sacrificial way of the cross, which is the way of the Spirit. The church discovers its identity in its role as the sanctified firstfruits in the image of Christ as the supreme offering to God for the redemption of the world. This church discovers its identity also in its practices, in the word of God, in adoration and prayer, in discipleship and missionary practice, and in the sacred meal, to name only several. All members share equally in the prophetic ministry to which the church is called. This is a humble church that hears the word of correction and recognizes only God as its strength in the midst of weakness. "Praise and glory and wisdom and thanks and honor and power and strength be to our God for ever and ever" (Rev 7:12).

Salvation

Revelation and Biblical Theology

How are we to describe salvation in the context of the NT, especially in Revelation? This question of salvation has emerged in certain eras of the church's history with a sense of urgency. Such was the case in 1937, four years after the Nazis had taken power in Berlin and as the German church tended in response to accommodate itself to this new situation and to proclaim a message that would not challenge this state of affairs. Shortly afterward, Dietrich Bonhoeffer penned his classic, *The Cost of Discipleship,* in order to describe the "gospel" of the church of his time and place as "cheap grace," the "deadly enemy" of the church. Cheap grace is the grace doled out without condition or limit by the established church, bourgeois Christendom. Bonhoeffer maintained that its opposite, costly grace experienced in the way of the cross, faded as the world was Christianized and as grace "became its common property." This ecclesiastical property was called "grace" but was in reality an abstract doctrinal principle or ecclesiastical system requiring only a confession or an accepted ritual. Cheap grace is "grace without discipleship, grace without the cross, grace without Jesus Christ, living and incarnate."[184] True grace is costly because it came in abundance in the Word made flesh (John 1:14-16) and was revealed in the cross, calling for our total allegiance. This grace opens and closes the battle for redemption that characterizes Revelation (1:4; 22:21). We will explore salvation in Revelation with this challenge in mind.

Revelation

Rev 7:10 declares, "Salvation belongs to our God, who sits on the throne, and to the Lamb." There is no question but that, according to Revelation, salvation is possible only by God's actions and grace. For this reason, declarations about salvation in Revelation are typically in doxological statements that praise God for divine victories over the dark forces (1:6; 5:9-10; 7:10; 12:10; 19:1-2). All things

---

184. Dietrich Bonhoeffer, *The Cost of Discipleship* (7th ed.; New York: Macmillan, 1976), 45-49.

are renewed only by God, because "God created all things," and by the divine will they were created "and have their being" (4:11). All things have their being in God, which means that there is no reality that exists apart from the creating and sustaining action of the Creator. Life already in some fundamental sense belongs to God in that it lives from God. There is no ultimate autonomy or capacity for life apart from the Creator, no autonomous secularity that can define itself wholly apart from the Creator. As Ps 104:30 notes, "When you send your Spirit, they are created, and you renew the face of the ground." Since all of creation has its being in the creating and sustaining power of the Creator, they can be redeemed, liberated, and made ultimately new only by this same God. In the light of what Revelation says about the creation in relation to the Creator, it is unimaginable that salvation could come from any other source than God.

Salvation in Revelation is further focused on the Lamb, who is slaughtered for the redemption of the world. Rev 1 gives a programmatic statement in this regard: Christ is the "firstborn from the dead . . . who loves us and has freed us from our sins by his blood, and has made us to be a kingdom and priests to serve his God and Father" (1:5-6). In the following verse, the redemptive work of Christ is fulfilled as he comes in the clouds to bring final judgment and salvation to the earth (1:7). Rev 5:9 and 14:4 add that Christ "purchased" us by his blood. These metaphors of ransom and purchase are closely related. The setting of Revelation involves the efforts by hostile powers to hold creation captive and alienated from the sovereign lordship of its creator. Ransom and purchase depict the Lamb as crucified to win the creation back to its creator, its rightful Lord. Though slain as a Lamb, Christ is also the Lion of Judah, risen for the redemption of creation. The rejection of God's grace by the powers of darkness that led to the crucifixion of the Lamb was turned by God into the means of victory over those very powers. Their decisive effort at victory has become the means by which they would lose their hold on creation, and creation would be restored to its God-intended destiny. This irony is especially clear in chapter 12, where the effort to devour the child by the dragon leads to the dragon's demise. In the cross and resurrection, God has used the enemy's attempt at victory to enact the victory of grace against it and for sinful humanity. God has overcome evil with good.

Salvation through the Lamb in Revelation is not only a ransom or redemption; it is also a form of liberation: "To him who loved us and *freed us from our sins* by his blood" (1:5). Not only is this salvation a personal liberation from the power, guilt, and judgment of sin, but it is also a larger historical and eschatological reality that leads to the heavenly city. A kind of exodus of the people of God is depicted in Revelation involving plagues and a journey through trial to the promised goal, a victory that is celebrated in the "song of God's servant Moses and of the Lamb: 'Great and marvelous are your deeds,

Lord God Almighty. Just and true are your ways, King of the nations'" (15:3). Salvation brings to realization the purposes of the kingdom of God, namely, the liberation of God's people from bondage to the dark powers and the establishment of God's just reign on the earth:

> The kingdom of the world has become
> the kingdom of our Lord and of his Messiah,
>   and he will reign forever and ever. (11:15)

Salvation as liberation in the service to the kingdom of God on earth implies a transformation of this present order not only socially and politically but in every way imaginable. The sanctifying presence of God purges and transforms all things into a place of God's dwelling. The saints have robes that are "fine linen, bright and clean," and nothing unclean will be allowed to enter their final dwelling in God's heavenly city (21:27). "Blessed are those who wash their robes, that they may have the right to the tree of life and may go through the gates into the city" (22:14). The heavens and the earth flee from God's holy presence at the time of final judgment (20:11). They are not merely abolished but are made new at the coming of God's holy city from heaven (21:1-2). The result is that "God's dwelling place is now among the people, and he will dwell with them. They will be his people, and God himself will be with them and be their God" (21:3). The time of war and judgment are over, and God comes close to wipe away every tear, as a parent cares for a weeping child. Indeed, "there will be no more death or mourning or crying or pain, for the old order of things has passed away" (21:4). The once-rebellious nations now walk in the heavenly city by the light of the Lamb (21:24).

Throughout redemption, liberation, and transformation, judgment, for Revelation, is the flip side of salvation. This is costly grace and not cheap grace. There are both a harvest and a winepress (14:14-20). In fact, judgment is vital to the fulfillment of salvation in Revelation. Judgment serves to free the world from evil. Death and Hades are thrown into the fire of God's eschatological judgment so that they can never torment and terrorize humanity again (20:14). Indeed, "God's creation, salvation, or justice or judgment, are closely aligned in the Apocalypse."[185] Divine justice is fulfilled in mercy, but it involves the exclusion of those who remain persistent in opposing it. Such exclusion includes upheavals and plagues involving the creation. Creation, however, is also used in rescue as well, since springs of water will nourish God's own (7:16-17), the

---

185. John A. du Rand, "Soteriology in the Apocalypse of John," in *Salvation in the New Testament: Perspectives on Soteriology* (ed. Jan G. van der Watt; Leiden: Brill, 2005), 479.

wilderness protects and nourishes the messianic mother and her child (12:14), and the earth comes to the woman's aid by opening up to devour the floodwaters (12:16). The creation that suffers trial while serving God's eschatological purposes will one day be liberated and transformed into the new heaven and new earth, providing a larger framework for the destiny of believers. Believers who also endure trial while serving God's purposes through their living witness will one day be raised to new life. The crucified and risen Christ in Rev 1 and 5 holds the hermeneutical key to understanding the destiny of both the church and the cosmos.

God does not just save from a distance in Revelation but invites us to partake of the divine life in being made new. The Shepherd will lead the sheep to streams of living water (7:17), and the new creation will involve drinking from "the free gift of the water of life" (22:17). The liberation and transformation of creaturely life comes from a partaking of the waters of God's Spirit, recalling how in the beginning the dust came to life as a living soul (Gen 2:7). God's putting the breath of life into the two witnesses in order to raise them up (Rev 11:11) is a potent foreshadow of the eternal drinking of the water of life that will characterize our eschatological future in God's presence (and that implicitly characterizes our partaking of the divine life penultimately in the here and now). The breath of life vindicated the truth of the testimony of these witnesses, "justifying them in the Spirit" in line with Christ's own vindication as the risen Lamb. For Revelation, one must partake of God in order to be vindicated and renewed by God. Revelation describes a gradual and immediate intimacy or union between Christ and his bride that leads ultimately to the saints being termed "sons" of God, a term reserved in the Johannine literature for Jesus as the Son of God (21:7). The saints partake of the divine nature.

Though salvation is possible in Revelation only by the work of the Lamb and the Spirit, believers must also by God's grace repent, obey, and patiently endure in order to overcome the forces of darkness. Grace is not the property of the church; rather, it is a precious pearl that one must be willing to give all to receive. The messages to the churches assume as much throughout chapters 2 and 3. Salvation is a past event and a present reality in Revelation, but it is also a future judgment by God given favorably only to those who overcome or are victorious (2:7, 11, 17, 26-28; 3:12, 21; 21:7), just as the Lamb has overcome (17:14). Those who overcome do so by patiently enduring (2:3), repenting (3:19), doing God's will to the end (2:26), and returning always to their first love (2:4). They overcome by the blood of Christ or by the same self-sacrificial love that constituted Jesus' own self-giving for the salvation of the world. Those who are redeemed by the Lamb become like the Lamb and follow him wherever he goes (14:4), and the clean linen of the faithful bride is adorned with righ-

Salvation

teous deeds (19:8). Works are important to salvation as an eschatological reality characterized as an overcoming to the end. The sanctifying union with Christ is dynamic and involves partaking of and conforming to Christ in all things, a living from grace in all of life. Works will also serve to condemn those who have not chosen the path of overcoming by the blood of the Lamb, for they will be judged "according to what they had done" (20:13). Though works are important to overcoming, they are part of the gift of grace given by God's renewing power. The fine, clean linen of the saints as the faithful bride represents her deeds, but these are given her to wear (19:8). Little wonder that the elders lay their crowns before the throne of God with the words:

> You are worthy, our Lord and God,
> to receive glory and honor and power,
> for you created all things,
>   and by your will they were created
>   and have their being. (4:11)

This dramatic redemption through the Lamb is not an afterthought in Revelation but was God's sovereign will from the very creation of the world (13:8). The connection between creation and redemption in God's sovereign will is thus sealed in Revelation. Creation occurs with the cross at its horizon. Rather than serving as an afterthought, the slain Lamb plays a vital role in the Creator's plan for the creation. The ancient Hebrew tendency to view redemption as connected theologically to creation is carried over into Revelation. Creation from the void and darkness in Gen 1 is replayed analogously in the redemption from the threats of a more sinister void and darkness in the form of the dragon and his followers in their goals for the world. In Revelation, the creation leads to the ultimate victory of redemption through the cross, which is where God reclaims rightful lordship over all things. "Creation finds its eschatological fulfillment in the new creation."[186] There is no possibility of a gnostic dualism here. This is not to say that salvation merely emerges from creation as a natural process in Revelation. The Lamb had to be slain and rise again in order to provide the power of abundant life needed for the captive creation to be redeemed, liberated, and renewed. Yet, there is still an overarching connection in Revelation between creation and redemption that is hidden in the elect will of God from all eternity.

As new creation, salvation in Revelation is not confined to the inner recesses of the pious life or to existential enlightenment. It is for the nations as well as for individuals. It has to do with the victory of the kingdom, or reign, of God

---

186. du Rand, "Soteriology in the Apocalypse of John," 498.

over all things, even the entire cosmos. Though inclusive of personal renewal, the soteriology of Revelation spills out over such confines to redeem, liberate, and transform all of creation. After all of the efforts of darkness to assert itself as the final reality, the Lamb remains the eternal light that has overcome the darkness and that will shine forever as the glory to be experienced in the renewal of all things. The victory of the Lamb and of the Spirit is for the blessing of all the nations and of the entire cosmos.

In the context of the Lamb's role as the elect one of God for creation, the names of the saints have been written in the Lamb's book of life (20:15). This book belongs to the *Lamb*, since he was the one chosen from the creation of the world (13:8), implying that all others belong to the book by belonging to the Lamb. It is the *Lamb's* book. The book of life is the Lamb's because the Lamb was the one who was slain and raised from the dead as the fountain of new life for others. Those bound to the Lamb receive the divine verdict of life rather than death. Those not written in the Lamb's book of life live under the reign of death and will worship the beast (13:8), having been astonished at seeing him (17:8). They will not be allowed to enter the heavenly city to partake of the waters of life (21:27). Is this book of life a fixed list predetermined by God from the creation of the world, without any significance granted to human responses to God or to the Lamb? In the history of salvation, are we merely dealing with the playing out of a divine script, or are those who are in the book there because they have chosen the Lamb and the path to life rather than the beast and the path to death? Revelation does note that those not found are "shameful or deceitful" (21:27), and those in the book are those who have overcome to the end (3:5). There is also the promise by God that those who are victorious to the end will not be blotted out from the book of life (3:5). Yet, this promise is conditioned on a faithful and patient overcoming by the grace of God. After all, the church of Ephesus was told that they were in danger of being removed as a lampstand if they did not repent (2:5). God remains sovereign over the content of the book, bound only to the Lamb and to the promise of life through him that is offered to all of humanity. The book in Revelation serves as a potent reminder that the direction of history is not unknown to God as something that can catch God by surprise. But this insight in no way eliminates the role that human responses to God play in the outcome of the drama and in the content of the book that lies behind it.

In conclusion, in the light of Revelation, cheap grace is the eclipsing of this human responsibility. It is "grace" without the crucified Lamb and without the victory of his blood as experienced in all things, in life and in death. The church of cheap grace has lost its first love and might drift to the place of desiring to live at peace with Babylon. The corresponding understanding of salvation is viewed in detachment from the rightful claims and judgments of the Creator, the self-sacrifice of the crucified Lamb, and the worldwide prophetic witness of the sevenfold Spirit. Bonhoeffer attempted to describe salvation in a way that would grant the church a clear understanding of the cost of following Christ in the midst of alien lures toward seemingly easier and secure paths. How do we describe salvation in our time and place in a way that resists cheap grace and opens us to the grand adventure to be experienced in the way of the cross and within the winds of the prophetic Spirit? Revelation dramatizes for us the challenges to be faced in answering that question.

Salvation in Revelation is costly grace. It is costly in the sense that God created all things with the cross of the Lamb at its horizon, knowing that the flourishing of the creation will come about only through conflict, wounding, and self-sacrifice. It is costly because the Lamb was slaughtered for its redemption and liberation and because the Spirit proceeds out from the crucified Lamb to take the victory of the Lamb to the furthest reaches of the earth and of human rejection in order to renew all things in the Lamb's image. It is costly because the people of God must be willing, while enjoying the blessings and promises of salvation, to follow the Lamb wherever he goes, even if this means the ultimate sacrifice of martyrdom. This grace is free, but it is not cheap, and it is certainly never to be taken for granted as an ecclesiastical property that is simply there at our disposal to claim without committing our entire lives to it. Salvation is God's provision from beginning to end, but it is also something that we actively receive and claim for both ourselves and the world. Salvation that occurs during this battle for God's reign over the nations is never something to take for granted. With these insights in mind, we will explore the meaning of salvation in the light of the larger NT witness.

Gospel of John and 1–3 John

The Gospel of John has a soteriological motive: "These are written that you may believe that Jesus is the Messiah, the Son of God, and that by believing you may have life in his name" (John 20:31). "Johannine thought, regardless of the specific topic, is always soteriological."[187] For John, salvation begins with the Father, who so loved the world that he sent the one and only Son into the world to save it (3:16). God did not send the Son to condemn the world but to save it. Only those who reject the light of the Son and choose the darkness will stand condemned and face death (3:16-20). But God is an eternal source of

187. Schnelle, *Theology of the New Testament*, 712.

life, love, and light. From the very beginning, the divine life was in the Logos, and the Logos was life, making him the means of creation and the light of all humankind. The hope of humankind rests in the fact that the darkness that rises up cannot destroy the light of the Logos: "The light shines in the darkness, and the darkness has not overcome it" (1:5). Though the world was made through the Logos, the world did not recognize him. Even his own within Israel did not embrace him. But those who receive the light and life of the Logos, who believe on his name, are born from above (1:9-13). This Word was made flesh and lived among us. The good news of John's gospel is that, because of the incarnation of the Word, followers of Jesus have seen the glory of the Word, "the glory of the one and only Son who came from the Father full of grace and truth" (1:14). This is the glory that the Son had with the heavenly Father from before the creation of the world (17:5). The victory of the Logos over the darkness is assured. The glory of his light has been seen, and the darkness cannot extinguish it.

Salvation is described in the opening verses of John's prologue in terms that recall creation. One finds a similar connection in John to the one found in Revelation between creation and salvation. "In the beginning," one finds the Logos of God creating all things. He is the light that overcomes the darkness and the life that gives life to all. The new creation through the light and life of the Logos is told in a way that causes one to connect it with the story of creation itself. New creation fulfills creation. Salvation is of the Jews (4:22), which means in part that it is to be read from the lens of the creation account given in the Hebrew Scriptures as the base of the hope for a new creation (foreshadowed in Ezek 37). The promises given to Israel are not taken back in John but are confirmed and fulfilled by the Jew of Jews, Jesus Christ. The law that came from Moses had its own glory but is now fulfilled by the even more abundant grace and truth of Christ (1:17), for "out of his fullness we have all received grace in place of grace already given" (1:16). The law of Moses is referred to as the witness to the "grace already given" or to the "grace after grace" that is now fulfilled by the fullness that belongs to Christ.

There is indeed a heavy accent in John's gospel on revelation as that which accounts for the fullness of grace that breaks in to the world through the coming of Jesus. The prologue stresses the Son as the Logos and the light of the Father that dispels the darkness. Jesus is the Savior in that he makes the Father known, for "no one has ever seen God, but the one and only Son, who is himself God and is in closest relationship with the Father" (1:18; cf. 6:46). The revelatory significance of Jesus continues on as an important part of his saving work. That Jesus called God his Father was itself an astounding claim rooted in his unique relationship with the Father introduced in the prologue (5:18; cf. 1:18). Jesus as the unique revelation of the Father represents a dramatic and decisive development in salvation history, for the Father was previously unknown in this way and is now so known only in Jesus (1:18; 17:25). Knowing Jesus will grant an open window to the Father: "If you really know me, you will know my Father as well. From now on, you do know him and have seen him" (14:7). Those who do not believe in Jesus do not have the Father's word in them (5:37-38). Jesus has disclosed to his followers all that he has learned from the Father (15:15). The Spirit who goes out from the Father does not represent a second truth detached from the one incarnated in Christ but, rather, will testify of Christ (15:26). The Spirit will take what is Christ's and make it known to his followers (16:15). Jesus is forever definitive and irreplaceable when it comes to knowing the Father.

But salvation is not reduced in John's gospel to enlightenment. Jesus gives *life* to the fullest (10:10). Jesus gives the water "welling up to eternal life" (4:14) or "crossing over" from death to life (5:24). Those who believe in him will have eternal life, the core of which is knowing the heavenly Father (3:15-16; 17:3). Those who refuse Jesus refuse life (5:40). Jesus is "the eternal life, which was with the Father and has appeared to us" (1 John 1:2). Jesus is the bread of God that gives life to the world (John 6:33), and those who feed and drink from him will never hunger or be thirsty (6:35). The Bread of Life is his flesh, which he gives "for the life of the world" (6:51), for he is the resurrection and the life, bestowing life on those who believe in him (11:25). Unless one eats his flesh and drinks his blood, one cannot have this life (6:53). Those who do eat and drink will be raised on the last day to life eternal (6:54). The very words of Jesus are "full of the Spirit and life" (6:63). Those who cling to their own lives will lose life eternal, but those who give of their lives for Christ will receive eternal life from him (12:25). He is the way, the truth, and the life, the only way to the Father (14:6). His authority to grant this life to others is granted by the Father (17:2).

Jesus gives life as the one who "takes away the sin of the world" (1:29). "The link between sin and the Lamb in this expression strongly suggests sacrificial atonement for sin."[188] The paschal lamb is in view here, especially in the light of Jesus being crucified at the time the paschal lambs are sacrificed in John. Indeed, this connection with sacrificial atonement is stronger in 1 John: "The blood of Jesus, his Son, purifies us from all sin" (1 John 1:7). "He is the atoning sacrifice for our sins, and not only for ours but also for the sins of the whole world" (2:2). Jesus' death, the beginning of his glorification as the Son of the Father, serves to "sanctify" his followers, which may be the meaning of John 17:19: "For them I sanctify myself, that they too may be truly sanctified."[189] Such

---

188. Jan G. van der Watt, "Salvation in the Gospel according to John," in *Salvation in the New Testament: Perspectives on Soteriology* (ed. Jan G. van der Watt; Leiden: Brill, 2005), 116.

189. van der Watt, "Salvation in the Gospel according to John," 116.

cleansing was foreshadowed in the footwashing ceremony, in which Jesus sets forth part of the ritual means by which his followers will communally accept the grace of cleansing (13:1-20). The Son of Man must be "lifted up" in crucifixion and resurrection as Moses' staff was lifted up for the healing of others (3:14). In being lifted up, he will draw all people to himself, implying that the impartation and witness of the Spirit that comes through him plays a role in salvation as well (12:32; cf. 15:26-27).

Salvation in the Spirit opens up the relationship of the Son with the Father to include others. Jesus reveals the Father to the disciples in order to extend the love that the Father has for the Son to them: "I have made you known to them, and will continue to make you known, in order that the love you have for me may be in them and that I myself may be in them" (17:26). This is the love that the Son uniquely shared with the Father before the worlds were made (17:24). This eternal depth of love is now opened to those who believe on Christ. The life that is shared in salvation is a dynamic communion, the very communion between the Father and the Son, in which believers may now partake: "that all of them may be one, Father, just as you are in me and I am in you. May they also be in us so that the world may believe that you have sent me" (17:21). This text makes it clear that the unity of believers is a dynamic communion that has its source in the communion of the triune God. This communion is to be a witness to the world that Jesus came from the Father, that is, from this communion of love that is now opened to the world. The rich depth of life enjoyed in salvation is thus not a closed circle but an open invitation that draws in others. Neither is evangelism a mere spoken word here, for it is rooted in the very quality of life that the loving community has in God. The community bears witness to the life in their life together.

Faith in Jesus and his work on behalf of the Father is essential to the reception of salvation from Christ. The entire gospel is written with this goal in mind (20:31). This challenge to believe is open to all, as implied, for example, by God's sending his Son out of love for the *world* so that "*whoever* believes" may have life. This programmatic statement of the universality of God's love sets the stage for numerous "whoever" statements in John's gospel (3:18, 21, 36; 4:14; 5:24; 6:35, 37, 54, 56, 58; 7:38; 8:12, 47, 51, 52; 10:9; 11:26; 14:12). A predestinarian implication is also given in statements like the following: "All those the Father gives me will come to me, and whoever comes to me I will never drive away" (6:37). But this giving of the faithful to the Son by the Father does not refer to a timeless decree as much as it does to an acknowledgment that the faithful remnant from Israel that accepts Jesus was viewed as a gift from the Father, who seeks to draw the elect people to Jesus (6:44). Salvation, after all, is first and foremost of the Jews in John's gospel. It also stresses the Father's enabling faith and hearing among those who believe: "Whoever is from God hears the words of God" (8:47), but the will to believe (or not to believe) is not necessarily canceled as insignificant from this process. Otherwise, the entire elect people of Israel would have been involved. God has not gone back on his promises to the nation. The crucial point is that those who believe are born anew: "No one can enter the kingdom of God unless they are born of water and the Spirit" (3:5). Those born anew in the Son will be raised on the last day. In the present time, they are in the world but are protected from the evil one. They are in the world but not of the world. They are sanctified by Jesus' own self-sanctification in his life and death on their behalf (17:15-18). Because the word of God lives in them, they will overcome the evil one (1 John 2:14). They can endure and bear fruit as they remain in Christ (John 15:4; 1 John 2:27). They will be like Christ when he appears: "We shall be like him, for we shall see him as he is." We are to purify ourselves in the light of this hope (1 John 3:2-3). We know that God lives in us "by the Spirit he gave us" (3:24; cf. 4:13) and by the love that we show (4:7, 16).

Matthew and Mark

Salvation in Matthew and Mark has to do with the coming kingdom, or reign, of God, "the coming of the one God in his royal power."[190] In both, the coming kingdom is a redefined story of the Jewish people, implying not only a return from exile but "that evil would be defeated and that Yahweh would visit his people."[191] Jesus' message was, Repent and believe the good news, for the kingdom is near (Mark 1:15; Matt 4:17). The Hebrew stress on steadfast loyalty now involves an accent on believing the good news, for the dramatic breaking in of the kingdom of God in Jesus' ministry has to be believed to be accepted and faithfully followed. This faith is not mere intellectual assent, since it includes sincere repentance, or a turning away from sin and toward God.

The central assumption of Jesus' proclamation in Matthew is that the kingdom of God is coming — in fact, is already near in the presence, preaching, and deeds of Jesus. The kingdom is present because of Christ, and it is powerfully felt in Jesus' acts of deliverance: "If it is by the Spirit of God that I drive out demons, then the kingdom of God has come upon you" (Matt 12:28). But the kingdom is also future, as Jesus prayed, "Your kingdom come, your will be done, on earth as it is in heaven" (6:10). The kingdom is present, but it is also

---

190. Schnelle, *Theology of the New Testament*, 87.
191. H. J. Bernard Combrink, "Salvation in Mark," in *Salvation in the New Testament: Perspectives on Soteriology* (ed. Jan G. van der Watt; Leiden: Brill, 2005), 43.

yet to come in fullness, like the way that a mustard seed hidden in the soil will burst through the surface of the ground in order to grow into a tree, or the way that yeast hidden within a loaf causes it to suddenly rise (13:31-33).

With regard to the kingdom, Matthew shows Jesus' effort to resist nationalistic political expectations, but the coming reign of God is still assumed to have larger social, political, and cosmic implications (24:29-31; 26:64). Matthew highlights Jesus as the Davidic Messiah, whom God commissioned to save Israel from its sins and to reign as Lord and King over those who follow the "law of the Messiah," the gospel of the kingdom. Not only communities but the entire world will never be the same because of the breaking in of the kingdom of God through the work of Christ and his outpouring of the Spirit. Christ will one day reign on the earth as the Danielic Son of Man (26:64). The coming of the Son of Man will involve cosmic upheaval as all things are brought into conformity to the victory of Jesus over the dark powers (24:29-31).

The basis for the victory of the kingdom of God over all things is located in the atoning death of Jesus and the victory of his resurrection. Mark highlights the necessary role of Jesus' suffering and death in the drama of redemption. From one angle, the journey to the cross is a victory over the devil. In Jesus' encounter with Satan in the desert, Jesus remains faithful with every temptation, which represented Satan's effort to redefine Jesus' sonship in ways that would involve disobedience to the will of the Father (Mark 1:12-13; cf. Matt 4:1-11; Luke 4:1-13). At Gethsemane, Jesus remains faithful as well, following the Spirit's lead to the cross in obedience to the redemptive will of the Father (Mark 14:32-42). From its Jewish background, the cup of Jesus' suffering implies the Messiah's taking the judgment for sins vicariously upon himself (10:38).[192] The effect is the deliverance of creation from the hold of evil. Mark 10:45 is key here: "The Son of Man did not come to be served, but to serve, and to give his life as a ransom for many." The figure of the glorious Son of Man from Dan 7 is here interpreted with the help of the Suffering Servant of Isa 53. He offers his life for the redemption and deliverance of humanity. Ransom related in the ancient world to deliverance from slavery or imprisonment (as with prisoners of war) through the making of a payment. The object of the payment is not the point stressed here (though it is obviously given to God); rather, it is the effect of the offering in the deliverance of creation. Jesus refers to his coming death as a ransom to set the captives of sin and death free from their imprisonment.

Atonement recruits those who receive it into its God-intended purpose of reconciling the world to God. Jesus tells his disciples that the Son of Man must give his life to ransom others in order to define for them the nature of discipleship

---

192. Combrink, "Salvation in Mark," 55.

(Mark 10:45). Mark stresses this fact, since the lesson of discipleship as following in the way of the cross forms the core of this gospel, occurring three times (once in each chapter) from chapters 8–10 (8:31-38; 9:30-36; 10:32-45). Following Jesus in the way of salvation is not confined to one's own blessings but, rather, opens one to journey with Jesus in the path of the cross and of the mission of God in the world. This path leads to glory, because Jesus' prediction of his coming death involves the prediction that he will rise again (8:31). In Matthew also, the new covenant of salvation will be sealed by Christ's death and resurrection, a sealing prefigured at the holy supper and to be enjoyed also in the future at the banquet of the kingdom of God (Matt 26:29). The rending of the curtain in the temple at Christ's death implies that Christ has now replaced the Jewish temple as the locus of God's redemptive presence in the world and as the place of atonement and reconciliation (Matt 27:51). Matthew's gospel shows the victory of the resurrection over sin and death to be prefigured already at the crucifixion, as theophanic signs appear along with the raising of some from the dead (Matt 27:51-54).

Divine favor in the kingdom of God involves forgiveness of sins. Jesus exercised the authority of forgiving sins, though this act met with resistance (Matt 9:4-6; Mark 2:5). He prayed the model prayer involving the petition for forgiveness, which included also the willingness to forgive others (Matt 6:12). "To receive forgiveness and to refuse to forgive others means excluding oneself from the reign of God."[193] Again, grace from God is not only an individual blessing but also a communal dynamic. Since humans have no capacity on their own to grasp the grace of God available in Christ, the witness of the Spirit is vital to salvation. All sins will be forgiven except blaspheming or finally rejecting the Holy Spirit (Matt 12:31; Mark 3:29; cf. Luke 12:10). Ultimately, Jesus defined the covenant he will make with his blood as "for the forgiveness of sins" (Matt 26:28).

Jesus' redeeming activity in all four Gospels involves healing and signs of God's favor that affects one's entire life in this world. Jesus' healing ministry is described in Matt 8:15-17 as the fulfillment of Isa 53:4:

> He took up our infirmities
> and bore our diseases.

The Messiah's ministry of bringing favor and wholeness to people was part of his redemptive mission, one that will involve his atoning death and resurrec-

---

193. Andries G. van Aarde, "ΙΗΣΟΨΣ, the Davidic Messiah, as Political Saviour in Matthew's History," in *Salvation in the New Testament: Perspectives on Soteriology* (ed. Jan G. van der Watt; Leiden: Brill, 2005), 16.

tion. In healing the sick and possessed, Jesus binds the strong man in order to bring the victory of the kingdom of God to earth as a force of deliverance among the captives (Matt 12:29). By bringing healing, Jesus foreshadowed the coming victory that he will bring in his death and resurrection. The challenge was to turn to Christ in faith. The connection between faith and healing is clear: "Your faith has healed you" (9:22). Healing was also given, however, in cases of weak faith, so long as a cry for mercy was involved (Mark 9:24). This faith involved acknowledging that Jesus spoke and acted with God's authority, an acknowledgment that was found surprisingly on the lips of a pagan centurion (Matt 8:8-9; cf. 27:54). There may even be a deep connection between healing and forgiveness (Mark 2:5). The redemptive power of God was not just a legal declaration but also a divine power that transforms all things in accordance with God's sovereign reign and its victory over the forces of darkness.

Jesus' resurrection granted him authority to reign on God's behalf (Matt 28:18). Even the gates of Hades will not overcome the church that he as the risen Christ will build (Matt 16:18). This inability of the gates of Hades to hold back the church of the risen Christ may imply that the saints will also rise from the dead and Hades will not be able to hold them captive. At any rate, the implication is clear that death and darkness have lost their hold on the people of the risen Christ. By implication, Christ's death and resurrection have burst through the powers of death and darkness in order to grant freedom to those who repent, believe, and follow Christ.

Luke and Acts

For Luke, Jesus represented and proclaimed God's eschatological favor for the poor and oppressed, "freedom for the prisoners and recovery of sight for the blind" (Luke 4:18). God will overturn the unjust social order in inaugurating the kingdom of God in Jesus, as Mary spoke prophetically in chapter 1:

> 50 His mercy extends to those who fear him,
>   from generation to generation.
> 51 He has performed mighty deeds with his arm;
>   he has scattered those who are proud in their inmost thoughts.
> 52 He has brought down rulers from their thrones
>   but has lifted up the humble.
> 53 He has filled the hungry with good things
>   but has sent the rich away empty.

Jesus was called to seek and to save the lost, including the outcasts of the household of Israel (Luke 15). The saving of the outcasts meets with resistance from the "righteous" as in the parable of the lost sons (15:11-32) and the story of Zacchaeus (19:1-10), or even the disciples as in the healing of blind Bartimaeus (18:35-43). The implication is that conversion is not only an individual but is also, in a sense, a communal reality in which the faithful must continue to change in order to receive all who respond favorably to the grace of God. Luke's story of justification brings out the communal dimension of salvation dramatically in the parable of the Pharisee and the tax collector. The Pharisee boasts of his superior status in relation to the tax collector and other sinners, while the tax collector can only beat his breast and ask God for mercy. The tax collector and not the Pharisee leaves justified before God (18:9-14). The way of justification for the Pharisee can come only in his humble acceptance of his own need of mercy alongside the tax collector. He must shed his sense of superiority altogether and accept the tax collector (18:9-14) as the crowd was encouraged to do in the salvation of Zacchaeus in the very next chapter (19:1-10). Forgiveness must be shared within community to be received from God. Jesus taught "forgive, and you will be forgiven" (6:37).

At Jesus' birth, the angels announce that peace will come on earth to those on whom God's favor rests (2:14). Such favor could be dramatic, such as casting out demons or raising the dead as a sign of Jesus' mission to bring the kingdom of God to earth. Later, God raises Jesus from the dead to inaugurate the era of the Spirit that will fulfill all that had come before. The two on the road to Emmaus are shocked to discover that they had journeyed and dined with the risen Christ. Their hearts burned when he opened the Scriptures to them, and he was revealed to them in the breaking of bread. This incident foreshadows how the risen Christ can be encountered in the fellowship of the saints who gather in his name (24:13-35).

Acts connects the issue of salvation to the mission of God in the world through Christ and a Spirit-empowered church. The challenge is to repent, believe, and be baptized (Acts 2:38). There is a fluid relationship between these elements throughout the narrative, though they are all connected together under what may be termed a complex initiation event. The soteriological focus of Acts, however, is not just one's personal initiation but, more broadly, the fulfillment of the kingdom, or reign, of God in the world through the witness of the promised Holy Spirit. The book opens with the risen Jesus teaching the disciples about the kingdom of God (1:3). When asked about the restoration of the kingdom to Israel, Jesus diverts the disciples' attention to the divine mandate for the fulfillment of God's reign on the earth, namely, the witness to the good news among the nations. The Spirit of the latter days will empower believers for this purpose (1:6-8). This mission will involve the breaking down of barriers between peoples and will climax with theophanic signs of the kingdom's coming fulfillment (2:18-20): "Everyone who calls on the name of the Lord will be saved" (2:21). The tongues of Pentecost are an initial sign of the vastly global reach of the Spirit in the world (2:4-12), and the key goal is the joining of Jew and Gentile in the one mission of the Spirit (ch. 10). The conclusion at the Jerusalem Council concerning the Gentiles was that God "showed that he accepted them by giving the Holy Spirit to them, just as he did to us. He made no distinction between us and them, for he purified their hearts by faith" (15:8-9). Acts sees continuity between the gospel and the Mosaic law (24:14; 26:22), though it is Christ and not the law that justifies (13:39), just as there is also continuity between the gospel and the implicit quest for God evidenced in the history of Gentile peoples (10:34-35; 17:26-28), though it is the gospel that will inform them about the mystery that they themselves have termed the "unknown God" (17:23).

Witness of what God has done in Christ is the soteriological accent of Acts. The believers bear witness that Jesus was the "righteous one" (22:14) anointed by God to bring salvation (10:38). The anointed one was condemned and executed unjustly but was vindicated in the Spirit through resurrection and exaltation by God (3:19-21; 4:27-31; 5:29-32; 7:51-53; 10:39-43). God did not abandon Jesus to the condemnation imposed on him by the world. Indeed, the apostles preached that Christ "was not abandoned to the grave, nor did his body see decay. God has raised this Jesus to life, and we are all witnesses to this fact" (2:31-32). This Christ who was condemned by the world but vindicated by God is now exalted as judge over those who unjustly condemned him (10:42). But the good news is that he turns with grace to his murderers.

Paul

The saving act of the triune God in Christ "is the beginning and orientation point of all Paul's thought, so that it bears a soteriological stamp throughout."[194] Salvation for Paul begins and ends in the heavenly Father. For Paul, there is "one God and Father of all, who is over all and through all and in all" (Eph 4:6). Almost always, the Father as the ultimate source of grace is connected with Christ as the one through whom the Father is revealed and the will of the Father is fulfilled: "For us there is but one God, the Father, from whom all things came and for whom we live; and there is but one Lord, Jesus Christ, through whom

---

194. Schnelle, *Theology of the New Testament*, 275.

all things came and through whom we live" (1 Cor. 8:6). Paul's favorite way of speaking about the saving significance of Christ is to say that God saves us in, through or with Christ. God "reconciled himself to us through Christ" (2 Cor. 5:18). God has adopted us as sons and daughters "through Jesus Christ" (Eph. 1:5). God has also given us spiritual new birth and "made us alive with Christ, even when we were dead in transgressions" (2:5). The fruit of righteousness comes forth in our lives "through Jesus Christ — to the glory and praise of God" (Phil. 1:11). This vision of salvation through Christ's mediation is common in the NT. Paul adds a colorful variety of metaphors to describe how this happened, as the above selection of verses illustrate. Reconciliation between enemies, adoption, awakening from a deep sleep, and the sprouting of fruit on a branch or vine all serve as metaphors for how Christ served to mediate between us and the heavenly Father in order to liberate and transform us by bringing us back to God from our captivity to sin and death. During Christ's role as mediator of salvation, the Father commits divine lordship to him, but after Christ destroys death, the final enemy, Christ will hand the kingdom back over to the Father (1 Cor. 15:24). The Son's reign does not cease, but there is a sense in which it has accomplished its redemptive purpose. The Father and the Son share lordship and are mutually dependent in how this lordship brings about the fulfillment of redemption for creation.

Paul tends to focus redemption on the death and resurrection of Jesus: "When I came to you, I did not come with eloquence or human wisdom as I proclaimed to you the testimony about God. For I resolved to know nothing while I was with you except Jesus Christ and him crucified" (1 Cor 2:1-2). He shared the ancient confession of the church that Christ was "delivered over to death for our sins and raised to life for our justification" (Rom 4:25). Paul thus passed on as of first importance "that Christ died for our sins according to the Scriptures, that he was buried, that he was raised on the third day according to the Scriptures" (1 Cor 15:3-4). The words "for us" imply some sense of substitution, even exchange — namely, that Christ entered into our situation of alienation and death in order to bring us into the riches of his communion with God: "For your sake he became poor, so that you through his poverty might become rich" (2 Cor 8:9). The ancient hymn as given by Paul in Phil 2:7-9 puts it this way:

> He made himself nothing
>   by taking the very nature of a servant,
>   being made in human likeness.
> And being found in appearance as a man,
>   he humbled himself

> by becoming obedient to death —
> even death on a cross!
>
> Therefore God exalted him to the highest place
> and gave him the name that is above every name.

In quoting from this ancient hymn, Paul joins his voice to the early Christian belief in Jesus as the one who partook of our death so that we could partake of his exaltation. The death and resurrection of the obedient Christ creates a new situation of righteousness between God and humanity for Paul, undoing the sin of Adam and rewriting the story of humanity in relation to God (Rom 5:12-21). The Pauline logic is clear: "For since death came through a man, the resurrection of the dead comes also through a man" (1 Cor 15:21).

Christ brings redemption by overcoming the dark forces: "And having disarmed the powers and authorities, he made a public spectacle of them, triumphing over them by the cross" (Col 2:15). Indeed, Christ "has destroyed death and has brought life and immortality to light through the gospel" (2 Tim 1:10). Paul also relies on the notion of atonement or reconciliation through the shedding of Christ's blood or through the sacrifice of the cross: "God presented Christ as a sacrifice of atonement, through the shedding of his blood — to be received by faith" (Rom 3:24-25). Through a conflation of images (redemption and sacrifice), Paul forcefully makes the case that Jesus' death fulfills the Jewish sacrificial system by winning freedom for humanity on the cross. Christ mediates and carries away our sins as the sacrificial Lamb by setting the captives free by his death and resurrection. Referring to the curse of not fulfilling the requirements of the law, Paul describes Jesus as redeeming us "from the curse of the law by becoming a curse for us" (Gal 3:13). Israel's occupation by the Romans made it clear that the elect people had not blessed the nations by fulfilling the witness of the law to the righteousness and goodness of God. Jesus bore the curse "in order that the blessing given to Abraham might come to the Gentiles through Christ Jesus so that by faith we might receive the promise of the Spirit" (Gal 3:14).

For Paul, the realm of the Spirit brings the blessings of salvation through Christ. Christ was raised from the dead "through the Spirit of holiness" (Rom 1:4). The love of God demonstrated in the cross and victorious in the resurrection "has been poured out into our hearts through the Holy Spirit, who has been given to us" (5:5). By bestowing the Spirit, the Father "has blessed us in the heavenly realms with every spiritual blessing in Christ" (Eph 1:3). Though the law is spiritual in its witness to the holy and just will of God (Rom 7:14), it cannot bring life, and thus we are justified through the death of Christ and the gift of the Spirit (8:31). "For if a law had been given that could impart life, then righteousness would certainly have come by the law" (Gal 3:21). Christ and the gift of his Spirit are needed: "You were washed, you were sanctified, you were justified in the name of the Lord Jesus Christ and by the Spirit of our God" (1 Cor 6:11). Christ was himself "justified in the Spirit" through his resurrection from the dead, bringing the blessings of God's righteous favor to those who receive the Spirit by faith (1 Tim 3:16). Paul's chief question to the Galatians was thus: "Did you receive the Spirit by the works of the law, or by believing what you heard?" (Gal 3:2). In Galatians, one is justified by faith (2:16) and receives the Spirit by faith (3:2). The blessing of Abraham involves both justification (3:8) and the gift of the Spirit (3:14). Ronald Y. K. Fung rightly notes that "the reception of the Spirit is in some sense equated with justification" in Galatians.[195] For Paul, it seems that justification and the gift of the Spirit are functionally equivalent (as well as substantially overlapping) realities.[196] Paul also wrote about the fruit of the Spirit that comes forth as one submits one's desires to the lordship of Christ and participates more fully in the new life to come. The process certainly involves a struggle whereby one must actively resist the desires of the sinful or fallen nature (Gal 5:13-26). The Spirit is the very nerve center of the Christian life for Paul.

In the Spirit, the death and resurrection of Jesus become more than distant historical events merely to be confessed as true. They become living realities that involve believers entirely: "We were therefore buried with him through baptism into death in order that, just as Christ was raised from the dead through the glory of the Father, we too may live a new life" (Rom 6:4). Paul elaborates two verses later: "For we know that our old self was crucified with him so that the body ruled by sin might be done away with, that we should no longer be slaves to sin — because anyone who has died has been set free from sin" (6:6-7). Paul claimed to be "crucified with Christ," so that "the life I now live in the body, I live by faith in the Son of God, who loved me and gave himself for me" (Gal 2:20). Paul's lifelong quest was to know Christ in "the power of his resurrection and participation in his sufferings, becoming like him in his death, and so, somehow, attaining to the resurrection from the dead" (Phil 3:10-11). Through the Spirit, we participate in Christ's sonship, crying Abba, Father, in worship, and are granted the hope that, just as Christ was vindicated as God's Son in resurrection, so shall we (Rom 8:11-16). Paul does use forensic terms, especially in speaking about justification, but he merges these with strongly

---

195. Ronald Y. K. Fung, *The Epistle to the Galatians* (NICNT; Grand Rapids: Eerdmans, 1988), 136.

196. See Macchia, *Justified in the Spirit*.

participationist language as well. E. P. Sanders thus notes: "In Paul's own letters, righteousness by faith, the Spirit by faith or sonship by faith mix indiscriminately with participationist language in such a way as to exclude the possibility of a systematic working out of righteousness as the forensic preliminary to life in Christ Jesus."[197] Another way of making this point is to note with Nils A. Dahl that "Paul makes no distinction between the forensic and the pneumatic."[198] One should keep in mind in this context that the Spirit functions for Paul (as for John) as intercessor and as the one who seals our experience of redemption (Rom 8:26; Eph 1:13), both of which were legal metaphors. For Paul, one has righteousness and life in Christ through the Spirit, in the place of sin and death (Rom 5:21).

Salvation for Paul is personal but not individualistic. Neither is the individual dissolved by the corporate *Geist*. Self-edification is preserved as a valid pursuit alongside the gifts used in the public gathering to bless the congregation (1 Cor 14). Paul's only qualification is that believers seek the gifts that edify others during public gatherings (14:26). In general, Paul viewed the redemptive drama as a grand plan to bring Jew and Gentile together into the one body under Christ. God relegated all under the judgment of disobedience (for all have sinned) in order to have mercy on all, Jew and Gentile (Rom 11:25-32). God effected redemption in order "to bring unity to all things in heaven and on earth under Christ" (Eph 1:10). Salvation is by grace so that the role of the law as a barrier between Jew and Gentile could be replaced by Christ as the one who united these two within his body (Eph 2). Justification has both a vertical and a horizontal dimension for Paul: "Accept one another, then, just as Christ accepted you, in order to bring praise to God" (Rom 15:7).

The unity envisioned by Paul is eschatological. The role of Christ as the last Adam and the eschatological horizon of salvation relate to the Holy Spirit in Paul's writings. Adam became a living soul, but Christ a life-giving spirit. By receiving life from Christ, we are destined as adamic dust to bear the image of the heavenly man, Christ Jesus (1 Cor 15:45-49). We groan under the burden of sin and death in this mortal body, seeking to be clothed with our heavenly body through resurrection. The Holy Spirit is the down payment of future immortal existence, "guaranteeing what is to come" (2 Cor 5:1-5). The Spirit is the down payment of future redemption and the seal marking us as belonging to Christ as we await the day of salvation (Eph 1:13-14). The entire cosmos groans

---

197. E. P. Sanders, *Paul and Palestinian Judaism: A Comparison of Patterns of Religion* (Minneapolis: Fortress Press, 1977), 506-7.

198. Nils A. Dahl, "Promise and Fulfillment," in *Studies in Paul: Theology for the Early Christian Mission* (Minneapolis: Augsburg, 1977), 133.

also under the burden of sin and death, waiting for the day when the Spirit will make all things new through Christ (Rom 8:18-25). We who believe in Christ are the firstfruits offering of a harvest that the Spirit is preparing in the image of the risen Christ.

The great work of redemption by the Father and through the Son and the Spirit was willed by God from before the time of creation. Christ was chosen to be "the firstborn among many brothers and sisters" (Rom 8:29). In choosing Christ, the Father thus chose us. In Christ, we were chosen to his sonship and to be holy and blameless (Eph 1:4-5). The purpose was to unify all things under Christ as their head, for all things made by and for him and in him "hold together," or have their unity and purpose (Col 1:16-17) in him. Redemption through Christ was thus willed by God "to be put into effect when the times reach their fulfillment — to bring unity to all things in heaven and on earth under Christ" (Eph 1:10). We were chosen by the Father in "conformity to the purpose of his will" so that we "might be for the praise of his glory" (1:11-12). "We know that in all things God works for the good of those who love him, who have been called according to his purpose. For those God foreknew he also predestined to be conformed to the image of his Son" (Rom 8:28-29). In Christ, nothing can separate us from God's love in Christ (8:38-39). Not even human rejection can thwart God's plan. When the Jews rejected their Messiah, God used their rejection to open the door of grace to the Gentiles. Then God will use the Gentile experience of grace to call the Jews back into the mission of God, which was fulfilled in Christ. Just as the Gentiles were shown to be sinners so as to be saved by grace, so too will the Jews be saved in the same way: "For God has bound everyone over to disobedience so that he may have mercy on them all" (11:32). Indeed, according to Rom 11, all are brought by the Spirit under the unity of Christ by grace:

> 33 Oh, the depth of the riches of the wisdom and knowledge of God!
>   How unsearchable his judgments,
>   and his paths beyond tracing out!
> 34 "Who has known the mind of the Lord?
>   Or who has been his counselor?"
> 35 "Who has ever given to God,
>   that God should repay them?"
> 36 For from him and through him and for him are all things.
>   To him be the glory forever! Amen.

For Paul, salvation is thus by grace and not works: "For it is by grace you have been saved, through faith — and this is not from yourselves, it is the gift of God — not by works, so that no one can boast" (Eph 2:8-9). Paul uses an analogy drawn from wages given to one who works: "Now to the one who works, wages are not credited as a gift but as an obligation. However, to the one who does not work but trusts God who justifies the ungodly, their faith is credited as righteousness" (Rom 4:4-5). Salvation for Paul is not analogous to a wage given for work. The logic of this kind of exchange works only in the realm of sin and death: "For the wages of sin is death" (6:23). When it comes to death, we have gotten what we had earned. But in the realm of grace, that rate of exchange does not apply. Paul makes this point clear: "The gift is not like the trespass" (Rom 5:15). Whereas many die through the trespass of Adam, so much more will the grace of Christ "overflow to the many" (5:15). If death reigned through Adam, "how much more" will those who receive "God's abundant provision of grace" reign through Christ (5:17). The language of abundance and "how much more" belongs to grace and not sin. Abundance implies that no amount of human work can account for it. For Paul, the language of abundance belongs only to grace because Christ is greater than Adam. The latter handed down death to us in a way warranted by human trespass (his and ours). But Christ, as the superior one in the comparison with Adam, hands down a saving grace that far exceeds anything we can do to warrant it. Grace cannot be measured according to what the recipient has done to warrant it but, rather, according to the overwhelming abundance of Christ, who gave all to offer it to us.

Granted only by the abundance of grace, salvation for Paul is received by faith in Christ rather than by one's own obedience to the law. The law is a holy witness to the justice of God (7:14), but it cannot atone for sin; only Christ can: "For what the law was powerless to do because it was weakened by the flesh, God did by sending his own Son in the likeness of sinful flesh to be a sin offering. And so he condemned sin in the flesh" (8:3). Also, the law could not impart new life; only Christ can: "For if a law had been given that could impart life, then righteousness would certainly have come by the law" (Gal 3:21). For Paul, to believe in salvation by works of the law is as foolish as believing that one could rise up from death to new life by the power of one's own faithfulness: "Flesh and blood cannot inherit the kingdom of God, nor does the perishable inherit the imperishable" (1 Cor 15:50). We are dead in trespasses and sins, awakened only by the grace of God as received in faith (Eph 2:1-5), for "faith comes from hearing the message, and the message is heard through the word about Christ" (Rom 10:17). The ancient formula applies: "If you declare with your mouth, 'Jesus is Lord,' and believe in your heart that God raised him from the dead, you will be saved" (10:9). Good works follow, because the grace of God "teaches us to say 'No' to ungodliness and worldly passions, and to live self-controlled, upright and godly lives in this present age" (Titus 2:12). Indeed, "we are God's handiwork, created in Christ Jesus to do good works" (Eph 2:10). For Paul, faith thus involves both love and hope (Rom 5:1-5). Without love we are nothing (1 Cor 13), and hope looks forward to the coming of Christ, at which time we will be raised from the dead and our adoption is made official (Rom 8:23). For Paul, it is not that we save ourselves by the power of faith; this response is itself grace-enabled. All things for Paul come from the hand of the one God, "who is over all and through all and in all" (Eph 4:6).

Other New Testament Voices

Hebrews seeks to restore a discouraged believing community to its early passion for salvation through Christ. The foundational soteriological point accents the giftedness of salvation through Christ as the only Son and heir (Heb 1:1–2:4). Soteriological imagery is drawn from Israel's exodus and journey to the promised land (2:10–5:10), the entry of the high priest into God's holy of holies (using also images of sacrifice and covenant; 7:1–10:39), and the heavenly city as the ultimate goal of the journey of faith.[199]

When it comes to salvation, Hebrews bases everything on the person of Christ, who stands utterly unique among the witnesses to God, for only he is appointed heir of all things (1:2). Only he is heir because only he is the Son, "the radiance of God's glory and the exact representation of his being, sustaining all things by his powerful word" (1:3). As such, he is the one appointed to provide purification for sins after dying and ascending to the right hand of the Majesty of heaven (1:3). All is thus based in the Father's vindication of the Son as the rightful heir:

> For to which of the angels did God ever say,
>   You are my Son;
>   today I have become your Father?

Or again,

> I will be his Father,
>   and he will be my Son? (1:5).

---

199. Craig R. Koester, "God's Purposes and Christ's Saving Work according to Hebrews," in *Salvation in the New Testament: Perspectives on Soteriology* (ed. Jan G. van der Watt; Leiden: Brill, 2005), 362.

After other divine statements exalting the Son, the chapter climaxes with the Father's commitment of divine lordship to the Son:

> Sit at my right hand
>   until I make your enemies
>   a footstool for your feet. (1:13)

God has redeemed humanity through the Son, who is appointed heir of all things and is himself the radiance of the Father's glory. For Hebrews, no one else could be the redeemer. No one else could share lordship with the Father except one who is the exact representation of God's being.

This redemption also involves the Son sharing in our humanity in order to "break the power of him who holds the power of death — that is, the devil — and free those who all their lives were held in slavery by their fear of death" (2:14-15). It also involves his role as the high priest being tested in every way but remaining faithful in order to make atonement for sin (2:17-18). The faithful high priest is able to help believers in time of trial (4:14-16). The Son's faithfulness in trial prepared him for the cross: "Son though he was, he learned obedience from what he suffered, and once made perfect, he became the source of eternal salvation for all who obey him" (5:8-9). His perfection under testing as the exalted high priest allows him to be the ultimate atoning sacrifice that is once and for all (7:27). It was not the ancient sacrifices but the obedience of the Son that brought redemption (10:4-10). By the eternal Spirit, Christ offered himself on the cross so that we may serve the living God (9:14). Those redeemed by the cross will have the law placed in their hearts, to which the prophets testified, and will know the forgiveness of sins (10:16-17). Salvation through the cross has a future horizon in Christ's coming: "Christ was sacrificed once to take away the sins of many; and he will appear a second time, not to bear sin, but to bring salvation to those who are waiting for him" (9:28).

Enduring and persevering faith is what is required to participate in the redemptive work of the faithful Son. Faith is the "confidence in what we hope for and assurance about what we do not see" (11:1). This faith also involves knowledge of God's deeds (11:3) and obedience to the will of God (11:8). The author of Hebrews wrote in eloquent terms of how people of faith endured great hardship out of faithful perseverance (11:32-38). The journey of the children of Israel to the promised land is the example for believers to follow as they "share in Christ" and hold the original conviction until the end (3:14). The believers are to persevere and obey until the end so that they do not perish during this time of testing, as the children of Israel did in the wilderness (3:15-19). They are to avoid falling from grace and putting the Son to open shame, for it is impossible to restore to repentance those who are doing so (6:4-8).

For James, all of life is a gift from the hand of the faithful, heavenly Father: "Every good and perfect gift is from above, coming down from the Father of the heavenly lights, who does not change like shifting shadows" (Jas 1:17). This grace surely involves salvation as well, as the next verse indicates: "He chose to give us birth through the word of truth, that we might be a kind of firstfruits of all he created" (1:18). Yet, for James, the journey of salvation still involves our willful obedience as well: "Therefore, get rid of all moral filth and the evil that is so prevalent and humbly accept the word planted in you, which can save you" (1:21). We must not only hear the word of truth but do it in relation to one another, especially those most in need (1:21-27). Just confessing the faith is not enough, for even the demons do that, and they do it with feeling (2:18-19)! Faith without corresponding deeds is thus "useless" (2:20). Indeed, for faith to be valid, it must be incarnated within flesh, within deeds, within the just community serving one another with humility: "As the body without the spirit is dead, so faith without deeds is dead" (2:26). One is judged just or righteous by both faith and deeds, for it is only by deeds that one's faith is vindicated as authentic (2:26).[200]

James advocates single-minded faith (1:2-7), which includes the discipline of the godly life as well: "Submit yourselves, then, to God. Resist the devil, and he will flee from you. Come near to God and he will come near to you. Wash your hands, you sinners, and purify your hearts, you double-minded" (4:7-8). One perseveres under trial in order to receive "the crown of life that the Lord has promised to those who love him" (1:12). Those who are burdened with sin and sickness should call upon the elders for prayer, "and the prayer offered in faith will make the sick person well; the Lord will raise them up" (5:15). More broadly, the church is admonished to "confess your sins to each other and pray for each other so that you may be healed" (5:16). This healing includes spiritual sickness as well as physical, for those who bring a wandering soul back to the fold cover a multitude of sins (5:19-20).

As for those who seek to use grace as an occasion to sin, Jude urges believers to contend (1) against them and (2) for the faith that has to do with our shared salvation (Jude 3-4). God is able to keep those who contend against them

---

200. It is an open question whether James is using the term "justification" or "righteous" in the technical Pauline sense, since Paul is referring to God's eschatological judgment declared and enacted in Christ, while James seems to be concerned with the vindication of one's faith within the just community. Also, James's "dead faith" is more of a confession than anything else, hardly the living faith by which alone one is saved in Paul's letters. Still, there is a creative tension between James and Paul here that urges the church to incarnate its faith in ever new ways.

from falling and to present them "without fault and with great joy" before the Lord (Jude 24).

For 1 Peter, salvation is in the triune God: We have been "chosen according to the foreknowledge of God the Father, through the sanctifying work of the Spirit, to be obedient to Jesus Christ and sprinkled with his blood" (1:2). We are chosen only because Christ "was chosen before the creation of the world but was revealed in these last times for your sake" (1:20). He was chosen as our redeemer, meaning that we are not redeemed through the laws of Israel but "with the precious blood of Christ, a lamb without blemish or defect" (1:19). Believing in Christ is to believe in the Father, who raised him from the dead, for through Christ "you believe in God, who raised him from the dead and glorified him, and so your faith and hope are in God" (1:21). Through the word of God, one is able to embrace Christ: "For you have been born again, not of perishable seed, but of imperishable, through the living and enduring word of God" (1:23). As newborn babes, we grow in salvation as we continue to drink from the word of God (2:2). We live as free people but also as "God's slaves" in the world (2:16). Christ set the example when he endured hardship and insults while sacrificing himself on the cross for our sins: "He himself bore our sins in his body on the cross, so that we might die to sins and live for righteousness; by his wounds you have been healed" (2:24). We are sheep who have gone astray, but Christ has become our shepherd, "the overseer" of our souls (2:25). We should be willing to suffer evil for the sake of a good purpose if God so wills, "for Christ also suffered once for sins, the righteous for the unrighteous, to bring you to God. He was put to death in the body but made alive in the Spirit. After being made alive, he went and made proclamation to the imprisoned spirits — to those who were disobedient long ago when God waited patiently in the days of Noah while the ark was being built" (3:18-20). How and why Christ proclaimed the good news to the disobedient spirits after his resurrection is unclear. The text implies a point, however, similar to the one made at the end of chapter 2, namely, that Christ set forth an example by his willingness to suffer hardship so as to bear witness according to the will of God. This text was mainly targeted to slaves who wondered about how to respond to ill treatment at the hands of masters. Peter points them to the cross as a way of viewing their unavoidable suffering within a larger context of faithful witness. As Christ endured pain to further the Father's will in the world, they may have to do the same. It is not slavery that is glorified here (or passively accepted) as much as what God can do through an unavoidably difficult situation. The conclusion is "therefore, since Christ suffered in his body, arm yourselves also with the same attitude" (4:1).

Second Peter begins with a description of salvation as the divine power given to us, granting us everything we need for the godly life. This power channeled to us through the divine promises causes us to participate in the divine nature: "He has given us his very great and precious promises, so that through them you may participate in the divine nature, having escaped the corruption in the world caused by evil desires" (2 Pet 1:4). For 2 Peter, perseverance comes as a result of the seeking after virtues, adding them to one another according to the analogy of building blocks: "For this very reason, make every effort to add to your faith goodness; and to goodness, knowledge; and to knowledge, self-control; and to self-control, perseverance; and to perseverance, godliness; and to godliness, mutual affection; and to mutual affection, love" (1:5-7). Faith is the foundation, and love the crowning, of one's edifice of virtues. By building up our lives in this way, we make every effort to confirm our calling and election (1:10). The assurance that the Lord will return unexpectedly to melt creation in the fires of divine judgment should cause us to engage in sober self-evaluation: "Since everything will be destroyed in this way, what kind of people ought you to be? You ought to live holy and godly lives as you look forward to the day of God and speed its coming" (3:11-12).

Conclusion

In sum, there are a few general remarks that can be ventured about salvation in the NT. Salvation is throughout by the grace of the triune God: the elect will of the Father, the redemptive story of the Son, and the eschatologically and cosmically vast perfecting work of the Spirit. Salvation takes the alienated creation up into the life of the triune God to participate in that life in all of its richness. This accent on the priority of grace does not mean that salvation becomes something to be taken for granted or manipulated according to our desires or plans. Salvation in the NT is under God's lordship and can be received and lived only in submission to that lordship in all things. The costly grace of God is defined by the divine self-giving and seeks to shape those who receive it as good news into its image. There are deep roots for this salvation in creation, for the Lord, who created all things to live from the divine Spirit and according to the divine will revealed in Christ, is the only one who can restore creation to its intended purpose. This purpose is foreshadowed in the election of Israel but is fulfilled in Jesus Christ and the Spirit's work in shaping all things in Christ's image. The cross becomes not only the focus of God's reconciliation with creation but also the pattern by which the creation moves in the power of the resurrection and Pentecost toward the fulfillment of God's eschatological purposes.

Revelation and Systematic Theology

We began our essay with Bonhoeffer's challenge concerning the need for a soteriology rooted in costly grace. One cannot read the book of Revelation without discovering rich resources for precisely such a view of salvation in our time. Salvation offered by God to a rebellious world captive to dark powers involves divine wounding and self-sacrifice, as the potent image of the slaughtered Lamb before the throne shows us. That God gave so much to give Godself to us in the midst of our rebellion is the very core of the gospel. This gospel once received cannot be mocked by taking it for granted. Grace lived out in resistance to the beast and in loyalty to the Lamb can hardly be viewed as cheap grace. Those churches among the seven addressed by Revelation that take the way to salvation lightly are sternly rebuked. Salvation is by the triumphant grace of God, but it is also by this grace through the patient and tenacious endurance of those determined to be faithful to the will of the Creator and the way of the cross. This general orientation to salvation has a number of implications for a constructive soteriology today. In a post-Christian world, where Christianity no longer has a vast hegemonic influence on Western culture, churches are being urged to rediscover anew the meaning of their sacred texts and the call of discipleship in relation to the challenges of our time.[201] The waning influence of the Bible and "Christian" culture in the public square is an opportunity for fresh thinking not bound by the accommodations of the past. Yet, reconstructions must not forget the wisdom of the past either. Revelation will help us not to forget.

Salvation, Trinity, and Divine Pathos

Costly grace is first a divine self-giving before it can ever become a human response. "Salvation belongs to our God, who sits on the throne, and to the Lamb" (Rev 7:10). This grace thus cannot be defined primarily in the service of a humanly conceived wish-fulfillment under the guise of either religion or morality. Salvation cannot be the end result of the human quest for meaning. Grace is free; it is a gift. Costly grace in Revelation is thus defined primarily from the divine pathos and action, especially as directed from the throne of the Father and revealed in the crucified Lamb (7:10). We are referring here to the priority of the divine to that which is human, of divine self-giving to human self-giving, of

---

201. See S. M. Schneiders's response to George Lindbeck in "Does the Bible have a postmodern message?" in *Postmodern Theology: Christian Faith in a Pluralist World* (ed. F. B. Burnham; New York: Harper & Row, 1989), 56-73.

revelation to religion and morality, of grace to human works. Broad ecumenical consensus was achieved in the twentieth century on this divine priority, in part because of the work of such great theological minds as Karl Rahner and Karl Barth. In order to preserve the integrity of human freedom in human responses to God, medieval scholastic theology posited a dynamic relationship between uncreated grace (the divine action through the Spirit) and created grace (the graced or elevated human capacities for God). In depictions of this dynamic exchange, the priority of the divine self-giving was obscured, giving rise to the criticism that grace is first a human possession that we utilize at our own discretion (a distortion of the medieval intention). Rahner wrote a seminal essay in 1939 responding to scholastic theology by clearly granting the divine self-giving in uncreated grace the priority in relation to created grace, or the graced capacity of humans to respond to God.[202] Created grace, or elevated capacities for God, function because of the priority of God's self-giving, "inasmuch as God's personal self-communication is permanently offered to man."[203] Rahner even saw ecumenical relevance to Luther's argument for salvation "by grace alone,"[204] a point affirmed jointly by the Vatican and the Lutheran World Federation in their 1999 *Joint Declaration on the Doctrine of Justification:* "Justification takes place solely by God's grace" (#19). More broadly, the declaration states:

> Justification thus means that Christ himself is our righteousness, in which we share through the Holy Spirit in accord with the will of the Father. Together we confess: By grace alone, in faith in Christ's saving work and not because of any merit on our part, we are accepted by God and receive the Holy Spirit, who renews our hearts while equipping and calling us to good works (#15).

This ecumenical consensus followed on the heels of decades of dialogue between Catholics and Lutherans both in the United States and in Germany. It found seminal support not only in Rahner but also in Hans Küng's book written as a doctoral dissertation in the late 1950s comparing Barth's theology of justification by faith to the core of Catholic tradition on the subject, in which Küng noted convergence especially between Barth's emphasis on the transformative power of the divine Word in the hearing of faith and the Catholic stress on

---

202. Karl Rahner, "Some Implications of the Scholastic Concept of Uncreated Grace," *Theological Investigations*, vol. 1 (Baltimore: Helicon Press, 1963), 319-46.

203. Karl Rahner, "Grace (II Theological, B Systematic)," in *Sacramentum Mundi: An Encyclopedia of Theology* (ed. Karl Rahner et al.; New York: Herder & Herder, 1968), 419.

204. Karl Rahner, *Foundations of Christian Faith: An Introduction to the Idea of Christianity* (New York: Crossroad, 1982), 357.

justification through grace as a transformative reality in the life of the believer.[205] Differences remain, of course, between Catholic and Protestant approaches to grace, but the *Joint Declaration* rightly concluded that enough consensus has been reached on the divine priority in salvation that such differences should no longer be viewed as church dividing in significance.

Extending the horizons of our discussion beyond human conversion to the larger framework of the biblical drama, Barth challenged liberal Protestant theology by clearly granting the divine action on behalf of humanity the priority in how one understands the divine-human relation at the core of the biblical message of salvation. In 1916 he gave an important speech toward this end entitled "The Strange New World within the Bible." In it, he responded critically to what his teachers had taught him about the results of historical criticism in unearthing the distinctive message of the Bible, which for them concerned human religion and morality. In his own reading of the Bible, however, Barth discovered that the Bible's core message was not about human religion and morality. The main actor of the biblical drama was not a mere human on a religious or moral quest but, rather, God's acting to address and redeem humanity. Barth noted that we may indeed linger in the Bible among various ancient religious or moral sensitivities, but at some point one may very well discover "a river in the Bible that carries us away, once we have entrusted our destiny to it — away from ourselves to the sea." This sea is the larger horizon of God's judgment and grace that qualify all else that is in the Bible.

> In it the chief consideration is not the doings of man but the doings of God — not the various ways which we may take if we are men of good will — but the power out of which good will must first be created — not the folding and fruition of love as we may understand it, but the existence and outpouring of eternal love, of love as God understands it — not industry, honesty, and helpfulness as we may practice them in our old ordinary world, but the establishment and growth of a new world, the world in which God and *his* morality reign.[206]

This priority granted to God's actions and self-disclosure when discerning the message of salvation in the Bible was essential to the Barthian revolution in contemporary theology.

---

205. Hans Küng, *Justification: The Doctrine of Karl Barth and a Catholic Reflection* (trans. Edward Quinn; Philadelphia: Westminster, 1981).

206. Karl Barth, "Strange New World within the Bible," in *A Map of Twentieth-Century Theology: Readings from Karl Barth to Radical Pluralism* (ed. Carl E. Braaten and Robert W. Jenson; Minneapolis: Fortress Press, 1995), 23, 26 (Barth's emphasis).

Barth's theocentric approach to the message of salvation in the Bible took on a Christocentric focus after 1936 because of the attention that he paid to a Christ-centered doctrine of election.[207] He ended up developing his theocentric vision of biblical salvation by maintaining that it is not the divine-human relation abstractly conceived that Christ ends up fulfilling in the story of the Bible. Such a vision of salvation results in shaping Christ in the image of our own version of human fulfillment. Rather, the biblical message posits the story of Christ as the fundamental key to interpreting the divine-human relation, against which the story of Adam is to be judged and understood.[208] Humanity and salvation are defined primarily from within the story of Jesus and not as a projection of perceived human wants and needs, for Christ reveals both the God who covenants with humanity and the ideal human servant who glorifies God and fulfills the divine will.

Barth's soteriology was thus developed with the help of his Christocentric doctrine of election. He criticized John Calvin's election doctrine because it was based on an eternal "absolute decree" concerning who will be saved, a decree that is "independent of Jesus Christ and is only executed by Him." Since in Calvin's theology Christ serves a subordinate and instrumentalist relationship to this decree, without having theological priority in a way that would fundamentally define it, "what an abyss of uncertainty is opened up!"[209] There is no way of determining the content or direction of this decree. Rather than following Revelation in defining creation and God's sovereign will for creation in relation to the crucified Lamb (13:8), we end up having to look elsewhere for guidance, which for Barth could very well be "nothingness, or rather the depths of Satan."[210] Barth wrote this extreme statement to make a point. For Barth, Jesus Christ serves as the Word of God that is prior to all others (subordinate to none other). He is eternally the Word of the Father, above which there can be no other word, no other divine decision for creation or its destiny. To create a decree, a divine elect will that is prior to and independent of Christ, both subordinates Christ in nature and function and causes one to fumble for criteria that might validate the content and direction of this decree. The Lamb was crucified from the very creation of the world, eternally being the Word that determines God's elect will for creation. Creation was made as the household

---

207. Bruce McCormick, "Seek God Where He May Be Found: A Response to Edwin Chr. Van Driel," in *Orthodox and Modern: Studies in the Theology of Karl Barth* (Grand Rapids: Baker Academic, 2008), 261-77.

208. See for, example, Barth's little classic *Christ and Adam: Man and Humanity in Romans 5* (Eugene, OR: Wipf & Stock, 2004).

209. Barth, *Church Dogmatics*, 2/2:65.

210. Barth, *Church Dogmatics*, 2/2:25.

of the Son, to bear his crucified and risen image. In the story of Jesus, we find the God who elects and the elect man in relation, through which God "took the author of evil to His bosom and willed that the rejection and condemnation and death should be His own."[211] We are elect only by being in Christ, the Son of Man, who partook of our condemnation in order that we could partake of his election: "It is the lost Son of Man who is partner of the electing God in this covenant."[212] In election, God elects Godself as our covenant partner and humanity as belonging to God. This is the meaning of Jesus Christ. There can be no election for Barth other than this.

Barth then developed his christological accent in the direction of a larger Trinitarian framework in support of an *analogia caritatis* (analogy of love, or communion) between God and humanity. Humanity is made to reflect the image of the triune God as revealed through Christ and in the power of the Spirit. "As and before God seeks and creates fellowship with us, He wills and completes this fellowship in Himself. In Himself, He does not will to exist for Himself, to exist alone. On the contrary, He is Father, Son, and Holy Spirit and therefore alive in His unique being with and for and in another."[213] God elected Godself to be the self-giving God who is there for humanity as a loving communion of persons.

This personal interrelation in its reciprocal relationality is especially poignant in the context of the biblical drama of redemption as a story of suffering. Moltmann explains:

> At the moments of God's profoundest revelation, there is always suffering: The cry of the captives in Egypt; Jesus' death cry on the cross; the sighing of the whole enslaved creation for liberty. If a person once feels the infinite passion of God's love which finds expression here, then he understands the mystery of the triune God. God suffers with us — God suffers from us — God suffers for us: It is this experience of God that reveals the triune God. It has to be understood, and can only be understood, in trinitarian terms.[214]

Moltmann sees God's act of creation as the place where God opens up the divine life to creation as the "other," as the Father binds creation to the Son. This binding of the Son to creation leaves God vulnerable to be wounded by the unfaithfulness and suffering of creation. In the cross, the Father hands the

---

211. Barth, *Church Dogmatics*, 2/2:167.
212. Barth, *Church Dogmatics*, 2/2:164.
213. Karl Barth, *Church Dogmatics*, vol. 2, pt. 1 (trans. G. W. Bromiley and T. F. Torrance; Edinburgh: T&T Clark, 1957), 275.
214. Moltmann, *Trinity and the Kingdom*, 4.

Son over to the abandoned creation, and the Son delivers himself up to this same fate. Through the solidarity of the Son with creation, the suffering of the world is taken up into the very core of God's being, and the story of redemption thus involves God's own journey toward freedom and self-reconciliation. In this light, the divine freedom is not one that can ever be exercised in any other direction than that of love. Yet, God does not love and suffer out of lack or need as we do but, rather, out of the infinite abundance of the divine life.

Costly grace is defined by the God who delivers up the Lamb to be crucified and by the path of the cross, trod by the Lamb, as well as by the Spirit, who proceeds from the Lamb to offer life to the rebellious nations. This grace is abundantly free, for it is given freely and without prior condition by the self-giving God, who will not let the nations remain captive to the dark powers without a fight. It is a fight that God is sure to win, but one that costs God dearly nevertheless. The image of the slain Lamb before the throne is a potent reminder of how deeply God took the wounds of Israel and the nations into the inner sanctum of the divine life. This is not a grace that humanity can accept as its own property to use at its own discretion and in fulfillment of its own plans and schemes. This grace is free, but it demands all from those who accept it joyfully and live by it. The Savor is the Lord of creation, and the kingdom is fulfilled through the victory of the crucified Lamb. The redeemed conquer by the blood of the Lamb and give themselves over to the divine will as offerings to God. They follow the Lamb wherever he goes. They can do nothing without the prior grace of God, but in God they are expected to hold nothing back but to give all in the power of the Spirit in service to God and the Lamb.

Atonement: Exclusion and Embrace

The central role that the crucified Lamb plays in the drama of redemption in Revelation calls for a theology of atonement. Part of the challenge in contemporary soteriology is to construct such a theology that is true to the great themes of Revelation but is also contextually relevant, especially with regard to the problems involved in reducing atonement to rational systems of exchange or in justifying unjust and destructive violence against others. In this light, atonement theology has become a fruitful area of theological reconstruction of late. Anselm has been the focus of attention because of the significant role that his atonement theory played in rejecting the penchant of some during the Middle Ages to understand the ransom won by Christ for creation as involving an offering given to Satan. Anselm on this score was right; the offering of atonement by the Lamb on behalf of creation is given not to Satan but to God.

As Revelation implies, God does not owe the dragon anything but judgment. The hold that the dragon has on creation is unjust, and God is fully just in reclaiming creation through judgment and redemption.

More elaborately, Anselm sought to explain atonement in a way that preserves the divine honor: "God maintains nothing with more justice than the honor of his own dignity."[215] By willfully placing themselves under the alien lordship of the devil, humans made God the "loser" and bruised God's honor and rightful claim over creation.[216] The moral balance of the universe was disrupted, and all of creation suffered as a result. The Creator/creature relation was fractured. According to Anselm, the need is for humanity to restore honor to God: "So then, everyone who sins ought to pay back the honor of which he has robbed God; and this is the satisfaction which every sinner owes to God."[217] If God overlooks this affront to the divine honor, "either God will not be just to himself, or he will be weak in respect to both parties; and this is too impious even to think of."[218] Besides, "God's compassion cannot contradict God's justice for God to be consistent with himself."[219] To preserve justice, God must punish the sinners unless they can restore the honor that they took from God. But how can humanity accomplish such an unreachable task? Doing so would involve breaking free of the devil's grip and redressing the moral imbalance of the creation. Humanity is the only one responsible to do this, but cannot. God is the only one who can, but is not properly responsible to do so.[220] This is the conundrum that humanity faces. The only way out is to have a Savior who is both divine and human. As human, Christ can represent the human race to pay the debt of honor owed to God; as divine, however, he is able to do so to the fullest extent.

Anselm's theory of atonement seemed quite compelling in its day, in the context of a social system in which an affront is best remedied by making a payment or satisfaction that restores proper honor and the delicate balance of a bruised relationship. It also made sense within a Neoplatonic worldview, in which the universe needed to exist according to a well-ordered harmony. One cannot deny that issues of honor, shame, and cosmic order are also at the heartthrob of Revelation. The captivity of creation under the dark powers is an affront to the Creator, whose acts of judgment and redemption to restore

---

215. Anselm, *Cur Deus Homo*, in *Saint Anselm: Basic Writings* (trans. S. N. Deane; La Salle, IL: Open Court, 1968), 1.13.
216. Anselm, *Cur Deus Homo*, 1.13.
217. Anselm, *Cur Deus Homo*, 1.11.
218. Anselm, *Cur Deus Homo*, 1.13.
219. Anselm, *Cur Deus Homo*, 1.24.
220. Anselm, *Cur Deus Homo*, 2.7.

creation to its divinely intended purposes for the divine glory are proper, just, and true.

But the heavenly Father in Anselm's essay plays a rather passive role of simply receiving honor through the cross. In accenting the cross as a place of offering ("satisfaction") to God in order to restore honor, caution must be exercised here so as to avoid the impression that the Father and the Son are at cross purposes during atonement, as though the Son intervened on humanity's behalf merely to assuage God's wrath against them. This addition of a penal doctrine of atonement through propitiation to Anselm's satisfaction theory is commonly found in popular evangelical preaching. In response, it is important to note that the Lamb is not merely seeking to save creation *from* God by assuaging divine wrath or restoring divine honor; rather, he is seeking to save creation *as* God, on God's behalf, "for God so *loved* the world that he sent his one and only Son" (John 3:16). "God was reconciling the world to himself in Christ" (2 Cor 5:19). There is indeed a sense in which God, in Jesus, overcomes divine wrath in order to extend mercy to sinful humanity; such is the suffering love of God, as Kazoh Kitamori saw so clearly.[221] But the Son bore our iniquity and the divine wrath in the sense that the Father delivered him up to the alienation and captivity that we have entered into in our fleeing from God:

> We all, like sheep, have gone astray,
>   each of us has turned to our own way;
> and the LORD has laid on him
>   the iniquity of us all. (Isa 53:6)

But the Father is motivated by love for humanity, and the Son delivered himself up in willful obedience to the Father's will. The triune love for creation occasioned the cross, God's love for the nations and for the suffering creation, and God is willing to suffer deeply to win them back. In the cross, God's wrath is not being assuaged by another party; God overcomes God's own wrath in suffering, or cruciform love.

Another problem to avoid in reading Anselm is the implication that God requires the divine honor to be restored as a precondition for offering grace to sinful humanity. Anselm's motive is that "God's compassion cannot contradict God's justice."[222] Justice in the sense of retribution must first be fulfilled before mercy can be bestowed. It is true that divine justice does involve judgment for sin. But divine justice in Scripture is fulfilled only in *mercy*. There is a harmony

---

221. Kitamori, *Theology of the Pain of God*.
222. Anselm, *Cur Deus Homo*, 1.24.

of divine compassion and justice in Scripture, but not in the sense that the latter is a precondition of the former. As Walter Brueggemann has shown, the Hebrew Scriptures do contain texts in which God is mainly concerned with maintaining divine honor (a kind of divine self-regard): God states that Israel was delivered so as "to gain glory for myself through Pharaoh" (Exod 14:4). Yet, in other texts God suffers humiliation and pain in pursuing unfaithful Israel, as one would go after an unfaithful spouse or a disobedient child (as in Hos 1–2 and 11:1-4), much in the same way that God more expansively goes after the rebellious nations in Revelation in order to win them back. This expansion from God's going after Israel to God's going after the nations is occasioned by the cross. Brueggemann notes that, in the OT, "Yahweh moves back and forth between self-regard and regard for Israel, sovereignty and pathos."[223] This tension leads to the faith of Israel being shaped by a convergence of these two, in which the divine honor or justice is fulfilled precisely in merciful acts of self-giving and redemption (Isa 45:8, 23-24; 51:6-8; Pss 71:19; 89:17; 96:13; 98:9; 111:3; Dan 9:16-18). Indeed, this "convergence of sovereignty and compassion is the staple of Israel's faith" and, in Brueggemann's judgment, "should be regarded as normative for theological interpretation and be allowed to govern other texts."[224] Thus, we cannot take from Anselm the idea that the restoration of divine honor in the cross was the necessary precondition for God's capacity to give of Godself graciously to humanity. The cross is precisely that divine self-giving, which is itself the means for the restoration of honor to God. Consistent with the OT convergence of sovereignty and pathos, God is glorified in Revelation for mighty deeds of redemption (Rev 5). Revelation follows the Hebraic notion that God is honored precisely in showing mercy. God is honored as just and true in acts of judgment as well, but even these have a redemptive purpose (11:13). God in Revelation, however, fulfills divine honor by going to the far country, not only in search of Israel, but also in search of the wayward nations to win them back through suffering love.

In restoring divine honor through redemptive acts, the Lord of creation is not bound to rules of honor or of cosmic order and harmony. As Gustaf Aulén wrote in his classic study *Christus Victor*, "The New Testament idea of redemption constitutes in fact a veritable revolution; for it declares that sovereign divine love has taken the initiative, broken through the order of justice and merit, triumphed over the powers of evil, and created a new relation between the world and God."[225] Aulén wrote his classic to restore atonement theory to its

---

223. Brueggemann, *Theology of the Old Testament*, 309.
224. Brueggemann, *Theology of the Old Testament*, 304, 309.
225. Gustaf Aulén, *Christus Victor: An Historical Study of the Three Main Types of the Idea of Atonement* (trans. A. G. Herbert; Eugene, OR: Wipf & Stock, 2003), 79.

proper description as a divine victory over darkness, sin, and death. In his view, both Anselm's satisfaction and Abelard's moral-example theories of atonement placed the weight wrongly on the cross as the place where humanity in Jesus wins salvation for itself.[226] For Aulén, the classical theory of atonement views the cross as the place of *divine* victory on behalf of humanity. In response to Aulén, we can note the importance of Jesus' obedience as a man to the Father in the atonement (e.g., Phil 2:8); yet, this was not just human obedience but, more deeply, the obedience of the divine Son to the heavenly Father, an obedience that involved the incarnation itself (Heb. 10:5-10). In Jesus, the divine Son took on flesh in order that all flesh could partake of the divine life. In Revelation, God triumphs over the dark powers in the crucifixion of the Lamb in order to bring the nations under his liberating reign. It is chiefly in this victory that God's rightful claim on creation is vindicated.

Rational systems of exchange cannot adequately explain the cross, because God's costly grace is excessively abundant and rich. Such is the reason that Revelation can properly speak adequately of these great redemptive deeds only in doxology or praise. Paul Ricoeur noted that the logic of exchange belongs to sin and death (the wages of sin is death) but that the logic of grace is surplus and excess (where sin increased, grace increased all the more). In Revelation, the trials of judgment result in incalculable multitudes coming to know God's grace (7:9-14), and the reign of peace towers over the time of trial in length of time (1,000 years compared to 3½ years). All of this is because of the love that God poured out abundantly for the nations in the figure of the crucified Lamb. Left to their own resources, humans would have caused history to end very differently. In effect, no atonement theory can explain the inexplicable outpouring of divine mercy in the cross for sinful humanity and God's decision to vindicate divine lordship over creation in precisely this way. Following the logic of excess in interpreting the atonement connects it not only to the resurrection of Jesus but also to the outpouring of the Spirit through Jesus upon all flesh. In terms of Revelation, the eyes of the crucified Lamb that proceed out into all the earth are the sevenfold Spirit. Jesus as the man of the Spirit entered into the depths of human alienation and darkness in order to bring humanity into the realm of his Spirit. In the words of Irenaeus, "The Lord, receiving this as a gift from his Father, does himself also confer it upon those who are partakers of Himself, sending the Holy Spirit upon all the earth."[227] The logic of grace and of abundant excess is precisely the logic of the resurrection, the logic of the Spirit of

---

226. We will not address here how accurately Aulén described Anselm's and Abelard's views.

227. Irenaeus, *Adversus Haereses* 3.17.2 (445).

life: "Let the one who is thirsty come; and let the one who wishes take the free gift of the water of life" (22:17). The Spirit is not only the means to salvation but is essential to salvation itself.

This emphasis on the excessiveness of grace would put an end to any illusion that salvation is something that one can merit through works. There is broad ecumenical consensus on this point. As noted above, the Catholic-Lutheran *Joint Declaration on the Doctrine of Justification* notes, "Together we confess: By grace alone, in faith in Christ's saving work and not because of any merit on our part, we are accepted by God and receive the Holy Spirit, who renews our hearts while equipping and calling us to good works" (#15). Even the Catholic use of the term "merit" for the Christian life stresses the fact that, in regarding human works as "meritorious," God is merely crowning divine gifts with rewards. Protestants understandably avoid the language of merit, though they do use the concept of the divine rewarding of human works, despite these works in and of themselves *not* being worthy of such excessive favor.

Yet, as Revelation shows, good works are still integral to the life of grace. Wesley avoids the concept of merit, though he does speak of works as a necessary "condition" of the justified life. Concerning salvation as an eschatological reality, he reminds us that, "in fact, every believer, till he comes to glory, works *for* as well as *from* life" (Wesley's emphasis).[228] Working "from and for" life summarizes well the absolute priority of grace in all things while still acknowledging the integral role of works in salvation. As Vladimir Lossky says from an Eastern Orthodox perspective, the issue of works is not "merit" but rather "cooperation" with grace (from grace) toward deeper union with God. He writes of "a synergy of two wills, divine and human, a harmony in which grace bears ever more and more fruit."[229] This "from grace, for grace" reminds us of Wesley's "from life, for life." Lossky elaborates: "Grace is a presence of God within us which demands constant effort on our part; these efforts, however, in no way determine grace, nor does grace act upon our liberty as if it were external or foreign to it." Rather, there is a mystery to the "coincidence of grace and human freedom in good works" that is directed to the glory of God.[230] Luther also made good works integral to the Christian life. In his 1520 *Treatise on Good Works*, he quotes John 6:28-29 to the effect that faith is the "first and the highest" of all good works (#2). Faith, as the first step of obedience, "lives and works" in all good works,

---

228. John Wesley, "Minutes of Several Conversations between the Rev. Mr. Wesley and Others, from the Year 1744 to the year 1789," in *Wesley's Works* 8:337.

229. Vladimir Lossky, *The Mystical Theology of the Eastern Church* (Crestwood, NY: St. Vladimir's Seminary Press, 1976), 197-98.

230. Lossky, *The Mystical Theology of the Eastern Church*, 198.

both great and small (#5). Though salvation is by faith alone for Luther, faith for him is always incarnated within good works.

The excessive grace of the cross has also been brought to powerful expression through the tendency of many to grant priority to healing over legal understandings of the atonement. The leaves of the tree of life in the heavenly city in Revelation are for the healing of the nations (Rev 22:2). Kimberly Alexander has noted that Wesley's healing metaphor for salvation provided the background for the later tendency for Holiness and Pentecostal groups to see in the atonement healing for both body and soul.[231] Morton Kelsey faults the West for not consistently supporting the implications in the atonement for healing, which resulted in the narrow identification between atonement and forgiveness. The grace of God that emerges from the atonement heals as well as forgives.[232] The power of the Spirit that brings the favor of God to the nations and that leads them to the eschatological fulfillment of salvation involves their healing in every dimension of human existence, including the realm of physical need.

Does the cross as the place of excessive grace and healing contradict the violence of the event? For some, our focus on the cross as the channel of excessive grace is haunted by the divine violence as implied by God's willing the Lamb to be slaughtered for the redemption of the world. For Friedrich Schleiermacher, to bring about redemption through such violent means implied "a conception of divine righteousness which has been transferred to God from the crudest human conditions."[233] More recently, this penal view of atonement has been described as a case of divine child abuse. The idea of Jesus' suffering innocently in order to satisfy the wrath of his Father implies a disturbingly oppressive, patriarchal view of God and would even indicate for some that violence is sanctioned by God so long as it is directed against evil for a good cause. We can take up our swords against the enemies after all.

J. Denny Weaver wrote his book *The Nonviolent Atonement* from the perspective of his Mennonite pacifist commitments against such implications. He takes Aulén's *Christus Victor* approach to atonement and reshapes it in the service of a pacifist vision that is drawn from Jesus' nonviolent ethic. He does so by removing the death of Jesus as the chief focus of Jesus' mission and replacing it with the inauguration of God's liberating reign in the world, which God intends to accomplish in Christ through nonviolent means. The death of Jesus was simply an unfortunate component of that kingdom mission because of the

---

231. Kimberly Alexander, *Pentecostal Healing: Models in Theology and Practice* (JPTS 29; Blandford Forum, UK: Deo Publishing, 2006).

232. Morton Kelsey, *Healing and Christianity* (Minneapolis: Augsburg, 1995).

233. Schleiermacher, *The Christian Faith*, 460.

violent response of the world to Christ's nonviolent mission. It was simply an "inevitable" result of Jesus' kingdom mission in the context of a violent world.[234] But it was not the violent death of Jesus itself that was willed by God; rather, it was the inauguration of the kingdom of God through Jesus. Weaver notes that God "does suffer with Jesus in making the reign of God visible in the world. But this suffering was not the specific purpose of Jesus' mission, nor was it required by a divine equation."[235]

Weaver is correct in the sense that the violence of Jesus' death was not something that God exercised directly at Jesus. Indeed, the cross was not the place where God crushed Jesus because Jesus joined himself to us as our representative. It is rather the case, as noted above when looking at Isa 53:6, that the Father laid *our* iniquities upon Jesus as the faithful Son stepped into our place (cf. Isa 53:5-6). In taking our place, the Son is crushed by participating fully in the consequences of our sin. As divine, the Son on the cross became the chief entry point for *God's* taking our sin and violence onto Godself and overcoming it through suffering love. Weaver is also right that the violence of Jesus' unjust death is laid squarely at the feet of the governing bodies who willed his demise (e.g., Acts 4:10). But the Bible also implies that, hidden beneath this reality, is the will of the Father to use this painful rejection of Christ by the world as the means of reconciling the world. There is thus a sense of destiny that Jesus shares in the Gospels that he "must go to Jerusalem and suffer many things" (Matt 16:21). Even his request to have that cup pass from him is quickly followed by a recognition that he is willing to accept the Father's will for him to go to the cross (Mark 14:36). It is true that the people killed Jesus, but it is also true that God led him to that point and, in the mystery of the divine will, chose to reconcile humanity through that event, the event of the Lamb slain from the creation of the world (Rev 13:8).

Using the work of René Girard on scapegoating, S. Mark Heim has recently helped us to understand the fittingness of the cross as the place of atonement. Heim notes that the Bible is unique in ancient literature in resisting the impulse to scapegoat or to obliterate the cries against injustice among victims. Scapegoating does so by transforming victims into noble martyrs or turning them into deserving villains. The Bible refuses to do this, as is shown in numerous Psalms or Revelation. The cries of the oppressed are recorded without alteration or cover-up. The texts about the cross do not scapegoat either, since the injustice of the event is not removed or glossed over. The brutality and injustice of the event must not be removed through scapegoating because it must

---

234. J. Denny Weaver, *The Non-Violent Atonement* (Grand Rapids: Eerdmans, 2001), 41.
235. Weaver, *The Non-Violent Atonement*, 226.

be shown how God met us precisely at the point of our worst rejection of divine grace. But rather than return in vengeance at his resurrection, the risen Christ appears to inaugurate a community and a mission of grace for the world.[236] This is a helpful lens for understanding the significance of Revelation for atonement theory. The martyrs' cry for justice is not silenced (6:10), and God responds with acts of judgment to end the violence and destruction (11:18). But the larger goal of judgment in Revelation is to bring about redemption.

Miroslav Volf offers us a theology of atonement that is even more directly sensitive to themes prevalent in Revelation. He asks how life under Caesar in a violent world is undone by the slaughter of the Lamb on the cross. Volf shows how an atonement theory that focuses only on removing the guilt of the sinners is one-sided. There is also the need to address the plight of the victims of sinful actions. True, all of humanity is to some extent guilty, as Revelation shows us (both the small and the great face judgment). This fact is especially clear in the world whenever the oppressed gain power over the oppressors and give them back a large dose of the injustice that the new holders of power had earlier received. The universality of sin is content-specific in such a way as to raise the question concerning how one breaks this cycle of violence. In terms of Revelation, the oppressed saints are not exhorted to take up arms in holy war so that they can join with other oppressed peoples in returning to the nations the violence perpetrated against them. Instead, the question raised in Revelation concerns how the nations are to be purged and converted so as to end the violence once and for all. Concerning the cross, Volf notes that, by taking in the violence of the aggressors but offering grace in return, the cross breaks the cycle of violence and resists allowing the aggressors to shape the future. Furthermore, by laying bare the mechanism of scapegoating, the cross does not allow Israel and the nations to cover their crime. They must face it if they are to understand their need for grace. When those who pierced Christ see him, "All peoples on earth will mourn because of him" (1:7). In this light, the cross is not a passive submission to violence but is part of God's struggle in a violent world for peace and redemptive justice. As to its goal, however, the cross is the place where God extends an embrace to a violent world. Unlike Weaver, Volf recognizes from Revelation the need for exclusion from God in purging the nations from their penchant for destruction. The plagues destroy those bent on destroying the earth (11:18). For Revelation, salvation involves judgment or "exclusion," but the goal of history or of divine justice is redemption and an end to violence, through God's never-ending "embrace." The saints hand cries for justice over to God, who alone can sanctify the nations and lead them to the fulfillment of

---

236. This is the central argument of Heim, *Saved from Sacrifice*.

justice in mercy.[237] Their role is to follow in the path of the crucified Lamb in order to overcome by his blood or self-sacrificial love in witness to the nations. This is costly grace, grace at great sacrifice, in which genuine loss is possible, but so also is a far greater triumph.

An Ecumenical Geometry of Salvation

The triumph of costly grace affects every dimension of life. How can it be otherwise? There can be no dimension of life immune from the joys and demands of grace. In Revelation, the grace of God overflows to reach all dimensions of life dramatically and thoroughly. The story of saving grace begins with the vision of the risen Christ and ends with the new heavens and new earth. Throughout the book, the Creator is seeking, through the Lamb, to reclaim the creation. If one remains true to the soteriology of Revelation, there is no possibility of holding to a gnostic dualism that reduces salvation to inner enlightenment and neglects the resurrection of the flesh in the fullest sense of this term. One must also reject Rudolf Bultmann's conviction that "only such statements about God are legitimate as express the existential relation between God and man. Statements which speak of God's actions as cosmic events are illegitimate."[238] Bultmann was attempting to avoid what he regarded as a mythological objectification of the divine action in literal cosmic upheavals such as one has in apocalyptic visions of end-time salvation. Though one must be cautious about interpreting such texts too literally, there is still the truth that lies within them, which points to a genuine remaking of the heavens and the earth that cannot be demythologized away. Such holism also involves the healing of the body. Bultmann referred to the healing ministry of Pastor Johann Blumhardt as an "abomination," to which Karl Barth replied in defense of Blumhardt that salvation highlights Jesus as "Victor" *(Sieger)* in the physical and social realms of life and not just in the realms of human spirit or consciousness.[239] Pentecostal and Charismatic groups have rightly noted that the gospel of salvation in the NT was proclaimed with signs and wonders of healing in order that faith would rest on the power of God rather than on human wisdom (1 Cor 2:4-5). The church is not to lack any spiritual gift while waiting for the Lord's return (1:7), including those that signal for us the "powers of the age to come" (Heb 6:5). There is no possibility here either of a pietistic confinement of

---

237. Volf, *Exclusion and Embrace*, 295-300.
238. Rudolf Bultmann, *Jesus Christ and Mythology* (New York: Charles Scribner's Sons, 1958), 69.
239. Rudolf Bultmann, *Kerygma and Myth* (New York: Harper & Row, 1953), 150; Barth, *Church Dogmatics*, 4/3, first half, 171.

salvation to personal conversion and going to heaven at death without a proper emphasis on the divine claim on communities, societies, and nations, against the background of the resurrection of the dead and the new heavens and new earth. In the last several decades, we have fortunately seen a dramatic turn among such authors as Jürgen Moltmann and Wolfhart Pannenberg in the direction of a view of salvation that accents new creation rather than an "eternal now" in the limited context of personal conversion or existential enlightenment. On a more popular level, N. T. Wright wrote *Surprised by Hope*, arguing that the NT speaks much more about a new body and a new world when it looks to the ultimate horizon of salvation than it does about going to heaven at death.[240] In Revelation, salvation is not fulfilled until the resurrection of the dead, the new heavens and new earth, and the walking of the peoples from among all nations by the light of the Lamb in the glorious heavenly city.

In Revelation, salvation is not an escape from the world into the inner recesses of one's soul or heaven above. The suffering saints are not encouraged to seek an escape from the earth, which has come under the domination of dark powers. These saints are given a vibrant hope of life with God in the new world that is to come. The depths of the soul are indeed taken up into the redemptive, liberating, and healing work of God, and heaven is an aspect of the Christian hope. But both of these are no escape from the new world that is to come.

Yet, neither is salvation to be reduced to vast corporate realities like social liberation, the transformation of the nations, or the new world to come to the neglect of one's personal relationship with God. Jan Milič Lochman wrote his *Reconciliation and Liberation: Challenging a One-Dimensional View of Salvation* in order to resist all reductionism, whether it be existential, social, or global. Lochman writes of an "ecumenical geometry of salvation" that tends toward a "comprehensive wholeness in this divided life." He concludes, "We understand salvation as newness of life — the unfolding of true humanity in the fullness of God. . . . It is salvation of the soul and the body, of the individual and society, mankind and the groaning creation."[241] Revelation offers us just such an expansive view of salvation that involves personal repentance and faith but also the sanctification of the nations, cosmic renewal, and new heavens and new earth.

Even on the personal level, it is important to seek an "ecumenical geometry of salvation." It is possible, for example, to reduce one's relationship with God to a rational acceptance of biblical truths in a way that neglects deeper

---

240. N. T. Wright, *Surprised by Hope: Rethinking Heaven, the Resurrection, and the Mission of the Church* (New York: HarperOne, 2008).

241. Jan Milič Lochman, *Reconciliation and Liberation: Challenging a One-Dimensional View of Salvation* (Philadelphia: Fortress Press, 1980), 28-29.

dimensions of experience in the Spirit. The legitimate Protestant response to medieval confusion over the priority of grace in all of our responses to God led to a *sola fides* (faith alone) doctrine meant originally to root the life of believers within a clinging to Christ and a daily dependence on him for all of the blessings and duties of the Christian life. The problem emerged, however, when faith came later to be defined largely as a rational affirmation of biblical truths or a proper confession formulated to secure Protestant ecclesial identity. The ancient way of viewing faith as essentially connected to love and hope (a way arguably present in the writings of the classical Reformers) was eclipsed in the process. For Revelation, however, faith is rooted in repentance and a constant return to the first love of a faithful bride (Rev 2:4-5). It involves a partaking of the springs of living water (7:17) and a sharing in the crucified and risen life of the Lamb (14:4). It involves a vibrant hope for the coming of the heavenly city but also a participation even now in its worship and experience of God. The wedding garment given to the faithful bride will be her righteous deeds, what the Reformers called "the obedience of faith" (19:8).

In Hebraic fashion, Revelation accents repentance, faithfulness, and works of love rather than believing. Its doctrine of faith (in the broader theological sense of the term) is implicitly a multidimensional reality that cannot be reduced to mental assent or verbal confession. Faith that is rooted in repentance and that is exercised in faithful endurance and good works cannot be cheap; it must be costly, a response to the costly grace of the divine self-giving. Yet, repentance itself must be viewed as integral to faith as a dependence entirely on the grace of God for all things, so that it does not get reduced to a human accomplishment, a kind of humanly achieved condition for affirming God's grace by faith. This is the great insight of the Protestant Reformation in relation to abuses of the penance doctrine in the late Middle Ages. So, how does one reflect on multidimensional "costly faith" in the light of Revelation?

Following Luther, Karl Barth sought to correct any potential one-sidedness by viewing faith as involved in a fundamental shift in loyalty toward Jesus as Lord or as the first step of obedience. Sanctification and vocation (discipleship), the distinctive accents of the Reformed[242] and Anabaptist traditions respectively, become the very goal of justification, the classically Lutheran focus. Faith comes to be viewed as a transformative and vocational reality that connects essentially with hope and love. As Barth noted, "Faith itself would not be faith if it did not work by love."[243] To connect Barth with the Catholic

---

242. We can add (especially) Wesleyan.
243. Barth, *Church Dogmatics*, vol. 4, pt. 2 (trans. G. W. Bromiley and Thomas Torrance; Edinburgh: T&T Clark, 1956), 627, see also 499-511.

tradition, Hans Küng wrote of faith as having the seeds of love within it (we could say the same of faith and hope).[244] Interestingly, Luther did not mind the "faith formed by love" idea of the scholastics, so long as the alternative would be viewed as false faith rather than "unformed" faith (which for Luther was not true faith, since faith for him was fundamentally a clinging personally to Christ rather than a metaphysical entity).[245] More recent ecumenical discussion has looked again at Luther and Calvin to discover a more robust understanding of faith as participation in Christ and in a life shaped by his crucifixion and resurrection. Luther wrote of faith as a taking hold of Christ in such a way that transforms life into a container of Christ in all his glory. Faith thus becomes a temple occupied by the presence of Christ.[246] As mentioned earlier, faith is also the first step of obedience for Luther, or that which finds expression in all good works. In conversation with the Russian Orthodox, the Finnish Lutherans mined such texts to connect Luther's understanding of faith with the Eastern Orthodox understanding of *theosis*, a transformative partaking of the divine nature. Tuomo Mannermaa notes that, for Luther, faith denotes "the full and complete divinization of the human being."[247] Luther considered that knowing Christ transforms the believer into becoming like Christ (knowing participates in the known), so that the believer can now become Christ to the neighbor.[248]

Union with Christ lies at the base and goal of salvation. Calvin based everything in union with Christ, a mystical union that involves Christ's presence in the human heart by faith: "Therefore, to that union to the head and members, the residence of Christ in our hearts, in fine, the mystical union, we assign the highest rank."[249] This union through faith comes by grace, or by the work of the Spirit: "Christ breathes into his people that they may be one with him."[250] The twofold benefit of this life-changing union with Christ is justification (knowing that we are accepted fundamentally because of Christ) and sanctification (set apart to function in Christ's image in the world). Though distinct, both bless-

244. Küng, *Justification*, 256.
245. Martin Luther, "Lectures on Galatians 1535," in *Luther's Works*, vol. 26 (ed. Jaroslav Pelikan; St. Louis: Concordia, 1963), 268-70. See my discussion of this remarkable admission in Macchia, *Justified in the Spirit*, 234.
246. Luther, "Lectures on Galatians 1535," 129-30.
247. Tuomo Mannermaa, *Christ Present in Faith: Luther's View of Justification* (Minneapolis: Augsburg/Fortress, 2005), 45.
248. Tuomo Mannermaa, "Why Is Luther So Fascinating? Modern Finnish Luther Research," in *Union with Christ: The New Finnish Interpretation of Luther* (ed. Karl E. Braaten and Robert W. Jenson; Grand Rapids: Eerdmans, 1958), 4-19.
249. John Calvin, *The Institutes of the Christian Religion* (2 vols.; Grand Rapids: Eerdmans, 1979), 2.3.11.
250. Calvin, *The Institutes of the Christian Religion*, 1.3.1.

ings are inseparable as branches of that one life-transforming union with (and participation in) Christ.²⁵¹ Calvin even gave a favorable nod to Martin Bucer's proposal accepted at the early Protestant-Catholic agreement at Regensburg (1541) that sought an integral and substantial connection between justification objectively secured by Christ alone and subjectively appropriated transformatively among believers.²⁵² As Veli-Matti Kärkkäinen has shown, the bridge for this integration within participatory and transformative understandings of faith has become the new ecumenical frontier for Protestants seeking to relate their *sola fides* (faith alone) doctrine to Catholic and Orthodox traditions.²⁵³ The multifaceted understanding of faith implied by Revelation can provide inspiration for this larger movement.

This holistic understanding of the life of faith is contextualized within a sanctifying and living union with Christ. As noted earlier, Revelation depicts an immediate union of the creature with God that has as its eschatological goal the partaking of the waters of life (Rev 7:17; 21:6; 22:1, 17) and the calling of the one who overcomes "son," a term reserved in the Johannine literature for Jesus as the Son of God (19:7). The base and goal of salvation is compatible here with a "deifying union" with Christ, in the words of Vladimir Lossky. This union is the context for a *theosis* of the creature that will be realized in the resurrection of the dead on the way to the coming of the heavenly city. This deifying union is also "to be fulfilled ever more and more even in this present life through the transformation of our corruptible and depraved nature and by its adaptation to eternal life."²⁵⁴ The way of union involves works: "prayer, fasting, vigils, and all other Christian practices," says St. Saraphim of Sarov.²⁵⁵ In his *Plain Account of Christian Perfection*, John Wesley described the process as that of the gradual perfection of the human will in conformity with the love of God: "Let your soul be filled with so entire a love to Him that you may love nothing but for his sake" (#6). He elaborates in #7:

O grant that nothing in my soul
    May dwell, but thy pure love alone!
O may thy love possess me whole,

---

251. Calvin, *The Institutes of the Christian Religion*, 2.3.11. See also my discussion of Calvin's debate with Osiander over mystical union with Christ, in Macchia, *Justified in the Spirit*, 55-62.

252. See Brian Lugioyo, "Martin Bucer's Doctrine of Justification and the Colloquy of Regensburg, 1541" (Ph.D. thesis, University of Aberdeen, 2007).

253. Veli-Matti Kärkkäinen, *One with God: Salvation as Justification and Deification* (Collegeville, MN: Liturgical Press, 2005). See also Macchia, *Justified in the Spirit*.

254. Lossky, *The Mystical Theology of the Eastern Church*, 196.

255. Quoted in Lossky, *The Mystical Theology of the Eastern Church*, 196.

> My joy, my treasure, and my crown!
> Strange fires far from my heart remove;
> My every act, word, thought, be love!

Quoting from one of his and his brother Charles's hymns, he continues by expressing what Revelation certainly assumes is to be the song of Christ's bride,

> Eager for thee I ask and pant,
>   So strong the principle divine,
> Carries me out with sweet constraint,
>   Till all my hallow'd soul be thine;
> Plunged in the Godhead's deepest sea,
>   And lost in thine immensity!

Once more, in #9:

> Heavenly Adam, life divine,
>   Change my nature into thine;
> Move and spread throughout my soul,
>   Actuate and fill the whole.

This sanctification process of the believer involves the transformation of the affections into "flames of holy love" (#8). Embracing the eschatological fervor of Pentecostal spirituality, Steven J. Land calls these transformed affections "passions for the kingdom of God."[256] This sanctifying grace is costly, for, as Wesley wrote of the believer in his *Plain Account*, "All the talents he has, he constantly employs according to his Master's will; every power and faculty of his soul, every member of his body" (#10). Such is the goal of Christ's bride in intimate union with her groom and in conformity to his image.

Conclusion

In the light of Revelation, costly grace in contemporary theology maintains its anchor in salvation being the work of the triune God. Salvation is wholly by God's excessive and overflowing self-giving, which no rational system of exchange can adequately grasp or explain. Costly grace overcomes resistance by the dark powers and shows their claims to creation to be false. Only the Cre-

---

256. Land, *Pentecostal Spirituality*.

ator's claims are just and true. Costly grace involves exclusion or judgment to be sure; it is not shallow sentiment. Yet, its assumption and goal are redemptive, offering creation a never-ending embrace that has its decisive occurrence in the cross. This costly grace that is so abundantly poured out will take up into itself all dimensions of reality. No dimension of existence can claim independence from its reach. One cannot play the personal off against the social or the existential off against the cosmic. One cannot play faith off against love or hope, for faith is participation in the life of God, a partaking of the divine nature. This costly grace is abundantly free, but it also cost God dearly and, as such, can never be taken for granted among the saints. Revelation is a potent reminder of this fact. "You have forsaken the love you had at first. Consider how far you have fallen! Repent and do the things you did at first" (Rev 2:4-5).

Eschatology

Revelation and Biblical Theology

Challenged and tempered by two world wars, Karl Barth sat at his desk to pen his lecture to be given at the University of Basel and included in his *Church Dogmatics* on the kingdom of God and "world occurrence," or the flow of history. Inspired in part by the image of the risen Christ in Revelation chapter 1, Barth wrote of his conviction that all of history falls under the judgment and is opened to the hope of the risen Christ. He wrote movingly:

> The point to be grasped is that in Jesus Christ we really do have the reality of world history. The great test of the relationship of the community and individual Christians to Him, of the genuineness of their existence, is whether they see and are sure and keep to the fact, and with child-like confidence avouch to the world, that it is in Him that world history really and properly takes place.[257]

World history has been changed by Jesus Christ (taken place in him), for in Christ, God has acted decisively to bring judgment and redemption for creation in all times and places. Everything is to be seen in a new light in the victory of Christ over sin and death. This insight informs the people of God as they approach the great challenges and the darkest moments of their times. They approach such moments through the lens of the risen Christ with the courage

---

257. Barth, *Church Dogmatics*, 4/3, second half, 712.

and renewing power of witness in the prophetic Spirit, who testifies of Jesus. In Christ they can see the new reality dawning already. Apart from Christ, "the new reality of history is still concealed," and the evil and confusion that reign within history seem to preclude any assumption concerning the divine providence that allegedly rules over it. All one can see is "the form of the history of a world which is yet unreconciled and far from the kingdom of God."[258] But the faithful community is not deceived or frightened by this surface picture of the world, for it sees a reality pictured before them "that is already outmoded and condemned to perish in virtue of the new reality even now present within it."[259] Thus, though the events of this passing world are taken seriously, the church "cannot fix its gaze on these pictures," for they are free from them, knowing that they are but fleeting. Only what God has done for the world in Christ will end up enduring and triumphing. Eschatology is the story of this triumph. We face challenges today of apocalyptic significance, not only in our nuclear weapons, but also in our continued destruction of our natural environment. Can we detect a new reality dawning in our midst in Christ? Will this new reality embolden our witness to the future of the world willed by God, a witness that not only hopes for a new world but seeks to create analogies of it that point to it in the here and now?

Revelation

The challenges that Revelation poses to this eschatological triumph, seen through the lens of the risen Christ, are stark and dramatic. Revelation makes the antagonist in the drama not only death or global catastrophe but also Hades and the forces of the dragon, which stand for the very absence of connection with the life-giving Creator. It is not just the first death that threatens the world but also the *second* with which the first is connected, namely, final alienation from the Creator. As such, the antagonist in Revelation threatens the creation with more than a sense of meaninglessness that may arise in response to a tragic end, but also with a perpetual state of alienation from God, who is the source of all life and joy. The Lamb in Revelation is slain. If this Lamb does not rise and if he does not come again to establish his reign over the nations and the entire cosmos, the Creator's rightful claim over the creation is nullified, and the creation remains captive to evil purposes. In Revelation, God has made the vindication and fulfillment of the divine claim to creation dependent on the missions of the Son and the Spirit. If the dragon, the beast, and the false prophet defeat them,

---

258. Barth, *Church Dogmatics*, 4/3, second half, 721.
259. Barth, *Church Dogmatics*, 4/3, second half, 721.

the Creator's claim to the creation is certainly nullified, and the creation itself along with it. This is the Abyss in Revelation, which threatens creation with a nightmare that is real and ultimate. Revelation raises the stakes of apocalyptic angst beyond what may be imagined within a secular context, while also elevating the assurance of divine victory along the way and at the conclusion of it all.

The threat of Death and Hades is confronted from the first chapter of the book by the vision of the risen Christ, the first glimpse that the audience receives of God's intended destiny not only for the saints but also for the heavens and the earth. Indeed, the resurrection of Christ initiates the time of the end and creates the conditions for both the final conflict and the assured victorious end. John stands before this blazing image of the risen Christ in chapter 1, anticipating the end, but also realizing that the end has still not yet come. It is soon to come, but it has not yet come. John has before him a foreshadow of the end and the very ground of hope, but the nations and the creation still lie in captivity to the dragon and in opposition to the crucified and risen Lamb. The end has begun in the risen Christ and now contradicts the present. But the nations have not yet been blessed. The Creator is not yet finished reclaiming divine lordship over creation. The Lamb has been slain and has risen again, but there are still a witness to give forth and a further battle to be won. The Spirit is being sent forth into all the earth in witness to the risen Lamb to prepare for the final triumph, but the triumph has not yet occurred. Christ has not yet returned. The end is delayed until these victories are fulfilled. Eschatology, as an accounting of God's ultimate purposes for creation, reaches its intense expression precisely within the drama of this battle of divine love to resolve the contradiction between the risen Christ and the world under captivity to the dragon and those who assist him. This is the context for Christian eschatology assumed by Revelation.

Christ's coming to set in motion God's final triumph is arguably a major focus of eschatology in Revelation. Chapter 1 notes, "Look, he is coming with the clouds" (v. 7). Soon thereafter Christ says, "I am coming soon" (3:11). The book gradually heightens the expectation of the audience that the Lamb will return in both judgment and triumph. With the sixth seal,

> there was a great earthquake. The sun turned black like sackcloth made of goat hair, the whole moon turned blood red, and the stars in the sky fell to earth, as figs drop from a fig tree when shaken by a strong wind. The heavens receded like a scroll being rolled up, and every mountain and island was removed from its place. (6:12-14)

This apocalyptic upheaval is followed by the efforts by the kings of the earth and people from all walks of life to hide from the wrath of the Lamb (6:15-

17). The seventh trumpet uses language that indicates even more explicitly the Lamb's final triumph:

> The kingdom of the world has become
>   the kingdom of our Lord and of his Messiah,
>   and he will reign for ever and ever. (11:15)

The elders elaborate in words of praise:

> We give thanks to you, Lord God Almighty,
>   the one who is and who was,
> because you have taken your great power
>   and have begun to reign.
> The nations were angry,
>   and your wrath has come.
> The time has come for judging the dead,
>   and for rewarding your servants the prophets
> and your people who revere your name,
>   both great and small —
> and for destroying those who destroy the earth. (11:17-18)

The final day of wrath and the final triumph coincide in Revelation as characteristic of the Lamb's second coming to earth. At a key point leading up to chapter 19, the Lamb's words remind the audience, "Look, I come like a thief" (16:15). Chapter 19 brings these themes together most clearly:

> I saw heaven standing open, and there before me was a white horse, whose rider is called Faithful and True. With justice he judges and wages war. His eyes are like blazing fire, and on his head are many crowns. He has a name written on him that no one knows but he himself. He is dressed in a robe dipped in blood, and his name is the Word of God. The armies of heaven were following him, riding on white horses and dressed in fine linen, white and clean. Coming out of his mouth is a sharp sword with which to strike down the nations. "He will rule them with an iron scepter." He treads the winepress of the fury of the wrath of God Almighty. On his robe and on his thigh he has this name written: KING OF KINGS AND LORD OF LORDS. (19:11-16)

After the vision of the new heavens and the new earth is given, the Lord assures the audience that he is indeed coming to bring about the day of judgment and the final triumph so as to set in motion the final series of end time events: "Yes, I am coming soon" (22:20). There is no question but that the second coming of Jesus, though not concluding all things, joins with the resurrection of the Lamb in forming the pivotal triumph that will bring about their fulfillment.

Divine sovereignty in Revelation thus does not preclude a real battle for victory. This battle is required because divine love does not prevent the rise of opposition but overcomes this opposition through the free witness of the saints and the conversion of the nations. In Revelation the conditions for eschatology consequently come to light in an interesting interplay of divine sovereignty and creaturely freedom. Since the creature is free to oppose the Creator's sovereign claim to lordship, the conditions are there for the playing out of a cosmic and personal battle for redemption. But since God is indeed Lord, the dragon cannot win. This tension between the divine love and its opposition in the world creates the conditions in Revelation for a dramatic battle that requires time and phases for its resolution. The divine reign has a history or a dramatic development within a redemptive battle that is won through the divine self-giving. This divine triumph takes the audience on a journey that has losses and gains, as well as a victorious climax. Such is the setting for eschatology in Revelation. Revelation thus makes it impossible to understand God or the God-world relation in anything other than eschatological terms.

A lot is at stake in this battle for redemption in Revelation, for God is personally involved in the outcome. God and eschatology are therefore integrally connected in Revelation, for God's very identity bears the stamp of eschatological fulfillment in time. The heavenly Father is identified as the one "who is, was, and is to come" (1:4, 8), and Christ, the firstborn from the dead, is the First and the Last (1:5, 17). Christ is the one who was dead but is now "alive forever and ever" as he holds the keys to "Death and Hades" (1:17-18). He is the triumphant one who is soon to return: "Look, he is coming on the clouds" (1:7). The Spirit is the one who goes forth from God's throne as the discerning eyes of the Lamb into the entire earth in preparation for the victory of God's love among the nations (5:6). This is the Spirit of global witness to all of the nations in preparation for the end, as well as the stream of life from which the redeemed are nourished. All of these references from chapter 1 and beyond already define God in strongly eschatological terms. God is described in such a way that believers who hold to the traditions of Israel and the earliest Christian proclamation, and also who experience God in power in the here and now, are made to fill out their understanding of God by looking also to the horizons of historical and global fulfillment in order to witness the completion of the work already accomplished. The Father, the Alpha and the Omega, "is to come"; the Son, the risen Lord, who conquered Death and Hades, "is coming"; and the Spirit before the throne is being sent "into all the earth" in witness to the coming Christ. This is the God of the past and of the present, but also of the future, who is about to bring to fulfillment globally and ultimately that which was accomplished in order to deliver the creation from the grip of evil and to bring creation into full participation in the divine life.

This eschatological fulfillment of the work of the triune God can be unpacked further. Concerning the heavenly Father, Revelation views the Creator as seeking to bring creation to its originally intended *telos,* or purpose. The heavens, the earth, and the seas, which witness such upheaval because of the invasion of evil, were created by God and have their reason for being in the Creator (10:6). The divine purposes for creation are found in the slain Lamb and the book of life (13:8), not in the schemes of the dragon, the beast, and the false prophet. The Creator will in no way resign these purposes and yield to the alien opposition. The Creator will not hand the divine lordship of creation over to the dragon. The Father is determined to defeat the opposition and to purge the creation from all evil in order to make it the divine dwelling place. After the final triumph, God draws near to dwell among the people, drying their tears and comforting them as a parent would a distressed child (21:3-4). The Lamb will be the light in which they walk, and the Spirit will be the water that sustains them (21:22-24; 22:17).

Christ is the focal point of this eschatological fulfillment for creation. His role was foreseen already at the very creation of the world as its implicit *telos* (13:8). He stands in triumph over sin and death already in chapter 1. He was born to rule and attained this fulfillment, even though the dragon sought to destroy him from his birth — but to no avail. The eschatological situation of the saints is described as a rejoicing that the dragon was defeated but also a warning that he is ferociously seeking to make war in the short time that he has left before the end (12:12). The church moves forward in witness, knowing that Christ is the one who has conquered Death and Hades; he directs the churches by his word and sends his Spirit into all the earth. He is coming again to reign over the nations. He will be the light of the heavenly city, by which the nations will walk (21:23). Since the saints conquer by his blood, they do not seek to identify eschatology with their own self-determined hopes and dreams but rather with God's redemptive purposes in the crucified Lamb (12:11). Eschatology is determined by Christology. This is eschatological Christology, which enfolds as a drama in which the end is already foreshadowed in him but is still yet to be fulfilled throughout creation. The person and work of Christ are discerned over the span of a redemptive drama, the fulfillment of which is both foreseen and yet to come. The Spirit who goes out into all the earth to witness of Christ to the nations through the prophetic mission of the churches is also the very promise of life offered in the Lamb, the waters to be drunk as the Shepherd leads the sheep to the streams of life (7:17; 21:6; 22:1, 17). This Spirit gives life to the dead (11:11) and brings fulfillment to the living. This is the Spirit of global witness, the Spirit of renewal, and the Spirit of life — the eschatological Spirit.

Since eschatology in Revelation has its context in the story of God's triumphant self-giving for creation in Christ, it centers on the story of the triune God; it cannot be preoccupied with future "end-time events." Revelation is not a crystal ball of future events; rather, it is a picturesque portrayal of the costly and triumphant self-giving of God for the redemption of the nations and of the entire creation. The story is told in a way that is not speculative but evocative: dramatic, conflict-ridden, redemptive, and transformative. The eschatological vision of the book is caught up in the battle of the Creator to maintain and to fulfill the divine claim on creation. This is a vision that inspires faithful and patient witness, a desire to fight on the side of redemption. The purpose of this vision is not to satisfy one's curiosity concerning the future or to round out one's theological system. The eschatology of Revelation answers the burning question of those caught in the throes of evil concerning whether there is indeed a higher and better purpose for the world, and it does so in the affirmative and in a way that calls the readers to enter the struggle and to experience the victory at the cost (and *fulfillment*) of their very lives.

The eschatological vision of the book is thus directed not only to the future but also to the present. There is an interesting eschatological tension in Revelation between that which is yet to come and that which is already. There is no question but that the book yearns for Christ's coming, which is explicitly announced no less than five times (1:7; 3:11; 22:7, 12, 20). Only then will evil be eradicated and the kingdom of God established on the earth among the nations. However, salvation is also a present reality to be experienced in the here and now. The creation that is yet to be delivered from evil already sings the song of victory at Christ's resurrection: "Then I heard every creature in heaven and on earth and under the earth and on the sea, and all that is in them, saying: 'To him who sits on the throne and to the Lamb be praise and honor and glory and power, for ever and ever!'" (5:13). Death and Hades will be thrown into the lake of fire before Christ's judgment seat at the end (20:14), but Christ is said to have already taken authority over them (1:17-18). The Christ who is coming again already comes to the churches in warning and fellowship (3:20). The Christ who will rule over the nations in the end (11:15) is already identified as "the ruler of the kings of the earth" (1:5). The glorified Christ that will appear at the end (19:12-13) already stands before John and in the midst of the churches (1:12-16). The kingdom is coming, but the saints are already redeemed from every nation

Eschatology

to be a kingdom (5:10). The New Jerusalem is yet to come, and yet the saints are already citizens of it (7:4-8; 21:12-13). The salvation that is yet to come is in some sense already present (1:5-6; 5:9-10; 14:3-4). More precisely, in Revelation, future events already determine the present because they are grounded in the eternal will of the Creator, in the crucifixion and resurrection of the Lamb, and in the witness of the Spirit throughout the earth. The past and the present are drawn into the future triumph, and the future triumph grows out of the redemptive events of the past and the present. This overlap of past, present, and future is because the God involved at every point of the redemptive drama is the one who was, is, and is to come.

The God of creation is active as the drama for redemption moves toward its climax and is foreshadowed at every step of the drama in a way that allows the faithful to experience the power of the end already, because they experience the God of the end. Believers in communion with Christ and God already partake of the life of the crucified and risen Lamb, already move out on the wind of the Spirit of prophecy, even while living in this present world. Eschatology has as its substance this partaking of the divine life in Revelation, an intimate communion in God that increases in its intimacy as the end draws near. The now and not-yet tension of the book is thus not static but dynamic and increasingly climactic. Though the book does not follow a neat or uninterrupted chronology, there is still a sense of movement toward a final climax. The readers are made to feel a sense of urgency from the rapid movement of God in the direction of the final conflict. The book is written to deal with "what must soon take place" (1:1). The time of the end is near (1:3), for Christ is "coming soon" (22:7, 12, 20). The audience is made to yearn for the coming Lord, as it is touched already by his final triumph. They are made to feel as though they are already standing at the threshold of that triumph and can see and experience something of the other side, because they are already standing in one sense within it.

The final triumph occurs as Babylon falls, the righteous dead are raised, the dragon is locked in the Abyss, and Christ establishes his kingdom on the earth. Christ reigns for a thousand years on the earth, a number of years that towers over the years of trial. A countless number of converts from all nations emerge from the time of trial to sing the song of the redeemed (7:13-14). Before the remaking of the heavens and the earth, the dragon and the opposition are ousted from the world in chapter 20, and Christ brings *this present earth* under God's reign. After the dragon is released to deceive once more at the end of the millennium, another rebellion is formed among the nations against Christ. This rebellion is crushed once more, which then leads to the final judgment. Finally, the dragon, the beast, the false prophet, and those who follow them are thrown into the lake of fire, God's eschatological judgment. They can deceive the nations no more. Death and Hades are themselves thrown into the fires of God's final judgment to torment humanity no longer. The heavens and the earth flee from Christ's judgment seat, for their purpose under Christ's reign has been served. They are to be remade for a new purpose, a new stage in the fulfillment of God's reign. The heavenly city will descend from heaven to earth, and the heavens and the earth are to be transformed to receive it.

The heavenly city is God's answer to the human need for *polis*, or structured community. It is fashioned from the communion of saints and is thus also called the bride of Christ (21:9). In Revelation, the glory of the heavenly city is marked by the presence of God as Father and Son (21:22-23) and Spirit (22:17). God is near, and the saints commune directly with the divine presence. They partake of this presence directly as they drink from the water of life, the Spirit of God (21:6; 22:1, 17). There is no longer need for the temple cult, for God and the Lamb is the temple (21:22), and in the presence of the Lamb "they shall see his face" (22:4). The glory of the new polis is like a garden, the fulfillment of the old Garden of Eden and of the original creation. The divine glory directly encountered takes the penultimate glory of the nations up into itself so as to fulfill it (21:26). Outside the gates of the New Jerusalem are the wicked who have been judged by the fires of eschatological judgment (22:15). But the open gates of the heavenly city point in the directions of the opposition and never shut, for there is no night or danger with which to contend; indeed, no one can enter who does not wash his or her robes by the atoning work of the Lamb (22:14; 21:13, 25). Those open gates are indicative in Revelation of a sovereign God who ultimately has nothing to fear from the opposition and who perpetually faces it with open doors. This is a divine exclusion that is overshadowed by an eternal yearning to embrace.

The sting of personal death is not overlooked in Revelation. The souls of the martyred saints recognize the injustice in how their lives were cut short and seek a just response (6:10-11). Their voices are not silenced by death, nor are they left out of the future victory of God's kingdom. Bound in the Spirit to the crucified and risen Christ, they continue to speak for themselves and to yearn for future justice. The future kingdom in Revelation does not relegate the dead to the trash bin of history or to the memory of voices who can no longer speak. They continue to speak, and in this case, divine judgment follows their speaking, but in a way that has the salvation of the nations as its overarching purpose. Death is in fact a grim reaper in Revelation, an enemy at war with the human race. Death has Hades following close behind in order to take hold of its captives once and for all (6:8). The grave danger is thus the first and the second deaths. The connection of Hades with death is significant, because it shows how death is symptomatic of a deeper alienation from the life of the Creator.

Eschatology

The second death, or banishment from God, is thus worse than the first death. Apart from divine grace, death in itself is by no means a friend, a normal part of life for Revelation. It is an enemy that has already been conquered by the risen Christ (1:18) and will one day fall victim to the fires of God's eschatological judgment (20:14). The ultimate hope of the dead in Revelation is resurrection or full participation in God's new creation. Even the souls of the departed before God's throne yearn for their ultimate vindication, which could come only in resurrection. This is the vindication of the witnesses in chapter 11. Ultimate victory does not come in the ascent of a disembodied soul in Revelation but rather in the remaking of creation into a vessel fit for the divine indwelling, the resurrected body and the new heavens and new earth.

Believers in Revelation patiently endure the trials and dangers that they face because the vision offered of God and the heavenly city gives them courage and hope. Believers who look forward to the glory of future resurrection do so as they follow the Lamb wherever he goes and, in obedience like the Lamb, give of their lives daily as an offering to God for the fulfillment of God's glory and purposes in the world (14:4). The path to glory is the cross, for they endure and overcome only through the blood of the Lamb (12:11). As the faithful bride, they keep themselves pure (14:5). They know that the faithless will be judged according to their works (20:12). They wish to commit their lives to the victorious blood of the Lamb. The vision of future glory for those who have done so is prefigured and experienced in the Spirit, especially in worship, as the doxological expressions of the book illustrate (e.g., 5:9-10). The vision of the nations as coming under the reign of the Lamb also drives the church's mission to the world. The mandate given to Israel is fulfilled in a way that does not leave Israel behind. The heavenly city, in which the kings of the nations walk in the light of the Messiah, has the names of the twelve tribes on its gates. The delay in the coming of Christ that characterizes eschatology in Revelation is thus also filled substantially with the missionary mandate of the Spirit first given to Israel and pursued in the latter days by the faithful bride. Those who belong to the Lamb enter the conflict between the world as it is and God's reign as revealed in the risen Christ, knowing that God will reign one day and, in fact, reigns already. The reign of God is the assurance of the churches as they face their darkest hours; indeed, no danger can befall them that can destroy the Father's elect purposes, their relationship with the Lamb, or their Spirit-empowered prophetic mission in the world. Any threat that might give rise to apocalyptic angst is answered by all of these divine purposes and assurances. The earth belongs to God, and nothing will be able to hold it captive for long. Christ is coming soon.

In sum, Revelation does not place the future in our grasp, but it does assure us that the future is in *God's* grasp. The future belongs to God, to the Creator, the victorious Lamb, and the missionary Spirit, who empowers Christ's church to bless the nations through the good news of the gospel. The future is wrought with conflict, threat, and suffering, but the spiritual insight, transformation, and empowerment to be had in the Spirit of the Lamb will grant the people of God the comfort and courage necessary to endure patiently and actively. This endurance is active, dynamic, and victorious, an aspect of their mission in the world while awaiting the fulfillment of God's kingdom. This endurance lives not only from the hope of this fulfillment but also from the foretaste of it that occurs in communion with Christ through the Spirit and, through Christ, with the heavenly Father. Eschatology in Revelation has as its substance this participation in God and the hospitality of this life offered to the nations through the Spirit of prophecy at work in the mission of the church.

John

Eschatology in John's gospel is well known for its emphasis on the present experience of eternal life or judgment: "Very truly I tell you, whoever hears my word and believes him who sent me has eternal life and will not be judged but has crossed over from death to life" (John 5:24). Those who reject the Son reject life and are condemned "already" because they do not believe (3:18). The prince of this world already stands condemned (16:11). As disbelief occasions existence within the wrath of alienation from life already, faith in Christ already confers participation in Christ and, through Christ, in the life enjoyed with the heavenly Father: "just as you are in me and I am in you. May they also be in us" (17:21b). We abide in Christ, and he in us: "Remain in me, as I also remain in you" (15:4). The believing community gathers together to feed from Christ as the Bread of Life (6:51). The Father's love is in us as Christ himself is in us, as Jesus prayed to the Father, "I have made you known to them, and will continue to make you known in order that the love you have for me may be in them and that I myself may be in them" (17:26). Through the Spirit, the Father and Christ take human life up into their loving embrace. The Spirit is the one who makes what Christ has from the Father known by us (16:15). We already know the Spirit of Truth, for he lives among and in us (14:17). This partaking of the divine life occasions a spiritual awakening. In Christ, believers are born anew of Spirit (3:5).

Life in the risen Christ sanctifies the saints, for Christ sanctified himself in his journey to the cross so that his followers will be sanctified in him as the Truth (17:19). They are not to be removed from this world but, rather, protected from the evil one, so that, while being *in* the world, they would not be *of* the world (17:14-19). The Paraclete, the Holy Spirit, will comfort them with the promise of Christ's coming:

> The Holy Spirit, whom the Father will send in my name, will teach you all things and will remind you of everything I have said to you. Peace I leave with you; my peace I give you. I do not give to you as the world gives. Do not let your hearts be troubled, and do not be afraid. You heard me say, "I am going away and I am coming back to you." (14:26-28)

Comforted by the Spirit of promise, the followers of Jesus will live the sanctified life in the world, bearing witness to the truth of Christ.

At the base of this new life in Christ is the momentous event of incarnation. Christ as the Word made flesh (1:14) represents the decisive occasion for participation in the life of God. He is the eternal Word of the Father made flesh, confronting humanity with eternal life and with the challenge to believe, which is the only means of receiving and participating in this life. The separated realms of "above" and "below," as well as "past," "present," and "future," are brought together in the Christ, who is the eternal Word ("from the beginning," 1:1) that comes to us in flesh (1:14).[260] Before Abraham was, "I Am," says Christ (8:58). Christ is already the resurrection and the life in his flesh (11:25), and eternal life is knowing the Father in the Son, already in the here and now (17:3). The offer of life in and through the Son brings the above below, and both the yearnings of the past and the fulfillment of the future into the present. Of course, rejecting this life has equally weighty consequences. If life is present now in Christ, so are death and alienation apart from Christ.

John thus pictures the present realization of the future as a meal in which we eat and drink from Christ as the source of life. Jesus explains that Israel's ancestors "ate the manna in the wilderness, yet they died," but "here is the bread that comes down from heaven, which anyone may eat and not die. I am the living bread that came down from heaven. Whoever eats this bread will live forever. This bread is my flesh, which I will give for the life of the world" (6:49-51). We can participate in life only as we eat his flesh and drink his blood (6:53). We remain in him and he in us if we eat his flesh and drink his blood (6:56). Future salvation is guaranteed to those who presently eat and drink from Christ: "Whoever eats my flesh and drinks my blood has eternal life, and I will raise them up at the last day" (6:54). The future resurrection is the culmination of the believers' partaking of Christ.

Yet, as implied in the text just quoted, we should resist any effort to re-

---

260. Schnelle, *Theology of the New Testament*, 742.

move from John the futuristic fulfillment of that which is present in Christ and through the Spirit. Jesus' statements in John's gospel of his future coming cannot be merely collapsed into the coming of the Spirit. Jesus himself will come back to take his followers with him where he is going (i.e., to the Father) so that they may be with him (14:3; cf. 14:12; 16:28). Jesus points also to the future resurrection of the dead: "Very truly I tell you, a time is coming and has now come when the dead will hear the voice of the Son of God, and those who hear will live" (5:25). The eternal life that we have in the Son does not preclude the experience of death or the need for future glorification. The paradox of saying that the "time is coming" and has "now come" may lie at the heart of Johannine eschatology.[261] The future is already experienced in the present within the believing community, but the future is not thereby collapsed into the present. There is still a future fulfillment that is lacking in the present. The dead are not yet raised, even though the reality of the resurrection already overlaps with the present because of the spiritually rich reality of abiding in Christ and living the born-again reality of life in the Spirit.

John's letters reveal this same paradox. The eternal life that comes to us in Christ is from the beginning and has appeared to us, occasioning our fellowship with God (1 John 1:2-3). Eternal life is now, experienced while remaining in the Son and the Father (2:24-25). So is the reality of alienation from life or judgment: "Whoever has the Son has life; whoever does not have the Son of God does not have life" (5:12). So also the spirit of anti-Christ, "which you have heard is coming and even now is already in the world" (4:3). Yet, the future fulfillment of Christ's coming is not collapsed into the present experience of believers in the Johannine letters. We also desire to be confident at Christ's future coming through the love and assurance in us now (2:28; cf. 4:17). The significance of future judgment and vindication is not eliminated, though these realities already shape our identity and hope in the present situation. In fact, present experience is moving toward future fulfillment, since "the darkness is already passing and the light is shining" (2:8).

In John's gospel the present experience of the future in Christ is marked by "signs through which he revealed his glory" (2:11). A sign that stands out on the path to Jerusalem is Christ's raising of Lazarus from the dead, a sure indication that Jesus is the Messiah and in his very being the resurrection and the life: "Jesus said to her, 'I am the resurrection and the life. The one who believes in me will live, even though they die; and whoever lives by believing in me will never die. Do you believe this?'" (11:25-26). Instead of convincing the Jewish leadership that he has come from God and is the key to their eschato-

---

261. Schnelle, *Theology of the New Testament*, 743-45.

Eschatology

logical destiny, this sign caused them to seek his death for fear that the masses would now turn to him and the nation be destroyed in the process (11:45-53). In making this decision, they were choosing a future characterized by fear and self-made efforts at security rather than by a trust in God and a willingness to follow divine revelation wherever it takes them. Ironically, God used their rebellion to bring about the fulfillment of the kingdom of God.

Matthew and Mark

As Ladd notes, "Most of the eschatology of Jesus as reported by the Synoptics has to do with the events attending the coming of the eschatological kingdom of God."[262] In Matthew, as noted above in our discussion of salvation, Jesus' acts of deliverance and healing through the Spirit of God cause the kingdom of God to come upon those who are present and receptive: "But if it is by the Spirit of God that I drive out demons, then the kingdom of God has come upon you" (Matt 12:28). The kingdom of God is based in the sovereignty of God, or God's lordship over creation, and is present through Jesus and his acts done in the power of the Spirit. The breaking in of the kingdom through Jesus and the Spirit does not refer fundamentally to a place but rather to something powerful and dynamic, to God's liberating reign that overthrows the opposition and brings about the conditions for a new life directed toward obedience to God's will. Jesus thus prays for God's kingdom to come, and for God's will thereby to be done on earth as it is in heaven (6:10). Jesus' entire ministry is marked by eschatological fulfillment, since the will of God is being fulfilled in and through him. The kingdom of God is experienced through repentance (3:2) and will lead to both restoration for those who repent and judgment for those who do not (3:12).

The sense of nearness of the kingdom in Jesus' ministry implies a realized eschatology. In Matthew, the demons say to Jesus just before he delivers a demon-possessed man, "Have you come here to torture us before the appointed time?" (8:29), a statement that "clearly supports the presence of the kingdom."[263] Jesus is identified as "Elijah who was to come" (11:14; cf. Luke 1:17), pointing to Jesus as an eschatological figure. He is the key figure, since the kingdom draws near in his coming. Jesus recognized the unprecedented eschatological fulfillment occurring in and through him, noting,

---

262. Ladd, *Theology of the New Testament*, 196.
263. Donald A. Hagner, "Matthew's Eschatology," in *To Tell the Mystery: Essays on New Testament Eschatology in Honor of Robert H. Gundry* (ed. Thomas E. Schmidt and Moisés Silva; Sheffield: JSOT Press, 1994), 52.

> But blessed are your eyes because they see, and your ears because they hear. For truly I tell you, many prophets and righteous people longed to see what you see but did not see it, and to hear what you hear but did not hear it. (Matt 13:16-17)

Those questioning whether Jesus fulfilled John's prophecy are told, "Go back and report to John what you hear and see: The blind receive sight, the lame walk, those who have leprosy are cleansed, the deaf hear, the dead are raised, and the good news is proclaimed to the poor" (11:4-5; cf. Luke 7:21-23). Though John was great, those least in the kingdom that Jesus inaugurates are greater than John (11:11; cf. Luke 7:28).

Jesus' baptism has apocalyptic overtones, with the heavens opening and God speaking (Matt 3:16-17; cf. Mark 1:10-11; Luke 3:21-22). In Matthew's gospel, Jesus' death is "unmistakably apocalyptic in character," described as accompanied by supernatural darkness, two earthquakes, and the descent of an angel from heaven (Matt 27:45-51; 28:4).[264] His resurrection indicates the divine glory revealed at the vindication of God's lordship and the establishment of the kingdom. The eschatological significance of the resurrection is obvious, accompanied by apocalyptic signs of an earthquake and an angel descending from heaven (his appearance being "like lightning" and "as white as snow," 28:2-3).

The kingdom of God in Matthew is not only present but also future. The parables of the kingdom of God like the mustard seed and the yeast imply a present reality that awaits future fulfillment (13:31-35). Jesus looks forward to those apocalyptic events that will consummate the age. Jesus anticipates the time when "many will come from east and west and sit at the table with Abraham, Isaac, and Jacob in the kingdom of heaven" (8:11). In reference to the time of eschatological blessings, the beatitudes promise comfort, inheriting the earth, eschatological mercy, and fullness in one's vision of God (5:3-12). Jesus promises his disciples: "Truly I tell you, at the renewal of all things, when the Son of Man sits on his glorious throne, you who have followed me will also sit on twelve thrones, judging the twelve tribes of Israel" (19:28). The decisive event in the fulfillment of the kingdom of God on earth is the coming of the Son of Man "on the clouds of heaven with power and great glory" (24:30; cf. Mark 13:26).

In Mark's gospel the reader is immediately confronted in the first chapter with the message that "the time has come." This remarkable announcement is followed by the proclamation that the "kingdom of God has come near. Repent and believe the good news" (Mark 1:15). Through a fast-paced series of

---

264. Hagner, "Matthew's Eschatology," 53.

Eschatology

dramatic events following this announcement, readers are meant to feel the eschatological urgency and significance of the moment. One does not leave the first chapter without learning that Christ has cast out demons and healed the sick. The eschatological breaking in of the kingdom requires radical changes among those caught up in its life. Believers are told that they must be made new to receive what the new era has to bring, much like old wineskins must be replaced by new ones in order to hold the new wine (2:21-22; cf. Matt 9:17; Luke 5:37-38). Beginning with chapter 8, Mark shows that the path to the kingdom is one of misunderstanding, rejection, and suffering. The power of the kingdom, dramatically felt in events of deliverance, does not preclude for Mark the weakness and vulnerability of life under the weight of such rejection. The result for Mark is the abandonment of oneself to the will of God in service to God and others, for "even the Son of Man came not to be served but to serve and to give his life as a ransom for many" (10:45).

Key to the coming time of renewal are the widespread rejection of the Messiah by Israel, God's judgment upon Jerusalem, and the blessing that will come to the nations before the fulfillment of the promises given to Israel are fulfilled. Tribulation signs of the end will occur in the days leading up to this fulfillment, as told in the Olivet Discourse. For the Synoptics (Mark 13; Luke 21; Matt 24), these tribulation signs of the coming end will include false messiahs, grand deception, and wars. Though one might regard such signs as connected with the arrival of the end, in Mark and the other evangelists Jesus cautions that, when such signs appear, the end is not yet or will be *delayed* (Mark 13:7; cf. Matt 24:6; Luke 21:9). These false messiahs and wars that initiate the latter days are but the beginnings of the birth pangs of the coming kingdom in the world. Such signs will come to involve greater wars and famine, persecutions, earthquakes, and, especially, the evangelization of the nations. The coming destruction of the temple and Jerusalem is connected to all of these events because the role of Israel in receiving the Messiah and in blessing the nations is vital to the eschatological drama of salvation. At Israel's rejection of the Messiah, God's turn to the nations through the remnant of Israel, represented by the twelve disciples and the rise of the community dedicated to Jesus, is crucial to the prophetic plan. Matthew notes that the judgment of the temple and Jerusalem is connected to the role of Christ and his kingdom replacing them as the center of God's eschatological blessings. Christ's return will catch those who are not faithful unawares, judging them for their unfaithfulness (ch. 25).

Especially in Matthew, however, Israel is not permanently removed from God's purposes for the world. Jesus weeps over Jerusalem but also implies that its rejection does not last forever: "For I tell you, you will not see me again until you say, 'Blessed is he who comes in the name of the Lord'" (23:39). This saying anticipates that, when God carries out final judgment and redemption, "a repentant Israel will welcome him."[265] Indeed, the names of the twelve tribes are given on the gates of the heavenly city in Revelation. At the end, a cosmic catastrophe occurs that is described in language similar to that found in Revelation: the darkening of the sun and moon, the falling of the stars, and the shaking of the powers of the heavens (Mark 13:24-25). This poetic language signifies the fact that the universe pales before God as the Lord steps forward to consummate salvation.[266]

Luke and Acts

Luke announces that, in the Spirit-anointed Christ, God has visited the poor and oppressed with striking signs of divine favor. The prisoners, the blind, and the oppressed are brought into the liberating power of the kingdom of God in ways that are tangible and that alter the conditions of their lives (Luke 4:18). Demons are cast out, the blind see, the lame walk, and the dead are raised as signs of the kingdom of God breaking in to the earth. This in-breaking of the kingdom will fulfill past mighty acts that result in a reversal of current worldly power structures:

> He has performed mighty deeds with his arm;
> > he has scattered those who are proud in their inmost thoughts.
> He has brought down rulers from their thrones
> > but has lifted up the humble.
> He has filled the hungry with good things
> > but has sent the rich away empty. (1:51-53)

The realization of the kingdom, however, is not only corporate but individual and personal. For Luke especially, the personal element is important. In terms of the final judgment, "one shall be taken and the other left" (17:34), and to the robber, Jesus said on the cross, "Today you will be with me in paradise" (23:43).

These great signs of the Spirit accompany the prophetic ministry of the Spirit through chosen servants (Mary, Elizabeth, Zechariah, Simeon, Anna), a latter-day gift that will be made available to all believers (12:11-12). The eschatological significance of this great move of the Spirit in the world is clear. In

---

265. Ladd, *Theology of the New Testament*, 201.
266. Ladd, *Theology of the New Testament*, 203.

Luke, Christ's "miracles and his own physical resurrection point to the new age as a *fulfillment,* a deliverance of the present material creation from the death powers of this age."[267] Jesus' resurrection is clearly eschatological in significance, as the risen Christ notes: "Everything must be fulfilled that is written about me in the Law of Moses, the Prophets and the Psalms" (Luke 24:44). Luke clearly distinguishes the resurrection from Pentecost and the fulfillment of the people of God as a missionary body. Luke's clear separation of the resurrection from the ascension and Pentecost was not to accent the heavenly over the material, since he preserves the materiality of Jesus' resurrection existence: "Touch me and see; a ghost does not have flesh and bones, as you see I have" (24:39). His purpose, rather, is to accent the distinction between Christ's act of inaugurating the kingdom in his life, death, and resurrection and the Spirit's act in witness to him in diversifying and expanding the kingdom in the world.

Luke is known for highlighting the delay of the kingdom's fulfillment so as to resist an overly enthusiastic apocalyptic expectation that ignores the mission of the Spirit in history. Luke especially draws out the implications of this delay, noting the need for a salvation history and, even more important, missional history of the church to occur before the end comes. Luke is unique in clearly separating those end-time signs connected to the historic fall of Jerusalem and those following "the times of the Gentiles" as final signs of cosmic upheaval (Luke 21:20-28). Indeed, the problem as Luke sees it is not the delay of the parousia, "but a false apocalyptic speculation that has misapplied the teachings of Jesus and threatens to pervert the church's mission."[268]

In the light of Luke, Acts seeks also to counter an enthusiastic apocalyptic expectation that abandons the full significance of the missional history of the people of God. According to Acts, the outpouring of the Spirit at Pentecost is preceded by the risen Christ's teaching them concerning the kingdom of God. The disciples are to wait for the Spirit in Jerusalem, the city connected with the fulfillment of the kingdom (Acts 1:3-5). The disciples then ask an eschatological question: "Lord, are you at this time going to restore the kingdom to Israel?" Jesus tempers their eschatological enthusiasm with two crucial eschatological insights. First, only the heavenly Father "has set by his own authority" when the end will come; this is not for them to know (1:7). Obviously, humans are not meant to have this kind of grasp of a future over which only God is meant to exercise lordship. Second, they are to concentrate instead on participating in God's eschatological goal of blessing the nations with the Word and Spirit of God. The Spirit is to be poured out upon all peoples, and the disciples are to

---

267. E. Earle Ellis, *Eschatology in Luke* (Philadelphia: Fortress Press, 1972), 14.
268. Ellis, *Eschatology in Luke,* 19.

be the first, spreading the good news under the empowerment of the Spirit as the firstfruits of the Spirit's outpouring on all flesh (1:7-8). For Luke, the Spirit is the eschatological blessing for all nations, for the "promise is for you and your children and for all who are far off — for all whom the Lord our God will call" (2:39).

For Acts, the eschatological blessing of the Spirit is rooted in the resurrection and vindication of the unjustly condemned Messiah. Though condemned to die a criminal's death, Jesus can still say to the Father:

> I saw the Lord always before me.
> > Because he is at my right hand,
> > I will not be shaken.
> Therefore my heart is glad and my tongue rejoices;
> > my body also will rest in hope,
> because you will not abandon me to the realm of the dead,
> > you will not let your Holy One see decay.
> You have made known to me the paths of life;
> > you will fill me with joy in your presence. (2:25-28)

With glad hearts and rejoicing tongues, the disciples are empowered to witness to the nations that God has raised this Jesus to life (2:32). In tongues understood by the nations, they declare the wonders of God (2:4-11). Gentile believers join their Jewish counterparts in speaking the tongues of Pentecost as an ongoing sign of the global reach of the Spirit (10:46). This witness to the vindicated Messiah includes miracles of healing as signs that Jesus is the Messiah come to bless the nations with the Spirit: "It is by the name of Jesus Christ of Nazareth, whom you crucified but whom God raised from the dead, that this man stands before you healed" (4:10). Ascended to the right hand of God, Jesus bestows the Spirit of life upon the world as the fulfillment of the promised blessing (2:33). The call is to repent and be baptized "every one of you" so that the promised Holy Spirit can be received (2:38).

The "all flesh" of the Spirit's global and eschatological reach is not generic but specific, personal, and social. Sons and daughters, young and old, and servants join the prophetic movement of the people of God in the world. Followers of John the Baptist join with the messianic movement devoted to Jesus' lordship, and a persecuted church comes to embrace its chief oppressor, Paul. Barriers of discrimination and suffering are crossed in the movement of the Spirit throughout the world in witness to the crucified and risen Christ. As the end draws near, the Spirit's witness includes cosmic signs, all sharing in the goal of the repentance and blessing of the nations:

> I will show wonders in the heavens above
> and signs on the earth below,
> blood and fire and billows of smoke.
> The sun will be turned to darkness
> and the moon to blood
> before the coming of the great and glorious Day of the Lord.
> And everyone who calls
> on the name of the Lord will be saved. (2:19-21)

All of the nations were created and had their unique journeys directed by God so that they would in their own unique ways seek after God (17:26-27). They stray toward idols, but they are drawn instead to the living God, who cannot be contained by human temples but who turns the entire creation into the divine dwelling place by raising the crucified Christ from the dead and pouring out the Spirit on all flesh (17:24-31). The God who draws them to seek thus fulfills their search in Christ and the gift of the Spirit, drawing them to the cross, the empty tomb, the missional empowerment of Pentecost, and the final renewal of all things. Eschatology for Luke spans creation and new creation and has its source and end in the miraculous power of God. All of human history has its beginning, substance, and *telos* in God.

Paul

In a way similar to Revelation, the symbolic universe of Pauline eschatology is shaped decisively by the crucified and risen Christ.[269] The future is experienced already through participation in the life of the Crucified and Risen One by the Spirit. In the Lord's Supper, we give thanks in "participation in the blood of Christ" (1 Cor 10:16b), or in union with his life-giving act, to the glory of the Father and for the redemption of the world. Even more seminally for our salvation, in baptism we are buried with the dead Christ in order to rise with him to "live a new life" (Rom 6:4). Even Christ's ascension and position next to the Father is now part of our experience in Christ (Eph 1:20). Our present life and future death are thus redefined by being brought into relation to the risen Christ. Buried with him and risen with him, we look at our future death as taking place in and with *him:* "If we live, we live for the Lord; and if we die, we die for the Lord. So, whether we live or die, we belong to the Lord" (Rom 14:8). Paul thus refers to believers as having "fallen asleep *in him*" (1 Thess 4:14).

---

269. Schnelle, *Theology of the New Testament*, 342.

In him, death is now stripped of its sting, which is sin and alienation (1 Cor 15:55-56). Death is now swallowed up in life and overcome (2 Cor 5:4). Since death is in Christ, it cannot separate us from the love of God given to us in relation to Christ (Rom 8:38-39). Death cannot remove us from being *in him.* To die is to "depart to be *with Christ*" (Phil 1:23), which allows Paul to say that dying is a "gain" to him (1:21). For Paul, the redefinition of death as a departing to be with Christ does not replace belief in the future resurrection. Believers will rise again with immortal bodies, when this mortal tent is exchanged for an immortal body (2 Cor 5:1-4; Rom 8:11). Paul stresses the spiritual nature of the resurrection body in order to note that "flesh and blood cannot inherit the kingdom of God" (1 Cor 15:50), or the kingdom is not the extension of human striving or evolution. Only at God's act of redeeming the body at resurrection do we cease waiting for our adoption as children of God (Rom 8:23). Yet, the fact that death cannot sever our relationship to Christ or occurs in him implies that deceased believers continue to exist somehow "in Christ," even before their future resurrection.

For Paul, death is thus not a natural part of life as God intended it. It is the final enemy to be defeated. It has to be transformed by being brought into relation to the crucified and risen Christ. Though Paul assumed that the risen Christ has conquered death for us all (and we all already redefine it as now *in Christ*), there is also a sense in which death as an enemy must still be overcome. We still die and grieve. We still groan for liberty from "this body that is subject to death" (Rom 7:24; cf. 8:23-25). In Paul's own sketch of his eschatology, he notes that Christ "must reign until he has put all his enemies under his feet. The last enemy to be destroyed is death" (1 Cor 15:25-26). After the last enemy is subjected to Christ by the Father, Christ then submits all to the Father so that God "may be all in all" (15:28). As the Father handed lordship over to the Son to fulfill the defeat of death, after the final victory, the Son hands lordship back to the Father. As the Father glorified the Son, the Son glorifies the Father.

Paul is insistent that the blazing glory of future resurrection not blind believers to the reality of the cross as the path to glory: "Now if we are children, then we are heirs — heirs of God and co-heirs with Christ, if indeed we share in his sufferings, in order that we may also share in his glory" (Rom 8:17). Paul wanted to know Christ personally in "the power of his resurrection and participation in his sufferings, becoming like him in his death and so, somehow, attaining to the resurrection from the dead" (Phil 3:10-11). It is not that suffering causes one to be worthy of resurrection; rather, the future glory grants one the power and courage of endurance in the present hardship. Enduring hardship courageously in this way helps one be faithful unto the end. Knowing Christ richly is impossible unless participation in both his sacrifice and in his glory is

Eschatology

involved, since Christ is both the Crucified *and* Risen One. Paul was crucified with Christ and lives according to the Son's faithfulness to the Father (Gal 2:20). Paul's entire life experience on the mission field of both hardship and victory is interpreted in the light of his living participation in the crucified and risen Christ. Those who sought to have eschatological glory without the self-giving and hardship of the way of the cross were rejected by Paul as gravely in error (1 Cor 4:8-13).

Life participation in the crucified and risen Christ occurs for Paul in the Spirit. Eschatological existence for Paul is also pneumatological existence. The love of Christ, from which we can never be separated, is imparted to us by the Spirit within, which is why hope will never put us to shame (Rom 5:5). The Spirit is the down payment of future redemption and the guarantee of future glory (Eph 1:13-14; cf. 2 Cor 1:22; 5:5). We are sealed for the future day of redemption by the Spirit (Eph 4:30). The Spirit is thus the great promise of the Christian life (Gal 3:14; Eph 1:13). The kingdom of God is currently experienced in the realm of the Spirit in joy, peace, and righteousness (Rom 14:17). We are the firstfruits of the future harvest through the sanctifying work of the Spirit (2 Thess 2:13). Yet, even having the firstfruits of the Spirit does not preclude weakness and groaning for future redemption (Rom 8:23). The Spirit helps us in our weakness (8:26). The spiritual gifts edify us as we see through a glass dimly (1 Cor 12–14). The church by the Spirit is "being built together to become a dwelling in which God lives by his Spirit" (Eph 2:22), growing "to become in every respect the mature body of him who is the head, that is, Christ" (4:15b). We wait patiently for future liberty and in the meantime "overflow with hope by the power of the Holy Spirit" (Rom 15:13). The resurrected body is called a body of the Spirit, a pneumatic body (1 Cor 15:44). Indeed, if we sow by the Spirit in following the Spirit's leading by bearing spiritual fruit, we will "from the Spirit reap eternal life" (Gal 6:8). In the meantime, the rise of spiritual fruit in us (love, joy, peace, forbearance, kindness, goodness, faithfulness, gentleness, and self-control) are the means by which we "keep step with the Spirit" (5:22-25) in our journey toward eschatological fulfillment.

Paul's understanding of the end involves a day of judgment, as well as salvation at the return of Christ. But first the rebellion must occur, along with the appearance of a "man of lawlessness" who is doomed to destruction because he opposes God and exalts himself above "everything that is called God or is worshipped," setting himself up in God's temple and claiming to be God (2 Thess 2:3-4). The secret power of lawlessness is already at work in the world but will appear with deceptive consequences at the end. In concert with Satan, using signs and wonders, the man of lawlessness will deceive those who are perishing (2:7-11). This sketchy and enigmatic outline of events is augmented positively by the conviction that the returning Christ "will come down from heaven, with a loud command, with the voice of the archangel and with the trumpet call of God, and the dead in Christ will rise first." At that time, those "who are still alive and are left will be caught up together with them in the clouds to meet the Lord in the air. And so we will be with the Lord forever" (1 Thess 4:16-17). The vindicated and risen Christ returns triumphantly over the opposition in order to vindicate through resurrection and ascension those who belong to him. This taking up of the saints into the clouds is no escape from the world, for the entire cosmos will be transformed along with the raised dead. As Paul notes, "The creation itself will be liberated from its bondage to decay and brought into the freedom and glory of the children of God" (Rom 8:21). We do not await escaping the world; rather, we hope for a new world to come and strive to be used of God to bring about signs of that coming liberty in the here and now through prayer and acts of justice and love.

That liberty will involve the removal of bondage to evil forces. For Paul, the day of salvation is also a day of judgment. God will judge people's secrets through Jesus Christ (Rom 2:16) as a payment for one's deeds (2:6). Salvation cannot be earned, since it is a gift granted to us out of the excessive abundance of God's grace. For Paul, the wrath of God, however, is earned as "wages," while salvation is not wages but a gift: "the wages of sin is death, but the gift of God is salvation through Jesus Christ our Lord" (6:23). Wrath will rest on Jew and Gentile alike if they disbelieve and fall short of God's eschatological glory (3:22-23). Israel has stumbled but in God's eschatological plan will not utterly fall (11:11). Reconciled with Gentile believers in the Messiah, "All Israel will be saved" (11:26). This is more than a missionary goal for Paul; it is an apocalyptic mystery. Even those who receive the free gift of salvation in Christ will have their works "revealed by fire" to bring them to light by testing their quality, especially as to whether or not they have built appropriately on the foundation that is Christ. If the work survives, it will be rewarded; if not, it will be burned up, the meaning of it nullified. If the works are consumed, "the builder will suffer loss but yet will be saved — even though only as one escaping through the flames" (1 Cor 3:15).

Paul writes with a sense of urgency about such matters, for he is convinced that the time of Christ's return is near: "The hour has already come for you to wake up from your slumber, because our salvation is nearer now than when we first believed" (Rom 13:11). Indeed, "the night is nearly over; the day is almost here" (13:12). The nearness of Christ's return should cause the saints to strive for holiness, clothing themselves with Christ and not gratifying the desires of the flesh (13:14). Yet, the nearness of Christ's return does not cause anarchy or the abandonment of life in this age. The saints are to occupy until

Christ comes, respecting human governments and paying taxes (13:1-7), as well as working for an honest wage (2 Thess 3:9-11). As in the Johannine tradition, the nearness of Christ's return increases one's passion to be a witness of Christ in the world, but it does not cause one to leave the world.

Other New Testament Voices

In Hebrews, Jesus became flesh in order to "taste death for everyone" so as to free them from fear of death. The devil is said to have the power of death and to keep his subjects in slavery through the fear of death. But Christ destroys the devil and sets his former subjects free from the slavery to fear (Heb 2:9, 14-15). His resurrection qualifies him to be the eternal high priest, since he attained this office "not on the basis of a regulation as to his ancestry but on the basis of the power of an indestructible life" (7:16). "He became the source of eternal salvation for all who obey him" (5:9). The resurrection shows his sacrifice to be eschatological in significance, for "by one sacrifice he has made perfect forever those who are being made holy" (10:14). His high priestly ministry was heavenly and eschatological, not earthly and bound by the limitations of time. After his ascension, he "sat down at the right hand of the throne of the Majesty in heaven . . . the true tabernacle set up by the Lord, not by a mere human being" (8:1-2). The earthly sanctuary of ancient Judaism was but an earthly shadow of the one established forever in heaven (8:5). Hebrews does not advocate an eschatology that forsakes the earth for heaven, for Christ who came to bear the sins of many is coming again "to bring salvation to those who are waiting for him" (9:28). His return will be victorious, since he presently waits "to make his enemies his footstool" (10:13). It is a "dreadful thing to fall into the hands of a living God" (10:31). Those who long for his return need to be patient,

> In just a little while,
>   he who is coming will come
>   and will not delay. (10:37)

Faith is thus eschatological, for through it we have "confidence in what we hope for" (11:1). By faith Abraham journeyed to the promised land like a stranger in a foreign country, "looking forward to the city with foundations, whose architect and builder is God" (11:10). All of the saints of old sacrificed greatly looking for the heavenly city, but none of them received it, "since God had planned something better for us so that only together with us would they be made perfect" (11:40). The eschatological heavenly city completes the saints of old in communion with all of the saints who later followed their example and inherited the eternal benefits of following Christ as the high priest. In our journey forward surrounded by a cloud of witnesses, we need to fix our eyes on Jesus, "the pioneer and perfecter of our faith" (12:1-2). Hebrews implores us to praise God for the coming kingdom, which will last forever as the sure foundation of this faith: "Therefore, since we are receiving a kingdom that cannot be shaken, let us be thankful, and so worship God acceptably with reverence and awe, for our God is a consuming fire" (12:28-29).

Salvation is eschatological in 1 Peter as well, since God in his great mercy "has given us new birth into a living hope through the resurrection of Jesus Christ from the dead, and into an inheritance that can never perish, spoil or fade" (1 Pet 1:3-4). This inheritance is preserved in heaven for the saints as they themselves "through faith are shielded by God's power until the coming of the salvation that is ready to be revealed in the last time" (1:5). For this reason, the saints rejoice even in great trials, knowing that the refinement of their faith will "result in praise, glory and honor when Jesus Christ is revealed" (1:7). Peter wrote to those who suffer: "Rejoice inasmuch as you participate in the sufferings of Christ, so that you may be overjoyed when his glory is revealed" (4:13). Those who suffer persecution should endure patiently, for "the Lord knows how to rescue the godly from trials and to hold the unrighteous for punishment on the day of judgment" (2 Pet 2:9).

In the light of their fervent hope, the saints are to struggle against the sin that wages war against their souls, living "such good lives among the pagans that, though they accuse you of doing wrong, they may see your good deeds and glorify God on the day he visits us" (1 Pet 2:12). Those who exercise leadership in the churches need to be servant leaders so that, when Christ the shepherd appears, they will "receive the crown of glory that will never fade away" (5:4). The risks are great, since the devil prowls as a roaring lion "looking for someone to devour" (5:8). But the divine power "has given us everything we need for a godly life through our knowledge of him who called us by his own glory and goodness" (2 Pet 1:3). We can "participate in the divine nature, having escaped the corruption in the world caused by evil desires" (1:4).

The attainment of self-control, perseverance, and mutual affection allows one to confirm one's election and avoid stumbling, receiving "a rich welcome into the eternal kingdom of our Lord and Savior Jesus Christ" (2 Pet 1:11). God is able to keep us from stumbling and to present us "before his glorious presence without fault and with great joy" (Jude 24). One is not to grow discouraged by the delay in the Lord's coming, for "with the Lord a day is like a thousand years, and a thousand years like a day" (2 Pet 3:8). The Lord is not slow in fulfilling promises, only patient in waiting on others to repent (3:9). But the Lord is coming in a way that is unexpected, like a thief. At that time, "the heavens will disappear with a roar; the elements will be destroyed by fire, and the earth and everything done in it will be laid bare" (3:10b). Since everything will be exposed and pass in this way, what sort of people ought we to be? Living holy and godly lives as we wait for the Day of the Lord "and speed its coming" (3:12). By holding fast to the promises, we look forward to the new heavens and new earth, in which righteousness dwells (3:13). Only that which is righteous will last. Everything else will be laid bare and destroyed.

Conclusion

To conclude, the NT highlights several eschatological themes. The God of Scripture is defined as the self-giving God who is involved at every point of the eschatological drama of salvation. This is the God who was, is, and is to come. The Creator sends Jesus Christ into the world to redeem the world by dying and rising again, and the Holy Spirit is sent to perfect salvation and to bear witness to the Son. All of God's eschatological purposes of all times take place within this Trinitarian framework. This drama describes the victory of God's eschatological purposes within the triune God's loving embrace of creation. These purposes are challenged at every point by the opposition of evil agents, but God's purposes are sure to prevail, have prevailed, and are prevailing already. The kingdom, or reign, of God that is yet to come is felt already as believers are drawn into God's life-transforming power. Through the Spirit of life, the death and resurrection of Christ have brought the future salvation into the present and set in motion the coming fulfillment. Those drawn into this life by faith are shaped fundamentally by it. Nothing can separate them from the love of God grasped in Christ; they die and rise *in him*. The final triumph comes at Christ's return, at which time Christ reigns over this earth and then turns the earth into the transformed place of his dwelling. The raising of the dead then leads to the new heaven and new earth, in which righteousness dwells.

Revelation and Systematic Theology

God reigns. The story of victory that culminates at the final triumph cannot be confined to "end times." We are in fact no longer accustomed to speaking of eschatology merely as "end times." Eschatology can no longer serve as nothing more than the closing chapter of one's understanding of history or of a theological system. The reason does not lie in a rejection of any connection between eschatology and the "end." Clearly, eschatology tends to highlight the end, or the ultimate fulfillment of God's purposes for history or for creation. The reason lies more substantially in the fact that eschatology is not primarily about times or events but rather about the God who takes creation up into the divine embrace through Christ and by the Spirit in such a way that creation is invited and empowered to participate. This embrace thus has a history and involves a struggle. Moreover, eschatology by implication is not a mere description of the end but informs history as a whole and the entirety of the various loci of the Christian faith. In other words, we have become aware in contemporary theological discussion that how everything ends influences the beginning and the middle as well. Eschatology casts its radiant light on the whole of Christian faith, directing it forward in an undying hope for the fulfillment of God's purposes for creation and granting an ever more powerful foretaste of this fulfillment that God arrives to bring about. Jürgen Moltmann's classic study *Theology of Hope* helped us all to view hope as part of the very fabric of Christian faith. His conclusion has now become widely accepted: "Eschatology is not just one element of Christianity, but it is the medium of Christian faith as such, the key in which everything else is set, the glow that suffuses everything here in the dawn of an expected new day."[270]

The Necessity of Eschatology

Christian eschatology deals fundamentally with hope, which is arguably widely desired in the world. The failures, tragedies, and injustices of history call for some kind of hope that something will occur to set things right and make the struggle for justice or salvation worthwhile. Revelation implies that all of creation yearns for salvation (5:13). Paul also spoke of the creation as under slavery, implicitly awaiting and groaning for final liberty (Rom 8:22). In Acts, Paul proclaims that God created all nations and determined their unique journeys so that they would seek after God (Acts 17:26-27). If humanity implicitly yearns for hope, it also implicitly fears or dreads its opposite, the dissolution of all hope. We have become accustomed to living with apocalyptic angst in our postnuclear age, in which we have become aware of other possibilities of global disaster such as global warming. Hope seems everywhere to be an essential ingredient of the human quest. But wherein is hope to be found?

The modern myth of progress has certainly drawn strength and relevance from the urgency of this question. Modernity has justifiably been character-

---

270. Jürgen Moltmann, *Theology of Hope* (Minneapolis: Fortress Press, 1993), 16.

ized as a celebration of the potential of human reason, science, and technology to take the human race beyond the reach of ignorance, war, disease, poverty, injustice, and even death itself. Utopian dreams of higher forms of consciousness and technology that will eventually grant humanity vast powers over the cosmos and human destiny have been nurtured in different ways. For example, physicist Michio Kaku writes and speaks tantalizingly of a "Type III civilization" at the horizon of human evolution, in which humanity might become "truly immortal." At this stage people could, through science and technology, achieve near-limitless power over the cosmos:

> They have exhausted the power of a single star, and have reached for other star systems. No natural catastrophe known to science is capable of destroying a Type III civilization. Faced with a neighboring supernova, it would have several alternatives, such as altering the evolution of a dying red giant star which is about to explode, or leaving this particular star system and terraforming a nearby planetary system.[271]

In line with this dream, many of us have been entertained by the *Star Trek* vision of the starship *Enterprise* and its mission to lead a potentially intergalactic federation to cosmic peace and justice. People dream of the day when disease and aging itself may be defeated. Indeed, those who drink from the great optimism of the Enlightenment see themselves as part of "the process of the world's inherent tendency toward the goal of human perfection and domination of the world."[272]

This is not to deny that humanity may very well experience significant moral and technological progress, and there is certainly a place for Christians and all people of good will to strive for it. But if history has taught us anything, it is that every step forward opens up new dangers and risks of tragedy and human depravity. In tension with a contagious optimism, the modern spirit has also interestingly cast its characteristic suspicion upon such dreams with equally compelling visions of human hubris, folly, and destruction. Science fiction is also haunted by apocalyptic visions of a dark and dismal future. The proposed dream of future perfection gives way to nightmares of final destruction. Such human nightmares are not without a basis in reality. The technology that has promised and brought so much hope to our contemporary world has

---

271. Mikio Kaku, "The Physics of Extraterrestrial Civilizations: How Advanced Could They Possibly Be?" http://mkaku.org/home/?page_id=246.

272. Trevor A. Hart and Richard Bauckham, *Hope against Hope: Christian Eschatology at the Turn of the Millennium* (Grand Rapids: Eerdmans, 1999), 12.

carried with it enormous risks that are now threatening us with oppressive and destructive possibilities. In fact, it "seems impossible to control the technological and economic juggernaut which seems now to be hurtling without a driver toward Armageddon."[273] The postmodern sensitivity to the dark side of the modern myth of progress as bent toward violence and destruction grows out from this modernist suspicion, chastising the naively optimistic side of the modern spirit. But what has postmodernism offered in its place? Wherein is there real hope to be found?

May we dream of such progress that the dangers of human depravity or tragedy are eventually overcome? Even if this dream of progress is realized one day, how is history thereby redeemed? How are justice and healing achieved for the countless souls who have been left out of the path to progress or even crushed beneath its wheels during the centuries leading up to the eventual utopia? What about the many who were marginalized by history, dumped within its many graves and forgotten? Even with regard to those who might have played a memorable role in the journey forward, is the only redemption available to them an honorable mention when those who occupy the future utopia celebrate the past? Are these remembered souls only to be viewed analogously as the ants that have sacrificed themselves in the building of a bridge to victory? Without denigrating the value of celebrating those who have left us a meaningful historical legacy, is such memory adequate for granting them a share in the kingdom to come? Why should they be left out simply because they were born too soon? Moreover, anything short of immortality will destine those who occupy the future utopia to be snatched from it all too soon as well.

The eschatology of Revelation speaks meaningfully to such troubling questions and inevitabilities. It features prominently the voices of those whose lives have been unjustly cut short in the battle for the victory of the kingdom of God over the agents of evil and oppression (Rev 6:9-11). Not only are these persons not forgotten, not only are their voices remembered, they continue to speak for themselves and to yearn for a fulfillment that they are sure to enjoy and, indeed, enjoy already. The passage of time has not left them in the graves of forgetfulness or stopped their right to address God, reducing them to the list of honorable mentions within the ever-more-dim annals of history. They are not left out. They are not cast into the darkness and alienation of Hades. The dragon has no power over them, cannot separate them from the Creator or their Lord. They continue to participate in the unfolding drama toward victory from the unbreakable bond that they have in the Spirit with the crucified and risen Christ, with the Creator of life, and with all those who have a share in God's

---

273. Hart and Bauckham, *Hope against Hope*, 17.

eternal salvation. What Revelation shows us, what the eschatology of the book reveals, is that "history cries out for redemption, and progress cannot provide it."[274] The eschatology of Revelation is needed because it opens redemption to all of history (to all peoples of all times), to the entire groaning creation from beginning to end. The God of Revelation is not only the God of a futuristic utopia but the living God of all times, who was, is, and is to come, the living God, who delivers creation from the crushing wheel of time and from the purposes of the dragon.

To incorporate a Pauline phrase at this point, "Neither death nor life . . . will be able to separate us from the love of God that is in Christ Jesus our Lord" (Rom 8:38-39). For Revelation or the NT, death is not a natural part of life. As Oscar Cullmann has shown, death in the NT is the final enemy of life.[275] God finally conquers it in order to liberate humanity and the entire creation (in all times and places) from its devastation and from the Abyss that lies behind its deepest threat. The good news is that death cannot separate us from the love of God in Christ. It cannot sever the bond that God has made with creation. By the grace of God, we "die in the Lord" (Rev. 14:13). To die *in the Lord* is to die within the inseparable bond that Christ has with his bride. Nothing can separate us from that bond. The dead still have their being in Christ. They still commune in him and express their yearnings to him. They journey with him toward the fulfillment of the kingdom of God. They will return with him to participate in the triumph of Christ's return. They will reign with him over the time of peace. They will walk by his light in the heavenly city, along with the kings of the nations. Nothing can take them from his hand.

The Question of Apocalyptic

Salvation comes by way of resurrection and new heavens and new earth. The saints conquer only by the blood of the Lamb, only by dying and rising with him and serving the redemptive purposes enacted through him. Eschatology is determined by the crucified and risen Lamb, which means that the kingdom of God cannot be merely the result of human progress. Such progress will never reach the promised land of immortality, for flesh and blood cannot inherit the kingdom of God. One can be born into it only by the God who raised the slain Lamb from the dead. The kingdom is not something of our own making. It can

---

274. Hart and Bauckham, *Hope against Hope*, 24.
275. Oscar Cullmann, *Immortality of the Soul or Resurrection of the Dead? The Witness of the New Testament* (Eugene, OR: Wipf & Stock, 2000).

result only from God's acts of self-giving, which take creation up into the divine embrace from the beginning to the end of the story of creation. Only then is real salvation possible: past, present, and future. We can then understand why the significance of the ultimate victory does not eclipse the participation of the past and the present in this final glory. We can comprehend why this triumph comes to us as a gift at every moment of time and is open to all peoples of all times, from those who are most visible to human remembering to those least visible and forgotten. They are not invisible or forgotten by God.

The reality of the kingdom of God as a gift of God is at the core of apocalyptic eschatology. Apocalypticism accents the coming of the kingdom as a divine action from above that brings a decisive end to human history and introduces something radically new. Any illusion that final salvation or justice can grow out from the historical present or from human strivings is to be judged as foolish and misdirected. As Paul Hanson has noted, apocalyptic eschatology gained prominence in Israel during the exile as the nation sought to come to terms with frustrated prophetic hopes for history. The disparity between the situation of exile and prophetic hopes tended to shift attention to a future kingdom to be fulfilled supernaturally on the ashes of human failure and tragedy. The question must be asked in this light as to whether apocalypticism does not lead communities devoted to it to a dualism between history and the kingdom of God, with the result that the prophetic witness or responsibility to history to which humanity is called in the here and now is discouraged. Martin Buber, for example, sharply criticized apocalyptic eschatology for removing from the people of God their prophetic responsibility for history in ongoing conversation with God, something he termed "prophetic reciprocity." He accused apocalyptic eschatology of eliminating this reciprocity and for being deterministic, as though all things are "inescapably destined." All one has to do within this determinism is to decipher the mysteries of the future through biblical texts that are made to function as a script of what will soon come to pass. One is otherwise reduced to passivity and resignation. The conviction that history is soon to come to an end prevents the kind of long-range planning and work necessary for dramatic turns and constructive change in the world of God's creation. The tendency is simply to wait for God to bring all things to an end so as to usher in the kingdom supernaturally from above. Creation and history are abandoned, and one simply waits for them to be replaced by something entirely new and different. Interestingly, Buber lays the responsibility for the reemergence of this Jewish apocalyptic eschatology in the world on the shoulders of Jesus and the witness of the NT. In making this charge, Buber contrasts the spirit of apocalyptic that arises through Jesus with that of the witness of the prophets:

Eschatology

After Jesus, and in like manner his emissaries had sounded the call afresh, the apocalyptics and their associates proceeded to disclose that there is no turning and no new direction in the destiny of the world that can issue from the turning. But the depths of history which are continually at work to rejuvenate creation, are in league with the prophets.[276]

Buber's critique needs to be taken seriously, since one could easily amass anecdotal evidence for escapist tendencies among Christian groups that favor the apocalyptic texts of Scripture in their understanding of the kingdom of God and its triumph in the world. The rapture doctrine, for example, has tended to replace the responsibility for social justice and renewal with a vision of widespread and impending global cataclysm and a desire to join the righteous elite in a quick escape from it all. The attempt to criticize utopian dreams as unrealistic expressions of human hubris has unfortunately made many vulnerable to the opposite quietist error of shirking their God-given stewardship of creation and historical destiny. There is a sharp tension detectable between apocalyptic doom and prophetic hope for renewal when one considers the negative possibilities of an eschatology devoted to a near-apocalyptic end to all things.

In response to Buber, however, one could point out, as did Leon Morris, that biblical apocalypticism (including that of the NT) does not preclude prophetic hopes for history.[277] As we saw in Revelation, though the kingdom comes in judgment upon the nations and their foolish efforts to build their own *polis,* the Spirit of prophecy implies that an alternative *polis* was open to human participation all along in God's salvific deeds, especially in the crucified and risen Christ and the bestowal of the Spirit. When God's *polis* comes, it will draw into it the splendor of the nations (Rev 21:24). Though the nations are judged in Revelation, they are also drawn into the kingdom of God quite dramatically, to the point where it seems at the end that God's grace has indeed converted the nations (15:4; 21:24-26). Though the kingdom introduces something miraculously new (resurrection and new heavens and new earth), the nations that walk in this newness bring their own splendor into it (21:24). This splendor is implicitly a gift from God as well, but one could well imagine that, in unique ways, it has also become their own as they have willfully cultivated it in response to God. Otherwise, it would not be *their* splendor. Moreover, the "critical function" of apocalyptic eschatology such as we find in Revelation rightly helps us to avoid any illusion that the kingdom of God can arise from

---

276. Martin Buber, "Prophecy, Apocalyptic, Historical Hour," in *On the Bible: Eighteen Studies* (Syracuse, NY: Syracuse University Press, 2000), 187.

277. Leon Morris, *Apocalyptic* (Grand Rapids: Eerdmans, 1972).

human efforts.[278] Again, apocalyptic in Revelation means that eschatology is determined by the crucified and risen Lamb. Moltmann notes eloquently in this regard: "Apocalypticism then means that the whole creation participates in Christ's tribulation and in the light of the cross is manifested in its forsakenness and havoc, so that it may be drawn into the cosmic resurrection and new creation."[279] This apocalyptic insight was the cradle of early Christianity (Käsemann) but not necessarily at the cost of prophetic responsibility for history, as Buber wrongly concludes. In Revelation, the apocalyptic and the prophetic are joined in the Spirit of the crucified and risen Christ.

In terms of Revelation, God acts to bring the kingdom, but human action is granted significance as well. While waiting for God, the saints are consequently called to both patience and obedient action in the direction of the fulfillment of God's will on earth. For example, 14:12 notes that "this calls for patient endurance on the part of the saints who obey God's commandments and remain faithful to Jesus." The following verse adds that they will rest one day from their labor, for their deeds will follow them (14:13b). They endure as they both wait on God and act in obedience to God's will. They will rest, but their deeds remain significant. This creative tension between waiting and action depicts an active waiting and a patient action. It depicts an eschatological salvation that belongs to God but that also invites and grants significance to human participation. Moreover, in Revelation God acts in history in ways fundamentally determined by the divine will but also in ways that respond to those who cry out for justice. One is reminded of how the divine response to the martyred saints in chapter 6 brings redemptive judgment upon the nations. Though God's overall goal of salvation for the nations remains unaltered, the path to that goal involves the justice called for by the martyrs. This reciprocity is also evident when the nations come into the heavenly city to walk by the light of the Lamb and to bring their own splendor into the city as well (21:24). Other NT voices may be cited in support of this reciprocity. One is reminded of 2 Pet 3:12, which refers to saints who "look forward to the day of God and speed its coming." This text does not imply that humans control the arrival of the future, but it does indicate that God brings the arrival in a way that responds to graced human action. Certainly one cannot identify God's kingdom with human actions, but neither can one radically separate the two. Human actions are by God's grace both a sign and an instrument of the coming kingdom in the world.

---

278. See Wolfhart Pannenberg, "Constructive and Critical Functions of Christian Eschatology," *HTR* 77 (1984): 119-39.

279. Jürgen Moltmann, *The Coming of God: Christian Eschatology* (Minneapolis: Fortress Press, 2004), 233.

Since apocalypticism tends to depict salvation as a wholly future reality, the presence of salvation in Revelation as a reality in which people can participate in history is relevant to this discussion as well. Though the kingdom is not the result of historical progress in Revelation, neither is it an eternal "now" that makes history insignificant as the arena of human existence and action. God acts in history in ways that are contextualized in faithful lives and communities. Such historical realities and moments then anticipate and lead to a future fulfillment. This fulfillment may also be said to draw those unique realities and moments forward so as to open up participation in that which is to come.

We may try to describe this divine-human interaction more precisely. Moltmann uses the concept of *conversion* to describe the relationship between the coming of God and the history of creation in its response to God. The kingdom does not just "break in" or interrupt the flow of history; rather more positively, it opens up history to new possibilities. He writes, "The future-made-present creates new conditions for possibilities in history. Mere interruption disturbs; conversion creates new life."[280] More elaborately, Moltmann writes: "God now already sets present and past in the light of his eschatological arrival which means the establishment of his eternal kingdom, and his indwelling in the creation renewed for that indwelling."[281] In fact, divine indwelling can be seen as the chief goal of eschatology and the reason why all things must be transformed, namely, to receive God.[282] God journeys with people through time toward final transformation, in which death is ultimately defeated by overwhelming life. This means that this future fulfillment is already "God's mode of being in history. The power of the future is his power in time. His eternity is not timeless simultaneity; it is the power of his future over every historical time."[283] The kingdom is not identifiable with historical progress, for in line with the crucified and risen Lamb, creation in its history must die to be reborn. But neither is the kingdom detached from history. It converts or transforms it by opening it up to participation in that which is to come. Such transformation is possible only through the divine presence. Through history, the present God opens up an experience of God's future arrival in glory. This power made possible by God's presence breaks open every moment in history beyond creaturely limits so as to make possible participation in something transcendent, something yet to come. As N. T. Wright notes concerning Rev 5, we may participate in a cosmic exaltation of the Lamb that is already occurring in some sense now in anticipation of the end.[284]

---

280. Moltmann, *The Coming of God*, 22.
281. Moltmann, *The Coming of God*, 23.
282. This is the major thesis of my *Justified in the Spirit*.
283. Moltmann, *The Coming of God*, 24.
284. N. T. Wright, "Revelation and Christian Hope: Political Implications of the Revelation

The thousand-year reign is not the end but will precede the final new creation. Interpretations of the millennial kingdom have at times been put forward from political or ecclesiastical efforts at domination out of self-serving purposes.[285] The millennium in Revelation, however, serves the reign of the crucified and risen Lamb. The saints reign only in service to him, in *his* justice and liberty. This reign is significant in that it takes place over *this* earth and in fulfillment of human history, before the final transformation of all things. It may thus be seen as a Sabbath rest for creation before the final transformation and another opportunity for the nations to repent. It brings to fulfillment the prophetic hopes for history but in a way that is determined by God and that sets the stage for the final transformation as the creation is reborn in order to receive the heavenly city. The goal is not escaping this world for heaven but, rather, a new world that receives God's heavenly presence and will on earth.[286] The future heavenly city is a reality to which the Spirit of prophecy opens John and the churches in their present moments in ways that introduce something new into those moments not otherwise possible, namely, a living witness to the kingdom of God. Apocalypticism and prophetic witness become mutually defining categories.

The Delay of Christ's Coming

Does the nearness of the end assumed in Revelation leave out adequate space for the prophetic witness to the kingdom in history? There is little question but that the final conflict and its resolution in history are near in Revelation. The urgency of the moment is signaled from the very first verse: "The revelation from Jesus Christ, which God gave him to show his servants what must soon take place. He made it known by sending his angel to his servant John" (1:1). That Christ is coming "soon" is mentioned in several other places in the book (3:11; 22:7, 12, 20). The dragon cast to earth knows that his time is short (12:12). Does this assumption exclude the significance of history as the arena of prophetic witness? Moreover, roughly two millennia have passed since the announcement of Christ's soon return was made. Is this announcement now null and void? Has too much time passed for the urgency of the moment to still be felt in our reading of the text?

In answer to the first question, it is apparent that the shortness of time

---

to John," in *Revelation and the Politics of Interpretation* (ed. Richard B. Hays; Waco, TX: Baylor University Press, 2012), 114.

285. See Moltmann, *The Coming of God*, 159-91.
286. Wright, "Revelation and Christian Hope," 110-14.

in Revelation does not nullify the significance of the prophetic witness of the people of God to the nations. The Spirit is not the realm of escape from history but, rather, the empowerment for prophetic witness in history in testimony to the crucified and risen Lamb. The Spirit is "sent out into all the earth" (5:6). John is told that he must still "prophesy again about many peoples, nations, languages and kings" (10:11). The people of God are represented by the faithful witnesses who give their lives in witness to Christ (11:1-14). Indeed, the Spirit "is the Spirit of prophecy who bears testimony to Jesus" (19:10). All nations will come to see the justice of God's judgments and will gather to worship the Lord (15:4). Though deceived and chastised, the nations will ultimately come to walk by the light of the Lamb in the heavenly city, bringing their own splendor into it (21:24). Multitudes from all nations will come out of the time of trial worshipping God (7:9-14).

All of this indicates that, before the end arrives, a missional history is to run its course that is to be dominated by the prophetic witness of God's people as empowered by the Spirit of Christ. The urgency of the moment as indicated by the message that the time is short is not meant to result in passive resignation. To the contrary, it inspires repentance, a fiery passion to join in God's desire to bless the nations, a holy resistance to the evil forces at work in the world, and an empowered witness to all peoples of the goodness of God in Christ. There is also the assumption that the work of God among the nations does not end with the coming of Christ. There is a millennium of peace intended to grant the nations another chance to recognize the justice and liberty of God's reign (ch. 20), and even after the onset of the new heavens and new earth, there are leaves for the healing of the nations (22:2). If one defines human history ultimately as a journey with God the Creator, history does not really come to an end with the coming of Christ or the arrival of the heavenly city. It is reborn in order to be taken up into God's eternity.

Considering the vastness of time indicated by Revelation in which the kingdom of God is to do its work, we are required by the text to view the urgency of the moment indicated by the shortness of time in a new light. The time is short until what? Until the narrative of end-time events has its beginning? Certainly the text implies that God is already taking matters into God's own hands when it comes to the presence of the kingdom in power. But the indication is also that the "shortness" of time is even more tellingly a quality of experience rather than simply a question of duration. The story of the coming conflict and triumph challenges the community of faith to yearn for the coming of Christ (22:20) as near at hand at every moment. The nearness of Christ's return is not the result of a scientific calculation or certainty but rather the result of a longing of a bride for her groom and for the justice of the kingdom. While yearning for Christ, believers are to feel already the winds of conflict, struggle, and change on the immediate horizon and to confront each moment as an arena of decision related to the final conflict and victory. The result is not passive resignation but loving action. The community is urged to have patience and to endure but also to engage in the prophetic witness that will be integral to the coming triumph.

The Ultimate Embrace

As implied by the discussion above, the rhetoric of Revelation concerning the destiny of the nations seems conflicted. On the one hand, judgment upon the nations seems widespread and devastating. They are angry at God's judgments (11:18) and will suffer the consequences of drinking the "maddening wine" of Babylon's idolatry (14:8), for their cities will collapse (16:19). The waters upon which the prostitute sits are the "peoples, multitudes, nations and languages" (17:15), for she will lead all nations astray (18:23). At the Lord's return, a sharp sword proceeds from his mouth to "strike down the nations" (19:15). When the nations are deceived again during the reign of peace, their rebellion and destruction involve numbers that are to be compared to the sands of the seashore (20:8). Yet, there is another side to this picture. Christ will rule the nations (12:5) or be their king (15:3). The numbers from all nations that will emerge from the time of trial as faithful to Jesus will also represent a number too staggering in size to count (7:9). There will be not only a winepress but a harvest (14:14-20). In fact, the text tells us that "all nations will come and worship before you, for your righteous acts have been revealed" (15:4). Christ strikes down the nations in 19:15, not to annihilate them, but in order to rule them in justice and peace! They reappear in the reign of peace in the following chapter, specifically with the promise that they will not be allowed to be deceived throughout the duration of Christ's reign on the earth (20:3). Even after the nations are tested and deceived again at the conclusion of Christ's reign and are judged, they reappear in the heavenly city walking by the light of the Lamb and bringing their former splendor into the city (21:24-26). The city also contains leaves for their healing (22:2).

What is one to make of this stark contrast between vast judgment and vast redemption? Can both be true? Are these alternative futures dependent on the response of the nations to God and the justice of God's kingdom? Not quite. In fact, the two "alternatives" are not equal. Grace towers over judgment in Revelation. Not only is the number from the nations that emerge from the short time of trial too great to count, but the reign of peace towers in duration over the brief time of trial or chastisement. It seems therefore that Revelation is seeking to highlight the magnitude of the deception and rebellion as a backdrop for the even greater magnitude of God's grace in extending to the rebellious nations the divine embrace. Despite the harshness of judgment assumed by the book, its fundamental conviction is that many nations will come to see the justice of God's ways. They will throughout their chastisement come to see the light and will eventually walk by that light in the heavenly city. In other words, they will come not only to see the light but to be fundamentally transformed by it so that they come to embody it in their walk. They are wounded in their journey, but the heavenly city also promises healing. Their walk by the light of the Lamb is the path to healing that they will take.

Does the grace of God triumph over all of the opposition? The existence of the lake of fire as God's final, eschatological judgment seems to indicate that those who oppose the divine embrace will be allowed to do so throughout eternity (14:11). C. S. Lewis proposed that the existence of hell as an eschatological judgment is required by the divine respect for human choice. Those who choose to spend an eternity fleeing from God are allowed to do so.[287] God does not force the nations to obey. Compulsion is the means of operation for the beast. There is a sense of finality about God's eschatological judgment in chapter 20, but the open gates facing in the direction of the opposition say something profound about the endurance of the divine offer of grace (21:25; 22:14-15). The glory of the nations will be brought into these gates (21:26). Those who enter in have joined the Lamb to walk in his light. Only those who have refused to follow him are unable to enter (21:27).

The dream of heaven in Revelation revolves around the presence of the Lamb. The greatest joy of heaven is to be where Jesus is (e.g., John 14:1-3). In Christ, one dwells in the embrace of the triune God. The light of God, the light of the Lamb, and the waters of the Spirit make up the essence of the heavenly city. In contrast to this vision of heaven, dreams of heaven drawn from human fantasy often include expressions of selfish wishes and even lusts. Dreams of eternal wealth, mansions, and political power hardly reflect the values of the kingdom of God. The beautiful designs of the heavenly city reflect the glory of the divine embrace, of holiness, of justice, and of love and communion. These are the weighty matters of divine law, as well as of the gospel. These are the joys of the coming kingdom as determined by the crucified Lamb.

Uttering the Unutterable

How can one adequately bring to expression the glories of the coming kingdom? Revelation seeks to bring to expression the inexpressible. Does this mean

287. C. S. Lewis, *The Great Divorce* (New York: HarperOne, 2009).

that it is impossible to bring to expression the coming kingdom? Is glossolalia the only language that is really proper to the kingdom of God to come? Of course, speaking in tongues is a powerful indication that the coming kingdom cannot be adequately expressed in rational language drawn from this mundane existence. Yet, the challenge still exists to express the inexpressible in understandable language as well. All of Scripture is faced with this enormous task, but the challenge involved is sharpened when one seeks to bring to expression the ultimate fulfillment of the kingdom of God. The language used in Revelation to describe the coming transformation of all things, though taken from this reality as we know it, cannot be limited to such language. Certainly the coming kingdom "transcends the language of our mundane speech."[288] The language is stretched imaginatively without being reduced to empty imagination without any real point of reference. It is figurative and imaginative, but it points the readers to a fantastic transformation of the creation that can be felt already in the here and now. The language of eschatology seeks to be evocative, opening up the audience to an experience of God that grants a foretaste of the coming kingdom. It strains "our imagination to the limits, leading us to the very brink of the unimaginable, peering into the brilliant darkness beyond."[289]

Through the evocative language of Revelation, "God's future reaches back into the present and bathes it in a quite distinctive light, transfiguring it and generating alternative ways of being in it."[290] The transformation of the present is the main goal of the language of Revelation, for only then can the future salvation be experienced in the here and now. The goal is not to satisfy one's curiosity about the future but to view and experience the present in a new way, in a way that is more open to God, open to the crucified and risen Lamb, as well as the life of the Spirit. The language of Revelation seeks to do so from the very beginning of the book, where the risen Jesus is described in dazzling language borrowed from such texts as Dan 7. The crucified Lamb that is risen strains this language to its limits. All of the other descriptions of the coming transformation in Revelation partake of this ultimate challenge. The description of the risen Lamb breaches the "otherworldliness of this world which scandalizes and turns our view of the whole of reality upside down."[291] For this reason, the language of praise in Revelation is more appropriate to God's future triumph than rational or scientific description. In the blazing light of the risen Lamb, death is viewed in a different light, as are sin and the claims that challenge the promises of re-

---

288. Hart and Bauckham, *Hope against Hope*, 81.
289. Hart and Bauckham, *Hope against Hope*, 100.
290. Hart and Bauckham, *Hope against Hope*, 83.
291. Hart and Bauckham, *Hope against Hope*, 103.

demption through Christ. This world in its present course is viewed in a new light, as is the life of the church, which bears the name of Christ. Listening to the language of this book does not leave us unchanged. Nothing remains the same.

Something more than mere perspective is changed through the evocative language of this book. Blessed are those who hear the words of this book and "take to heart what is written in it" (1:3). Taking the message to heart means allowing it to affect one's worship and practice in ways that leave an impress on one's entire life and on the communities dedicated to the mission of Christ in the world. One worships in a way that anticipates the kingdom to come. One exercises stewardship over creation in a way that honors the Creator and the renewal of all things that will come at the end. One lives in relation to others in a way that anticipates the reign of the crucified Christ in the world. One fulfills one's vocation in a way that honors the mission of the prophetic Spirit among the nations.

Conclusion

Eschatology means that hope is not put to shame, because it is rooted in the Creator's faithfulness to the creation, the crucified and risen Lamb's victory, and the Spirit that pours the triumphant love of God realized in Christ into our hearts. The Father has elected to gather up all things in the crucified and risen Lamb, and the Lamb has faithfully given of his life toward this end. The Spirit creates a bond with Christ and with God that is unbreakable by the threats of death and evil. The story of this triune embrace is focused on the person of Jesus, who reflects the sovereign will of the Father for all of history, as well as the substance of the prophetic Spirit's witness. Eschatology is determined christologically and not humanistically, as that term is sometimes understood. It is humanistic only in its conformity to Christ. Eschatology cannot be the result of human progress, though the kingdom calls forth progress and takes it up into the divine fulfillment in a way that can transform it into a witness to God's justice for the world. As the story of this triune embrace, eschatology is concrete, dynamic, and evocative. It involves past, present, and future, though it moves forward and culminates at the ultimate coming of God. It shows how God takes those of the past and the present into the future fulfillment, both in time and at the end. Eschatology tells of the coming triumph in a way that can already be felt as dawning in our midst. This story thus comforts the fearful, motivates the discouraged, chastises the lazy, and counsels patience to the zealots. As the German pietists Johann and Christoph Blumhardt saw so clearly, the kingdom of God is experienced in our "waiting and hurrying" in response to it.[292] Eschatology encourages faithful obedience to the Lamb and in patient waiting in hope for the Lamb who was slain but is alive for evermore and is coming again to reign over the nations.

"Even so come quickly Lord Jesus!"

---

292. See my *Spirituality and Social Liberation: The Message of the Blumhardts in the Light of Wuerttemberg Pietism* (Metuchen, NJ: Scarecrow Press, 1991).

Bibliography

Alexander, Kimberly. *Pentecostal Healing: Models in Theology and Practice*. JPTS 29. Blandford Forum, UK: Deo Publishing, 2006.
Allo, Ernst-Bernard. *Saint Jean: L'Apocalypse*. Paris: J. Gabalda, 1921.
Anselm. *Cur Deus Homo,* in *Saint Anselm: Basic Writings*. Translated by S. N. Deane. LaSalle, IL: Open Court, 1968.
The Ante-Nicene Fathers. Edited by A. Roberts and J. Donaldson. Vols. 1, 7. Grand Rapids: Eerdmans, 1989.
Apocalyptic Spirituality: Treatises and Letters of Lactantius, Adso of Montier-en-Der, Joachim of Fiore, the Franciscan Spirituals, Savonarola. Translated by B. McGinn. New York: Paulist Press, 1979.
Apostolic Faith. Edited by William J. Seymour. Los Angeles, CA. 1.8 (May 1907): 2.
The Apostolic Fathers: Greek Texts and English Translations. Edited by Michael W. Holmes. Grand Rapids: Baker, 1992.
Archer, Melissa L. "'And the Seventh Angel Trumpeted': A Literary Analysis of Revelation 11:15-19." Th.M. thesis, Columbia Theological Seminary, 2006.
Aulén, Gustaf. *Christus Victor: An Historical Study of the Three Main Types of the Idea of Atonement*. Translated by A. G. Herbert. Eugene, OR: Wipf & Stock, 2003.
Aune, David E. *Revelation 1–5*. WBC 52A. Dallas: Word, 1997.
———. *Revelation 6–16*. WBC 52B. Dallas: Word, 1997.
———. *Revelation 17–22*. WBC 52C. Dallas: Word, 1998.
Bacchiocchi, Samuele. *From Sabbath to Sunday: A Historical Investigation of the Rise of Sunday Observance in Early Christianity*. Rome: Pontifical Gregorian University Press, 1977.
Ball, David. *"I Am" in John's Gospel: Literary Function, Background, and Theological Implications*. JSNTS 124. Sheffield: JSOT Press, 1996.
Barr, David L. "The Apocalypse of John as Oral Enactment." *Int* 40 (1986): 243-56.
Barth, Karl. *Christ and Adam: Man and Humanity in Romans 5*. Eugene, OR: Wipf & Stock, 2004.
———. *Church Dogmatics*. Vols. 1/1-2, 2/1-2, 3/3, 4/2-4. Edited by Geoffrey William Bromiley and Thomas Torrance. Edinburgh: T&T Clark, 1956-69.

Bibliography

———. *Protestant Theology in the Nineteenth Century: Its Background and History.* New ed. Grand Rapids: Eerdmans, 2002.
———. "Strange New World within the Bible." Pages 21-30 in *A Map of Twentieth-Century Theology: Readings from Karl Barth to Radical Pluralism.* Edited by Carl E. Braaten and Robert W. Jenson. Minneapolis: Fortress Press, 1995.
Barth, Marcus. *Israel and the Church: Contribution to a Dialogue Vital for Peace.* Richmond, VA: John Knox Press, 1969.
Bauckham, Richard. *The Climax of Prophecy: Studies on the Book of Revelation.* Edinburgh: T&T Clark, 1993.
———. *Jesus and the God of Israel: "God Crucified" and Other Studies on the New Testament's Christology of Divine Identity.* Grand Rapids: Eerdmans, 2008.
———. "Monotheism and Christology in the Gospel of John." Pages 148-68 in *Contours of Christology in the New Testament.* Edited by Richard N. Longenecker. Grand Rapids: Eerdmans, 2005.
———. *The Theology of the Book of Revelation.* Cambridge: Cambridge University Press, 1993.
Bauckham, Richard, and Trevor A. Hart. *Hope against Hope: Christian Eschatology at the Turn of the Millennium.* Grand Rapids: Eerdmans, 1999.
Beale, Gregory K. *The Book of Revelation: A Commentary on the Greek Text.* NIGNT. Grand Rapids: Eerdmans, 1999.
Beasley-Murray, George R. *Revelation.* Grand Rapids: Eerdmans, 1981.
Bede, The Venerable (Venerable Beda). *The Explanation of the Apocalypse.* Translated by E. Marshall. Oxford: James Parker, 1878.
Benson, Edward White. *The Apocalypse: An Introductory Study of the Revelation of St John the Divine.* New York: Macmillan, 1900.
Berkhof, Hendrikus. *Christian Faith: An Introduction to the Study of Faith.* Grand Rapids: Eerdmans, 1991.
Biguzzi, Giancarlo. "The Chaos of Rev 22,6-21 and Prophecy in Asia." *Biblica* 83.2 (2002): 193-210.
Blake, William. *The Complete Poetry and Prose of William Blake.* Edited by D. V. Erdman. New York: Doubleday, 1988.
Bloom, Harold. *Blake's Apocalypse: A Study in Poetic Argument.* Garden City, NY: Doubleday, 1963.
Boesak, Allan A. *Comfort and Protest: Reflections on the Apocalypse of John on Patmos.* Edinburgh: St. Andrew Press, 1987.
Bonhoeffer, Dietrich. *The Cost of Discipleship.* 7th printing. New York: Macmillan, 1976.
———. *Letters and Papers from Prison.* London: SCM Press, 1967.
Bonino, José Míguez. "Fundamental Questions in Ecclesiology." Pages 145-49 in *The Challenge of Basic Christian Communities.* Edited by Sergio Torres and John Eagleson. Maryknoll, NY: Orbis Books, 1988.
Bosch, David. *Transforming Mission: Paradigm Shifts in Theology of Mission.* Maryknoll, NY: Orbis Books, 1991.
Bowman, John W. "The Revelation to John: Its Dramatic Structure and Message." *Int* 9 (1955): 436-53.
Bredin, Mark. *Jesus, Revolutionary of Peace: A Non-violent Christology in the Book of Revelation.* Paternoster Biblical Monographs. Waynesboro, GA: Paternoster, 2003.

Brewer, Raymond R. "The Influence of Greek Drama on the Apocalypse of John." *ATR* 18 (1935-36): 74-92.
Brown, Raymond E. *The Epistles of John*. Garden City, NY: Doubleday, 1982.
Brueggemann, Walter. *Theology of the Old Testament: Testimony, Dispute, Advocacy*. Minneapolis: Augsburg/Fortress, 2005.
Bruns, J. Edgar. "The Contrasted Women of Apoc 12 and 17." *CBQ* 26 (1964): 459-63.
Buber, Martin. *Der Jude und sein Judentum*. Hessen: Melzer Verlag, 1963.
———. "Prophecy, Apocalyptic, Historical Hour." Pages 172-87 in his *On the Bible: Eighteen Studies*. Syracuse, NY: Syracuse University Press, 2000.
Bugliosi, Vincent (with Curt Gentry). *Helter Skelter: The True Story of the Manson Murders*. New York: Norton, 1974 (1994).
Bultmann, Rudolf. *Jesus Christ and Mythology*. New York: Charles Scribner's Sons, 1958.
———. *Kerygma and Myth*. New York: Harper & Row, 1953.
Caird, George B. *The Revelation of Saint John*. London: A&C Black, 1966.
Callahan, Allen D. "The Language of the Apocalypse." *HTR* 88 (1995): 453-70.
Calvin, John. *The Institutes of the Christian Religion*. 2 vols. Grand Rapids: Eerdmans, 1979.
The Cambridge Companion to Handel. Edited by D. Borrows. Cambridge: Cambridge University Press, 1997.
Charette, Blaine B. *The Theme of Recompense in Matthew's Gospel*. JSNTS 79. Sheffield: JSOT Press, 1992.
Charles, J. Daryl. "The Apocalyptic Tribute to the Lamb (Rev 5:1-14)." *JETS* 34 (1991): 461-73.
Charles, Robert Henry. *The Revelation of St. John*. Vol. 1. ICC. Edinburgh: T&T Clark, 1920.
Cheung, Paul W. "The Mystery of Revelation 17:5 and 7: A Typological Entrance." *Jian Dao* 18 (2003): 1-19.
Childs, Brevard. *Biblical Theology in Crisis*. Philadelphia: Westminster Press, 1970.
———. *Biblical Theology of the Old and New Testaments: Theological Reflection on the Christian Bible*. Minneapolis: Fortress Press, 1992.
Cloete, G. Daan. "'And I Saw a New Heaven and a New Earth, for the First . . . Were Passed Away' (Revelation 21:1-8)." *Journal of Theology for South Africa* 81 (December 1992): 55-65.
Collins, Adela Yarbro. *The Apocalypse*. NTM 22. Collegeville, MN: Michael Glazier Press, 1979.
Collins, John J. "Toward the Morphology of a Genre." *Semeia* 14 (1979): 1-20.
Colson, F. H. "Triangular Numbers in the New Testament." *JTS* 16 (1915): 67-76.
Combrink, H. J. Bernard. "Salvation in Mark." Pages 33-66 in *Salvation in the New Testament: Perspectives on Soteriology*. Edited by Jan G. van der Watt. Leiden: Brill, 2005.
Cone, James. *God of the Oppressed*. Maryknoll, NY: Orbis Books, 1997.
Court, John. *The Book of Revelation and the Johannine Apocalyptic Tradition*. JSNTS 190. Sheffield: Sheffield Academic Press, 2000.
Cullmann, Oscar. *Christology of the New Testament*. Translated by Shirlie C. Guthrie and Charles A. M. Hall. Philadelphia: Westminster, 1963.
———. *Immortality of the Soul or Resurrection of the Dead? The Witness of the New Testament*. Eugene, OR: Wipf & Stock, 2000.
———. *Peter: Disciple, Apostle, Martyr*. Translated by Floyd V. Filson. Waco, TX: Baylor University Press, 2011 (1953).
Dabney, D. Lyle. "Naming the Spirit: Towards a Pneumatology of the Cross." Pages 28-58 in

Starting with the Spirit. Edited by Stephen Pickard and Gordon Preece. Task of Theology Today 2. Hindmarsh, Australia: Australian Theological Forum, 2001.
Dahl, Nils A. "Promise and Fulfillment." Pages 121-36 in his *Studies in Paul: Theology for the Early Christian Mission*. Minneapolis: Augsburg, 1977.
Dansk, En. *The Drama of the Apocalypse*. London: T. Fisher Unwin, 1894.
Day, John. "The Origin of Armageddon." Pages 315-26 in *Crossing the Boundaries: Essays in Biblical Interpretation in Honour of Michael D. Goulder*. Edited by S. E. Porter, P. Joyce, and D. E. Orton. Leiden: Brill, 1994.
Deppermann, Klaus. *Melchior Hoffman: Social Unrest and Apocalyptic Visions in the Age of Reformation*. Edited by B. Drewery. Translated by M. Wren. Edinburgh: T&T Clark, 1987.
Deutsch, Celia. "Transformation of Symbols: The New Jerusalem in Rv 21:1–22:5." *ZNW* 78 (1987): 106-26.
Draper, Jonathan A. "The Heavenly Feast of Tabernacles: Revelation 7:1-17." *JSNT* 19 (1983): 133-47.
Dunn, James D. G. "The Question of Anti-Semitism in the New Testament Writings of the Period." Pages 177-211 in his *Jews and Christians: The Parting of the Ways, A.D. 70-135*. Grand Rapids: Eerdmans, 1999.
du Rand, John A. "Soteriology in the Apocalypse of John." Pages 465-504 in *Salvation in the New Testament: Perspectives on Soteriology*. Edited by Jan G. van der Watt. Leiden: Brill, 2005.
Eichrodt, Walther. *Theology of the Old Testament*. Vol. 2. Philadelphia: Westminster, 1972.
Ellis, E. Earle. *Eschatology in Luke*. Philadelphia: Fortress Press, 1972.
Elwell, Walter. "The Deity of Christ in the Writings of Paul." Pages 297-308 in *Current Issues in Biblical and Patristic Interpretation: Studies in Honor of Merrill C. Tenney Presented by His Former Students*. Edited by Gerald F. Hawthorne. Grand Rapids: Eerdmans, 1975.
Eusebius. *The Ecclesiastical History*. Translated by K. Lake. 2 vols. London: Heinemann, 1926-32.
Farrer, Austin M. *The Revelation of St. John the Divine*. Oxford: Clarendon, 1964.
Fee, Gordon D. *Revelation*. NCCS. Eugene, OR: Cascade Books, 2011.
Feuillet, André. "Les martyrs de l'humanité et l'Agneau égorgé: Une interprétation nouvelle de la prière des Égorgé en *Ap* 6:9-11." *NRT* 99 (1977): 189-207.
Frey, Jorge. "Erwägungen zum Verhältnis der Johannesapokalypse zu den übrigen Schriften des Corpus Johanneum." Pages 326-429 in *Die johanneische Frage: Ein Lösungsversuch*. By Martin Hengel, with J. Frey. Tübingen: J. C. B. Mohr [Paul Siebeck], 1993.
Fung, Ronald Y. K. *The Epistle to the Galatians*. NICNT. Grand Rapids: Eerdmans, 1988.
Gaechter, Paul. "The Original Sequence of Apocalypse 20–22." *Theological Studies* 10 (1949): 485-521.
Gause, R. H. *Revelation: God's Stamp of Sovereignty on History*. Cleveland, TN: Pathway, 1983.
Giblin, Charles Homer. "Revelation 11:1-13: Its Form, Function, and Textual Integration." *NTS* 30 (1984): 433-59.
Gieschen, Charles A. "Sacramental Theology in the Book of Revelation." *Concordia Theological Quarterly* 67.2 (2003): 149-74.
Girard, René. *The Scapegoat*. Baltimore, MD: Johns Hopkins University Press, 1989.
Glancy, J. A., and S. D. Moore. "How Typical a Roman Prostitute Is Revelation's 'Great Whore'?" *JBL* 130.3 (2011): 551-69.

Grubb, Nancy. *Revelations: Art of the Apocalypse*. New York: Abbeville Press, 1997.
Griffiths, J. Gwyn. *Plutarch's De Iside et Osiride*. Cambridge: University of Wales Press, 1970.
Gundry, Robert H. "The New Jerusalem: People as Place, not Place for People." *NovT* 29 (1987): 254-64.
Guthrie, Donald. *New Testament Theology: A Thematic Study*. Downers Grove, IL: InterVarsity Press, 1981.
Hadorn, Wilhelm. "Die Zahl 666, ein Hinweis auf Trajan." *ZNW* 19 (1919-20): 11-29.
Hagner, Donald A. "Matthew's Eschatology." Pages 49-71 in *To Tell the Mystery: Essays on New Testament Eschatology in Honor of Robert H. Gundry*. Edited by Thomas E. Schmidt and Moisés Silva. Sheffield: JSOT Press, 1994.
Harper Collins Study Bible. New York: HarperCollins, 1993.
Hauret, Charles. "Ève transfigurée: De la Genèse à l'Apocalypse." *Revue d'histoire et de philosophie religieuses* 59 (1979): 327-39.
Hays, Richard B. "Faithful Witness, Alpha and Omega." Pages 69-83 in *Revelation and the Politics of Interpretation*. Edited by Richard B. Hays. Waco, TX: Baylor University Press, 2012.
Heim, S. Mark. *Saved from Sacrifice: A Theology of the Cross*. Grand Rapids: Eerdmans, 2006.
Hemer, Colin J. *The Letters to the Seven Churches of Asia in Their Local Settings*. JSNTS 11. Sheffield: JSOT Press, 1986.
Hengel, Martin. *Die johanneische Frage: Ein Lösungversuch*. Tübingen: J. C. B. Mohr [Paul Siebeck], 1993.
———. *The Johannine Question*. London: SCM Press; Philadelphia: Trinity Press International, 1989.
———. *Studies in the Gospel of Mark*. Translated by J. Bowden. Philadelphia: Fortress Press, 1985.
Herms, Ronald. *An Apocalypse for the Church and the World: The Narrative Function of Universal Language in the Book of Revelation*. BZNW 143. Berlin: Walter de Gruyter, 2006.
Heschel, Abraham J. *The Prophets*. 2 vols. Peabody, MA: Hendrickson, 2003.
Hick, John. *The Center of Christianity*. New York: Harper & Row, 1978.
———. *Evil and the God of Love*. New York: Palgrave Macmillan, 2010.
———. *The Metaphor of God Incarnate: Christ in a Pluralist Age*. Louisville, KY: Westminster John Knox Press, 1983.
Hiers, Richard H. "'Binding and Loosing': The Matthean Authorization." *JBL* 104 (1985): 233-50.
Hill, David. *New Testament Prophecy*. Atlanta: John Knox Press, 1979.
Hillyer, Norman. "'The Lamb' in the Apocalypse." *EQ* 39 (1967): 228-36.
Holwerda, David E. "The Church and the Little Scroll (Revelation 10,11)." *CTJ* 34 (1999): 148-61.
Hort, F. J. A. *The Apocalypse of St. John*. Vol. 1. London: Macmillan, 1908.
Hunt, Anne. *The Trinity and the Paschal Mystery*. Collegeville, MN: Liturgical Press, 1997.
Hurtado, Larry. *Lord Jesus: Devotion to Jesus in Earliest Christianity*. Grand Rapids: Eerdmans, 2005.
Hütter, Reinhard. *Suffering Divine Things: Theology as Church Practice*. Grand Rapids: Eerdmans, 1999.
Irenaeus. "Adversus Haereses." Pages 309-567 in *The Apostolic Fathers: Justin Martyr and*

Irenaeus. Edited by Alexander Roberts and James Donaldson. Revised by A. Cleveland Cox. Ante-Nicene Fathers 1. Peabody, MA: Hendrickson, 1984.

Jauhiainen, Marko. "The Measuring of the Sanctuary Reconsidered (Rev 11:1-2)." *Biblica* 83 (2002): 507-26.

———. "The OT Background to Armageddon (Rev 16:16) Revisited." *NovT* 47.4 (2005): 381-93.

Jenson, Robert W. *Systematic Theology*. Vol. 1: *The Triune God*. Vol. 2: *The Works of God*. New York: Oxford University Press, 1997-99.

Joachim of Fiore. *Expositio in Apocalypsim*. Frankfurt: Minerva, 1964.

Johns, Loren L. *The Lamb Christology of the Apocalypse of John*. WUNT 2.167. Tübingen: Mohr Siebeck, 2002.

Johnson, Elizabeth. *She Who Is: The Mystery of God in Feminist Theological Discourse*. Chestnut Ridge, NY: Crossroad, 2002.

Kaku, Mikio. "The Physics of Extraterrestrial Civilizations: How Advanced Could They Possibly Be?" http://mkaku.org/home/?page_id=246.

Kärkkäinen, Veli-Matti. *One with God: Salvation as Justification and Deification*. Collegeville, MN: Liturgical Press, 2005.

———. *The Trinity and Religious Pluralism: The Doctrine of the Trinity in the Christian Theology of Religions*. Hants, UK: Ashgate, 2004.

Kelsey, Morton. *Healing and Christianity*. Minneapolis: Augsburg, 1995.

Kiddle, Martin. *The Revelation of St. John*. New York: Harper, 1941.

Kinnamon, Michael, and Brian E. Cope, eds. *The Ecumenical Movement: An Anthology of Key Texts and Voices*. Grand Rapids: Eerdmans, 1997.

Kitamori, Kazoh. *Theology of the Pain of God*. Richmond, VA: John Knox Press, 1965.

Koester, Craig R. "God's Purposes and Christ's Saving Work according to Hebrews." Pages 361-88 in *Salvation in the New Testament: Perspectives on Soteriology*. Edited by Jan G. van der Watt. Leiden: Brill, 2005.

———. "The Message to Laodicea and the Problem of Its Local Context: A Study of the Imagery in Rev 3:14-22." *NTS* 49 (2003): 407-24.

———. *Revelation and the End of All Things*. Grand Rapids: Eerdmans, 2001.

Kovacs, Judith, and Christopher Rowland. *Revelation*. Oxford: Blackwell, 2003.

Kretschmar, Georg. *Die Offenbarung des Johannes: Die Geschichte ihrer Auslegung im 1. Jahrtausend*. CTM 9. Stuttgart: Calwer, 1985.

Küng, Hans. *Justification: The Doctrine of Karl Barth and a Catholic Reflection*. Translated by Edward Quinn. Philadelphia: Westminster, 1981.

LaCugna, Catherine M. *God for Us: The Trinity and Christian Life*. San Francisco: HarperOne, 1993.

Ladd, George Eldon. *A Commentary on the Revelation of John*. Grand Rapids: Eerdmans, 1972.

———. *Gospel of the Kingdom: Scripture Studies in the Kingdom of God*. Grand Rapids: Eerdmans, 1959.

———. *A Theology of the New Testament*. Rev. ed. Grand Rapids: Eerdmans, 1993.

Land, Steven J. *Pentecostal Spirituality: A Passion for the Kingdom*. JPTS 1. Sheffield: Sheffield Academic Press, 1993.

Lee, Pilchan. *The New Jerusalem in the Book of Revelation: A Study of Revelation 21-22 in the Light of Its Background in Jewish Tradition*. WUNT 129. Berlin: Mohr Siebeck, 2001.

Levison, John R. *Filled with the Spirit*. Grand Rapids: Eerdmans, 2009.
Linton, Gregory. "Reading the Apocalypse as an Apocalypse." Pages 161-86 in *SBL Seminar Papers*. Atlanta: Scholars Press, 1991.
Lochman, Milič. *Reconciliation and Liberation: Challenging a One-Dimensional View of Salvation*. Philadelphia: Fortress Press, 1980.
Lohse, Eduard. *Die Offenbarung des Johannes*. NTD. Göttingen: Vandenhoeck & Ruprecht, 1960.
Longenecker, Bruce W. "'Linked like a Chain': Rev 22:6-9 in Light of Ancient Translation Technique." *NTS* 47.1 (2001): 105-17.
Lossky, Vladimir. *The Mystical Theology of the Eastern Church*. Crestwood, NY: St. Vladimir's Seminary Press, 1976.
Lugioyo, Brian. "Martin Bucer's Doctrine of Justification and the Colloquy of Regensburg, 1541." Ph.D. thesis, University of Aberdeen, 2007.
Lumen Gentium: Dogmatic Constitution on the Church, §9.
Luther, Martin. *Lectures on Galatians, 1535*. Vol. 26 in *Luther's Works*. Edited by Jaroslav Pelikan. St. Louis: Concordia, 1963.
Macchia, Frank D. *Justified in the Spirit: Creation, Redemption, and the Triune God*. Grand Rapids: Eerdmans, 2010.
———. *Spirituality and Social Liberation: The Message of the Blumhardts in the Light of Wuerttemberg Pietism*. Metuchen, NJ: Scarecrow Press, 1991.
MacKenzie, Robert K. *The Author of the Apocalypse: A Review of the Prevailing Hypothesis of Jewish-Christian Authorship*. MBPS 51. Lewiston, NY: Edwin Mellen Press, 1997.
Mangina, Joseph L. "God, Israel, and Ecclesia in the Apocalypse." Pages 85-103 in *Revelation and the Politics of Interpretation*. Edited by Richard B. Hays. Waco, TX: Baylor University Press, 2012.
Mannermaa, Tuomo. *Christ Present in Faith: Luther's View of Justification*. Minneapolis: Augsburg/Fortress, 2005.
———. "Why Is Luther So Fascinating? Modern Finnish Luther Research." Pages 4-19 in *Union with Christ: The New Finnish Interpretation of Luther*. Edited by Karl E. Braaten and Robert W. Jenson. Grand Rapids: Eerdmans, 1958.
Marshall, I. Howard. *New Testament Theology: Many Witnesses, One Gospel*. Downers Grove, IL: InterVarsity Press, 2004.
Martin, Clarice J. "Polishing the Cloudy Mirror: A Womanist Reading of Revelation 18:13." Pages 82-109 in *From Every People and Nation: The Book of Revelation in Intercultural Perspective*. Edited by David Rhoads. Minneapolis: Augsburg/Fortress, 2005.
Martin, Lee Roy. *The Unheard Voice of God: A Pentecostal Hearing of the Book of Judges*. JPTS 32. Blandford Forum, UK: Deo Publishing, 2008.
Mathewson, Dave. "The Destiny of the Nations in Revelation 21:1–22:5: A Reconsideration." *TynB* 53.1 (2002): 121-42.
———. "New Exodus as a Background for 'The Sea Was No More' in Revelation 21:1c." *Trinity Journal* 24 (2003): 243-58.
Mayo, Philip L. *"Those Who Call Themselves Jews": The Church and Judaism in the Apocalypse of John*. PTMS. Eugene OR: Pickwick Publications, 2006.
Mazzaferri, Frederick David. *The Genre of the Book of Revelation from a Source-Critical Perspective*. Berlin: Walter de Gruyter, 1989.
McCormick, Bruce. "Seek God Where He May Be Found: A Response to Edwin Chr. Van

Driel." Pages 261-77 in his *Orthodox and Modern: Studies in the Theology of Karl Barth*. Grand Rapids: Baker Academic, 2008.
McIlraith, Donal A. "'For the Fine Linen Is the Righteous Deeds of the Saints': Works and Wife in Revelation 19:8." *CBQ* 61.3 (July 1999): 512-29.
Mealy, J. Webb. *After the Thousand Years: Resurrection and Judgment in Revelation 20*. JSNTS 70. Sheffield: JSOT Press, 1992.
Melito of Sardis. *On Pascha and Fragments*. Edited and translated by S. G. Hall. Oxford: Clarendon Press, 1979.
The Methodist Hymn-Book. London: Wesleyan Conference Office, 1904.
Metzger, Bruce M. *Breaking the Code*. Nashville: Abingdon, 1993.
———. *The Canon of the New Testament: Its Origin, Development, and Significance*. Oxford: Clarendon Press, 1987.
Meynet, Roland. "Le cantique de Moïse et le cantique de l'Agneau (Ap 15 et Ex 15)." *Gregorianum* 73 (1992): 19-55.
Michaels, J. Ramsey. *Interpreting the Book of Revelation*. Grand Rapids: Baker, 1992.
Miles, Barry. *Paul McCartney: Many Years from Now*. New York: Henry Holt, 1997.
Miller, Kevin E. "The Nuptial Eschatology of Revelation 19–22." *CBQ* 60.2 (1998): 301-18.
Moltmann, Jürgen. *The Coming of God: Christian Eschatology*. Minneapolis: Fortress Press, 2004.
———. *God in Creation: A New Theology of Creation and the Spirit of God*. Translated by Margaret Kohl. New York: Harper & Row, 1985.
———. *The Spirit of Life: A Universal Affirmation*. Minneapolis: Fortress Press, 1992.
———. *Theology of Hope*. Minneapolis: Fortress Press, 1993.
———. *The Trinity and the Kingdom*. San Francisco: Harper & Row, 1981.
———. *The Way of Jesus Christ*. Philadelphia: Fortress Press, 1992.
Moo, Douglas J. "The Christology of the Early Pauline Letters." Pages 169-92 in *Contours of Christology in the New Testament*. Edited by Richard N. Longenecker. Grand Rapids: Eerdmans, 2005.
Moore, Rick D. "Joel." In *The Book of the Twelve*. Edited by J. C. Thomas. Blandford Forum, UK: Deo Publishing, forthcoming.
———. "The Prophetic Calling: An Old Testament Profile and Its Relevance for Today." *JEPTA* 24 (2004): 16-29.
Morris, Leon. *Apocalyptic*. Grand Rapids: Eerdmans, 1972.
Morton, Russell. "Glory to God and the Lamb: John's Use of Jewish and Hellenistic/Roman Themes in Formatting His Theology in Revelation 4–5." *JSNT* 83 (2001): 89-109.
Mounce, Robert H. *The Book of Revelation*. NICNT. Grand Rapids: Eerdmans, 1977.
Moyise, Steve. *The Old Testament in the Book of Revelation*. JSNTS 115. Sheffield: Sheffield Academic Press, 1995.
Murphy, Frederick J. *Fallen Is Babylon: The Revelation to John*. Harrisburg, PA: Trinity Press International, 1998.
Musvosvi, Joel N. "The Song of Moses and the Song of the Lamb." *Journal of the Adventist Theological Society* 9.1-2 (1998): 44-47.
Newbigin, Lesslie. "The Evangelization of Eastern Asia." *International Review of Mission* 39 (1950): 137-45.
Newport, Kenneth G. C. *Apocalypse and Millennium: Studies in Biblical Eisegesis*. Cambridge: Cambridge University Press, 2000.

Niebuhr, H. Richard, Wilhelm Pauck, and Francis Miller. *The Church against the World*. Chicago: Willet, Clark, 1935.

Nostra Aetate: Declaration on the Relationship of the Church to Non-Christian Religions, §4.

Osborne, G. R. *Revelation*. ECNT. Grand Rapids: Baker, 2002.

Ozanne, C. G. "The Language of the Apocalypse." *TynB* 16 (1965): 3-9.

Pannenberg, Wolfhart. "Constructive and Critical Functions of Christian Eschatology." *HTR* 77 (1984): 119-39.

———. *Jesus: God and Man*. Philadelphia: Westminster Press, 1968.

———. *Systematic Theology*. Translated by Geoffrey W. Bromiley. Vol. 2. Grand Rapids: Eerdmans, 1994.

Pattemore, Stephen. *The People of God in the Apocalypse: Discourse, Structure, and Exegesis*. SNTSMS 128. Cambridge: Cambridge University Press, 2004.

The Pearl: Mediaeval Text and Notes. Translated and edited by S. Deford et al. New York: Appleton-Century-Croft, 1967.

Pelikan, Jaroslav. *The Emergence of the Catholic Tradition (100-600)*. The Christian Tradition 1. Chicago: University of Chicago Press, 1971.

Peters, Ted. *God as Trinity: Relationality and Temporality in Divine Life*. Minneapolis: Westminster John Knox Press, 1993.

Philonenko, Marc. "'Dehors les Chiens' (Apocalypse 22:16 et 4QMMT B 58-62)." *NTS* 43.3 (1997): 445-50.

Poirier, John C. "The First Rider: A Response to Michael Bachmann." *NTS* 45 (1999): 257-62.

Poucouta, Paulin. "La mission prophétique de l'Église dans l'Apocalypse johannique." *NRT* 110 (1988): 38-57.

Prigent, Pierre. *L'Apocalypse de Saint Jean*. CNT 2.14. Geneva: Labor & Fides, 2000.

Provan, Iain. "Foul Spirits, Fornication, and Finance: Revelation 18 from an Old Testament Perspective." *JSNT* 64 (1996): 81-100.

Putter, Ad. *An Introduction to the Gawain-Poet*. London: Longman, 1996.

Rahner, Karl. *Foundations of Christian Faith: An Introduction to the Idea of Christianity*. New York: Crossroad, 1982.

———. "Grace (II Theological, B Systematic)." Pages 419-20 in *Sacramentum Mundi: An Encyclopedia of Theology*. Edited by Karl Rahner et al. New York: Herder & Herder, 1968.

———. "Some Implications of the Scholastic Concept of Uncreated Grace." Pages 319-46 in his *Theological Investigations*. Vol. 1. Baltimore: Helicon Press, 1963.

Ramsay, William. *The Seven Letters to the Seven Churches of Asia and Their Place in the Plan of the Apocalypse*. London: Hodder & Stoughton, 1904.

Resseguie, James L. *The Revelation of John: A Narrative Commentary*. Grand Rapids: Baker, 2009.

Rissi, Mathias. *Die Zukunft der Welt: Eine exegetische Studie über Johannesoffenbarung 19,11 bis 22,15*. Basel: Verlag Friedrich Reinhardt, 1966.

Rowe, Christopher Kavin. *Early Narrative Christology: The Lord in the Gospel of Luke*. BZNW 139. Berlin: Walter de Gruyter, 2006.

Rowland, Christopher C. "The Book of Revelation: Introduction, Commentary, and Reflections." Pages 501-743 in *The New Interpreter's Bible*. Vol. 12. Edited by L. E. Keck. Nashville: Abingdon, 1998.

Royalty, Robert M., Jr. "Don't Touch This Book! Revelation 22:18-19 and the Rhetoric of Reading (in) the Apocalypse of John." *Biblical Interpretation* 12.3 (2004): 282-99.

Ruiz, Jean-Pierre. *Ezekiel in the Apocalypse: The Transformation of Prophetic Language in Revelation 16,17–19,10*. EUSST 23. Frankfurt: Lang, 1989.

Sanders, E. P. *Paul and Palestinian Judaism: A Comparison of Patterns of Religion*. Minneapolis: Fortress Press, 1977.

Schilling, Paul. *God and Human Anguish*. Nashville: Abingdon, 1977.

Schimanowski, Gottfried. *Die himmlische Liturgie in der Apokalypse des Johannes: Die frühjüdischen Traditionen in Offenbarung 4–5 unter Einschluß der Hekhalotliteratur*. WUNT 2.154. Tübingen: Mohr Siebeck, 2002.

Schleiermacher, Friedrich. *The Christian Faith*. Philadelphia: Fortress Press, 1976.

Schneiders, Sandra M. "Does the Bible Have a Postmodern Message?" Pages 56-73 in *Postmodern Theology: Christian Faith in a Pluralist World*. Edited by F. B. Burnham. New York: Harper & Row, 1989.

Schnelle, Udo. *Theology of the New Testament*. Translated by M. Eugene Boring. Grand Rapids: Baker Academic, 2009.

Schroder, Joy A. "Revelation 12: Female Figures and Figures of Evil." *Word and Witness* 15 (1995): 175-81.

Schultz, F. LeRon. *Reforming the Doctrine of God*. Grand Rapids: Eerdmans, 2005.

Schüssler Fiorenza, Elisabeth. *The Book of Revelation: Justice and Judgment*. Philadelphia: Fortress Press, 1985.

———. *Revelation: Vision of a Just World*. Minneapolis: Fortress Press, 1991.

Sellers, O. R. "Weights and Measures." Pages 828-39 in *The Interpreter's Dictionary of the Bible*. Edited by G. A. Buttrick. Vol. 4. Nashville: Abingdon, 1962.

Simoens, Yves. *Apocalypse de Jean: Apocalypse de Jésus Christ*. Paris: Éditions Facultés Jésuites de Paris, 2008.

Skaggs, Rebecca, and Priscilla Benham. *Revelation*. PCS: Blandford Forum, UK: Deo Publishing, 2009.

Skehan, Patrick W. "King of Kings, Lord of Lords (Apoc. 19:16)." *CBQ* 10.4 (1948): 398.

Slater, Thomas B. *Christ and Community: A Socio-Historical Study of the Christology of Revelation*. JSNTS 178. Sheffield: Sheffield Academic Press, 1999.

Smalley, Stephen S. *The Revelation to John*. Downers Grove, IL: InterVarsity Press, 2005.

———. *Thunder and Love: John's Revelation and John's Community*. Milton Keynes, UK: Word, 1994.

Smith, Christopher R. "The Portrayal of the Church as the New Israel in the Names and Order of the Tribes in Revelation 7:5-8." *JSNT* 39 (1990): 111-18.

Smith, D. Moody. "Judaism and the Gospel of John." Pages 76-99 in *Jews and Christians: Exploring the Past, Present, and Future*. Edited by James H. Charlesworth. New York: Crossroad, 1990.

Stevenson, James. *The Catacombs: Life and Death in Early Christianity*. Nashville: Thomas Nelson, 1985.

Stronstad, Roger. *The Prophethood of All Believers: A Study in Luke's Charismatic Theology*. Cleveland, TN: CPT Press, 2010.

Suetonius. *The Lives of the Caesars*. Translated by J. C. Rolfe. Vol. 2. London: Heinemann, 1965.

Sweet, John. *Revelation*. London: SCM Press, 1990.

Swete, Henry Barclay. *The Apocalypse of St. John*. London: Macmillan, 1909.

Tacitus. *Histories and Annals*. Translated by J. Jackson. Vol. 4. London: Heinemann, 1962.

Tertullian. *The Writings of Tertullian*. Edited by A. Roberts and J. Donaldson. Vol. 1. Edinburgh: T&T Clark, 1869.
Thayer, Joseph Henry. *A Greek-English Lexicon of the New Testament*. Grand Rapids: Zondervan, 1973.
Thielman, Frank. *Paul and the Law: A Contextual Approach*. Lombard, IL: IVP Academic, 1995.
Thomas, John Christopher. *The Devil, Disease, and Deliverance: Origins of Illness in New Testament Thought*. Cleveland, TN: CPT Press, 2010.
———. *1 John, 2 John, 3 John*. London: T&T Clark International, 2004.
———. *Footwashing in John 13 and the Johannine Community*. JSNTS 61. Sheffield: JSOT Press, 1991.
———. *The Spirit of the New Testament*. Leiderdorp, Neth.: Deo Publishing, 2004.
Tillich, Paul. *Systematic Theology*. Vol. 2. University of Chicago Press, 1957.
Tobin, John. *Handel at Work*. New York: St. Martin's Press, 1964.
van Aarde, Andries G. "ΙΗΣΟΥΣ, the Davidic Messiah, as Political Saviour in Matthew's History." Pages 7-32 in *Salvation in the New Testament: Perspectives on Soteriology*. Edited by Jan G. van der Watt. Leiden: Brill, 2005.
Van Buren, Paul M. "Israel and the Church." Pages 536-37 in *Dictionary of the Ecumenical Movement*. Edited by Nicholas Lossky et al. Grand Rapids: Eerdmans, 1991.
van der Meer, Frederick. *Apocalypse: Visions from the Book of Revelation in Western Art*. New York: Alpine Fine Arts, 1978.
van der Watt, Jan G. "Salvation in the Gospel according to John." Pages 101-32 in *Salvation in the New Testament: Perspectives on Soteriology*. Edited by Jan G. van der Watt. Leiden: Brill, 2005.
Vanhoozer, Kevin J. *The Drama of Doctrine: A Canonical-Linguistic Approach to Christian Doctrine*. Louisville, KY: Westminster John Knox Press, 2005.
Volf, Miroslav. *Exclusion and Embrace: A Theological Reflection on Identity, Otherness, and Reconciliation*. Nashville: Abingdon, 1996.
Vriezen, Theodorus C. *An Outline of Old Testament Theology*. Oxford: Basil Blackwell, 1958.
Waddell, Robby C. *The Spirit of the Book of Revelation*. JPTS 30. Blandford Forum, UK: Deo Publishing, 2006.
Wainwright, Arthur W. *Mysterious Apocalypse*. Nashville: Abingdon, 1993.
Wainwright, Geoffrey. *Doxology: The Praise of God in Worship, Doctrine, and Life*. New York: Oxford University Press, 1980.
Wall, Robert W. *Revelation*. NIBC, NTS 18. Peabody, MA: Hendrickson, 1991.
Wall, Robert W., and E. E. Lemcio. *The New Testament as Canon: A Reader in Canonical Criticism*. JSNTS 76. Sheffield: JSOT Press, 1992.
Walsh, Richard. "On Finding a Non-American Revelation: *End of Days* and the Book of Revelation." Pages 1-23 in *Screening Scripture: Intertextual Connections between Scripture and Film*. Edited by G. Aichele and R. Walsh. Harrisburg, PA: Trinity Press International, 2002.
Weaver, J. Denny. *The Non-Violent Atonement*. Grand Rapids: Eerdmans, 2001.
Weinrich, William C. "Death and Martyrdom: An Important Aspect of Early Christian Eschatology." *Concordia Theological Monthly* 66.4 (2002): 327-38.
Welker, Michael. *God the Spirit*. Minneapolis: Fortress Press, 1992.
Wesley, John. *Wesley's Works*. Vol. 8. Grand Rapids: Zondervan, 1979.

Whealey, Alice. "The Apocryphal Apocalypse of John: A Byzantine Apocalypse from the Early Islamic Period." *JTS* 53 (2002): 533-40.
Williams, George H. *The Radical Reformation*. Philadelphia: Westminster, 1962.
Williams, John. *The Illustrated Beatus: A Corpus of the Illustrations of the Commentary on the Apocalypse*. 5 vols. London: Harvey Miller Publishers, 1994-2003.
Wojciechowski, Michael. "Apocalypse 21:19-20: Des titres christologiques cachés dans la liste des pierres précieuses." *NTS* 33 (1987): 153-54.
Wright, N. T. "Revelation and Christian Hope: Political Implications of the Revelation to John." Pages 105-24 in *Revelation and the Politics of Interpretation*. Edited by Richard B. Hays. Waco, TX: Baylor University Press, 2012.
———. *Surprised by Hope: Rethinking Heaven, the Resurrection, and the Mission of the Church*. New York: HarperOne, 2008.
Yong, Amos. *Hospitality and the Other: Pentecost, Christian Practices, and the Neighbor*. Maryknoll, NY: Orbis Books, 2008.
Zimmerman, Ruben. "Nuptial Imagery in the Revelation of John." *Biblica* 84.2 (2003): 153-83.

Index of Names

Alcmeon, 246
Alexander of Alexandria, 462
Allo, E.-B., 73, 146, 166, 178, 202, 216, 231, 239, 252, 263, 266, 330, 332, 339, 345, 357, 362, 374, 377
Ancus Marcus, 300
Andrew of Caesarea, 230, 290
Andrew of Crete, 49
Anselm, 569-71
Antiochus the Great, 112, 115
Antipas, 22-23, 100, 160, 190, 201, 205, 237-38, 261, 303, 336
Archer, M. L., 210-11, 213
Aristotle, 419
Athanasius, 420, 463
Augustus, 27-28, 98, 301
Aulén, Gustaf, 572-73
Aune, D. E., 2, 27, 29, 33, 76, 87, 90, 92, 94, 99, 107, 111, 116, 126, 128-29, 139, 145-46, 148-49, 156, 158, 160, 162, 170, 176, 181, 185, 193-94, 198, 203, 209, 212, 215, 220, 222, 234, 236-38, 241, 243, 252, 256-57, 260-61, 264-65, 276-77, 281, 283, 286, 292-95, 297, 299-301, 305, 307, 310-11, 317, 319, 321, 325, 327, 329, 333, 342, 345, 347, 355-58, 362, 364, 367, 370, 375, 377-78, 381-83, 385-86, 388, 391, 396, 398

Bacchiocchi, A., 35, 81
Balaam, 100-102, 106, 109, 111, 191, 295
Ball, D., 78

Balz, H., 117, 123, 146, 182
Barr, D. L., 7
Barth, Karl, 405, 421, 430, 432-33, 458-59, 488, 566-68, 578, 580, 584-85
Barth, Marcus, 534
Bauckham, R., 2, 8, 11-13, 25, 29, 37, 76, 110, 137, 139, 141-42, 147-49, 151, 153, 167, 175, 178, 191-92, 194, 198, 202, 206, 209, 211, 222, 246-47, 253, 255-56, 258, 264, 269, 301, 313, 315, 337, 366, 368, 380, 385, 394, 400-401, 440, 441
Bauer, J. B., 218
Beale, G. K., 13-14, 28, 33, 38, 41, 74-75, 77, 84, 103, 108, 121, 130, 139, 142, 150, 155, 158, 161, 172, 177, 181, 186, 192, 198, 203, 216, 219, 242, 251, 258, 261, 278-79, 283, 302, 305, 335, 344, 368
Beasley-Murray, G. R., 73, 99, 188, 203, 205, 233, 239, 260, 267, 276, 285, 289, 300, 310, 326-28, 334, 339, 341, 343-44, 350, 359, 364, 366, 368-69, 372, 378-81, 385-86, 393, 399, 401
Beatus, 52
Beckett, Samuel, 428
Bede, 66-67
Benham, P., 81, 111, 194, 281, 301
Benson, E. W., 8
Berkhof, Hendrikus, 467
Beyer, H., 105, 230
Biguzzi, G., 399
Bloom, H., 59

Index of Names

Blumhardt, Johann, 578
Bocher, O., 183
Boesak, A. A., 69-72, 161
Bonhoeffer, Dietrich, 430, 527
Bosch, David, 527-28
Bowman, J. W., 8
Braumann, G., 330
Bredin, Mark, 471
Brewer, R. R., 8
Brown, C., 374
Brown, R. E., 19
Brueggemann, Walter, 410, 571-72
Bruns, J. E., 295
Buber, Martin, 469, 614-16
Bugliosi, V., 45
Bultmann, Rudolf, 577-78

Caird, G. B., 41, 112, 125, 137, 140, 147, 165-66, 206, 209, 224, 237, 241, 269, 272, 276, 283, 297-99, 314, 325, 331, 335, 337, 341, 356-57, 360, 367, 369, 372, 378, 385, 389, 402
Callahan, A. D., 40
Calvin, John, 582
Charette, B. B., 212
Charles, J. D., 150
Charles, R. H., 40, 103
Cheung, P. W., 295
Childs, Brevard, 405, 407-8, 429
Cicero, 158
Claudius, 28, 295
Clement of Alexandria, 33, 41
Cloete, G. D., 370
Collins, A. Yarbro, 112, 115, 119, 127, 135, 158-59, 191, 198, 251, 253, 257, 263, 312
Collins, J. J., 12
Colson, F. H., 249
Cone, James, 435
Constantius, 69
Court, J., 47-49
Cyprian, 49
Cyril, 33
Cyrus, 47, 112, 115

Day, J., 288
DeCaro, S., 86
Deford, S., 59

Deissmann, A., 245
Deppermann, K., 45
Deutch, C., 374
Domitian, 33
Donaldson, J., 33, 141
Draper, J. A., 173

Eichrodt, Walther, 410
Eusebius, 31, 33, 38, 41, 43, 255

Farrer, A. M., 194
Fee, G. D., 43, 90, 111, 138, 141, 170, 263, 364
Feuillet, A., 160
Folger, A., 45
Frey, J., 19, 40
Frykowski, V., 45

Gaechter, P., 354
Gaius, 27-28
Galba, 27-28, 66, 70, 301
Gause, R. H., 96, 175, 188, 192, 201, 217, 226, 231-32, 234, 236, 238, 253, 262, 267, 273-74, 284, 294, 297, 305, 307, 317, 324, 328, 332, 340, 347, 349, 351, 354, 356-57, 359-60, 363, 366, 376, 378-80, 383, 387
Giblin, C. H., 203
Giesen, H., 115
Glancy, J. A., 292
Goedt, M. de, 97
Goldingay, J., 329
Gregory, 33, 52, 491
Griffiths, J. G., 249
Grubb, N., 51
Gundry, R. H., 366, 370

Hadorn, W., 246
Hall, R. G., 140
Handel, 53-54
Hanson, Paul, 614
Harrison, R. K., 86
Hartman, L., 234
Hauret, C., 216, 229
Hegel, G. W. F., 421, 423
Heim, S. Mark, 443, 576-77
Hemer, C. J., 32, 86, 94, 98, 118, 339
Hengel, M., 19-20, 38, 461
Herms, R., 385

Index of Names

Herod, 69
Herodotus, 379
Heschel, A. J., 11
Hick, John, 468-69
Hicks, A., 54
Hill, D., 21, 74
Hillyer, N., 148
Hippolytus, 41
Hoffman, M., 44-45
Hofius, O., 236
Holmes, M. W., 33
Holwerda, D. E., 198
Horace, 299
Hort, F. J. A., 40
Howell, V.W., 46, 47
Hunt, Anne, 420
Hurtado, L., 138, 440-41

Irenaeus, 33, 141, 247, 573

Jackson, J., 30
Jauhiainen, M., 200, 288
Jenson, Robert, 426
Jezebel, 21
Joachim, 68-69
Johns, L. L., 146, 149
Johnson, Elizabeth, 427
Josephus, 290
Julius Caesar, 301
Jungmann, Josef, 464
Justin Martyr, 32, 41
Juvenal, 295

Kaku, Michio, 611
Kärkkäinen, Veli-Matti, 524, 582
Kiddle, M., 117, 136, 145, 154, 159, 166, 187, 206, 227, 231, 238-39, 242, 273, 301, 324, 329, 339-40, 347, 361, 363-64, 378, 381, 388
Kitamori, Kazoh, 429-30
Koester, C. R., 57, 86, 118, 128, 135, 141, 154, 197-98, 202, 205, 209, 221, 247, 258, 261, 276, 278, 284, 287, 309, 315, 336, 340-41, 344, 354, 357, 378, 390
Koresh, D., 46-47
Kovacs, J., 69, 156, 201, 217, 340
Kretschmar, G., 67

Kretzer, A., 316
Küng, Hans, 565-66, 581

Ladd, G. E., 146, 176, 237, 258, 261, 276, 283, 293, 298, 300, 304, 315, 327, 340, 345, 351, 353, 355, 359-60, 365, 371, 380, 387, 398
LaHaye, T., 64
Lake, K., 31, 33, 42
Lampe, P., 167
Land, Steven J., 424
Lee, P., 364, 376
Légasse, S., 268
Lemcio, E. E., 15
Levison, John, 497-98
Lewis, C. S., 621
Lichtenberger, H., 176
Linton, G., 12
Livia, 112
Lochman, Jan Milič, 579-80
Lohse, E., 145
Longenecker, B. W., 394
Lossky, Valdimir, 582
Lucian, 241
Luther, Martin, 433, 581

MacKenzie, R. K., 38
Mannermaa, Tuomo, 581
Manson, C., 45-46
Marcellus of Ancyra, 463
Marshall, I. Howard, 405
Martial, 299
Martin, C. J., 315-16
Martin, L. R., 75, 140, 213, 376
Mathewson, D., 366-67, 384, 388-89
Mayo, P. L., 96, 121, 388
Mazzaferri, F. D., 2, 11, 36, 336
McIlraith, D. A., 332-33, 338-39, 341
Mealy, J. W., 345, 352-53, 355, 358, 362, 380
Melito of Sardis, 31
Merkel, F., 327
Mesomoth, 69
Methodius, 33
Metzger, B. M., 15, 141, 148, 150, 165, 180, 206, 245, 287, 331, 341, 356, 361-63, 382, 389, 397
Meynet, R., 270
Michaels, J. R., 18, 147, 149, 154, 177-78, 180,

639

Index of Names

182, 211, 231, 256, 275, 284, 286, 289, 312, 319, 333, 335-36, 346, 348, 361, 370, 379, 386, 389, 393-94, 396, 399-401
Miles, B., 46
Miller, K. E., 335, 337
Moltmann, Jürgen, 419, 430, 469-70, 473, 568-69, 610, 616-17
Monachus, G., 42
Moore, R. D., 11, 14, 35, 40
Moore, S. D., 292
Morton, R., 141
Mounce, R. H., 98, 101, 112, 118, 124, 132, 145, 158, 165, 170, 177, 186, 193, 196, 230, 260, 278-79, 301, 308, 311-12, 315-16, 324, 328, 339, 347, 351, 357, 359, 361-62, 365, 369, 371, 373, 379, 381-83, 397-98, 403
Moyise, S., 14, 39, 86
Murphy, F. J., 14, 27, 94-95, 103, 106, 110-11, 121, 127, 147, 150, 161, 172, 175, 177-79, 187, 190, 211, 213, 215, 228, 241, 254, 265, 286, 289, 293, 299, 301, 304, 310, 312-13, 319, 324, 328, 330, 334, 336, 346, 356, 360-61, 368, 370, 375, 383, 387, 389, 391
Musvosi, J. N., 270

Nero, 25-31, 66, 69-70, 240, 246-47, 249, 295, 299
Nerva, 28, 66, 68
Newbigin, Lesslie, 527-28
Newport, K., 46, 54
Numa Pompilius, 300
Nutzel, J. M., 122

Orestes, 246
Origen, 34-35, 166, 340, 462
Osborne, G. R., 40, 74, 78, 82, 84-85, 87-88, 90, 95-96, 106, 129, 132, 136-37, 139, 142, 144, 146, 164, 173, 183, 185, 189-90, 201, 205, 231, 239, 257, 282, 285, 305
Otho, 28, 66, 301
Ovid, 299
Ozanne, C. G., 40

Painter, J., 15
Pannenberg, Wolfhart, 459, 579
Pattemore, S., 160-61, 165, 170, 173, 206, 234, 237, 253-54, 281, 352, 366, 371, 385, 398
Pederson, S., 397
Peters, Ted, 422
Philonenko, M., 397-98
Philostratus, 30
Pilate, 132
Pliny, 31-32, 295, 300
Plotinus, 419
Plutarch, 249
Poirier, J. C., 156, 159
Poucouta, P., 21
Prigent, P., 2, 97, 99, 104, 113, 121, 127, 133, 148-49, 170, 176, 186, 188, 204, 216, 218, 233, 238, 257, 266-67, 274, 279, 282, 285, 290-92, 295, 304, 309, 318, 320, 324-25, 327-28, 331-33, 338-39, 345, 351, 355, 362, 368-69, 371, 375, 377, 380, 383, 395
Primasius, 283
Provain, I., 315
Putter, A., 57

Radl, W., 182
Rahner, Karl, 422, 565
Ramsay, W., 17, 86
Resseguie, J. L., 3, 40, 74, 76, 95, 113, 124, 132, 140, 143-44, 149, 152, 158, 162, 165-66, 169-70, 176, 178, 180, 183, 185, 189, 193-94, 201-2, 204, 206, 228, 230-31, 242, 266, 269, 272, 283, 300, 302, 305, 315, 346, 350, 361, 376, 383, 388-89
Rissi, M., 339, 351
Roberts, A., 32, 141
Rolfe, J. C., 30, 246
Romulus, 300
Rowland, C. C., 69, 156, 201, 217, 340, 346
Royalty, R. M., Jr., 401
Ruiz, J.-P., 9, 20, 40

Saladin, 69
Sand, A., 180, 318
Sanger, D., 134
Saraphim of Sarov, 582
Schimanowski, G., 147
Schleiermacher, Friedrich, 420, 466-67, 488
Schneider, C., 284

Schneider, G., 73, 291, 299, 373
Schroder, J. A., 218
Schussler Fiorenza, E., 12, 14, 140, 161, 170, 177, 288, 297, 310, 344, 364, 394
Schwarzenegger, A., 62
Seabring, J., 45
Sellers, O. R., 379
Servius Tullius, 300
Shepherd of Hermas, 13
Simoens, Y., 19, 75, 85, 110, 138-40
Skaggs, R., 81, 111, 194, 281, 301
Skehan, P. W., 343
Slater, T. B., 338-39, 343, 345, 348
Smalley, S. S., 7-8, 10, 74-75, 79-80, 82, 84, 86, 108, 115-16, 120-21, 126, 132-33, 135-37, 142-43, 145-46, 148, 157-58, 160, 164-65, 168-69, 174, 177, 181-82, 184, 186-87, 195, 197-98, 201, 204, 210, 213, 220, 224, 233, 236, 244, 250-51, 256-60, 262-63, 265, 268-70, 274, 276-79, 283-86, 291-92, 295-96, 299, 304-5, 307, 309-10, 313-15, 321, 326-28, 330, 333-34, 337, 342-46, 352, 356, 359-63, 365-66, 368-69, 374, 376, 378, 381, 383, 386-87, 394, 396-97, 399-400
Smith, C. R., 168
Smith, E., 53
Stenger, W., 184
Stevenson, J., 50
Strabo, 128
Suetonius II, 30, 240, 246
Sweet, J., 12, 16, 122, 151, 157, 165, 181, 185, 189, 193, 203, 232, 238, 241, 243, 252, 254, 262, 283, 285-87, 308, 310-11, 313, 318, 320, 329, 333-34, 339, 341-42, 346-47, 351, 353, 358, 361, 363, 367, 369-70, 372, 374, 376, 379-81, 386, 388-89, 396, 398, 401
Swete, H. B., 305

Tacitus IV, 30
Tarquinius Superbus, 300
Tertullian, 31
Thayer, J. H., 189
Thomas, J. C., 16, 19, 42-43, 88, 107, 110, 116, 119, 130, 244, 293, 356-57, 388, 391, 397, 401
Tiberius, 28, 30, 118, 301

Tillich, Paul, 467
Titus, 28, 65, 301
Tobin, J., 53-54
Trajan, 27-28, 31, 33
Trummer, P., 143
Tyconius, 52, 67, 69, 258

Untergassmair, G., 107

Valeria Messalina, 295
Van der Meer, F., 51-53, 159
Vanhoozer, Kevin J., 421, 489
Vespasian, 28, 66, 118, 301
Vettius, 255
Victorinus, 37, 65
Vitellius, 28, 66, 301
Volf, Miroslav, 433-34, 436, 577-78
Vriezen, T. C., 410

Waddell, R. C., 16, 38, 192, 200, 205, 320, 337
Wainwright, A. W., 45, 69
Wainwright, Geoffrey, 424, 461, 468-69
Wall, R. W., 9, 15-16, 103, 137, 155, 158, 178, 185, 197, 202-4, 207, 258, 278, 294, 300, 310-11, 331, 355, 382
Wallis, R. E., 65-66
Walsh, R., 63
Weaver, J. Denny, 575-76
Webster, J. S., 94
Weiser, A., 104
Welker, Michael, 485-86
Wesley, C., 54-58
Wesley, J., 499, 574-75, 582-83
Whealey, A., 47
Williams, G. H., 45
Williams, J., 52
Wojciechowski, M., 381
Wren, M., 45
Wright, N. T., 579

York, M., 63

Zimmerman, R., 323, 365
Zmijewski, J., 29

Index of Subjects

666. *See under* Mark of the beast
144,000, the. *See before* OT in NT

Abyss, 23, 46, 62-63, 183, 186, 204-5, 229, 235, 298-99, 300, 348-51, 357-59
angels, 4-7, 10-11, 13, 26, 36, 46, 49-52, 57, 61, 74, 76, 84-86, 94, 98, 102-3, 112-13, 115, 117-18, 126, 135, 145, 152-54, 165-67, 171, 174, 176-84, 186-88, 191-97, 210-11, 213-15, 220-21, 223, 225, 256-60, 263-67, 271-72, 274-79, 281-84, 288-89, 291, 294, 297-99, 304-8, 311-13, 316, 321-22, 329, 332-35, 341, 343-44, 346-50, 360, 362, 373-80, 385, 391-94, 399, 401, 408-9, 440, 455, 463, 494-95, 526-27, 551, 559, 598, 606, 618
apocalyptic tradition, 11-13
apostles, 25, 27, 29, 32, 41-43, 45-46, 49, 53, 58-59, 69, 87-88, 91, 95, 106, 121, 134, 138, 319-20, 337, 371, 377-78, 399, 483, 488, 492, 502, 507, 512-14, 516-18, 522, 532, 534, 552

Babylon, 4-5, 11, 14, 21, 24-28, 42, 44, 47, 52, 68-69, 97, 191, 205, 216, 230, 258-59, 261, 265, 288-89, 291-92, 295-96, 305-14, 317-26, 328, 330, 333-34, 342, 344, 351, 365, 367-68, 373-74, 379, 382, 384, 386, 391, 442, 445, 460, 502, 542, 591, 620
beast(s), 6-7, 15, 22-27, 29-31, 44, 46-47, 51, 60, 62-66, 68-69, 71-72, 92-93, 140, 159, 202, 204-7, 217, 227-52, 255, 257-62, 265, 267-69, 272-74, 277-78, 280-87, 289, 291, 293-307, 311, 313-14, 318-19, 329, 335-36, 339, 344-50, 352-54, 358-60, 362-63, 370-72, 380, 386-87, 390, 392-94, 398-99, 411-12, 433, 441-42, 445, 477, 487, 494, 496, 500, 502, 505, 522, 526, 531-32, 542, 564, 585, 589, 591, 621
beatitudes, 7, 75, 396, 598
blood, 22, 24, 46, 52-53, 56, 58, 62, 64-65, 77, 102, 109, 151-52, 157, 159-61, 163, 166, 172-73, 179-80, 182, 202, 204, 206, 224, 236, 265-66, 272, 278-82, 292, 296-97, 320, 323-27, 329, 331, 336, 340, 342, 353, 387, 409, 431, 440, 443, 445, 463, 471-72, 484, 508-9, 511, 533, 538, 542, 545, 549, 554, 558, 562, 578, 586-87, 595, 603-4, 613
blood of the Lamb, 54, 77, 151, 163, 166, 172-73, 224, 229, 241, 253, 266, 281, 314, 333, 396-97, 431-32, 441, 495, 502, 507, 509, 517-18, 522, 524, 540-41, 545, 562, 569, 593, 603, 613
book of life, 116-17, 236, 241, 251, 254, 284, 298-99, 361, 363, 367, 371, 386, 398, 521, 542, 589
bowls, seven, 3-4, 5, 214, 266, 271, 275-89
bride of Christ, 4, 21, 394, 397, 505, 592

canonical location of Revelation, 15-16
Christ, 2, 4, 5-6, 12, 19, 21-22, 25, 31-32, 36, 39, 41, 47, 50, 53, 58-59, 63, 65-66, 68,

Index of Subjects

73-76, 80, 82, 88, 103, 120, 134, 154, 192, 210-11, 223, 231, 319, 334, 338-40, 343, 345, 348, 352-56, 358, 364, 382, 394, 397, 399, 402-3, 437-74; baptism of, 449-50; Book of Revelation, 437-45; Christological method, 459-60; death of, 450, 452, 455-56; deity of, 462-67; and the Father, 445-46; functional Christology, 465-66; Gospel of John and 1–3 John, 445-47; Hebrews, 454-55; and Israel, 469-70; as the Lamb, 4-5, 7-8, 16, 19, 22-24, 29, 40, 42, 47-48, 52-54, 56-61, 71, 77, 93, 96, 135, 141, 146-57, 159-64, 166, 170-74, 176, 185, 191-92, 196-98, 208, 210, 212, 221-24, 229, 231-36, 238, 241-43, 250-57, 259-60, 262-63, 266, 268-70, 279, 281, 284, 291, 294, 296, 298-99, 301-4, 306, 312-14, 319-21, 323-25, 328, 330-35, 337-44, 346, 348, 356, 358-60, 365, 368, 370-74, 377-78, 382-84, 386-92, 394-99, 406-11, 422, 425, 427-29, 431-36, 438-45, 447, 455-64, 466-77, 486-88, 490, 492-97, 499-500, 502-3, 505-8, 520-32, 534-43, 545, 554, 562, 564, 567, 569, 571, 573, 575-80, 585-94, 613, 616-24, 627, 629-30, 632; as Lion, 93, 146-49, 156, 167-68, 174-76, 193, 270, 313, 325, 399, 410, 422, 428-29, 438-43, 457, 469, 471, 497, 538; Luke-Acts, 451-52; Matthew and Mark, 447-50; mediation, 438-42, 461-62, 466; messiah, 447-48, 469-70; non-violent, 470-72; Paul, 452-54; 1–2 Peter, 455-56; and pluralism, 468-69; Prophet, Priest, King, 460; resurrection of, 426, 443-44, 450, 452-53; return of, 473-74; as Rider on the white horse, 93, 164, 205, 340-41, 355, 368, 385; Son of God, 449-50; Son of Man, 447-48; and the Spirit, 443-44, 451, 460, 472-74; Word, 445-46, 472-74; worship of, 438, 461-63, 468-69
church(es), 2-4, 8-10, 17-18, 21, 23, 25-27, 31-33, 41-43, 47-48, 57-59, 62-63, 65, 67-68, 70-72, 75-76, 79, 82, 84-92, 94-118, 120-35, 138, 141, 149, 151-53, 167-69, 172, 198, 202-5, 208, 219-24, 226, 228-30, 237, 239, 257, 261, 267-68, 273, 286, 292, 298, 305, 309, 327, 330, 334-37, 339, 342, 349, 351-52, 356, 371-72, 374, 385, 387, 392, 395, 397-403, 407, 415, 420-21, 424, 429-30, 432-35, 438, 440-41, 444, 447, 450-51, 453, 458-59, 461-62, 464, 466-67, 469, 472-73, 475-78, 481-93, 495-97, 500-537; Book of Revelation, 501-9; election, 522; Gospel of John and 1–3 John, 509-11; Hebrews, 518; Israel, 532-36; James, 519; Luke-Acts, 513-15; *Lumen gentium*, 525, 533; martyrs of, 529-32; Matthew and Mark, 512-15; mission of, 526-29; *Nostra aetate*, 533-34; Paul, 515-18; 1–2 Peter, 518-19; and pluralism, 524; sanctified, 523-24; spiritual gifts, 523; and the Trinity, 520-25; worship of, 525-26
color(s), 8, 103, 116, 119, 137, 155-58, 161, 216, 293-94, 360, 381

Death and Hades, 84, 97, 119, 158-59, 183, 184, 362, 444, 539, 586, 588-92
dragon, ix, 5-6, 23-24, 26, 31, 44, 51, 63, 69, 212, 214, 216-35, 238-41, 255, 258-59, 261, 268, 272-74, 284-86, 293, 295, 297-98, 302, 306, 308, 313, 335-36, 339, 346, 349-52, 354, 358, 362, 372

eschatology, 584-624; apocalyptic, 613-18; Book of Revelation, 585-94; delay, 618-21; Gospel of John, 594-97; Hebrews, 607-8; hell, 621; language of, 621; Luke-Acts, 597-600; Matthew-Mark, 600-602; millennium, 617; and the nations, 620-21; necessity of, 610-13; Paul, 603-7; 1–2 Peter, 608-9
eternal life, 75, 89, 94, 102, 114, 120, 164, 236, 256, 263, 354, 356, 388, 397, 402, 531, 545, 594-96, 605
Eucharist, 132, 453, 510, 517, 523

faithful witness, 8, 22-23, 76-81, 95, 97, 100, 104, 107, 116, 127-34, 138, 146, 149, 172, 197-98, 204-6, 224-25, 229, 237-38, 261, 268, 280-81, 296-97, 310, 320-21, 327, 333, 335-38, 341, 344, 353-56, 359, 362-63, 370, 372-73, 384-87, 392-94, 400, 403, 406, 411, 460, 471, 494-96, 505, 507, 509
false prophecy, 26, 307

Index of Subjects

footwashing, 397, 401, 510, 523, 546

gematria, 63, 245-50
genre of Revelation, 7-13
God, 2, 4-6, 10-11, 16, 19-24, 36, 39, 49-50, 53-57, 60-61, 63, 65, 70-78, 80-84, 87-90, 94-97, 99, 102-4, 106, 108-9, 112-15, 117-19, 121-28, 131, 133, 135-46, 148-57, 159-88, 190-203, 205-16, 218-39, 241-43, 251-61, 263-98, 301-14, 316-20, 322-96, 398-99, 401, 405-37; Book of Revelation, 405-12; classical theism, 419-22; creator, 415; election of, 416, 458; eternality of, 406, 415; and evil, 411-12; feminist understanding of, 427; Gospel of John and 1–3 John, 412-13; Hebrews, 417; holiness of, 431-33; James, 417; judgment of, 412-14, 418; justice of, 408-9, 432; kingdom of, 413-15, 425; love of, 409-12, 423; Luke-Acts, 414-15; Matthew and Mark, 413-14; mystery of, 412; Paul, 415-17; 1–2 Peter, 417; sovereignty of, 407, 410-11, 423, 425-37; suffering of, 428-30; violence of, 433-34; worship of, 423-24. *See* Trinity
great whore, 21, 26-27, 291, 308-18, 321, 324, 326-336, 344-48, 365, 370-72

hymns, 8, 54-57, 141-44, 151, 210-12, 223-29, 232, 253, 270-74, 279-82, 461, 505, 553-54, 583

intertextuality. *See* OT in NT
Israel (transformed), 122, 125, 137, 167-75, 215-21, 226, 251, 358, 366, 369, 376-78

judgment, 16, 48, 50-51, 87, 90, 102, 107, 110-11, 113, 115, 119, 127, 137, 139, 149, 161-62, 178-80, 184-85, 188-90, 194, 199, 201-3, 207-9, 212-13, 222, 257, 259-68, 271, 274, 276-78, 281-86, 289-92, 295, 297, 304-7, 310-32, 338, 340, 342, 344, 347, 349, 352-55, 359-64, 368, 373, 386, 392, 395, 402

kings of the earth, 24, 76, 78, 110, 119, 127, 133, 163, 272, 285, 287-88, 291-92, 296, 303, 305, 308, 310, 313, 343, 344, 345, 347, 371, 384-86, 390, 398, 406, 475, 503, 524, 586, 590

mark of the beast, 24, 242, 251, 277-78, 295, 345-46; as 666, xv, 24, 63, 243-44, 246-50, 301, 380
martyrs, 53, 71, 281-82, 335, 409, 411, 429, 433, 435, 502, 507-8, 524, 529-31, 576-77, 616
millennial kingdom, 64, 66, 69, 358, 436, 591, 618-19

New Jerusalem, ix-x, 4-5, 7, 21, 29, 42, 45, 67, 76, 94, 103, 124-25, 215, 291, 325, 358, 363-68, 370, 373-76, 379-80, 383, 387-91, 397-98, 402-3, 409, 436, 438, 469, 495, 500-502, 504, 506-7, 518, 532, 534, 536, 591-92, 628-30
Nicolaitans, 25, 91-92, 100-102, 106, 109, 259, 305, 309

144,000, the, 16, 45, 164, 167, 169, 171, 175-76, 182, 184, 186, 201, 242, 250-56, 262, 269, 285, 303, 336, 341, 369, 376, 378-79, 441, 501, 506, 527, 530, 532
OT in NT, 14, 20, 34, 37, 39, 76, 81, 97, 101, 119, 202, 277, 287, 315, 321, 323, 354, 381
overcome(rs), 22, 24, 79-80, 85, 93-94, 98-99, 102-3, 110-11, 113, 116, 117, 124-25, 133, 136-38, 143, 146-47, 152, 155-156, 162, 170, 172, 174, 199, 204-5, 212, 218-19, 224-25, 228, 231, 235-36, 238, 251, 261, 263, 267-69, 272, 274, 282, 291, 298, 302-4, 325, 328, 335, 338-39, 341-342, 352-56, 361-372, 383, 388, 393-94, 397, 400, 422, 429, 431, 434, 444, 451, 495, 538, 540, 542, 544, 547, 550, 571, 578, 582-83, 588, 593, 604, 612

Pentecostals and Revelation, xv, xvi, 39, 61, 528, 575, 578, 583
people of God, 70, 96, 160-61, 165, 171-73, 198, 200-201, 206, 221, 234, 237, 253-54, 280-81, 285, 320, 329, 352, 357-59, 364-66, 371, 374, 377-79, 385, 395, 398, 407, 431, 476, 478, 481, 484, 488, 492, 494-95,

Index of Subjects

497-98, 502, 512-14, 517-18, 520, 524, 532-33, 535-36, 538, 543, 584, 594, 601-2, 614, 619, 633
persecution, 22-23, 29-31, 39, 69, 80, 89, 95, 97, 100, 117, 124, 126, 130, 134, 200, 226-27, 256, 349-50, 359, 444, 470, 473, 514, 608
pneumatic discernment, 79, 112, 220, 237-38, 243-45, 247, 253, 261, 280, 298-99, 337, 351, 382, 391-93, 400, 403
prayer, 77, 118, 150, 153, 160-62, 177-79, 187, 199, 260, 264, 271, 275-76, 280-81, 292, 294, 297, 327, 402-3, 409, 417, 434, 440, 461-62, 496, 503-4, 516-17, 519, 525-26, 536, 549, 561, 606
prophecy, 2, 10-11, 13, 26, 37-38, 75, 93, 111, 134, 196, 201, 204, 237, 305, 335-37, 346, 369, 384-85, 392-97, 400-403

repentance, 21, 49, 85, 87, 89-91, 93, 96, 102, 106-7, 112, 114-15, 118, 123-24, 131-32, 134, 159, 179-80, 185, 189-91, 202, 209, 232, 254, 257-58, 260-61, 263, 265, 268, 271-72, 278, 283-84, 286, 290, 292, 303, 323, 338, 341-42, 345, 358, 371, 386, 395, 398, 401, 409, 412-13, 435, 451, 476, 480, 487-89, 494, 503, 505, 508, 510-12, 514, 520, 528, 533, 540, 542, 547, 550-51, 561, 579-80, 584, 597-98, 600, 602, 608, 618-19
Revelation and the Johannine Community, 39-41
rewards, 56, 59, 87, 96, 110, 116, 124, 143, 212-13, 257, 269, 280-81, 289, 329, 331, 340, 373, 384, 395-97, 408, 417, 574, 587, 606
Rome, 25, 27-31, 65, 72, 258, 299-300, 441

salvation, 170-71, 223-24, 285-86, 297, 326-27, 333, 383-88, 537-84; and atonement, 450, 452, 455-56, 569-78; Book of Revelation, 537-43; faith, 580-82; Gospel of John and 1–3 John, 543-47; grace, 564-66; Hebrews, 559-61; James, 561; justification, 565-66, 574-75, 580; Luke-Acts, 550-52; Matthew and Mark, 547-50; multidimensional, 579-80; Paul, 552-59; 1–2 Peter, 562-63; sanctification, 580, 582-83; theocentrism, 566-67; Trinitarian, 568
sanctification, 118; and cleansing 54, 172, 285, 374, 397, 431, 546
scroll, 13, 36, 65, 69, 71, 135, 144-45, 154, 163, 191, 196, 198, 267, 338, 425, 430, 438-44, 457, 461, 463, 470-71, 494, 507-8, 527, 531, 586
scroll of God, 13, 36, 71, 144-45, 191, 196, 267, 338, 425, 430, 438, 439-40, 444, 457, 461, 463, 470-71, 494, 507-8, 527, 531
seals, seven, 135, 144-47, 151-52, 154-66, 175-82, 191-94
666. *See under* Mark of the beast
sounds, 6, 24, 51, 81, 83, 139, 145, 156, 159, 175-76, 178-79, 182, 186, 189, 193, 195, 210, 242, 251-53, 277, 288, 321-23, 325, 329-30, 365, 370, 373, 402
Spirit, 2-11, 205-10, 237, 400-402, 475-500; Book of Revelation, 475-78; and Christ, 472-74, 476-78, 479-80, 482-84; deity of, 476, 489-94; discernment of, 485-89; filioque, 493-94; Gospel of John and 1–3 John, 479-80; Hebrews, 483-84; and the kingdom of God, 480-82; of life, 496-99; Luke and Acts, 481-82; Matthew and Mark, 480-81; and the nations, 494-96; Paul, 481-82; personhood of, 492-93; 1–2 Peter, 484; of prophecy, 11, 337, 391-92, 476-78, 484; sanctification, 482-83; as the seven Spirits, 2, 21, 76, 112-14, 139, 145, 148-49, 203, 475-76; "in the Spirit," 2-11, 38-39, 79-84, 92-93, 135-36, 297, 325, 373-74; spiritual gifts, 483
star(s), 65, 83-87, 89, 111-12, 117, 163, 181, 183, 195, 197, 215-17, 348, 393, 399-400, 586, 600, 611
sword, 6, 82-83, 98, 102, 157, 159, 203, 205, 216, 221, 237, 240-41, 247, 263, 285, 303, 341-43, 347-48, 351, 362, 388, 392, 433, 470, 495, 575, 587, 620

Trinity, 420-22, 430; and Christ, 472-73; and the church, 520-25; and modalism, 420, 463; and salvation, 568; and the

645

Index of Subjects

Spirit, 475-76; and subordinationism, 420, 463-65
trumpets, 3-4, 7, 51, 67-68, 81, 135-36, 139, 147, 154, 156, 176, 179-84, 187-89, 191, 193-95, 203, 209-11, 213-14, 217, 242, 267-68, 275-76, 278-79, 282-84, 289-90, 321-22, 348, 401, 587, 606
two witnesses, 22-23, 64, 191, 201-8, 212, 219, 220, 225, 228, 231-32, 235, 241, 285, 298, 350, 355, 359, 441, 477, 494, 496-97, 508, 530, 540

violence, 44, 63, 160, 409, 411, 427, 428-36, 443-45, 470-71, 495, 529, 531, 569, 575-77, 612

war, 22, 46, 102, 186, 203-6, 220-21, 226, 228-30, 232-33, 235, 239, 241, 244, 250, 253-55, 261, 263, 268, 272, 280, 284-89, 295, 298, 302-3, 312, 318, 337-42, 344-45, 347, 351, 357-59, 376, 392, 411, 418, 433-34, 445, 470-71, 474, 539, 577, 587, 589, 592, 599

woman clothed with the sun, 21, 23, 51, 63, 214-20, 226, 228, 260, 268, 294, 296, 349
women in Revelation, 21
works, 10, 25-26, 77, 85, 87, 89-93, 104-11, 113-15, 118, 120, 127-28, 130-31, 133, 172, 189-91, 209, 212, 261-62, 271, 284, 287-88, 305, 311, 333, 361-63, 371, 395-96, 398, 401, 499, 504-5, 519, 524, 541, 555, 557-59, 565, 574-75, 580-82, 593, 606
worship, 8-9, 23-24, 26-27, 31, 37, 39, 48, 52, 64, 74, 77, 83, 105-6, 121-22, 141-44, 149-55, 171, 189-90, 194, 198-200, 203, 208-9, 211, 215, 232-33, 235-36, 238-44, 257-62, 265, 268, 271-74, 277-78, 281-84, 286, 289, 296-98, 304, 307-9, 318, 324, 326, 328-29, 334-36, 345-46, 349, 352-54, 358, 360, 369, 371, 378, 384-86, 388-89, 392-94, 398-99, 402-3, 406, 408-9, 413, 416, 423-26, 438-41, 444-45, 457-58, 460-64, 466-69, 474, 478-79, 482, 484-85, 487, 489, 491-93, 496, 499, 504-6, 513-14, 520-22, 525-27, 535-36, 542, 555, 580, 593, 605, 608, 619-20, 623

Index of Biblical and Other Ancient References

OLD TESTAMENT

Genesis
1:1-13	407
1:10	193
1:26-28	355
2:7	445, 476, 497, 540
2:9	94
2:10	387
3:1-7	222, 349
3:5	445
3:15-16	217
3:15	216, 228
3:16	216, 218, 231, 349
3:19	498
3:22	94
3:22-24	388
3:23-24	94
4:15	166
9:8-17	137
10:2	357
12:1	310
15:18	187
16:10	192
18:18	495, 501
19:1-29	260
19:24	178, 347
19:28	260, 313, 328
22:2	374
22:11-18	192
22:18	501
24:7	192
31:11-13	192
37:9	215
49:8-12	146
49:9	147
49:10	147

Exodus
1:22	227
3:2-12	192
3:14	406
7:13	283
7:14-24	278-79
7:17	204
7:20-21	179-80
7:22	283
7:24	279
8:5	285
8:15	283
8:19	283
8:32	283
9:7	283
9:12	283
9:22-26	179
9:34-35	283
10:1	283
10:4-20	184
10:20	283
10:21-23	182
11:9-10	283
12	166
12:23	187, 348
13:21-22	358
14:4	283, 572
14:4-7	410
14:19	192
14:21-22	284
14:31	269
15	269
15:6	408
15:11	270-72
15:11-12	233
15:25	181
16	102
17:9-10	374
19	374
19:4	226
19:16	139
20:13	190
20:14	190
20:15	190
21:24	213
22:18	190
24:15-18	408
25:31-40	139
28:17-21	137, 375
28:36-38	125
31:16	408
32:31-33	116-17
33:20	164, 389
34:29-35	375
40:4	139
40:24-25	139
40:34-35	276

Leviticus
11:9-12	285
11:41-47	285
24:20	213
26:8	185
26:11-12	366

Index of Biblical and Other Ancient References

26:12	366	5:31	82	9:30-37	305
26:21-24	267	6:22	192	10:1-11	108
		9:7	374	18:12	269
Numbers		13:20-22	192	19:4	165
1:1	188	15:11	213	19:16	165
12:7	269	16:13-22	186	21:8	269
16:23	310	18:30-31	168	21:13	199
16:30	346	20:40	260	23:5	215
16:31-33	228			23:29	287
22–24	100	**Ruth**			
24:17	111, 400	4:11	512	**1 Chronicles**	
25:1-2	100			16:9	271
31	167	**1 Samuel**		16:31	272
31:16	100	4:8	204	24:4-6	138
35:30	201	7:6	277		
		21:5	254	**2 Chronicles**	
Deuteronomy				7:1-3	276
3:24	233	**2 Samuel**		24:9	269
4:16	240	5:7	250	36:16	323
4:19	215	7:14	369		
12:32	401	8:2	199	**Ezra**	
13:1-5	239	11:11	254	9:6	310
17:3	215	14:25-26	186		
17:6	201			**Nehemiah**	
19:15	201	**1 Kings**		1:8	269
19:16-19	320	5:17	381	9:33	279
19:21	213	6–7	380		
23:9-10	254	6:20	379	**Job**	
23:18	398	6:30	382	1:16	178
28:42	184	8:9	274	2:1-10	277
29	401	8:37	184	18:15	260
29:23	260	8:53	269	26:6	186
31:26	274	8:56	269	28:22	186
32:4	271, 273	10:14	244	31:12	186
32:11-12	226	12:25-33	168	31:26	215
34:5	269	16:31-32	105	33:4	476, 497-98
		17:1	204, 239		
Joshua		18:13	220	**Psalms**	
1:1	269	18:15	239	2:6	250
1:4	187	18:20-46	374	2:8-9	111
1:15	269	18:36-40	178	6:3	270, 272
3:14-17	285	18:38	239	7:10	108
5:12	102	18:42	374	7:11	279
8:20	260	19:18	209	7:14-16	213
8:31	269			9:4	279
9:24	269	**2 Kings**		9:11	250, 495, 501
10:11	290	1:10	178, 203	11:6	178, 260
		1:12	178	11:7	389
Judges		1:14	178	13:1-2	160
1:7	213	9:7	327	15:1	270, 272
2:1	192	9:22	105	17:15	389
5:19	287	9:27	287	18:31	233

18:49	495, 501	98:1	150	6:2	141
22:16	398	98:1-2	271	6:3	141, 406
22:20	398	98:1-3	253	6:8	406
22:28	272	98:5	150	6:13	208
28:5	512	98:9	410, 572	10:5	182
29	193	99:2	272	11:1-10	147
29:10	292, 312	104:29-30	498	11:2	147
33:2	150	104:30	538	11:4	147
33:3	150	105:26	269	11:6-8	147
38:11	313, 317	106	326	11:10	147, 501
40:3	150	106:48	329	11:15	285
42:2	389	111–113	326	12:4	495, 501
45:17	495	111:1-2	271	13	288
46:10	495, 501	111:3	410, 572	13:13	162, 289
47:8	272	112 (LXX)	329	21:9	307
47:9	501	113:5	233	21:17	156
49:15	426	115:3-8	190	22:12	202
67:2	495	117	326	22:22	119
67:4	495	118:1	271	23:16	292
68	188	118:22	512	24:23	250
68:17	188	119:103	197	25:7-10	250
69:9	131	132:13	250, 358	25:8	174
71:19	410, 572	135	326, 329	26:16-17	216
72:11	495	139:14	271	27:1	216
72:17	495	144:9	150	28:16-17	199
74:10	160	144:9-10	253	30:33	260
74:14	216	144:17 (LXX)	273	34:4	163
75:8	260	145:17	271	34:9	260
76:2	250	146–150	326	34:10	313
77:18	139	147:7	150	34:11	199
78:46	184	148 (LXX)	329	34:11-15	308
79 (LXX 78)	160	149:1	150	34:12	323
79:3-6	277	150 (LXX)	329	38:18	426
79:5	160			40:18	272
82:2	160	**Proverbs**		40:18-20	190
86:8	233	8:15-16	323	40:25	270, 272
86:9	495	15:11	186	40:25-26	233
87:2	358	30:27	186	40:31	226
88:11	186			41:2	470
89:8	233	**Ecclesiastes**		41:6-7	190
89:17	410, 572	2:16	426	42:1	495, 501
89:46	160			42:9	407
90:13	160	**Isaiah**		42:10	150
91:13	189	1:4	182	42:10-13	253
92:5	271	1:21	292, 331	43:3-4	121
94:3	160	2:2	501	43:18-19	407
96–100	258	2:2-4	273, 374	44:6	369, 396, 406, 439
96:1	150	2:4	495	44:7	233
96:2	258	2:10	163	44:9-20	190
96:3	510	2:19	163	45:8	410, 572
96:10	272	2:21	163	45:14	121-22
96:13	410, 572	6:1-4	276	45:20	386

Index of Biblical and Other Ancient References

45:22	386	10:25	277	2:8–3:2	196
45:23-24	410, 572	11:15	358	3:12	293
45:24	386	11:20	108	3:14	293
46:10	407	12:7	358	5:9	294
46:13	407	13:27	294	5:11	294
48:20	310	14:16	277	5:12	165
49:2	83, 342	15:2	159, 237	6:9	295
50:3	163	16:9	323	8:3	293
51:4	501	16:18	311	9:1-11	166
51:6-8	410, 572	17:10	108	9:11	83
51:17	260	20:12	108	10:2-8	178
51:22	260	23:1	182	11:1	293
52:11	310	23:15	181	11:24	293
53:4	572	24:6	512	16:15	292
53:5-6	576	24:7	366	20:41	410
53:6	571, 576	25:10	323	23:1	292
53:7	148	25:17	260	23:1-49	304
54:1	216	25:28	260	23:31-33	260
54:11	381	28:34 (LXX)	218	24:6	182
55:1	369	31:4	512	26:3-4	292
55:1-3	129	31:38-40	199	27:12-24	315
57:6	277	32:35	294	27:27	318
57:15	409	33:7	512	28:13	94, 381
60:1-22	121	43:11	237	29:3	216
60:3	384, 501	44:22	294	31:8-9	94
60:11	386	46:28	279	32:3-16	216
60:19-20	383	49:12	260	36:23	410
62:2	125	49:36	165	37	241
63:9	428	50:8	310	37:1	293
65:16	126	50:11 (LXX)	237	37:3	172
66:6	277	50:29	156	37:5	207
66:7	218	51:1-2	156	37:10	207
66:7-9	216	51:3	94, 156	37:13-14	426
66:18	501	51:6	310	38–39	288
		51:7	260	38:2	357
Jeremiah		51:9	310	38:6	357, 376
1:2	74	51:13	292	38:22	290, 359
1:2-3	35	51:25	300	39:6	359
1:4	74	51:34	216, 218	40–48	28, 199
1:10	512	51:45	310	40–46	383
1:11	74	51:59-64	321	40:1-2	374
2:2	331			43:5	293
4:8	202	Lamentations		44:4	276
4:11-12	165	2:4	277	45:2	378
4:24	163	2:8	199	47:1-12	387
5:14	203	4:21	260	47:12	388
7:20	277			48:8-9	378
7:34	323	Ezekiel		48:30-35	376, 378
8:2	215	1:4-28	140		
9:15	181	1:13	139, 178	Daniel	
10	190	1:16	82	1:12	97
10:7	272	2:3	35	1:14	97

Index of Biblical and Other Ancient References

2:24	323	**Joel**		**Zephaniah**	
3:6	82	1:1	74	1:7	175
3:22	283	1:3	35	3:13	256
3:27	283	1:4-7	185		
4:33	323	1:19-20	180	**Haggai**	
4:34-37	295	2:1-11	185	1:1	35
5:1-3	323	2:10	162	1:15	188
5:9	323	2:31	163	2:6	162
5:23	323	3:13	263, 265	2:6-7	289
6:17	323				
7	230	**Amos**		**Zechariah**	
7:7	217	1:1	35	1:1	35
7:7-23	204	3:7	196	1:7	188
7:9	82, 139, 439	3:8	193	1:8	155
7:10	361	3:13	271	1:16	199
7:13	82, 263	4:13	271	2:1-2	199
7:13-14	438, 448, 451, 486	5:3	208	2:6-7	310
7:14	535	5:8	271	2:11	386
7:20	233	5:14-15	271	2:13	175
7:21	204, 230	5:16	271	3:3-5	115
7:23	230	5:18	182	3:3-7	395
7:24	302	5:27	271	3:4	115
7:25	200, 227, 234-35	7:7-9	199	4	202
8:10	217	9:5	271	4:1-14	139
8:11-14	200	9:6	271	4:2	76, 82
9:14	279	9:7	410	4:6	202, 477, 522
9:16-18	410, 572	9:11	512	4:10	148, 475
10:4-6	82	9:15	271	4:14	202, 477
10:8-17	197			6:2-6	155
10:13	221	**Obadiah**		6:5	165
10:21	221	16	260	8:23	386
12:1-2	172			10:3	455
12:4	13, 394	**Jonah**		12:2	260
12:7	200	1:2	310	12:3	199
12:9	13	2:2	426	12:10-12	78
		3:6-8	202	12:11	287-88
		3:7	323	13:8-9	180
Hosea				14:4-5	289
1:1	35, 74	**Micah**		14:11	389
1:2	410	1:1	35		
2:7	331	2:5	199	**Malachi**	
4	410	4:1-3	374	1:11	272-73
5:3	292, 410	4:9-10	216	3:2	164
5:14-15	410	7:18	233, 270, 272	4:4	269
7:13	182				
11:1-4	572	**Nahum**			
11:10	193	1:6	164	**NEW TESTAMENT**	
12:5	271	3:4	292		
12:8	128			**Matthew**	
13:4	407	**Habakkuk**		1	16
13:14	426	2:15-16	260	1:18-20	447, 480
		2:20	175		

Index of Biblical and Other Ancient References

Ref	Page	Ref	Page	Ref	Page
2:2	447	16:21	576	2:21-22	599
2:5	447	16:22-23	449	2:33-35	512
3:1-2	413	17:5	449	3:11	449
3:2	480, 511, 597	17:12	450	3:11-12	449
3:11-12	449, 480	19:28	511, 598	3:20-21	512
3:12	414, 597	20:18-19	450	3:29	549
3:16	480	21:5	447	4:21-25	512
3:17	449	21:9	447	5:7	449
4:1	481	21:39	265	8:22-26	513
4:1-11	548	22:32	413	8:27-38	448
4:17	547	22:41-46	447	8:31-33	449, 549
5:3-12	598	22:44-45	448	9:7	449
5:20	413	23:23	450, 528	9:12	450
5:45	414	23:37-39	511	9:24	550
6:9	414	23:39	599	9:30-36	549
6:10	547, 597	24–25	16	9:31	540
6:12	549	24:6	599	10:15	413
6:19-34	414	24:14	495, 512	10:32-45	549
6:26-27	414	24:29-31	548	10:33	450
6:33	413	24:30	598	10:38	548
8:8-9	550	24:43	114	10:39	42
8:15-17	549	25:34	414	10:43-44	513
8:29	597	25:41	414	10:45	413-14, 448, 450, 513, 548-49, 599
9:4-6	549	26:28	450, 549		
9:10-13	511	26:29	414, 549	12:26-27	413
9:17	599	26:41	481	13	16
9:22	550	26:61	511	13:7	599
10:2	29	26:64	448, 548	13:24-25	600
10:28	414	27:11	447	13:26	448, 598
10:29	414	27:40	449	13:38	450
11:4-5	598	27:45-51	598	14:24-25	450
11:11	598	27:51	549	14:32-42	548
11:14	597	27:51-54	448, 549	14:36	414, 576
11:20-24	414	27:54	511, 550	14:38	481
12:6	511	28:2-3	598	14:58	448-49, 511
12:18	480	28:4	598	15:33-34	414
12:22-32	480	28:8-10	450		
12:28	413, 448, 480, 511, 547, 597	28:16-20	450	**Luke**	
		28:18	550	1:15-17	481
12:29	550	28:18-20	448	1:17	597
12:31	549	28:19	492, 495, 512	1:35	449, 451, 480
13:16-17	598			1:40-42	481
13:24	600	**Mark**		1:50-51	414
13:31-32	413	1:1	449	1:51-52	414
13:31-33	548	1:8	449	1:51-53	600
13:31-35	598	1:10-11	480, 598	1:53	414
13:38	450	1:11	449	1:54	414
13:43	414	1:12	481	1:67	481
15:24	511	1:12-13	548	2:14	551
16:16	447, 449	1:15	512, 547, 598	2:25	481
16:18	512, 550	2:5	549-50	2:52	498
16:18-19	512	2:13-17	449, 511	3:15-18	480

Index of Biblical and Other Ancient References

3:16-17	449, 451	1:1-18	74, 341	3:2	106, 386
3:21-22	451, 598	1:2-3	144, 445	3:5	480, 510, 547, 594
3:22	449, 480	1:3	623	3:5-8	509
4:1	481	1:4	83, 94, 412, 445-46	3:6-8	480
4:1-11	548	1:4-5	323, 446	3:7	297
4:1-13	449	1:5	383, 386, 544	3:10	106, 167
4:12	468	1:5-7	510	3:14	113, 220, 263, 293, 546
4:18	451, 481, 513, 550, 600	1:6	88	3:15-16	545
4:18-19	414	1:7-9	323	3:15-17	412
5:37-38	599	1:9	119, 307	3:16	77, 89, 309, 316, 479, 510, 543, 571
6:37	551	1:9-13	544	3:16-17	447
7:21-23	598	1:11	341	3:16-18	104
7:22	451	1:12	89, 509	3:16-20	543
7:28	598	1:13	480	3:17	88
9:1	29	1:14	75, 119, 142, 219, 234, 271, 366, 412, 446, 510-11, 544, 595	3:17-21	510
9:10	513			3:18	412, 510, 546, 594
10:1-24	513			3:19	418
10:17-19	451	1:14-16	403, 537	3:20	92
12:10	549	1:16	75, 544	3:21	274, 546
12:11-12	513, 600	1:17	75, 229, 271, 412, 544	3:24	97, 307
12:12	481			3:29	114, 331
12:32	511	1:18	73, 104, 389, 412, 446, 509, 544-45	3:33	166, 271, 350
12:39	114-15			3:34	479
15:11-31	511	1:20	99, 117, 447	3:35	104, 412, 479
15:11-32	551	1:23	220, 293	3:36	164, 412-13, 546
17:5	513	1:29	16, 40, 77, 148, 447	4	171
17:25	450	1:31	167, 274, 508	4:7-15	369
17:34	600	1:33	88, 449	4:8	151
18:9-14	551	1:34	104	4:10-24	498
18:35-43	551	1:37	75	4:12	400
19:1-10	551	1:37-38	254	4:13-15	174
21	16	1:38	106	4:14	174, 181, 545-46
21:9	599	1:40	75, 254	4:19	207
21:20-28	601	1:41	447	4:20-24	122, 199
21:26	469	1:42	103, 303, 334	4:22	171, 509, 544
22:14	29, 513	1:43	254	4:23	199
22:30	511	1:47	76, 167	4:23-24	479
23:43	600	1:49	76, 104, 106, 167, 303, 343, 509	4:24	413, 479, 491
24:10	513			4:26	426
24:13-35	513, 551	2:1-11	254	4:27	232, 297
24:39	601	2:1-12	218	4:29	344, 447
24:44	601	2:2	303, 334, 545	4:31	106
24:49	481, 513	2:4	115	4:34	88, 195, 271
24:52-53	513	2:11	142, 274, 303, 334, 596	4:35-38	264
John		2:14-15	199	4:36	212, 331, 344
1:1	127, 445-46, 491, 595	2:16	309	4:38	88, 262, 320, 377
		2:17	196	4:42	75, 171
1:1-2	446	2:19	449, 511	4:46-54	388
1:1-5	412	2:19-21	199	5:1-18	388
1:1-14	458	2:23	207	5:2	186

653

5:5	104	6:49-51	595		217, 222, 255, 316, 349, 371, 398-99, 413
5:12-14	510	6:50-51	102		
5:14	107, 199	6:51	545, 594		
5:16	226	6:53	263, 545, 595	8:47	75, 547
5:18	446, 544	6:53-56	77	8:48-49	190
5:19	446	6:53-58	102, 510	8:50-54	142
5:20	232, 271, 291, 297, 373, 412	6:54	545-46, 595	8:51	120, 546
		6:56	546, 595	8:51-55	75, 114
5:21	445	6:58	546	8:52	190, 546
5:22-23	446	6:59	106	8:56	331
5:24	75, 545-46, 594	6:61-66	100	8:58	426, 595
5:24-28	132	6:63	479, 545	8:59	199
5:25	75, 104, 596	6:66	116, 384	9:1-41	129, 388
5:26	445	6:67	29, 377	9:2	106
5:27	263	6:69	118	9:3	274
5:28	75, 232, 297	6:70	303, 377	9:3-4	271
5:28-29	355	6:70-71	29	9:4	386
5:30	271	6:71	377	9:5	323
5:35	322, 331	7:3	271	9:6	130
5:36	195, 271	7:4	254, 274	9:22	117
5:37-38	545	7:6	299	9:34-38	200
5:40	545	7:7	92	9:35	263
6	94	7:12	222, 240, 351	9:38	122
6:2	207	7:14	106, 199	9:39	352
6:3	374	7:15	232, 297	10:1	115, 191, 200
6:5	151	7:18	142	10:1-21	174
6:6	123	7:20	190	10:3	75
6:12	316, 348	7:21	232, 271, 297, 594	10:3-5	132
6:12-13	344	7:21-22	412	10:4-5	254
6:15	219, 303, 343, 374, 447	7:24	271	10:7	119
		7:28	106, 199, 271	10:7-10	119
6:17	386	7:30	115, 345	10:8	75, 115
6:19	207	7:31	447	10:9	546
6:19-20	83, 96	7:32	345	10:10	115, 191, 316, 479, 545
6:20	426	7:33	255		
6:25	106	7:35	106	10:11	159, 447
6:27	166, 263, 316, 350, 446	7:37	479	10:11-15	510
		7:37-39	174, 401, 498	10:11-17	225
6:28-29	574	7:38	174, 181, 387, 546	10:12	219
6:29	102, 271	7:38-39	478-79	10:14-18	229
6:31	220, 293	7:44	345	10:15	159, 447
6:32	119	7:47	222, 240, 351	10:16	75, 132, 200
6:33	102, 545	8:12	254, 323, 384, 386, 546	10:17	159, 412
6:35	102, 174, 545-46			10:17-18	447
6:37	546	8:14	255	10:18	447
6:38-40	144	8:16	119	10:20-21	190
6:39	316	8:20	106, 115, 199, 345	10:23	199
6:40	207, 445	8:21-22	255	10:25	271
6:44	546	8:24	113, 426	10:27	75, 132, 254
6:45	106	8:26	271	10:28	316
6:46	389, 446, 544, 546	8:28	73, 106, 447	10:28-29	219
6:49	220, 293	8:44	88, 96-97, 121, 190,	10:30	446

10:32	271, 373	12:43	142	14:28	75, 331
10:33	271, 291	12:45	207	14:30	210
10:36	104, 118	12:46	323, 386	14:31	229
10:37-38	271	12:49-50	73	15:1	119, 447
10:38	446	12:50	229	15:1-5	510
10:39	345	13:1	77, 89, 110, 115	15:2	105
11:1-57	388	13:1-11	447	15:4	547, 594
11:4	104, 142	13:1-20	510	15:6	264, 344
11:8	106	13:2	97, 132, 334	15:9	412, 479
11:9-10	384	13:3	255, 446	15:10	75, 114, 120, 229
11:10	386	13:4	132, 334	15:11	114
11:15	331	13:8	356, 401, 458	15:12	229
11:25	445, 545, 595	13:10	77	15:13	159, 225
11:25-26	596	13:13-14	106	15:15	73, 510, 545
11:26	546	13:16	29, 88, 377	15:16	89, 303
11:27	104	13:18	114, 303, 510	15:18–16:4	93
11:28	106, 299	13:19	262	15:18	92
11:31	146, 313	13:20	88	15:18-19	92
11:33	146, 313	13:26	340	15:20	75, 114, 226
11:35	174	13:27	222, 349	15:20-21	89
11:40	142	13:29	151	15:23-24	92
11:43	291, 373	13:30	357, 386	15:23-25	92
11:44	187	13:31	263	15:24	271
11:45-53	597	13:33	255	15:25	114
11:47	344	13:34	90, 229	15:26	545
11:47-48	447	13:35	90, 104	15:26-27	546
11:48	105	13:37-38	159, 225	16:1	100
11:50	316	13:38	99	16:1-4	39
11:52	344, 509	14:1-3	621	16:5	255
11:54	220, 293	14:2-3	159	16:8-11	131, 149
11:56	199	14:3	596	16:10	255
11:57	345	14:4	254	16:11	93, 210, 222, 594
12:2	104, 132, 334	14:6	83, 94, 119, 271, 446, 468, 545	16:13	174, 479, 480
12:6	115, 191			16:17	255
12:13	167, 170, 303, 343	14:7	262, 264, 545	16:20	207, 313, 331
12:15	303, 343	14:9	291, 373, 446	16:21	79, 95, 172
12:20	122	14:10	73	16:22	331
12:23	115, 263	14:10-12	271	16:23-24	89
12:23-28	413	14:12	546, 596	16:24	114
12:24	447	14:13-14	89	16:26	89
12:25	92, 104, 225, 316, 545	14:15	120, 229	16:27	412
		14:15-24	75, 114	16:28	446, 596
12:26	104	14:16	480	16:33	79, 95, 133
12:29	193	14:17	207, 479, 594	17:1	115
12:31	221	14:18	480	17:2	111, 545
12:31-32	115	14:19	207	17:3	119, 271, 545, 595
12:32	447, 509, 546	14:21	229	17:4	195, 271
12:33	74, 215	14:23-24	120	17:5	142, 153, 236, 446, 544
12:34	263	14:26	88-89, 106, 479, 509		
12:35	384, 386			17:6	75, 114, 123, 274, 510
12:38	114	14:26-28	595		
12:42	117	14:27	76	17:7-8	510

655

Reference	Pages
17:8	73
17:9	510
17:11	118, 142, 510
17:11-15	75, 114
17:12	114, 316
17:13	114
17:14	73, 92
17:14-15	122-23
17:14-19	595
17:15-18	547
17:16-19	510
17:17	118
17:18	320, 377
17:19	119, 510, 545, 594
17:20-21	528
17:20-22	510
17:20-23	479
17:21	412, 446, 510, 546
17:23	77
17:23-24	412
17:24	159, 208, 236, 412, 446, 510, 546
17:25	271, 545
17:26	546, 594
18:2	344
18:5	426
18:6	426
18:8	426
18:9	114
18:11	260
18:12	187
18:14	129
18:15	199
18:20	106, 199
18:24	187
18:25	99
18:32	74, 114, 215
18:33	303, 343
18:36	210
18:36-37	447
18:37	132, 303, 343
18:39	303, 343
19:2	294
19:3	294, 303, 343
19:5	294
19:7	104
19:12	303, 343
19:13	186
19:14-15	303, 343
19:17	186
19:19	303, 343
19:20	186, 265
19:21	303, 343
19:24	114
19:25	44
19:25-27	218, 228
19:28	351
19:30	195, 305, 351
19:31	148
19:33-34	40
19:34	77
19:36	114
19:37	78
19:39	386
19:40	187
20	354
20:11	146, 313
20:13	146, 313
20:14	82, 208
20:15	146, 313
20:16	106
20:17	369
20:19	76
20:19-20	383
20:19-23	450
20:20	291, 331, 373
20:21	88, 320, 377, 479
20:21-23	510
20:22	114, 445-46, 497
20:24	29
20:26	76
20:26-27	447
20:27	97, 371
20:28	446, 491
20:29	510
20:29-31	447
20:31	89, 104, 543, 546
21	354
21:1	274
21:3	345
21:7	129
21:10	345
21:11	248
21:14	274
21:19	74, 215
21:19-22	254
21:20	132, 334
21:23	79
Acts	
1:1-8	451, 481, 513
1:3	551
1:3-5	601
1:6-8	552
1:7	601
1:8	481, 495, 514
1:9	451
2:4	514
2:4-11	602
2:4-12	552
2:5	469
2:11	486
2:17-21	414, 514
2:18-20	552
2:19-21	603
2:21	552
2:22-36	415
2:25-28	602
2:30-32	451
2:31-32	552
2:32	602
2:33	451, 481, 602
2:38	515, 551, 602
2:38-39	414
2:39	602
2:42-47	481
2:44-47	514
2:47	514
3:13	415
3:19-21	552
4:10	576, 602
4:12	451
4:24	415
4:27-31	552
4:30-31	514
4:31	482
5:1-5	491
5:29-32	552
5:41-42	514
7:51-53	552
7:52	451
8:4	514
8:14-17	515
10:28	514
10:34	414, 552
10:38	552
10:38-39	451
10:39-43	552
10:41-43	514
10:42	552
10:44	514
10:44-46	482
10:44-48	515
10:46	602
11:17	414
11:28	215

Index of Biblical and Other Ancient References

12:24	514	6:2	483	15:7	517, 556
13:17	415	6:4	555, 603	15:13	605
13:39	552	6:4-5	453	15:19	453
13:49-52	514	6:6-7	555	16:16	453
15:8-9	552	6:11	453		
15:8-10	514	6:12	483	**1 Corinthians**	
17:22-34	451	6:16	470	1:2	515
17:23	552	6:23	453, 606	1:3	453
17:24	415	7:14	452, 554	1:7	578
17:24-28	435	7:24	452, 604	1:9	515
17:24-31	603	8:3	452, 483, 558	1:10	517
17:25	415	8:9	454, 482, 491-92	2:1-2	553
17:26-27	514, 603	8:11	483, 604	2:1-5	483
17:26-28	552	8:11-16	555	2:4-5	482, 578
17:28	498	8:15	414, 482, 515	2:10	482
17:29	415	8:15-16	515, 518	2:12	482-83
17:31	451	8:17	604	3:10-14	517
19:4-6	515	8:18-25	452	3:15	606
19:5	451	8:22	610	3:16	483
19:6	482, 514	8:23	483, 559, 604-5	3:16-17	517
20:27	414	8:23-25	604	4:8-13	605
22:14	552	8:26	556, 605	6:11	482, 555
22:16	452	8:28-29	557	6:20	491
24:14	552	8:29	557	8:6	415, 553
26:22	552	8:30	518	9:1	452
		8:31	555	10:16	603
Romans		8:31-39	517	10:17	517, 453
1:4	415, 482	8:32	416	10:25-30	101
1:7	470	8:33-36	557	10:32	515
1:18-23	416	8:38-39	557, 604	11:12	415
1:19-20	415	8:39	613	11:16	515
1:24-28	418	9:13	415	11:17-34	517
2:6	453, 606	11	557	11:22	515
2:16	606	11:5	515	11:26	517
3:19	415	11:11	416, 606	11:29	517
3:22-23	606	11:15	453	12:1-3	516
3:23-24	416	11:17-21	515	12:3	453, 482
3:24	452	11:17-24	533	12:4-6	415, 454, 482, 490, 493, 516
3:24-25	554	11:25-32	556	12:13	453, 483, 515, 517
4:4-5	558	11:26	606	12:15-19	516
4:17	415, 426	11:29	416	12:23	516
4:25	416, 453, 553	11:32	416, 557	12:26	516
5:1-5	559	11:33	416	12:28	515
5:1-9	426	11:36	415	13	516
5:5	482, 554, 605	12:19	418	14:1	516
5:6	515	13:1-7	607	14:4	516
5:10-11	453	13:10	452, 482	14:5	483
5:12-21	554	13:11	606	14:6	73
5:15	558	13:12	606	14:17	516
5:17	558	13:14	606	14:17-18	483
5:20	409	14:7	605	14:18	516
5:21	452, 556	14:8	603		

14:19	185	2:16	555	4:14-16	483
14:26	516, 556	2:20	453, 483, 555, 605	4:15	515-17, 605
14:27-28	516	3:1-2	453	4:15-16	516
14:36-40	516	3:2	482, 555	4:30	518
14:39	516	3:7	533	5:18-21	517
15:3-4	453, 553	3:8	555	5:21	516
15:7	483	3:13	554	6:10-20	517
15:8	452	3:13-14	452		
15:9	515	3:14	482, 554-55, 605	**Philippians**	
15:10	453	3:15	231, 349	1:11	553
15:12-19	415	3:21	483, 499, 554, 558	1:21	604
15:20-28	415	3:21-22	452	1:23	604
15:21	554	3:26-28	517	2:4-11	453
15:24	553	3:28	516	2:7-9	553
15:25-26	604	4:6	414, 482	2:8	573
15:28	604	5:8	416	2:9-11	416
15:44	605	5:13-26	555	2:12-13	483
15:44-49	518	5:16-25	483	3:4-11	452
15:45	453	5:22-25	605	3:6	515
15:45-49	556	5:23	483	3:7-11	452
15:50	604	5:25	483	3:10	453
15:55-56	604	6:7	416	3:10-11	555, 604
		6:8	605	3:20	453
2 Corinthians				4:20	515
1:1	515	**Ephesians**			
1:2	453	1:1	416	**Colossians**	
1:3	416	1:3	515, 554	1:4	453
1:22	482-83, 605	1:3-4	453-54, 515	1:12	515
2:16	416	1:4	454	1:13	453
3:6	483	1:4-5	557	1:16-17	557
3:18	482, 491, 523	1:5	553	1:18	515
4:1	416	1:10	500, 515, 556-57	2:15	554
4:6	415, 452	1:11-12	557	2:19	516
4:7-12	523	1:13	482, 556, 605	3:3	453
5:1-4	604	1:13-14	483, 518, 605	4:13	18
5:1-5	518, 556	1:17	482	4:16	17
5:4	498, 604	2:5	553		
5:5	483, 498-99, 605	2:8-9	558	**1 Thessalonians**	
5:18	553	2:10	559	1:1	515
5:18-19	453	2:11-18	453	1:10	415
5:19	571	2:14-18	517	2:14	515
8:9	453, 553	2:18	482	4:8	482
11:4	482	2:20-21	517	4:14	414, 603
12:4	483	2:21	517	4:16-17	606
12:4-10	487	2:22	605	5:2	115
12:6-10	483	3:9	415	5:9	416
		3:15	515		
Galatians		4:3	518	**2 Thessalonians**	
1:2	515	4:4-6	415, 454, 482, 490, 493	2:3-4	605
1:6	416			2:7-11	605
1:12-16	452	4:6	552, 559	2:12	416
1:13	515	4:14	603	2:13	482, 605

Index of Biblical and Other Ancient References

3:9-11	607	8:5	607	1:26	519
	5:24	8:10-13	455	1:27	519
		9:7-9	483	2:1-4	519
1 Timothy		9:12	417	2:14-26	519
3:16	555	9:14	455, 484, 560	2:18-19	561
		9:15	455	2:20	561
2 Timothy		9:16-28	518	2:26	561
1:10	554	9:24	455	3:3-12	519
1:13-14	516	9:28	455, 560, 607	4:7-8	561
		10:1-4	455	4:11	519
Titus		10:4-10	560	5:8	113
2:12	559	10:5-10	455, 573	5:13-18	519
2:13	491	10:13	607	5:15	561
3:5	482	10:14	607	5:16	561
		10:16-17	560	5:19	519
Hebrews		10:19	518	5:19-20	561
1:1–2:4	559	10:22	417		
1:2	454, 559	10:28-30	484	**1 Peter**	
1:3	454, 559	10:31	417, 607	1:2	484, 490, 518
1:5	559	10:37	607	1:3-4	608
1:5-6	417	11:1	444, 518, 560, 607	1:5	608
1:13	560	11:3	560	1:7	608
2:4	483	11:6	417	1:10-11	484
2:9	607	11:8	560	1:13	417
2:10–5:10	559	11:10	607	1:15-16	519
2:14-15	455, 607	11:32-38	560	1:17	417
2:17-18	560	11:40	607	1:18-20	455
3:1	518	12:1	455	1:19	562
3:6	518	12:1-2	608	1:20	518, 562
3:7	483	12:1-3	518	1:21	417, 562
3:12	417	12:2	455	1:23	519, 562
3:14	560	12:4-12	47	1:27	417
3:15-19	560	12:9	417	2:2	562
3:16-19	518	12:12	518	2:4-7	456
4:12	417	12:28-29	608	2:5	417
4:13	417	12:29	417	2:12	608
4:14-16	455, 560	13:8	406	2:16	562
4:16	417, 518	13:12	265	2:24	456, 562
5:8-9	455, 560	13:17	518	2:25	417, 456, 562
5:9	607	13:20	417	3:12	417
6:4	484			3:18-20	484, 562
6:4-8	561	**James**		4:1	562
6:5	578	1:2-7	561	4:13	608
6:13	617	1:6-8	519	5:4	608
6:18	417	1:9-10	519	5:7	417
7:1–10:39	559	1:12	561	5:8	608
7:16	455, 484, 607	1:17	561	5:9	417
7:21	417	1:18	519, 561	5:10	417
7:27	560	1:19	519	5:11	417
8:1	607	1:21	561	5:13	28
8:1-2	455	1:21-27	561		
8:3-6	518	1:22-25	519		

Index of Biblical and Other Ancient References

2 Peter	
1:3	608
1:4	563, 608
1:5-7	563
1:10	563
1:11	608
1:12	484
1:16-18	519
1:19	519
1:21	484
2:2-5	484
2:4-9	417
2:9	608
2:10	519
2:24	456
3:8	608
3:9	608
3:10	115, 456, 609
3:12	609
3:11-12	563
3:11-13	519
3:12	616
3:13	608

1 John	
1:1-4	511
1:2	20, 94, 412, 545
1:2-3	596
1:3	79, 104
1:4	114
1:5	386, 413
1:5–2:2	397
1:6	255
1:6-7	79, 116, 384
1:7	104, 172, 545
1:7–2:2	77
1:8	106, 222, 240, 351
1:9	117, 172, 271
2:1	271
2:2	545
2:3	229
2:3-4	120, 229
2:3-6	510
2:5	89, 195
2:6	120, 384, 447
2:7-8	229
2:8	119, 596
2:8-9	386
2:9	92
2:11	92, 129, 384, 386
2:12	89
2:13-14	93
2:14	547
2:15-16	510
2:16-17	316
2:20	118, 131, 244
2:21	255-56, 371, 399
2:22	106
2:22-23	99
2:22-24	104
2:23	117
2:24-25	596
2:26	106, 222, 240, 351
2:27	114, 244, 255-56, 371, 399, 547
2:28	130, 299, 596
2:29	271
3:2	354, 389, 511
3:2-3	547
3:3	119
3:4-10	77, 397
3:7	106, 222, 240, 271, 351
3:8	77, 104, 222, 349
3:12	160
3:13	92
3:15	92
3:16	77, 89, 159, 225
3:16-18	90
3:19-24	397
3:22-24	120, 229
3:23	89, 104
3:24	480, 547
4:1-2	391
4:1-3	511
4:1-6	88, 308
4:2	447
4:2-3	117
4:3	596
4:4	93
4:6	106, 223, 391, 479
4:7	89, 547
4:7-8	412, 447
4:7-12	511
4:7–5:5	90
4:8	412
4:9	412
4:9-10	89, 104
4:10	412
4:11	412
4:12	89, 195, 389, 412
4:13	479
4:14-15	104
4:15	117
4:16	89, 547
4:17	596
4:17-18	89, 195, 412
4:18	511
4:19	90
4:20	92
4:21	229
5:1	104, 510
5:2-3	229
5:3	120
5:4	93
5:4-5	99, 133
5:5	93
5:6	113, 479
5:6-7	77
5:6-12	20
5:9-13	104
5:10	510
5:12	596
5:13	89
5:14-17	397
5:20	104, 119, 244, 271

2 John	
1	303
3	104
4	114, 116, 384
4-6	229
6	384
7	106, 117, 223, 240, 357
8	212, 316
9	104, 106
11	79
12	114
13	303

3 John	
3	20
3-4	116, 384
6	20
12	20

Revelation	
1–8	80
1–3	136, 293, 339, 374
1	85, 136
1:1	36, 74, 136, 162, 166, 192, 196, 198, 213, 291, 320, 329, 368, 373, 377, 391, 438, 493, 591, 618

Index of Biblical and Other Ancient References

1:1-2	399	1:9	36, 38, 74, 89, 95, 97, 105, 107, 122, 160, 162, 172, 183, 224, 238, 261, 272, 303, 334, 336, 353, 393, 444, 507, 522, 529		177, 294, 339, 368, 384, 493
1:1-3	5, 36, 84			2:1-7	4, 85, 87
1:1-8	4, 67, 73			2:1–3:22	3-4, 10, 79, 85
1:1–3:22	68			2:2	25, 29, 42, 87, 89, 91, 95, 104-5, 121, 123, 255, 298, 320, 362, 371, 377, 395, 399, 504, 522
1:1–19:9	334				
1:2	36, 74, 82, 160, 177, 201, 224, 336, 393, 507				
		1:9-10	136, 293		
1:3	2, 6, 10, 74, 75, 93, 110, 120, 176, 201, 226, 286, 305, 334, 339, 392, 394, 501, 504, 591	1:9-20	4, 36, 79	2:2-3	89, 105, 122, 261, 262
		1:9–3:22	4, 67, 79		
		1:10	2, 34-35, 48, 79-81, 93, 136, 139, 160, 176, 182, 252, 322, 438, 476, 486, 492, 505, 526	2:2-6	87, 89
				2:3	22, 39, 87, 89, 99, 113, 120, 298, 504, 522
1:4	2, 9, 36, 82, 93, 111-12, 136, 139, 211, 239, 256, 280, 298, 339, 352, 391, 400, 403, 407, 537, 588				
		1:10-11	82	2:4	90-91, 104, 505, 540
		1:11	9, 36, 84, 86, 146, 193, 339, 394	2:4-5	580, 584
1:4-5	75, 406, 475, 490, 493	1:12	82, 130	2:5	87, 90-91, 102, 106, 110, 112, 114, 123, 487, 542
		1:12-13	147, 252, 294, 441, 503		
1:4-6	336, 520	1:12-16	444, 501, 590	2:5-6	87, 362
1:4-8	521	1:12-20	35, 81, 135	2:6	25, 87, 89, 91, 92, 102, 305, 308
1:5	22, 54, 90, 97, 100, 110, 127, 131, 133, 160, 163, 173, 201, 224, 272, 280, 303, 338, 343, 347, 385, 387, 407, 493, 503, 505, 588, 590	1:13	87, 130, 177, 263, 275, 460		
				2:7	20, 22, 92-93, 102, 106, 111, 132, 156, 205, 224, 268, 334, 336-37, 369-70, 388, 397, 400, 438, 476, 503, 540
		1:13-16	103		
		1:14	6, 103, 116, 130, 155, 161, 173, 225, 263, 268, 339, 360		
1:5-6	77, 236, 336, 538, 591	1:15	191, 252		
1:5-7	505	1:16	6, 87, 98, 159, 191, 203, 231, 263, 285, 341, 383, 433	2:8	97-98, 113, 148, 339, 346, 353, 354, 368, 396
1:6	77, 79, 104, 125, 138, 154, 169, 173, 199, 223, 251, 257, 272, 306, 312, 328, 356, 383-84, 389, 407-8, 460, 537				
		1:17	83, 94, 96, 135, 143, 171, 334-35, 396, 403, 438, 461, 505	2:8-10	22
				2:8-11	4, 94
				2:9	23, 25, 96-97, 105, 113, 129, 152, 167, 222, 230, 283, 349, 502, 535
		1:17-18	588, 590		
		1:18	83-84, 94-95, 97, 113, 119, 148, 183, 185, 346, 362, 444, 593		
1:6-7	126, 154, 171			2:9-10	39, 79, 107, 172, 234
1:7	55, 78, 81, 83, 91, 122, 191, 208, 263, 281, 313, 341, 402, 443, 471, 538, 577, 588, 590				
		1:19	36, 82, 193, 339, 368, 394, 493	2:10	23, 25, 88, 96-98, 110, 123-24, 138, 149, 155, 183, 185, 215, 222, 225, 263, 302-3, 307, 338, 349, 350, 370
		1:19-20	400		
		1:20	20, 130, 177, 195, 202, 294, 295, 502		
1:7-8	35				
1:8	10, 78, 83, 108, 119, 142, 211, 271, 280, 282, 298, 303, 330, 340, 343, 353, 367-68, 396, 406, 411-12, 467, 501, 588	2–3	9, 17, 22, 25, 27, 32, 59, 67, 86, 92, 94-95, 139, 148, 169, 237	2:11	20, 22, 93, 113, 156, 185, 205, 224, 268, 336-37, 356, 363, 369-70, 394, 400, 438, 476, 487, 540
		2	85, 224		
		2:1	85, 87, 99, 124, 130,		

661

Index of Biblical and Other Ancient References

2:12	6, 99, 263, 339, 342, 368, 433, 493	2:26	87, 212, 229, 231, 353, 505, 540		263, 392, 586, 590, 618
2:12-17	4, 98	2:26-27	6, 156, 251	3:12	22, 93, 125, 156, 173, 199, 205, 224, 251, 268, 339, 358, 365, 369-70, 389, 506, 540
2:13	22-23, 39, 89, 96, 99, 100, 103-4, 113, 120, 160, 190, 201, 222, 238, 261, 280, 303, 336, 338, 349	2:26-28	22, 93, 156, 205, 224, 268, 335, 369-70, 393, 540		
		2:27	174, 218, 342		
		2:28	104, 181, 400	3:13	20, 336-37, 400, 438, 472, 476, 487
2:13-15	87, 124, 370	2:29	20, 336-37, 400, 438, 476, 487		
2:13-17	99			3:14	6, 127, 154, 160, 171, 224, 271, 303, 338-39, 368, 402, 493
2:14	100-101, 115, 167, 191, 239, 243, 254, 287, 292, 309, 371, 398, 441	3	85, 224		
		3:1	87, 112-13, 116-17, 139, 339, 368, 395, 438, 472, 475-76, 493		
				3:14-22	4, 126
2:14-15	25, 92			3:15	87, 128, 362, 395, 504
2:15	106, 259	3:1-2	362		
2:16	6, 90-91, 106, 110, 123, 203, 205, 210, 221, 263, 285, 303, 339, 342, 392, 433	3:1-6	4, 112. 115	3:16	183
		3:2	87, 113-15, 183, 239	3:17	128-29, 153, 305, 309
		3:3	90, 93, 114, 123, 191, 229, 286		
				3:17-18	95, 287
2:17	20, 22, 93, 103, 111, 113, 120, 125, 132, 155-56, 205, 224, 263, 268, 334-37, 340, 360, 369-70, 393, 400, 438, 476, 487, 540	3:4	87, 103, 115-16, 130, 142, 254, 281, 286, 336, 384, 395	3:18	103, 129, 131, 151, 155, 161, 244, 263, 268, 294, 314, 360
		3:4-5	155, 161, 263, 360	3:19	90, 131, 134, 172, 540
		3:5	22, 93, 103-4, 112, 116-17, 138, 156, 205, 224, 236, 239, 251, 254, 268, 294, 298, 361, 367, 369-70, 386, 542	3:20	128, 132, 334, 403, 473, 506, 523, 590
				3:21	22, 93, 104, 111, 133, 137-38, 146, 156, 174, 205, 219, 224, 231, 251, 268, 303, 335, 352-53, 369-70, 387, 393, 540
2:17-18	339				
2:18	6, 108, 268, 339, 368, 493	3:6	20, 336-37, 400, 438, 476, 487		
		3:7	127, 132, 142, 147, 150, 160, 183, 204, 271, 338-39, 350, 368, 399, 493, 504		
2:18-29	4, 103				
2:19	87, 104, 107, 110, 114, 122, 261, 362, 395, 504			3:21-22	394
				3:22	20, 336-37, 400, 438, 476, 487
2:20	11, 21, 37, 113, 166, 196, 222, 240, 243, 254, 287, 292, 324, 351, 371, 398, 441	3:7-13	4, 118	4–16	293, 374
		3:8	22, 87, 89, 120, 122, 125, 135, 229, 231, 362, 395, 504	4–5	51, 137, 155, 211
				4	136, 194, 211, 214, 225, 267
2:20-21	259, 296, 309	3:8-9	239	4:1	64, 67, 73, 81, 135-36, 176, 178, 198, 208, 291, 322, 337, 373, 439
2:20-23	215, 327	3:9	23, 25, 96, 121-22, 124, 131, 167, 190, 222, 232, 255, 349, 371, 399		
2:20-25	26				
2:21	10, 185, 191			4:1–5:14	4, 135, 288
2:21-22	90			4:1–7:17	67
2:21-23	292			4:1–8:1	68
2:22	87, 254	3:10	88, 104, 122-23, 183, 206, 229, 235, 238, 261, 292, 307, 336, 504	4:1–11:19	214
2:22-23	362			4:1–16:21	4, 6, 135, 154, 156, 288, 368
2:22-25	107, 109, 110				
2:23	87, 110-11, 159, 212, 262, 395, 444, 505				
2:24	23, 96, 222, 349	3:11	87, 91, 123-24, 138, 156, 185, 210, 215,	4:2	2, 136, 139, 293, 476, 486
2:25	87, 124				
2:25-27	152				

Index of Biblical and Other Ancient References

4:2-6	352	5:3	145, 439		306, 312, 328, 352, 360, 406, 440, 590, 610
4:3	191, 214, 375, 380-81, 407	5:3-4	145		
		5:4	146, 313, 439		
4:4	138, 155-56, 162, 177, 185, 215, 263, 294, 328, 352, 360, 375, 378	5:5	93, 147, 156, 193, 205, 250, 303, 313, 350, 399, 439	5:14	54, 83, 171, 190, 199, 211, 232, 275, 328, 334, 335, 402
		5:5-6	252	6–9	192
4:5	6, 139, 155, 178, 181, 193, 203, 214, 252, 268, 288, 391, 400, 475-76	5:6	16, 40, 77, 96, 161, 174, 236, 269, 275, 298, 320, 324, 337, 339, 361, 377, 387, 391, 400, 409, 433, 439, 472, 476, 494, 503, 527, 535, 588, 619	6	64, 67, 155, 164, 170, 182
				6:1	252, 275, 350
				6:1-2	338
4:5-6	139-40, 239			6:1-8	159
4:6	60, 268, 364, 375, 387			6:1-17	4, 154-55
				6:1–8:5	3-4, 135, 154
4:6-9	275			6:2	93, 156, 164-65, 185, 205, 263
4:7	182, 186, 189, 226, 328	5:6-7	352		
		5:6-10	502	6:3	275, 350, 408
4:8	78, 141, 150, 154, 211, 224, 232, 261, 271, 273, 280, 282, 298, 303, 330, 343, 360, 386, 409, 411, 423	5:7	149, 191, 406	6:4	156-57, 216, 407
		5:8	83, 150, 171, 177, 211, 239, 252, 260, 269, 275-76, 280, 294, 320, 322, 328, 334, 375, 378, 441, 502	6:5	350
				6:5-7	275
				6:6	394
				6:7	350
				6:7-8	313
4:8-11	505			6:8	84, 107, 159, 164, 180, 184-85, 190, 231, 278, 362, 407, 592
4:9	142, 153-54, 171, 209, 257, 272, 294, 306, 312, 326, 331, 384, 386	5:8-9	150		
		5:8-10	253, 255		
		5:8-14	461		
		5:9	151, 160, 170, 173, 198, 224, 235-36, 253, 257, 269, 304, 314, 324, 340, 350, 366, 384, 387, 432, 445, 476, 502, 538	6:9	74, 159-60, 187, 199, 224, 241, 264, 281, 324, 350, 353, 441, 507
4:9-10	142, 165, 276, 346, 352, 354, 390, 406				
4:10	83, 156, 171, 185, 190, 199, 211, 215, 232, 239, 328, 334, 375			6:9-10	71
		5:9-10	77, 152, 232, 440, 460, 508, 537, 591, 593	6:9-11	22, 170, 173, 177, 195, 276, 335-36, 508, 612
4:11	141, 144-45, 151-53, 194, 209, 211, 223, 231-32, 257, 272, 294, 303, 306, 312, 326, 343, 384, 386, 406-8, 439, 526, 531, 438, 541			6:10	177, 180, 182, 206, 216, 235, 271, 273, 280-82, 292, 296, 307, 313, 320, 326-27, 335, 338, 340, 409, 411, 504, 577
		5:9-14	141, 269, 505		
		5:10	169, 173, 199, 200, 223, 272, 353, 356, 383, 389-90, 443, 502, 504, 591		
		5:11	188, 275, 352	6:10-11	592
5	29, 67, 150, 155, 192, 196-97, 211, 225, 269-70, 306, 330	5:11-12	171, 210	6:11	103, 177, 183, 237, 281, 360
		5:11-14	505		
		5:12	70, 154, 160-61, 171, 182, 221, 223, 231, 243, 313, 324, 326	6:12	180, 208, 350, 586
5:1	165, 191-92, 339, 352, 406			6:12-13	216
				6:12-14	65, 162
5:1-2	350			6:14	163
5:1-10	425	5:12-13	53, 209, 232, 257, 272, 294, 306, 312, 384, 386, 408	6:15	95, 272, 285, 303, 343-44, 385, 395
5:2	77, 145, 153, 160, 182, 191, 195, 221, 313, 321			6:15-16	323
		5:13	71, 141, 153, 171,	6:15-17	586

663

6:16	164, 185, 208, 212, 352, 361, 389, 406	7:13-14	360, 591		206, 226, 235, 256, 292, 307, 317, 344
		7:13-17	55	9	46, 209
6:16-17	40, 260, 268	7:14	79, 103, 172, 216, 224, 234, 236, 241, 333, 340, 396, 431, 441, 495, 506	9:1	81, 322, 348, 407
6:17	164, 212, 216, 258, 260, 443			9:1-2	183, 349
				9:2	216
7	16, 45, 67, 171, 174-75, 184, 200			9:3	231
		7:14-17	22	9:4	166, 178, 242, 295, 350, 389, 394
7:1	87, 141, 166, 178, 187	7:15	173, 199, 224-25, 239, 352, 360-61, 366, 383, 386, 389, 406, 431		
				9:5	186, 207, 216, 260, 312, 314, 317, 407
7:1-3	176				
7:1-8	251, 358, 369			9:6	185
7:1-17	3-4, 154, 164, 255	7:16	282-83	9:7	188, 205, 220, 294, 332
7:2	182, 194, 216, 346, 350, 352, 407	7:16-17	369, 539		
		7:17	174, 342, 352, 409, 540, 580, 582, 590	9:8	189
7:2-3	394			9:9	205
7:3	166-67, 178, 196, 242, 251, 295, 329, 389	8	67	9:10	217, 231, 394
		8:1	67, 178, 276, 350	9:11	186, 246, 287, 348-49
		8:1-2	3, 252		
7:3-5	350	8:1-5	4, 7, 154, 175, 394	9:12	187, 316-17
7:3-8	184	8:1–11:18	67	9:13	81, 199, 239, 264, 294, 378, 441
7:4	167, 188, 252	8:2	51, 81, 176, 322, 407		
7:4-8	215, 254, 375-76, 591			9:13-21	209
		8:2-4	239	9:14	77, 81, 187, 199, 216, 341
7:4-9	251	8:2–11:18	68		
7:5-8	168, 378	8:3	177, 187, 199, 238, 264, 294, 352, 378, 441	9:15	77, 188, 220, 332, 366
7:7	169				
7:9	103, 170-71, 173, 198, 235, 239, 251-52, 257, 263, 268-69, 294, 304, 360, 366, 384, 508, 620			9:16	188
		8:3-4	280-81, 320, 441, 502	9:16-19	341
				9:17-18	265, 268, 283, 347
		8:3-5	276, 409	9:17-19	285
		8:4	261, 328	9:18	312, 366
		8:5	6, 178-79, 193, 214, 252, 265, 268, 283, 503	9:19	217, 231, 394
7:9-10	325, 445, 493, 524, 535			9:20	67, 87, 190, 232, 271, 294, 307, 312, 335, 362, 441
7:9-11	352				
7:9-14	573, 619	8:6	81, 188, 332		
7:9-17	409, 524	8:6-8	81, 322	9:20-21	90, 191, 209, 254, 283, 286
7:10	182, 210, 216, 223, 232, 326, 329, 406-7, 535, 537, 564	8:6-11	203		
		8:6–9:21	4, 179, 267	9:21	191, 371, 398
		8:6–11:19	3-4, 135, 154, 179	10	36, 195, 306
		8:7	305	10:1	153, 191, 221, 263, 268, 294, 313, 383
7:10-12	141	8:7-8	265-66, 268, 283, 340		
7:11	83, 190, 199, 211, 232, 239, 328, 334-35, 408, 505			10:1-2	215
		8:7-12	141	10:1–11:13	209
		8:8	216, 340	10:1–11:14	3-4, 191
7:11-12	275, 360	8:8-9	278	10:2	192
7:12	153, 209, 211-12, 221, 223, 231-32, 243, 257, 294, 306, 312-13, 326, 384, 390, 402, 406, 408, 526, 537	8:9	327	10:3	216
		8:10	81, 183, 216, 322	10:3-4	3, 252
		8:10-11	183, 197, 279	10:4	196, 339, 350, 394
		8:11	366	10:5	229
		8:12	182, 386	10:6	346, 354, 390, 407-8, 589
		8:12-13	81, 322		
7:13	103, 263, 272, 294	8:13	81, 183, 187-88,		

Index of Biblical and Other Ancient References

10:7	11, 20, 81, 195, 256, 269, 281, 295, 305, 320, 322, 329, 351	11:11-12	472, 491	12:4-5	442
		11:11-14	355	12:5	219, 342, 352, 442, 620
10:8	192, 277	11:12	210, 263	12:6	202, 220, 227, 293, 332
10:8-9	36	11:13	209, 216, 257, 272, 283, 306, 312, 326, 331, 384, 408-9, 505, 508, 572	12:7	221, 302
10:9-10	219			12:7-9	225, 349
10:9-11	409, 522			12:7-12	23, 226
10:10	507	11:14	202, 209, 316, 317	12:8	228, 313
10:10-11	487	11:15	53, 81, 211, 223, 232, 272, 283, 303, 322, 328, 330, 343, 360, 390, 406, 445, 474, 492, 500, 504, 539, 587, 590	12:8-12	221
10:11	36-37, 196, 198, 201, 206, 213, 235, 257, 272, 303-4, 306, 343, 384, 406, 494, 527, 619			12:9	23, 96, 222, 240, 302-3, 324, 334, 349-51, 359
				12:10	223-24, 231, 239, 262, 319, 325-26, 360, 386, 537
11	28, 36, 60, 64, 258, 320	11:15-18	141, 272, 505		
		11:15-19	3-4, 210, 267	12:10-11	225
11:1	27, 199-200, 232, 265, 335, 378, 441	11:16	83, 199, 211, 232, 239, 312, 328-29, 334-35, 352, 375, 500	12:10-12	141, 223, 232, 272
				12:11	93, 224-25, 229, 236, 268, 303, 336, 340, 409, 431, 442, 507, 522, 589, 593
11:1-2	200-201, 213, 342				
11:1-13	22	11:16-18	211		
11:1-14	619	11:17	78, 223, 231, 271, 280, 282, 303, 326, 330, 343, 390, 406, 411, 526		
11:2	201-2, 204, 233, 265, 350, 364			12:12	23, 225, 234, 238, 259, 300, 308, 319, 364, 589, 618
11:3	196, 220, 294, 336				
11:3-4	337	11:17-18	232, 272	12:13	226
11:3-13	225, 230, 238, 255, 310, 395, 400	11:18	11, 37, 67, 164, 196, 208, 212, 228, 257-58, 260, 272, 280-81, 292, 313, 320, 327, 329, 361, 382, 384, 409, 411, 424, 432-33, 442, 445, 577, 620	12:13-17	220
				12:14	227, 293, 349, 540
11:4	203, 239, 303, 343, 445			12:15	227, 285
11:5	196, 203, 219, 268, 285, 359, 394			12:17	22, 74, 212, 235, 241, 261, 296, 302, 336
11:6	231-32, 340, 342, 350				
				12:18	358
11:7	22-23, 93, 197, 205, 228, 230-31, 235, 245, 280, 298, 302, 305, 336, 349, 351	11:19	3, 6, 193, 214-15, 217, 252, 274-75, 290, 338, 383	13	27, 46-47, 64, 235, 237, 247, 250, 259, 300
11:7-12	280, 441	11:19–14:20	68, 214	13:1	6-7, 23, 229-30, 233, 244, 249-50, 256, 263, 266, 274, 283, 293, 302, 339, 364
11:8	20, 217, 222, 225, 287, 303, 305, 328, 334, 337, 343, 376	11:19–15:8	67		
		12–14	3, 6, 230, 267, 275		
		12	21, 63, 68, 219-20, 229		
11:8-10	289, 347			13:1-2	412
11:9	206, 224, 235, 257, 304, 350	12:1	6, 214, 221, 266, 294, 375, 383	13:1-18	5, 229, 245, 346
		12:1-6	226, 296	13:2	23, 233, 239, 244, 284, 306, 326, 349, 352
11:9-13	384	12:1-12	412		
11:10	11, 196, 216, 235, 260, 281, 292, 307, 312, 314, 317, 319-20, 331	12:1-13	23		
		12:1–13:1	5, 214	13:3	24, 29, 235, 244, 297, 298
		12:1–14:20	4, 135, 214	13:3-4	26, 239-40, 298, 335, 393, 497
11:11	208-9, 217, 241, 257, 272, 353, 476, 497, 498, 540, 590	12:2	216, 260, 314, 317		
		12:3	221, 302, 339, 349	13:4	23-24, 141, 233, 239, 244, 252, 272-
		12:4	196, 217, 349		

665

	73, 297, 302, 318, 335, 349, 412	14:1-20	5, 250	14:20	340
		14:2	150, 252, 269, 322	15–16	401
13:4-5	239	14:3	253, 255, 269, 275, 294, 352, 375	15	51
13:5	202, 233, 300, 302, 350, 354, 390	14:3-4	314, 591	15:1	3, 6-7, 214, 266, 271, 274-77, 305, 312, 351
13:5-6	241, 283-85	14:3-5	505	15:1-4	7, 394
13:6	225, 234, 244	14:4	21-22, 54, 254-55, 277, 280, 296, 334, 336, 341, 353, 441-42, 502, 508, 523-24, 527, 538, 540, 580, 593	15:1-8	5, 266
13:6-8	445			15:1–16:17	68
13:7	93, 239, 257, 280, 284, 304, 320, 347, 384, 407, 504			15:1–16:21	3, 5, 135, 214, 266
				15:2	6-7, 24, 93, 150, 229, 268, 269, 322
13:8	240-41, 250, 272-73, 284, 292, 297-98, 307, 324, 335, 339, 361, 386, 427-28, 442, 459, 471, 522, 534, 541-42, 567, 576, 589	14:5	285, 372, 399, 593	15:2-4	280
		14:6	7, 256, 263, 265-66, 274, 304, 494	15:3	78, 87, 271, 279, 281-82, 303, 310, 326, 330, 338, 343, 362, 395, 411, 439, 502, 505, 532, 620
		14:6-7	272, 308, 344, 409, 505		
		14:6-11	263		
13:9	22	14:7	141, 208, 258, 264, 283, 292, 306, 312-13, 326, 329, 331, 335, 384, 526	15:3-4	141, 279, 303, 332, 343, 384, 406
13:9-10	10, 20, 337			15:3-5	505
13:10	237, 240-41, 243, 261, 277, 280, 320			15:4	208, 272, 310, 312, 334-35, 409, 424, 504-5, 526, 615, 619-20
13:11	7, 23, 250, 256, 263, 266, 274, 346	14:8	277, 287, 292, 295, 307-8, 384, 620		
		14:9	166, 261, 273, 295, 335		
13:11-15	24			15:5	274, 338, 366
13:11-17	24	14:9-10	289, 346	15:6	294, 312, 316, 332
13:12	29, 239, 244, 273, 292, 297, 307, 335, 383	14:9-11	24	15:6-7	294, 378, 383
		14:10	164, 212, 260, 265, 267-68, 277, 283, 312	15:7	277, 346, 354, 390
				15:8	277, 305-6, 312, 326, 351, 383
13:13	305				
13:13-14	286	14:10-11	312, 314, 317	16–21	198
13:13-15	497	14:11	260-62, 273, 328, 335, 360, 386, 421	16:1	278, 383
13:14	24, 292, 297, 307, 324, 351			16:1-21	5, 67, 277
		14:12	22, 261, 281, 320, 616	16:2	24, 283-84, 316, 335
13:15	273, 280, 296, 335, 347, 371, 398, 412			16:2-9	141
		14:13	6, 10, 22, 75, 87, 262, 281, 286, 333-34, 339, 362, 368, 396, 493, 505, 613, 616	16:3	278
13:15-16	329			16:3-4	340
13:15-17	346			16:4	283
13:16	95, 166, 295, 361			16:4-5	408-9
13:16-17	24			16:4-6	282
13:17	314	14:14	7, 263, 266, 274, 294, 360, 378	16:5	273, 280, 282, 292, 310, 313, 338, 395, 406, 409, 504
13:18	20, 24, 65, 153, 243, 247, 261, 299, 337				
		14:14-15	264		
		14:14-16	266, 524		
14	45, 269, 308	14:14-20	539, 620	16:5-6	411, 505
14:1	7, 104, 166, 250-52, 256, 263, 266, 274, 295, 339, 375, 389, 506	14:15	263-64, 383	16:5-7	141
		14:17	383	16:6	11, 22, 116, 196, 296-97, 319-20, 340, 504
		14:17-20	266		
		14:18	265, 268, 283, 441		
14:1-2	141, 252	14:19	265, 267, 277	16:7	78, 281-82, 292, 303, 310, 313, 326,
14:1-4	378	14:19-20	342		
14:1-5	303				

Index of Biblical and Other Ancient References

	330, 338, 343, 395, 406, 411, 441	17:4	24, 296, 312, 315, 317, 321, 371, 375, 382	18:10	205, 319
16:8	283, 407			18:11	317
16:8-9	283	17:4-5	371, 386, 398	18:12	315, 321, 375, 382
16:8-11	413	17:5	20, 167, 295, 339, 371	18:12-13	323
16:9	90, 283, 306, 312, 331, 384, 505	17:6	22, 24, 26, 298, 320, 327, 335-36,	18:13	445, 460, 502
16:10	24, 352		340, 504	18:15	95, 323
16:10-11	284	17:6-7	26, 393	18:16	205, 321, 375, 382
16:11	87, 90, 362	17:7	20, 24, 302, 305, 335	18:17	318-19
16:12	302-3, 305, 332, 343	17:8	24, 298-301, 307, 339, 349, 361, 386, 542	18:18	153, 328
16:12-14	286			18:18-19	205
16:12-16	376	17:8-18	298	18:19	95, 319
16:13	23-24, 37, 295, 346, 349, 487	17:9	20, 65, 153, 261, 299	18:20	11, 29, 42, 141, 196, 319, 320, 324, 326, 329, 352, 377
16:13-14	307-8, 445	17:9-10	301, 337	18:21	153, 205
16:14	78, 123, 286, 295, 302-3, 330, 343-45, 357, 411	17:9-11	27	18:21-23	367
		17:10	25, 302	18:21-24	334
		17:10-11	65	18:22	322
		17:11	24	18:22-23	325
16:15	6, 10, 22, 75, 91, 286, 305, 334, 356, 384, 396, 587	17:11-14	24	18:23	191, 323, 331, 351, 365, 371, 373, 384, 398, 620
		17:12	298, 302, 314, 317, 350, 354, 390	18:24	11, 22, 37, 196, 206, 324, 340, 504
16:16	37, 288, 303, 334, 344, 345	17:13	314, 317, 326	19	21
16:17	6, 352, 367-68, 383	17:14	93, 302-3, 334, 338-41, 343, 540	19:1	330, 384, 505
16:17-21	295	17:15	298, 312, 620	19:1-2	537
16:18	193, 289	17:16	295, 298, 313, 318, 344, 371, 398	19:1-8	141, 505
16:18-21	6, 368	17:16-17	24, 308, 314, 317, 367	19:1-10	5, 291, 325
16:18–19:21	68	17:17	74, 345, 351	19:1–21:8	5, 325
16:19	164, 205, 212, 287, 289, 295, 308, 312, 342, 373, 384, 620	17:18	205, 298, 305, 385	19:2	22, 327, 329, 338, 340, 371, 395, 398, 406
		18	24, 25		
16:21	312	18:1	312, 337	19:3	360
17–18	21, 62, 365	18:1-24	5, 291, 306, 325	19:4	83, 328, 334-35, 375, 402, 406
17	XV, 24-25, 27, 46, 74, 293, 306, 308	18:1–19:8	11	19:4-5	352
17:1	4, 73, 292, 304, 308, 312, 334, 352, 373	18:2	153, 313	19:5	208, 330, 361
		18:3	24, 95, 309, 312, 314, 317, 326, 371, 385, 398	19:6	53, 78, 153, 330, 411
				19:6-8	335
17:1-2	371, 398			19:7	384, 582
17:1-3	4	18:4	312	19:7-8	365, 373, 400
17:1-18	5, 291, 325	18:4-5	311	19:7-9	506
17:1–18:24	67, 345	18:5	311	19:8	287, 504-5, 524, 541, 580
17:1–19:2	374	18:6	87, 362	19:8-9	356
17:1–19:9	334	18:7	312-14, 317, 326	19:9	6, 74-75, 333-34, 338-39, 393, 396, 493
17:1–21:8	4-6, 291, 306, 368, 374	18:7-8	314, 317		
		18:8	314, 328	19:9-10	337, 394
17:2	296, 307, 313, 385	18:9	313, 371, 385, 398	19:10	36, 74, 333, 337, 346, 353, 393, 400,
17:3	2, 4, 24, 291, 293, 302, 374, 400, 476, 486				

667

	438-39, 441, 445, 461, 471, 485-86, 493, 507, 529, 619	21	48, 67	22:1-2	53
		21:1	60, 367	22:1-5	373
		21:1-2	374, 539	22:2	409, 436, 442, 495, 575, 619-20
19:11	103, 338, 343, 348, 352, 360, 368, 395, 470	21:1-6	408		
		21:1-8	5, 291, 325, 363, 379, 383	22:3	389
				22:4	167, 506, 592
19:11-16	5-6, 325, 337, 587	21:2	125, 332, 365, 374, 381	22:6	11, 37, 73, 196, 377, 391, 393, 400, 507
19:11-21	291				
19:12-13	590	21:3	225, 366, 388, 539		
19:13	74, 470, 445, 506	21:3-4	369, 409, 589	22:6-7	5, 6
19:14	103, 360	21:4	428, 539	22:6-9	391, 394
19:15	78, 164, 212, 342, 351, 384, 433, 620	21:5	391, 406, 411, 493, 507	22:6-11	7
				22:6-21	4-5, 391
19:16	53, 439	21:6	6, 368, 387, 396, 499, 582, 590, 592	22:7	6, 10, 75, 91, 305, 392, 395, 402, 590, 591, 618
19:17	344, 347-48, 383				
19:17-21	5, 325, 343, 347	21:7	93, 540		
19:18	344, 348, 361	21:8	67, 113, 386, 397-99, 441		
19:19	347-48, 385			22:7-20	10
19:20	24, 37, 346, 348, 351, 359, 372	21:9	4, 373, 390, 592	22:8	36, 73, 83, 393
		21:9-10	4, 73	22:8-9	333, 438, 441, 461
19:21	348, 351, 355, 433	21:9-12	502	22:9	11, 37, 196, 507
20:1	67, 348	21:9-21	373	22:9-10	305
20:1-6	5, 66, 291, 325, 348	21:9-22:5	4-6, 373, 391, 397	22:10	10, 13, 226, 394
20:1-10	68, 364	21:10	2, 4, 125, 373-74, 400, 476, 486	22:11	395-96
20:2	23, 87, 187, 349			22:12	87, 91, 402, 590, 591, 618
20:3	23, 77, 351, 357, 359, 384, 620	21:11	383, 387		
		21:12	379	22:12-20	400
20:4	24, 74, 166, 352-53, 507-8	21:12-13	215, 388, 591	22:14	6, 75, 396, 402, 506, 592
		21:13	383-84, 409, 592		
20:4-6	22	21:14	27, 29, 43, 377, 502, 507, 522	22:14-15	621
20:5	67			22:15	397-98, 441, 592
20:6	6, 61, 75, 77, 113, 363, 383, 389	21:15	378	22:16	9, 400
		21:16	383	22:16-20	445, 492, 493
20:7	62, 77, 187	21:19	381	22:17	445, 472, 479, 498-99, 504, 540, 574, 582, 589, 590, 592
20:7-8	23	21:19-20	381		
20:7-10	5, 23, 291, 325, 357	21:21	294		
20:8	141, 357, 376, 384	21:22	78, 411, 592		
20:9	196, 620	21:22-23	592		
20:10	24, 37, 352, 372, 386	21:22-24	589		
		21:22-27	373	22:18	402
20:11	103, 360, 364, 389, 539	21:23	441, 589	22:18-19	10, 37, 305
		21:23-25	438	22:19	401, 504
20:11-15	5, 291, 325, 360	21:24	76, 87, 384-85, 524, 539, 616, 619	22:20	54, 91, 402, 588, 590-91, 618-19
20:11–22:21	68				
20:12	50, 361, 362, 386, 593	21:24-25	495	22:21	9, 537
		21:24-26	388, 615, 620		
20:12-13	87, 396	21:25	390, 409, 592		
20:13	362, 541	21:26	435, 524, 592, 621	**PSEUDEPIGRAPHA**	
20:13-14	84	21:27	386, 398, 539, 542, 621		
20:14	113, 539, 590, 593			3 Maccabees	
20:15	386, 542	22:1	73, 389, 582, 590, 592	2:28-30	242
21–22	60				

JOSEPHUS

Jewish Wars
5.270	290

APOSTOLIC FATHERS

Didache
14.1	34

Ignatius
To the Magnesians
9:1	34

EARLY JEWISH AND CHRISTIAN AUTHORS

Andrew of Caesarea
Commentary on the Apocalypse
13.2	230

Apocalypse of St. John Chrysostom
1-4	48
5-10	48
8-19	48
20-51	48

Clement of Alexandria
Who Is the Rich Man That Is Saved?
42	33, 41

Coptic Apocalypse of John
2	49
3	49
7	50
13	50
14	50
18	50

Eusebius
Ecclesiastical History
1.243	33
3.19-20	31
3.23.5-6	33
3.34.2	43
3.39.8-17	43
4.26.9-10	30
5.24.3	38
7.25.1-27	41
7.25.2-3	41
7.25.7-8a	42
7.25.8b-11	42
7.25.17-24	42
7.25.25-26	42
7.25.27	42

Gospel of Peter
35	34
50	34

Hippolytus
De Antichristo
18	41
36-42	41

Irenaeus
Against Heresies
1.26.3	41
2.22.5	33
3.3.4	33
4.14.2	41
4.20.11	41
5.26.1	41
5.30.3	33

Justin Martyr
Dialogue with Trypho
81.4	32, 41

Primasius
Commentary on the Apocalypse
16:9	283

Second Apocalypse of John
2-3	48
7	48
8	48
10-11	48
17	48
18-19	48
20	48
24	48
27	48

Sibylline Oracles
5.343	30

Tertullian
Against Marcion
3.14.3	41
3.24.4	41

Apology
5.4	31

Third Apocalypse of John
1	49
2-10	49
11-35	49
23	49
23-27	49
24	49
25	49
26	49
27	49
35	49

CLASSICAL REFERENCES

Cicero
Ad Att.
6.5	299

Verr.
3.81	158

Herodotus
Hist.
1.178	379

Horace
Carm.
7	299

Martial Epigrams
4.64	299

Ovid
Trist.
1.5.69	299

Index of Biblical and Other Ancient References

Philostratus

Life of Apollonius

4.38	30

Pliny

Letters

10.46-47	31

Natural History

34.139	300

Plutarch

Nicias

29	242

Suetonius

Nero

16.2	30
39	246
49	240

Tacitus

Annals

3.37	98
3.72	300
4.30	80
15.44	29

Virgil

Aeneid

6.783	299

Geor.

11.535	299

www.ingramcontent.com/pod-product-compliance
Lightning Source LLC
Chambersburg PA
CBHW031537300426
44111CB00006BA/90